山东华侨史研究丛书

Chinese Labourer's Diaries
Journal des travailleurs chinois dans la Première Guerre mondiale

华工日记

山东华侨会馆　编
山东华侨博物馆

吴桂金　王敬群　译

山东画报出版社
济南

图书在版编目（CIP）数据

华工日记 / 山东华侨会馆, 山东华侨博物馆编; 吴桂金, 王敬群译 .— 济南 : 山东画报出版社, 2024.1
　　ISBN 978-7-5474-3394-2

Ⅰ . ①华… Ⅱ . ①山… ②山… ③吴… ④王… Ⅲ . ①第一次世界大战 – 华工 – 史料 Ⅳ . ①D634.31

中国版本图书馆CIP数据核字(2022)第033177号

HUAGONG RIJI
华工日记
山东华侨会馆　山东华侨博物馆 编
吴桂金　王敬群 译

责任编辑　怀志霄
装帧设计　王　芳

主管单位　山东出版传媒股份有限公司
出版发行　山东画报出版社
　　　　　　社　　址　济南市市中区舜耕路517号　邮编 250003
　　　　　　电　　话　总编室（0531）82098472
　　　　　　　　　　　市场部（0531）82098479
　　　　　　网　　址　http://www.hbcbs.com.cn
　　　　　　电子信箱　hbcb@sdpress.com.cn
印　　刷　山东临沂新华印刷物流集团有限责任公司
规　　格　160毫米×230毫米　32开
　　　　　　20.25印张　42幅图　693千字
版　　次　2024年1月第1版
印　　次　2024年1月第1次印刷
书　　号　ISBN 978-7-5474-3394-2
定　　价　98.00元

如有印装质量问题，请与出版社总编室联系更换。

山东华侨会馆
山东华侨博物馆

《华工日记》编委会

主　任：邢红霞

副主任：刘登峰

委　员：常　珑　张　岩　李　翔

　　　　David Moore（法）马京东

　　　　孙光隆　孙肇永　蒋德山

　　　　齐德智

主　编：邢红霞

副主编：李　晓

编　辑：邵明娟　杨梦冉

孙干
Sun Gan

孙干全家福
A family portraits of Sun Gan.

孙干故居和尚坊村
Sun Gan's former residence Heshangfang village.

孙干在家乡威望极高，和尚坊的村碑写有"此乃博山知名人士孙干之故里"。（图为孙干长孙孙光隆驻足观看）

Sun Gan has a high reputation in his hometown, the stele of Heshangfang village said" This is the hometown of renowned figure Sun Gan from Boshan". Sun Gan's eldest grandson Sun Guanglong stopped to watch.

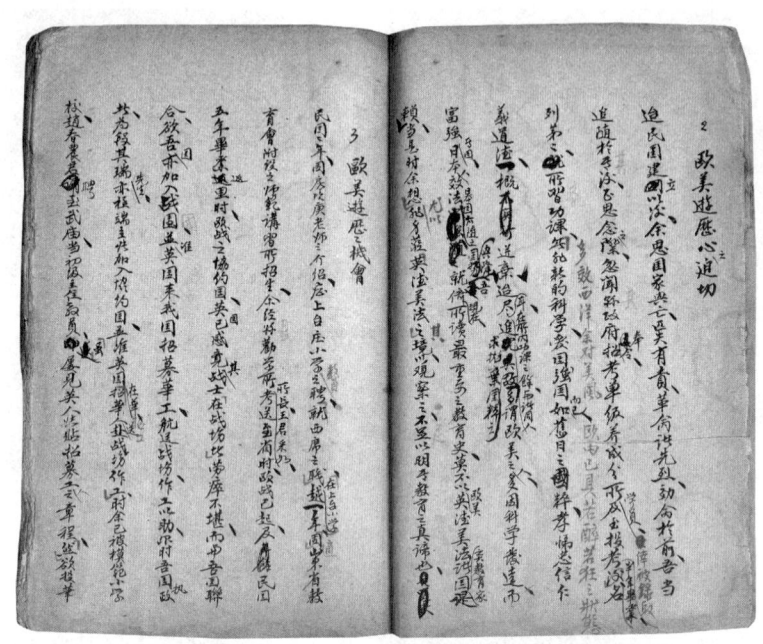

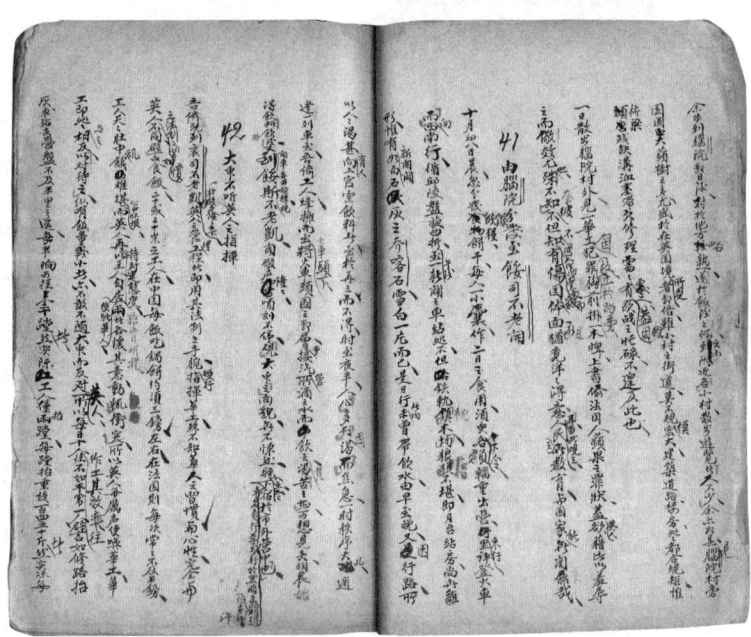

孙干日记手稿

The manuscript of Sun Gan's diary.

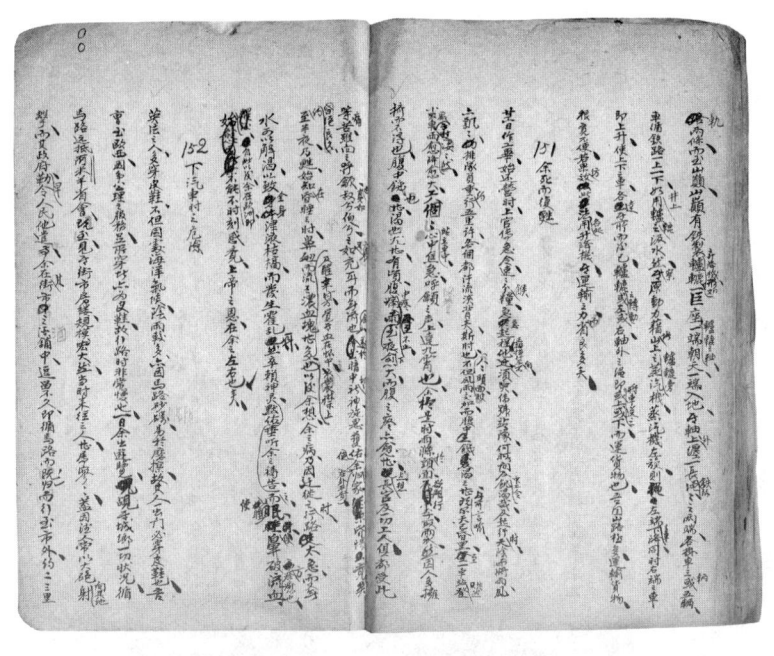

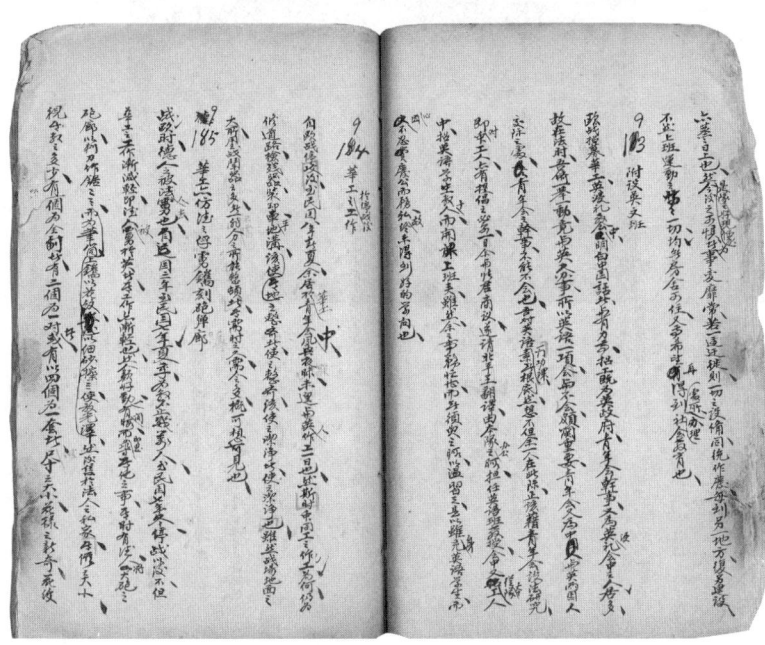

孙干日记手稿

The manuscript of Sun Gan's diary.

马春苓

Ma Chunling

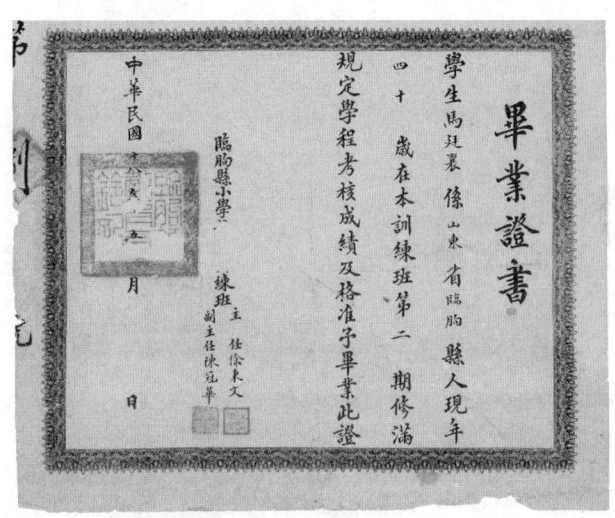

马春苓毕业证书
Ma Chunling's diploma.

马春苓日记手稿

The manuscript of Ma Chunling's diary.

马春苓日记手稿

The manuscript of Ma Chunling's diary.

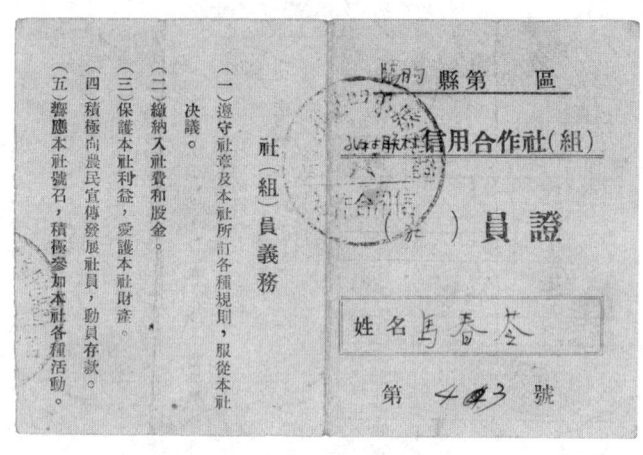

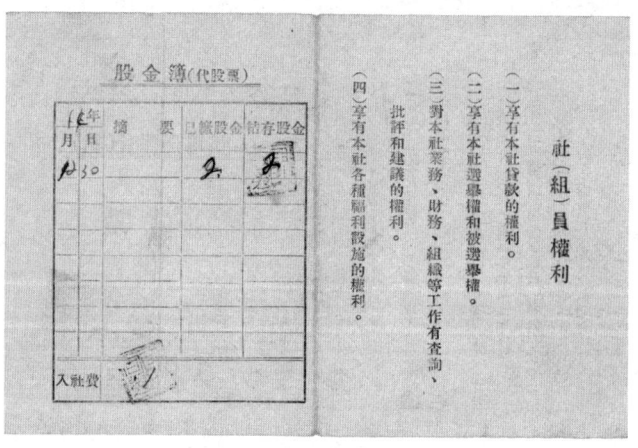

马春苓社员证

Ma Chunling's membership certificate.

蒋镜海画像
Portrait of Jiang Jinghai.

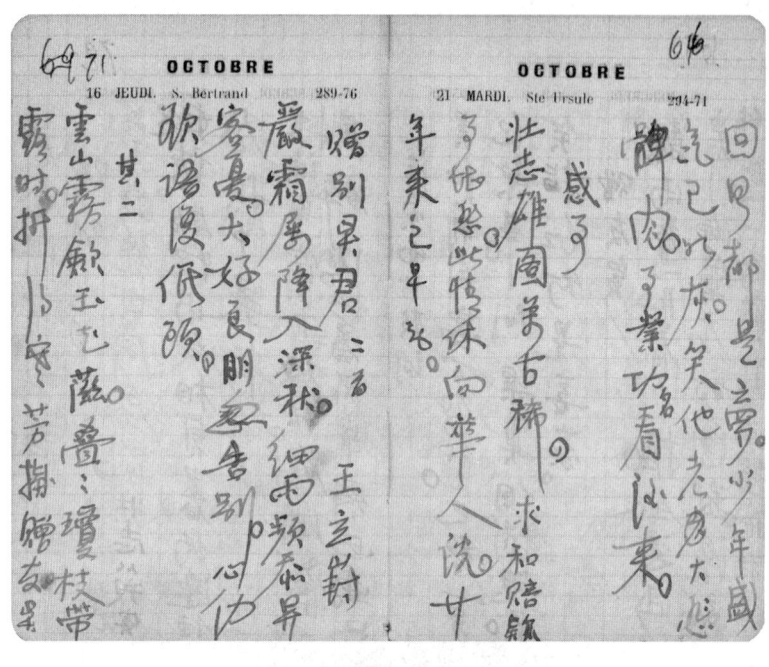

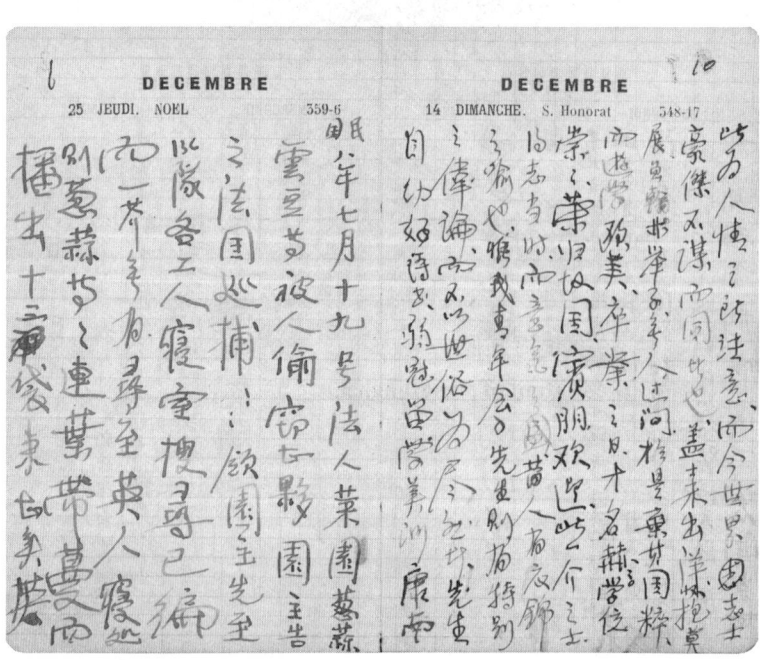

蒋镜海日记手稿

The manuscript of Jiang Jinghai's diary.

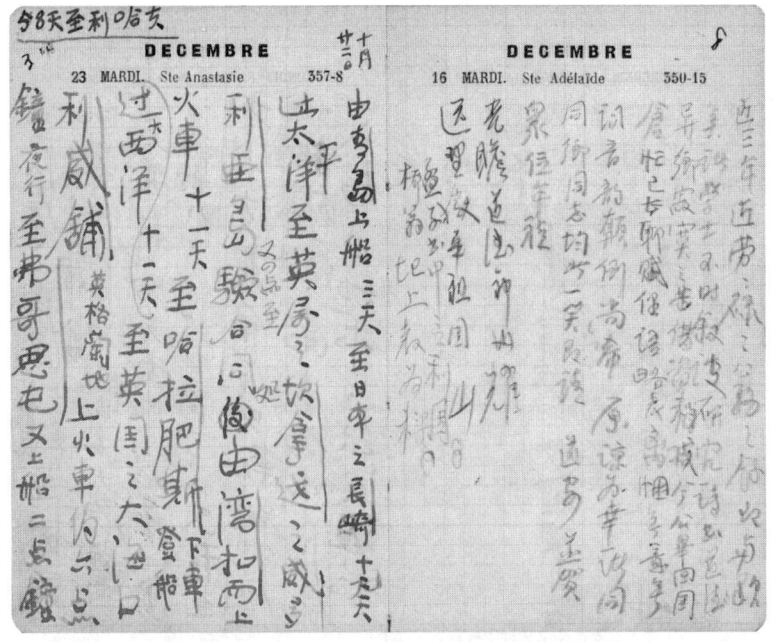

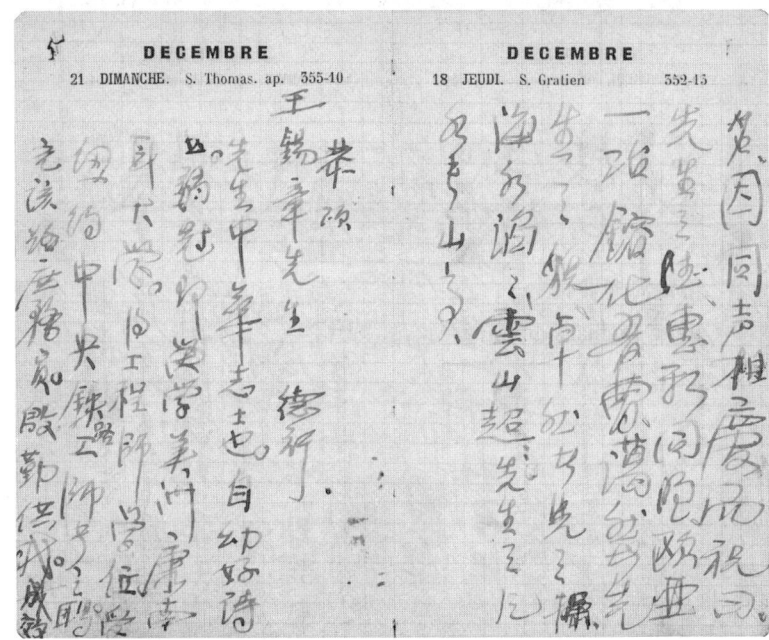

蒋镜海日记手稿

The manuscript of Jiang Jinghai's diary.

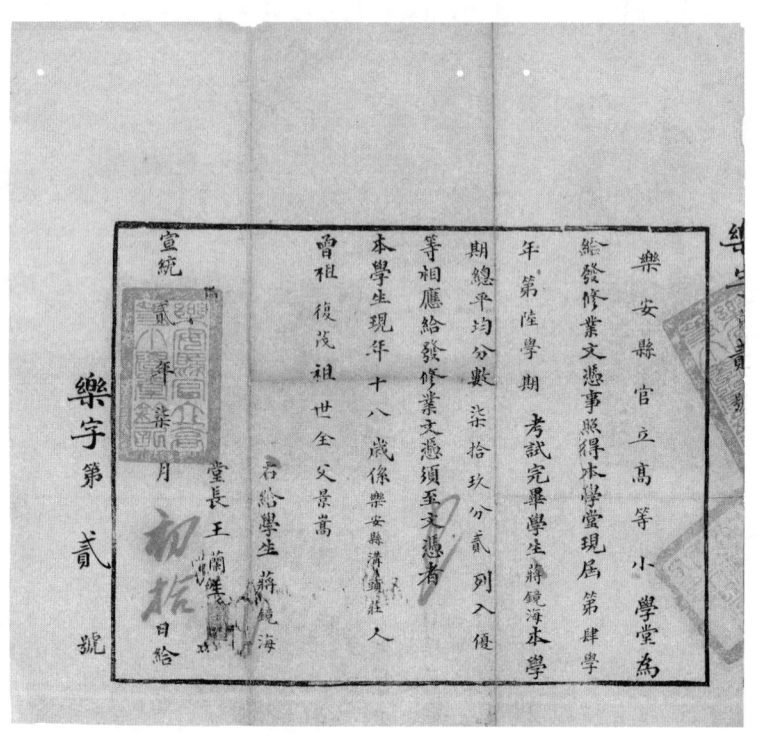

蒋镜海毕业证

Jiang Jinghai's diploma.

顾杏卿
Gu Xinqing

1917年顾杏卿拍摄于比利时
Gu Xinqing, filmed in Belgium, 1917.

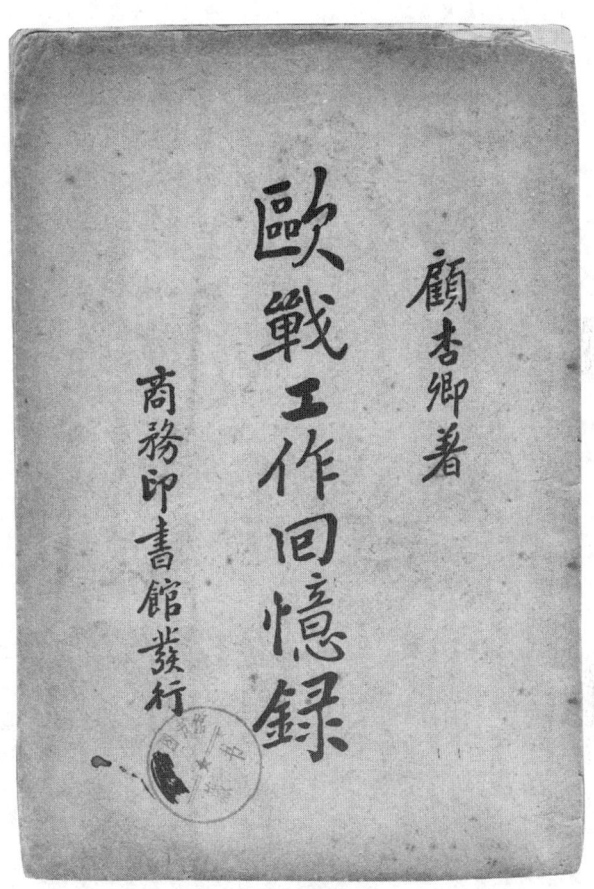

顾杏卿著《欧战工作回忆录》
Reminiscences on My Work during European War by Gu Xingqing.

六　駐英福克斯登（Folkestone）

同始來此之大隊華工亦於此次呼號中離舟登岸並由英政府招派之幹事人員禮任招待董此次華工之由英赴法前聯絡服務者上實際上為赴前線服務耳英軍持此戰鬥上助力或可俟估勝勢彼國政府與歐美歐戰之熱烈歡迎自屬應有之表示

登岸後由利物浦上車此地工廠林立一入煙囪密佈此地為廣派中樞軍官管理其事之福克斯登地方福克斯登者由英赴法輪埠之一此地工廠林立一入煙囪密佈此地為廣派中樞軍官管理其事曉市面已蕭條一象漢語有英人煽市有軍行十二小時乃抵英吉利海峽並棧漢華工數百名留以此地為華工休息之營合由英此法者留以此地為華工休息之營合

余等與歐華工末圖在此暫宿，次發官查驗結果患有耳腺典病者曾即搭輪赴法，次發官查驗結果患有耳腺典病者有一千

四百名以上之多，較扣留屆此者凡一月因余聞此地特懷覽此地之風景亦可謂非旅途中之眼福也

此千餘人在客人之目光一無患病之廠者人一無異現被英警官指得有疾可鬼 醫驗之廠者人在英欽一無異現城奧務常在暗之日光一無患病之廠者人在英欽一無異現被英警官指得有疾可鬼 飛彈不斷落瞪邑首卿此余正驚詫之際別英軍官有餘無事之態已一次之彈中繼甚惨之馬此（時間約在晨間二時）余室聞何故英軍官又大鬧不已逐出出餘聞何故英軍官又大鬧不已逐出出餘起來融為大驚不可說…… 余室聞何故英軍官又大鬧不已逐出出

出時繼夏天氣寒冷一如我國之冬天余出後見其同營之隊伍皆已飛矣此間雖方知此時有大事發生此危懼吧地者紛紛女幼稚之受傷者百七十四人余當以為急奔走未見急奔走未見傷亡毫未余嚴厲此危懼吧地者紛紛爆線外一無所事……一月有餘每日除以急奔走未見傷亡毫未余嚴厲此危懼吧地者紛紛閒戰時社會機能之紛亂也

一三　大戰中之民衆

一般普通民衆在軍事舉動抱之態度以缺乏軍事學識無助戰之能力於是袖手旁觀者實之速而避之者也能於戰事勝利時為於色性於戰的勝利時為於色性惟在大規模之戰爭為大規模之戰爭不明近代戰爭性所致要之各項工作的為大規模之戰爭不明近代戰爭性所致要之各項工作的於戰爭方能事無論何時期戰之勝敗無關何人在前線如亦士之奮勇殺敵在後方為幾百萬工人之餘幾百萬工人之餘續不斷之精神地心身在後方為幾百萬工人之餘幾百萬工人之餘續不斷之戰軌則就比較為宣地身處事物之請求等必增列其之充實以及文字之引證於其事以見民衆對戰事之方力於此戰勝兵一家關係統言之勢甚重要性戰爭與持久戰無異即一一項言每天烘焙數百萬枚以供戰地需要不斷者一萬五千名婦女日夜縫合飲以供戰地前線需要不斷者即不不項所餘數男女擔任之勤務者則不計其數其擔任直接戰爭者以外亦多所餘數男女擔任之勤務者數萬有功於前方誠非淺鮮余數此頃所餘數男女擔任之勤務者數萬有功於前方誠非淺鮮余欲戰一役面盡信

一四　軍官與華工

查我華工隊中之官員考其來源有在吾國傳教之牧師有在吾國營業之商人有歐美軍隊調而來者至於暫待華工以各員性質之優劣及資格不同各區別施性性也以余深知一般軍官對待華工人員皆有之以人道待之與一般軍官實格亦有之以余深知一般軍官對待諸工人之無顯色待人即多與諸工人訓話時始終不忘彼等命其言其受彼鞠雖聞而有英政府特先派官員共約十餘人內面有一軍中生長吾國善探傳教以宗優委養華藝皮對待工人大漠不忍耐者一名一名有一軍官生長吾國善探傳教以宗優委養華藝皮對待工人大漠不忍耐者一名一名有一軍官生長吾國善探傳教以宗優委養華藝皮對待工人大漠不忍耐者一名一名另有一名馬太斯（Matheus）者余自英軍中見喚多另英政府特先派官員共約十餘人內面命其任服務於華工隊以宗優委養華藝皮對待工人大漠不忍耐者一名一名此人毫無怪異發現此人毫無怪異發現此人毫無怪異發現此人毫無怪異發現殊求受高等教育使然歟余留有良命但至翌日置膽虔祝見到被殊發現此人毫無怪異發現殊求受高等教育使然歟余留有良報告隊長使其了悟優委養華藝皮對待工人大漠不忍耐者必命但至翌日置膽虔祝見到被殊發現此人毫無怪異發現殊求受高等教育使然歟余留有良

顧杏卿著《歐戰工作回憶錄》

Reminiscences on My Work during European War by Gu Xingqing.

一六 死裏逃生

余隊在法工作約有三載然並未常駐一地各地調動頻先後有之多受遷調之原因有時因處境危險工人自動要求避居他處有時因敵人猛衝而後退不得不遷徒後方以避危險每次遷營命令一到立即出發並且命令之發出無分晝夜往返及一九一八年三月某晚因句鐘余等正在酣睡忽接軍工團工作處通知程夜間隊出發乘軍用小火車向後方遷避時敵人行攻甚急不容坚然每次團事不必用之衛生隊將全營清潔後面列隊開拔英人之甚重視清潔與戰備之精神亦由此可見一班

余隊離往在戰線後方工作但距離前線僅有數英里之遙故敵砲彈轟炸之危險隨時可以發生為令回憶前情猶覺不寒而慄

某日余隊駐在此地時正與同事戚君步雲暢話國事忽聞頂穿下砲彈碎片者干始知德軍用大砲轟擊其時又借助中有難民夫婦二人及小兒（一年約四五歲）一年約十二三歲）被砲彈傷重不治而死余等深為戰時工作而不幸已而留此但君等向何最隱佳之處乃法語言語彼夫婦工人不諳為何亦能脫險

又聞大砲轟炸附近比國民家地窖中有難民夫婦二人及小兒（一年約四五歲）一年約十二三歲）被砲彈傷重不治而死余等深為戰時工作而不幸已而留此但君等向何最隱佳之處乃法語答彼夫婦工人不諳言語彼夫婦工人不諳為何亦能脫險

此時期危亂點甚有記載因一二六關北之戰復某月余隊俯聽此地附近有德國火車站所為第一聲中箭敵均不時來於所能想像萬一某夕開始在余隊當彼地生活時大如皋桌食物時來拉彈故此每夜余被驚醒數次日開聞正舊余在余隊過身之後園梅克在地中營時項稱此二夫人如大火如皋桌食物如大桌深上面裏以蛾蟲必當下力勇動彈不得不安頓此余隊下所給余寒熱之病嗣於下列當時隊長梅克在倫（Nice Ffiane）為主教徒陣風因此罷動彈不得不安頓處余隊下所給余寒熱之病余處慰問余將生實萬寫彈炸力之大此種炸彈體積其大亦有於當時余隊所安頓處如皋桌深上面裏以蛾蟲必當下力勇動彈不得不安頓此余隊下所給余寒熱之病嗣於下列

二四 休戰日之狂歡

一日午前十一句鐘余發任在歐戰與歐唱聲兩時並往 Rouen 油廠工作之時忽聞教堂鐘聲工廠汽笛聲以及廠外獻呼聲與歐唱聲兩時並起不知敵人業已簽訂休戰條約戰事從此可以終止矣此何日也即余永久不忘之一九一八年十一月十一日也是日各地戰事竟一律停止余送聚七點鐘為即出外遊一起巴地街皆日人山人海男女老幼軍工人種混雜一起互相擁抱親吻歐洲戰情況造行至街市間已人山人海男女老幼軍工人種混雜一起互相擁抱親吻歐洲戰情況造行至街市間已人山人海男女老幼軍工人種混雜一起互相擁抱親吻歐洲戰情況造行至街市間已人山人海男女老幼軍工人種混雜一起互相擁抱親吻歐洲戰情況造行至街市間已人山人海男女老幼軍工人種混雜一起互相擁抱親吻歐洲戰情況

二五 德國致敗之由

歐戰日一九一四年八月初爆發後直至一九一八年十一月十一日始告休戰計四年零三月之久在此長久時期中德國始終未被擊敗至於一兵一卒侵入其大批殺殺德國之本土故在法比南國境內是德國之兵甚實軍事上之失敗乃外交上以及其他方面之種種錯誤因而戰略失敗全

比利時於一九一四年八月內即強佔領比國全部其意雖欲威嚇法國一月之內即佔領巴黎然則德國雖必不致加入戰團而勸阻比利手可得也此雖比國意與小國德國之威脅而全國上下一致抗拒絕力抵抗實出德國意料之外此雖比國雖於一星期內全佔領比國雖於在此短短七日內予英法兩國益致敗力預備從容渡此不辭犧牲抗絕假設實為聯軍勝利之第一功也

顧杏卿著《歐戰工作回憶錄》
Reminiscences on My Work during European War by Gu Xingqing.

顾杏卿手稿

The manuscript of Gu Xinqing.

前　言

本书出版的是"小人物"的"大历史"。

2018年11月11日，在法国巴黎举行的第一次世界大战停战100周年纪念仪式上，一位华裔女生用中文朗读了一段记录停战日当天欢庆场景的日记，引发极大关注："忽闻教堂钟声、工厂汽笛声，以及厂外欢呼声与歌唱声同时并作，余辈惊问何故？始知敌人业已签订休战条约，战事从此可以终止矣！此何日也？即余永久不忘之一九一八年十一月十一日也……"日记作者是时年25岁的中国人顾杏卿，他是一战期间英法在华招募的华工翻译之一。1936年，顾杏卿的《欧战工作回忆录》由商务印书馆发行，是公开出版的第一本一战华工亲历者记述，也是现今所知为数不多的华工文字遗存之一。

一战期间，英法两国在中国招募14万劳工赴欧洲西线战场，其中约8万为山东人。他们在残酷的战场上从事搬运武器、制造枪械、修筑工事、挖掘战壕、清理战场等艰辛繁重的后勤保障服务工作，用苦力和牺牲为一战的提早结束和战后家园重建做出了贡献，但这段历史在很长时间内却被忽视和遗忘。

近年来，随着中国国际地位的提高以及相关研究的深入，一战华工的作用与贡献逐渐得到更多的关注。作为8万华工的家乡人，我们走访华工后裔，打捞有关华工的史海遗珠，推动一战华工历史研究，在海内

华工日记
Chinese Labourer's Diaries

外举办史料图片展览。越来越多华工史料遗存被发现，特别是华工孙干、马春苓、蒋镜海百年前的日记手稿，记录了华工招募、远渡重洋、战地劳作、战后遣返的全过程及其家国情怀，揭示了战争的残酷和人们对和平美好生活的向往，帮助我们进一步还原一战华工这段"被遗忘"的历史，是我们了解一战华工和一战华工历史的"金钥匙"，也为研究中国与一战的历史添补了宝贵的文物素材和历史佐证。

为铭记华工历史，缅怀华工贡献，我们编辑出版这本中英文对照的华工日记。希望以此启迪后人，铭记历史，珍视和平，共襄发展！

前 言
Foreword

Foreword

This book is about the "big history" of "little people".

On the 100th anniversary of the armistice of the First World War on 11 November 2018 in Paris, France, a diary recited by a Chinese girl that recorded people's celebrations on the day when the armistice was signed in 1918 attracted great attention. It read as follows: "All of a sudden, we heard the sound of church bells, factory sirens, cheers and singing outside the factory. Greatly surprised, we asked each other what had happened. Only then did we learn that the enemy had signed the armistice agreement and the war was finally over! What was the date? It was 11 November 1918, a date I would never forget...." The diary was written by 25-year-old Gu Xingqing, one of the Chinese interpreters recruited by Britain and France in China during the First World War. His book *Reminiscences on My Work during European War* was published by the Commercial Press in 1936. It is the first publication recording Chinese labourers' experiences during WWI and also one of the few existing works by Chinese labourers during this period.

During the First World War, 140,000 Chinese labourers, among which about 80,000 were from Shandong Province, were recruited by Britain and France to work on the battlefields of the western front in Europe. They

华工日记
Chinese Labourer's Diaries

engaged in various hard jobs of logistical support services in brutal battlefields such as carrying weapons, manufacturing firearms, building defense works, digging trenches, and clearing battlefields. With their hard work and sacrifice, they made great contributions to the end of WWI and the post-war home reconstruction. However, this history has been ignored and almost forgotten for a long time.

The role and contributions of Chinese labourers in WWI have come to receive due attention in recent years with the improvement China's international status and the deepening of relevant research. To promote the research on the history of Chinese labourers in WWI, we, as town fellows of the 80,000 labourers, endeavour to discover the neglected historical relics by interviewing many of their descendants and holding exhibitions of historical materials and pictures at home and abroad. More and more historical items of Chinese labourers in WWI have been found, especially the manuscripts of diaries written by Sun Gan, Ma Chunling and Jiang Jinghai, which recorded the whole process of Chinese labourers' recruitment, across-ocean travel, battlefield work, and post-war repatriation as well as their feelings about home and country. These manuscripts also revealed the cruelty of war, expressed people's yearning for a peaceful and happy life, and helped us to restore the "forgotten" history of Chinese labourers in WWI. They are not only the golden key for us to understand the Chinese labourers and their history during WWI, but they can also provide precious cultural relics and historical evidence for the study of the history of China and WWI.

To remember the history of the Chinese labourers and cherish the memory of their contributions during WWI, we publish this Chinese-English book of *Chinese Labourer's Diaries*, in the hope that our future generations can remember history, cherish peace, and work together for better developments.

目 录

孙干：欧战华工记　　　　　　　　　　　　　1
马春苓：游欧杂志　　　　　　　　　　　　379
顾杏卿：欧战工作回忆录　　　　　　　　　437
蒋镜海：旅欧文集（摘要）　　　　　　　　551

附　录
回忆祖父蒋镜海　　　　　　　　　　　　　599
我的爷爷是一战华工　　　　　　　　　　　605

后　记　　　　　　　　　　　　　　　　　615

华工日记
Chinese Labourer's Diaries

Contents

Records of Chinese Labourers in European War by Sun Gan   1

Miscellaneous Records of Travel to Europe by Ma Chunling   379

Reminiscences on My Work during European War by Gu Xingqing   437

Collected Works on Travel to Europe (Abstracts) by Jiang Jinghai   551

Appendix

Recollections of My Grandfather Jiang Jinghai   600

My Grandfather Was a Chinese Labourer in WWI   608

Afterword   616

孙干：欧战华工记

Records of Chinese Labourers in European War
by Sun Gan

华工日记
Chinese Labourer's Diaries

孙干，1882年生，山东省淄博市博山区和尚坊村人，自幼接受传统教育，1916年于山东师范讲习所毕业后，任博山县武庙小学教员。19世纪末20世纪初，西风东渐，志士仁人皆求新求变，孙干亦被先进思潮所吸引，渴望有朝一日能亲临欧洲学习西方教育理念。1917年，英国"华工招募处"沿着胶济铁路线设招工点，孙干认为这是出国考察的绝好机会，不顾战争危险，毅然决定应募。1917年9月9日，孙干怀着考察西方教育和周游世界的梦想，从青岛码头乘船启程，奔赴欧洲西线战场。

在华工队伍里，孙干文化程度高，又有一定的组织能力，不久就当上了小队长。当时的华工队伍，人员参差不齐，大多数是目不识丁的农民，他们在劳作之余，常以聚众赌博为乐。为遏制这种恶习，孙干自发在华工群体中以各种形式宣传赌博的危害，告诫华工远离赌博，勉励华工多学习，增长见闻，日后报效祖国。孙干还被时任中国基督教青年会干事张翕如邀请担任基督教青年会教师，一起为华工开设汉文班、英文班、算术班等，充实华工业余生活。为了考察国外教育，孙干在艰苦和繁重的劳作之余，常常深入法国当地学校考察学习。法国的乡村教育模式对孙干产生极大影响，促使他萌生了回国办学的强烈愿望。在欧期间，孙干根据所见所闻写下的《欧战华工笔记》《世界大战战场见闻记》两本日记，共计8万多字，真实记述了一战的惨烈、华工的艰辛、东西方文化的冲突以及对祖国前途命运的思考。

1920年1月6日，孙干回归故里，复职教学工作，并与夫人在家乡和尚坊村创办乡村女子学校，后又在博山考院小学、博山矿业小学、博山进德小学多所学校任教。孙干时常向学生介绍他在欧洲的所见所闻，将其在欧洲带回的头盔、防毒面具等物品作为教学用具，甚至自己动手制作飞机模型，鼓励学生努力学习，为国家富强贡献力量。此外，他还向乡民传播新文化、启迪新思想。孙干在家乡享有极高的威望，和尚坊的村碑写有"此乃博山知名人士孙干之故里"。

孙干：欧战华工记
Records of Chinese Labourers in European War by Sun Gan

新中国成立后，孙干当选山东省淄博市博山区第一届人民代表大会代表，淄博市第二、三届人民代表大会代表，还担任过第一、二届淄博市政协委员、常务委员。

Sun Gan was born in 1882 in Heshangfang Village, Boshan District, Zibo, Shandong Province. He received a traditional education during his childhood. After graduating from Shandong Teachers Training Institute in 1916, he worked as a teacher in Wumiao Primary School in Boshan County. At that time, people with high ideals began to seek change and innovation as many Western thoughts came to China at the end of the 19th and early 20th century. Attracted by the advanced ideas of the West, Sun Gan also longed to travel to Europe and learn more about the Western ideas on education. When the British "Recruitment Bureau of Chinese Labourers" set up a recruitment office along the Qingdao-Jinan railway in 1917, Sun Gan thought it would be a great opportunity to study abroad and decided to apply for the recruitment regardless of the danger of war. With his dream of studying the Western education and travelling around the world, Sun Gan set sail from Qingdao wharf to the battlefields in the western front of Europe on 9 September 1917.

For his better education and organising ability, Sun Gan was soon selected as a team leader among the Chinese labourers. Because the majority of Chinese labourers were illiterate farmers, they often gathered to gamble in their spare time. To curb the bad habit of gambling, Sun Gan voluntarily publicised the dangers of gambling in various forms among the Chinese labourers. He admonished them to stay away from gambling and encouraged them to learn more things so that they could serve their motherland better in the future with their knowledge. He was also invited by Zhang Xiru, a secretary of the Chinese YMCA at that time, to be a YMCA teacher. Together, they set up classes of

华工日记
Chinese Labourer's Diaries

Chinese, English, arithmetic, and other subjects to enrich the spare time of Chinese labourers. To explore foreign education systems, Sun Gan often went to visit local schools in France after completing his hard work in the daytime. Greatly influenced by the educational modes of rural schools in France, he got a strong desire to run a school when returning to China. During his stay in Europe, Sun Gan wrote *Notes on Chinese Labourers in European War* and *Battlefield Sketches of World War*, two diaries with a total of more than 80,000 words, recording the cruelty of the First World War, the hardships of Chinese labourers, the clashes between Eastern and Western cultures, and his reflections on the future and fate of China.

After returning to his hometown on 6 January 1920, Sun Gan resumed his teaching work and, together with his wife, established the Rural Girls School in Heshangfang Village. Later, he also taught in Kaoyuan Primary School, Kuangye Primary School and Jinde Primary School in Boshan successively. In his teaching he often introduced what he had seen and heard in Europe, using the helmets, gas masks and other items he had brought back from Europe as teaching aids. He even made his own aeroplane models on his own in an attempt to encourage his students to work hard and make contributions to the strength and prosperity of their country. He also actively spread new cultures and edified new ideas to the villagers around. Sun Gan enjoyed such high prestige that on the village monument of Heshangfang Village were engraved words "hometown of Boshan celebrity Sun Gan".

After the founding of the People's Republic of China, Sun Gan was elected as a representative of the first People's Congress in Boshan District, Zibo, Shandong Province, and a representative of the second and third People's Congress of Zibo, as well as a member and standing member of the first and second Zibo Chinese People's Political Consultative Conference (CPPCC).

孙干：欧战华工记
Records of Chinese Labourers in European War by Sun Gan

1. 思想之嚆矢

余自学校肄业后，因家境窘甚，大兄复业入课书院于济南，二兄、四弟均就商在外，自己在家不得不暂就农业，借奉高堂。暇尝看《西游记》以作消遣，其中一语云："鱼生三日，游遍江湖。"余心亦恻然动，想到："人生三日，应游遍五洲也。"自此游历全球之念，无时或忘。更加近数年来，政府对于招考留学生送至外洋去求学者，欧美各国无论。最近之往日本者，多至数千人。迨清光绪念八年，余大兄又赴日本，间接研究西洋各种科学。余游欧美之心，因之亦益坚决矣。

First Thoughts of Travelling Abroad

I was born into a poor family. When I finished my studies in high school, I had to stay at home and help my parents to do some work in the field because my eldest brother had just resumed his studies in an academy in Jinan and my two other brothers had left home to do business. In my spare time I often read *Journey to the West* for amusement. One day, I read a sentence that "A fish can travel all over the rivers and lakes within three days after its birth". It touched me deeply and it was at that time that I first had the impulse to "travel all over the world during my lifetime". From then on, the thought of travelling around the world took root in my mind. Later, the government began to recruit students and send them to countries in Europe and America for further study.

Many people had already been sent to Japan in the past few years. In 1902, the 28th year of the reign of Guangxu in the Qing Dynasty, my eldest brother also went to Japan to study Western science and technology. All these reinforced my determination to travel to America and European countries in the future.

2. 欧美游历心之迫切

迨民国建立以后，余思国家兴亡，匹夫有责，革命诸先烈，效命于前，吾当追随其后。正思念之际，忽闻县政府奉令招考单级养成分所学员。及至投考，幸被录取，半年毕业，名列第二。所习功课多效西洋，余对美风欧雨已具若醉若狂之状态。尤以非身莅其境，以观察之，不足以明其教育之真谛也。

Burning Desire to Travel to America and Europe

After the establishment of the Republic of China, I thought that since each of us was responsible for the fate of our nation, I should follow the example of those revolutionary martyrs who had devoted their lives to the cause of the revolution. Just as I was thinking of doing something, the news came to me that Sun Yatsen's Government was recruiting students for the single-level teacher training substation. I applied and was fortunately admitted as a candidate. I studied there for six months and graduated as a top student with the second place in academic performance. As most of the courses I studied there followed

孙干：欧战华工记
Records of Chinese Labourers in European War by Sun Gan

those taught in schools of Western countries, I became more and more obsessed with Europe and America. We could not well understand the truth and essence of their education unless we could observe their education in person by being in those countries.

3. 欧美游历之机会

民国二年，因房次庚老师之介绍，应上台庄小学教员之聘。越一年，适山东省教育会附设之师范讲习所招生。余经县劝学所所长王君采如考送至省时，欧战已起。及民国五年毕业返里时，欧战之协约国英国已感觉其战士劳瘁不堪，而与吾国联合，欲吾国亦加入战团，并准英国来我国招募华工，航送战场，作工以助。尔时吾国执政者，为段祺瑞先生，亦极端主张加入协约国，并准英国在华招工。

时余已被模范小学校赵春农君聘至武庙，当初级主任教员。屡见英人张贴招募工人之章程，欲投笔应募工者屡次，反因余父母之年俱近七秩，兄弟又多在外，无人侍养，于是迟迟而又秘密。卒至民国六年六月，英人之招募愈急，余欲代国家出而帮忙英国之意已定。遂于本月念四日，由学校托故，毅然决然而行。乘车到周村，下榻英国招工局以旁之某店中，预谋从事应募矣。

Opportunity of Travelling to Europe and America

With the introduction of my teacher Fang Cigeng, I began to teach in

华工日记

Chinese Labourer's Diaries

Shangtai Primary School in 1913, the second year of the Republic of China. After teaching there for over a year, I was recommended to the Teacher Training Institute affiliated to Shandong Provincial Education Association by Wang Cairu, the director of the Department of Education in my county. At that time, the European War had already broken out. By 1917, the fifth year of the Republic of China, when I returned to my hometown after graduation from the Teachers Training Institute, the war-torn Britain, one of the Triple Entente nations of the European War, had formed an alliance with our country. According to the alliance, China joined the fighting forces of the European War and Britain was permitted to recruit labourers in our country and send them to work in European battlefields. Duan Qirui, the ruler of our Chinese government at that time, strongly advocated China's joining the Triple Entente, and given Britain the permission to recruit labourers in China.

At that time, I was already a junior head teacher in Wumiao Model Primary School at the invitation of Mr. Zhao Chunnong. When seeing the recruiting notice, I came up with the idea of giving up teaching to become a labourer in the European battlefields. However, considering my parents, who were already in their late sixties and needed my care because all my brothers had left home, I had to postpone my secret recruitment. Till June of 1917, with the call for Britain's recruitment of labourers becoming more urgent, I finally made up my mind to help Britain on behalf of our country. So I asked for leave from the school and left resolutely for Zhoucun by train on 24 June 1917. On arrival, I stayed in a small hotel next to the British Recruitment Bureau and made full preparations for my recruitment.

孙干：欧战华工记
Records of Chinese Labourers in European War by Sun Gan

4. 周村招工局首次应募之经过

当余赴周村英国招工局应募时，适值余四弟在家，即同乘火车往。甫下车，即见车站附近，大街小巷，行者坐者，谈者卧者，颇形拥挤。既至旅店，细问始知其人，皆来应募者也。

英人在华所设之招工局，分总局与分局。总局在山东沧口，其余烟台、坊子、周村、济南皆设分局。总局司定详细合同，及管衣食住宿，并编制工程队，天天加以徒手操之训练。工人入局出入不能自由，惟训练徒手操外，有传耶稣道者可随便听道而已。

First Experience at Zhoucun Recruitment Bureau

When I left for the British Recruitment Bureau, my younger brother happened to be at home. So we left together for Zhoucun by train. The moment we got off the train we found that the streets and alleys nearby the railway station were crowded with people who were either walking or talking, either sitting or lying. Later, when we arrived at the hotel, we knew from the mouth of the hotel keeper that all these people came for labourer recruitment.

The head office of the British Recruitment Bureau in China was located in Cangkou, Shandong Province, while its branch offices scattered in Yantai, Fangzi, Zhoucun and Jinan. The head office was responsible for formulating detailed contracts, providing clothing, food and accommodation, organising engineering brigades, and training labourers with free-standing exercises every day. Once recruited, labourers were not allowed to get in or out of the bureau freely, but they could listen to the sermons given by Christian missionaries when they finished their drilling of free-standing exercises.

5. 局长挑选应募之工人

周村之分局不独不能司工人应募之合同,即衣服、训练等概一不管。其办招工之手续,亦分初步(初步不用言语,只用木签)与第二步(用言语讯问)。初步为凡欲应募之工人,令都早到火车站东一空旷场内,排为长行而站立。排齐后,以待局长率其伙计,挟木签多根而至。从排此端,挨个观察,适一入选者,即给一木棒,且看且挑、且挑且走,以至彼端。各行挑毕后,即令未得木棒者各还家。凡持木棒者均跟随入局,再经局内之人,从第二步手续讯问。当工人甫入局,问即着其按先后排队,从头至尾,一一审问其姓名、年龄、籍贯、职业等,书写于草合同簿及按手印。倘有应对不适之处,立即令出,仍不能入选也。

余当日到周村探明应募手续,本日已晚。翌日晨,余亦早起到车站东,厮入工人队内,伫立以待。须臾,工局局长率挟木签者至,从排首逐一察看,被选者约六十余人,竟不耳余,余心顿觉怃然。及旷场内手续完毕后,凡入选者均随局长蜂拥而入招工局。余思之再三,而亦随之而入,视其办理手续。俟完毕后,始出局而归旅店。

孙干：欧战华工记
Records of Chinese Labourers in European War by Sun Gan

Director's Selection of Applicants

Without the right to sign recruitment contracts, the Zhoucun branch office did not take charge of such affairs as clothing and training. Its recruiting procedure consisted of two steps: the preliminary step (with pegwood rather than language) and the second step (inquiry with language). In the early morning, all applicants were asked to stand in line in an open field on the east side of the railway station. The selection began when the branch director and his attendants with pieces of pegwood arrived. The director observed the applicants one by one from one end of the line and gave pieces of pegwooden to those who met his requirements. In this way, all those qualified applicants were picked out as he walked along the line from one end to the other. While those failed applicants were asked to return to their respective homes, those applicants with pegwood in their hands followed the director into the bureau for the second step: being interviewed by people inside the bureau. They were asked about their names, ages, birthplaces and occupations and all the information was recorded in the draft contracts that were fingerprinted by them. If there was something improper in their answers, they were ordered to get out immediately, meaning that they failed in the second step.

When I learned about the recruitment procedures on my arrival at Zhoucun, it was already very late. The next morning, I got up early and went to the open field on the east of the railway station, standing in the line of applicants and waiting for the selection. A few minutes later, the director and his attendants with pegwooden arrived and began to inspect people in the line one by one. More than 60 people were picked out whereas I failed to be selected. Disappointed, I watched all the selected applicants flock into the bureau after the director and his attendants as soon as the preliminary procedure was over. After thinking for a while, I followed them in to see what formalities they would go through. I did not return to the hotel until all was completed in the bureau.

6. 虽落选，心终未死

余翌日复往挑选旷场，伫立队中等候，及至挑毕，仍未被挑。俟人尽散去后，又入招工局观察其办理一切手续。是日，被选者草合同书写完竣，余乃到主事者之前曰："余亦愿赴法，为协约国英人帮忙。"彼答曰："现招送欧之工人，皆系身体强壮，能推车、担担作苦工者，汝之身体孱弱，如此焉能作苦工也？"余即应之曰："无论推车、担担，即再苦加倍之工，余亦能作。"彼又曰："以前所招之工人送往欧洲者，现有来信云：'现在赴欧做工危险万分，懊悔无及。'即最近所招已入局之工人中，其家中亦有持钱来赎者。汝勿以为吾不愿汝去，吾恐汝真去后，在外水土不服，生长疾病，不得归来也。"余又答曰："余之身体，素日异常健壮，乞先生毋庸过虑。谢谢费心。"于是，彼即慨然应允，执笔将余姓名、年龄、籍贯等书于草合同簿，然后加盖大拇指印。

彼书名事毕，则曰："凡验中者，均须住于此处，有出外自由找宿者，听，每人每日只发给馒头六个。再隔一日，第三日早八点钟，各人只穿单衣一身，齐集车站，等由济往东车来时，一齐坐火车赴沧口。"余听罢乃出局而回旅店。

孙干：欧战华工记
Records of Chinese Labourers in European War by Sun Gan

Persistent Aspiration to Go Abroad

Early the next morning I went to the open field and waited in the line for selection again. Unfortunately, I was still not selected this time. When people left, I followed into the recruitment bureau again to see how the selected people went through the formalities. When all the selected ones had signed their contracts, I went forward to the person in charge and said, "I also want to go to France and do something for Britain and their allied countries!" On hearing my words, he said, "All the labourers we are recruiting are those who are strong enough to do hard manual work such as pushing carts or carrying heavy equipment. But you look so weak. How can you do any hard labour?" I answered immediately, "I can push carts and carry things. Whatever hard work there is, I can do it." He then said, "Among the previously recruited people that we have sent to Europe, some have sent letters home saying, 'it is extremely dangerous working in Europe, but it is too late for regret.' Even among the recently recruited people, some are ransomed by their families with money. It is not that I would not like you to go but that you might not become accustomed to the life there and fall ill, unable to come back home again." I responded again quickly, "Thank you, but there is no need to worry about that. I have been extraordinarily healthy and strong all the time." Thus, he consented to my request, wrote down my personal information such as my name, age and place of birth on the draft contract, then sealed it with my thumbprint.

After the contract was signed, he said to me, "All the recruited people should live here. Only a few can find their own accommodation should leave. Now listen carefully: every day we give only six steamed buns to each person. We'll all gather at the railway station at 8 o'clock on the day after tomorrow, each with a single unpadded garment. When the eastbound train from Jinan pulled in, we'll get it on and going to Cangkou." After the announcement, I left the recruitment bureau for the hotel.

7. 由周村乘车到沧口招工局

六月廿七日，着余四弟由周村带余一切衣物还博山。余于翌日早到车站候车，来既至，见同伴约百余人。当时大雨沛然，个个遍身淋沥，登车后雨始少杀。到沧口日已暮，宿局外一大厦中。及晚，局中食之以米饭、咸菜，并云翌日始正式检验。

Leaving Zhoucun for Cangkou Recruitment Bureau

On 27 June, I asked my younger brother to take all my spare clothes back to Boshan from Zhoucun. On the next day, I went to the railway station in the early morning. When I arrived there, I found there were already over one hundred people waiting for the train. It rained heavily and we were all soaked through to the skin. It did not stop raining until we boarded the train. When we arrived at Cangkou, it was already dark, and we lodged in a building outside the recruitment bureau. For supper we were given rice and pickles and we were told that the official examination would begin the next day.

孙干：欧战华工记
Records of Chinese Labourers in European War by Sun Gan

8. 沧口招工局应募检验之经过

沧口总局总办以下职员甚夥，中英人兼用为医生也、书记也、量高也、称重也、书姓名也、书号头也、砸手镯也、编排也、检理洗澡也、司厨也、剪发也，一切应用之物，无不俱备，而一切办事之人亦俱有专责。检验时，有大厦数间，只留二门一出一入。工人由入门鱼贯而入，经过职员书写合同一切手续而出，遂易新衣，编排为工程队矣。

Examination Process in Cangkou Recruitment Bureau

In the executive office of Cangkou General Recruitment Bureau, there were a great many both Chinese and British clerks serving as doctors and secretaries or taking charge of weighing and measuring, writing down names and numbers, putting bracelets on labourers, making arrangements, checking for baths, cutting hair, cooking meals and every other kind of necessary activity. All daily necessities were available here and each staff member had his own responsibilities. The examination was made in a building with several rooms. But only two doors were left open, one for entrance and the other for exit. Labourers filed into the entrance to go through the formalities and left through the exit as members of the engineering brigades of the Chinese Labour Corps with new clothes on after signing the contracts.

华工日记
Chinese Labourer's Diaries

9.

余之被检验时,初由大厦出,即到一小门前,见有多人相待。及至入门,闻传令将各人所着之单衣脱去。余既脱衣,医生着手检验,并问答如眼也、口也、皮肤也、肺脏也、肛门也、阳物也,一一详看,并问诘有无宿病,余以真诚无病以对。彼则令再由此内入,先到剪发房剪发,复到澡塘洗澡,以后始入大厦经司量高处量高,司称重处称重,问姓处报姓,问名处记名,问兄问弟、问姊问妹、问父母妻子等,及年龄、职业无不详详细细,书之于合同之上,然后按以大拇指印。至合同事书写完毕,最后将出门时,并将其所预备之上书六万三千四百八十四号之铜镯,砸于余之手腕上。然后出后门,穿新工人衣,而又编制为一百零二队第三排第一棚矣。

When it was my turn to be examined, I got out of the building at first and went to a small door many people were waiting. After entering the door, I was told to remove my single-layered garment. I followed the order and took off all my clothes. Then a doctor gave me a physical examination whilst asking questions about my health. He carefully checked many of my organs such as my eyes, my mouth, my skin, my lungs, my anus, and my penis. He also asked me about my medical history, asking whether I had suffered from any diseases. I told him frankly that I had never had any disease. I was then instructed to go inside to the next room to have my hair cut and take a bath in the common bathing pool. Upon completion of all these, I was directed into the building to get my weight and height measured, and to confirm and write down my name. I was also asked in detail about my family, including my parents, my brothers and sisters, my wife, and their respective ages and professions. All the information was recorded in the contract, which was then impressed with my thumbprint. When the contract had been completed and I was about to get out of the building, a copper bracelet with the number 63484 was fastened onto my wrist. Then I left the building through the exit door, put on my new uniform and was allocated into Tent 1, Row 3, of Brigade 102.

10.

余在沧口报名入局等手续办妥后，知英人办事井井有条。驻沧口念余日，天天除米饭两餐菜为青鱼与咸菜外，并发给铜元六枚。所给铺盖惟每人线毯一床，每日所事即学徒手操。至临开船之日，每人又发给各人之合同及大洋二十元，以备船上零用。此后余书家信一封以慰高堂。

Having gone through all the procedures of registration in Cangkou, I knew that the British did things in a well organised way. We stayed in Cangkou for over 20 days. Every day we were given six copper coins besides two meals of rice, fish and pickles. Each of us was also given a cotton blanket for the bedding. We did nothing but learning the new physical exercises. On the day we got aboard the ship, we were given our own contracts and 20 silver dollars each to cover any expenses on the ship.

17

华工日记
Chinese Labourer's Diaries

11. 开船出东海及过日本津清海峡

七月念三日，忽闻英国送工人之专船已到青岛靠岸等候，午后英人率众工人遂乘车到青岛大码头。先每人领到棉衣服及被褥包一个，然后登船。既上船，一入门即每人领太平带一条以备不虞。当晚开船后，余即口占俚句如下：

一离青岛四无山，绿浪白花远连天。
同伴千余相欢呼，共祝前途康且安。

余从未习诗，平仄韵字，均属茫然，特触景情生，任口读去，聊以破闷耳。

第一夜，船在东海颠簸亦甚，余默想自己性命如能平安到欧，惟赖神灵默佑耳，默祷者再三。明日早饭为大米，菜为猪肉与白糖。吃饭后到舱外远眺，海中石峰矗立，上戴茂草，罗列于海中者，数见不鲜。惟北望则高丽之岗峦纠纷，极高处竖有高杆数见，至天晚又口占俚句如下：

绿波一片水漫漫，海上风云近日边。
五百童男女不见，疑其桃园已为仙。

孙干：欧战华工记
Records of Chinese Labourers in European War by Sun Gan

Sailing Out of East China Sea and Passing by Tsugaru Strait of Japan

On 23 July, news came that the British transport ship for Chinese labourers had already pulled in to shore in Qingdao. So on that afternoon, the British officers led all the labourers to the large wharf of Qingdao where each of us received cotton clothes and a bedding pack before boarding the ship. As soon as we got onboard, each of us received a lifebelt in case of emergency. When the ship set sail that evening, I composed an impromptu poem.

> Together with Qingdao the mountains are in view no more,
> Green waves and white foams are what our eyes reach all.
> Over a thousand of companions onboard hailed loud and long,
> Wishing a safe and sound voyage to all the passengers young.

I had never learned poetry composition and had no idea about the rhyme. Inspired by the vastness of the sea, I just blurted out whatever came into my mind to drive the boredom away.

On the first night, the ship bumped along on the East China Sea. Thinking to myself that whether or not we could safely arrive in Europe depends on the blessings of God, I prayed in silence again and again. Our breakfast the next day included rice, pork and white sugar. After breakfast I went out of the cabin and looked far into the distance. I found that in the sea scattered numerous standing peaks covered with lush weeds. Only when I looked far to the north could I see mountains and hills of Korea in the distance, with tall posts on the top of some peaks. In the evening I composed another poem:

Green waves rolled on and on in the vast sea,
Clouds connected with the sun seemed to be.
With not a woman but only five hundred men,
Reclusive immortals might they become then.

12.

在东海中第三天与第四天，船向东北。因风浪较大，人多半晕船，呕吐者甚多，余身亦不适，故只好躺卧舱中耳。

On the third and fourth days on the East China Sea, our ship kept heading northeast. For the large wind and waves, most people onboard got seasick and began throw up. I felt quite uncomfortable too and had to lie in the cabin most of the time.

13.

第五日晨早起，到甲板上，遥遥望见东方缥渺，仿佛山岭重叠。至天将午时，恰好到了日本之津清海峡，两岸苍松翠柏为数甚多，北岸尤盛。海峡之北岸有商埠，岸之附近，海中椿浮灯塔，满目皆是，遥望远山之上，亦有高粱生焉。彼时抒诗一首如下：

孙干：欧战华工记
Records of Chinese Labourers in European War by Sun Gan

七月念八日，夙兴观海洋。
南北山对峙，丛树皆苍苍。
人云至长崎，余心以为妄。
往来划如鹜，东西任飞扬。
波涛与鸥戏，浮椿亦供忙。
太平已不远，秋水共天长。
胆大船犹稳，何畏万里浪。
逢此无限乐，谁肯念家乡。

On the fifth morning, I got up early and went out onto the deck. I saw a hazy outline of mountains in the distance to the east. At around midday we arrived in the Tsugaru Strait of Japan. Large numbers of luxuriant pines and cypresses stood on both banks of the strait, but the north bank seemed to enjoy more exuberance. There was a trading port on the north bank, nearby which one could see buoys and lighthouses in the sea everywhere. Looking into the distance, people could see sorghum crops on the mountains. Inspired by this, I composed a verse as follows:

> On the early morning of twenty-eighth July
> Rose I and observed the ocean with my eye.
> Mountains in north and south opposite stands,
> Lush clusters of trees and bushes cover all lands.
> In Nagasaki they say we are arriving,
> But what a delusion it is I'm thinking.
> Like swimming ducks are boats and ships,
> Coming and going any way the foams whips.
> Surging waves with flying seagulls play,

Up and down float buoys in a busy way.
Not far is awaiting a quiet and peace,
On horizon are water and sky in one piece.
With boldness and stability our ship sails,
Fear of surging waves always fails.
What a good time with infinite gaiety,
Who shall miss hometown in eternity?

14. 过太平洋到加拿大

第六天，已出日本津清海峡，偶见船工急疾，绸缪舱口及一切绳索，殆如巢处者之知风将至也。遂又作诗一首如下：

飞鸟提提如雪白，天光云影共徘徊。
万顷一色明若镜，惟无苍葭红蓼开。

至晚上，官亦发散各种闲书，如《三国》《列国》等等数箱，又有乐器，如锣、鼓、笙、箫等等亦数箱，盖以备工人之在船中消遣以解闷也。至夜间，忽阴风怒号，人多因船行不稳显晕船状，一概加穿棉衣矣。

第七日又抒诗一首如下：

七伏昏昏向奎星，既到水国无蓼逢。
未至一日已膺发，疑是寒带又无冰。

孙干：欧战华工记
Records of Chinese Labourers in European War by Sun Gan

酸风侵人人面白，棉衣有钮钮扣红。

欧人待余真可笑，衷情满腹对谁倾。

Crossing the Pacific Ocean to Canada

On the sixth day, after we had left the Tsugaru Strait of Japan, I noticed by accident that the sailors hurried back and forth, taking precautions at the hatchway by fastening the ropes against storms just as those living in nests had the hunch of coming storms. So again, I composed the following verse:

> Snow white birds flying leisurely in the sky,
> Sunlight and cloud shadows hover together high.
> As a large mirror the waters in view are bright,
> But there are no green reeds or red flowers in sight.

On that evening, several boxes of books for light reading such as *Three Kingdoms* and *Annals of the Kingdoms in the East Zhou Dynasty*, and several boxes of musical instruments such as gongs, drums, *sheng* and *xiao* were distributed for us to while away the time. Later at night, a cold wind began to blow suddenly and the ship began to toss. As a result, most people became seasick again and everyone put on their cotton-padded clothes for warmth.

I composed another verse on the 7th day:

> While sailing northward on gloomy dog days,
> We encountered no knotweed along our ways.

华工日记
Chinese Labourer's Diaries

Freezing cold winds came in less than a day
Did we enter the iceless frigid zone along the way?
Acid winds blew into faces bleached white,
We put on cotton coats with red buttons held tight.
How ridiculously we are treated by Europeans
But nowhere can we tell our heartfelt feelings.

15.

自船入太平洋后，风大而浪高，人多呕吐。余几乎不能进饮食，斯时方知平日在旱地之平安也。至第十二天时，又抒诗一首如下：

开船至此十二天，约行水程万八千。
风激桅杆绳索啸，人疑何处匿猴猿。
只艘颉顽轻若叶，大浪崎岖高如山。
当午日月低已甚，所以令人倍觉寒。

From the moment our ship arrived on the Pacific Ocean, the winds had been strong and the waves high. As a result, many people got seasick again. I was unable to eat and drink almost anything. It was at this time that I realised how much safer it was to live on dry land. On the 12th day, I composed another poem as follows:

Twelve days we've been out on the sea,

孙干：欧战华工记
Records of Chinese Labourers in European War by Sun Gan

With a voyage of about ten thousand *li*.
Against the mast clashed wind and ropes,
Just as sounds from monkeys and apes.
The ship tossed up and down like a leaf in the sky
By waves as huge as mountains we were lifted high.
The sun hangs low in the sky at noon,
We all feel the chill in cold and gloom.

16. 经过太平洋伤叹工人被殴

船自到太平洋中，日夜向东北奔，然非一直前行，总是左偏一程再右偏一程，令人不解其故。半月以后，人皆因呕吐而口中无味，腹又觉饥，所以各人将在沧口所得到之大洋，在船上随意买烟卷、糖果、鱼虾、葱蒜等，花之殆尽。

当是时，余亦尝和山东淄川县西山中河石坞庄同乡李君守顺合伙贩卖黄豆，遍船舱中优游叫卖，且叫且跑，藉是以免去晕船之苦。尔时，见工人中有在船上不守规则，而窃人细物被船主捉住殴打，极为可怜。余回想吾国民之无教育，不第被外国人轻看己也。遂口占俚句如下：

　　　　吾国教育何其衰，官学两界互相猜。
　　　　西席与东鲜接洽，家庭对校多隔阂。
　　　　就吾一般工人看，在内强悍出外呆。
　　　　时常犯规被殴打，吞声忍气不敢哀。

华工日记
Chinese Labourer's Diaries

Sailing through the Pacific Ocean and Lamenting over Labourers Being Beaten

After entering the Pacific Ocean, our ship had sailed fast in the direction of northeast day and night. Rather than following a straight route, it kept deviating to the left and then to the right all the time, which puzzled us all. After two weeks, because of vomiting, people had completely lost their appetite but felt hunger in their stomachs. To alleviate the situation, they bought cigarettes, sweets, fish and shrimps, onions and ginger, with the money they had been given at Cangkou.

At that time, I once sold soybeans in partnership with Li Shoushun, a fellow countryman from the village of Heshiwu, in Zichuan County, Shandong Province. We ran and hawked throughout the cabins, by means of which our seasickness could be alleviated a little bit. While running and selling on the ship, I sometimes saw some poorer labourers were caught and beaten by the ship owners for not obeying the rules and stealing articles from others. This made me think a lot about our countrymen's lack of education, for which they were despised by foreigners. So, I composed another poem as follows:

> So poor our country's education remains,
> No trust between Government and academics.
> With few contacts with countries in west,
> Huge gaps arose in families and schools.
> Our ordinary fellow labourers seem to be,
> Tough at home but slow-witted abroad.

孙干：欧战华工记
Records of Chinese Labourers in European War by Sun Gan

Often as they are beaten for breaking rules,

They dare not complain but just bear insults.

17.

自从青岛开船，东北行至十五日之后，船近北纬五十度之际，天渐晴朗，不同初入太平洋时之霾雨连连。而人人之乘船亦有习惯性，精神渐见恢复，盖因天时地带凉爽之故也。天天除在甲板上按一定时间作徒手操外，非看闲书，即弄些箫、笛。惟余因未得闲书与乐器，独长在舱外闲眺，见海上之天朗气清，水天一色，众鱼跃于海面，白鸥时飞翔于空际，时栖憩于水中，亦万金难买之大观也。

Since departing from Qingdao, we had sailed toward northeast for 15 days. When our ship was approaching 50 degrees north latitude, the weather began to clear up, which was quite different from the continuous rainy days when we first sailed in the Pacific Ocean. During this period, people seemed to have adapted to the life onboard and gradually became high-spirited due to the milder weather. Every day, except for the regular free-standing exercises on the deck, they just read books or played the *xiao* or *sheng*. With no books to read or musical instruments to play, I spent most of my time on deck looking into the distance. The sky over the sea was so clear and bright that it seemed to have been integrated into the water. Fishes jumped out of sea while white gulls flew in the blue sky or perched on the water every now and then. Such a view was a grand and priceless one.

华工日记
Chinese Labourer's Diaries

18.

　　余既天天常到甲板上盘桓优游，有时见海中有大块黑物，飘浮海面，徘徊不定，有时见大鱼成群，比赛跃梁。总觉船不稍停，难得所见者之真为何物，鱼之大者，究竟不知有多大也。乃船上之工人，天天忙于刷洗，盖因所载人众，特别注重卫生也。

　　一日，忽闻上官传令，船快到码头矣，谁愿给家中书回信者，可随便到各人排头处，领取信封与信纸也。各人闻之，莫不欣欣雀跃，盖因苦于晕船者，至众且久之故也。

I often wandered leisurely on the deck every day. Sometimes I saw large black objects floating and lingering on the sea, while at other times I saw schools of fish jumping competitively in front of the ship. However, it was always hard for me to identify them because the ship kept moving all the time. Therefore, I only knew they were big fish but never really knew how big they were. Because of the large number of people onboard, special attention was paid to hygiene, and the labourers on the ship were always busy washing and cleaning every day.

One day, an order from the officer came that our ship was approaching a dock, and that anyone who wanted to write home could go to their respective platoon leaders to get envelopes and writing paper. Everyone jumped with joy because most of us had suffered from seasickness for such a long time.

孙干：欧战华工记
Records of Chinese Labourers in European War by Sun Gan

19. 航海亦用寒暑表

航海所使用之什物不独用经纬镜、航路图、指南针、路程轮、风雨表、救生带、救命圈等，即寒暑表区区之小物，亦时刻不能无也。当民国六年八月中旬，余乘船过太平洋时，船至北纬五十度左右，见船工屡屡将沉于海水中之寒暑表提出察看。余因不解其故而问之，彼曰："船行海中，若距寒代近，不以寒暑表时刻察之，恐遇冰山之来，以触船也。"余始知寒暑表虽区区之小物，亦为航海家所须臾不敢离者也。

Thermometers Used in Navigation

In sea voyages not only such instruments as the sextant, routing charts, route wheel, compass, weather-meter, lifebelt, and lifebuoy, but also even small thermometers are required all the time. When we sailed at about fifty degrees north latitude on the Pacific Ocean in the middle of August 1917, the sixth year of the Republic of China, I noticed the sailors frequently took out the thermometers which had been lowered into the seawater to read and record the temperatures. I was so puzzled that I asked them why they did so. They told me, "When a ship sailing in the ocean is close to the frigid zone, the temperature of sea water should frequently be observed in order to avoid crashing into an iceberg." Till then, I knew that small as the thermometers are, they were indispensable necessities for navigators.

华工日记
Chinese Labourer's Diaries

20.

第十九日,天气清明,无风无浪,饭后人多半在舱外眺望谈天。忽又传令云:"工人们快下船矣。各人所写之家信,速速交来,以备船到码头,即给转送。"于是众人烦人写信之声一时大作。殆因中国工人多系不识字者,不能自写家信故也。竟有一人信内,只写数人之名即代数人之信者。其求人不得,而卒不写者,盖多多也。

On the nineteenth day, it was clear and there was no wind or waves. While most people were gazing at the sky or chatting on the deck after dinner, an order came suddenly: "Attention please. All labourers shall get off the ship soon. Hand in your letters quickly so that they may be delivered promptly as soon as the ship arrives at the wharf." So for a while afterwards, I could hear the voices of people frantically asking others to write letters for them. It was because most of the Chinese labourers were illiterate and unable to write letters on their own. In some letters there were even the names of many people so that they could also stand for their letters. Many people did not write a letter at all because they failed to find someone to write for them.

孙干：欧战华工记
Records of Chinese Labourers in European War by Sun Gan

21. 游维多利亚岛

第二十天早，在船上东望，隐约见山。至傍午，见高山积雪，山高不啻数千尺者。傍晚水平如镜，船至维多利亚岛，众皆下船，在岛上一游。见海湾澄清，鱼游海带之间，历历可数。岛上无甚高山，蔚然茂密者多为灌木。及日落将黑之际，始登船入舱。

第二十一天寅时，船又开往北行，半日见北方尽是崇山峻岭，正北之山巍然独放白光，而无苍翠之色。及日夕，船抵山之附近，始知山无杂树，除山崖之外，亭亭竖立者，尽为已枯之干松柏也。

Visit to Victoria Island

On the morning of the twentieth day, I looked eastward from the ship and could see the faint outline of mountains in the distance. By noon, I saw high mountains covered with snow, which were thousands of feet high. At dusk, the sea became rather quiet and smooth, and our ship arrived at Victoria Island. Everyone disembarked from the ship to take a tour of the island. The water in the Bay was so clean that we could see quite clearly the fish swimming between the kelp. There were no really high mountains on the island, and those that we could see were covered with bushes. We did not get back aboard the ship until it became dark at sunset.

On the twenty-first day, our ship sailed northward again. Half a day later, we saw lots of high mountains and lofty hills in the north, but the majestic mountain in the north due had green colour at all. Only later when our ship sailed nearby this mountain at sunset, did we know that it was because the whole mountain was covered with some dry pines and cypresses except the cliffs.

22. 到加拿大之温古洼

中秋节前一日，下午到温古洼。船进口后，即见商埠在北面山上，电车行人往来如织。口占俚句如下：

中秋滨临加拿大，水平山苍景倍佳。
仰见高山多积雪，转瞬下船温古洼。
大船汽笛威逾虎，洋楼灯盏艳于花。
岸上妇孺摇巾帽，欢迎口中乩喧哗。

Arrival at Vancouver, Canada

On the day before Mid-Autumn Festival, we arrived at Vancouver in the afternoon. After the ship was berthed, I noticed that this commercial port, located on the hill in the north, was very busy with the coming and going of trams and pedestrians. I composed an impromptu poem as follows:

Our ship approached Canada on Mid-Autumn Festival,
Where landscapes of waters and mountains are beautiful.

Admiring the snow atop high mountains that covers,

Very soon we disembarked at Vancouver with others.

Sirens from ships sounded louder than the roar of tigers And lanterns of mansions shine brighter than flowers.

Women and kids on the shore waved hats and scarves,

Shouting words of sincere welcome from their mouths.

23. 交涉入口加拿大及乘火车

中秋节在船上休息一日，盖因工人入口之检查身体、衣物、乘火车之一切手续，至翌日晚始办理妥善。于是按次各背各人衣包下船后，先入关隘之办公室，一一被检验后，当晚登火车开往东行。当夜未阑，则火车转入山谷之中，有时钻深谷，行数折，而复入山下之石穴，有时从山下石穴中钻出，驶于大河之上。当时余以为火车所经之路，危险万分。口占俚句如下：

> 开车沿河（夫拉塞河）溯流行，两岸巉巉皆高峰。
> 仰见高山俯绿水，时穿石洞时腾空。
> 此地森林何所自，养成松柏蔽苍穹。
> 火车站处繁华地，只见农夫数十丁。

Negotiating Entry to Canada and Taking Trains

On the Mid-Autumn Festival, we spent the whole day resting on board awaiting the formal procedures for our entry into Canada to be completed. All the necessary checks and train travel arrangements were not finished until the evening of the next day. We then disembarked from the ship with our clothes and bags on our backs in an orderly fashion and entered the customs office. After being inspected one by one, we boarded an east-bound train that very night. In the early morning, our train descended into a valley. Sometimes it wound in and out of deep valleys, while at other times it entered tunnels below mountains. Occasionally it got out of the tunnels and passed on bridges over rivers. For me, the route of the train was extremely dangerous, so I composed the following poem:

Along the river (Fraser) went the train upstream,

Dangerously steep peaks on both sides.

With mountains above and water below,

It passed out of tunnels and soared high.

From where came the forest of pines and cypresses That grew into a canopy of evergreen against the sky.

A prosperous place the railway station must be,

But only a few dozens of farmers we could see.

24.

自乘加拿大火车，饭食改换好的面包，间或吃大米饭，菜多系鱼与猪、牛等肉。车中之座位也是两用，可拉开坐，亦可推合作在上边卧。

孙干：欧战华工记
Records of Chinese Labourers in European War by Sun Gan

车中两侧并有吊铺，故乘车时十分舒服也。

行三日后，始见车道两旁有果园。至第四日到温尼伯地方，盖此地为自温古洼东来之第一繁华地。故吾侪一到，即有人呼之为已到了天堂焉。中国人在此作工者甚多。又东行两日到苏必略湖滨，见湖中水平若镜，一碧万顷。又东行一日到魁伯克，为加拿大最大之市场。

又东行一日，达加拿大之东岸大商场哈勒法。总观英属加拿大之东西大铁路之行车在西段，有时如蛇钻之穴洞，有时如虎之由穴出而跃梁，又有时如蜂蝶串花枝左右盘旋，莫得一直线。至几里路者，至温尼伯以东，皆经邱陵地带，绝无险峻可言。森林之大，莫可言喻，有时见铁路旁斩伐森林数顷，而仅住农夫一二户，其人烟稀少，可想而知矣。

Since we boarded the Canadian train, our food had changed into good bread and occasionally rice while the dishes were mostly fish, pork or beef. The seats in the train were made for dual purposes. They could be pulled apart for passengers to sit on or pushed together for people to lie on. There were also hammocks on both sides of the compartment, making it very comfortable to ride in the train.

After travelling for three days on the train, I began to see orchards on both sides of the railway. On the fourth day, we arrived at a place named Winnipeg, which was the first prosperous place east of Vancouver. It was acclaimed by some of us a paradise. Many Chinese people worked here. After travelling eastward for another two days, we arrived at the shore of Lake Superior, where the clear water was as smooth as a mirror. After another day of eastbound travel, we arrived at Quebec, the largest market in Canada.

After another day's eastbound travel, we arrived at Halifax, a trading centre on the east coast of Canada. The train we took never travelled in a straight line along the western section of the East-West Railway in British

Canada. Sometimes, it travelled downhill into a tunnel like a snake burrowing through a cave sometimes or upward into the sky like a jumping tiger leaping out of a den. At other times it wound all its way in circles like dancing bees and butterflies. After travelling few miles to the east of Winnipeg, the train passed through a vast area of hilly land without any steep peaks. The forests there were indescribably large and the area so sparsely populated that only one or two households of farmers could be found in the clearings of hectares of forests along the railway.

25. 游欧美所乘最大之船只

自温古洼乘车东行，逾八昼夜，达哈利夫哀凯司。车甫停，上官急亟传令各负包挨次下车。下车行数武，众皆询问何所往。排长对之曰："不可随便他往，先从队长入客栈也。"于是循一户梯盘旋而上，既入则见此客栈之楼房上，尚有街巷数层通，无论街道房间，整洁异常。众工人之房间安排既定，时已下午五点矣。遂即开饭，此次所食之饭，不但米饭好，即所分之菜，较前亦异常美香也。饭后余出住房散步，时见天色已晚，想远游不便，不如以待明天，另邀同知己者三五人，一同到哈勒夫哀凯司街市中一游，以扩眼界，购买点纪念物，较为有趣也。思想至此，遂不游而归矣。

至翌日早起，随人出门一望，四面汪洋，水天一色，遂自惊讶曰："余等昨晚非下榻于哈利夫哀凯司之客栈欤？"他人有答曰："昨晚初下车，即登之楼房，即现在吾等所乘之大船也，此船今夜已离开哈利夫哀凯司百余里矣。"余又继问之曰："何昨晚上此船时，人多不能看出为

孙干：欧战华工记
Records of Chinese Labourers in European War by Sun Gan

船？"彼答曰："哈利夫衷凯司是水旱码头，火车站与登船处紧紧相靠，无空隙之地可见海水，故余等昨晚下车，又接上船而不之觉也。"余听罢始知外国人对于商埠码头之建筑，其严密与便利，诚有出人意外者。昨晚以为住宿客栈之错误，斯时始恍然矣。

Largest Ship Taken by Chinese Labourers to Europe

After eight days of travelling eastward by train from Vancouver, we arrived at Halifax. As soon as the train pulled in, we were ordered by the officers to get off with our baggage. After walking for a while, we asked where we were going. The platoon leader told us, "We shall not go anywhere else. We just follow the Captain to the inn first." So, we went upward following a winding staircase and saw that there were still more alleyways upon the building of this inn. Both the alleys and rooms were very clean and tidy. When all the accommodation arrangements were completed, it was already 5 pm. Then the meal was served. Both the rice and the dishes were more delicious than ever before. After dinner, I went out of my room for a walk. Seeing that it was already too late for a long walk, I thought it would be a better idea to invite three or four of my friends to take a trip around the streets of Halifax tomorrow to broaden our horizons and buy some souvenirs. So I returned to my room without going any further.

The next morning I got up early. When I went out of the room with others, I found we were surrounded by the ocean on all sides. I was surprised and asked, "Did we stay in the inn at Halifax last night?" Someone answered, "The building we ascended into last night when we got off the train is this large ship we are on now and it has left Halifax many miles behind tonight." I then asked, "Why was it that so many of us did not recognise it as a ship when we got on last night?" He answered, "Halifax is a port city where the railway station is so closely connected to the boarding place that there is no space to see the water. Thus, we did not realise that we had boarded the ship immediately after leaving the train." After hearing his words, I learned that the construction of foreign commercial ports and wharfs were so well-conceived and complicated that they were quite beyond our expectations. And till then I realised what a mistake I had made about the inn last night.

26. 是船之伟大

余等之登是船也，见其上有街有巷，来往之人又多，故初不拟为船，盖因当上船时又未看见海水之故也。是船之身阔约三丈左右，长约里许，从底至顶共有十八层，每层高约七尺左右，其中除特别舱与通舱外，游戏场、澡堂、厕所、洗脸房等，其中皆是汉白玉制成。装以自来水、电灯、肥皂、手巾、纸等，应有尽有，其洁净之状，出人意外也。容货仓、官室、医院等等，应有尽有。

Large Size of Ship

When we boarded the ship, we did not notice any sea water around it, only streets and alleys with many people coming or going, so we thought it could not be a ship. The ship was actually about 50 feet wide and 600 feet long. There were 18 decks from top to bottom and each deck was over six feet high. Apart from the officers' quarters and the cabins, there were communal areas, bathhouses, toilets and washrooms, all of which were made of white marbles. Equipped with tap water, electric lights, soaps, towels, paper and other life necessities, the ship was so clean that it was really beyond our expectations. It also had a variety of other facilities such as warehouses, offices, and hospitals.

27. 在海面等候美国之赴法军舰

船在哈利夫哀凯司海湾外等候二日后，有美之军舰一十四艘驶至船之两旁。虽较之是船都小，然观其形式，则威望万分。盖因其船上除将士而外，皆载武器，特惊人者为其黑塔。塔之巨炮，不但伟大而数目又多也。

隔一日军舰均齐，列于余乘之大船左右。余船主亦按人数给太平带一条（亦名救生带），一齐鸣笛向东北开驶。余在船上四望，见军舰左七只，右亦七只，俱颉顽上下，先后不紊。余乘之船虽行，却若不动者，然非如在太平洋时之颠簸也。吾侪在船上，除每日按时作徒手操外，优游而休而已，渡大西洋之安乐竟如是也。

Waiting for American Warships to France at Sea

We waited outside Halifax bay for two days. Then 14 American warships arrived on either side of our ship. Although smaller in size than our ship, they looked very majestic in appearance. There were not only military officers and soldiers but also weapons on these warships. The most impressive weapon was the black tower cannons, whose great number and large size were really amazing.

Another day passed before all the warships were deployed on either side of our ship. Each of us were given a safety belt (also known as lifebelt). Then all the ships whistled to the northeast. When I looked around our ship, I saw seven warships on its left and seven on its right, all sailing forward smoothly and orderly. Although our ship was also moving forward, it moved so smoothly that it seemed to be still and we could not feel any shaking as violent as it was on the Pacific Ocean. Every day, besides the regular free-standing exercises, we had nothing to do but take good rests and enjoy our leisure time. We had never imagine it was such a great pleasure to sail on the Atlantic Ocean.

28. 大西洋船中工人之哭泣

至开船之第六日,九月初三日,上官忽传令曰:"凡工人均站队听上官讲话。"工人皆如令以待。英人三人,一为长官,其二,一持快枪与刺刀,一持一手枪而至。长官曰:"自是之后,务各时刻小心,各人之救生带,务要昼夜紧束于身。无论睡卧,即出恭之时,亦不能解去。因为德人在大西洋海面之潜水艇到处皆是,倘一遇着我们所乘之船,如被潜击,万余人之性命危险万分也。是船之主人,亦有预备诸多小船,挂于大船之外。每营每排之人,各有定座。若果大船不幸遇打击,我们均出而上小船,将小船送下海面,人在小船中即无危险矣。倘人人处处小心,将

孙干：欧战华工记
Records of Chinese Labourers in European War by Sun Gan

各人之太平带紧束，敢保不伤一人也。

"虽然，吾侪最可虑者，倘一遇此船被潜水艇中之人用炮一击，船中之人心一慌，都想快快逃出。然门小人多，争先恐后，彼时将门塞住，不能出入，船中必没秩序，斯时全船人之性命，乃危险立至矣。所以希望你们当排头者，可详细告诉众位弟兄，不但所发给各人之太平带，要时时紧束身上，即吃饭、睡觉，或出或入，人人须按各人号码先后，依次行动。倘万一遇事，即着是等兵士，在各门上监视，何人争先，立即用枪击毙，或用刀杀死。"即万一是船遇击，亦不一定能沉。因为船中诸舱，均有严密之门，并有至死不去之负责兵士看守。纵有三几舱被击破坏，水入一二，尚无大碍。即船舱俱坏，亦须需时四点钟，方能全沉。吾们如按次向外出走，不到一点钟，乘小船平安到海面上，即可完竣。你们自是以后，务要谨守秩序，倘在舱中无事，可常到船之上面，观察海中有无潜水艇。如看得见者，可速速报与船主，果所报真实者，赏洋三百也。"

长官言罢而去。众工人多半面皆失色，吁嗟叹息，放声痛哭者，亦不少也。口占俚句如下：

哈利夫凯司初离岸，人人常戴"救命船"（亦曰太平带）。
西洋鱼大船犹稳，日日直奔国尼兰。
德国潜艇真可惧，合众援艘十余丸。
海水温度无大异，何故身热心里寒。

Labourers' Weeping on the Atlantic Ocean

On 3 September, the sixth day after our ship departed, an order from the chief officer came suddenly that all labourers queue up to listen to him. All labourers followed the order and lined up immediately. In a little while, a

华工日记
Chinese Labourer's Diaries

British officer accompanied by two soldiers, one with a long rifle and bayonet and the other with a pistol in his hand, arrived. The officer said, "From now on, all of you must take great care at all times. The lifesaving belt must be worn day and night, even when you are sleeping or going to toilets. German submarines are everywhere in the Atlantic Ocean. If our ship was attacked by one of them, the lives of over ten thousand people onboard would be in great danger. The owner of the ship has prepared many small boats, which are hung outside the ship. There is a seat for each member in each battalion and platoon. If the ship is unfortunately attacked, we should all go out to the small boats, which would be lowered onto the sea. Once we get into the small boats, there is no danger any more. If all of you are careful enough and fasten your lifesaving belts tightly, I assure you that no one would be injured.

"What worries me most is that all people on the ship might hurry to escape in panic once our ship is hit by cannons from the submarines. Because the exit door is small, it would soon become blocked if everyone hurried to get out. In that case, the ship would be in disorder, which would put all people on the ship at stake. Therefore, I hope all platoon leaders should tell your men in detail that they should not only have their lifesaving belts fastened all the time, they should also act in turn according to their numbers in doing everything, including eating, sleeping, going in or out onto the deck. If an attack did happen, there would be soldiers to watch over the doorways and hatches. Anyone who fails to obey the order would be shot with a gun or killed with a bayonet immediately. Remember this, even if the ship were hit, it might not necessarily sink because all cabins in the ship have waterproof doors and are guarded by dare-to-die soldiers. Even if several cabins were damaged and some water entered into them, it would still be all right. In fact, even if all the cabins were damaged, the ship would not sink completely until four hours later.

If we leave the ship in an orderly and organised manner, it will take no more than one hour for all of us to get off the ship and into the small boats safely. From now on, all of you must obey these orders strictly. You can go out onto the upper deck to observe whether there are submarines in the sea if you have nothing important to do in the cabins. As soon as you see a submarine, you must report it to the ship owner immediately. If your report is true, you can get a reward of 300 silver dollars."

The officer left after he finished his words. With faces turning pale and sad sighs, most of the labourers were greatly scared and some even began to cry loudly. I composed a poem to record the scene.

Once departing from Halifax, all onboard were ordered to fasten "lifebelts" (also known as the Safety Belts).

Still as it is on the Ocean, our ship headed for France both days and nights.

So formidable were German submarines, fourteen naval vessels came to escort.

Nearly no difference in sea temperature, why I've a cold heart in a body so hot.

29.

九月初四日天阴，下午风又作，雨渐大。初五日，风雨愈大，浪之高非在太平洋时所能比，盖不仅几百尺也。至夜，海雾尤浓，两侧之美

华工日记
Chinese Labourer's Diaries

国军舰，均被雾隐不见，但闻汽笛之声呜呜不断耳。直至初六日午后，忽闻上官英人宣布云："德在大西洋中之潜水艇，下令全然收回。我们大家尽可放心，我们之船不久即可入口也。"满船之人闻之，均欣欣然有喜色矣。

是船本身之重量，有若干万吨。万余人及各人之行李、饮食等之重量，又有若干万吨。往来行驶于大西洋中，风平浪静时，无所感觉。即如此次之渡大浪，一纵而高约数百丈，一俯而低亦数千尺。一上一下，昼夜不停，在其中者，并不觉丝毫之颠簸。

On 4 September, it was cloudy. Wind began to blow in the afternoon and the rain was getting heavier and heavier. On the next day, the storm raged even more violently, and the waves were many feet high, incomparable to those in the Pacific Ocean. The sea fog grew even thicker at night. Completely unable to see the American warships on either side, we could only hear the sound of their ceaseless whistles. This situation continued until the afternoon of 6 September when the British officer announced that the German submarines in the Atlantic Ocean had been ordered to withdraw and that we could all rest assured that our ship would soon enter the port. Hearing this news, all the people onboard became delighted.

The weight of our ship itself was tens of thousands of tons while the weight of more than 10,000 people and their baggage, food, and other things was also tens of thousands of tons. We could hardly feel any movement on the ship while it sailed on the calm Atlantic Ocean. During this storm, the ship rose hundreds of feet high occasionally and then the next minute it dropped a hundred feet down. However, even with the rise and fall of the waves like this day and night, we did not feel too much bumping inside the ship.

孙干：欧战华工记
Records of Chinese Labourers in European War by Sun Gan

30. 大西洋海浪之高

在太平洋时，船为风浪所飘，颠簸颇甚。其浪之大，有时从船之左侧起而到达船之右侧，察其面积，不过几十丈而已，能一目竟之。而在大西洋中之海浪常如是也，浪之高不过三五丈耳。余此次在大西洋所经之大浪，海水一逛不啻几十里路之遥，虽数十分钟，而始一次。然船随之一起时，几乎高欲蠹天，而一落时，若沉于深谷者半日。其浪之大，真可谓令人不能计算者也。

High Waves on the Atlantic Ocean

While sailing on the Pacific Ocean, our ship was tossed up and down by the wind and waves. The big waves sometimes started from the left side of the ship and ended at the right side. The area the wave covered was only about 100 yards, which could be completed at a glance. For most of the time, waves on the Atlantic Ocean were just like these, with a height of about fifteen to thirty feet. However, the waves I experienced on the Atlantic Ocean during a storm were so large that each wave continued for hundreds of yards in distance and completed only dozens of minutes later. When our ship rose together with the waves, it seemed to have risen all the way into the sky and when it fell back down with the waves, it seemed to have fallen directly into a deep valley and remain there for hours. The waves were so large that it was impossible for me to calculate their size.

华工日记
Chinese Labourer's Diaries

31. 到英之利物浦

初七日午后,船平安到利物浦。英人持火鞭一只,出而向吾侪曰:"中国人真有福,此次船平安到此,托中国人之福也。"遂将火鞭燃放半响。

在船上住二日,又换乘小船,始得近岸。

Arrival at Liverpool, England

On the afternoon of 7 September, our ship arrived safely at Liverpool. A British took a string of firecrackers and said to us, "So blessed are the Chinese! Thanks to the blessings of the Chinese, our ship has arrived here safely." Then he set off the firecrackers and the noise continued for quite a while.

After staying for two days on the ship, we were put onto smaller boats and taken ashore.

32. 过英京而至豆付耳(杜佛)

在船中休息一礼拜余,至九月二十日上午十时,由利物浦乘火车过伯明翰、曼撒斯特,而达英之京都伦敦。即见烟囱林立,楼房之建设,道路之修整，无一而不整齐秀丽，宜乎有世界第一大都会之名称也。当夜由伦敦又南开，翌日晨至杜佛（豆付耳）。

Crossing London and Arriving at Dover

After resting on the ship for over a week, we took the train from Liverpool and arrived in London via Manchester and Birmingham at 10 a.m. on 20 September. With numerous factories with high chimneys, tall buildings and clean streets, London really deserved its fame as the world's largest metropolis. The train left London that same night and arrived at Dover the next morning.

33. 初见飞机

处豆付耳郊外野营帐棚中，忽闻嗡嗡之声，众仰视之，高约千丈，如蜻蜓者，英国之飞机也，盘旋空际，岂非防德飞机来袭击者欤？

自利物浦登车后，一路见铁路两旁，畎亩道路无不整齐，园圃中之苹果树极为繁茂。更足令人羡慕者，其专修筑之国道，虽当野外，而两边树木齐整，间有以柏作墙，草地如茵者。想在吾国，真不易保护也。

First Sight of Aircraft

While we were in tents in the suburb of Dover, a sudden buzzing sound came to our ears. Looking up, we saw something like a dragonfly hovering at the height of over ten thousand feet. Was it a British aeroplane ready to prevent the attack of the German ones?

During our journey by train from Liverpool, we noticed that along both sides of the railway were neat roads and farmland, and the apple trees in the orchards were particularly flourishing. Even more admirable were the specially-built country roads, which were neatly lined with trees or walls of cypresses and large open grass fields, even though these roads passed through wild areas. If it was in China, such things would be difficult to protect.

34. 初见轻气球

在豆付耳野外休息数日，念五日下午起程，五句钟到达豆付耳海岸，遂随英之兵士上船。初入船门，人人多半面带恐怖色，所预备之太平带亦随人自取。队长排头等，各只顾自己，不暇过问他人矣。至日将落时，忽见天空有如一丈余长之大鸡卵者光滑明润，盘旋而至，询之，乃轻气球也。须臾又有飞机数架，亦自东来，盘旋数匝，偕往正北飞去，其距地约皆千余尺焉。

First Sight of a Light Balloon

We rested for several days in the fields near Dover before we set out again on the afternoon of 25 September. About five hours later, we arrived at the coast of Dover, where we immediately boarded a ship along with British soldiers. Most of the men looked scared when they first set feet on the deck, where each of them was given a lifebelt. All were busy sorting out their own stuff and even the captains or platoon leaders had no time to take care of others. At sunset, I suddenly saw a bright egg-shaped craft of over ten feet long hovering toward our direction in the sky. After inquiry, I knew that it was a light balloon. Soon afterwards, I saw several aeroplanes also flew toward our direction from the east and went away to the due north after performing several circles overhead, all about one thousand feet above the ground.

35. 夜过豆付耳海峡

过英国海峡所乘之船虽小，而航行极快，因其机轮露在船之两侧外也。由是赴法，危险万状，莫可言喻。在未开船之前，峡中小舟，由英海岸接连不断，或距五六丈一只，或距十数丈一只。在远望之，如一线然，似在海面而不动者。盖皆监察德之潜水艇，而防其袭击英之战舰在海峡往来者也。

至天色黑定，余乘之船即开往南行。约二十分钟，船忽又北返，将到北岸，又折回南行，如是者往返数次。据人云，平日用是等快船，不逾两点钟，即南抵法境，今则用七八点钟始达。所以当时之人，因船小且快而又旋转之故，头晕呕吐者不少。至翌日上二点，始到达法国北方之喀离。渡此海峡，不惟中国之工人，人人惧甚，即英之兵士，亦莫不惴惴焉。其船冒险之甚，不言可知。斯时也，余等多云，听天由命，靠神而已。

华工日记
Chinese Labourer's Diaries

Crossing Strait of Dover at Night

When we crossed the English Channel, the ship we took was small but sailed very quickly because its engine wheels were exposed on both sides of the ship. Going to France like this was inexplicably dangerous. Before the ship set sail, we saw numerous small boats in the Channel. They were either 50-60 feet or over 100 feet apart from each other, forming a continuous line along the British coast. Looked from distance, these boats seemed still on the sea. They monitored German submarines in real time and prevented the passage of warships intending to attack Britain through the English Channel.

When night fell, our boat began to sail southward, but it changed its voyage to the north about twenty minutes later. Then as it got nearer to the northern coast, it suddenly began to sail toward the south again. In this way, it sailed back and forth for several times. It was said that clippers were usually used, which could sail down to the border of France within two hours. But that day it took us seven or eight hours. Due to the small size, fast speed and constant direction change of the boat, many people felt dizzy and became sick. At two o'clock the next morning, we eventually arrived at Calais in the north of France. Crossing the Straight of Dover was not only a frightening experience for Chinese labourers but also for the British soldiers. It was extremely dangerous and at that time most of us could only resign ourselves to fate and rely on the blessings of the Gods.

孙干：欧战华工记
Records of Chinese Labourers in European War by Sun Gan

36. 乘车到工人总驻所脑院

九月二十六日，天尚未明，由法之喀离乘火车至明天下晚，始到脑院，住于帐棚中。此两昼夜，虽多半趁火车，然处处禁止点灯，天又阴雨，黑暗泥泞，人不无痛苦。

脑院大约数顷，其中之帐棚，能容万余人。在脑院休息两日，上官下令，明天饭后到野外某地，都听讲话，届时不准不到云云。

Taking Train to Noyelles, the Base Depot of the Chinese Labour Corps

On 26 September we set out by train from Calais at dawn and arrived at Noyelles the next evening, where we lived in the tents at night. During those two days and nights, although most of the time we were on the train, it was really miserable because lighting was forbidden, and we had to proceed in darkness in the mud due to the rainy weather.

Noyelles was a place with an area of dozens of hectares and filled with tents that could accommodate more than ten thousand people. After two days' rest in Noyelles, we received an order from the British officers that we should all listen to speeches in the field after breakfast the next day. Everyone should be present without exception.

华工日记
Chinese Labourer's Diaries

37. 工人赴法初次领英人之告诫

九月卅日，饭后排队出，到野外一大旷场中，先排队报齐，然后英人站在场中，令众工人绕之作一圆阵。英人曰："汝等此次应募来此作工，除路费、医药、衣服俱有规定而外，对于饮食之规定，恐有诸多人不明了。今天特别对大家说，你们大家在中国时，虽然是居住不在一省，大概吃饭，多是任其肚量。现在英人之对于你们的饮食，却不然了。每日三餐，譬如面包，每人每饭只吃每个之三分之一。菜有时牛肉或猪肉，每餐一碗，每日必有肉一次，其余两次，非奶油即吉司（亦油制成）或鱼。其余如蒸面卷、焖米饭或分饼干，均有一定之数目，不能任各人之量多吃。你们大家在中国之时，有的吃糠、有的咽菜、有的竟吃胡萝卜，都是任吃，习惯既久，多变为草包肚子了。今英人所预备之食物，量数虽轻，均系有养料者，倘汝等尽量多吃，肚腹亦不能消化。若吃入肚内消化不了，就必泻肚。泻肚生病，殊非汝们千山万水出门之人之所宜也。倘以后汝等由此发到他处作工，或因工头作弊，或因作饭之工人作梗，致令你们饭食大差，逐日挨饿，可写信寄来，详细报告，吾们亦能给你们查办。以上之言，望你们切记之。"云云。

First Warning to Chinese Labourers in France

On 30 September, we formed up and walked to a large open field as soon as we finished our breakfast. After counting off in lines, we were ordered to form a circle with a British officer standing in the centre. The officer said, "As recruited workers, you may have already known the regulations on transportation fares, medicines and clothing, but I believe most of you are not clear about the regulations on food. Today I would like to make this clear to all of you. When you were in China, most of you were accustomed to eating as much as you liked. But now the British meals for you will be different. For the three meals a day, each person can only eat one third of his bread for each meal. Every day, you can have a bowl of dish for each meal, but only one meal with meat, either beef or pork. For the other two meals you will have cheese (made of animal fat) or fish. As for other food such as steamed dough rolls, steamed rice or biscuits, each has his ration and no one can eat to his heart's content. In China, some of you ate bran; others ate noodles; and still others ate vegetables. Whatever you ate, there were no limits to how much you could have. Therefore, the long-established eating habits have made your stomachs large. Now, although the meals prepared by the British are smaller in amount, all are very nourishing. If you eat as much as you can, your stomach will not be able to digest properly, which will lead to diarrhoea and sickness. I don't think that after travelling such a long distance to work here, any of you wish to suffer from sickness. Also, I want you to bear in mind that when you are sent to work at other places away from here, if you think you are being starved by the inferior quality of your food due to the cheating of the foremen, or the neglect of duty of the cooks, you can write to us and send detailed reports, we can then investigate and deal with it accordingly. I hope all of you will remember my words today."

华工日记
Chinese Labourer's Diaries

38. 工匠之挑选

十月初一日,又下令云:"俟翌日复排队到野外旷场,将各排中之各种匠人,一一着其自行报名。"于是我们工人纷纷议论,有人曰:"余本是石匠,但余不报名。"亦有人曰:"余本甚么不会,但余报是修铁路的。"又有一临朐人曰:"余报木匠。"与之同来之邻人止之曰:"汝本不会,焉可胡来耶?"有人怕拔出使去当兵,有人怕拔出逼作苦工,其说不一。

至翌日饭后,偕往站队,排列整齐,英人数名亦至。一英人对大家曰:"凡是在家时当木匠者都出本队,另成一排。"排毕,令一官员领到他处。再如是挑石匠、铁匠、瓦匠、鞋匠、邮差、铜匠、银匠、当兵的、修铁路的、当巡警的、一一挑毕,并将其各人手镯上之写码数,一一登记于工人簿。然后告之曰:"凡被挑者,俟明日随余到各项工厂考试。"言罢,令排队而归。

Selection of Craftsmen

On 1 October, another order came, "All labourers should muster again tomorrow and all craftsmen in each platoon should register their specialized trade. This caused much discussion among us labourers. Someone said, "I am a stonemason, but I will not sign up." A man from Linqu county said, "I will sign up as a carpenter." But another man who came from the same place stopped him, "You know nothing about carpentry. How come you can do that? Some people were afraid that they would be picked out to serve as soldiers while others feared to be singled out for hard labour.

After breakfast on the next day, we all formed up in order in the open field and several British officers also came. One officer called out, "All who worked as a carpenter in your home county stand out of the line and queue up here." After the men stepped forward and stood in another line, he asked another officer to lead them elsewhere. In this way, all those who had worked as stonemasons, blacksmiths, bricklayers, shoemakers, postmen, railroad builders, soldiers and policemen were all picked out one by one. These men had their bracelet numbers registered one by one in the labourers' book. Then the officer told everyone, "All that have been selected shall be tested in different workplaces tomorrow." After this we all returned to our camp.

39. 考验华工中各有手艺者

当华工在法国脑院华工总分发处时，知英人对于已赴法之华工，必先告之饭食之规定，及考验各人之特长。盖一方恐华工后日到各作工地，为饭食发生争执，有碍工作。一方又恐不考验各人之特长，不明华工之用项，而不易使唤，又各工程无正当人去作。所以凡华工一到总局，必先宣讲吃饭问题，与考验其各人之手艺也。

迨十月初三日，始闻吾侪被编为一百零二队矣。余等无手艺者，都在营中休息，凡报有手艺者，是日都从英人到各行工厂中去考试。据临朐县华工某人云，彼在中国之时，无甚手艺，既应募到法，亦报为木匠。及至被英人领到木工厂考验时，彼则高高兴兴，与厂中之木工抬木、竖

华工日记

Chinese Labourer's Diaries

板、拉锯，都是殷殷勤勤。厂中之司木工职员，即报知英总华工分发处云："此人真木匠，可多为之开工价。"此人既考验毕，却无适当木工为之作，仍归还本营将其考验。木工已成，及多得工价情形告知同伴者，同伴皆甚羡慕之云。

Testing the Craftsmen Among Chinese Labourers

When they were in the General Distribution Camp for Chinese Labourers in Noyelles, France, Chinese labourers had already known that the British would first inform them of the regulations on food and then test their trade specialities. The British did this for two main reasons; Firstly, they feared that when Chinese labourers were sent to their workplaces later, disputes would arise among them on food, which might hinder their work. Secondly, the British were afraid that without testing the specialities of these Chinese labourers, they would not know exactly what kind of work should be distributed to them. Besides, various projects needed to be undertaken by professional labourers. This explained why Chinese labourers were told of the regulations on food the first thing they arrived at the General Camp and then tested their craftsmanship and professional skills.

On 3 October, I heard that I became a member of Brigade 102. While labourers with no skills like me rested in the camp, those who had signed up as craftsmen were taken by the British to various factories to be tested. It was said that a Chinese labourer from Linqu signed up as a carpenter even though he had no trade at all while he was in China. When he was taken to the woodworking factory to be tested, he was cheerful and polite to everybody, helping the carpenters in the factory to carry logs, erect boards and saw wood diligently. At the end of the day, the foreman of the factory reported to the British officer, "This man is a real carpenter, and he deserves to be paid more." Thus, he passed the test. But he was brought back to his original camp for further tests since there was no suitable carpentry work for him to do for the time being. When he told his companions about how he passed the carpentry test and how he was to be paid more, they were all very envious of him.

40. 脑院村之近郊

　　余等到脑院数日后，对于地方略熟，饭后多至附近小村散步游览，余亦如是。见脑院村旁园圃中大苹果树之多，尤盛于在英国境所见者数倍。虽小村之街道，莫不规模宏大，建筑道路、楼房，处处都合规矩。惟桥梁残缺，沟洫塞滞，欠修理处，处处有之。盖因欧战之忙碌，不遑及此也。

　　一日散步脑院村外，见一华工立于路旁，胸前挂一木牌，上书："偷法国人苹果之罪状。"盖英人欲借此以羞辱之，而儆效尤也。奈彼不但不知一人作恶，即有伤国家体面，且犹觉洋洋得意。由此观之，人民之无教育，与国家能无关系哉！

Outskirts of Noyelles Village

After a few days' stay in Noyelles, we became somewhat acquainted with the place. Most labourers would like to take a walk to the nearby village after dinner. So did I. There was an orchard near the village of Noyelles, where the apple trees seemed even more abundant than those I had seen from the train in Britain. Small as the village was, all the streets were very wide; all the roads and houses were well-built. But many bridges were old and damaged; many ditches were blocked; and many places were in need of maintenance. Perhaps it was because the men were busy with the European War and had no time to take care of them.

One day as I took a walk around the village, I saw a Chinese labourer standing by the roadside with a board on his chest that read "guilty of stealing French apples". I thought the British must be trying to send a warning to others by humiliating him. However, the labourer seemed unaware that his wrongdoings not only affected his own reputation, but also hurt the dignity of our country. In this sense, individuals' lack of education had much to do with the country.

41. 由脑院分发至馁司不老开（阿兹布鲁克）

十月初八日晨，忽分发糇粮、饼干，每人一小囊，作二日之食用。须臾下令，各负辎重出营。东行里许，登火车向西南行。循邱陵盘旋曲折，午后至一新辟之车站处，不但铁轨枕木狼藉不堪，即月台站房，尚无雏形，惟有新开辟如白石灰之乔喀石雪白一片而已。是日，行者均未曾带饮水，由早至晚，又因行路，所以人人渴甚，有人向上官索饮料者，至于再三而不得。

时至夜半，人多因渴焦急，一时秩序大乱。适逢一列车至，吾侪工人蜂拥而至火车头下，将火车头围之数层，争接汽管所滴之水而饮之。

孙干：欧战华工记
Records of Chinese Labourers in European War by Sun Gan

其渴可想见矣。明晨始得饮，又开车委曲婉转，晚到馁斯不老凯。闻炮声隆隆，顷刻不停，大众面貌，无不悚然。晚八点，令下车，各负行李步行于黑暗之路约十里许，始得宿于市外营中。

Distribution from Noyelles to Hazebrouck

On the morning of 8 October, each of us was suddenly given a small sack of dry provisions and biscuits as food for two days. This was followed quickly by an order that we leave the camp with our baggage. We walked eastward for about 0.3 miles and then boarded a southwest-bound train. After travelling on a winding track through an undulating landscape, we arrived at a new station where the rails and sleepers lay in a mess. There were no platforms or station buildings completed, but only a newly-developed white landscape. On that day, we travelled from morning to night without any water. Extremely thirsty, some of us asked the officers for drinks but in vain.

Due to thirst and anxiety, most people got into a total disorder at midnight when a train arrived. All of my fellow labourers flocked to the locomotive and fought to get the water from the steam pipes to drink. Hundreds of people clambered over and under the locomotive for the water. So you could imagine how thirsty they must have been! We still did not get any fresh water to drink until the next morning. We then took the train again and after winding for many hours, arrived at the town of Hazebrouck. Hearing the ceaseless rumbling of artillery, everyone became terrified and horror came onto their faces. At eight o'clock that evening, we were ordered to get off the train. Then, we marched in the darkness with our bags on our backs for about three miles before we finally arrived at a camp outside of the town.

华工日记
Chinese Labourer's Diaries

42. 大众不听英人之指挥

吾侪既到哀司不老凯，于炮声隆隆之下，英人之管理工程者，即用其法制之手腕，硬行指挥华工。殊不知华人之习惯与心性，完全与英人之法制之习惯不同。譬如食饭，二十或三十岁之工人，在中国每饭吃锅饼约须三镑左右，在法国则每次常常不及半镑。工人天天肚中饥饿难堪，心中怀恨。而英人再持封建态度，谁肯听从？所以英人每厉声使唤华工，华工即处处与之相反。纵有饭量较小者，亦不敢不随大众而反对英人。所以每日十人作工，其效率往往不如平常一人。譬如修路抬灰，车站去营盘不及半里之遥，每半晌可往来二十趟者，然实际工人仅抬两趟。每趟抬重该百四五十斤者，然实际每趟仅抬七八斤。是以管理工程者，有时大声吵闹，华人更相率罢工，连营门不出。英人催之再三，众则一口同音，以肚子里饿答之。有时英人以调军队来打威吓工人，工人亦毫不惧怕。余因是作《饭食歌》一则如下：

在营盘，二十五人一顿一桶饭。一人仅分小半碗，菜蔬葱地蛋。有肉常缺盐，分回纪司隔数天。饭量大的，饿的头晕眼花无人管。

（纪司是油制之饼饵）

Disobedience to the British Command

From the day we arrived at Hazebrouck, where the sound of artillery

孙干：欧战华工记
Records of Chinese Labourers in European War by Sun Gan

fire never stopped, the British officers had begun to command us Chinese labourers with their strict rules and regulations. However, they were not aware that due to different customs and temperaments, Chinese labourers had rather different habits from those of the British. For example, a labourer in his twenties or thirties would eat about three pounds of wheat cakes per meal in China, whereas they were given less than half a pound per meal in France. Being hungry every day, the labourers were full of hatred for the British. In this case, who would follow their orders if the British continued to treat us with their tyrannical attitude? Therefore, whenever the British ordered about them, Chinese labourers tended to do the opposite. Even those with small stomachs did not dare to go against the general opinion of the labourers and had to disobey the orders of the British. As a result, even if there were ten labourers working every day, the efficiency of these ten labourers was often lower than that of one person under normal circumstances. For example, the station was only about 250 yards from the barrack and labourers could have made 20 trips carrying cement for road construction in about two hours, but the reality was that they only made two trips. Those who could have carried more than 100 pounds per trip carried only 10 or 15 pounds per trip. This sometimes resulted in the British officers' yelling, which would in turn lead to the repeated strikes by Chinese labourers at the camp. Upon the repeated urging of the British, all Chinese labourers would respond the same that they had no food in their stomachs and were hungry. Sometimes the British would threaten the labourers by deploying armed soldiers around the camp, but the labourers were not afraid of this threat at all. In view of this, I composed a "Song of Diet" and it goes as follows:

In the military camp, twenty-five people were given only one bucket of rice. This meant less than half a bowl for each, with rice, greens, potatoes and onions. The meat often had no salt and the cheese was only distributed several days apart. Those with big stomachs were starved to dizziness, but no one cares about us.

(Cheese is a cake made of animal fat.)

43. 在哀司不老凯之工作

吾侪一营五百人，分为四大排，大致每一三道杠（即大工头），每日率领出营到工厂作工，约四五点钟即归。除整理各人之床铺、衣服、盥洗、澡身外，余则休息而已。然不得随意出营游览，殊觉不快。

倘有身体不适，不能随众出营作工者，即许其挂病号，在营中休息。如果身体有病，天天亦有医生乘摩托车至，为之查看治疗。轻则当时诊治，重则乘车随之而往大战地医院医治。凡挂号者即无工钱。

每一三道杠（大工头）带领其下三排之各棚，或斩伐森林辟为道路，或浚疏路旁之水渠，或装卸火车之煤炭，或修新敷之铁路，或到各工厂作大扫除。近则步行，远则乘摩托车。所做完之工程，有专官验看，不中者则再另作。

一日火车装有鱼盒、牛肉盒、果子酱桶、饼干箱等多箱，吾工人间有私启箱而取食者。后英人察觉，欲罚工人之工价。吾出而与之理论曰："吾侪华工本知仁义，因汝等供给之饭食不足，他人上书又不之听，而使其不得不偷食，非汝英人之过欤！"彼闻之默然。

孙干：欧战华工记
Records of Chinese Labourers in European War by Sun Gan

Working in Hazebrouck

There were 500 labourers in our battalion, which was divided into four platoons. Every day the foreman of the platoon led us out of the camp to the designated work area and we returned to camp at four or five o'clock in the afternoon. For the rest of the time, we made our beds, cleaned or repaired our clothes, washed our hands and faces, took baths or just had a rest. However, we were forbidden to leave the camp for any reason, which made us sad and angry.

If a person was not well enough to work, they could register as sick patients and stay at the camp. If they were sick, doctors would come by motor vehicle each day to give check-ups or treatments. If they were not seriously ill, the doctors would gave them immediate diagnoses and treatment. If they were seriously ill, they would then be sent to a large field hospital for further treatment. Any labourers registering sick did not get paid for that day.

Each foreman of the platoon led the labourers of three rows of tents to cut down trees in the forests for road building, to dredge ditches, to load and unload coal from trains, to repair newly-laid railways, or to clean up at the factories. We walked to the working site if it was near, but we usually travelled by motorcycle if it was far away from our camp. Once a project was completed, it would be inspected by the officers. If it failed to meet the requirements, labourers would be ordered to do it again.

One day some of our labourers took a box from a train packed with boxes of fish, beef, jam, and biscuits and opened it secretly to get the food. When it was found out later, the British intended to punish the labourers by not giving them wages. I came up and argued with them, "Our Chinese labourers also have a sense of righteousness, but you refuse to give us sufficient food and never respond to our petitions at all. It is you that have forced us to steal food. So, isn't it the fault of yours?" Hearing my words, they became silent.

44.

　　每队中雇用翻译一人，常常随从队长到工场往来传话。然工场繁多，每队翻译一人，何克有济！所以遇翻译不到之处，英人即利用绘画，画图以指示工人作工。

Each brigade had an interpreter, whose job was to pass on messages between the officer and labourers at each working site. However, we had so many working sites that it was far from enough to have only one interpreter in each brigade. So when the interpreter was not available, the British officer instructed labourers by drawing pictures.

45. 华工之衣服

　　吾侪之衣服，每人发给。除由青岛领得之灰色棉袄、棉裤、灰色小褂、裤各一件、褐色帆布雨衣一件、布鞋、洋袜各一双、水壶一把、饭碗、筷子各一具外，既到法后，在哀司不老凯又发给青色大氅一身、灰色线毯二床、皮靴一双、针线包一个、蓝夹洋制服裤袄各一件、卫生衣

孙干：欧战华工记
Records of Chinese Labourers in European War by Sun Gan

毛与线各一身、裹腿一付。衣服遇有小破绽，自己缀缝，有大撕裂，即褂号另易之。对于皮靴，另有鞋匠天天在营中专司修理。总之英人对于华工衣服，可谓用心周至。然华工中之少数作弊者，将好衣盗卖，而诚实之人倒领不到好衣服穿，彼亦无可奈何也。余有《衣服歌》一则如下：

投顾主，三年之间身穿西洋服。毛毯三床作被褥，破坏挂号另取，小人把弊舞。十回八回向外估，正道君子倒反，常常穿的破如苏。

一日，三道杠韩某带工人一群，至一车站工作，遇英人验工程。英人苛甚，使反复另作者数次。而英人尚不满意，屡训大工头韩某，使之以严厉之言训众工人。工人时已都觉疲乏已极，及归营时，未暇吃晚饭。遂有一人出大声曰："当打死大工头韩某。"一人喊打，全营之工人齐出相应，遂蜂拥往捉韩某。不意韩某早已闻讯，抱头鼠窜，不知去向。众工人复质问营长。英人因众以索韩某而欲打死之，乃曰："汝等欲打韩某，系为何故？可告诉我。"在前者无言以对，在后者之工人中，有一人从衣囊中取出小刀一把，立将其膝上之裤来往平刮数刀。裤断膝出，彼遂趋营长之面前曰："余之衣破裂如此，与大工头韩某语者数次，伊并不理，不将其打死，留之何为？"英人曰："汝等勿着急，先各回棚休息休息，待余令其速速为汝等换之。"众工人始徐徐而散。自是之后，英人待遇华工之封建态度，始渐杀矣！

Clothes of Chinese Labourers

Our clothes were distributed by the British. In addition to what we were given in Qingdao, including a set of grey cotton-padded jacket and trousers, a set of grey shirt and pants, a brown canvas raincoat, a pair of cloth shoes,

华工日记
Chinese Labourer's Diaries

a pair of woollen socks, a kettle, a bowl, and a pair of chopsticks, each of us was given in Hazebrouck a green overcoat, two grey cotton blankets, a pair of leather boots, a pack of needles and thread, a suit of foreign uniform, a sweat shirt, a cotton underwear and a pair of leg wrappings. If the clothes had some small holes, we would mend them on our own, but when they were badly damaged, we would register to change them. For leather boots, there was a professional shoemaker (cobbler) to repair them in the camp. In short, the British were very good with clothing supply to the Chinese labourers. But a few Chinese labourers would cheat by stealing and selling the good clothes so that some honest labourers could not get good clothes to wear and they could do nothing about it. Hereupon I wrote a poem entitled "Song of the Clothes" as follows:

With the British as their employers, our workers had the chance to wear foreign clothes for three years. Each was given three blankets, which, if damaged, could be exchanged for new ones, resulting in the cheatings of some villains. They sold to outsiders the good ones, leading to the sufferings of honest workers, who often had only worn-out clothes as beggars.

One day, a group of labourers were led by Foreman Han to work at a railway station, when the British happened to come to inspect the project. The officer was very harsh and ordered them to redo the job for several times. However, the officer was still not satisfied and reproached Han repeatedly and asked him to reprimand the labourers with strict words. When they returned to the camp, all the labourers became extremely exhausted and had no time for supper. Suddenly a man shouted, "We should kill Foreman Han." With these words, the labourers of the whole platoon flocked to find him. But Han had heard of the news earlier and already fled to somewhere else. So the labourers went to ask the battalion commander for Hans' whereabouts again. The British officer asked about the reasons, "Why do you want to kill Han? Please tell me your reasons." While the labourers at the front did not know how to respond, one of the labourers standing at the back took a knife out of his pocket and scraped his trousers on the knee. The trousers were ripped, and his knee was exposed to the air. He went up to the battalion commander and said, "My clothes are torn open like this. I have told Han many times about it. But he does not care about me at all. Since he has neglected his duty, why should we keep him as our foreman?" The officer said, "Don't worry. Please go back to your tents and have a good rest. I will ask him to give you better ones soon." Hearing this, the labourers began to disperse slowly. From then on, the British gradually changed the way they treated the Chinese labourers.

46. 亦分发给白糖与葡萄干、枣子、烟卷等

华工一百零二队之工人，容有时粮台不能按期照发，然白糖和烟卷是照常所发给者。每礼拜约六两左右，以备饮茶时用焉。枣子亦有时发给，若以全数华工计之，每次亦须得枣子一万五千斤之左右。若连英人、南非人、印度人总计，尚不知须几百万斤也。

Distribution of Sugar, Raisins, Dates and Cigarettes

On some days, the food would fail to be delivered to Chinese labourers of Brigade 102 on time, but sugar and cigarettes were always distributed to every one of us on time. Each week about 10 ounces of sugar was given to each labourer for tea drinking. Dates were also given sometimes. If all of the Chinese labourers were counted, about 15,000 pounds of dates were needed every time. If the British, South Africans and Indians were also counted in, the total amount of dates should be millions of pounds!

47. 支搭帐棚

吾侪自到欧洲战场，夜间所宿之处，虽有时住于以铁瓦构成房内之木板上，然因常常迁徙，故不如宿帐幕以内之时为多也。帐幕之住，每迁至一地，必另支搭，故每次必众工人轮流执行支搭之。棚之内，撑之以杆，棚之外，系之以绳。绳复系于棚四周，埋于地内之木橛上，使之松紧适度，方能不畏刮大风急雨也。吾祖国之人若多练习之，将来亦有时用之也。我对此学习锻炼愈觉有趣也。

Setting up Tents

Since our arrival at the battlefields of Europe, we had slept in tents for most of the time due to frequent moving although we occasionally slept on wooden floors of huts built with iron and tiles. Every time we moved to a new place, we had to set up our tents again. So the labourers took turns to set up the tents. Inside the tents poles were used as supports, while outside ropes were used to fasten them. The ropes were also used around the tent to be fastened to the wooden pegs hammered into the ground. In this way, these ropes were made neither too tight nor too loose so that they could not be blown during storms. If people in our motherland could practice setting up tents more, it would be useful for them in the future too. I found such learning and exercises more and more interesting.

48. 同工多人不愿余作苦工

不识字之人，常在家中，则无甚难。若出门焉，一遇有事，非通信不可，所以处处常求人也。余佣工于一百零二华工运输队，常觉工作不苦，一有暇焉，不但本队中之同工来祈为之写信。所以到法以后不数月，而天天来祈余为之写书家信者，前后拥拥不退。或有人云，将余应作之工，大家代余。余不之允，以抽暇代为写信，亦应尽义务也。多见多闻，于人之经验，更为有益也。

My Colleagues' Unwillingness for Me to Do Hard Work

For illiterate labourers, there was nothing difficult if they stayed at home. But once they had left their homes, they could only communicate with their families by letters if something happened to them. Therefore, they had to ask others to write letters for them. While working in Transportation Brigade 102 of the Chinese Labour Corps, I often wrote letters for my fellow workers in my spare time at their request. So a few months later, workers came in flocks to ask me to write letters for them every day. Some suggested that the work I was supposed to do during the day should be done by them. I did not agree because I thought writing letters for them in my spare time was my duty and pleasure. After all, keeping well-informed is more beneficial to one's experience.

49. 大家议余代众写信

华工往家写一信，求人花费往往有多至数元者。一日本队之同工，公议云："吾曾未有不向家中写信者，每至欲写信时，不但借笔、借墨、买信封、买信纸，往往有因烦人买物附带所花之钱，多至数元。不如将买信纸与信封之钱，交于孙先生，烦其乘暇为大家书写之为愈也。"大家曰："善。"余亦遂答应大家之决议而照办。所以自是以后，余常于工作之余，为大家写信。自是大家每写一信，仅费法币五分耳，免去自买信纸信封、操笔操墨之一切麻烦耳。

Public Resolution on My Writing Letters for Them

Usually it took a Chinese labourer several yuan to have a letter written by others. One day, a fellow worker in my brigade put forward a suggestion, "All of us need to write letters to our families. Every time we attempt to write a letter, we not only have to borrow pens and ink, but we also need to ask others to buy envelopes and paper for us. The total cost will be as much as several yuan. It's better to give the money for buying envelopes and paper to Mr. Sun and ask him to write letters for us in his spare time." All my fellow workers agreed, "Good idea." I also agreed to follow the public's resolution. So from that time on, I always wrote many letters for my fellow workers in my spare time. They spent only five cents of the French currency for each letter and spared themselves all the trouble of buying envelopes and paper as well as the costs of pens and ink.

50. 华工工作时之饭食

吾侪每晨约三四点钟即起床，吃饭、站队、出营盘后，往往天始放亮。每日三餐，第一顿在夜间，第一顿常是米饭，每人仅分半碗。菜为牛肉，熬地蛋或熬葱头亦有半碗，较在祖国饭食内之养料真不算少。不过按其重量体积，不止小于在祖国者四五倍也。工人习惯之食量，大于所食之食物四五倍。食欲方兴，食物已罄。正在饥痛难言、无人可诉之际，英人即以哨吹催促站队，赴场作工。午餐常是面包，约重五两左右，带至作工处，及时而食。菜非奶油即纪司块（奶油为油质之黄酱，纪司如中国之豆腐干，亦带油性），约一二两。第二顿食物之体积小于第一顿，亦小于第三顿。晚饭回营盘，或分三四两饼干，或分上白面自蒸之面卷一枚，约重六七两。菜或牛肉与地蛋，或牛肉盒或鱼盒等，每人约分重三两左右。

观每日三餐之养料，实不为少。奈多数华工之大肚食量，确凿不能充实其饥。伙友黄世恩、刘希瑞云彼是石匠，在祖国时每餐每人吃干粮

华工日记
Chinese Labourer's Diaries

重二斤左右，每日三次。现今来此不吃饭时，饥尚是小饥，一吃米饭半碗，食欲方兴，则觉大饥，更难过矣。一顿如是，一天三顿均如是，奈何奈何。

Chinese Labourers' Food While at Work

Every morning, our Chinese labourers got up at about three or four o'clock. It did not light up until we had left our camp in line after breakfast. We had three meals a day, the first of which was usually eaten in the night time. The food for the first meal was usually half a bowl of rice and half a bowl of beef, boiled potatoes or onions. Compared with the food we had in China, there were more nutrients in the meals here, but the amounts were four or five times less. Hardly had the appetite of labourers was satisfied when their food had run out. We would often be left still feeling hungry, but nobody would listen to our complaints. The British just blew the whistle to urge us to line up for work. For lunch we usually had bread, which was about 8 oz. The bread was usually brought to our work site so that we could eat it while still at work. The dishes were 3 or 4 ounces of either cream or cheese (cream was thick yellowish fatty liquid while cheese was like Chinese dried bean curd, but also fatty). The amount of the second meal was smaller than that of both the first and the third meals. We had dinner after we returned to the camp. For dinner we were usually given 5-7 oz of biscuits or 10-12 oz of steamed wheat flour rolls while the dishes were usually about 8-10 oz. of either beef and potatoes, or fried beef dumplings or fish dumplings.

The nutrients in the three meals each day were really sufficient. But they could hardly satisfy the hunger of most Chinese labourers due to their large stomachs. My friends Huang Shien and Liu Xirui said that while working as stonemasons in China, they ate about two pounds of dry food for each of the three meals per day. But now they might not feel so hungry when they did not have meals. However, they would feel even hungrier once they had eaten half a bowl of rice because their appetite for food was aroused at that time. It was all right for just one meal like this, but all three meals every day were the same. What could they do?

51. 华工之做饭者

华工每营有一造饭室，人名之曰饭房。饭房亦以工人组织之。饭房棚头一人，司做菜汤者几人，做米饭或面卷者几人，汲水烧火及打扫者几人，共十数人至二十人不等。除饭房头较多得工价外，其余不过较普通工人，得着饱饭吃而已。

饭房除司涝米饭、蒸面卷、熬菜、冲茶外，其余工人之事，一概不管。工人对于饭房不能随便出入，或呼唤。饭房所用之水均须好水，如其近无好水，即以水车从远方拉来饮用。所以工人对于水土不服，致生疾病之事，未之有也。英人之饭食，另以华工二三人，特别立一饭房为之服役。

英人对华工除饭食而外，尚有白糖，每日每人约两许；烟卷，每礼拜约四五盒，或烟丝一两包。虽非按天发给，多为每礼拜发给一次。此外糖浆、枣果等间或发给，无一定时也。倘遇食物不适口时，或因疾病不能吃所分之饭时，亦可自己买点材料，生火另做，然非在闲暇时不可能也。

华工日记
Chinese Labourer's Diaries

Cooks of Chinese Labourers

In every Chinese labourer camp, there was a cooking tent known as the meal room, which was also organised and run by the labourers. For each meal room, there were altogether a dozen or a score of workers, including a head, cooks taking charge of preparing dishes and soups, cooks responsible for preparing rice or steamed rolls, and scullions in charge of carrying water, making fires, and cleaning rooms. The head received higher wages, but others were just ordinary workers and the only advantage for them was that they could have full meals.

Apart from cooking rice, steaming rolls, stewing dishes and making tea, those working in the meal room did nothing of what other ordinary labourers did. Ordinary labourers were not allowed to enter or shout at the meal room. All the water used in the meal room should be of good quality. If there was no water of good quality nearby, water from elsewhere would be brought in by a water cart. Therefore, no labourers had ever had illness because of the water they drank. There was also a separate meal room exclusively serving the British by two or three Chinese labourers.

Apart from the meals, the British also provided about four ounces of sugar for each Chinese labourer every day. Besides, there were also about four or five packs of cigarettes or one or two packs of cut tobacco each week. Although these things were not distributed to us on a daily basis, most of them were usually given to us once a week. In addition, syrup, dates and fruits were distributed too, not on a regular basis but occasionally. If one found the food unpalatable or had no appetite for the distributed food because of illness, he could also buy food materials and cook them by himself. But this was only possible during leisure time.

孙干：欧战华工记
Records of Chinese Labourers in European War by Sun Gan

52. 华工之睡眠

华工需用之帐棚，以白帆布为之，顶高约五六尺，中以木杆直立撑其顶。杆之下端，地面周出约四尺左右，围以宽尺许之布缘，上连缀于棚顶，周留一缝作棚门，可容八九人，或十人睡眠。夜则共铺各人之毯，而成一铺；出则各卷其铺，使之整齐洁净。夜间所燃之灯，为上等洋烛，每两晚发给一支。用之不足者，往往将发给作食菜之黄油，燃之作灯。即自购洋烛，亦无不可。

Sleeping of Chinese Labourers

The tents of Chinese labourers were made of white canvas. The ceiling, supported by an upright wooden pole inside the tents, was about five to six feet high. At the lower end of the pole, about four feet high above the ground, a cloth of about one foot wide was used to enclose the edge and was attached to the ceiling at the top with an opening left as its entrance. Generally, such a tent could accommodate 8-10 people. At night, the blankets of all labourers were laid together to make a large bed and each labourer would roll his own blanket up when they left the tent to make it neat and tidy. First-rate foreign candles were distributed to be used in the lamps at night, one for every two nights. Sometimes, when the candles were not enough for use, the butter which was often given us for food would be used in the lamps. Labourers could also buy foreign candles with their own money.

53. 华工之卫生

每队中挑出十几人或二十几人,天天整理厕所,使其毫无臭味外,又常常打扫院子,使院子之中不见污秽。英人对于华工之卫生可谓至注意焉。

Sanitation of Chinese Labourers

Toilets were cleaned and emptied every day by a dozen or score of specially-chosen labourers from each brigade. This prevented the area from becoming smelly. The courtyard was also cleaned frequently so that no dirt could be found in it. The British paid special attention to maintaining the hygiene and sanitation of the Chinese labourers.

54. 带领华工之英国长官

由青岛带领华工赴法之长官,至脑院后,即因另编制工人之队而又易人。吾等自脑院开至哀司不老凯,不匝月而又将长官调换。盖因役使华工为之效力,非易事也。营长亦谓之队长,英文谓之哈夫塞队长。以下又有副队长一人，再下有撒侧迷侧（即大工头）、靠八（即两道杠）若干人，皆奉队长之命，协同中国工头管理华工者，亦常常调换。

British Officers Leading Chinese Labourers

The British officers that came with us to France from Qingdao were transferred to other places during the reorganisation of brigades after we arrived at Noyelles. Our officers changed again within a month when we moved from Noyelles to Hazebrouck. It was actually not an easy thing to command Chinese labourers to serve them. The battalion commander was also known as Officer in English. Under the Officer was assistant Officer, under which there were several sergeants and captains, all of whom were responsible for the management of Chinese labourers together with the Chinese foremen. These sergeants and captains liaised with the interpreter and foremen but were often changed from time to time.

55. 队长欲令余充大工头，余固辞去

吾侪至哀司不老凯，不久队长欲吾充大工头。余思赴法初志，本欲参观西欧之风俗及学校教育，若一就大工头之职，天天公事在身，上有上司，下有工人，何暇参观其他？至于中国工人多半素无程度，开口即带着骂人，难于管理，又其余事。充大工头，固然有益，究不若做点教育事工，学点英语，到各处参观风俗、教育之更有益也，是以将大工头之职辞去。

77

华工日记
Chinese Labourer's Diaries

My Refusal to Be a Foreman

Soon after we arrived at Hazebrouck, the Captain wanted me to become a foreman. My original purpose of coming to France was to learn about the customs and school education in Western Europe. If I were a foreman, I would be busy with various official duties, dealing with affairs from both the supervisors and labourers. In that case, how could I have time to visit other places? As for the Chinese labourers, most of them were poorly educated. They often spoke using bad language and were hard to manage. Of course, it would be beneficial to be a foreman, but it was more beneficial to work on my education, to learn some English and to learn about the customs and education of the region by visiting various places. Taking all of this into consideration, I refused the job of a foreman.

56. 觇法国人之信仰

吾侪至法之哀司不老凯，初无礼拜日之休息。盖因雇主与工人心情尚不相融洽，事功无甚可观耳。后渐臻融洽，乃有安息日焉。一日，安息停工。早饭后，余到哀司不老凯街市，见市内阒其无人。及到大高崇天之一礼拜堂前，始闻堂内塔上铃声当当，盖将到礼拜上帝之时矣。

须臾，由各街各巷，男女老少，均衣冠整齐，屏气而入是礼拜堂。余亦随之入。入后，见初入门之左右，各有如盘大之小水池，内盛清水，凡入堂者均以指蘸水点于额上及胸之两旁，然后进内室，跪于椅

孙干：欧战华工记
Records of Chinese Labourers in European War by Sun Gan

上，俯首作祷。将至午时，有神父领跪，或唱诗或讲解《圣经》，严肃异常。礼拜毕后，余亦随之徐徐退出。斯时也，余想于平日繁华异常之大街市，一至礼拜日，则寂然无声。法人于礼拜日，不但将一切工作停止，且人人更换新衣帽，入堂敬祷于此。可见其信仰上帝之虔诚矣。

Faith of the French

During the first days in Hazebrouck, we did not have weekends because the employers and the labourers could not get along with each other and the work efficiency was not very high. But later, as the relationship between them became more harmonious, we began to have our weekends. One Sunday, we had the day off and I went into the downtown of Hazebrouck after breakfast. The streets were very still with no one there. As I approached a large church, I heard the strike of the clock from the tower inside it. Only then did I realise that it was time for the local people to worship God.

In a short time, neatly-dressed people of all ages came out from the streets and alleys into the church quietly. I followed them and entered the church too. As I went inside, I found a small pool on both the right and left side of the entrance with clear water in it. All the people dipped their fingers into the water and then put it onto their foreheads and both sides of their chests while they were entering the church. Then they entered the inner chamber, knelt down on chairs, bowed their heads and began to pray. Towards noon, the priest led them to kneel down to sing psalms or explain the Bible solemnly. After the service, I followed them out of the church slowly. At that time, I couldn't help thinking that it was very pious of the Frenchmen to stop all their work and put on their new clothes and hats to pray in the church on Sundays, leaving the busy and hustling streets extraordinarily quiet.

57. 法国道路旁亦有小庙

法人多半信天主教，敬圣母马利亚。通都大邑，矗天之礼拜堂，毗连一方公共之墓田者，为数不止三五座已也。即偏僻乡村、道旁路口，也往往有建筑极简单之小庙焉。小庙之内塑有男女神像三五尊，此亦欲令行路之人触目惊心者欤！其对于信仰尊崇之神，用意亦大矣哉！

Small Roadside Temples in France

Most of the French were Catholics and worship the Virgin Mary. In each city, there were usually more than three or four imposing churches adjoining the public cemeteries. Even in remote villages, roadsides and intersections, there were often small temples of very simple construction, inside which stood three or four statues of gods and goddesses. This sight often shocked passers-by, but these temples had great significance to the worship of the gods or goddesses that the local people believed in.

孙干：欧战华工记
Records of Chinese Labourers in European War by Sun Gan

58. 华工信件之往来

吾侪往来之书信，英人但发给信封，信瓤归各人自备。各人家中去信，大约半年左右始可收到，由法寄回中国之信，不过三四个月，家中即可收到。然一队之中，挑选写信明白者，不过五六人，仅能达意者，亦只有七八人。与英国兵士之都能写信一较，其高低奚啻天壤。

某休息日，忽一人从他队至，因其亲见余曰："烦先生写一家信可否？即花二十日之工价，亦所不惜。"余曰："可，只有信纸、信封足矣。"当时他人借与信纸一张，余即为之写一信持去。此可见赴法华工大多数之程度矣。

一日工毕归营，忽来一年幼者向余曰："请先生为余写一家信。"问其何县，曰："不知也。"余曰："汝既不知家住何县，信即不能写。"彼又曰："先生行行好吧，既会给他人写信，亦当会给予写也。"余遂问之曰："汝在家时都作何事？"曰："下庄稼地。"曰："进过城里否？"曰："未也。""赶过集否？"曰："咱是下庄稼地之人，欲赶集何为？"余知此人真一庄稼老斗，遂令去问其亲朋，彼是何县，先问明后再来，余即为汝写信。彼始唯唯而去。呜呼，中国人民教育之程度如是，可胜叹哉！

Correspondence of Chinese Labourers

For the correspondence of our fellow workers, the British provided us with only envelopes and we had to buy the paper on our own. For the letters we wrote home, it took about six months to arrive in China from France. Then, the letters would be received by our families in China in three or four months. However, in our brigade there were only five or six people who could write and only seven or eight people who could read or basically express their thoughts. In comparison with the British soldiers, most of whom could both read and write letters, it was not hard to see the great difference in literacy between China and Britain.

On a day off, a man suddenly arrived from another brigade. He came to find me directly and asked, "Would you please write a letter to my family? I'm willing to pay you 20 days of my wages." I said, "OK. But I only need a piece of paper and an envelope." Then someone lent him a piece of paper and I wrote a letter for him. This incident reflected, in a sense, the low literacy level of most of the Chinese labourers in France.

One evening, when I had just returned to the camp after a day of hard work, a young man came up suddenly and said to me, "Please write a letter for me, sir." I asked what county he was from, he said, "I don't know." I told him, "If you don't know your home address, there is no way for me to write a letter for you." He said again, "Sir, please do me a favour. Since you can write for others, you must be able to write for me." So, I asked him, "What did you do when you were at home?" He said, "I worked in the fields." I asked again, "Have you ever been to the city?" He answered, "No." I asked, "Have you ever been to any market fair?" He replied, "We are farmers, why should we go to a fair?" Knowing that this young man was really an out-and-out farmer, I told him to ask his friends or relatives about the place he was from so that I could write the letter for him when he came back the next time after knowing his address. Only then did he leave. Alas, it was really sad to see such a low level of education of Chinese people!

孙干：欧战华工记
Records of Chinese Labourers in European War by Sun Gan

59. 华工之赏罚

此次华工赴欧帮助协约，无所谓求赏。然英亦无甚明显之赏也，至于挞罚，则不能无者。因华工多半未受教育，不作工者、打架者、偷窃者、作弊者处处难免。如事小队长就地站队讯问，轻则罚钱，重则押至黑屋禁拘数日。非遇关系重大之案件，不能将犯人发送脑院，使进大牢。所以当时之工人皆曰："下外洋来打官司，不跪不打真算便宜之至矣！"

Rewards and Punishments of Chinese Labourers

The Chinese labourers who went to Europe to help the Entente countries did not intend to get rewarded. Although the British did not give obvious rewards, punishments were unavoidable because of the idleness, fights, thefts and cheatings of some Chinese labourers, most of whom were uneducated. In cases of such trivialities, the British Captain would investigate by asking us to stand in a line on site. The violators would be fined or detained in a dark room for several days. Only when it was a case of great importance, would the violators be sent to Noyelles for imprisonment. Therefore, all the labourers at that time said, "It would be light punishment without being forced to kneel or beaten in a lawsuit abroad!"

华工日记
Chinese Labourer's Diaries

60. 法国乡村之住户

法国北方乡村之住户，建筑房舍，不论东西南北之方向，此家与彼家距离甚稀。其住房多是一座大楼，楼傍一大泥湾，其中多泥水与麦穰，盖如中国农家之积攒肥田粪也。楼下为地窖数间，以备盛物用也。二层楼上有许多房间，以备一家之分处睡眠也。惟一进门之较大之房间，如中国人家之庭院，不仅全家之人吃饭时尽聚于其中，即宾朋之来，亦系在此招待。

住户之种地者，或用马耕，或用机器耕，所种大概以麦子、地蛋为大宗，次则为甜萝卜、白菜或荞麦。各家养奶牛数头，故家家有养牛之草地。牛奶煮熟加白糖，为其长年之饮料。如宾朋至，亦以此应酬之。乡村住户之果树多葡萄、苹果，苹果树几成森林，所以家家都贮藏果子酒、葡萄酒。其余榆柳等树虽有，极寥寥也。

Rural Residents of France

Households in the rural areas of northern France were usually very far apart from each other. Most of the households lived in their own tall buildings. Nearby each building was a large muddy bay filled with muddy water and stalks of crops, which was much the same way that Chinese farmers accumulated manure for their fields. Under the ground were cellars for the purpose of storing materials or food. On the first floor there were many rooms for family members to sleep in. Downstairs was a very large room leading to the entrance, which was like the Chinese courtyard, where the whole family gathered to have meals or entertain their friends and guests.

Farmers here cultivated their land either by horse or by machinery. Wheat and potatoes were their major crops and secondary to them were crops like turnips, cabbage or buckwheat. All households raised cows and each of them had large tracts of grasslands. Milk, to which sugar was added after it was thoroughly boiled, was their main drink all the year round. It was also used to entertain visiting friends and guests. Apples and grapes were the major fruits of rural households, which were widely planted by farmers in the rural areas. As a result, each household would store large amounts of fruit and grape wine. There were also other trees such as elms and willows but very few.

61. 农户之割麦

法人割麦之小机械如二轮之马车，然一马拉之，一人在车上两手持鞭与缰御之。马走车行，车前有如剪发刀之齿，车一前行遇麦，则左右推剪，剪下后另有一机随之而捆。捆成个后，从车后落地，毫不用人之力。一人一马，一日可割几十亩，若用较大之机械，其快又当如何耶！

Wheat Harvesting by Farmers

For wheat harvesting, the Frenchmen used small machinery such as the two-wheeled carriage, which was pulled by a horse. A person stood on the carriage and controlled the horse by holding a whip and the reins in his hands. With the moving of the horse and carriage, wheat on the left and right sides of the carriage was cut quickly by the sharp blades in its front like hair shears. Another machine followed to bundle the sheared wheat. After the wheat was bundled up, it was dropped onto the ground behind the carriage. No great human efforts were needed. With one person and one horse, several acres of wheat could be harvested in only one day. Suppose larger machinery was used, how fast would the harvesting be!

62. 妇女结队锄田

法国妇女，虽文明而有学识，然亦有时结队而至田间从事农作。按次排列，各持长铲，将田间之草一一戳死，此亦善良之风也。近吾祖国妇女之稍有学识者，其亦有是美德欤！

Women Hoeing in Groups

Although French women were civilised and educated, they sometimes came in groups to work in the fields. Standing in line and each holding a long shovel, they removed all the weeds in the field. Such was also the virtue of Frenchwomen. It made me wonder whether those women in our motherland with the same level of education could have such virtues!

孙干：欧战华工记
Records of Chinese Labourers in European War by Sun Gan

63. 割麦后之打场

法人割麦后，将麦个运至田间之一处。以摩托车将打麦机器拉来，燃火于机器中，后即将麦个从上边一一投入打麦机，麦粒即从机下流出，麦穰即已捆成个，从旁送外。所以观其用打麦机打麦之时，围打麦机数人合作，有向里投麦者，有从下用袋装麦粒者，有在旁垛麦穰者。一时齐忙，未及半日，千余麦个之粒，即都装入麻袋中矣。顾西人之收获打麦用机器，而不用场与碌轴，其省人工不止数十倍也。

Wheat Threshing after Harvest

After the wheat was harvested, the Frenchmen carried all the bundles to a certain place in the field. Then the machine for wheat threshing was brought along by a motor vehicle and was started to work. The bundles of wheat were put into the machine one by one. The wheat grain flowed out from below the machine while the bundled stalks were ejected from the side. Therefore, in threshing wheat with a machine, the cooperation of people around the machine was needed, with some in charge of throwing bundles inside, some in charge of sacking the grains below, and others in charge of piling the stalks nearby. With the effort of several people, more than a thousand bundles of wheat were threshed and put into sacks in less than half a day. Compared with grain threshing using stone mills on the threshing floor in China, the foreigners' harvesting and threshing of wheat with machines saved dozens of hours of labour.

64. 到法人学校参观其教授法

一日工毕,到哀司不老凯街市里之学校。其中学生数百,先生十余,都在院中游戏。余遂向其一主任交涉,愿参观其上班教授,彼即慨然应允。

刹那间摇铃上班,余亦随其师生登楼而入教室。学生甫坐定,先生登讲坛,先领学生肃立合目低头,同声祈告。约近五分钟,始坐。所授为算术,其教授之际,学生之求知心,无一或懈,争先恐后,无暇及他。因想己在祖国教授学生为时不少,未曾得有一次,如法人之使学生如此之用心努力也,不禁汗颜。旋闻铃声,余遂辞出。又至一室,与其先生数人一一寒暄,所恨者为余不谙法语,不能答意,惟以少微之英语,加以手势形容而已。

Visit to French School

One day after work I went to a school in the city of Hazebrouck, where hundreds of students and more than ten teachers were playing games in the schoolyard. When I explained my intention of seeing their teaching in classrooms, the head teacher among them agreed to let me observe.

Soon the bell for class rang and I followed the teacher and students into their classroom. As the students got themselves seated, the teacher walked onto the platform. He asked the students to stand up and prayed together with their heads down. Five minutes later, they finished their prayers and sat down again. It was an arithmetic class and all students showed great eagerness for learning. Although I had taught in my motherland for quite a few years, never once did I make my students work so hard as the French teacher did. Thinking of this, I could not help feeling ashamed of myself. After a while, the bell rang, and the class was over. I left the classroom and came into another room where there were several teachers. Because I knew little French, I could only greet them one by one with simple English words and a few gestures.

65. 华工队中之赌风已萌芽

安息日为西欧大多数人之圣日，一方礼拜真神上帝，因是学习耶稣暨圣母马利亚，一方学爱人负十字架之苦，以锻炼至善之精神教育。而华人既根本无此真神上帝观之信仰，又多无普通教育之知识，只知惟利是视。若一时无强制之法律管束之，则不能安分守法。一不使之得暇则已，一使之有暇，非四处扰乱，或窃或掠，即聚众作赌矣。余之一百零二队中之同伙，即表现此等现象也。以后渐赌渐热，虞诈更多。甚或在聚赌时数人暗中朋比为奸，而用诡计陷害一人，使其将在法所挣之工钱，全数输尽外，再输欠数月之工价之债。不但一棚如是，全队莫不如是。察之他队，亦莫不尽然。自此以后，赌风之盛愈演愈烈矣。华工中多系敦厚农夫，自赴法后，天天在工头借英人威权驱使之下，不敢不处处听从。工头亦借顺从之故，遂邀善于诡诈作弊者，为之作伥，与极老实之农夫聚赌。农夫之任其宰割，不问可知也。

华工日记
Chinese Labourer's Diaries

Gambling among Chinese Labourers

For most Europeans, Sunday was a holy day when they worshipped God to learn the spirit of Jesus Christ his son and the Virgin Mary on the one hand, and they learnt about the suffering of the Cross to cultivate the spiritual education of the supreme good on the other hand. However, because Chinese labourers did not have the belief in God and lacked the knowledge of general education, profit was their only consideration. As a result, they would not abide by the law once there was no compulsory law to discipline them for a time. It was all right if they were not given free time. But once they had got time, they would either steal or plunder in the camp or gather together to gamble. The phenomenon of gambling was prevalent among our fellow workers in Brigade 102. Later, as gambling became increasingly popular, there were more and more cases of cheating. Sometimes several people would secretly conspire to cheat a person in gambling so that all the money he had earned in France and even the wages for the next few months would be lost. Such a phenomenon was common not only in one tent but across the whole brigade. As far as I knew, labourers in other brigades also did the same. From then on, gambling became more and more popular. Most of the Chinese labourers were honest farmers who, driven by the foremen under the authority of the British officers, had become submissive in everything they did since they arrived in France. Taking advantage of their obedience, the foremen, together with other cunning individuals, incited these honest farmers to gamble. Thus, the poor farmers were reduced to the victims of gambling without even being aware of it.

孙干：欧战华工记
Records of Chinese Labourers in European War by Sun Gan

66.

时余棚之棚头刘成德（长山县人）者，于一晚间亦用此赌博诈财之手段，联络余赌。余再三谢绝，卒不罢休，并邀数人相劝，以稍作消遣为名。遂出宝而令众人押，余不得已遂之坐，每次只押一佛郎，约至半夜，未输一次。彼等云须多押，余即于幺与三各押一佛郎，虽有一输，而亦有一赢也。输赢相抵者良久，仍是未有输赢。彼又劝余不必如此，可再多押。时余因不能熬夜，甚觉精神疲乏，而生气矣。遂于每次十余佛郎，而渐输渐气，而每次押数百或数千佛郎矣。至斯时也，天将平明，而彼不敢再出，将账总算，余欠彼八百多佛郎也。彼欲作罢，余与之理论曰："余本不会赌博，原为汝强逼余赌，余输款至巨时，余不得先言作罢，还须再赌。俟余赢汝后，余言罢赌方可。不然汝与吾同去见长官再打官司，再不然余不能还汝钱也。"卒至经众人调说曰："出外与小人遇，稍花几钱，免有性命之忧也。"余遂应允还彼三分之一而始完结。于此可知，华工队中，老实忠厚之农夫，不会赌博而吃此等亏者，为数岂少也欤。

One evening Liu Chengde, head of our tent, tried to entice me into gambling by such cheating means. I declined again and again, but he did not give up and asked several other people to persuade me to join their gambling in the name of recreation. Then he tossed some dice and asked the others to bet the total points on the dice. I had to sit with them and bet. At first, I only bet one franc at a time and made it to midnight without losing. Then he and the others told me to bet more, so I bet a franc on the number of one and three each. Although I had one loss, I had one win as well. This situation continued for a long time. Then, he said there was no need for me to be so cautious and advised me to bet more money. Because I could not want to stay up too late into the night, I was already very tired and angry at that time. So I began to bet more than ten francs at a time. Every time I lost, I became angrier and gradually began to bet tens and even several hundred francs at a time. Till then, it was already dawn and he did not dare to continue. After the final account was figured out, I owed eight hundred francs to him. I did not intend to give him the money and argued with him, "I had no intention of gambling at all, it was you who forced me to gamble. When I lost so much money you should not end the gambling. We should not stop until I've won you and say it's time to stop. Otherwise, I would go to see the officer together with you and make a complaint against you. I will not give you any money." Hearing this, other people said to me, "It is unavoidable for us to encounter some bad guys. You had better give some money for the sake of your own safety." Finally, it was settled after I promised to give him one third of the money. From this event, we could see that there must be many other simple and honest farmers in the brigade of Chinese labourers, who suffered such losses in gambling because of their ignorance of it.

67. 余在队中寄禁赌告白于各队

余想华工中之素日会赌、好吃、好嫖者固不少，然忠厚善良之不

孙干：欧战华工记
Records of Chinese Labourers in European War by Sun Gan

会赌博者，仍占多数。若任会赌博者之用种种方法，将忠厚者工价使其输尽，使原不会之良善分子，而渐学成会赌之坏习惯，亦良可惜也。况使欧美人士见之，将使堂堂华民贻笑大方，余又安肯坐视？于是余于作工之暇，除想提倡社会教育外，即书写告白纸多张，以寄在法华工各队中，俾张贴于各队之冲要处，以儆醒赌博者。其告白之文如下：

告白

众位弟兄知悉：

　　吾们千山万水，远涉重洋来到欧洲，实在不易。各人家中父母妻子，现在正希望我们在外赚几元钱，寄到家中，方能度日。我们在此千万不可赌博。若一赌博，将钱输尽，不但将来自己乏钱使用，即归家之后，邻里子侄，亦都看我不起也。

华工一百零二队工人孙宝桢敬启

My Initiative to Ban Gambling among Chinese Labourers

Although quite a few of Chinese labourers were fond of gambling, good food and whoring, most of them were honest, kind and loyal individuals and disapproved of gambling or other vices. It would be a great pity if these honest labourers were cheated into gambling and lost all their money to those gamblers who cheated with various tricks. Also, if such bad behaviours were seen by the Europeans and Americans, our Chinese labourers would become a laughingstock of them. How could I just sit back and do nothing about it? After some thought, I decided to advocate social education in my spare time. So I wrote several notices and sent them to various brigades of Chinese labourers in France to be posted on prominent places to warn against gambling. The warning notice read as follows:

NOTICE

My dear fellow labourers,

It is not easy for us to travel across the oceans to Europe. Our parents and wives at home are expecting us to send the money we earn here to make a living. So, we must not gamble here. If we do, we will lose all our money. Not only will we have no money ourselves in the future, but we shall also be looked down upon by our relatives, our neighbours and even our own children when we return home.

Sun Baozhen from Chinese Labourer Brigade 102

68. 寄给各队翻译及大工头书

某队翻译员、大工头诸位先生仝鉴：

现今，我们远离祖国来至此地，同工等有赌钱者，有格外好穿自买衣服及食物者，又有好喧闹滋事者。作以上种种，不惟无益而有害，且徒使他国之人见之，更加耻笑也。现今，我们祖国正待积极振兴，即我等在外，当如何保全祖国之名誉，如何广求振兴国家之学问，如何学得技巧之艺术，如何储蓄应得之金钱，至三年还家以后，以学问与技艺帮助我们国家，以储蓄之金钱捐输我们国家，以作恶之力量勇于为善，使不善之名誉变为令名。望以此意，彼此互相劝勉，个个努力，外人不但

孙干：欧战华工记
Records of Chinese Labourers in European War by Sun Gan

不耻笑，且能重视。若在法国同胞，各队都能如此做去，对国家之帮助，岂曰浅鲜。今另有告白若干张，收到后分贴贵队之冲要处，是幸，专此候覆。

　　敬讯

旅安

　　　　　　　华工一百零二队　　63484　　孙某　　敬启

Letters to Interpreters and Foremen

Dear interpreters and foremen,

　　Since arriving in France, some of our Chinese labourers have been addicted to gambling; others have been fond of buying food and clothes by themselves; and some have made troubles constantly. However, it is of no benefit for people to do all the things mentioned above. As a matter of fact, not only is it harmful to our labourers, but it also makes foreigners look down upon us. Today, our motherland is waiting to be revitalised. For us who are working in foreign lands, what we should do is to learn how to preserve the reputation of our motherland, to seek knowledge for the revitalisation of our country, to acquire new skills, and to save the money we have earned. Only in this way can we help our country with our knowledge and skills, contribute to our country with our savings, do good deeds by fighting against the evils, and turn the bad reputation into a good one when we return to our motherland three years later. I hope all of us can encourage each other to work hard so that we will not be looked down upon by and even win the respect of the foreigners. If all brigades of our fellow countrymen in France can do so, it will be of great help to our country. Enclosed are some notices and I hope they can be posted on prominent places within your brigades for the labourers' attention.

Best wishes to you. I am looking forward to your reply.

Yours sincerely,

No. 63484 Labourer Sun from Brigade 102

69. 劝告在法华工勿学赌博书

华工众位同胞知悉：

我们千山万水来到法国，大英政府之待遇我们，衣暖食美，可谓周到。我们当尽心竭力，好好做工。千万莫要学习赌博，赌博之人往往打架，不惟弟兄彼此伤情，尤能坏人之品行也。当时赢者无非挥霍，输者能不愈输愈罄。且我们家中谁无父母，谁无妻子。三年还家，手中有钱，阖家欢喜；手中无钱，阖家愠怒。语云："贫则父母不子，富而亲戚畏惧。"尔时懊悔，岂不晚哉！岂不晚哉！

中华民国七年正月

工人63484　孙某某　敬白

Notice Warning Chinese Labourers Not to Gamble

My dear fellow Chinese labourers,

We have come all the way to France after undergoing many difficulties and the British government have treated us well by providing us with warm clothes and good food. In return, we should take pains to work hard. Never try to learn gambling. Those who gamble will fight with others, which will hurt the relationship between our brothers and lead to bad conduct. While gambling, winners tend to squander what they have got while losers will lose all their money. All of us have parents, wives and children at home. All the family will be happy if we return with lots of money three years later. However, they will get infuriated if we return without money. Just as the saying goes, "A poor man will not be disowned by his parents whereas a rich man will be dreaded by relatives." At that time, it will be too late for you to repent. Too Late!

July 1918

No. 63484 Labourer Sun

70. 在法华工中提倡社会教育

  余在工程队中，见工人多数于作工之暇，聚于帐棚内出宝、看牌作等等有害之事。遂想到向来所学之教授法中，有言云："人性好动，幼儿尤然。"遂又想华工者，年龄虽然不幼，而其程度仍如年幼者也。利其好动之性，教以识字，以代学赌，现则正逢其时矣。遂到各棚中演讲读书之益，其后工人有反对者，颇多赞成。问余者曰："若学读书，当先读何书？"余以其皆无程度故，即以读百家姓与之相商，愿者甚多。于是余即预备黑板一页，每于晚间授以数字。

华工日记
Chinese Labourer's Diaries

Advocating Social Education among Chinese Labourers in France

When I was in the engineering brigade, I often saw labourers gathering in their tents and gambling in their spare time. It made me think of the words in Teaching Methodology I had learned that "Human beings are born to be restless, especially for young children". Although these Chinese labourers were not children, their education level was nearly the same as that of children. It was a good time to take advantage of their restless nature and teach them to read and write instead of gambling. So I went to different tents to tell them the benefits of reading and writing. Some labourers objected to my proposal, but most of them approved of it. They asked me, "What book should we use if we learn to read?" Considering that they had received very little education, I recommended the *Book of Family Names*. After explaining the reasons for my choice, they all agreed. So I prepared a blackboard and taught them several characters from the book every evening.

71. 参观哀司不老凯市东某小村之小学校

余工作，往哀司不老凯之东分运大炮弹，于郊外往来已数日焉。一日作工之余，到某小村之一小学校内参观。其教师为夫妇二人，均年在三十左右，有子女各一。校内附有教员家属室，二人均极谦和。余向之说明愿参观彼校之意，彼亦问及余赴法时所经之路径，一一问之。

孙干：欧战华工记
Records of Chinese Labourers in European War by Sun Gan

及摇铃上班，学生男女仅十数人，所授之教材为猛虎，为师者先抱一猫来，使学生观察，并逐一问答。继则使猫去，而用绘画，如画虎头，又画虎眼、虎眉、虎须、虎牙、虎爪等等，一一画出，并书其名字。其画不但迅速而且逼肖，学生之注意力无稍懈者。以后授课文时，肃静之精神乃不如前，盖因学生本性喜常动不喜久静也。须臾下班，排队出校而散。

其教师曰："校有十岁之学生，每天清早骑自行车背饭包，从十数里外来上学。是时亦自骑其车而归。"观其好学之心，良可嘉也。时将近下四点钟，余亦辞出。吾想，法之充教员者，其绘画之程度，真为吾侪所望尘莫及，宜乎欧美之人民，对于绘画均甚迅速也。

Visit to a Village Primary School in Eastern Hazebrouck

I once carried cannonballs in the east of Hazebrouck. After spending several days in the suburbs, I went to visit a primary school in a small village after work. The only teachers at the school were a couple, both in their thirties and with a son and daughter. Inside the school, there were separate rooms for their family. Both of them were very kind and modest. After I told them my intention of visiting the school, they agreed and asked me about the route I took during my travel to France.

When the bell rang for class, I found there were no more than ten students, including both boys and girls. The teaching content was fierce tigers. The teacher first brought a cat into the class for students to observe and answered the students' questions one by one. Then, he let go of the cat and began to teach

99

by painting. He painted the head, eyes, eyebrows, and whiskers, teeth, claws of tigers, and wrote their respective names. He soon finished the painting which was very true to life. The students were very attentive all the time. However, when the teacher taught the text later, the atmosphere was not as quiet as before. This was because the children were inherently restless and found it difficult to keep quiet for a long time. The class was over a while later and the students left school in an orderly manner.

The teacher said to me, "There are some ten-year-old students who ride bicycles and carry lunch bags to school from their homes over ten miles away every morning. And now they also return home by riding their bicycles." It was really admirable that these students had such inquiring mind. Soon, it was nearly 4 o'clock in the afternoon and I left the school. I thought to myself that the painting level of the French teachers was so high that we could never catch up with them. It was no wonder that Europeans and Americans were able to paint so fast.

72. 赴法华工之工资

英人对于赴法华工之工资，普通者，在中国每人每月发给其家中大洋十元，特别者即翻译，暨工头、匠人等，每月每人发给其家属自十余元至数十元不等。在法国者，普通工人每月每人发给法国纸币三十佛郎，特别者亦分匠人、小工头、大工头、翻译等，自四十五佛郎至八九十佛郎亦不一。每至月稍发给纸币时，工人先站队，按次领取。如各工人或有不愿工作，或挂号不能作工者，即无工资。每日工头持大家之工牌，

孙干：欧战华工记
Records of Chinese Labourers in European War by Sun Gan

按日作工者，即按日画到。每到月稍，视工牌有无旷工、挂病号等情事。无旷工者，每人应支给洋三十佛郎，如工人心不愿当时领出，复交队长，队长即为之收存，入于存款账上。察英人为华工储蓄之用意，亦恐多数华工之无程度者，钱一到手，就任意挥霍，或喝酒或赌博作无益之消耗，其用意亦美矣哉。然当时亦有多人，对于每日只给一佛郎之数极不满意。余为之作歌一则如下（用祖国歌长江谱子）：

贪财：外洋来，多半指望到此发大财。那知按月领工牌，一天一佛郎开，次第往下挨。若挂病号工钱裁，再遇花销，手中还是分文不能存。（每佛郎抵法之铜元十枚）

Wages of Chinese Labourers in France

For ordinary Chinese labourers, the British paid ten silver dollars to their families in China every month. For some special Chinese labourers such as interpreters, foremen, and craftsmen, the British government gave wages ranging from over ten silver dollars to dozens of silver dollars to their families in China every month. In France, the ordinary labourers received 30 francs every month while those special labourers, who were again divided into craftsmen, assistant foremen, chief foremen and interpreters, received 40 or 50 or 80 to 90 francs every month. At the end of each month when paper money was distributed, all labourers would stand in line to get their wages one by one. For those labourers who had been absent from work or registered unable to work, there were no wages. Every day, the foremen recorded the attendance of those who came to work on the work card of each labourer. At the end of every month, they would see from the work cards of each labourer whether or not there were any absences. Those without any absence, would each receive 30 francs as pay. If the labourer did not want payment at that time, they could return their pay to the Captain, who would take the money back and place it in a deposit account. I think the British officers were afraid that the uneducated Chinese labourers would waste their wages on gambling or drinking once they had money in their pockets. It was out of good intention that the British saved the wages of the Chinese labourers. However, there were many people who were very dissatisfied with the amount of only one Franc per day. I composed a song for them as follows (with the tune of *Yangtze River*):

Greed for money: When coming to foreign countries, they mostly expected to make great fortunes. Out of their expectations, they were paid only one franc a day at the end of the month. At the end of the month, according to their work cards, wages would be subtracted if they had any days off to see a doctor, meaning there is no money left in their pocket if other expenses had to be paid. (One franc equalled ten copper coins)

73. 西欧之人长于绘画之我见

西欧人士之教育，其对于绘画一科，在学校中之教授儿童，盖与文字并重也。有一次余往法人学校中参观，见为教师者，于教授时随手绘出课内之主要处，使学生一见明瞭，于此可见绘图之有价值，而代替语言之讷讷半天矣。一次，又往法人另一小学校参观，见群生于正课之余，争绘法国兵士之头盔，个个绘出快而且肖。即吾侪华工队中，数十英人与数百工

孙干：欧战华工记
Records of Chinese Labourers in European War by Sun Gan

人之言语交际，用翻译只有一人，翻译除应付队长，暨几大工头以外，无暇及其他人。所以数十英人与数百工人，语言不通之处，多半利赖绘画。譬如英人欲建筑房屋，绘以简单之几线而成屋形，然后书明高与长宽之尺数以示华工工头，几乎不用语言，亦能将屋建成。一事如是，他事亦能如是。余赴法后，愿学英语，未学法语。所以在法国街市中，买物、问路甚觉不便，遂亦仿英人之用绘画，如欲买鱼，即先画鱼。无论法人、英人或美人，无不知之者。由此观之，西人教育之重看绘画，可知其故矣。回想吾国教员，对于绘画不甚重视，宁非一大缺点？

My View on Western European Painting Techniques

The subject of drawing was given the equal importance with writing in the education of western Europeans. When I visited a French school one day, I saw the professor sketched out the main points of his lesson quickly on the blackboard so that the students could see them clearly. Thus, the value of drawing was evident. A good drawing could replace a long explanation with words. On the other day, I went to visit another primary school and saw a group of students were drawing the helmet of French soldiers during their playtime break. All their drawings were completed quickly and were true to life. In our brigade of Chinese labourers there was only one interpreter who had to communicate with dozens of British soldiers and hundreds of Chinese labourers. As a matter of fact, he did not have enough time to talk to anyone except the Captain and several foremen. Therefore, whenever there was something hard to explain with language, the dozens of British officers and hundreds of Chinese labourers had to rely on drawings to communicate. For example, when the British wanted to build a house, they would draw a shape of the house with several simple lines and then show the required length and width to the Chinese foreman. In this way, a house could be built even without any verbal communication. Other things could be done similarly. Because I hadn't learnt any French after I arrived in France, although I had learnt some English, it was very inconvenient whenever I went shopping or asked directions on French streets or markets. So I followed the example of the British by taking advantage of drawing. For example, I would draw a fish if I wanted to buy fish so that everyone, whether he was a Frenchman, an Englishman or an American, would know what I meant. From these examples we could understand why Western education attached so much importance to drawing. However, teachers in China usually failed to see the importance of drawing. Was it a great disadvantage of Chinese education?

74. 法人之买卖铺

余因欲提倡社会教育，使华工认字，华工即多欲买铅笔、石笔、石板、纸张，以便仿写。然在队中不能随便出入，对于所需之物，求之不得也。一日，众工人烦余设法为其买购一切文具，余遂向上官索护照一张，持而之哀司不老凯之街市，为之购求。此处之街道宽约两三丈，或有更宽而至四丈五丈者，大街旁之小巷宽亦一二丈。其房屋尽为楼房，通常皆五六层，有高至十余层者，规模之宏大，不言可知也。店员多是少妇与小学生，间或有年至五十或六七十之长者在其店中坐，若皆理事者。然余至一文具店中，见有四人，小孩二人，俱束发辫，盖女学生也，约七八岁。其余二人为年在二十岁左右之少妇，一见余至，逢迎极有礼

孙干：欧战华工记
Records of Chinese Labourers in European War by Sun Gan

貌，余亦用恭敬之言语答之。

以后彼询余之所购求，余即一一指其货架上之物。两学生知余之所欲买者为何物焉，遂即一一取来以纸包好，又将货单书写清楚，而递余手。其余少妇二人，笑而不言。余接货单一一察看，见文具列一行，价目列一行，遂后即交钱携物而归。知法人之教育儿女，盖有素也。

French Stores

Now that I advocated social education and offered to teach the Chinese labourers to read and write, many of them wanted to buy pencils, slate pencils, slates, and paper for writing. However, because we were not allowed to leave the camp freely, we could not get these things easily. One day, the labourers asked me to buy all the stationery they needed for them. So, I asked the British officer for a pass and went to the marketplace in Hazebrouck to buy all these items. The streets were about twenty to thirty feet wide, or even forty to fifty feet wide. The alleys beside the streets were about ten to twenty feet wide. All the houses were magnificent buildings of five to six storeys or even as high as ten storeys. The store assistants were mostly young women and primary school students. Occasionally there were elders in their sixties or seventies sitting inside the stores. However, in the stationery store I entered there were altogether four assistants: two were schoolchildren, seven- or eight-year-old girl students with braided hair, and the other two were young women in their twenties. As soon as they saw me enter the store, they greeted me politely and I returned their greetings with respect.

When they asked me about the goods I intended to buy, I pointed at the items on the shelves one by one. The two students understood what I meant,

105

and took all the items I wanted from the shelves and wrapped them in paper. They also wrote a list of the items clearly and then handed them to me. The other two young women smiled at me but said nothing. I took a look at the list and saw that on the paper there were two columns, with one being the items of stationery and the other being the prices. After paying the bill, I returned to the camp with all I had bought. From this experience in the store, I realised that the French children were well-educated by their parents.

75. 华工之自由

吾国既加入协约，许英招募华工，吾华工等亦愿撇家舍业，帮忙英人赴法作工。此乃彼此同意，无可仇视者也。只要彼尽主人之责，我辈尽工人之力，不但吾侪之所甘心，亦英人之所乐意也。然华工工作以外，往往不得自由，营盘出入，极不随便，其故何也？果英人之苛虐乎？余曰不然。

华工工队初至法时，除工作外，出入行动，极其自由。时日既久，工人有至法人家中，见其什物随便持去者；有至法人家中，终日呆坐，不回营作工者；甚至掠物住宿，处处出人意外。索酒喝、打苹果皆其小焉者也。于是法人之至各华工队中，与英人交涉。于是英人始在队中出告示，或面谕，常常演讲，终仍无济于事。殊不知华工，虽多忠厚农夫，而流氓匪类亦为甚多。如是之流氓匪类，若一时不用严厉之刑律绳之，徒以善言相劝，岂非对牛弹琴乎？所以卒至各队禁止华工出入营门，以前之自由遂失矣。

孙干：欧战华工记
Records of Chinese Labourers in European War by Sun Gan

Freedom of Chinese Labourers

After China joined the Entente Countries, Britain was allowed to recruit Chinese labourers who were also willing to leave their families for France to work for the British. This was a mutual agreement and there was no enmity. As long as they took their responsibilities as employers and we did our best to work as labourers, not only would our workers be willing, but the British would also be delighted with it. However, in reality the Chinese labourers often had no freedom to leave their camp after work. Why was this? Was it because the British were too cruel? I would say "No".

When brigades of Chinese labourers first arrived in France, our labourers could move in or out of the camps freely in the spare time after work. But everything turned to be very different later. After being in France for a while, some of our workers went into the houses of the French and took their belongings away; some kept sitting in the French houses and refused to go back to work; some even grabbed the belongings of the French and lived in their houses; and still many others asked the French for wine or picked their apples from their orchards. As a result of all these types of incidents, the French came to the camps to complain to the British. The British then began to post notices around the camps, talk with our workers face to face, or give speeches to the whole brigade, but nearly all their efforts were in vain. Little did they know that there were some bad guys among the Chinese labourers although the vast majority were honest and hardworking farmers. For these few bad guys, any attempt to persuade them without severe punishment in accordance with strict laws would be like "casting pearls before swine." As a result of their actions, Chinese labourers in all brigades were prohibited from going in and out of their camps other than to work, thus losing their former freedom.

华工日记
Chinese Labourer's Diaries

76. 法国野外之饼干肉盒

欧战一起，各洲各国，运往欧洲之一切什物至夥。除快枪、大炮、小皮靴之使用与身着者外，又有食料焉。法国田野间抛弃之食物，如饼干也、牛肉盒也、面包也、糖酱也，或成箱焉，或成盒焉。不弃之于道，即弃之于沟洫；不藏之于洞中，即藏之于土下。饼干、肉盒多盛以大小之洋铁箱，糖酱、面包或盛之以大小木箱，或盛之以大小纸盒。观盒上制造之年月，有已三年、五年者，亦有十年、二十年者，甚有已五十余年者。吾侪之食量大者，每遇之即喜出望外，盖借之得一饱也。

Biscuits and Meat Cans in French Fields

During the European War, large numbers of materials were transported to Europe from countries on all continents. In addition to objects for use and wearing such as fast guns, cannons, and boots, there were various kinds of foodstuffs. In the fields of France people could often find abandoned food such as biscuits, bully-beef cans, bread and sugar, all in boxes or packets. They were abandoned either beside roads or in ditches, either in caves or in dugouts. Biscuits and meat boxes were usually filled with foreign metal containers of various sizes, while sugar and bread were in wooden boxes or paper sacks. From the date printed on the boxes, it could be seen that some food was three or five years old, others ten or twenty years old, and still others even more than fifty years old. Some of my fellow labourers who had great appetite would be overjoyed whenever they found food because they could eat to their heart's content.

77. 法人之茔田

余赴欧战作工以助协约国，借观西人之教育与风俗习惯焉。法人之习惯，与中国人之不同者，如守安息日也、接吻也、跃舞也、收获庄稼也，等等一切，各有各之方法，各有各之习惯。今就法国人之墓田言之，其墓田多系靠近其一村之人常作礼拜之礼拜堂后，且一小村庄公共只用一处。非若吾国之设立茔田，一家一族，各不相混也。

French Cemeteries

While I worked in Europe helping the Entente countries in the war, I took the opportunity to observe the education and customs of the westerners. The French had some customs and practices that were different from those of the Chinese, such as observing the Sabbath day, kissing, dancing, and the methods of harvesting crops. Each had their own habits and ways of doing things. In terms of cemeteries, the French usually built their cemeteries behind the churches, where villagers often went on Sundays, and each village had only one cemetery for public use. It was quite different from the practice in China, where every family had its own burial plot that would never be mixed with others.

华工日记
Chinese Labourer's Diaries

78. 英人与法人举动不同

或有问于余曰："近百年来，英法两国在向外开拓殖民地方面极端挟手合作，汝此次至欧洲战场协助又是英人，所到又是法地，对于英法两国人之接触既多，观察其举止，或同或异，心中更当明了也。"余必应之曰："是。"

世界之人，凡居于优胜，或居于失败者，人往往另有一心以审察之。英法近百年来，国势极盛，所以余早以有是心焉。英人与法人在先曾有百年战争，而今则无之，其已过去者，有下数端焉：

一信仰，英人是新教，法人是旧教，新旧两教不能合一也。一地势，英人所居近寒带，法人所居近热带，热带人活动，寒带人沉静也。一种族，英人系条顿后裔，法人系拉丁后裔，显明英法两国非一种族也。其他尚有国体，如英为君王，而法为民主。而即现在余所见英人与法人，英人诚实小心，法人清高易动；英人尚坚忍，法人爱美观。然观察其现在之所以能合作者，盖因其国民教育至高，而不致以近邻自相残杀也。

Difference between British and French Behaviours

Sometimes people would ask me, "In the past one hundred years, Britain and France have both closely cooperated in the expansion of their colonies.

孙干：欧战华工记
Records of Chinese Labourers in European War by Sun Gan

Since your arrival to assist the British in the battlefields in France, you must have had a lot of contact with both the British and French people. Therefore, from your observations, you must be more aware of the similarities and differences in their behaviours?" I would always answer "Yes."

People in the world would like to study the behaviour of other nations who were either winners or losers of conflict. Both Britain and France had enjoyed great national powers for over one hundred years, and I had intended to study them long ago. Britain and France had fought the Hundred Year's War (1339–1453) in history, but they had not fought against each other in recent times. Some of the differences between them are as follows:

One difference was religion. The British believed in Protestantism while the French believed in Catholicism, which could not be unified. Another difference was climate. The British lived near the cold zone while the French lived close to the tropical zone. People in colder zones preferred a less active lifestyle while people in the warmer zones enjoyed more outdoor activities. The third difference was ethnicity. The British were of Teutonic descent while the French were of Latin descent. Obviously, the British and the French did not belong to the same ethnic group. The fourth difference was their systems of state. The state system of Britain was a monarchy while the state system of France was democracy. From my observations, the British were honest and steadfast while the French were self-contained and emotional; the British were perseverant while the French loved beauty. As for the reasons for their cooperation in contemporary times, it was because both of them had good education and were well aware that it was not wise for them to fight with their neighbours.

79. 法地之运河

余自民国六年冬月到法国以后，回想吾国之人享受自由，不为不多。何以言之？中国不但住房、道路随人民之心意，任其自由，即溪涧、湖沼、江河、海洋，亦莫不任人出处，毫无限制也。而余到法国，不但道路、房屋处处按法制之须使之整齐，即其河流也必条条浚之疏之，令其有用也。

当余在法之东北部，马尔内河及疴易斯河、索美河三流域往来作工之时，于田野间，尝见有不少之河流从地内流往他处，如火车之入隧道然。河身之上以石筑建之穹窿高起，上复覆之以厚土，数里而留一洞，盘旋上通地面，以备河中乘船之人便于上行或下行者。察闻其长度，或几里或几十里不等，盖为其露天运河之另培土，可谓之地里运河者也。观其治理之齐整，其有益于交通也，亦大矣哉。想吾国之治河者，盍亦仿效之也。

Canals in France

After arriving in France in the winter of 1917, I often thought that compared with the French, people of our country enjoyed much more freedom. Why would I say this? Because in China not only could people build their houses and roads as they liked, but they could also have free access to streams, lakes, rivers, seas and oceans, without any restrictions. In France, however, not only should roads and houses be built in order according to the nation's laws, but all their canals and rivers should also be dredged to keep them useable by the people.

When I worked in the reaches of the rivers of Marne, Oise and Somme in the northeast of France, I often noticed that many rivers flowed from the land to other places just as the train the tunnels. Over the river, there was a stone vault with a thick layer of soil upon it and a hole was left every several miles, which circled up to the ground for the ascending and descending of boat riders. Varying from a mile to dozens of miles, these ground canals were actually open canals built with soils upon them. Seeing the uniform governance of these canals, which was of great benefit to the boat traffic, I could not help thinking that governors in our country should follow their examples in the governance of rivers and canals.

80. 医院之多

欧战一役，劳民伤财，不徒直接加入战争者被害，即不加入战争者，国中什物缺乏，物价昂贵，感觉心中之不快，其人数亦多多也。

民国七年一月六日，余因苦工而手皲裂，至一大镇市中，哀斯不老凯医院中诊视，见医院中之大夫、护士及一切作工服事病人者，莫不谦和恭蔼，言语忠实，举动宜人，其设备药物之完备，更属见所未见。自是以后，余之驻所，又迁徙数次，而至八宝林池野外，见野外之医院所占之地约大数亩。英人之战地医院，不独大城市有之，即田野间亦随处多有。

Numerous Hospitals

The European War brought about a great loss of resources in the countries that joined the war directly. Even in countries that did not join the war, countless people suffered a lot from it due to the shortage of necessities and high prices of goods in their own countries.

On 6 January 1918, I went to a hospital in the centre of Hazebrouck because my hands became chapped from the hard work. The doctors, nurses and all other people working in the hospital were courteous and friendly and the equipment and medicines in the hospital seemed very complete and advanced. From then on, we moved several times. When we were encamped in the fields near Boulogne, I saw a field hospital which covered an area of several acres. There were numerous British field hospitals, not only in big cities but also everywhere in the fields.

81. 欧美妇孺亦开摩托车

吾人一到欧美,即自以为欧美各国之强盛,绝非中国一时所能及。单即其交通一观,无论都会乡村,其道靡不修理整齐,使摩托车之往来迅速也。余至法见欧美之摩托车,种种不一,即实用方面观之,有载重者,有乘客者,有稍迟者,有极速者。迟者日行数百里,速者日行数千里,马路之上往来驰骋,交通之便不但成人能驾驶之,妇孺之能驾驶者,亦极其普通之事。

孙干：欧战华工记
Records of Chinese Labourers in European War by Sun Gan

European Women and Children Riders of Motorcycles

As soon as we arrived in Europe, we realised the power and prosperity of the European countries and America, which was something that China could not catch up with for many years. All the roads, in cities or in countryside, were paved and tidy, where motorcycles moved back and forth at fast speeds. I had seen a great variety of European and American motorcycles since I arrived in France. From a practical point of view, some motorcycles were used for carrying materials, while others were used for carrying passengers. In terms of speed, some motorcycles could travel only at a low speed while others could travel at a high speed. The low-speed motorcycles could travel tens of miles a day while the high-speed ones could travel hundreds of miles a day. They could be seen moving back and forth on the roads every day. For their convenience motorcycles were greatly liked not only by men but also by women and children. It was quite common to see women and children riding motorcycles.

82. 余于工作以后之工作

中国之文弱，实因读书之人以不作劳力之事为上等人。积之久，全国人亦俱陷于文弱矣。今余思将此恶习改之，自到法作工，无时或懈也。暇时，除私自教授数十工人读百家姓外，又常书写禁赌告白，四出张贴。一日余出张贴时，在野外路中，忽遇一形似豺狼之赌鬼，那人说："执令

华工日记
Chinese Labourer's Diaries

汝作我们的首领和审官，管辖我们呢（《创世纪》二章十四节）。我们赌博非输他人之钱，汝四出张贴布告何为？以后不改，吾等群起殴之。"余曰："劝大家不学赌博，乃善意也，汝爱赌可以随便，千万不可见怪。"同伴亦以婉言相劝，彼始行去。同伴向余曰："人心叵测，莫若华工。劝勿赌博，虽属善意，而吾闻华工队中之反对汝劝阻赌博之告白者，实大有其人。以后出贴告白，当慎之也。"

My Work in Spare Time

Most Chinese seemed to be frail-looking in that Chinese scholars considered themselves superior and were unwilling to do manual work. With this thought in people's mind for a long time, the whole nation had gradually become weak. In an attempt to change this bad habit, I had worked tirelessly every day since my arrival in France. In my spare time, I taught dozens of labourers to read the *Book of Family Names*. Besides, I often wrote anti-gambling notices and posted them everywhere. One day, when I was out to post the notices, I met a tough-looking gambler on a field road. He said to me, "Who makes you our leader and the judge and ruler over us? (Exodus 2:14) We gamble with our own money. Why do you put up posters everywhere? If you go on doing it, we will beat you up!" I replied, "I discourage people from gambling out of my own good intentions. If you like gambling, that is your right, and you can do as you please." He left only after my companions had persuaded him for a while. My companions then said to me, "Chinese labourers are unpredictable. Although it is your goodwill to advise them not to gamble, we hear that there are quite a few people opposing your anti-gambling advice amongst the brigades of Chinese labourers. You should be cautious when you go out to post them later."

孙干：欧战华工记
Records of Chinese Labourers in European War by Sun Gan

83. 在欧战时华工到处之天空

自到哀司不老凯，即见有形似雁行之大鸡卵遍空皆是者，轻气球也。轻气球虽不时被炮打，被飞机至燃火焚烧，然缺者立补，仍无害于在空中观察敌情也。轻气球之制，外为胶质之皮，以绳联络为网围于其外，内充以较空气更轻之轻气，是以易于上浮。下端系以乘人之小艇，球升而人艇随之，顷刻升至云霄矣。艇中之人以望远镜视敌人，敌人之行止历历可见也。

欧战时，法境天空之飞机，无日无夜，无早无晚而不见也。有时似闲暇而三五架回还往复，学习打靶；有时反复上下，各显武艺；有时德机飞来数十架而聚为一团，翱翔战斗。机关枪声彼此交加，吸引地上之大炮，隆隆不绝，其形可观，其危险亦可悯也。

Light Balloons and Aeroplanes in the Sky during the European War

From the time we arrived in Hazebrouck, we often saw countless enormous egg-shaped crafts flying in the sky like flocks of flying geese. They were light balloons used to observe the enemy from the sky. Although some of them were bombarded from time to time or attacked and burned by aeroplanes, new light balloons were sent up to replace them. The outside of the light balloon was made of rubber and its inside was filled with hydrogen, which was lighter than air so that it could float in the sky. It was surrounded by a net or ropes and at the lower end was a small boat like basket for people, which would go up as the balloon went up. Light balloons could fly high into the sky in an instant. With telescopes, people in the basket could clearly observe any movement of the enemy.

During the European War, aeroplanes in the sky of France could be seen every day, from morning until night. Sometimes, several aeroplanes flew back and forth in the sky leisurely, seeming to be practicing shooting and sometimes they flew up and down repeatedly, seeming to show off their skills. At other times, dozens of German aeroplanes flew amongst them and they fought fiercely in the sky. Combined with the sound of machine-guns and the rumbling artillery on the ground, the situation was very impressive, but the danger was also considerably great.

84. 英人之载重摩托车及法之马路

战场所需之子弹枪械、粮台用具，除少数由火车运输外，其大多数尽赖于载重摩托车。车每辆能容六七十人，每点钟能行三四十里。其所以惊人者，犹不在其行驶之快，而在其辆数之多。由法之北部之马路分数条，远于战场，每一条马路一来一往，两行之摩托车，亦直达战场，并不间断。察其数目之多，则有十几万辆之数焉，而昼夜往来，运输不已。

孙干：欧战华工记
Records of Chinese Labourers in European War by Sun Gan

British Heavy-duty Motor Vehicles and French Roads

Only a few of the bullets, firearms and food supplies needed by battlefields were transported by trains and most of them were transported by heavy-duty motor vehicles. Each lorry could accommodate 30 to 60 people and could travel 15 or 20 miles an hour. What astonished us was not their high speed, but the great number of them. There were several roads in the northern part of France leading to the battlefields and the two lines of motor vehicles on either side of the road coming to or from the battlefields never ceased. These thousands of motor vehicles came to and from the battlefield continuously both day and night.

85. 哀司不老凯东郊分卸炮弹

一日早饭后，工头中英两国之三道杠，率领出营后，路逾哀司不老凯，至东郊外二里许之野地中。忽见一巨栋铁梁之长廊，铁板为顶，顶上盖以尺余厚之土一层，内所藏尽炮弹也。弹形圆而有蒂，蒂之长约寸许，弹圆之直径约尺许，重约三四十斤，铁皮之厚约指许。外表之色为土黄、草青及灰色，无次相间，以色涂抹后，似以桐油涂之者。工人有将火车上新运来者，往地上卸，而跌破之，见其内包有白细粉末与黄细末。洋工头见其破状甚惊愕，迅速抱去埋于秘密处，盖不但恐其上司知之有罚，亦恐发生不测也。

华工日记
Chinese Labourer's Diaries

吾侪数十人从长廊运出之炮弹，距约半里许，即垛一垛，每垛千枚。一日即运出数垛，都使边层整齐，井井有次。然连运数日，长廊中之未运出者，尚余大半数也。以后英人又以火车继续运至一列车。是故余因是想，此次欧战，英人在法预备之各种子弹，处处山积，其用心之深，能不出人意外耶？祖国之当政者为国之预备，亦如是之用心欤？

Unloading Cannonballs in Eastern Suburb of Hazebrouck

One day, the British officer and Chinese foremen led us out of our camp after breakfast and arrived at a field in the eastern suburb about one mile away from Hazebrouck. Suddenly we saw a long corridor of huge iron beams. The top of the corridor was a thick iron plate which was covered with a layer of earth about a foot deep. The inside was full of round cannonballs, each with a pedicle of about two inches in length. The diameter of each cannonball was about 12 inches and they weighed about 30 or 40 pounds. Its iron casing was as thick as a finger, with the surface colour painted yellowish brown, grass-like green and grey alternately, and it seemed that a layer of Chinese wood oil was painted over the colour coats. The labourers unloaded the newly-arrived cannonballs from the train. When one was broken after it was dropped onto the ground, I saw the inside of it was filled with white and yellow fine powders. Greatly shocked by the scene, the British officer carried it away and hurriedly buried it somewhere because he was afraid not only that he would be punished by his superiors if they knew it, but also that something more dangerous might happen.

The cannonballs unloaded from the long corridor by dozens of our labourers were piled up into a stack every 250 yards, with each stack containing a thousand. By the end of the day, we had unloaded several stacks of cannonballs and arranged them into neat piles. However, after several days of continuous work, there were still many cannonballs inside the corridor. Later, the British transported another train of cannonballs here. From the mountains of ammunitions of the British during the European War in France, it could be seen that the British really had prepared well for the war, which was something really beyond all expectations. Could it be possible for the rulers of our motherland to get well-prepared for her defence like this?

86. 作华工者之生气，因之而怨伤

华工到法，论种族既与欧人不同，而言语规矩，风俗习惯，亦都各异。所以一举一动，无不枝节随之丛生。况人人之往往因自私自利行事而违背公理，于是交际一出，猜忌随之。虽每队中有翻译员，然只一人而对众工人之一切，焉能一一尽及之？所以众工人每与英人接触，即发生反抗生气等等争执矣。

在一百零二队中，余之友张蕤庄君（山东高密县人）即常常对英人生气、悲伤。余为之作歌二则，使之讽诵，以舒解之。其歌词如下：

第一则　生气　混洋事，挣几元钱实在真不易，规矩风俗各都异。言语不懂的，行动请翻译。少有因为打官司、回话不听，被屈受罚，无足异。

第二则　悲伤　莫怨伤，应募作工劳苦理应当。骗江过海下外洋，

华工日记
Chinese Labourer's Diaries

安家工钱偿。米面不吃糠，医药白给，供衣裳。报酬不薄，莫谓出来上了当。

Anger and Resentment of Chinese Labourers

When Chinese labourers came to France, troubles arose everywhere due to the differences between Chinese and Europeans in race, language and culture. Besides, because people tended to behave selfishly regardless of justice, misunderstandings arose whenever they communicated with each other. Even though there was an interpreter in each brigade, he was unable to deal with every request from both sides. Therefore, every time the labourers came into contact with the British, there would be resistance, anger and disputes.

In Brigade 102, Zhang Ruizhuang, one of my friends from Gaomi County in Shandong Province, often felt angry and was saddened by the British soldiers. I wrote two songs for him to recite and relieve his resentments. The lyrics were as follows:

Song I: Anger   It is really hard to earn money by working in foreign countries, since both rules and customs vary too much. Unable to understand their language, we have to ask the interpreter to help for every one of our actions. So, it is no surprise that we are sometimes wronged and punished because of misunderstandings in language.

Song II: Grief   There is no need to be sad and resentful since it is our duty to work hard as recruited labourers. We are paid for our crossing oceans and working in foreign countries. We are given food, medicine and clothes, all free of charge. So, it is unfair to say we are deceived because we have such good payments.

87. 作洗机关车

华工一百零二队，尽作浚水沟、修马路、修铁路、伐森林、装卸火车、挖战壕等等工作。一日，大工头率往营北之火车站洗涤火车头，火车头英语为因谨。初至车站，见火车头，有完整者，有破坏者，共二十余个，盖从他处拉来之待修理者。洗涤时，各以线团一把，蘸油揩拭，使之明润光泽始罢。然于揩拭之时，往往其火仍炽，恒烙手足。

作工数日，一天傍午，忽有人传德之飞机至，几乎不闻其声，更难辨认其体，盖其高不知数千尺也。一刹那间，见站西铁工厂中之众工人，纷纷逃向四野。不须臾，从天空落一炸弹，恰好坠于工厂墙外之水沟深泥中而未爆炸。一时欢声雷动，人人称幸，厂中工人又徐徐归厂复工矣。

Washing Locomotives

What the Chinese labourers of Brigade 102 did most was dredging ditches, building roads and railways, chopping wood in forests, loading and unloading trains, and digging trenches. One day, the foreman led us to the railway station located in the north of Hazebrouck to wash locomotives, namely, engines in English. When we first arrived at the station, we saw there were more than twenty engines standing there, some of which were in decent condition while others were damaged. They had been brought here from other places for service and repair. While cleaning them, each labourer wiped the engine with a reel of thread, which was first dipped into oil to make the engines bright and glossy. But as we were wiping, some of the engines were still operating and it often burned our hands and feet.

We worked there for several days. One day, news came suddenly before noon that a German airplane was to arrive. But because it was flying at a height of thousands of feet, we could barely hear any sound of it, nor could we recognise its shape. All of a sudden, the labourers in the iron factory located in the west of the railway station fled to all directions. Shortly afterwards, a bomb fell from the sky and landed into the deep mud of the ditch outside the factory wall, but it did not explode. People gave a thunderous applause for a while and then the labourers in the factory returned to their work again.

88. 在法华工之沽酒

法国城市、村镇，随处有卖牛奶及各种酒类者。盖因其地多养牛，又多苹果与葡萄树也。家家饲牝牛取其奶以作饮料，为普遍之习惯，与其植苹果与葡萄树酿为各种酒之习惯正相同。吾侪在战争环境之中，习焉既久，又按月开薪俸，于是渐渐有人谓在法之饭食有不合华工之口者。或自买食，或沽各种美酒，任意以脍炙其口。然因聚赌而手中乏钱者，其人更多，其中之乘工人有钱之机作种种买卖，所以华工队中饮酒之风一时极盛。余亦作歌一则以志之。歌词如下：

孙干：欧战华工记
Records of Chinese Labourers in European War by Sun Gan

嗜酒　在工场，一阵风吹鼻孔酒味香。手中乏钱不能尝，快把买卖想。五郎赚三郎，挣些麻内囊里藏。晚间各棚，非喝啤印即是弯薄郎。（麻内即钱。郎即佛郎，钱名。啤印及弯薄郎皆法国人之酒名也。）

Chinese Labourers Buying Wines in France

Milk and alcoholic beverages were sold everywhere in cities or villages in France because many cows were raised and many apples and grapes were planted. It was a common custom for every household to keep cows to get milk as drinks. Similarly, the French grew apples and grapes to make various kinds of wines. Having become accustomed to the war environment as well as the customs of the local people and getting their monthly pay regularly, some of my fellow workers began to complain about the food they were given by the British. As a result, some began to buy their own food, or all kinds of wines to satisfy their appetites. However, many of the labourers had no money due to their gambling. So, some of them started to make various kinds of deals with those who still had money in their pockets. The result was the great popularity of drinking wines among the Chinese labourers for a time. To commemorate it, I wrote a song as follows:

Wine Addiction: In working places, a gust of wind blows the smell of wines into people's nostrils. Unable to taste it for lack of money, labourers were eager to do some business. With five francs they tried to make three francs more in their pockets. In the evening people in camps drink wines of various types.

华工日记
Chinese Labourer's Diaries

89. 英法及俄与德停战讲和，华工放假一日

一日炮声忽停，英人向吾侪曰："协约与联盟双方诸国，欲罢战讲和，吾侪亦停工一日。"工人闻之，莫不喜形于色。饭后，有洗衣服者，有写家信者，有往他队视亲朋者，有读书识字者，有聚赌奕棋者。余亦出队而至一乡，察其风俗，觇其人心。

甫进庄，见一门半开，余遂入内。有法之少妇一人，又有华工一人，将法人之屋内用具一一翻动，妇人对彼华工只是微笑。有顷，华工又入其内房，将立橱、抽屉中之物取置桌上。法妇心虽不愿，而口未敢说。余遂劝阻吾华人，然后同去。吾想法之妇人和蔼待人，盖亦受教育而有程度者也。

A Day off during Peace Negotiations

The gunfire stopped suddenly one day, and the British officers told us, "The Entente Powers and the Central Powers wanted to end the war and negotiate peace. All labourers could have a day off." Hearing these words every labourer's face lit up with pleasure. After breakfast, some labourers washed their clothes; some wrote letters home; some went to other brigades to visit their relatives or friends; some read books; and some gathered to gamble or play chess. I went out to a nearby village to learn about the customs and practices of the local people.

孙干：欧战华工记
Records of Chinese Labourers in European War by Sun Gan

As soon as I arrived at the village, I saw a half-opened door and entered it. Inside the house were a young French woman and a Chinese labourer. The labourer was turning over all the articles in the house, but the French woman only smiled at him. After a while, the Chinese labourer went into the bedroom and placed the objects he found in the cabinets and drawers onto the table. Dissatisfied with his behaviour, the Frenchwoman did not dare to say anything. I dissuaded the Chinese labourer and left together with him. I thought the woman's politeness and kindness must be the result of good education.

90. 被炮击之深坑

哀司不老凯既为一省会，其街市之繁华，无待于言。然英人常常出示禁华人入市，其故何也？盖德之飞机炮弹常轰击之，不独市中之房屋被毁不堪，而市外之深坑，深七八尺者，亦到处皆是。深坑周围之大，余曾周游之，恒五十余步。炮弹溅击之土块，往往远出数丈，德之武器亦烈矣哉。

Deep Shell Pits

Hazebrouck was a large French provincial town and the prosperity of its streets and markets were beyond description. However, the British often prevented Chinese labourers from going into the town. But why? It turned out that the German aircraft and artillery often bombarded the area. Not only were the houses in the town badly damaged, but the deep pits, usually seven or eight feet deep, could be found everywhere around the town. I once walked around some of these deep pits and found that in most cases the circumference was often over 50 steps. The shells sent huge clods of earth about 30 feet away, which also reflected the incredible power of German weapons.

91. 年假与法人斗殴

民国七年元旦，队长赐给些猪肉及各等食物外，并放工一日，使华工随便出外游散。上午十二时，华工有游于法人之火车站旁者。法人与之口角，且欲以枪击之。华工见势不支，遂归而号召多人蜂拥而至，欲与法人斗殴。法人知不敌而遁，于是众工人要求工头，递呈以告法人，非使法人与华工道歉不可。大工头遂令余写呈一张，呈词如下：

具呈人：

华工一百零二队众工人等，既应英国招募来法，加入协约以助战争，被英人处处保护，极为周到。今因阳历新年节，各队放假，许工人等出外游览。是日，华工一百零二队有一工人出外闲眺，至法人之铁路旁。忽遇一野蛮法人，强向工人勒索银钱。工人囊中本有佛郎票若干，却不愿给。法人初以刺刀威吓，继即强行掠夺，将工人之钱票劫去。工人与之理论，被彼殴打一顿以后方遁。工人随后穷追，彼又发放数枪，幸未伤人。此等凌辱，不独我华人不能忍受，谅大英国贵国亦不能坐视也。在当时倘我华人以众武力及之，不惟吾中法两国有伤人性命、有伤邦交，

孙干：欧战华工记
Records of Chinese Labourers in European War by Sun Gan

即在贵国不但耽误工作，即来往交涉，而亦无甚面目也。

谨望大英欧战司令大人钧座，速将此事与法人交涉，使法人向我工人道歉，并登报宣布，以警效尤。工人等则感德无既矣。

中华民国柒年戊午正月元旦日

驻法华工一百零二队全体工人谨呈

自一百零二队中之华工与法人斗殴，英人与法人交涉，彼此互相谅解后，不久，吾侪即迁移，去战线较近之处。盖因不但华工与法人彼此有隙，而战争之猛烈视前为甚。并传闻德人在两月内，要取巴黎也。自是以后，吾曹每迁一处，或住三日五日即迁。较以前，真可谓疲于奔命矣。

Fighting with a Frenchman on New Year's Day

On New Year's Day of 1918, the seventh year of the Republic of China, the British Captain gave us pork and other good food and had one day off for us Chinese labourers. Some took the opportunity to have a look around the town. At about midday, a Chinese labourer came to a place nearby the French railway station, where he got into a dispute with a Frenchman who threatened to shoot him with a gun. Seeing that he was not a match for the Frenchman, the labourer ran back to the camp and called upon a group of his fellow labourers back to the station in an attempt to fight with the Frenchman, who, on seeing the large group, fled the scene. As a result of this incident, the labourers demanded that their foreman write a letter of complaint, asking the Frenchman to for make an official apology to the Chinese labourer involved. The foreman asked me to write the complaint. The following was just the complaint I wrote.

华工日记

Chinese Labourer's Diaries

To whom it may concern.

The men of Brigade 102 of the Chinese Labour Corps, who were recruited by Britain to work in France and participate in the Entente countries to help the war, are protected by the British military law. Because today was New Year's Day, all brigades of Chinese labourers were given one day off and permitted to go out for sightseeing. On this day, one labourer from Brigade 102 came to a place nearby the railway station, where he was blackmailed for money by an aggressive Frenchman. Although the labourer had several francs in his pocket, he was unwilling to give them to the Frenchman. The Frenchman intimidated him with his bayonet at first and then brutally plundered all his money. Our worker tried to argue with them, but was beaten by the Frenchman and forced to run away in a hurry. Some Chinese labourers from the camp accompanied him back to the scene to look for the Frenchman. But on seeing them, the Frenchman fired several shots at the Chinese labourers. Fortunately, no one was injured. This act of humiliation is unacceptable, not only to the Chinese but also to the British and we firmly believe Britain would not refrain from taking strict actions in response. If the Chinese labourers had used force to attack the Frenchman during this incident, serious injury would have been unavoidable on both sides and there could even be a possibility that the diplomatic relations between China and France would be damaged. Even if the work in France were not delayed for it, the friendly exchange and negotiations would be affected in the future.

I sincerely hope that the British commanders in the European War will negotiate on this matter with the French as soon as possible and urge the Frenchman to apologise to our worker and publish this apology in newspapers as a warning. The Chinese labourers would be very grateful for that.

1 January 1918, the 7th year of the Republic of China

Submitted by all members of Brigade 102 of Chinese Labour Corps in France

孙干：欧战华工记
Records of Chinese Labourers in European War by Sun Gan

Later, the British negotiated with the French on the fight between the Chinese labourer in Brigade 102 and the Frenchman, and a mutual understanding between them was achieved. Soon after that, we moved to a place closer to the battlefront, not only because of the frictions between Chinese labourers and the French but also because of an escalation of the war not seen before up to that point. There was a rumour that the Germans planned to seize Paris within two months. After that we had to transfer frequently and in every place we moved to, we stayed only three or five days. Compared with the past, we were really kept on the run at that time.

92. 华工之懒惰者

民国七年春，法地阴雨连连，道路泥泞，时常迁徙，帐棚支搭之烦琐，可谓无人不以为苦。一次住于野外坡上，忽传令站队分发臭帽，并听训话，与看表演。站队后，各给一如囊之帽一具，外装一小布包，偶嗅之，其臭不可当。继令大众列为圆阵，队长英人在中阵，谓大众曰："此后战事愈急，恐德违背公法，发放臭炮。刚发之帽，防臭炮者也。汝等可谨保存之，德人放臭炮时，另有专人司之，及时即发号令。各队之工头如闻号令，即都喊盖施，即臭帽。汝大家可将臭帽速戴于头上，自闻令至戴毕，时间不过一分钟者，方能于各人之性命无虞。今余令一撒针（即大工头）先做表演，汝等可细观之。"即令一大工头，亦列阵之中央，肩负一臭帽。队长手持时表，待大工头立定后，大声曰："盖施。"大工头即忙将所负之臭帽帽包仓皇摘下，解扣取出带于头上。自发声至带讫，时止四十余秒。演毕，工人遂散。

华工日记
Chinese Labourer's Diaries

自发臭帽之后，大家多有不愿作工。所以挂病号者，往三日多至数十人。甚有取野中之毒草，就身上或臂上一搓，则其皮肤立即红肿，以待医生至时之检查，被检查无病而受罚也。口占俚句如下：

一日迁徙二日挪，隆隆雷电何其多。
伟大蜻蜓蔽天日，尾泻青烟快于梭。
空中行列如蚁卵，时遭焚毁遇天火。
物质文明二十世，竞争生存赖勤学。

Idlers among Chinese Labourers

In the spring of 1918, it rained continuously in France and the roads were muddy for most of the time. Besides, we also had to suffer from the cumbersome process of putting up our tents during our frequent moving. Life at that time was really annoying for all of us. One day, while we were encamping on a slope in the countryside, a sudden order came that we should queue up for the distribution of anti-gas hoods, for listening to instructions and for watching a demonstration. After queuing up in line, each of us was given a bag-like hood with a canvas sack outside, which gave off an unbearable stink. Then we were ordered to stand in a circle with the British Captain standing in the centre. He said, "From now on, the war will become fiercer. We are afraid that the Germans will ignore the international law and use gas shells in battles. The hoods we gave to you just now are specially made to prevent the effects of gas. Be sure to carefully keep your hoods. When the Germans fire the gas shells, we will have specifically-assigned persons to take charge and they will give you orders to follow. When the foreman of each brigade hears the order, please shout 'gas' loudly. As soon as you hear the shout, you should put the hoods on your head as quickly as possible. Only those who do it within a minute after hearing the order can have their lives guaranteed. Now I shall ask the sergeant (that is, the big foreman) to show you how to do it. Please watch it very carefully." A sergeant with an anti-gas hood on his shoulder was asked to come to the centre of the circle. When the sergeant arrived at the centre, the Captain with a watch in his hand shouted 'Gas' loudly. The sergeant immediately opened the bag of the anti-gas hood, took the hood out and put it on his head. It took him forty seconds to complete this. After the demonstration, labourers were dispersed.

Many labourers did not want to work after we were given the anti-gas hoods. As a result, dozens of labourers registered at hospital in the next three days. Some labourers even picked poisonous weeds in the field and rubbed them on their bodies or arms, which became red and swollen immediately. However, when the truth was revealed by doctors after an examination, they would be punished for their deception. I composed a poem as follows:

> We migrated to different places every one or two days,
> While rumbling thunderstorms occurred in many waves.
> Aeroplanes obscured the sky like giant dragonflies,
> Which poured from their tails black smoke of fires.
> Like ants' eggs they flew in procession in the high,
> But would be destroyed down on fire from the sky.
> In the material civilisation of the 20th century,
> Competition and survival depend on hard work and study.

93. 英炮误击英飞机

一日午后，闻空中嗡嗡之声。翘首一望，一飞机东来。顷刻闻高射炮声，隆隆四起，竟将飞机击落。群往视之，乃一英国之飞机也，所幸者，司机之人跌伤而未致死。

Mistakenly Hitting a British Aircraft

One afternoon, a buzzing sound came to our ears from the air. Looking up, we saw an aeroplane flying towards us from the east. In an instant we heard a burst of anti-aircraft artillery and the aeroplane was knocked down from the sky. We all went close to have a look and it turned out to be a British aeroplane. Fortunately, the pilot was only slightly injured with no life-threatening injuries.

94. 坦克车之行动

当欧战时，论车辆与战争之效用，莫如坦克车。坦克车之形，如一蛤螺蚘，所以亦有人谓之蛤螺蚘车。其构造法，车身自带铁轨，行时随到随铺，过后随去随带。外为钢甲皮，虽以小炮击之，而弹不易入。内虽仅容数人，而钢炮之猛烈异常。无论行于山林，入于沟渠，无不驾驶自如也。

Action of Tanks

During the European War, no vehicles were more effective in battles than tanks. The tanks were just like clams in shape and some people even called them clam vehicles. They had rails of their own and the rails were paved in front as they moved forward and rolled back on again at the rear. The exteriors of the tanks were made of steel armour, which prevented the bullets from penetrating when they were attacked by small cannons. Although a tank could only accommodate a few people, its cannons were extremely powerful. The tanks could be driven with great ease over any terrain, whether they are in mountains or in ditches.

95. 余在法之野外亦学打靶

余于欧战战线后防，工作之暇，有时散步野外。常见英人以饮罢之空酒瓶为的，练习打靶。一日，余亦持路旁之枪，作数次练习，始知虽距三四十步之近，而亦不易取中也。非亲手经过，乌知其难！

My Shooting Practice in Fields of France

While I was working in the rear areas of the frontline during the European

War, in my spare time I often took walks in the fields. I often saw the British soldiers practicing shooting with their empty bottles as the targets. One day, I was allowed to fire a rifle and practiced my shooting several times. From this experience I realised that it was in no way an easy thing to hit the target even though it was only 30 to 40 steps away. Thus, it was impossible to know the difficulty of shooting if one had never had such experiences.

96. 到法人某女校参观

一日下午，余作工毕，到一村中，探其村有数百女生之一较大女子小学校焉。及至到是校门口，要求参观时，见年十五六岁之女生由课室出，成群而至。继则有女教员数人，亦随后赶来。其中一人问余来故，余告以参观。彼曰："此为一女子学校，从来无论欧洲人、美洲人都不承认入校参观。今先生之来，亦如是拒绝。"余听其语意，观其举止，与吾国男女有别之见不惟相同，且为尤甚。

Visit to a French Girls' School

One afternoon, I walked to a village after finishing my work and found that there was a large girls' school with hundreds of female students. When I arrived at the school gates to ask for permission for a visit, I saw girls aged 15 or 16 walking in groups from their classrooms followed by several female teachers. One of them asked me what I was doing there, and I told her that I wanted to pay a visit. She said, "This is a girls' school, and no one is allowed to enter the school, whether they are people of Europe or people from the Americas. We have to refuse you entry too." From the tone of her voice and from her demeanour, I realised that the difference between treatment of boys and girls at school was similar, or even more severe, than in our country.

97. 法国之学校教育亦有时用体罚

余在祖国学校中充小学教员数年，常常见诸教育书籍中，赞许欧美教育家不体罚学生。及至来法，暇暂到法校参观。一日，至一镇中之学校。始至校外，闻校中上课，对浮躁之学生，亦以教鞭责打。及至入校参观时，亦睹面见有学生，就以鞭楚绝不听命者。盖人之生性，良莠不齐。无论欧美亚东，学生之教授不从，继之以责罚，则立用心，其理一也。

Physical Punishment in French Schools

I had taught as a teacher in a primary school in China for several years. At that time, I often read books on education praising educators in Europe and America for not punishing their students physically. Since my arrival in France, I took the opportunity to visit French schools whenever it was possible. One day, I went to a particular school in the town. As I was still outside the school,

I heard that teachers in class would also beat impertinent students with a whip. When I entered school, I saw with my own eyes that some students were whipped for not obeying the teacher's orders. It is a fact that human beings are all born different. Whether in Europe, America or Asia, students who failed to follow the instructions of teachers would receive physical punishment to encourage them to study harder in the future. It could be seen that the intentions of teachers everywhere were based on the same principle.

98. 冬夏之天气

余自民国六年冬季到法时，虽阴雨绵绵，天气却不甚冷。已近阳历十二月，而苹叶尚未尽凋。惟至冬至节后，半月至一月之时，则天气感觉最寒。过此时期，则天气又清凉如故。直至夏至节后，半月至一月之时，则天气感觉极热。过此时期，则天气又清凉如故。

若按诸纬度，在暑季固较中国奉天、吉林两省为凉爽。若按诸寒季，则较中国奉天、吉林两省为更寒也。然观其果树之果或叶，与园圃之草，青枝绿叶，碧色如茵，则竟不寒而反暖。其亦为大西洋中之温流所激荡，而致气候反温和如是欤。

Weather in Summer and Autumn

I arrived in France in the winter of 1917, and it was not very cold despite the continuous rain. Even by the end of November, there were still leaves that had not withered. The coldest days were felt only at some point after mid-December and the winter solstice and continued until after late February. From then, it would be as cool as before. The hottest days were felt one month after the summer solstice and continue again until November. After that, it would be as cold again as before.

In terms of latitude, the weather in France was cooler in summer than that in the provinces of Fengtian and Jilin in China, while it was colder in terms of cold seasons. However, when we looked at the fruit and green leaves on fruit trees as well as the green grass in the gardens, we might find that it was not really cold at all, but actually rather warm because of the influence of the warm currents from the Atlantic Ocean.

99. 法国妇女之灵活

法国妇女眉目之秀，神气之清，态度活泼，不独通都大邑者如是，而偏僻村庄，亦莫不如是。其教育之有素欤，抑种族之特殊欤？

Nature of French Women

French women in both large cities and remote villages looked beautiful in countenance, graceful in manners and outgoing in personality. Was this because of the better education they received or because of the uniqueness of their ethnicity?

华工日记
Chinese Labourer's Diaries

100. 挖深地洞

欧洲战场现因双方炮火之烈，不得不挖掘种种战壕、种种隧道与地洞，以求避免大炮、机枪之袭击。是以欧战开始以后不数月，双方战地穴洞之多，尽如蜂房矣。其挖深洞之法，自地之表面起斜向下凿，遂凿遂以木框镶齐之。有深数尺者，亦有深至丈余者。其中之土石，均以麻袋装出之。其不斜下而直下者，亦遂挖遂镶，使洞内之上下四方，均为木板，毫不见土也。深至丈余者，至其底，则分挖为若干间，装置电灯、电话与床铺焉，其便利为何耶！

Digging Deep Trenches

Because of the fierce fighting in the European battlefields, trenches, tunnels and dugouts had to be excavated to avoid the constant artillery shells and the fire of machine guns. Therefore, in just a few months since the beginning of the European War, the tunnels and trenches of both sides had been as many as beehives. The way they dug deep holes was to start diagonally downward then chisel sideways underground from a suitable depth, framing with wood as they go along. Some tunnels were several feet deep while others were tens of feet deep. The excavated earth and rocks were carried out in sacks. Another way was to dig directly downward instead of sloping from the ground by means of digging the edges and boundaries neatly. There were wooden boards in all directions of the tunnel, and no earth could be seen. At the depth of three yards was the bottom, where a few rooms were dug and they were equipped with various convenient facilities such as lights, telephones, and beds.

101. 作告白以告同工个个留心技术

中国众位同胞弟兄知悉：

我们大家既由祖国平安来到此地，亦为极可庆幸，极不容易之事。至于我们做工，那是我们的本分。凡我们当作之事，我们就尽上力量好好去做，因为将来我们的工价是从作工得来也。将来我们要想多得工钱，现在大家都应当好好作工。不特此也，我们现在不但好好作本分以内之工，即本分以外之技能艺术，我们也当处处留心，处处学习。

譬如大家会木作者，凡是西人以木作之器具为何种样式，何种制造，处处留心学习仿造。又如会铁作者，凡见西人以铁作之器具，是何等样式，为何等构造。此外自行车、摩托车、汽车、电车等等，用什么物造成，以什么法使用，在得暇时一一学过明白。以后回国时，不但挣些钱回家，还能会些艺术。将来国家一旦有事，便能请你帮忙。你到那时，一定有名有利也。

旷观世界，自古之有本实者，未有不于事前处处留心，处处学习，以备后日之所需用者也。今日我们在此，所作之工分门别类，可谓不少。所见之器具与事物，尤其是多。若果人人用心，处处留意，昼夜学习，将来回国以后，一定大有用处。那时不但自己直接得益，即国家亦间接得莫大之利益焉！甚望大家处处乘早留心也。

驻法华工一百零二队工人　63484　孙某某敬白

华工日记
Chinese Labourer's Diaries

Announcement for Fellow Labourers to Learn New Techniques

For the attention of all my fellow countrymen:

It was a great blessing but not without difficulty that we arrived here safely from our motherland. It is our duty to work hard. Whatever we were asked to do, we should try our best to do it well because the wages we shall receive later depend on the work we did. If we want to get more money in the future, we should work diligently. Not only should we do our own work well, but we should also keep an eye on the techniques outside of our own work and try to learn new skills all along the way.

For example, if we are carpenters, we should pay attention to what styles those woodenwares of the westerners are and how they are made. At the same time, we should try to learn from and imitate them. If we are blacksmiths, we should pay attention to what styles the ironwork of the westerners is and what structures they have. In addition, during our spare time we should try to learn about and understand the processes used in making vehicles such as bicycles, motorcycles, automobiles, and trams. In this way, when we return home in the future, we will not only have money but also new crafts and skills. If something happens to our motherland, we will be able to help with our new skills and then you will have both fortune and fame.

If we observe men of great ability in our history, we will find that all of them are people who are observant and good at learning new skills from others everywhere for later use. Today we do a great variety of work here and we see a great many new tools and objects. If each of us can work diligently, keep our eyes open and learn new things day and night, it will be of great use when we go back home. When that time comes, not only will we benefit directly from our new skills, but our country can also profit from it indirectly. Therefore, I sincerely hope that all of us can become observant people and try to learn new skills whenever we have the opportunity.

No. 63484 Labourer Sun from Brigade 102 of Chinese Labourers in France

102. 木板之预备

欧战后防之路旁，除栉比大垛之子弹外，有时亦见木板如山。其木板之厚薄长短不一，厚自三分、五分而至三寸；宽自二寸至五、六寸，长自五、六尺至丈许。从英运来，以备挖深地洞，镶缘隧道，构造木房，修筑道路及作为种种家具之用者也。

Preparations of Boards

During the European War, mountains of shells were piled up along the roadsides in the rear of the frontlines. Besides shells, there were sometimes mountains of wooden boards on the roadsides too, ranging from 1 to 6 inches in thickness, 2 to 6 inches in width and from 6 to 10 feet in length. These boards were shipped from Britain to be used in tunnels as supports, in the construction of trenches, in the building of houses and roads, and in making various kinds of furniture.

103. 红十字会之表面观

基督教徒于欧战之最大贡献，厥惟红十字会。红十字会所设立之医院，凡战场后防，随处皆有。其规模之大者，不止能容数千人，即规模之较小者，亦能容数百。至于红十字会所用之汽车与摩托车，往来不绝，为数盖不止数万辆也。其服务之人，或男会员，或女会员，或在战地，或在医院，忙碌异常，劳苦颇甚。

Overview of the Red Cross Society

The most important contribution to the European War made by Christians was that of the Red Cross Society. Hospitals set up by the Red Cross Society could be found all along the rear of the battlefronts. There were both large-scale hospitals which could accommodate thousands of patients and smaller ones which could accommodate hundreds. Hundreds of automobiles and motorcycles of the Red Cross Society came and went ceaselessly. All the labourers of the Red Cross Society, both men and women, worked constantly and tirelessly on battlefields or in hospitals.

孙干：欧战华工记
Records of Chinese Labourers in European War by Sun Gan

104. 法人丧事之一瞥

一日工暇，出游法村，见一家老少，面颜凄怆。或人曰："此家乃为一遭丧事者。"至翌日午后一时出殡，又见柩前为孝子，孝子前有衣裳楚楚之宾客。盖亦与我国丧事之有亲朋祭客挽柩送葬之意，正相同也。其不同之处，不但孝子不大声哭，而亦不衣白孝衣也。

A Glimpse of French Funerals

One day, I went out to visit a French village after work. During the trip, I encountered a family all with sorrowful looks on their faces. I was told that this family had just lost one of its members. The next day, at one o'clock in the afternoon, a funeral procession was held. During the procession, I saw a filial son walking in front of the coffin and other family members and relatives in front of the son. This scene was similar to Chinese funerals where friends and relatives accompanied the coffin to the burial place. The only difference lay in the fact that the son of the deceased did not cry nor wear white clothes.

105. 为挖战壕使英之大工头大哭

英大工头老实异常，殊不和气。工人与中国大工头均甚恶之，凡对其所言，皆故意不懂，与之相反。挖掘战壕又为重要工作，就其地势，按其方向，敌人之在左方者，将掘出之土常摊于左；敌人之在右方者，将掘出之土常摊于右，用以护身。英大工头言土应左者，偏右之；土应右者，偏左之。工作将毕，英检点工程之上官至，见数十丈之重要战壕，均将掘出之土误置，遂勃然大怒，立时质诸其大工头。大工头讷讷数语，眼泪滂沱而大哭矣。素抱封建态度者，就此可以鉴也。

British Foreman Crying during Trench Excavation

The British foreman was very honest but unsociable. Both the labourers and the Chinese foremen disliked him, so they often pretended that they did not understand his orders and did the opposite deliberately. Excavating trenches was also a very important task. According to the terrain and the position of the enemy, the excavated earth was to be placed on the left side if the enemy was on the left or on the right side if the enemy was on the right. The purpose of doing so was to protect those in the trench from the enemy. So, when the British foreman said the earth should be put on the left, the labourers deliberately put it on the right. When he asked them to put the earth on the right, the labourers put it on the left side. At the end of the day, when the British officer came to inspect the work and saw that the excavated earth along dozens of yards of important trenches was misplaced, he flew into rage and blamed the British foreman who then burst into tears and began to cry loudly after saying only a few words. Perhaps those who held a feudal attitude could learn from this incident.

106. 故饮火酒几乎致死

法之葡萄酒，世界著名。欧战兵将，嗜饮自多。坡野饮罄各种之玻璃酒瓶，弃之逦迤，到处皆是。华工之狡黠者，将有酒之瓶窃来饮者，亦不少也。

一日值天雨，而又迁徙，道路泥泞。行李尽被雨淋，栉风沐雨之苦况，不言可知。既至一地，在泥泞中支搭帐后，始得避雨休息。斯时也，有一工人从路旁之众瓶中，捡来数瓶，视之内尚有酒。以火燃烧，炎状似酒。尝之，果酒也。有二三人因不奈霆雨酸风之苦，围而饮之。酒未及半，数人即醉。吾乃劝之少饮，彼亦让余饮，余饮不一杯，不须臾而亦觉醉。自是以后，数人都酩酊大醉、不醒人事者数日。余虽以少许一尝，而亦醉醺半日也。或曰："此战士熨饭之有毒火酒也，岂可饮乎？"遂弃之。

Drinking Poisonous Alcohol

French wine was famous all over the world and many European generals and soldiers were addicted to drinking wines. The empty glass bottles of wine discarded all over the field. Many crafty Chinese labourers often picked up some of the bottles that they found and drank the little wine that was left in them.

One rainy day, as we marched along the muddy roads, all of our equipment had become soaked. We experienced unbearable hardships while moving especially during bad weather. When we arrived at our destination, we set up the tents in the mud and could take shelter from the rain till then. One of the labourers picked up some bottles with a little wine in, from a pile of bottles nearby. When it was burnt, the flames were just like those of wine. He had a taste and it proved to be wine. Because of the bitterness of the wind and rain, several other labourers sat around and drank from the bottles too. A few people got drunk before half of the wine was drunk. I advised them to drink less but they suggested me drinking a cup of it too. A short while after drinking a cup of it, I felt drunk as well. Later that day, many more people were very drunk and some of them remained unconscious for several days. Although I only tasted a little, I was drunk for half a day. Later we were told, "It is the poisonous alcohol used for making fire and it is not meant for drinking!" Therefore, we discarded the rest of the bottles of alcohol.

107. 法商家反对华工入市

余在法，既见众工人之工作甚宽，又恶忠厚农夫之渐渐学为赌博鬼。遂天天于工作之余，即再上班教工人识字，或有时持护照，到哀司不老

孙干：欧战华工记

Records of Chinese Labourers in European War by Sun Gan

凯为读书之工人买文具。

哀司不老凯市，有一文具铺。其中之店员，为年在二十一二岁之少妇二人、十一二岁之幼女二人。余因数次往买其物，渐渐熟识。一日余于作工之暇，欲参观哀司不老凯市内之学校，而至其店铺中，探询学校之所在。一少妇欲与吾牵手同往。余因己之生性固执，不乐同妇人携手，祁其在前以作向导，彼亦不愿。正商谈间，此少妇突跑入后宅，彼少妇仓皇将其前门紧紧关闭。余心愕然，追问其故，彼虽呢喃相告，余仍不解。急牵余手，促进后宅。时余更不解其意，挣扎欲向外出。见门又紧闭，遂想素无仇怨，当无恶意，遂从之入。既至其内院，余始知彼欲送余从小门出也。余出，见门小巷窄，知为后门，然终不解为何事。乃再从旁而转至大街，以求其故。至其门前，始见有华工四五人，正在敲其门。余始恍然大悟，彼与余出其后门者，极不愿他华工复入耳。

翌日，余复还至其铺店买物，并察前日不令他工人入门之故。甫入门，彼二妇人从其架上取下数本新成之纸簿，在框台上一一指示。余见簿中之纸，多为工人污秽之手指所沾染。自是以后，哀司不老凯之街市中，凡商店之门上，均写"禁止华工"之纸条。有正贴者，有反贴者，亦有倒贴者，令人见之，不惟无礼之华工使人气，而书之反贴倒贴法人，亦使人笑也。哀司不老凯人对华工反对入其市也，可想而知之。无程度者之到外国，惹人厌恶，竟尔如是。

Objection to Chinese Labourers' Entry to French Stores

When I was in France, seeing that our labourers had some spare time and fearing that the honest farmers might be gradually reduced to gamblers, I taught them to read and write after work every day. Sometimes I also went to

华工日记
Chinese Labourer's Diaries

Hazebrouck to buy stationery for them with my passport.

In Hazebrouck there was a stationery store, where worked two young women in their early twenties and two teenage girls. Because I often went to buy stationery from their store, I became acquainted with them gradually. One day, as I was planning to visit some schools in Hazebrouck in my spare time, I stopped by their store and asked for the location of schools. One of the young women wanted to hold my hand and go with me. Because of my stubborn nature and my reluctance to hold the hand of a woman, I asked her to walk in front of me instead. Just as we talked, the young woman suddenly rushed into the back of the store and the other young woman hurried to close the front door. Astounded by all this, I asked what had happened. She murmured something to me, but I still remained confused. She grabbed my hand hurriedly and pulled me into the back of the store. More puzzled than ever, I struggled to get out, but the door was closed again. Realising that there had been no animosity between us and that they had no ill intentions, I followed her through the door. Only when we had arrived at the inner courtyard did I realise that she wanted to send me out through a back gate. I stepped out into the narrow alley and she closed the gate. I still did not understand what had happened, so I returned to the main street to find out what was going on. When I came to the front door, I found four or five Chinese labourers were knocking at the door. Suddenly it dawned on me that she sent me out from the back door because she did not want to let other Chinese labourers in.

The next day, I went to their store again to buy some stationery and to investigate why they would not allow other Chinese labourers to enter their store. As soon as I walked in, the two women took several new paper books from the shelf and put them on the counter for me to see. I saw that most of the books were stained with the dirty fingerprints of Chinese labourers. From that day onwards, nearly every store in Hazebrouck had a poster on the door stating, "No entry to Chinese Labourers". The signs on some of the stores were posted and spelt correctly, but others were posted reversely or even upside down. Seeing these signs, one would not only became angry with the impoliteness of Chinese labourers, but he would also feel funny at the way the French posted these signs. Sadly, it also reflected the opposition of these stores in Hazebrouck to the entry of Chinese labourers. I had never imagined that Chinese labourers would be so badly behaved in foreign countries that they would be unwelcome or even viewed with disgust by the local people.

108. 华工之卫生

吾侪华工，每队中挑扫地夫十余人，或二十余人，按天打扫，使营中洁净。英人又常常更换吾人之内衣及铺毯，以蒸溜锅蒸溜，以防蚤虱传染疾病。并催促工人按时洗澡。洗澡之器，有大池焉，有木盆、铁盆、磁盆焉，有挂于高处之喷壶焉。工人中虽有对卫生不甚注意者，而大多数皆极清洁。所以天天虽有医生诊病，而队中之人，除故意言有病而挂者外，其真有病者，为数甚寥寥也。

Hygiene of Chinese Labourers

Over ten or twenty people were selected in each brigade to carry out cleaning duties and every day the camp and tented areas were cleaned thoroughly. The British also ensured that we had a regular change of underwear and bedding, which were usually put into pots to steam so as to prevent the spread of fleas or lice. They also urged each labourer to bathe regularly. There were various types of facilities used for bathing such as large pools, wooden baths, iron baths, hand basins, and showers hanging on high places. Although some labourers did not pay much attention to their hygiene, most of us kept clean every day. Therefore, although doctors came to examine us every day, very few were diagnosed as sick except those who falsely claimed to be sick to avoid work.

109. 飞机之种类

欧战时除炮声隆隆外，其在空嗡嗡者，为飞机也。英德飞机，形状相同，而内容之构造与外面之符号各异。英属纽贼尔之飞机，与英本部飞机大致相同，惟其头端之旋转页为二铁条所合作十字形也。德机又更有分三头者，盖其上有机器三部，飞起时三驾驶员须同开，而后方可观。法之飞机，只有骨架，其飞亦若行倒耳。余初见英之飞机时，即作《飞机说》一篇，其文如下：

飞机说

论语云："工欲善其事，必先利其器。"所以轩辕氏造舟车，有巢氏构木为巢，此皆今人所利用之器，创自古人者也。今余佣工于太西，见战场利用之器，以飞机为巨擘焉。飞机之制，各国不同。所常见者为英人所造，以铁质为骨，以木为肉，以油为血，以火为气，以布为皮，以

孙干：欧战华工记
Records of Chinese Labourers in European War by Sun Gan

铜丝为筋，以望远镜为目，以机关枪为其爪牙。有首，有尾，有身，有翼，有腿。以轮为足，中空而外丽，体大而质轻。人乘诸其胸部，拨弄其机关，先使其头部之火油机燃烧，则其顶端之旋转页或一或二，因之旋转，激动空气而成巨风，风至迅速，全体振动，初虽就地而驶，极则腾空而上矣。其小者仅容一人，其大者能容三五、八九人，此皆余所亲眼目睹者也。

飞机之用，于国家闲暇之时，人乘之送信也，馈亲朋也，优游也，观海洋也，反复空际，凌驾云霄，无不自如。人瞻仰之，恰如伟大之蜻蜓，提提飞舞。其行之速，较汽车不啻天壤。国家扰攘之秋，不独便于觇窥敌人之行动，即敌国之城邑也、舟车也，输送之兵士，驻扎之将校，无一而不能借飞机之扔炸弹，为之焚毁焉。是故太西各国之有飞机者，早为他洲戍卒之所极畏惧矣，飞机之用不綦大欤！

Types of Aircraft

In addition to the constant rumbling of artillery during the European War, there were thundering aircraft in the sky. The British aircraft and the German aircraft were the same in shape, but different in internal structures and external symbols. The aircraft of New Zealand, one of the member countries of the British Commonwealth, was similar to that of the British and the only difference was that the rotating leaves on the front end of the aircraft were cross-shaped with two iron bars. Some German aircraft were three winged because there were three engines on the aircraft. To get it to take off, three pilots were needed to drive it at the same time. The French aircraft looked like a skeleton and it flew in a backward direction. When I saw the British aircraft for the first time, I wrote an essay entitled "On Aircraft" as follows:

华工日记
Chinese Labourer's Diaries

On Aircraft

The Analects of Confucius says, "A workman who wishes to do his work well must first sharpen his tools." Xuanyuan's building chariots and boats and You Chao's building wooden houses are both examples illustrating that the implements people make use of today are the same as those created by our ancestors. Now we were working in Europe, we saw that the largest implements used in warfare were aircraft. The making of aircraft varied from country to country. The most commonly seen aircraft was the British aircraft, which had iron as its bone, wood as its meat, petroleum as its blood, fire as its energy, cloth as its skin, copper wire as its sinews, telescopes as its eyes, and machine guns as its claws and teeth. Thus, the aircraft had its head, tail, body, wings and legs. With wheels as the feet, the aircraft was hollow inside but looked beautiful outside, large in size but light in weight. The person inside the aircraft started the engine in its head by handling some organs to make the one or two rotating blades on top of it turn around, which then excited the air to create a large and fast wind to make its whole body vibrate. Although at first it ran on the ground, it soon rose up into the sky. The smaller one could only accommodate one person while the larger one could accommodate three to nine people. All these were what I saw with my own eyes.

In peaceful times, aircraft could be used to deliver mails, to visit friends and relatives, to go sightseeing, and to observe the ocean. The aircraft could fly freely in the sky above the clouds. Looked up from the ground, it resembled a giant dragonfly in the sky. Compared with automobiles, it travelled at a much faster speed. In wartime, aircraft could not only be used to observe and supervise the actions of the enemy, but it could also be used to destroy the enemy's cities, automobiles and ships, the soldiers being transported, and the stationed generals and officers by dropping bombs from it. This was why troops and soldiers of other continents had long been terrified by those European countries which had aircraft. It was evident that aircraft was of great use.

110. 英人在法飞机场之布置

英在欧战时,于法境布置之飞机场,距战场约数十里。其地基之大,一处约数十顷,其中除工人所住之木房,或小铁瓦房外,其余均为帆布帐棚。帐棚之大者长数丈,宽高均丈余,其中均容一飞机。其排列之次序亦与军人帐棚之行列相同。其余之小棚,则为每驾驶员一人住一帐棚也。

至于飞机之起飞,亦按其预定之次序,先令工人整理飞机上之一切,如内部之座位、地图及机关上之一切,外部之机关枪与炸弹等等。何处当灌水者灌水,何部应灌油者灌油,一一检点,都须妥当。驾驶员饱饭后,衣皮袄、皮裤、戴皮帽,检点机已齐备,然后登梯上机。坐定后,开机前行,围机场或一周或半周,即离地而盘旋上升矣。

此第一机起三五分钟后,第二机亦随之而起,第三机、第四机,或多至数十机陆续上升。均起后从远方观之,如鸿雁之往来。其降落时亦盘旋而下,始着地绕场旋转,渐行渐迟,徐徐而停止也。

British Airfield in France

During the European War, Britain set up an airfield in France, which was about dozens of miles away from the battlefield. With an area of dozens of hectares, the airfield had very large foundations. Besides the wooden huts where the soldiers lived or in the iron tile-roofed shelters, all the rest were canvas tents. Some tents were dozens of feet long, over ten feet wide and high, which could accommodate an aeroplane. These tents were arranged in the same order as the military tents. There were also some small tents for the pilots, who had one tent each.

The take-off of aircraft would follow strict orders. First, workers were required to put every item on the plane in order, including the internal seats, maps and all other things, and external guns and bombs. They should also make sure that water and petroleum were filled to the maximum. After all the inspections were finished, the pilots in their leather jackets, trousers and hats would climb into the plane after the meal. After sitting down on the seat, the pilot would drive the plane forward and eventually left the ground up into the sky after running on the ground around the airfield for half or one full circle.

A second aircraft would then take off three or four minutes after the first one. Then the third and the fourth followed. Sometimes, dozens of aeroplanes would take off successively. Looked afar after the aeroplanes had taken off, the group of aeroplanes seemed like a group of wild geese. When the aircraft landed, it would also first hover over the airfield and then keep running along the ground for a while until it slowed down and eventually stopped.

111. 余在飞机场上之工作

飞机场宜于平坦，辄用华工平其不平。余在其中作工数月，常见

孙干：欧战华工记
Records of Chinese Labourers in European War by Sun Gan

飞机之行止，时亦登机览其设备与构造，中设驾驶员座位，座位对面有天文图，其下面足踏处排列脚踏磴数块，座旁有或开或停，或升或降，及左右旋转之机关把柄数根。观其大概，与摩托车上之设备大略相似。

一日余在机场，见英之机工向汽缸灌油，遂询其所用者为何种油。彼答云："盆嗤儿。"为石油中之挥发极快者，并解桶倾出少许，以手掌受之。将手掌一覆反间，其手立干矣。

My Work at Airfield

Because airfields should be flat and smooth, Chinese labourers were asked to level off the ground. I had once worked on a British airfield for several months. During this period, I often saw the take-off and landing of the aircraft. Sometimes, I also climbed onto the aircraft to see its equipment and structure. Inside the aircraft there was the pilot's seat and an astronomical map on its opposite. Under the seat were some foot pedals and beside the seat were some buttons or handles for switching on or off, for ascent or descent, or for turning left or right. According to my observation, the equipment of the aircraft seemed to be roughly the same as that of motorcycles.

One day, I saw a British mechanic was filling the aeroplane tank with oil. I asked what kind of oil he was filling, He answered, "Petroleum." He told me that petroleum could vaporise very quickly, and he poured some of it into his palm. Just as he turned his palm up and down, the hand had already become dry.

华工日记
Chinese Labourer's Diaries

112. 飞机上人员之工作

驾驶员须先有强健之身体与强健之精神,再有良好之学识,然后入航空学校练习数年,方能胜任。

在欧战时,英之飞机场上驾驶员特多,通常之人皆称之曰哈夫赛,盖如中国之称官也。其责任在平常时,司交通最敏捷之飞机于空中,俯仰盘旋,真凌空而上,抱青云之志,而不虚传焉。

一至战时,其品格更使人尊重。因其工作,非远扬侦探敌情,即挟种种炸弹与机关枪,与敌人战斗。每一机上或乘一人或乘三五人不等,盖亦视其飞机之大小也。

Work of Aircraft Personnel

Pilots should first be physically and mentally strong. Besides, they should have a good deal of knowledge and have several years of professional training in aviation schools.

During the European War, there were many pilots at the British airfield. They were commonly called "Officers", which was just like saying "Officials" in Chinese. In ordinary times, the responsibility of these pilots was to control the flying of the aircraft when it pitched or hovered in the sky. They were people who deserved their reputation for rising up over clouds and had the aspiration to soar high into the blue sky.

孙干：欧战华工记
Records of Chinese Labourers in European War by Sun Gan

In wartime, the aircraft played a very important role. It was greatly respected because it could observe the enemy or carry various bombs or machine guns to fight against the aircraft of the enemy. The aircraft could have from one to five people in it, depending on the size of the aircraft.

113. 南斐洲人之运输

一日余在外工作，于路旁忽来运输大车一大队。在车上御车之人，其面黑而放光，其目白者雪白，睛则漆黑，其唇与舌鲜红，而牙亦雪白。乍见其凶恶之状，无异食人之兽，不止一人如是，大队之人个个如是。初余以为印度人，问之英人，英人言为阿斐利喀也。印度人以红巾缠头，而此斐人无之也。余闻此之后，遂快然曰："不加入欧战，何克见斐人之真如火烧耶！"

Transport of the South Africans

One day, a large group of transport vehicles came by the roadside while I was working outdoors. The driver of the lorry had a black shiny face with large white and black eyes, red lips and tongue, and very white teeth. His appearance instantly reminded me of the cannibals I had read about. He was not the only one with such an appearance. Everyone in the brigade was like him. At first I thought they were Indians, but the British officer told me that they were Africans. Indians often wrapped their heads with red scarves, but these Africans did not. On hearing this I said jokingly, "How would I ever have known that Africans were as black as charcoal if I had not joined the European War?"

114. 遍地高射炮

欧战时英兵在法境，最能维持后防安宁之武器，惟赖高射炮。英之高射炮常见者身长七八尺，底周约二尺许，口径约二寸左右，不独山野旷地遍处皆是，即田畔村头、大街小巷，亦几乎为之杜塞。其为数之多，盖可想见。是以日日除闻战场炮声隆隆之外，则为遍地之高射炮声。故德之飞机，昼至时则往往高至数千尺，使人目几不见。纵扔下炸弹，十不中一也；夜至低甚，虽上下诡谲，计谋多端，亦常常为炮击落。

Numerous Anti-aircraft Guns

During the European war, the anti-aircraft guns were the most effective weapons the British had in maintaining the peace of the rear defence in France. The British anti-aircraft guns were usually seven or eight foot long, about three foot in circumference and about three inches in calibre. These anti-aircraft guns were scattered everywhere, not only in the hills and countryside, but also in the villages, city streets, and alleys. One could never have imagined there being such an immense number of them. Besides the constant rumble of artillery in the battlefield, it was the sound of these anti-aircraft guns that we heard the most. As a result, during the daytime the German planes often flew thousands of feet high in the sky so that they could hardly be seen with naked eyes. Because of this, even if they dropped some bombs, nine out of ten of them would fail to hit the target. During the night however, the German aircraft flew very low. Even though they frequently changed up and down, they were often shot down by these anti-aircraft guns.

115. 安南之战士

余因助战作工，至法国地驻扎良久，但未见法人之武器与其战士。惟有时或在车站，或在道路，见安南之战士焉。安南人之身体，较吾华人稍短，而颜色略黑，虽不懂吾国语言，却多识吾国文字。

一次余队他迁，在车站遇数法人率安南之战士甚多。余与之谈，用中国话不懂，又与谈英语，亦不懂。以后余书汉字与之相谈，不但书写极快，且亦明白晓畅。其文云："吾安南与中国，不独同文，人亦同种。今后深望复与中国合而为一。吾因很爱中国人之和平，后日回国，如得机会，愿到中国内地各处一游也。"彼方书写至此，遂闻令站队。彼始向余辞去，吾于是知安南人之读汉文者，现在仍有多数也。

Soldiers of Vietnam

During the long time I worked for the British in France, I had never seen any French weapons or soldiers. But occasionally, I could see the Vietnamese soldiers on the road or at railway stations. These Vietnamese were a little shorter than Chinese but darker in skin colour. Although they could not speak Chinese, most of them could read and write Chinese characters.

On one occasion when our brigade moved to another place, I met many Vietnamese soldiers at the railway station. I tried to talk with them in Chinese at first, but they did not understand. I then tried to talk with them in English, but they did not understand that language either. Later, I talked with them by writing Chinese characters and found that they were not only able to understand me but that they could also write very fast. They wrote, "The Vietnamese not only have the same written language as the Chinese, but also are of the same kind in race as Chinese. We hope we can be reunited with China again one day. We love the peace of the Chinese people very much and would like to travel around China when we return home in the future." Just as he had finished writing these words, an order came that they stand in line because they had to leave. It was only after this encounter that I realised that there were still many Vietnamese that could read Chinese.

116. 法境之照空灯

华工到法国作工，一到夜间，无不黑瞳瞳而无丝之光见。惟德之飞机来时，则一道一道明光四起者，乃英人设备之照空灯也。英设照空灯于法境，其数盖不减于高射炮。观其设置之法，于平地先掘一坑，深约四五尺，坑之周约丈二三尺。其中灯状之机器如镜头，然而能旋转。看守人昼则以布蔽之，夜闻敌机一至，立使白光高射，照中飞机，人皆立

孙干：欧战华工记
Records of Chinese Labourers in European War by Sun Gan

见。斯时也，高射炮一齐猛击，敌之飞机十之七八被击而降下也。

一夜德之飞机至，照空灯由四方一齐高射者，有十有四条之多。而德之飞机反覆上下，终不能逃避所射之光矣。于是高射炮声，哄然齐发，卒将德人之飞机击毁而坠落。翌日余往观其机，始知其木架之掌，亦为四页薄板所合成，如鸟羽之中空然。由此可知，其重量定然较轻不鲜也。

Searchlights in France

In France it became completely dark when night fell. Only when the German aircraft approached did beams of light brighten the sky from all around. They were the British searchlights and there seemed to be as many of them in France as that of the anti-aircraft guns. To set up a searchlight, a pit was first excavated in the ground, which was about four or five feet deep and about three feet in circumference. The lamp-like machine sited inside the pit could rotate just like lens. The soldiers covered the light with cloth in daytime, but once the enemy aircraft approached at night they were unveiled immediately and made it shine brightly towards the aircraft so that people could see it clearly. At the same time, the anti-aircraft guns were targeted at the aeroplane, and many were successfully shot down with this method.

One night, as many as fourteen searchlights lit up the sky when a German aeroplane was approaching. Although it attempted to escape the bright rays of these searchlights by flying up and down repeatedly, it failed and was shot down by the anti-aircraft guns that had all started firing at it. The next day I went to have a look at the crashed aeroplane and discovered that it only had a wooden frame made of four thin wooden boards which were just like the feathers of a bird. Obviously, its weight must be very light.

华工日记
Chinese Labourer's Diaries

117. 英人之巨炮

一日,余等排队往野中挖战壕时,路过一铁工厂。适遇炮车五套,分拉一巨炮将入铁厂,盖从战场拉来修理者。炮身分为五节,每节之长约四五尺,底巨梢细,巨者略短,细者稍长,若连成一炮则长约两丈,炮底之粗处约有三抱左右。拉炮之车亦极特别,又非载重摩托车所能比,前行则以自带相联分节之铁轨,先铺于地为道,车过遂又将分节铁轨,复由车上而转至车前,以备再铺,节节相连。所以车之行时,全赖车之外面分节而又相联之铁轨,如一长带。车之前方遂行遂铺,车之后方遂行遂起,循环不已也。余因是车从前未之见,故今名之为特别炮车。

一日,余驻在阿米阳近旁之郊外遥望车站,有一巨炮为一长火车挽至。至车站之旁,吾侪多人相率往观,约距是炮二里许,即有英兵拒余等曰:"此炮一响,不但能将人震聋,而恐有震死之虞。故非吾炮队中之英人,不准入近也。汝等俱视余之耳。"余等视其耳塞以絮,余等亦以棉絮杜之。及余等归,炮声一响,众帐棚上下鼓当不停,并闻炮弹在空中吼声大作,直至远甚,始不得闻。是巨炮约十余分钟而发一响,迨共五六发,后火车引之而又他去矣。吾侪当时不但被震惊惧,且共赞叹不置。

Gigantic Cannons of Britain

One day, on our way to the field for trench excavation, we passed by an ironworks where I saw five giant cannon carrying vehicles were sent for

孙干：欧战华工记
Records of Chinese Labourers in European War by Sun Gan

repairs from the battlefield. The body of the gun was divided into five sections, each being about four or five feet long. The base of the gun was large, but the tip was small. The large section was slightly shorter while the thinner section was somewhat longer. If all the sections were connected together, it was about twenty feet long and the circumference at the thickest part of the gun, near the base, was about three arms thick. The vehicle that carried the cannon was very special, quite different from the heavy-duty motor vehicles. When moving forward, the vehicle first laid its own connected segments of track on the ground. As each plate passed underneath, these segments were transferred from the top of the vehicle to its front and then continued laying the joined plates for further travel. Thus, the movement of the vehicle depended entirely on the segmented but interconnected belt-like rails outside it and the cycle continued ceaselessly as the vehicle moved. I had never seen such vehicles, so I called them special cannon vehicles.

On another day, when I looked out towards the railway station from the suburb of Amiens where we were encamped at the time, I noticed a giant cannon carried by a long train had arrived. When I came near the railway station, I followed many of my fellow workers to have a look at it. But when we were about two hundred and fifty yards away from it, we were stopped by some British soldiers, who said, "People can be deafened or even killed by the noise of this cannon when it is fired. So no one except members of our brigade is allowed to go near to it. You can look at my ears." When we looked at his ears, we found that they were filled with cotton, so we all put cotton in our ears too. Afterwards, when we had returned to the camp, the cannon was fired, and the tents vibrated up and down ceaselessly as the sound of shells roared across the sky. The sound disappeared gradually as it travelled further away. The giant cannon fired once every ten minutes or so. After it had fired five or six times, the train moved on towing the giant cannon. We were not only shocked and frightened, but also amazed at its great power.

118. 夜间至战线近旁参观空中之灯

余之至友，石匠黄世恩君一夕谓余曰："战事如是殷，吾恐后日之还祖国也难矣。吾侪在此，虽不怕死，而父母老幼日望回归，良可闵也！"言至此，一旁呆坐数人，有啜其泣者，有声泪俱下者。有顷，又谓余曰："祝忱兄，余有一事，愿与汝商。"吾二人由棚中出，彼曰："今夕往战线一观，汝愿冒此险乎？"余立答曰："欲往参观，久蓄此意。何惮之有？"彼又曰："吾二人倘一遇险，当如何？"余曰："如余遇死，乞将余之衣物，费心携归，交于吾家中。汝有不测，余亦如是照办。如俱遇不测，可俱作罢论。汝以为何如？"彼曰："只好如此。"

于是吾二人初由灌木丛中盘旋东行，又上一丘岭，将及巅，岗警渐密。恐被阻挡，余二人乘夜昏黑，窜默行旁，逾岭而过，见处处皆为兵士所踩躏者，山石荦确，土径坎坷。既至岭下，屡见明光四出，没知所以，并渐闻英兵攒簇愈密，约行里许而英人则更多矣。余二人以为吾侪虽非英人，而于夜间混入，英之将士亦未必觉也。

然闻枪声已近，而炮弹又屡屡发来。复前行，地势渐低，危险亦更大，而不如在此高处一观，以为有益，遂同坐于乱石之上。斯时也，细察其枪炮之射击，及兵士之动作，大约距德人之战壕不过二三里路而已。甫坐定，即见战线天空，忽飘飘而出一红灯，其光明亮而且大，徐徐下坠。同时较低处又有较小之灯数点，亦俱散布空中，复徐徐下坠。其大者自起至落，约时数十分钟方灭；其小者自起至落，约需时亦十余分钟

孙干：欧战华工记
Records of Chinese Labourers in European War by Sun Gan

即息。不独吾所相对之处如是，而由南而北以及远处，莫不如是，盖由其兵士射起之照空灯也。于是吾想欧人能由心理而明物理，使黑暗战场变如明亮白昼，若复由物理而求得天理，方可谓真文明也。感慨不已，良久始归，至营已逾夜半矣。

Observing Searchlights Near Battlefield at Night

Huang Shien, a stonemason and one of my best friends, said to me one evening, "The War is very intense now and I am afraid that we may never return to our homeland. Although we are not frightened of death here, it would be a pitiful thing if we were killed because our parents and children are looking forward to our returning." Upon hearing his words, some labourers sitting nearby began to sob and some even burst into tears. After a while, he said to me again, "Brother Sun, there is something I want to talk to you about." So, the two of us went out of the tent and he said, "I have decided to go and have a look at the front lines this evening. Would you like to take a risk and come with me?" I answered at once, "I've long had the intention to do so. Why should I be afraid?" Then he said, "If one of us were in danger, what should we do?" I said, "If I died, I hope you could take the trouble of taking my clothes back to my home. If anything happened to you, I would do the same. If we were both to be killed, we could do nothing about it. What do you think of it?" He said, "I agree, that is what we shall do."

So, we both headed eastward from the bushes and then went up a hill. When we arrived at the top we found more and more guards. Afraid of being blocked we moved silently by the roadside and climbed over the ridge in the darkness of the night. Along the way, we saw there were traces

华工日记

Chinese Labourer's Diaries

of war everywhere, large, jagged rocks blown up by the bombardments or the rough earth paths that were once roads. When we came to the foot of the ridge, we could see bright lights appear frequently all around us. We did not know what was happening. Then we heard more and more soldiers moving. After walking forward for another five hundred yards, the number of British soldiers became increasingly larger. We both thought that we might not be noticed if we mixed amongst them under the cover of the night, even though we were not British.

However, we could hear the approaching gunfire and the repeated cannonballs. Thinking that we would be in greater danger if we went forward any further because the terrain got lower and flatter, we decided to sit on the rocks and observe the frontlines from a higher place, which turned out to be a better choice. At that time, from the sound of the guns and the movement of the soldiers, we estimated that we might be one or two miles from the trenches of the German troops. As soon as we sat down, we saw a large, bright red light fluttering in the sky above the battle front and then fell slowly. At the same time, several smaller lights in the lower areas also went up into the sky and then fell slowly. It took the large light many minutes to go up and then fall into darkness again, as did the smaller lights. The lights were not only scattered into the sky we faced, but also to the skies all around us and far beyond. It turned out that these were the searchlights that the soldiers were manipulating. Seeing all this made me realise that the Europeans were good at human's psychology and the law of physics so that they could change the dark battlefield almost into a bright day. If they could have more reason from the law of physics, then their civilization would be a true civilisation. After seeing the battlefront and sighing with emotion for a long time, we began to return and it was already midnight when we arrived back at our camp.

孙干：欧战华工记
Records of Chinese Labourers in European War by Sun Gan

119. 印度人之运输

印度人到法境当兵者有之，充医士者亦有之，而御马车作运输队者，为数则更多也。其面目虽与阿斐利加人同，其习惯却与之异。印人之首，虽暑甚，往往以红巾裹之。食饭时不用箸叉刀匙，而以手指抓之。其身躯之伟高，亦多为斐人所不及。

Transport of the Indians

There were many Indians in France. Some of them served as soldiers and some worked as doctors, while the majority of them worked as drivers of carriages in the transport brigades. Although they were similar to Africans in appearance, their customs and habits were quite different from those of Africans. Despite the hot weather, the Indians usually had red scarves wrapped around their heads. While eating meals, they would take food with their hands instead of using knives, forks and spoons. Besides, they were usually taller than Africans.

华工日记
Chinese Labourer's Diaries

120. 战地子弹之种种

英人自他处运来之子弹，或在道旁，或在车站，处处山积，种类繁多，最大者可数百磅。一日，余询英人曰："一切子弹均为贵国所自造欤？"曰："不尽然。"指路旁之灰色、形如棒槌之炸弹曰："是为结拉骂呢（Germany德国人）所造。此细绳，由柄之内部联于弹内之发动机。掷时，一手持柄，一手用两指将珠捻紧而用力猛一挣，使弹内之火燃烧机关发火，谅火已燃，然后持把之手用力向敌人抛掷。德人安以长把者，以其能抛掷较远也。英国人之炸弹，弹外之发条，自此端强逼之使至彼端，并用一钉紧别之。掷时，先以一手将弹握紧，一手将紧别之铁钉抽去，然后用力向敌人掷去也。"英人言至此，遂手取一英人之炸弹，先以右手紧掘，又将弹上之铁钉抽下，抛出数丈，弹落即炸。余等往观，其地炸有小坑深数寸。询其能伤几人，云多者二三十人也。

Bombs in Battlefields

The munitions that the British transported to the battlefronts were usually piled either by the roadside or at the railway depots. They were great in number and variety. The largest could be as heavy as several hundred pounds. One day, I asked a British officer, "Are all these munitions made in your country?" He answered, "Not all." Pointing to the grey, hammer-shaped bombs by the roadside, he said, "These were made by Germany. This string is connected to the trigger inside the grenade through the handle. When throwing them, you should hold the handle with one hand and pull it forcefully by twisting the beads tightly with the other hand to ignite the fuse-burning mechanism inside the grenade. When the fuse has been ignited, you should throw it at the enemy and be as far away as possible. The German grenades with long handles are designed to be thrown at a greater distance. However, in the British grenade, there is a spring connected to the handle outside and fastened with a pin. When throwing, you should hold the grenade tightly with one hand and pull the pin out, then throw it forcefully at the enemy." With these words, the British soldier took a grenade, held it tightly with his right hand, then pulled out the pin with the other hand and threw it out several yards away. As soon as it dropped on the ground, the grenade exploded. We went to look and found a hole several inches deep in the ground. When I asked how many people could be injured by a grenade, he said about twenty or thirty people by just one grenade.

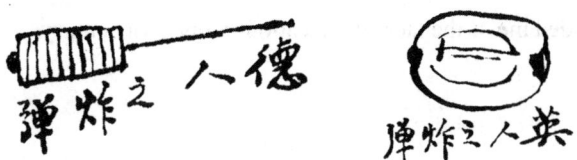

My Drawing of German & British grenades

121. 西欧之犬与鸽

　　法地不但人有教育，而禽兽亦有受教育而供人役使者。某日，无事出游，见坡下一荆棘为篱之营盘，帐棚数座，余则有小木屋若干间，每一木屋内有犬一只，守一小盆。余不解其故，询诸他人，乃知为受训练、受编制之送信犬队也。素知其鸽能送信，今又知其犬亦能至战场服务，回想吾亚东病夫人之无教育者，竟多多焉。

Dogs and Pigeons in Western Europe

In France, not only were the people educated, but even their animals were also well trained to serve as messengers. One day, while wandering about in my spare time, I came across a small camp fenced by thorns on the slope of a hill. In addition to some tents, there were a number of small cabins, inside each of which was a dog and a small basin. I did not understand what they were doing, so I asked someone, and he told me that they were trained and prepared messenger dog teams. I knew that pigeons could deliver messages, but it was not until then that I found that dogs were also used in the battlefields. This again reminded me of the lack of education in my own country.

122. 法地之电线遍地

欧战后防，电话既多，电线必密，既不能一一架于洋灰杆上，有时埋于地内，有时置放地面。所以后防电线之密，遍地皆是。其战场消息之灵通，非吾辈之思想之所能及也。

孙干：欧战华工记
Records of Chinese Labourers in European War by Sun Gan

Widely Scattered Wires

In the rear defence of the European War, due to the great number of telephones used for communication, there were densely arranged wires everywhere. Some of them were buried underground while others were just laid on the ground because not all of these wires could be erected on posts. As a result, the wires were scattered everywhere. The fast speed of information delivery in the battlefields was quite beyond imagination.

123. 法境之森林

华工到法，除修路挖壕外，多伐森林。法南部固多庄田、桑麻，北部、东部多半丘陵起伏，除少数之麦田、菜圃及苹果行外，多是森林之区。庄村极稀，各村房舍，相距亦极疏远，其它之地非自然森林即人造林也。法之人造林多在平地，每林之大，有长十数里者，其中树株大致可分为二，即白苦栗与松柏也。白苦栗林之树，大者小者各都成行，其间杂有其它之小树甚多，盖因年久之自生者。白苦栗之大者，粗及数抱，高亦凌空。路人入此，空气凉爽，精神焕发，真不知赤日之将午。人造松柏林，面积较其它小甚。其中，除杉、桧等不甚高者外，即荆、棘、樗、梂等，亦并不生。观其林内之状况，迥与苦栗林之中杂树郁菀者不相同也。至丘陵起伏处之自然林中，任何种树都有所生，其枝叶之条达茂密。

华工日记
Chinese Labourer's Diaries

Forests in France

In addition to road building and trench digging, the Chinese labourers in France worked as lumbermen chopping down trees in forests for most of the time. The southern part of France was mainly covered with farmland while the northern and eastern parts of the country were mostly covered by forests on the undulating hillsides, along with a few wheat fields, vegetable gardens and apple orchards. There were few villages, which were often far away from each other. Most of the land was covered with either natural woodlands or man-made forests. Most of the planted forests in France were on flat land. Each forest was often larger than five square miles. There were mostly two types of planted forests, those with chestnut trees and those with pine trees. In the chestnut forests, all of the trees whether big or small were planted in rows, between which grew other self-seeded smaller trees. The big chestnut trees were as thick as several arms rising high in the sky. It could make walkers in the woods forget it was a hot day because the air was so cool and fresh. The planted pine forests were much smaller in area and most of the pines were intermingled with spruce and juniper trees and no other trees or bushes such as thorns and brambles were growing in amongst them. These planted forests of pines and cypresses were quite different from the forests of chestnuts, where there were numerous types of trees and bushes growing. As for the natural forests on the hills, there are many varieties of trees growing there and all are very thick and dense with undergrowth.

孙干：欧战华工记
Records of Chinese Labourers in European War by Sun Gan

124. 橡皮胶质之利用

　　欧战时，战场前后拥拥护护，各国之摩托车，为数不知多少。观摩托车上之重要部分，虽赖其头上之汽缸，然亦全靠车下以橡皮制之胶质轮也。今仅就英之摩托车言之，其摩托车约数也有二十万辆之多，每车有橡皮轮四个。若一车之轮以百斤重计之，则英之车即胶质橡皮，有其车辆之数百倍，二千万余斤之多也，其余各国尚不与焉。又如战场上之胶皮靴、胶皮雨衣，或以之作枕，或以之作澡盆与饮马槽等等一切。细察其橡皮胶质之为用亦大矣哉，宜乎各国争制造之。吾侪之抱爱国心者，不可不留意焉。

Utilisation of Rubber

　　During the European War, numerous motorcycles from various countries travelled back and forth from the battlefields. An important part of the motorcycle was its cylinder above its head and the rubber wheels underneath it. There are about two hundred thousand motorcycles from Britain alone and for each motorcycle there were four rubber tyres. Suppose the weight of each tyre was 100 pounds, the weight of rubber on the thousands of vehicles would be over twenty million pounds, let alone the vehicles of other countries. There were also rubber boots and rubber raincoats as well as rubber pillows, bathtubs and mangers used on battlefields. Rubber was really of great use and was suitable for all countries to manufacture. Thus, the great use of rubber should not be neglected by our own patriotic Chinese labourers.

125. 队长借与余英汉单字注解

一百零二队工人，自开至战线后防作工，自冬至春为队长者更易数次。自英人潘尔恩至队，队长暨工头等，与众工人始渐臻融洽，盖因潘队长会说中国话故也。一日在野外掘战壕工毕，余询其赴巴黎之路程，及请假买英汉书籍。彼不之允曰："巴黎之城，法人之巴黎，非英人余之巴黎也。英人欲去者，须先向法政府交涉，方可出入。吾等欲去极不随便，况汝中国人耶？汝欲学习英语甚好甚好。俟余归队后，借与汝一本可也。"以后果借与余英汉单字注解一册，余借之且学且书，对于英语始稍有进步矣。

Annotated British-Chinese Book Lent to Me by Our Captain

From last winter to this spring, the captains of Brigade 102 of Chinese Labour Corps had changed many times since we arrived at the rear of the battlefront. However, ever since the Englishman Captain Paine came to our brigade, the relationship among Captain, foremen and labourers had become quite harmonious. This was mainly due to the fact that Captain Paine could speak Chinese. One day, after we had finished our work of excavating trenches in the field, I asked him about the route to Paris and asked him for leave to buy English-Chinese books. He did not agree and said, "Paris is a French city rather than a city of Great Britain. Even if the British officers want to go to Paris, they can only enter the city with the permission of the French government, which requires us to apply to the French government first. It is very difficult for us to go to Paris, let alone you Chinese. You want to learn English. That is a very good thing. I'll lend you a book when we return to our camp." Later, he gave me his annotated English-Chinese vocabulary book, with which I learnt to read and write in English. From then on, my English began to improve.

126. 华工工作之进步

华工到法，因英人所发之粮不足，好事者常常胡闹。久之，队中之忠厚良农，都知天天所食之饭论数虽不多，养料实不少。工作既不甚勤，而各人之身体亦渐见肥胖。是以对于作工，大半勤勤苦苦，又因会说中国话之队长潘尔恩到队，处处都能与工人直接谈话，工人之素甚狡猾者，亦无从捣乱。自是而后，上下融洽，工人工作处处较前为妥善矣。余因之作歌一则如下：

作生活　讲干活，会洋话的先去来往说。吾侪排队后跟着，用具挑巧拙。你抢我也夺，不得车辆摸锹镢。一人瓦喀胜于欧人作工三倍多。

（瓦喀即生活也）

华工日记
Chinese Labourer's Diaries

Progress of Chinese Labourers in Work

When Chinese labourers first arrived in France, some of them often made some troubles because of the insufficient food given to them. Over time, honest labourers in the brigade realised that although the food provided every day was not too much in amount, it contained adequate nutrition. Since the work was not too heavy, each of us even began to gain some weight. Therefore, labourers began to work harder. Besides, ever since the Chinese-speaking Captain Paine took his office, he would come to talk things over directly with the labourers. So, even the cunning labourers had no reason to make trouble again. It was since then that the labourers began to make much greater progress in their work than ever before. Hereupon I wrote the following poem:

On Work: In terms of work, the Chinese-speaking British Captain would negotiate. In line we just followed, and picked out the ingenious working equipment. All competed to work, with either a vehicle or shovel and spade. One Chinese labourer could work three times more than the workers of Europe.

127. 掘深战壕

近年，欧人物质进步甚速。故此次欧战杀人利器，实令人惊惧。然使人人能避之者，惟赖战壕。法地之战壕，可谓不少。如深一费忒（英尺名），无整齐边缘者，可曰临时战壕。深三费忒，宽下底三费忒，上

孙干：欧战华工记
Records of Chinese Labourers in European War by Sun Gan

口四费忒，而边缘整齐，并有伏台者，可曰普通战壕。是等战壕，其弯曲度或左或右，视地势方向而定。战士在内可坐可卧，放枪时不止击一方面，而左右均可击之。敌人以枪炮射来时，亦不止避一面也。即运送子弹及饭食汤水等等者，由其中行，虽不能站，然匍匐行之，无甚险也。深六费忒，宽亦如之者可曰深战壕。其弯曲且左且右，一如普通之战壕，边缘亦使整齐，惟其底部一边有阶路，司射击之兵士常立其上，以伺敌人。彼一边则为往来者之路，壕身既宽且深，故行其中者，虽骑马往来，而亦无惧敌人视之也。是类战壕，不惟如普通之战壕容纳战士，运输往来又可通行已也。如敌人之骑兵及其坦克车至，又可阻之使其陷入不能前进。至于炮队所需之战壕、所藏之地窖，又为特别之形势矣。

Deep Excavation of Trenches

Europeans had made rapid progress in materials in the past few years. As a result, the killing weapons used in this European War were really frightening. It was the trenches that enabled people to escape these frightening weapons. There were countless trenches in France. Those that were one foot deep and had no neat edges were called temporary trenches. Those that were three feet deep, three feet wide at the bottom, four feet wide at the upper and had neat edges and platforms were called ordinary trenches. These kinds of trenches were either left or right bended depending on the direction of the terrain, in which soldiers could sit or lie and could shoot from both sides. When the enemy's bullet came, soldiers in it could also avoid being shot from both sides. Munitions, food and water could be transported along these trenches and even though people could not stand up in the trench, they could crawl forward without fearing that they would be injured. Trenches that were deeper than six feet and up to six feet wide were called deep trenches. Like the ordinary trenches, they would curve either left or right and had neat edges. The difference was that there were steps at the bottom on one side of the trench, on which the soldiers could stand and shoot the enemy. On the other side of the trench was a pathway for people, which was both deep and wide. Even those who rode horses could move along them without being detected by the enemy. Therefore, compared with the ordinary trenches, this type of trench could not only accommodate soldiers, but they could also be used by traffic and transport. If the enemy's cavalry and tanks arrived, these trenches could also trap them in and hinder them from moving t forward. There were also special trenches and shelters for artillery emplacements.

128. 骑士之留踪迹

一日，余与同工数人出游，行至一丘陵之曲阿，见其中园圃整齐，苹果树多而且大，地面虽大，而人家止一。可想知其地之景致清幽，鸡犬安闲矣。迨余数人前行逾其路之大半，见一切园门，虽尽柴扉而无不整理，视其路阶，虽尽石砌而无一不坚固。吾与同工且观且行，同声赞叹。有顷，忽从后方有一骑兵策马奔至，肩上负枪，肩下附有白纸屑小包壹个，一手持缰，一手将纸包内之白粹纸下扬而其行也。飞窜柴扉，即跃篱墙，不一刻，自其斜坡而去，形影即眇不之见。当时余等咸怪其愚，盍由正路平坦而易行，偏找其有障碍之柴门与偏僻耶？正言之际，从后方又有骑兵五人，循前人所撒下之纸屑，过柴门跃篱笆，匆匆而至。观其马不但骁勇，而又驯良。骑者命之速跑则速跑，命之高跃则高跃。

孙干：欧战华工记
Records of Chinese Labourers in European War by Sun Gan

不须臾，而又沓然不之见矣。斯时也，余始知先奔之兵士所撒之白纸屑，乃留后之来者追赶彼之踪迹也。观其人与其马，非教之有素，临阵能如是耶？吾国善骑之士对国家之有志者，其亦当取法也。

Traces of Cavalrymen

One day, several labourers and I travelled out to a large house at the bottom of a hillside. Although there were neat gardens and numerous large apple trees, it seemed that only one family lived there. It could be imagined what a quiet and beautiful place it was. When we had walked along most of the road leading to the house, we noticed that all the garden gates and fences were neatly arranged, and all the stone steps were well presented. Seeing the neatness, my fellow labourers and I could not help admiring it very much. Suddenly, a cavalryman on a horse rushed up from behind, with a gun over one shoulder and a small bag of white paper scraps over the other. The cavalryman held the rein in one hand and threw the white paper scraps to the ground with the other hand. Flying through the wooden gates and jumping over the fences, he soon disappeared from view in an instant. At that time, we all thought the cavalryman was so stupid that he chose to jump over wooden gates and fences rather than ride on the flat ground. Just as we were talking with each other, another five cavalrymen appeared from behind. They all passed through the gate and jumped over the fences, obviously following the scraps of the first cavalryman in a hurry. I thought that the horses they rode were not only brave but also very agile. They ran as fast or jumped as high as they were commanded to by their riders. In a short time, all of them had disappeared from our view. We then realised that the white scraps of paper spread by the first rushing cavalryman were actually traces left for those who came after him. From the performance of both the cavalrymen and their horses, we could see that all of them had received excellent training. Otherwise, they would not be able to ride so well. Cavalrymen with great aspirations in our country should also learn from them by imitating this method of training.

129. 吾侪之住宿

华工到法宿于帐棚，一百零二队之到战地后防，时适霪雨，虽在冬季，天天零零然，犹如中国夏季也。而十数人住一帐棚之内，同时不能尽入，其中之容量狭小可知，况且人人足穿庞然之皮靴乎？其后迁移渐多，或二三礼拜而始一迁，或在一礼拜而往他处数迁，一行一拆，一止一撑，天天雨水淋漓，泥涂殆遍，真有令人不胜其烦劳者。及至夏季，每棚之中，人数渐减，盖因气候渐热也。

民国七年夏，天气渐渐清和，支搭帐棚，亦不如前之泥泞，帐棚杆都易高者，欲搭帐棚之处，先掘去其土使之深二三尺，然后将棚支于其上，适天晴，即将棚周之缘挂起。人在中卧，望四面如开亮窗，然倘遇敌人之飞机至，身卧深地，亦较他日免却一些危险耳。然工人中往往有不住棚中，自寻一地挖为深窖，而睡眠其中者，英人亦不禁止也。

Accommodation of Our Labourers

Chinese labourers lived in tents in France. When Brigade 102 arrived in the rear of the battlefields, it was the season of heavy rain. Although it was already winter, it rained every day, just as what it was like during the summer in China. More than ten people lived in a tent, which was so small that they could not enter together at the same time. And conditions were made more difficult because everyone wore huge leather boots. Before too long, we began to move camp frequently. Sometimes we moved once every two or three weeks but at other times we would move several times within a week. Every time we moved, we needed to dismantle our tents and as soon as we arrived, we needed to set them up again. With rain falling every day and mud everywhere, the setting up and dismantling of tents was really annoying. When summer arrived, the number of people living in a tent was reduced because of the increasingly hot weather.

In the summer of 1918, as the weather became gradually warmer, the way of establishing and dismantling of tents was not the same as before. All tent poles were changed into higher ones. Before setting up the tent, we usually dug a pit about three feet in depth and then set the tent up over the pit. If it was sunny, we would hang up the edges of the tent. While we lay inside and looked around, it was very bright just as if we had windows. When the enemy aircraft attacked, lying in the deep pit could also help us avoid any danger. However, some labourers chose not to live in the tents, they preferred to dig a deep hole and sleep in them alone. This was not forbidden by the British.

130. 四月挖战壕于白唐高来寺之所见

七年四月，迁至白唐高来寺时，挖掘战壕之工，更行紧张，所以天

华工日记
Chinese Labourer's Diaries

天在野外，抗洋镐者，每日不止数百人。其忙之甚，何待于言？而在野四望，上有伟大之蜻蜓，回环往复，往来上下，有低飞像练习打靶者，有高飞而伺敌机之来袭击者，亦有成行成群，而来去不停，而掩护其步兵者。下有苍然之松柏森林，望之由蔚然之中，形如窜梭之各种车辆，如载长官也、子弹也、工人也、邮差也，自晨至夜，无一时不轰烈。一日余于作工之余，口占俚句如下：

白唐高来寺远眺

白唐高来寺为家，
时正清和感物华。
余握战壕密如网，
人乘蜻蜓上云霞。
森林往来人急回，
车马驰骋力尤加。
精神竞争贵合群，
确实胜利是何家。

Digging Trenches in Bertangles in April

The work of digging trenches became increasingly heavier when we moved to Bertangles in April 1918. Every day, hundreds of labourers were kept busy digging trenches with their pickaxes, staying in the fields all day long. The hardships they had to suffer were beyond words. Looking around in the fields, we could see aircraft flying back and forth, or up and down in the sky like giant dragonflies. Some flew very low as if they were having shooting practice; others flew very high waiting for the attack of the enemy aircraft;

still others flew in groups back and forth to cover the marching infantry. We could see forests of pines and cypresses below. Amidst these lush forests came and went all kinds of vehicles carrying officers, munitions, labourers and also letters and parcels from morning until night. I composed a small poem after work one day:

A View from Bertangles

We moved to Bertangles around Tomb-sweeping Day,
When everything in nature began to grow fast and lushly.
I excavated deep trenches as part of the dense network,
Seeing people soar into the sky in aircraft like the dragonfly.
Amidst the forest below soldiers rushed back and forth,
While horses and vehicles moved with their full strength.
Cooperation and solidarity counts most in competitions,
I wondered who would be the ultimate victor of the war.

131. 异地之风俗

年龄至幼之稚子，不但色白而且胖。最亲切之尊长，见之辄以嘴衔其唇、舌或其腮、耳，盖亲切爱情之表现也。余到欧西，见英法城市中之大人，往往行谓之接吻。余初见之，以为是礼也，吾国不行之于成人，而行之于婴儿。西人不但行之于幼儿，而又行之于成人；不但行之于其家，而行之于其街市。盖非极亲切者，而仍不行。在吾国，此举甚轻；在西欧，则行之极重。可见异地之风俗，与吾国之不同也矣。

华工日记
Chinese Labourer's Diaries

Different Customs

Young European children were usually fat and white. Their closest elders would often kiss them on their lips, cheeks or ears to show affection. When I first arrived in Europe, I noticed that adults would also often greet each other with kisses. I knew it was a greeting etiquette, but in our country such greetings could only be applied to babies and never to adults. In contrast to our customs, this style of greeting occurred not only at home but also in streets and markets. Kissing as a social etiquette would occur only between people who were very intimate. In our country, people seldom greeted each other by kissing but in the West Europe, kissing as a way of greeting was very common. From this it can be seen that the Europeans had different customs from those in our country.

132. 英飞机之自焚

欧战时，英之飞机有时被德人之高射炮击之下落，不但被德人之高射炮击之下落，亦被英人之高射炮误认而击落之。

一日，余在野外，见空中有一飞机翱翔甚高。正盘旋间，忽见机之头部火起。不须臾失其前行之效力而下坠，尚未及地，飞机上燃烧之物，已成灰烬。及地时惟余寥寥之金属物与驾驶员半焦之尸体而已。睹其莫不恻然也。

孙干：欧战华工记
Records of Chinese Labourers in European War by Sun Gan

Self-Burning of British Aircraft

During the European War, British aircraft were sometimes shot down by German anti-aircraft artillery or even by the British anti-aircraft artillery occasionally because they were mistaken for enemy aircraft.

One day, I saw an aeroplane flying very high in the sky while I was in the field. Suddenly, its engine caught fire and it began to fall towards the ground. But the whole plane had been burnt to ashes before it could landed on the ground. Only a few metal objects and the half-burnt body of the pilot could be found at the wreckage site. Such a terrible scene filled everyone with deep sorrow.

133. 英法之气候

英法两国都居于北温带，北纬五十度左右，而中国北部，亦同是居于北温带，北纬五十度左右者，其天气却大不相同也。盖中国北部全靠大陆，常旱干，故人谓之大陆气候。英法两国虽处温带，然四面全靠海洋，常常潮湿，故人谓之海洋气候也。

凡华工被招而赴英法者，多山东与河北二省人，原无海洋气候之习惯，赴法日久，自以为自冬徂秋常度清凉阴湿之时日，终觉无寒，无暑，无春，无秋也。余尝自其植物之生长观之，一一都较中国为宜人。华工多数言论，则又以不及吾国之天气也远甚，此乃华工以其主观与其习惯片面之论也。

华工日记
Chinese Labourer's Diaries

Climate in Britain and France

Located at about 50 degrees north latitude, both Britain and France belonged to the North Temperate Zone. North China, also located at about 50 degrees north latitude and belonging to the same North Temperate Zone, has quite different climate from that in Britain and France. Because North China was bordered entirely by land and was often dry, the climate there was called the continental climate. Although Britain and France were in the same temperate zone, their climate was called marine climate because they were mostly surrounded by sea and quite humid.

Most of the Chinese labourers recruited by Britain and France were from Shandong and Hebei, where there was no knowledge of the marine climate. When they came to France, they found all the days from winter to autumn were cool and humid, almost as if there were no extremes in the seasons. The climate of both Britain and France was better than that in China from the viewpoint of plants' growth, but most Chinese labourers thought the climate in Britain and France was not as comfortable as that in China, which was, of course, just the slightly biased view because most of them were missing home.

134. 法人之耕田

法人耕田，普通用一犁一马耕之深，较中国之用四牛者，过之。至于用机器耕至何等，快及几倍，尚未之见。法国养牛，牡者惟食其肉，牝者兼饮其乳，此外则无大用焉。非如中国之养牛，令代农夫之耕田效劳也。

Ploughing by Frenchmen

The Frenchmen ploughed fields with a horse and a plough. When compared with the Chinese way of ploughing with four oxen, the French ploughing was simpler. As to how fast and how many times the plough could be used for farming, I had no idea because I had not seen it in person. The purpose of raising cattle in France was to eat their meat and drink their milk, with no other great use. However, in China the main purpose of raising cattle was to plough the fields for the farmers.

135. 出外应有之现象

水土不服，此人人出门必有之心理，亦往往必有之现象也。中国人平常在家，对饭食有数目、论好歹者，即不甚多。若一出门，非味不适口，即多少无度。时日既久，则身心不快，岂非水土不服之现象乎？华工到法所食之饭，养料非不多，顿数亦不少，然未及半年往往厌而不食，复另买食物，或自己再另煎熬烹煮，而后适口。所以日思中国之味者，人人皆是，盖因烹调之不同也。

一日，余因欲买中国食物，而出远寻华商在法所做之豆腐乳，方寸

华工日记
Chinese Labourer's Diaries

之盒约花洋一元二角，尚不惜其价之贵。及买食之，然后始口适而心快，其他之人亦多如是。于此可见，烹调饮食之习惯，不可不注意也。

Essential Experience for People Travelling Abroad

Be unaccustomed to the local food and climate was something indispensable for people away from home. While at home, few Chinese were particular about either the amount or taste of their food, but once they had left home, they felt that the food had no taste, or the amount of food was either too much or too little. Before long they would become unhappy both mentally and physically. Was it culture shock? The food for Chinese labourers in France had enough nutrition and the meals they had were plenty, but they became dissatisfied and refused to eat the food they were given. They began to buy their own food or cooked with their own ingredients, which they felt tasted better. As a result, people began to miss both their home and its food. This was simply because Chinese people and the Westerners had different ways of cooking.

One day because I wanted to buy Chinese food, I travelled quite some distance looking for fermented tofu made by Chinese businessmen in France. A small box of the fermented tofu cost me one *yuan* and two *jiao*, but I did not mind paying the high price. After buying and eating the food, I felt happy and contented. The others had the same experience. It would be wise for us all to remember the importance of paying attention to our cooking and eating habits.

孙干：欧战华工记
Records of Chinese Labourers in European War by Sun Gan

136. 德国大炮之厉害

一日，与同工数人，于工作之余时，散步于法野间。至一地，见丘陵起伏处，被炮火轰击。原为岗峦者，现则变为丈余之深井。不惟一地如是，约有数十亩之地当如是焉。观其地在德人未轰以前，盖为英人重要机关之所在也。今观山崩地裂之惨状，德国大炮之厉害，可见一斑矣。

Power of German Cannons

One day, I was walking across the fields with some fellow labourers after work when we came across an area heavily bombarded by German shellfire. What was once a hill had been transformed into a well over 10 feet deep and this was not the only place with such serious damage. As a matter of fact, it looked the same over many acres of the surrounding land. The place had been an important position for the British before it was bombarded by the Germans. From the tragic state of this place, we could fully appreciate the great power of the German cannons.

华工日记
Chinese Labourer's Diaries

137. 地雷之厉害

自美国加入协约，调兵赴欧参战以后，德人屡有败北。在民国七年秋后一战，德人败退时，将一村口之马路以地雷轰毁之，盖以阻止英之追兵也。观其所轰之处，既为马路要口，其坑之深约两丈有余，其面积之大约周数百步，故当时从四方开来之摩托车、马车等聚集于此，一时不能前进，地雷之厉害，竟至如是。然英人工程队赶修之速，不半日而使来往之车，又通行无阻矣。

Power of Landmines

Since the United States joined the Entente countries and sent troops to fight in Europe, the Germans had been repeatedly defeated. During the battle in the autumn of 1918, the Germans destroyed a road at the entrance of a village with landmines as they withdrew to prevent the chase of the British troops. The place the Germans had bombarded was the only entrance road to the village. The pit was 20 feet deep and its circumference about one hundred steps. Therefore, motorcycles and carriages from all directions were stuck there for some time and could not advance until it was repaired. It was hard to imagine that landmines were so powerful. The British engineering brigade came to repair the road and in no more than half a day's time, the traffic returned to the normal.

孙干：欧战华工记
Records of Chinese Labourers in European War by Sun Gan

138. 美国之军队

美自一千九百十七年四月六号，以总统威尔逊之演说对德宣战后，又捐七十万万美金，以作战费。更召集年在二十一岁至三十一岁之青年，约一千万余名，教练从军。良足使协约国之经济力及战斗力，大见增加。所以余等自中国上船，逾加拿大时，适美国发百万战士，由哈里夫哀开斯上船，同时渡大西洋，而向欧洲战场。自是以后，由英至法往来路途间，常见美军矣。

观美国之行军也，军队之举止，行时步伐整齐，纪律严肃，军乐悠扬，其欢乐之状，为英法等国之所无。若一休息，则在田野言语坐卧，嬉笑自由，毫无阶级状态，更为各国之所不能。盖因其一切上官，素日既有耶酥博爱熏陶，即靡封建之恶习。是以现在，虽然作行军之事，而无丝毫专制之表现耳。有时吾侪与之接谈，俱表现美国与中国极亲爱、极厚道之状态。其国民之程度，能不令人羡慕乎？余每一遇此国人时，不禁为吾祖国忧也！

American Army

After President Wilson declared war on Germany in his speech on 6 April 1917, the United States donated another seven trillion dollars as war expenses. More than 10 million young men aged 21 to 31 were recruited to be soldiers after training. All these greatly increased the economic strength and combat effectiveness of the Entente countries. When we arrived in Canada from China and boarded the ship to England, millions of soldiers sent by the United States boarded their ships from Halifax and sailed for the European battlefields across the Atlantic Ocean. Since then, many thousands of young American soldiers have sailed this route to and from Britain and France.

When the American troops marched, the uniform and neat steps, the serious disciplines, the melodious music, and the joyful morale could not be found in the British and French soldiers. When they took a rest, the American soldiers would sit down in the field and laughed freely, showing no distinction of class or status, which was much less likely to be found in soldiers of other nations. Because all their superior officers were influenced by the fraternal love of Jesus, they had no bad habits of feudalism. Although they marched toward battles, there was no sign of authoritarianism at all. When our labourers talked with them sometimes, they all expressed their wishes to have friendly relations between China and America. How can we not admire the extent of their nationality and their degree of education? Every time I met people from this country, I could not help feeling worried about our motherland.

139. 学习英语

余在欧日久，常与英人接触，故不得不学习浅薄之英语，又见华工赌风日盛，深为之忧。故于读书外，兼提倡复学英语。遂请本队翻译龚哲夫先生为英语研究社之老师，又邀工人若干组织一英语研究班也。其时拟以研究英语，使众工人忘却赌博，故又书告白数张，贴于各处，其文如下：

孙干：欧战华工记
Records of Chinese Labourers in European War by Sun Gan

告白

中华众位同胞知悉：

敬启者，人生于世，当上念先祖之恩爱，下顾子孙之荣辱，务期后世子孙，日见发达，方不失其为人之道也。然为人之道，又当如何？即书云作善降祥，作不善降殃。及尔为德罔小，万邦为庆；尔为不得罔大，坠厥宗易。亦曰"天道福善祸淫"是也。

弟今想，吾曹在此人人于尽职务之余，做些何事，方能使后日有益？其非学习英语乎。譬如大家就吾现在组织之研究英语班，若将各人学习赌博之心思，不学习赌博，而学习英语；将赌博后日之累累欠债，而不赌博，转为后日无债；将作不善之工夫，易为作善。若果如此，不但现在被队长高看，即对祖国之同胞，亦必落一好名誉也。对学习英语一事，或因无书本而不学习者，或因不识字而难以学习者，或因学之有限而竟不学习者。以我观之，无论有何难处，均能学习也。

今余有编就之浅显英语一本，已将吾祖国之注音字注于英语之旁，拟于下午七点钟乘作工之暇，大家愿学者同在一处，口诵心维而练习之。能写字者记之书本，不能写者，即单记话。一日一句，百日百句，不到三年如此浅显之英语一定可以读熟。若能与英人对谈，比较赌钱，一日只输一佛郎，十日即为十佛郎，久而久之，不但无毫益处，惹得这弟兄向之要钱，那朋友对之讲债，一见了面，面上虽然极好，心里却是为钱怨恨，先为彼此相好，后则彼此都恼。从此看来，赌博与求学，孰好孰歹，孰益孰乖，熟为能合乎人道，真能于后日有益也？若人人果将此书读熟，真不亏来到外洋三年帮助英法之工夫也。

今天正逢端阳佳节，愿学习者，可于下午七点钟，都到研究处一同研究。以后除礼拜日停课外，其余每天照常上班，切切此告。

中华民国七年六月十日
63484　山东博山工人　孙某某　敬启

华工日记
Chinese Labourer's Diaries

Learning English

Having been in Europe for some time, I had to resume my learning of English for the frequent contact with the British officers. I was still deeply concerned about the increasing gambling among Chinese labourers, therefore, besides my own study, I also advocated more group learning. I asked Mr. Gong Zhefu, an interpreter in our brigade, if he would become the teacher of our English Study Group and invited some of the labourers to form an English study class. My purpose at that time was to make labourers forget gambling by studying English. So I posted the notice on English study everywhere. The notice was as follows.

Notice

To all Chinese compatriots,

As human beings living in this world, we should respect the love and sacrifice of our ancestors and try to honour rather than disgrace our descendants. Only when we work hard will our offspring be able to prosper. It can then be said that we have followed the rules of conduct of good human beings. What are the rules of conduct then? They are just what was said in our *Book of History*: good acts will be rewarded whereas evil acts will be punished. If you cultivate morality, no matter how small it may be, all the people in the world will rejoice; but if you do evil deeds, even if the deed was small, you will lose your way. In other words, "God blesses the good and punishes the evil."

It is time for us to think of this question now: What can we do here after we have done our work well so that we can benefit from it in the future? In

孙干：欧战华工记
Records of Chinese Labourers in European War by Sun Gan

my view, it is learning English. For example, if you participate in our English study class and put your energy into learning English instead gambling, we will change our situation from heavy debt into no debt at all, and also change the time for evil doings into the time for good doings. If so, we will not only be respected by the Captain, but also have a good reputation among the compatriots of our motherland. Some people may be afraid to learn English, either because there are no textbooks or because they are illiterate and find it difficult to learn, or because they think they will make little progress. However, from my experience, everyone is capable of learning English despite whatever difficulties he has.

I have a book of simple English and I have written the Chinese phonetic characters beside the English words. It is planned that all the people who would like to learn English meet at 7 p.m. after work to learn and practice. You can write down what you learn in a book if you can write; if not, you can just remember the pronunciations. If we learn just one sentence a day, we could learn one hundred sentences in one hundred days. So, it could be easy for us to memorise all these simple sentences and maybe even talk with the British officers in less than three years. However, if you gamble and you lose only one Franc a day, you will lose ten francs in ten days. Over time it will do you no good at all. On the contrary, it will make you lose friends and brothers. Some will ask you for money and others will ask you to pay the debts. Whenever you meet with them, they will resent you because of money, even though they act as if they were still your friends. In this way, your former friends or your brothers will turn into people who dislike or even hate you. By comparing learning English with gambling, we can see which one will be best for us, which one brings us the most benefit, which one is humane, and which one will be of most use in the future. If everyone can learn this book well, it will have been worth our being abroad and working for Great Britain and France for three years.

Today is the Dragon Boat Festival. Learners can come to the Study Office at 7 p.m. to learn English together. In the future, except for the suspension of classes on Sundays, we will learn every day at the same time. Please inform everyone about this notice.

10 June 1918

No. 63484 Labourer Sun from Boshan, Shandong Province

140. 飞机夜用之暗号

大战之利器，其最巨者，除大炮外，即为飞机。所以近今之人，一讲各国之兵力，莫不曰："有飞机若干架也。"白昼飞机，其多蔽天，然其胜负，亦视其驾驶者之技术而已。观其技术之娴熟者，其飞机有时若上而忽下，有时若降而又腾，旋转反覆，往来上下。一遇作战，彼此用枪射击，其危险不啻逾于地上之战士百倍千倍也。

飞机在白昼时优游空际，而不迷途，固赖其中之地面。然一到黑夜，地上之光线已失，地面之设备罔效，又将如之何？其人又有法焉，以各红黄紫绿色之火药，造为爆竹，临放时，先将其爆竹安置枪内，再以火燃其枪内之火药，而使爆竹远射。所以一到夜间，飞机场中时刻预备各色火药所造之爆竹，以伺候之。一闻本场之飞机从他处飞至，立时即将爆竹以枪射出。爆竹爆炸，而现其或红或黄之色，机上人见即知其所示之意矣。不独飞机场上，夜间伺候各色之爆竹，至临时而向高空射击。即飞机之上，遇夜间腾空，亦必预备是项爆竹。一遇有事，亦先将其爆

孙干：欧战华工记
Records of Chinese Labourers in European War by Sun Gan

竹置于枪内射出，而发现各色之光。地上人见之，立能晓其意焉。其用是灯，以作夜间之暗号，亦善矣哉。

Night-time Signals for Aircraft

Apart from the artillery, aircraft was the most powerful weapon of the largest size. That was why people today would say, "We've a great number of aeroplanes" when asked about the military force of their country. During daylight there are so many aeroplanes that almost covered up the sky. However, their success depended not only on the number of aeroplanes but also on the flying skills of the pilots. For those skilled pilots, their aeroplanes could fly up and down sometimes while at other times they seemed to be coming down but was actually taking off. They could rotate repeatedly in the air or fly up and down freely. During combat, they would shoot each other with guns and the danger they faced was even greater than that faced by the soldiers on the ground.

During the daytime, an aeroplane could fly in the sky without losing its way by observing certain points on the ground but when night came, how did the aeroplanes fly without the ability to observe the ground? They had a special way of doing this. The British made a great many firecrackers containing red, yellow, purple and green gunpowder. To ignite them, they would first place the firecrackers in a gun. With the firing of the gun, the firecrackers would shoot far away. At night, the airfield would prepare firecrackers of various colours of gunpowder. When they received a message that a plane was coming into land, a firecracker would be shot into the air. The pilot would see the coloured light and understand its meaning. The plane would then land at the airfield between lights that marked the landing area. Firecrackers of various colours were often shot into the sky, not only on the airfields but also in the battlefields. Even the aeroplane pilots used them to communicate with the ground, especially at night. Also, with the soldiers on the ground, if something happened during battles, the firecrackers were shot out from the guns and the light of a certain colour was given out, the soldiers on the ground would know what each colour meant when seeing them. Therefore, firecrackers were actually very useful when used as lights for sending signals.

141. 华工割麦

　　法人之割麦，有用机器者，亦有用删刀与镰刀者。余一百零二队住白唐高来司时，常作战壕工，亦曾于德人新退之区割麦数日。一日往麦田时，见马路之旁，以大炮所击之大树，倾倒甚多，其树身之巨细不一，有一抱或二抱者。田中之麦与小蓟菜多寡相间，盖因当春日应锄之时，因作战场而未得锄也。麦田中几乎不得见其土，细审之有大者小者，有扁者圆者，又有黄者黑者，尽为枪炮子弹之实与皮也。于极厚处，以手拢之，不一方尺而盈两捧。想其战争之时，枪炮射击之猛，子弹爆炸之多，可想而知矣。

Chinese Labourers Reaping Wheat

　　In France, people usually reaped wheat with machines, but some people were still reaping with cutters and sickles. When our Brigade 102 encamped at Bertangles, we mainly worked in the trenches, but we also once harvested wheat for several days in an area from which the Germans had recently retreated. One day, as I was going to the wheat fields, I saw many tall trees attacked by the artillery lying at the roadside. The trunks of these trees were of varying sizes, most of which would take one or two arms around. The fields were full of both wheat and thistles because it had been a battlefield and had not been hoed in the springtime. The soil could hardly be seen in the field, but on closer inspection we realised that it was covered with bullet and shell cartridges, large and small, yellow and black. If we tried to collect them with our hands in the thickly-covered areas, we could pick up two handfuls of them within an area of no less than one square foot. From this we could only imagine how fierce the fighting had been and how many explosions there were.

142. 英设战士之墓田

欧战伤亡人数共约三千万，即英一国之死亡者计之，约二百万左右。此巨大之数，任在战场风化欤？——运之回英欤？抑是均不然。即在战线后防，——寄埋于特别设备之墓田中。余侪在法之东北部，在头一年，迁徙无常，而对英人所建之新墓田在各处，亦常常见之。观其新建之墓田，每坟之大，仅占地约三方尺左右，每坟之前，有木制之十字架一个，上书以英文，盖为死士之名也。按次葬埋，每一冢间约隔尺许，不仅坟冢行列整齐，而十架之大小及颜色俱都划一。每人若以六方尺之葬地计，总计亦须需地一千万余方尺，为死亡人数之六倍也。其整齐划一之设立，令人一见而亦起钦敬之心焉。

华工日记
Chinese Labourer's Diaries

Cemetery of British Soldiers

The total number of casualties in Europe so far was about 30 million, among which Britain's total deaths were 2 million. How could Britain deal with so large a number of dead bodies? Leave them exposed to the weather? Or transport all of them back to Britain? Neither answer seemed workable. Therefore, special cemeteries were set up in the rear of the battlefront to bury the dead bodies of the British soldiers. During my first year in north-eastern France, we moved frequently, and during these moves we saw many newly-built British cemeteries at different places. In these new cemeteries, the size of each grave was about three-square feet and in front of the grave stood a wooden cross with the name of the dead on it. All the graves were neatly arranged in rows and columns, about a foot apart from each other, even the size and colour of the crosses in front of the graves were the same. Imagine that the burial place for each person was 6 square feet, the total area for the cemetery would be over 10 million square feet of land, nearly six times the number of deaths. The sight of all these neat and uniform British cemeteries really aroused our great admiration.

143. 幸甚之驾驶员

一日在野外修筑铁路时，飞机成群往来空际。忽有一机从远空飞至，将至余等之上空，骤然失其前行之效力，正欲左歪，遂又右倒，进退上下，悉不自如。不须臾，遂下降而坠于森林中矣。及吾曹趋而视之，行尚未至，而驾驶员已由林中循木而下，步行而出矣。

Fortunate Pilot

One day, while building a railway in the countryside, we saw a group of aeroplanes flying above us in the sky. Suddenly, another aeroplane flew overhead from the distance and lost its power. It tilted first to the left and then to the right; it flew upward one minute and dropped downward the next. It seemed that it had lost control. After a while, it dropped abruptly and fell into the forest. We rushed to see what had happened, but before we arrived at the scene the pilot had already walked out of the forest.

144. 法境昼长夜短

法之北境，在北纬线四十七度至五十度。同中国之蒙古、吉林等地。其在夏日，日之出没，晨则在四点钟前出，昏则八点将半没。昼约长十六点钟，夜约长八点钟，昼夜相较，夜仅有昼之二分之一也。如至冬季，则又昼夜相反，长短各异于夏季矣。中国山东夏季日出之时，在四点钟后，日没在七点钟前。昼长约十四点钟，夜长约在十点，昼夜相较，昼长于夜仅四点多钟也。

华工日记
Chinese Labourer's Diaries

Long Days and Short Nights in France

The northern boundary of France was located between 47 and 50 degrees in the northern latitude, the same latitude as Mongolia and Jilin provinces of China. In summer, the sun rose at four o'clock in the morning and set at half past eight in the evening. The day was about sixteen hours long and the night about eight hours long. Thus, the night was only half as long as the day. In winter things were the opposite. The day was only half as long as the night. In Shandong Province of China, the sun rose after four o'clock in the morning and set before seven o'clock in the evening. The day was about fourteen hours long while the night was about ten hours long. Thus, the day was only four hours longer than the night.

145. 西人之夫妇

吾国之人，自男女授受不亲及夫妇有别之说盛行后，除夫妇外，不惟男人一遇妇女不肯以正眼视之，即妇女因以躲避男人之故，而往往不敢出门，此亦矫枉过正者乎？西欧则不然，余在欧战之时，协助协约于法国，常见法人之街市，有夫妇之偕行者，莫不牵手扪肩，齐步前行。倘有从两方而至，邂逅相遇者，则为夫者，速速向前用力紧抱其妇，然后恳切与之接吻，而表显其夫妇爱情之深厚。华人骤见，辄非笑之。余则以为东亚古人之立言，取敬意也。西欧信神之主义，取爱人也。取敬意者，习焉既久，有矫枉过正之习。想彼爱人者，亦不能免使人讥诮无礼也。惟取敬与爱彬彬然行之，而致中和者，为吾侪之所当效法也。

Western European Couples

In our country, since the ideas prevailed that it was improper for men and women to touch each other and that couples should be separated, a man should not look directly at a woman on their encounter unless they were couples. To avoid meeting men, many women did not even dare to go outside of their homes. These things were quite different in Western Europe. While I was in France helping the Entente countries in the European War, I often saw French couples walking in the marketplace, hand in hand or arm in arm with each other. If a couple met each other from a distance, the husband usually ran quickly to the wife, embraced her passionately and kissed her sincerely to show their deep love. Upon seeing such a scene, our Chinese labourers would laugh at them. But, in my opinion, what our ancestors in East Asia valued was respect whereas the Western European religion stressed was the importance of love. Too emphasis on showing respect for others would lead to hypercorrection after it was practiced too long while those who openly showed affection would be ridiculed as being inappropriate. For us Chinese labourers, we should follow the example of only those who could strike a good balance between respect and love.

华工日记
Chinese Labourer's Diaries

146. 英印兵士之角力

英印人群聚旷场角力。吾各队华工，相率参观。见英印之人，各于马上额手相见后，即回环往复，往来上下，有时纵其马向前猛撞，用力将对方猛推；有时扯对方人之臂而后一拉，有人若坠而又起；有时若东而忽西，卒至此方之人将彼方之人拉之下马，此方即为胜利矣。参观者见一方胜利，全都鼓掌。继则以一骑而御两骑，而决胜负；或同时数骑而与数骑，合力相竞。在其相竞之前，俱先以礼相见。以后又为二人之摔跤，一英人一印人脱去衣服，彼此握手，然后二人一齐用力，或抱其头，或抓其臂，正左转而复右转，方猛牵手而又插脚，卒至一方无力而失败，倒于地上。听罢鼓掌，然后额手告别。斯举也，无分长官，不论兵卒，既去尊卑之畛域，亦免贵贱之界限。吾观英人对印度人之用意，美且深矣。

Wrestling between British and Indian Soldiers

The British and Indian soldiers gathered in an open space to wrestle with each other and many Chinese labourers went there to watch. Both the British and Indian soldiers rode on their horses. Firstly, they greeted each other by putting their hands on their foreheads and then the wrestling began immediately. They went back and forth repeatedly. Sometimes they reined their horse forward to have a hard collision and pushed the other with great force. Other times, they pulled each other's arms backward which almost forced them to fall from their saddles, or they pretended to ride in one direction but suddenly turned the other way. The soldier who first made his opponent fall down from his horseback would win the victory. When one side defeated the other, all spectators applauded loudly. Then, one rider of the winning side would compete again with two riders of the defeated side for the final victory, or several riders on both sides would compete together for the final victory. Before they competed against each other, all of them greeted each other with courtesy. After the horseback competitions, normal wrestling began. A British soldier and an Indian soldier took off their clothes and shook hands with each other before they began to exert all their strengths to either hold their opponents' heads or grasp his arms. They turned each other left and then right again or they seized the other's hands suddenly and then tripped the other with their feet. The wrestling finished only when one was forced to fall to the ground and failed to stand up again. They then bid a farewell to each other after the applause had stopped. Anyone could take part in the competitions no matter whether he was an officer or a soldier, totally regardless of the boundary between superiority and inferiority. In my view, the British's intentions towards Indians were sincere and profound.

147. 法国之牛与豕

法人之牛以牝者为多，盖因家家咸赖牛奶为饮料也。牛之牡者，除杀之食其肉外，无他用焉。法人之养牛，每家必有一园，园边皆以铁丝

华工日记
Chinese Labourer's Diaries

为篱。数口之家，必养奶牛数头。不独一家如是，各城各村家家如是。所以一到法国，欲饮牛乳，随处皆可买也。法人之养豕，黑白两种俱有。惟白者，为数特多，常纵放院外，任其自寻食物。

法国北部养牛之草圃特多，若按其纬度，一到冬天，应为寒冷之区，然其地之天气，因靠海洋，反极温润，不但宜人与畜，即树木花草，无不冬夏如常。所以一到法之北部者，便觉碧油油之绿草一望无际，不止其景致堪入画也，于其人民养牛之更多，盖亦可想见矣。

French Cows and Pigs

Most of the cattle in France were cows because every household took milk as their drink. A cow had no other uses unless they were killed for meat. In France, every household raised cows in a field surrounded by wire fences. In general, a household with several people would raise more than one cow. This was true not only for just one household but for every household in every village or town. Therefore, whenever one wanted to drink milk in France, he could buy it everywhere. As for the pigs the Frenchmen raised, there were both white ones and black ones, but the white pigs accounted for the majority, which were often raised outside the confines of their yards where they moved around freely to find food.

There were many grass fields for raising cows in the north of France. Although it should be very cold in winter according to the latitude, because of the influence of the ocean, the climate was rather warm and mild, which made it suitable not only for people and animals but also for the growth of trees, flowers and plants, making no difference between winter and summer. When one arrived in the north of France, what first came into his view were the vast

孙干：欧战华工记
Records of Chinese Labourers in European War by Sun Gan

green grass fields, which not only constituted the picturesque landscape of France but also helped one to have an idea of the huge number of cows raised by the French people.

148. 就什物始悟亚东人之虚伪

　　自民国以来，国人之日日趋于西人之科学不已，而吾滥竽教育界，亦不得不随潮流，而处处模仿如英文也、算术也、物理也。诸种学术之外，又如洋帽也、洋衣也、洋鞋袜也。而私人所需之物，及洋车、电报、洋楼、洋房等等一切均为西人之所制出，甚不奈久，甚不坚固，无不日日在研究学习之中。后虽历时数年，而终无得于其奥，不独无一得其奥，而更有手中当时虽勉强用其物，而心中却极不赞成之。

　　及至欧西，不但察西人之对于英文、算术、物理、图画种种科学，无一不精，而对于洋衣、洋帽、洋楼、洋房亦无不坚实也。不观其洋火柴乎，每盒之重量约较在中国所造者之重量每盒加倍，而其数仅有四十余根；其洋衣、洋袜，每件着数月而不破；其盛物之箱与楼房门之框，其坚牢，实非在中国时所见之洋衣、洋袜及洋楼、洋房之用数日即破，不能奈久者所可比也。于是始知前在祖国所见所需之洋货，皆亚东之号称文明先进国，模仿西人所造之洋货也。其形虽似，其实则材料轻薄，只知哄人而取利者之所造，实非西人之所造者也。细察彼仿造物者，所造坏物，本无坏心。为人心坏，其身其家，而至其国，岂不更危险耶，嗟夫！

　　前余在祖国时，在学校中见新建筑之洋楼、洋房，其门其窗，往往不满一年即破坏颓废。又如穿洋袜时，购一双穿不满一礼拜，而即破坏。

华工日记
Chinese Labourer's Diaries

如此种种之不能奈久者，指不胜屈，然皆自西欧之人已为先导，而亚东人之自仿造者也。及至余在法日久，尝执铁镢以拆法人之门户，始知其门户之坚固异常，即西人发给之毛袜，亦穿数月而未破。即此以观，对亚东人之诡谲，造物之不可靠者，恍然不可信任矣。

Understanding of East Asians' Hypocrisy

Since the founding of the Republic of China, Chinese people had become increasingly attracted by western science and technology. As a member of the Chinese educational circles, I also had to follow this trend and tried to imitate the western approach towards teaching subjects such as English, arithmetic and physics. Besides the imitation of academic subjects, there were imitations of other aspects such as foreign hats, dresses, shoes and socks. In addition, many personal daily necessities as well as foreign cars, telegrams, buildings, and houses were all made by imitating the western styles, but all these things were not very strong or durable by comparison. I have studied them day after day and several years passed, but I still could not find their secret eventually. Despite my use of these imitations, I often disapproved of them at the bottom of my heart.

When I came to western Europe, I found that the westerners were not only good at English, arithmetic, physics and painting but also at making dresses, hats, buildings and houses, all of which were very solid and durable. For example, each box of the foreign matches weighed twice that of those matches made in China and had only 40 matches in a box. The foreign clothes and socks kept wearable for months. The boxes used for packaging of possessions and the frames of the buildings and doors were very solid. Their construction could not be compared with the copies that we made in China as those would break after being used for just a few days. I began to realise that the foreign goods we had seen and used in our motherland were all imitations of goods made by westerners and that they had been produced by the so-called "advanced civilised country" in eastern Asia. Similar as they were in looks or style, the products were actually made from lighter and thinner materials, all for the purpose of making profits by cheating people into believing that they were made by westerners. After examining their imitated products, I found that the badly-imitated products actually had no bad intentions. If a person had bad intentions, alas, what a danger it would be for himself, for his family and even for his country!

While in my motherland, I had noticed that the doors and windows of newly-built houses in schools were often broken or decayed in less than a year. The foreign socks would become worn out after they were worn for no more than a week. There were countless other examples of goods with no durability. All of these products supposedly originated from western countries but were really imitations made by eastern Asians. After having been in France for some time, I had once tried to use an iron spade to dismantle the door of a French house. It was then that I learned of the firmness of the doors! Even the woollen socks distributed by the British were durable enough to still be intact after several months of wearing. From these examples, it was evident that the eastern Asians were not so trustworthy considering their deceitful intentions and the unreliability of their products.

华工日记
Chinese Labourer's Diaries

149. 民国七年六月望日驻白唐高来寺盛掘战壕，口占俚句如下：

在野花中遍掘战壕

一片红花一片黄，
百锦铺地任吾镶。
瓦根撒空驰骋速，
松柏森森望无疆。
此处原昔谁作主，
养成百卉正菲芳。
诘诸考八与撒金，
彼虽呢喃仍未详。

（考八、撒金：英国之官吏名；镶：法地去土不深，即为石灰岩之白垩土，挖掘战壕所掘出之白土，委曲婉转于黄花红花之旷野，故诗曰任吾镶也。）

While digging trenches in Bertangles on 15 June 1918, I composed the following poem:

Digging Trenches among Wildflowers

Blooming are red and yellow flowers,
In wild fields embedded with various colours.

The brocade of field tapestry I spread

Speedily roll wagons back and forth on roads,

With thick pine and cypress trees on either sides.

We wonder who was in charge of the land in the past,

That gives us this fragrance of flowers at their best.

But when we enquire of our captains and sergeants,

They murmured something without distinctive details.

(Captain and sergeant are the titles of British soldiers. The chalky limestone soil below the surface soil, unearthed by us while digging trenches, was laid tortuously upon the red and yellow flowers in the wild, just like a belt embedded in the flowers.)

150. 英法妇女之装束

英法妇女均有程度，中学、大学毕业者，为数甚多。不但人人酷好学问，而更酷好清洁，尚美观也。今就其普通妇女之装束言之，头部之发，顶后梳髻，与中国妇女之装束无大异。冬戴各种棉帽，帽下围以各样毛巾，夏则戴夏帽，外罩以薄纱罗，盖防尘埃污其面也。身之上部，穿夹袄及小褂，下继之以青裙，此乃普遍之装束。至于脚部除裤之外，鞋与靴，或以草制，或以麻制，或以木制，或以布制及革制，又有少数尚讲究者，帽插鸟羽而项围狐皮，以作围巾也。

华工日记
Chinese Labourer's Diaries

Clothing of British and French Women

Both British and French women were educated and most of them were graduates of high schools or universities. They not only loved learning but also loved cleanliness and beauty. The ordinary women would comb their hair back into a bun, which had no great difference from that of Chinese women. They wore cotton hats of various types on their heads and scarves of various types around their necks in winter. In summer, they wore summer hats and veils of gauze to protect their faces from dust and dirt. They wore jackets and shirts on the upper part of the body and blue skirts on the lower part, which was the common attire of women. Their feet were covered by trousers. They wore shoes and boots which were made of grass, linen, wood, cotton or leather. A few of tasteful women wore feathers on their hats and fox furs as their scarves.

151. 火车之上山

一夜他迁，登厂车，遇天雨，车行至夜半，入于炮火之下，雷声炮声隆隆莫辨。风雨交加，天黑异常，惟在电光一闪之际，瞥见道旁之营垒泥沟，木梁参差错落，杂沓之状，莫可言喻。

吾曹之在厂车上，一任夜雨淋沥。天近晓，雷罢雨霁，至一山下，车乃停。停片刻，有机关车二辆，一在前，又一在余等之车之旁。二辆齐开，前挽后拥，循路而上至山角，又盘旋而逾山岭。至山之后，车乃停。余等华工本系一队，所乘之火车原为十数辆，及至上山之时，将人

孙干：欧战华工记
Records of Chinese Labourers in European War by Sun Gan

乘之车分为若干次，而送上山，较之令工人自负行李登山，省力多矣。

一日，余等作工至一山下，见英人将山下之煤，以小火车运输上山。他项什物，由山上送下。细观其法，先自山下敷铁轨两条，而至山巅、山巅有铁制之升降机，形如轳辘一巨座。轳辘之轴一端朝天一端入地，其轴上外缠一长铁丝绳，绳之两端，各挂车三辆或五辆，车循铁路一上一下，如井下用轳辘之汲水。然察其原动力，借诸山上轳辘旁之蒸汽机。蒸汽机左旋则绳左端之车下降，同时右端之车即上升，使上下之车各达其所而后已。轳辘之转动或左或右，轴外之绳即将车送之或上或下而运货物也。吾国山路极多，运输货物很觉不便，若果仿效此法，各处用升降机，其运输之力，省良多矣。

Trains Moving Uphill

Late one night, we boarded the factory coach to move to another place. It rained heavily as we drove through the night and we could hear loud explosions and gunfire along with the rumble of thunders. It was extraordinarily dark, and we could only glimpse our surroundings when the lightning flashed. With wooden beams scattered everywhere, the chaotic mess was beyond description.

It rained throughout the night as we journeyed in the factory coach. At dawn, the rain ceased and it cleared up. The coach stopped at the foot of a large hill. After a while, two locomotives came alongside us: one stopped ahead of our coach and the other was behind. We were transferred onto the train and the two locomotives set out together. They moved uphill along the line to a corner of the hillside and then wound their way to the top where they finally stopped. There were so many labourers in our brigade that it had taken dozens of train journeys to reach the top. We had been subdivided before being sent uphill, which saved a lot of effort compared with climbing to the top with luggage.

One day, while we were working at the foot of a mountain, we saw the British soldiers transporting coal uphill from the foot of the mountain by a small train and then other things being transported downhill. I observed carefully how it was done. First, two rails were laid down from the foot of the mountain and there was large windlass-shaped iron lifts at the top and the ridge of the mountain. One end of its axle faced toward the sky and the other was buried into the ground. Around the end of the axle was wrapped a long wire rope, on either end of which hung three or five cars. These cars went up or down the rails in the same way we collected water from a well with windlass. However, when I examined it closely, I found that its power was generated by a steam engine alongside the windlass on the hill. When the steam engine was turning, the car at one end of the rope fell while the car at the other end rose. When both the upward and downward cars reached their respective destinations, the engine stopped. With the leftward or rightward rotation of the windlass, the off-axle rope would send the cars up or down. In this way, the cargos could be transported by the cars. There were many mountain roads in our country and it was very inconvenient to transport goods in these mountainous areas. If we could follow this method and use these types of elevators everywhere, a great amount of energy would be saved in transportation.

152. 余死而复苏

某日作工毕，始还营时，上官传急令速速分馊粮，急急起程他迁。正掤挡行李间，不须臾，传号站队，何暇问及众工人之饥渴哉！及起行

孙干：欧战华工记
Records of Chinese Labourers in European War by Sun Gan

时，天阴将雨，风亦飘飘，排队负重，约行五里许，各个都汗流浃背矣。斯时也，不但风雨交加，而腹中饥渴之甚，无可言喻。

既尔天已昏黑，至一车站，哄然登小车厂，其时雨愈降愈大。工人站立车中，心中焦急，呼吁之声，上达九霄也。余于是时，雨涤于头面，欲解行李取雨衣，然因人多拥挤而不得也，腹中饥渴尤甚。有顷，腹中疼痛不止。至夜，雨下愈大，而腹之疼亦愈甚。默想长官及一切工人，俱都受此等痛苦，虽向之呼吁也，真如叔兮伯兮，又如充耳而无济也。

余遂于暗中切切祈神施恩护佑，使余在外平安以至归家，昏愦而觉矣。约至半夜乃苏，始知在昏睡之时，鼻衄而流之浓血块甚多，及醒来时方觉其血在怀中之衣襟上也。以后余想，余之病乃因迁徙之时，行路太急而又无水可以解渴，以致全身津液枯槁，而发生霍乱耳。然卒赖神灵垂听余之祷告默佑之，而使睡眠，使鼻破流血方痊愈也。自此以后，余在欧洲即不能不时刻感觉上帝之恩在余之左右也矣。

My Revival after Death

Just as we returned to the camp after work one day, an urgent order came from the Captain that we should be given our food provisions in no time and set off for other places. We were still packing our luggage when we were ordered to line up immediately to commence the move. Nobody had taken the time to ask whether our labourers were hungry or thirsty. When we set off, the weather was terrible. It was cloudy and rainy and the wind was about to blow. With our heavy loads we marched in line for about 5 miles and everyone was sweating and exhausted. Just then, it rained heavily with a strong wind blowing into our faces. We suffered not only the heavy rain and strong wind but also the great hunger and thirsty. Such agony was completely beyond word.

华工日记
Chinese Labourer's Diaries

It was nearly dark when we arrived at a rail station and we all rushed to board the carriages. The rain was getting heavier and heavier at that time. Standing amount the cars, the labourers were became so anxious that they began to shout loudly. At that time, I was completely exposed to the rain and I tried to get my raincoat from my luggage. However, I could not get it due to the crowdedness. What made it even more intolerable was the hunger and thirst in my stomach. After a while, I began to feel great pain in my stomach. As it rained more heavily, the pain became worse. Thinking that all our officers and labourers would be suffering the same pain, we protested against it. But the protests were useless as we were so humble and helpless.

I prayed quietly for God's grace and protection to allow me to return home safely, but I began to feel dizzy and soon after I fainted. Only when I came to, at about midnight, did I realise that my nose had been bleeding heavily while I was in deep sleep and had stained my coat. Later, I thought my illness might have been gastroenteritis caused by the loss of fluid in my body due to the rapid marching and having no water to relieve my thirst. Fortunately, with God's blessing, I had fell asleep after saying my prayers and it was with God's blessing that I had recovered from my illness by bleeding from my nose. From that point onwards, I felt that the grace of God would be with me wherever I was in Europe.

153. 下汽车时之危险

英法之人，多穿皮鞋，不但因处海洋气候，阴雨较多，亦因马路砂砾易于磨擦，故其人一出门必穿皮鞋也。吾曹至欧西，因争公理之服务，

孙干：欧战华工记
Records of Chinese Labourers in European War by Sun Gan

足所穿者亦为皮鞋，故行路时非常慢也。

一日，余出游览，觇其城乡一切状况，循马路远抵阿米羊省会，见其街市、房楼规模宏大，然当时来往之人，甚属寥寥。盖因德人常以大炮向其地射击，而其政府早勒令人民他遭也。余在其街市酒铺中，逗留不久，即循马路而归，行至市外约二三里之遥，回首一望，见由市内之英人摩托车蠕蠕而来。不多时，车即随后而至。当时路上有法之数人云："此尽空车，吾侪可上此，借乘一程。"言罢，遂纷纷由车之后方上升。

余闻既为空车，吾一人借坐一程亦无妨也。由一车后方，攀援而上。吾等乘车，开汽车者，在前或未之知也。约前行十余里，余谅距自己所驻之营不远，即由车后倒退而出，然后使足徐徐下垂，谅足去地不远，乃将手用力一推，车去，余由车而下矣。余因不谙于车不停时上车下车之法，是以余身一下，而即被前行猛力拉倒在地，两手掌上之皮，俱为马路之砂石抢去少半，当时余昏卧良久始起。此次余所幸者，后边无继来之汽车也。如有汽车复从余身上压过，其危险不更大耶！

Dangerous Jumping off Vehicles

People in Britain and France often wore leather shoes not only because of the marine climate which brought about frequent rain, but also because of the road gravel which gave more rubbing to shoes. Thus, people there were accustomed to wearing leather shoes whenever they went out. Out of fairness, our labourers were also given leather boots after we arrived in Europe. As a result, we often walked very slowly.

One day, I went out to have a tour around the city and the countryside. I walked along the road and soon arrived at Amiens, the capital city of the Somme region. I saw many large buildings, but few people were walking in the streets. Because the Germans used to shell the area, the government had ordered its residents to leave for somewhere safer. Having lingered in a street wine shop for a while, I began to return by walking back along the road. Looking back after walking about half a mile, I saw some British motorcycles moving slowly from the city. After a short time, these motorcycles travelled past me. At that time, some French people on the roadside said, "They are all empty motorcycles and we can take a ride from here." With these words, they jumped on the motorcycles from behind one after another.

Hearing that the motorcycles were all empty, I thought I might as well take a ride too. So I climbed up onto one of them from behind. After travelling on the motorcycle about three miles, I thought that I must be close to the camp and decided to get off the motorcycle. I lowered myself out of the motorcycle by dropping my feet slowly from the back and when they were close the ground. Then I jumped off by pushing away hard with my hands. However, I was not familiar with the way of getting on or off while the motorcycle was still moving. Therefore, I was pulled to the ground by the forward force as soon as my feet touched the ground. Nearly half of the skin on both my hands was rubbed away by the road gravel and I lay on the ground for a long time before I could rise to my feet. Fortunately, there were no other motorcycles behind me. Otherwise, I would have been ran over by the following vehicles. What a dangerous situation it would have been!

154. 尸横遍野中之睡眠

民国七年九月，战事愈烈。一日，忽传令迁徙，无论长官工人，所

孙干：欧战华工记
Records of Chinese Labourers in European War by Sun Gan

有一切均以摩托车载之。午前十点钟起行，下午四点经过德人新战败地，所见如毛毯也、被褥也、床铺也、小枪也、大炮也、炮弹也、手榴弹也，莫不成堆成垛抛弃遍地。及日向暮，路过一斜坡，及一东西之谷。骤远望之，谷之两旁，尽为已枯之黄蒿，南北之阔约三里许，东西之长遥无边际。及至就近细观，乃知系德人所设，以铁丝撒拉之障碍物，而阻挡英兵之前进者也。及所乘之车，委曲婉转，从其中过时，则见其中有木桩，有铁桩，高低相间排列，以带刺之铁丝，回环往来撒于其上，间留弯曲之道，另有活动障碍物，以为道路之间。噫！德人对于战斗之设备，可谓出人意外也。

过此复前行，迨日西下时，至一马路之旁，见德人之尸体三个一攒，五个一簇，脑白血红，淋沥遍地。吾侪至此，天将昏黑，遂下车而择一尸体较少之地而宿焉。是时也，同工之面莫不气象愁惨，急忙支搭帐棚，仓皇欲睡，不遑复谋及饮食矣。

Sleeping among Dead Bodies

In September 1918, the war became more intense. One day, all officers and labourers were ordered to move to other places and everything was to be carried by motorcycles. We started out at ten o'clock in the morning. At four o'clock in the afternoon we travelled past a battlefield where the Germans had recently been defeated. Piles of discarded blankets, beddings, small guns, artillery, cannonballs, and grenades scattered everywhere. At dusk, we passed across a slope of an east-west valley. Looking into the distance, we saw what seemed to be dried and withered artemisia plants on either side of the valley, which was about a mile wide and endlessly long. However, as we got closer, we could clearly see that these were the wire obstacles set up by the Germans to block the advance of British soldiers. As our motorcycles wound their way among these obstacles, we could see that there were both high and low wooden and iron pickets arranged alternately with barbed wires entwined upon them. Even on the winding roads were other movable obstacles in the middle. My goodness! The fighting equipment of the Germans was really beyond our expectations.

We continued our journey after passing by this place. Just as the sun set, we came to a roadside where we saw the bodies of many German soldiers, with three or four bodies in a pile, their brains out and blood all over the ground. At this point, because it was nearly dark, we got off the motorcycles and chose a place with fewer dead bodies as our camping site. At that moment, all our Chinese labourers, with a look of disguise and sadness on their faces, set up their tents hastily and hurried to sleep, having no appetite for any food.

155. 德意志之俘虏

自一九一七年美国对德宣战后，协约方面战场兵士之心志，为之一振。至翌年下半年，战斗益烈，双方之死亡既多，被人之俘虏尤众。

德人之被英人俘虏者，自开战之日起二年之后，即有二十四万五千之多。英人将其编为俘虏队，日使作工，给以半数饷糈，并给以少数工资。观其工作之寥寥，盖因其糇粮之太轻也欤？吾曹每在马路作工，常见英人监视大队德国俘虏，自战场归来，不但其衣服琐兮猥兮，即其饥饿之状，亦常常视吾侪，而手指其口以乞饮食焉。

一日，余等数十人，在一大路之旁休息。适英人荷枪押大队德俘至。

孙干：欧战华工记
Records of Chinese Labourers in European War by Sun Gan

观其衣帽之泥泞、驰驱之疲乏，盖由战场上之所获者。向余等乞水乞食者甚多，吾辈有以自己之糇粮与之者，有以自己之茶水饮之者，英人虽屡屡禁止，德俘亦往往不顾。

今将欧战前二年兵士之伤亡一览表列下：

国名	死亡	受伤	俘虏	合共
英	205447	512465	109358	827270
法	870000	2704000	400000	3974000
德	893211	3163334	245000	4301545
奥	523125	1775125	591000	2889250
布	7500	35000	6000	48500
土	127000	550000	70000	747000
俄	1360000	4720000	3420000	9500000
意	105000	245000	55000	405000
塞	60000	140000	200000	400000
比	50000	110000	40000	200000
总共	4201283	13954924	5136358	23292565

此表自一千九百十四年八月一号起，至一千九百十六年七月三十一号止，由丹国京城哥卑纳结之研究欧战损失社所核算（见一千九百十六年九月二十二号之《华盛顿日报》）。

Prisoners of Germany

Since the United States declared war on Germany in 1917, the morale of soldiers of the Entente countries in the battlefield had been greatly boosted. By the second half of the next year, the battles had grown much more in intensity. A great number of soldiers on both sides were killed in battles and the number of prisoners taken during this period was especially great.

There had been more than 245000 German prisoners captured by the British within the first two years of the war. The British organised them into captive brigades and ordered them to work every day. They were given half the amount of food and low wages. However, I found that they worked very inefficiently. Was it because of the small amount of food they were given? While working on the roads, I often saw large groups of German prisoners supervised by the British coming from the battlefields. The clothes of these prisoners were dirty or torn and because of their great hunger, they often begged our labourers for food by looking at us and pointing to their mouths with their fingers.

One day, dozens of our labourers were taking a rest on a roadside when a large group of German prisoners came past under the supervision of the armed British soldiers. From their muddy clothes and caps as well as the fatigue shown in the way they were walking, we knew that they must have been recently captured in the battlefield. Many of them begged us for food and water. Some of our labourers gave their own food and others gave their own tea to the German captives. Although the prisoners were prohibited by the British from asking for food and drinks repeatedly, they often ignored these orders.

The casualties of soldiers in the first two years of the European War were listed below:

Country	Dead	Wounded	Prisoner	Total
Britain	205447	512465	109358	827270
France	870000	2704000	400000	3974000

孙干：欧战华工记
Records of Chinese Labourers in European War by Sun Gan

Country	Dead	Wounded	Prisoner	Total
Germany	893211	3163334	245000	4301545
Austria	523125	1775125	591000	2889250
Bulgaria	7500	35000	6000	48500
Turkey	127000	550000	70000	747000
Russia	1360000	4720000	3420000	9500000
Italy	105000	245000	55000	405000
Serbia	60000	140000	200000	400000
Belgium	50000	110000	40000	200000
Total	4201283	13954924	5136358	23292565

The figures in the table were calculated by the Copernicus Institute for the Study of European War Losses in the capital city of Denmark from 1 August 1914 to 31 July 1916 (see *Washington Daily*, 22 September 1966).

156. 欧战众尸体中之捡拾纪念品

吾侪在此战争正殷之际，不挖深洞，即掘战壕；不修垫路，即装卸车。所以每天一到野外，地下除沟壕以外，即为洞穴；地上除枪刀以外，即为炮弹。

一日，数同人忽语曰："现在德人尸横遍野，人多从众尸体中捡其手表或金钱，以作回国之纪念。汝盍亦捡一二也。"余曰："捡人之物，以为己之纪念，义乎不义乎？"彼等答曰："德人之蛮横，挑出如此之大战，何义之有耶？"言罢而去。至翌日饭后，余从营中出，观众德人之

225

华工日记
Chinese Labourer's Diaries

尸体，坐者、倾者、仰者、俯者、切齿者、瞪眼者，种种惨状，无一不使人见之伤心也。

Collecting Souvenirs from Corpses in the European War

In the midst of the European war, our Chinese labourers were engaged in various types of work such as digging caves and trenches, repairing roads, or loading and unloading vehicles every day. Therefore, working in the fields every day, we saw only trenches and caves below ground or guns, shells and bayonets above ground.

One day, one of my fellow workers said to me, "The field was littered with German dead bodies, and many people are collecting watches or money from these dead bodies as souvenirs when they return home. Why don't you try to get some?" I replied, "Is it righteous to pick up dead people's belongings as souvenirs?" He answered, "The Germans were so cruel that they started the European War. Where is their righteousness?" With these words, he went out to join the others to search the dead. The following day, I went out of the camp after finishing my meal and saw the horror of the German dead bodies, either in sitting or leaning positions, lying with faces either upward or downward, with gritting teeth or staring eyes.

孙干：欧战华工记
Records of Chinese Labourers in European War by Sun Gan

157. 战壕内之铁路

英人之战壕，有窄而浅，仅容一人卧者；亦有宽与深俱数尺，能容多人，并能从其中输运粮饷与子弹者；又有深可从中骑马往来者。而独德人之战壕中，敷设大铁路焉。

于此可知，不但德之将士乘火车往来，极其迅速，极其便利；即子弹之运输，亦极其敏捷，极其充足矣。况在其战壕铁路之旁，更有不数丈即砌地窖一处，以作储蓄子弹之用。德人对于欧战之布置，往往出人意外也。

Railway within Trenches

Some British trenches were narrow and shallow, large enough for only one person to lie in. Others were several yards wide and deep, large enough to accommodate many people and to transport food and munitions. Still others were deep enough for people to ride through on horseback. But it was only in the German trenches that I ever saw railways laid down.

With these trains, it was fast and convenient not only for the travel of German officers and soldiers but also for the sufficient transport of munitions. In addition to the rail lines, there were numerous dugouts along the trenches for the storage of bullets and bombs. The German dispositions of supplies and storage often shocked us.

华工日记
Chinese Labourer's Diaries

158. 德人设备之炮战线

民国七年下半年时，德人着着失败。吾侪华工亦随英军逐渐前进，整理道路，搬运子弹。一日，余等数人于工作之暇，观德人建筑之大炮战线，莫不赞叹不已，今将其大概情形略述于下：

德人将其炮安置妥当后，炮身之上架以铁梁，铁梁之上覆以铁板，然后盖土尺许，最上掩之以青苔，盖蔽敌人侦察也。自其炮口之一方观之，如大炮之容藏于一大厦，复由炮身之两旁地下，斜向深处挖掘隧道。至深丈余后，复使隧道平行，平行三二丈后，又向上挖，及至地面，适遇第二大炮之所在。不独炮之一边如是，炮之他边亦如是，是以由此隧道之此一端入，可自隧道之彼一端出也。在隧道之深处，两旁更另挖为房间若干，以备放炮职员之栖憩。战线后方，距数丈而置一炮，当时欧战战线之长数百里，而炮数随之亦数千门。其大炮门数之多，令人闻之，亦可惊矣，况复有第二防线，为数岂不更多耶！

Artillery on the German Front

In the second half of 1918, the Germans were destined to be defeated in the war. The Chinese labour brigades also advanced together with the British army to maintain the roadways and transport munitions. One day, some of our labourers and I went with to see the German artillery at the front in our spare time. We were greatly amazed by the artillery disposition of Germans, which was roughly described as follows:

After a cannon was properly placed in the required position, the Germans set up an iron frame above it and covered the frame with heavy iron plates, which were then covered with a thick layer of earth and moss in case of being found by the enemy reconnaissance. Viewed from one side of the muzzle, the cannon seemed to be hidden within a large building. Tunnels were also excavated into the ground on both sides of the cannon. At the depth of about ten feet, the tunnel was made to be parallel to the ground for about 30 feet. Then the tunnels were sloped upwards to the ground, where another cannon was located. In this way, one could enter from one end of the tunnel and exit from the other end of it. In the depth of the tunnel, a number of rooms were excavated on both sides to provide shelter for cannon personnel. In the rear of the front line, there were many more cannons, each being set up at an interval of dozens of feet. At that time, the European front was hundreds of miles long and so there were thousands of cannons. The number of cannons was truly amazing. Beyond these, there was still the second front. So one could imagine how many cannons the Germans actually had.

159. 枪炮形式之种种

欧战所用之枪类，各国式样多有不同，与吾国相同之花枪，虽亦有之，殊不多见。至于大小不等之炮，如迫击炮、开花炮、小钢炮、高射炮、机关快炮等等，大者以火车载之，小者以马车拉之，此外海军之所用者，尚不与焉。

华工日记
Chinese Labourer's Diaries

Various Types of Cannons and Guns

The types of guns used in the European War varied greatly from country to country. Although there were the types of gums used in our country, their number was rather small. There were also cannons of different sizes, including mortars, flamethrowers, small steel cannons, anti-aircraft cannons, and machine guns. There were large ones that were carried by trains and there were also small ones that were carried by carriage. There were also cannons used by the navy, which were not quite the same.

160. 为收见家书领薪不妥上书英人

具禀：山东省博山县六万三千四百八十四号工人某某，今收到家中来函二封，内皆云，家中往周村大英招工局领取上年十二月份之工钱，招工局并不发给。今工人想本人在此天天作工，并无请假旷工、犯规等等一切，何故周村招工局不支付十二月份之工钱也？

望督办费大人，为工人费心清查，寄信周村招工局，饬其将工人上年十二月份之工资，如数发给工人家中，以便养老顾少，工人感德无既矣。

一千九百十八年十二月十八号
华工一百零二队63484工人孙某某上

孙干：欧战华工记
Records of Chinese Labourers in European War by Sun Gan

为呈请由法转送英国学校求学：

具禀：山东博山县工人63484孙某为恳求由法送英求学事。窃前在中国，原是教育界人。今既来此作工，无不尽心竭力，以助贵国之战争。而贵国之兵事，现在既已了结。闻不久即将吾敝国之工人，完全送回中国。工人家中本极窭贫，本拟还中国后，再赴贵国师范学校学习英文，以期深造。然因往来路途之遥，势出万难，定难办到。是以今不得不具呈前来，恳求费心，将工人就近由法国转送贵国，入师范学校。俾工人一半求学，一半作工。工人异日之深造，实费大人今日费心之所赐也，专此敬恳，千祈赐准。

中华民国七年十二月二十一日

一百零二队工人63484　某某谨上

Petition to the British for Not Receiving Pay at Home

To whom it may concern,

 I am the Chinese labourer No. 63484 from Boshan County, Shandong Province. I received two letters from home, both of which mentioned that when my family went to the British Recruitment Bureau in Zhoucun to get my pay for December last year but was rejected by the Bureau. I have been working every day without any absenteeism or poor discipline since I arrived in Europe. But why did the Recruitment Bureau refuse to pay me any money for December?

 I hope that the supervisor in charge of wages will take the time and trouble to check this for me and send a letter to the Recruitment Bureau in Zhoucun, urging them to distribute my wages for December of last year to my family because they are in need of the wages for a living. If this matter can be solved successfully, I would be very grateful to you.

18 December 1918

No. 63484 Labourer Sun from Brigade 102 of Chinese Labour Corps

Application for being transferred from France to British schools for further study:

To whom it may concern,

Labourer Sun, No. 63484, from Boshan County, Shandong Province, respectfully requests to be sent from France to Britain for further study. I was originally a teacher before I left China. Since arriving here in Europe, I spared no effort to help your country in the war against Germany. Now that the military affairs of your country have been over, I hear that all our labourers will soon be sent back to China. I had planned to study English in one of the normal schools in your country after my return to China. However, due to the great distance and the costs involved, my family would find it almost impossible to send me to your country from my home. Therefore, I am submitting this application to ask you to take the trouble to transfer me from France to your country to study in normal schools. I would take a work-study program. My further education in the future will depend on the careful consideration you give to me today. I sincerely hope you can give me permission. Looking forward to your reply.

21 December 1918

No. 63484 Labourer Sun from Brigade 102 Chinese Labour Corps

孙干：欧战华工记
Records of Chinese Labourers in European War by Sun Gan

161. 捡取避氯气炮之帽作纪念品

民国八年八月初旬，黄君世恩语余曰："快还国矣，回国之纪念物已预备齐乎？"余遂诘之曰："君所备者，金镑欤，戒指欤，抑金表欤？"黄君曰："敝舍本农家也，金镑既无钱买，金表、戒指又是无用。虽然，余所备者，乃将德国之钢盔与众一看耳。吾知先生素亦不尚浮华，却不知将图回国，以示众者为何物？"余答曰："吾祖国现在所缺少之物实多，如飞机、大炮、战舰、快车。然而非吾祖国之所缺少。其最缺少者，惟天道也。不然，纵有一切武器，必至自相残杀，又何益耶？"彼又曰："在吾祖国罕见之物，从此稍带一二回国之后，以作标本无妨也。"于是，余遂捡取德人之所造避氯气炮之帽子一具，以携归焉。

Getting a Chlorine-proof Hood as Souvenir

In the early August of 1919, Huang Shien asked me, "We'll return to China soon. Have you got any souvenirs to take back with you?" I responded to him, "What have you prepared? Pounds? Gold rings? Or gold watches?" Mr. Huang said, "I'm just an ordinary farmer. I've no money to buy pounds, and gold rings or watches are useless for me. What I've prepared is just a German steel helmet to show to others. I know you don't like flashy things. So what do you plan to get and show to others when you return to China?" I answered, "There are too many things that our motherland lacks at the moment, such as aeroplanes, artillery, warships and express trains. However, all these things are not what our motherland really lacks. What she needs most is faith. Otherwise, even if we had all the types of weapons, which would result in self-destruction, what good would they be without faith?" Then he said to me, "We might as well bring one or two things that are rarely seen in our motherland as reminders when we return home." So, I picked up a chlorine-gas hood made by the Germans as the souvenir to take when I return home.

162. 李大工头几乎被炸

华工一百零二队中国最高之大工头，人公称之曰"李四道"。其人极爱秩序，故工人有时无理争斗，辄严厉训之，训之罔效，则继之以鞭楚。一日晨早，彼从帐棚中出，见帐棚外四周绳上，各系炸弹一枚，幸未牵动其绳，未曾爆炸。后虽经英人侦察者再三，卒未获得系炸弹者为何许人也。

Foreman Li Almost Blown up

The foreman with the highest rank within Brigade 102 of Chinese labourers was a man known as "Li Sidao". He loved to put everything in order. Thus, sometimes when labourers fought without good reason, he would reprimand them harshly first and if the reprimand failed, he would give them a beating with a whip. One early morning, when he came out of the tent, he found four bombs tied to the ropes that secured the tent. Fortunately, he did not touch the rope and the bombs did not explode. Although the British soldiers made a thorough investigation into it, they failed to find out who did it.

163. 法人之跳舞

　　法国街市中，与吾国不同之现象，除夫妇相遇接吻外，又有跳舞。其跃舞之法，一人在场，手舞足蹈，俯仰进退，颇按规矩。或舞者自唱，或众与和唱，或一女单舞，或二女双舞，或男女对舞，如吾国市场上之耍拳比武者。然吾国市场上之打拳者，多为卖艺获利，而欧美人士之跳舞者，多取技巧欢乐；吾国市场之打拳卖艺，多系专门人为之，而法国街衢之跳舞者，则人人可参加，极为公开。

Dance of French People

　　Unlike in China, the French couples would kiss each other when they met in streets. Another French custom that was very different from those in China was that people danced in streets. When a person danced, he moved his hands and feet together with different movements of his body in accordance with the type of dance they were performing. Sometimes, the dancers would also sing aloud while at other times the crowds would sing in chorus. Sometimes a woman would dance alone, while at other times two women, or a man and a woman would dance together. This was somewhat like boxing or martial art displays in Chinese streets. But most boxers in Chinese streets performed for the sake of money whereas most dancers in European streets showed their dancing skills for the sake of pleasure. Also, most boxing or military arts shows in Chinese streets were done by professionals while the dancing in French streets was open to all, and everyone could join it.

164. 火药之种种

火药之形式，有如中国旧式之烟袋杆者，其粗如指，其长尺许，一捆数根，外装以布袋，有如中国药铺中之清宁药片者，以刀切之，或长或方。以袋装之，每袋重约四两，有如中国之牛皮弓弦，长约七八寸，数十根而为一束者。又有以棉絮制之，如农家手工纺纱之布绩者，此皆以木箱盛之，散见于战场之野地者也。其燃烧之性，有极迟者，如烟袋杆与弓弦形者是也；有极速者，如药片与布绩者是也。至于大炮弹内所装之火药，有如硫磺细面者，又有如黄香者，其形状颇不一致也。

Various Kinds of Gunpowder

The form of gunpowder used by the British was similar to that of the long stems of old-fashioned smoke pipes in China. They were about a foot long and as thick as a finger. Several gunpowder pipe-sticks were bundled together and then packed within a canvas bag. Just like the *Qingming* tablets in Chinese pharmacies, they could be cut with knives into long or square segments, which were then packed in bags, each weighing about seven ounces. Like Chinese cowhide bowstrings, each of the sticks were about 10 inches long and several dozens of them formed a bunch. Others were made from cotton floss and were contained in wooden boxes like hand-spun yarns, which were scattered in the battlefields. Some types of gunpowder burned very slowly just like the stems of smoke pipes and bowstrings while other types burned very rapidly just like the tablets or yarns. As for the gunpowder loaded in the artillery shells, some was similar to the fine sulphur flour and others was like yellow incense. They were quite different in shape.

165. 法国牧羊人之犬

民国七年冬，一日余散步野外，见一法人牧羊一群，并带领一长毛犬，羊数约二百只。其始也，羊散于野，约在半里之内，牧羊人坐于草地上，其犬亦卧其侧。以后羊四散渐远，约至里半以外，然牧人仍坐不动。余遂呼之曰："忙尔斯以厄。"并以手示其羊已远去。牧人仍卧不动，只以法语语其犬，其犬乃跑至羊所到处，将羊围绕狂吠，使之尽归。及羊至牧人前，牧人仍以法语止其犬，其犬方罢。

Dog of French Shepherds

One day in the winter of 1918, while walking in the field, I saw a shepherd herding about 200 sheep with a long-haired dog. At first the sheep scattered in the field about 250 yards away from the shepherd, who sat on the grass with a dog at his side. Later, the sheep moved further away, but the shepherd still sat there without any movement. So I shouted, "Mind your sheep!" and motioned with my hand to him that his sheep had gone. The shepherd still remained motionless and said something in French to his dog. Then, the dog ran to the place where the sheep were grazing and barked continuously around them to make them come back. When the sheep came near to the shepherd, he spoke something again to the dog and the dog stopped barking.

166. 以炸弹捕鱼

战地之各种炮弹、枪弹、炸弹到处皆是。吾一百零二队之工人，有时为之装置，有时为之拆卸，有时为之运输，有时为之整理。为日既久，渐习其性。同工等有在索美河中抛掷炸弹而捕鱼者，将炸弹按法掷于河内，炸弹一响，水被猛震，而鱼即从河底飘浮于水面矣。

Fishing with Bombs

Everywhere in the battlefields were all kinds of shells, bullets and bombs, which my fellow workers in Brigade 102 installed, disassembled or transported, or sorted out sometimes. Working with them for a long time, we gradually became acquainted with their design and power. Some of our labourers even discovered how to fish with bombs. They threw bombs in the

孙干：欧战华工记
Records of Chinese Labourers in European War by Sun Gan

Somme River and the fish would float on the surface of the water when the bombs blew uo.

167. 两种望远镜

余等在欧战已过之地，作运输工作之时，尝见军人使用之望远镜弃于野地者。其镜身之长约尺许之管状物也，其中空杜以玻璃片数页，然此为圆筒形之直形者也。此项望远镜之用，为看对方者，如飞机上、轻气球上、大炮队中、高山上多用之也。此外尚有曲头望远镜，其镜身亦为直筒状，惟其末端，则倾于旁边，并使其能周围旋转。此项望远镜为窥四旁及上下者，如战壕内也、船中也、墙后也，人不用露头，只将此镜伸出，即可见周围之一切。由此观之，光学之发明，亦妙矣哉！

Two Types of Telescope

When we did the transportation work in the places where the European War took place, we once found an abandoned telescope used by soldiers in the field. The body of the telescope was a tube about a foot long. Fixed within the tube were several pieces of glass. This type of telescope, with lenses in a straight line, was usually used by artillery teams or on hilltops for watching the enemy aeroplanes or light balloons. There was another type of telescope with an angled lens. Its body was a straight tube, but it leaned to one side at the end and could rotate around. This type of telescope was used for observing objects from below ground level and could be angled in any direction. It was very useful in trenches and from behind walls as objects could be seen clearly through the telescope without the exposure of your head. From the telescopes, we could see how ingenious the optical inventions were!

168. 检理氯气炮弹而被害

欧战告终，吾侪挖掘战壕之工程遂亦停止。所作者非修理道路，即检理武器。民国八年一月，吾曹数十人在疴易斯河流域之野，捡拾炮弹。其地乃为德人之久占新退者。一日晨，初至一地，见岗峦起伏之处，德人所遗之军器，遍地皆是。吾侪将所遗之枪支子弹，应排者排，应垛者垛。一一整理时，其中有德人之氯气炮弹，分散各处，群相负荷，垛于路旁。当时同工数人欲将是等炮弹之螺栓取下，以观其中之构造。英人见而禁之者再三，同工等卒不听从。及至以石将炮弹砸破时，其中之毒质已化，而一人立即仆倒，不能言语者。余二人，目亦无见矣。吾侪之乘早遁去者，幸未遭此毒气也。以后有十字会之车，将受氯气毒者送往医院去矣。中国同工之无知，可笑又可怜也。

Getting Killed While Checking Chlorine Shells

With the end of the European War, our labourers stopped our projects of digging trenches and began to do some work on the former battlefields such as maintaining roads or collecting munitions and picking up weapons. In January of 1919, dozens of our labourers were collecting artillery shells in the fields around the Oise River Basin, an area which had been occupied for a long time by the Germans but abandoned only recently. One morning, we arrived at a new place where weapons abandoned by the Germans scattered all over the hills and ridges. We collected the abandoned guns and bullets and put them in rows or stacks. While sorting them out one by one, we found the chlorine shells of the Germans scattered everywhere. So we collected and stacked them at the roadside. As we were collecting them, some of the labourers wanted to unscrew the bolts of the shells to see how they were constructed. When the British saw what they were doing, they abruptly ordered them not to do it. However, our labourers did not listen. They smashed up the shells with rocks and the poisonous gas inside leaked out, causing one of our labourers to fall down immediately and lose the ability to speak and two others to become blind. Fortunately, for those who fled quickly enough, there were no further casualties by the poisonous gas. Later that day an ambulance from the Red Cross Society came and took the other labourers poisoned by the chlorine to hospital. The ignorance of our Chinese labourers really was ridiculous but pitiful.

169. 以炸弹作戏嬉而被害

欧美军人，争战之暇，仍常运动游戏。然皆不同我中国未受教育者之无理游戏也。吾一百零二队之同工，每于作工之暇，或用饭以后，亦

华工日记
Chinese Labourer's Diaries

常常集于一处，作种种之嬉笑，使大家快乐。一日饭后，同工素好玩笑者，手持炸弹一枚，初与三四人聚作圆圈形，互相谈天，且谈且掷。继则加入之人渐多，而传递之炸弹，亦愈扔愈快。最后炸弹在人圈之手上旋转迅速之时，人皆极呼，勿令炸弹落地。正在传递速度极快之时，炸弹果然坠地而响，伤三人，轻伤者二，重伤者一。

Getting Killed While Playing with Bombs

In their spare time, the European and American soldiers still enjoyed playing sports and games. These games were quite different from the dangerous games of the uneducated Chinese labourers. For example, every day after work or after meals, my fellow labourers in Brigade 102 often gathered somewhere and tried to make each other happy with playful antics. One day, just after the meal, a labourer who used to play jokes held a bomb in his hand and stood in a circle with three or four other people. At first, they just stood there chatting and throwing the bomb from one to the other. Then, more and more people joined them, and the bomb was passed from one to the other more and more quickly. Finally, as the bomb was being passed rapidly between the hands of the circle, all the men cheered loudly to keep the bomb from falling to the ground. Just as it was being passed at a very fast speed, the bomb fell to the ground and exploded. As a result, three people were injured, one seriously and the other two slightly.

孙干：欧战华工记
Records of Chinese Labourers in European War by Sun Gan

170. 以火药取暖被烘而死

德人败绩，宣告停战。德军一退，吾曾即进至战场，整理一切。所见火药，形形色色，或盛于大箱之内，或零碎装一袋、捆一捆者，随处有之。为数之多，出人意外。有人焉，因天寒冷，而将野外之火药箱负于帐棚之内燃以取暖，卒至药箱烘炸，人被轰死，亦惨矣哉！

Deaths Caused by Gunpowder Used for Heating

The Germans declared a truce when they were defeated. As soon as the Germans withdrew, we were sent to the battlefield to tidy things up. Everywhere on the ground scattered a great variety of gunpowder either in large boxes, small bags or in bundles. The great amount of gunpowder shocked all of us. Because it was so cold, some of our labourers carried some gunpowder boxes into their tent and lighted them for heating. Unfortunately, the boxes exploded and they were all killed in the explosion. How sad it was!

171. 英人亦愿华工娶法妇女

欧战猛烈时，法国国内之成年男子，后防并不多见。而华工经济之

华工日记
Chinese Labourer's Diaries

较宽裕者，亦有人同法之妇女结为夫妇焉。英人于一九一八年初，宣告吾等曰："倘华工队中有人欲与法国妇女结婚者，英人亦赞许之。但必先由其家属，从中国政府领得原无妻子之认可证书，寄至法地，交之于英人。然后英人始准与法之妇女实行结婚也。"观法人之与中国人结婚，其种族之见，似较英人为浅也。

Encouraging Chinese Labourers to Marry Frenchwomen

When the war raged fiercely in Europe, very few grown-up Frenchmen could be found in the rear towns or villages of France. As a result, some wealthy Chinese labourers married Frenchwomen. In early 1918, the British Captain made an announcement to us saying, "The British will give permission to those Chinese labourers who would like to marry Frenchwomen. However, their family in China must first send official certification from the Chinese government, proving that they are not married and hand the certificates to the British officials. Only in this way can the British permit them to marry Frenchwomen." It seemed to me that the French did not have the same racial prejudices against Chinese as the British when it came to the marriage between Chinese labourers and European women.

172. 应基督教之请

余于欧战服务之暇，则常教本队同工读书识字，代为写信。余则

孙干：欧战华工记
Records of Chinese Labourers in European War by Sun Gan

出外参观法人之教育、建设、风俗、武器等等。一日，一工头向余曰："英人将以汝为教师，汝以为如何？"余答之曰："不知也。"有顷，又一工头，亦如此询问。余曰："欲余作何教师也？"彼答以本队将欲设基督教青年会，办理工人教育也。至翌日，一英人与华人张鸣镛先生至。英人向余曰："汝不作工，充当教员，教授众工人读书可乎？"尚未及答，英人又曰："汝若在青年会教授工人读书，虽不作工，余仍按日支给应得工资也。"张鸣镛先生曰："我们中国耶稣教会，欲在此法境战线后防，办理社会教育，帮助工人识字，愿请孙先生出来帮忙。"余曰："先生为耶稣教人，所办之事，须耶稣教人方能胜任。余向虽滥竽教育界者，然对耶稣主义，又丝毫不明，焉能胜任？"张先生曰："一定胜任，保无难处。"余曰："俟余斟酌之，待改日另行规定可也。"二人辞去。

翌日饭后，工头传令命余不与众工人一同出外作工。余询其故，答曰："基督教青年会张鸣镛先生，欲请汝为本队中之青年会副干事，帮办社会教育也。"余曰："余恐不胜任，可请其另请他人。"既而，张先生亦至，余向之坚辞。张先生亦曰："其他无人可行，请孙先生勉为之耳。"于是不得不应其请焉。

Being Invited by YMCA to Be a Teacher

When I worked hard during the European War, I often taught my fellow labourers to read and write and wrote letters for them in my spare time. With the rest of my spare time, I went out to look around the local areas in order to learn more about French education, architecture, customs, and weapons. One day, a foreman asked me, "I hear that the British want to ask you to be a teacher, what do you think of it?" I replied, "I have no idea of it." After

华工日记
Chinese Labourer's Diaries

a while, another foreman asked me the same question. So, I asked him, "What do they want me to teach?" He said that our brigade planned to set up the YMCA (Young Men's Christian Association) to educate our workers. The following day, a British officer and Mr. Zhang Mingyong, a Chinese representative, came to me. The officer said, "If I ask you to teach the labourers to read and write rather than do the manual work, would you like to do it?" Before I had time to answer, he continued, "If you agree to teach with the YMCA, I'll pay you the same wage as you receive each day for doing the manual work." Mr. Zhang Mingyong said, "Our Chinese Church of Christianity plans to establish a social education system in the rear of the battlefields of France to help teach our labourers to read and write. And we'd like to ask you, Mr. Sun, to help us." I said, "You are a Christian, and what you are going to do should better be done by Christians too. Although I had worked in the field of education, I know nothing about Christianity. How can I do it?" He replied, "I'm sure you can. I promise you can do it without any difficulty." I answered, "Let me think about it carefully. I'll tell you my decision later." Then they left.

The next morning, the foreman ordered me not to go out to work with the other labourers after breakfast. I asked why and he answered, "Mr. Zhang Mingyong from the YMCA would like you to be the deputy secretary of the YMCA for our brigade to assist in social education." I said, "I'm afraid I'm not up to it. Please tell him to let someone else do it." After a while, Mr. Zhang came, and I told him of my decision. He said to me, "No one else can do it. I sincerely hope, Mr. Sun, you can accept the job." So I had to accept his invitation.

孙干：欧战华工记
Records of Chinese Labourers in European War by Sun Gan

173. 张鸣镛之为人

欧战之际，华工在后防服务，中国基督教青年会干事张鸣镛先生又为华工服务。其人，字翕如，年二十余岁，中国奉天本溪湖人，举动不苟，丰采异常。不惟于食饭时，先切切感谢上帝，即于早晚间，或睡或起，每必祷告。可知其处处靠神，而不徇私也。虽是奉天大学毕业，而又留学东洋，然于劳力苦工，尽与工人同作，毫无贵族封建习气。其未到法境之前，一百零二队中之工人，醵赌者比比皆是。甚至将将来之二年工价，早已输罄。一时赌风之盛，不言可知。自先生一到，天天讲道，天天教书，不一年而队中赌博者殊不多见。工人之原不识字者，被其循循善诱，亦渐渐能自写书信。不惟其学问，对人则有若无，实若虚也，观者言谈，亦无不娓娓动听。

其尤使人佩服者，以未曾识字之一群工人，授以算术，不一年，而工人之算术程度之进步，骎骎乎已为余学数年之程度所不及也。其能真本基督之牺牲精神，而帮助华工，使华工之恶劣者，渐渐变为良善，愚昧者徐徐化为聪明。至于领人诵诗，引人祈祷，工人因之守本分、要体面、乐合群、爱国家等等，亦吾曹一生所不能及也。宜乎于华工之将欲回国时，因彼此分离之故，使众工人则依依在旁，不忍去也。

Mr. Zhang Mingyong

During the European War, the Chinese labourers served the British

华工日记
Chinese Labourer's Diaries

in the rear while Mr. Zhang Mingyong, secretary of the Chinese YMCA, served the Chinese labourers. Born at Benxihu of Fengtian (today's Liaoning Province) in China, Zhang Mingyong, courtesy name Xiru, was a handsome and charismatic young man in his twenties. Before every meal, he would thank God sincerely for the food. Besides, he would also pray before he went to bed in the evening and the first thing after he got up in the morning. It was obvious that he did everything according to the will of God and would never show any favouritism. He graduated from the University of Fengtian and then studied in Japan, but he kept working tirelessly alongside the Chinese Labourers, displaying no feudal aristocracy at all. Before he arrived in France, many labourers in Brigade 102 were heavily indulged in gambling and some had even lost their future wages for the next two years! It was evident that gambling was very popular at that time. However, few workers in Brigade 102 would gamble again a year later after Mr. Zhang's preaching and teaching every day since his arrival. With his patient instruction, even the most illiterate labourers were gradually able to write letters by themselves. He won the respect of labourers not only for his extensive knowledge but also for his honesty and his modest personality. As a result, his manners and words deeply impressed all of us.

What I admired most about him was his ability in arithmetic teaching. He once taught arithmetic to a group of illiterate labourers who made so much progress in less than one year that their arithmetic was nearly as good as what I had learned for many years. Truly following Jesus Christ's spirit of sacrifice, he served the Chinese labourers wholeheartedly. Under his guidance, the wicked ones in the Chinese Labour Corps gradually became righteous and the ignorant ones gradually became wise. By teaching them to sing hymns and pray to God, he made our labourers honest, polite, cooperative and patriotic people. All the things he did were what I could never achieve during my whole life. Thus, it was understandable why the Chinese labourers were reluctant to part with him when they were going to return to China.

174. 张君翕如来法之原因

欧洲大战，死伤几三千万人。在其五年之间，战士之苦，犹堪问乎！观各国之战地后方，各有其本国基督教青年会为之服务，以帮助其战士。而独吾侪华工赴战线后方服务，以助协约，而无人为之服务，以帮助之乎？是又不然。吾国基督教青年会，虽在幼稚之期，论人才较各国为少，经济视外人尤弱，然有人焉见报端所登载赴法华工之苦状，而亦不得不本基督耶稣之使命，多言牺牲，尽量服务之旨，亦有多人欲设法招人送入法境战地后防。遂经开会议决，一方劝募经费，以备服务人所需之一切什物，而一方搜罗能牺牲、有才学之人才，以使赴法实行援救。

是以自民国六年冬发起，至民国七年秋季，而即实行招赴法青年会干事若干人，而陆续送至欧洲。是事之前，张君翕如在日本留学，常见报端登载华工之在法，不但有时受苦，无人过问，即聚赌方盛，将流而为盗贼者，正待人救。教会既请其赴法，而彼亦甘心为华工服务，所以乃由日本归国，暂停留学，而返祖国，又由祖国摒挡一切，偕其同工者数人，经月余而抵法也。张君等之来法服务，不但恐华工之在法者，天天赌博，渐渐流为盗贼，以害其各人之身家，而亦恐其在外殃及外人，而遗笑于世界各国也。

249

华工日记
Chinese Labourer's Diaries

Reasons for Zhang Xiru's Coming to France

As many as 30 million people were killed or injured during the European War. During the five years, the suffering of soldiers in the war was unimaginable. The YMCA of different countries served in the rear of battlefields, providing help for their soldiers. Was it true that the Chinese labourers went to Europe to work in the battlefields for the Entente countries and had no one to help them? No, it was not. It was true that the YMCA in China was still in its infancy and that it had fewer representatives and less local funding compared with those in other countries. However, after reading about the sufferings of Chinese labourers in France in the newspapers, many people in the YMCA in China would like to provide assistance for them by following the example of Jesus Christ's spirit of devotion and sacrifice. Some even managed to recruit more people and send them to the rear of the battlefields in France. Therefore, decisions were made after meetings that funds should be raised to prepare necessary stuff and more talented and dedicated people should be recruited and sent to France for assistance.

From the winter of 1917 to the autumn of 1918, the YMCA in China recruited several people as senior representatives and sent them to Europe. At that time, Mr. Zhang Xiru was studying in Japan. From newspapers, he learned about the sufferings of Chinese labourers in France. He learned that many of the Chinese labourers had been indulged in gambling or reduced into thieves for lack of care from others and that they were in urgent need of help. When the Church asked him to go to France, he was also willing to serve the Chinese labourers. Therefore, he suspended his studies in Japan and returned to China. He was soon accepted by the YMCA and enrolled for service overseas. About a month later, after overcoming many difficulties, he and a group of other suitably qualified people arrived in France. Mr. Zhang and his colleagues came to France to serve the Chinese labourers not only because they were concerned that the labourers were at risk of ruining their lives by gambling and stealing, but also because they were afraid that the behaviour of the Chinese labourers could harm innocent people and give China a bad reputation, making them a laughing-stock throughout the world.

175. 青年会之设备

  青年会者，本耶稣基督之救人主义，而帮助社会人群，使个个人人，将其天良从心而发，及其天才从身而现。所以凡是人类向善之举，如其分德育、智育、体育、群育等，无不尽其心力，而提倡之，而协助之。

  欧战之际，中国青年会赴法之干事，驻于各处华工队中，在各队之队长观之，盖视青年会之干事为宾客也。客之住于主家者，一切举动皆赖主人，如欲行其所行，必先达知主人，然后方可作也。主人既承认青年会为其至友，则青年会如有其至大之利害，而各队之主人间接负其责任也。

  至于一百零二队中青年会之设备，其一切用具极为简单。关于德育之演讲，或阅览者，有《圣经》《青年诗歌》等数十本而已；关于智育之演讲或阅览者，有地球仪、地图，及新闻纸各数份而已；关于体育之演讲，或实用者，除兵士在野外，抛掷之枪支，外有秋千绳、秋千架、摔跤衣等。其余则有大帐棚一座，木椅数十把，盛物箱数个也。每晚众工人有暇时，将铃一摇，惠然肯来而坐时，余之心中天天觉得颇不寂寞也。

华工日记

Chinese Labourer's Diaries

YMCA Facilities

As an association following the doctrines of salvation of Jesus Christ, the YMCA aims to provide help for all people, attempting to evoke the conscience and stimulate the full potential of every individual. Therefore, the YMCA advocates and assists in all human acts of kindness and benevolence such as moral education, intellectual education, physical education, and collectivistic education.

During the European War, the secretaries of the Chinese YMCA in France lived in the same camps as the brigades of Chinese labourers in various areas and were treated as distinguished guests. As people living with their hosts, the guests would depend on their hosts for whatever they would do. The YMCA secretaries would inform their hosts of what they intended to do before they actually did anything. Since the hosts accepted the YMCA as their best friend, the leaders of each brigade were therefore jointly responsible for it if vital events occurred to the YMCA.

The facilities of the YMCA in Brigade 102 were very simple. For moral education and reading, there were dozens of books such as *Bible* and *Youth Hymn;* for intellectual education and reading there were several terrestrial globes, maps and newspapers; for sport or physical education, there were swing ropes, climbing frames and boxing gloves, as well as guns that had been abandoned by enemy soldiers in the battlefields. In addition, there were also a large tent, dozens of chairs, and several boxes to store things. Every night when the labourers came and sat in the tent on hearing the bells, the loneliness I felt during the daytime would begin to disappear in an instant.

孙干：欧战华工记
Records of Chinese Labourers in European War by Sun Gan

176. 青年会在欧战时初步之工作

余既应青年会副干事之职，则日日与张君翕如在一起。其初步所作之工，为先与工人联络感情。所以先将从中国带来之花生瓜子、笙笛管箫、锣鼓胡琴等等一切之玩具，于工人作工之暇，与工人开娱乐会。除其自己，拜托他人为之调查华工队中之会唱戏者、会唱曲者、会拳术者、会玩魔术者外，并设茶点瓜子、枣栗、花生等等之食物，以真诚相款待之。所以当时一百零二队中之工人，素恶赌博鬼之包围者，一时欢呼，以为基督教青年会来此服务，真使吾辈乐不可当也。

然每晚之间，唱二黄者有之，唱笛梆者有之，其余如大鼓小调、昆古昆曲，每唱及一阙，则张干事起立，对之招待一次，或遂继之以智育演讲，或德育演讲，或时事或新闻等演讲，然后始散。不独一晚如此，天天晚上莫不如此也。余于是将以前英人派与极少之工作，暂置不作，而到青年会帮张翕如君作招待、作文牍、作会计、作教员及店伙、作学生等等之工作，身体遂孜孜不已，劳苦终日，心思却以为乘机服务，洋洋然而快乐也。此即青年会到欧之初步工作也。

茅屋是吾居。休想华丽的、画栋的，不久居；雕梁的，有坏期。只求他能克遮蔽风和雨，再休想高楼大厦，但得个不漏足矣。疯人草于柿岩

Preliminary Work of YMCA during the European War

Since I agreed to be the deputy secretary of the YMCA in our brigade,

华工日记

Chinese Labourer's Diaries

I could work with Mr. Zhang Xiru every day. The first thing he did was to make friends with all the labourers. He organised recreational parties in their leisure time. He provided snacks such as peanuts and melon seeds at the parties. He also provided musical instruments such as the *sheng, xiao*, gong and drum, which he had brought over from China. He sought out people good at singing or asked others to look out for those who were good at singing traditional Chinese operas or songs, or performing magic or boxing, or any other educational sports or entertainment among the labourers. He treated them with respect and sincerity, offering them tea, melon seeds, dates, peanuts and kind words. Thus, those labourers in Brigade 102 who had always resented about constant gambling cheered for these activities organised by the YMCA. They were happy that the service of the YMCA brought delight to the Chinese labourers.

From then on, there were performances every evening among the labourers. Some sang traditional Chinese operas such as the *Erhuang* melodies, *Bang* drama and *Kun* opera, while others played various musical instruments such as the flute or the drum. After every performance, Mr. Zhang would stand up and applaud the performer. He would then give a speech on moral or intellectual education and on about current affairs or the latest news before people left to sleep. Such activities were held every evening, not just one evening per week. So I put aside the little work the British has assigned to me and went to the YMCA to help Mr. Zhang with miscellaneous duties as a receptionist, secretary, accountant, teacher, clerk, and student. I worked hard from morning until night, but I was as happy at the bottom of my heart for this opportunity to serve others. These were what the Chinese YMCA did in Europe at the very beginning.

A simple thatched cottage is my dwelling. Never have I wished to live in a magnificently decorated building, which, because of its short-time endurance, is not suitable for long living. My sole wish is a shelter that can keep me out of the wind and rain.

It was written by Crazy Man from Shiyan, Shandong Province.

177. 青年会亦为华工备饮料

华工之食物，多半觉每顿饭不足，不为大害也。所最感不便者，实为汤水。汤水每餐分茶水一铁碗，天凉尚无大碍。一遇天热，或行路迁徙时，则人人费力较多，其渴也实甚。苟非亲自备壶煮水，又焉得水以解其渴耶？一百零二队中，自青年会至，知工人之需茶水，故每日按其相当之时，制备茶水，以供工人之用。工人一时咸称便焉。

青年会为工人之制饮料也，用烧锅一口，内添好水。先以火将水烧开，然后取可可（另一种茶水粉）半磅和入，再加牛奶一桶，白糖一磅，亦都调入。调匀后，烧之使沸，即可饮矣。若用咖啡，以代可可亦可，不过咖啡价贵而味清，不若可可之能香甜适口而养人也。当时凡工人之渴者，持碗而至，每碗售其铜元二枚。工人至此，遂购遂饮，较以前便利多矣。

YMCA Offering Drinks to Chinese Labourers

For most Chinese labourers the food rationed for each meal was not sufficient. But it was not a big problem when it was compared with the insufficiency of water. Each labourer was given an iron bowl of tea for each meal. It was all right when it was cool. But when it was hot or when we moved a lot, we would suffer unbearable thirst mainly because we sweated so much. How could thirst be quenched if there was no way to boil water for making tea? Knowing of the labourers' need for boiled water, the YMCA prepared tea for the labourers at certain times every day. For a long while, all the labourers praised the YMCA for the great convenience it brought them.

When preparing drinks for labourers, the YMCA first boiled the water in a large pot and then added half a pound of cocoa powder (another kind of tea powder), a barrel of milk and a pound of white sugar into the boiling water. After thorough blending, the mixture was boiled again. Cocoa could be replaced by coffee in preparing the drink. Coffee was more expensive and had a mild taste while cocoa was sweet and was more to the taste of the labourers. At that time, any thirsty labourer could get a bowl of cocoa to drink at the cost of just two copper coins. Labourers could buy hot drinks whenever they were thirsty, which was much more convenient than ever before.

178. 青年会对华工之本意

一日，询张君翕如曰："青年会对华工之本意如何？"张君答曰："青年会本基督耶稣服务于人之旨，使人渐渐认识上帝。譬如余之来法，负有服务华工同胞之职，使其在此于作工之余，彼此常在一处，开一娱乐会，借以免却各人心中之痛苦。以后逐渐帮助其德育、体育、智育、群育，使人人具有高尚之志操、强健之身体、丰富之智识、大同之团契也。吾既负

孙干：欧战华工记
Records of Chinese Labourers in European War by Sun Gan

此等使命而来，不得不请孙先生亦尽心尽力来作辅助。"余闻之，遂欣然答曰："余自来至欧洲战线后方不久，即见诸同工中，有时有抗枷者，有时有被殴者，有时有坐黑屋者，有时有罚款者，诸如此类，现象丛生。弟始不得不提倡教书，使华工之不识字者，令其识字，并书写诸多告白，四出张贴，甚或遭些毁谤，亦所不计。所恨者，余一人方浅力薄，一时不能挽回大多数华工之颓风。今先生既负救人救国之大任，不远重洋而来，正为余一所馨香祷祝者也，敢不聊尽棉薄。"彼曰："善。"余自是以后，将余在各人棚中教书与代人写信之举遂停，而渐移于青年会中矣。

张君问于余曰："众弟兄在此最大之难处为何？"余曰："饭量较大者，其所食不足，饥饿似有可怜。"张君曰："吾侪代买饼干几箱，以供其饭食之不足者，与队中生病而不能进食者之用，可乎？"余曰："可。"张君即乘摩托车，往巴黎中国总青年会商议其事。翌日购来饼干、牛奶、糖果、玩具、信纸、信封数箱。自是日，余兼为青年会之店员及会计，逐日按时将货外售所收款项按时交代。然一日一次点货清算，起初为数尚少，尚不麻烦，其后为数至多，货物一日一点，账目一日一清算，而又加之演讲、写信，及时常随队迁徙，其忙碌之甚，真有令人不堪言状者也。

Original Intention of YMCA for Chinese Labourers

One day, I asked Mr. Zhang Xiru, "What is the original intention of the YMCA for the Chinese labourers?" He replied, "YMCA aims to help people come to know God gradually, which is in conformity with the spirit of Jesus Christ. For example, I came to France with the mission to serve Chinese labourers. By helping labourers to have gatherings for recreation in their leisure time, I want to help reduce their pains of being away from home and to gradually help them in moral, physical, intellectual and collectivistic education so that everyone can develop their aspirations as well as becoming strong in body, mind and spirit. This is why I have asked you, Mr. Sun, to do your utmost to assist me to achieve this mission." On hearing his words, I replied with enthusiasm, "Since arriving at the European front, I have often observed many awkward things happening among Chinese labourers. For instance, sometimes some of our labourers were put on shackles or shut in dark rooms. At other times some of our labourers were beaten or heavily fined. Because of this, I have tried to advocate teaching the illiterate labourers to read and write. I wrote many notices and posted them everywhere. I don't care too much about my being slandered. What I hate most is the fact that I can't change the decadence of most Chinese labourers with just my own efforts. From your words, I see that you came here with very good intentions to save both our people and country from suffering. You are just the person I have been praying for all the time. I'm far too glad to make my humble efforts to help you." He said, "Fine." From that day on, I quitted my job of teaching and writing letters for others and directed all my energy towards the work of the YMCA.

Mr. Zhang asked me, "What is the greatest difficulty for our labourers here?" I replied, "Those people with bigger appetites cannot get enough food to eat and have to remain hungry all the time." Mr. Zhang said, "How about me buying a few boxes of biscuits for those big eaters and those who are too sick to eat?" I said, "Good idea." The next day, Mr. Zhang rode a motorcycle to the YMCA headquarters in Paris to discuss the matter. He returned with boxes of biscuits, milk, sweets, toys, letter paper and envelopes. From then on, I worked both as a clerk and accountant for the YMCA, timely figuring out the money we got from the sale of our goods every day. At first, the work of taking account of the stock and clearing account every day was not too hard due to the small number of goods. However, as the number of goods increased day by day, the work of taking an account of stock and clearing account required increasingly more efforts. What's more, I had to give speeches and write letters. The frequent moving together with the brigade also added to the difficulty of my work. I became extremely busy and such situations were beyond description.

179. 剑桥大学学生

中国基督教会虽人才济济，而欧战华工之赴法者，亦二百余队。所以当时考选青年会干事，送法服务者，殊觉不敷分配，故常以英人代之。英国剑桥大学毕业学生某君，至一百零二队帮办青年会。月许，又往海洋洲担任政治工作而去。其未去时，天天除工作之外，常与余出外散步。一日到野外，见死马数匹，马车数辆，机关枪数杆，大炮数门，地上血肉到处不少。余一一问之，彼谓为结拉骂你（即德人也）所遗弃者。观其野中现象之惨，无以言喻。余指马问之曰："此马是谁打死者？"彼曰："德人退却之至急时，不能复牵之去，故一一打死之。不但马也，此大炮数门不皆德人临逃时，而以火药炸毁者也？"当时余观被毁之大炮，长约丈许，口径约一英尺，由被毁处观之，炮筒之内层，为生铁质，其外绕以红铜丝甚厚，铜丝之外，方为熟铁，坚固之状可想知矣。

Cambridge University Student

Although Chinese YMCA had many talents, the number of YMCA secretaries selected and sent to France was still not enough because there were more than 200 brigades of Chinese labourers in France during the European War. For lack of Chinese YMCA secretaries to be sent to France, some British representatives were selected to make up the shortfall. A graduate of Cambridge University was sent to Brigade 102 to help with the YCMA. After working there for about a month, he was sent to Oceania to carry out some political work. Before he left, we took a walk together every day after work. One day, when we walked across a field, we saw many dead horses, carriages, machine guns and broken artillery guns scattered on the ground, which was heavily stained with flesh and blood. I asked him for the reason and he told me that all these had been abandoned by German soldiers. The scene was too cruel to express in words. Pointing at the horses, I asked him, "Who killed the horses?" He replied, "The Germans did. When they retreated the Germans were in too much of a hurry to take the horses with them, so they killed all of them. Not only did they kill the horses, but they also blew up all the cannons as they fled!" On closer inspection, I found that the destroyed cannons were about 10 feet long and the diameter was about one foot. Seeing from the part destroyed, I found that the inner layer of the barrel was made of cast iron while the outside was surrounded with thick red copper wire. Outside of copper wire was wrought iron. You could imagine how strong they were.

180. 坎亭

坎亭者，如吾中国之店铺也。一百零二队青年会，既处处想与工人以便利舒适。故凡工人之所需者，莫不竭力代办。华工到法，对食物久而厌生，每思不食，久则疾病随之。吾与英人既为工人服务，即渐渐添购种种食物及糖浆、果品等，为一坎亭矣。众工人对此坎亭，不特代买文具已也，凡遇一时口味不适或生病者，购求所需或食物，甚觉便利焉。

Canteen

The YMCA canteen was something similar to a store in China. Intending to provide convenience and comfort for labourers, the YMCA in Brigade 102 made every effort to supply whatever the labourers needed. Many of the Chinese labourers in France had been tired of the local food for a long time since their arrival in France. Some of them even fell ill due to having not appetite for a long time. With the purpose of providing a good service for the labourers, we, together with the British, bought more and more kinds of food such as syrup and fruits. Gradually a canteen was established. Not only could labourers buy stationery from it, those who had no appetite or fell ill could also buy food or other things they needed. The canteen provided great convenience for Chinese labourers.

181. 有人反对青年会

基督教青年会，虽费巨款，派干事赴法服务，而华工亦有蛊惑工人，结成团体反对者。一百零二队中亦有此现象也。奸人聚赌，不但期将工

华工日记
Chinese Labourer's Diaries

人现钱一网打尽，未来之三年工钱，亦将设法使之输尽。居心之恶，至于此极。青年会到，常常演讲赌博之害，即自然为合局者之所嫉。始也忿愲毁谤，继也至夜偷窃，甚或偷斫什物，割其帐棚。《圣经》云："善人如入恶人之群，如羊之入狼群也。"信哉斯言！

Opposition to YMCA

The YMCA had spent a lot of money sending its secretaries to France for the purpose of providing services for Chinese labourers. However, some men among the Chinese labourers gathered to incite other labourers to oppose the YMCA. Brigade 102 was no exception. By organising labourers to gamble, some villainous people not only cheated the labourers out of all their current earnings, but also managed to leave them indebted of all their wages for the next three years. How treacherous they were! When the YMCA arrived, its secretaries often gave speeches on the dangers of gambling to the Chinese labourers, which naturally resulted in the hatred of these gambling organisers. They got so annoyed about the YMCA's tactics that they began to spread vicious slanders everywhere at first and then they stole things or even cut the YMCA stuff and destroy its tent furtively at night. Just as the *Bible* says, "A good man in the midst of the wicked is like a sheep in the midst of the wolves". It was just the case.

孙干：欧战华工记
Records of Chinese Labourers in European War by Sun Gan

182. 余学耶酥道

余既与张君翕如常常同处，彼即常引余诵赞美诗，有时率领祷告。渐明了其教中之底蕴，此余信奉耶稣之初步也。

Learning Doctrines of Christianity

When I stayed together with Mr. Zhang Xiru, he often taught me to sing hymns and sometimes led me to pray. Gradually I knew about Christianity and began to believe in Jesus.

183. 英之长官亦常到中国青年会作礼拜

余观世间公事之大者，莫大于国家之战争；已事之要者，莫要于时刻不离乎上帝。中国青年会自到法境后，常有英国之长官，每至礼拜日，必邀约数人或数十人到余等青年会，与凡信基督耶稣者一同作礼拜，以敬上帝。

余初至青年会，每至礼拜日，既不知作礼拜者之本意，又不解英人之语言，所以只知观其行动，听其嗫嚅而已。对于其言语之意义，尽茫

华工日记
Chinese Labourer's Diaries

然也。然为时既久，询诸懂英语之人张禽如先生。彼答曰："西人之亲近上帝，真如祖国《中庸》书所说：'道也者，不可须臾离也。'如今之战争杀敌人，虽极要紧，而礼拜日之敬神，却私心，彼英人以为更要紧也。"

British Officers Visiting YMCA for Worship

As far as I could see, for a country nothing was more important than war while for an individual nothing was more important than to be with God. After the arrival of the Chinese YMCA in France, British officers often invited many people to the YMCA for worship on Sundays. They prayed together with others who believed in Lord Jesus.

When I first began working with the YMCA, I knew little about the meaning of Sunday worship or about the language of the British soldiers, so I just watched their actions and listened to their mumblings. But I was totally at loss and did not understand anything they said. After a few weeks, I asked Mr. Zhang Xiru, because he knew about religion and also understood the English language. He told me, "Westerners are close to God, just as what is said in the Chinese classic of *The Doctrine of the Mean*, "'The Way may not be left for an instant.' At the moment, it is extremely important to kill enemies in battles, but for those British it is even more important to worship God on Sundays and get rid of selfishness on Sundays.

孙干：欧战华工记
Records of Chinese Labourers in European War by Sun Gan

184. 张干事之演讲

华工一百零二队青年会干事张翕如君，为一善演讲者。彼自到队后，天天晚间，与众工人接谈，而观众工人，逐渐与之融洽矣。一日向余曰："咱们提倡使工人识字或学算术可乎？"余曰："可。"于是至本日下午众工人工罢而归，余乃开门招之，工人哄然而至。甫坐定时，张君曰："大家在此天天作工，使吾中华民国工界之好名誉，远播于全世界，此亦大家劳苦之功也。虽然吾想大家只知作工，得些工钱，固甚美也；若人人再多读些书，识些字，或学习些算术，而会算账，那才不愧远游外洋一趟。譬如大家一日识一个字，学到一年，则识三百余字。若每天学五个字，十天即为五十个，一月即一百余。如此算之，每年识字一千余个，与普之当先生者，相去不甚远也。现在吾闻大家之工作亦不甚忙，劳力亦不算多，如果愿学，余即可以招生五六十名。如果读书一年后，即可学着写信。来往之信，自己会写，毋用再烦他人矣。大家想想，咱们大家在此地，同有工夫，如你一旦回国，回到家中，那时各人想再读书，即自己请先生，每月用钱十元，恐亦无有工夫得读书矣。大家想想，彼时懊悔，岂不晚哉。倘大家愿意，可先报名一试也。"张君言毕，而其中亦有人言学之寥寥，无甚大用。然众工人中纷纷报名愿学识字者，共六十余人也。

Mr. Zhang's Speeches

Mr. Zhang Xiru, secretary of the YMCA in Brigade 102, was a good

华工日记
Chinese Labourer's Diaries

public speaker. He talked to the labourers every evening after his arrival in this brigade. Thus he gradually got along with the labourers very well. One day, he asked me, "What do you think of the idea of teaching labourers to read or to learn arithmetic?" I said, "A good idea." Later that day when the labourers came back from work, I opened the door and called them all in. They all came along noisily. As soon as everybody was seated, Mr. Zhang said, "I know all of you work hard every day. It is because of your diligent work that the good reputation of the Republic of China can be spread throughout the world. I know you only want to work hard to earn more money, which is of course very noble. But I think it would be even better if all of you could learn to read more books and know more Chinese characters or learn some arithmetic and do accounts. For example, if you can learn to read just one character a day, you will learn over 300 characters in a year. If you can learn five every day, you will learn fifty in ten days and maybe over one hundred in a month. In this way, you can learn more than 1,000 characters a year, making you as good as a teacher. Now that you aren't very busy and do not have too much manual work to do, I'd like to recruit fifty or sixty students if you want to learn. After learning for one year, you'll be able to write letters by yourselves without asking a favour of others. You can begin this now, while we are all here and have the time to learn. Suppose you wait until you return to your homes in China, you'll have to find a teacher on your own and pay ten yuan every month if you want to learn to read. What's more, I don't think you'll have time to learn. By then it would be too late to regret. So, if you like, you can sign up and give it a try here first." As soon as Mr. Zhang finished his remarks, more than sixty labourers signed up for the class although some labourers still felt that it was useless to try and learn.

孙干：欧战华工记
Records of Chinese Labourers in European War by Sun Gan

185. 兼作青年会之会计

余本不谙簿记之法。青年会至法之后，因干事人少，不敷分配，不得不兼用华工中之可靠者以助之。一百零二队中青年会干事张翕如君之请余帮助一切，盖如此也。余在青年会中，既积极代之管理，而其中之最关心者，厥为新式账簿耳。新式账簿之管理法，大概亦分为出入两项。每项之中，又分若干条，每条分若干数目。譬如每日所入之款，五十元之纸票若干张，共数若干；十元之纸票若干张，共钱多少；五元之纸票若干张，共钱多少；三元、二元、一元、五佛郎、三佛郎、两佛郎、一佛郎，以下至一分半分等等，均一一登记。其总数于账簿之分格中，然后再将各项之总数，总共之，登记于总格。其详细也既如此，其麻繁也，自然知之。

然战地青年会，随工程队之三日一迁，五日一挪，所以天天须将其坎停中一日所销之货价算讫，以后再将所余之货，一一点数清算。日日如此，乃可谓之其麻繁矣。当时余觉吾二人只办白天之事已觉不胜其烦，至夜晚，则算账也，点货也，一一整理完毕，然后方得睡眠。所以当时余觉受人之托，殊不易也。

Working as an Accountant for YMCA

I knew little about accounting. Because there were not enough secretaries, the YMCA in France had to ask some reliable Chinese labourers for help. I became one of them when Mr. Zhang Xiru, secretary of the YMCA in Brigade

102 asked me to assist him with his work. Of all the work I did for the YMCA, the book-keeping accounts were my biggest concern. The management of the account books could be roughly divided into two categories: income and expenditure. Within each category there were several other entries, each of which was further divided into sub-items. For example, under the item of income of every day, there were sub-items of number and total for fifty-yuan notes, ten-yuan notes, five-yuan notes, three-yuan notes, two-yuan notes, one-yuan notes, five-franc coins, three-franc coins, two-franc coins, one-franc coins and half-franc coins. I had to record all these items one by one. Tables were made in the account books, and then the totals for each item were calculated and registered in the total cell. It was obvious that the work of accounting was rather tedious.

However, the battlefield YMCA had to move every three or four days with the engineering brigades. So I had to settle the daily sales of the canteen each day and counted the goods in stock one by one. It was really tedious to do this day after day. During this period, Mr. Zhang and I felt extremely tired after completing our full day's work. But we had to settle the accounts and could not go to bed until everything was done. My only thought at that time was that I could not fail to live up to the trust of others, but it was really a hard time for me at that time.

186. 又招算术二班

一百零二队中之华工，虽因其无教育、无程度，故不免有反对青年会者。然吾侪因招识字工人两班，以不识字者为一班，为张君禽如教授之；以稍有程度者为一班，为余担任教授之。而张君以为人之性情个个不同，不喜学文字者未尝不愿学算术也，故又对余曰："咱们明天再招算术二班，使工人学习算术，免得彼作工之后，空费其光阴也。"余应之曰："可。"

至翌日，张君又于下午演讲，对众工人曰："余此次之来，为竭力帮忙大家，虽然招汉文学员两班，已经天天上班，学习认字，然汉文非余之所长也，余在大学之功课特别见长者为算术也。余毕业时，校长于算术一门，给余以特别文凭耳。世间之人，不会算账者，人多半视之为愚人。大家工作之暇，愿学算术，可速速来此报名。大家若学习半年后，通常账项，可毋庸求他人算也。"言尚未毕，众工人中有人曰："吾对于汉文不愿学，而对算术愿学焉。"一时报名者纷纷而至。不一刻，人数即达六七十矣。

Recruitment of Two Arithmetic Classes

For lack of education and illiteracy, some labourers among Brigade 102 opposed the YMCA. Even so, we had still managed to recruit two literacy classes, one for literate labourers and the other for illiterate labourers. Mr. Zhang taught the class of illiterate labourers while I taught the class of labourers with some literacy. Mr. Zhang then had another idea. He thought that since each person had a different temperament, those who did not want to learn to read might have an interest in learning arithmetic. He said to me, "Let's recruit two arithmetic classes tomorrow so that the labourers can learn arithmetic instead of just wasting their time after work." I replied, "All right."

Mr. Zhang gave a speech to labourers again on the afternoon of the following day. He said, "I've come here to help you as much as possible. As you all know, we have two Chinese literacy classes which have already begun to learn how to read. However, Chinese is not my speciality. When I was in university I learnt how to teach arithmetic. When I graduated from university, the president gave me a special Diploma for my excellence in teaching arithmetic. In the world today, people who are incapable of arithmetic are usually considered to be foolish. So, if you are willing to learn arithmetic after work, please sign up as soon as possible. When you have studied for six months, you will be able to settle your own accounts without asking others for help." Before he had finished his words, one of the labourers shouted, "I don't want to learn to read, but I'd like to learn arithmetic." Many labourers signed up for the class and the number of applicants quickly reached sixty to seventy soon.

187. 华工学地理者之踊跃

吾侪所招之汉文两班，算术两班，按日上课。一日，张君又对众人演讲曰："大家在此工作之暇，不但能学些文学，并能学些算学，此真是些好的事情。如此学去，将未回国到家之时，不但手中能积些钱还家，而亦得些学问还家。那时到家，真能使人人高看哩。若是大家再有地理知识，于一到家时，这亲戚请吃饭，那朋友请喝酒，到那时人家一定先问您说：'你出门多年，都是走到些甚么地方呢？现在请你对我们说一说罢，我们很愿意听呢。'然而大家到那时，若能对着人说，必须自己预先知道。大家若想预先知道，必然得学地理。现正是当学地理了，若是乘早在此将地理学学过明白，到那时，一定能对答如流，有些话说，使人家拿着当人呢。现在大家若想学地理时，余有地图，亦有地球仪，如我

孙干：欧战华工记
Records of Chinese Labourers in European War by Sun Gan

们之来法国，由我国而向何方，行船而至多少日，中国距法国地，有多少路程，一一学之，以后自然即明白矣。"众人听罢，愿报名者，纷纷然多至三十余人焉。

Chinese Labourers' Enthusiasm for Learning Geography

Thus, we now had two literacy classes and two arithmetic classes, and we gave them lessons every day. One day, Mr. Zhang gave the workers a speech again, "It is a very good thing for you to learn how to read and to count in your spare time. If you continue to learn like this, when you go back home, you will not only have money for your family, but also knowledge for yourself. With your new knowledge you will be respected by everyone. However, if you can also learn some geography, when your friends and relatives invite you for dinner and ask you, 'Where have you been during these years? Please come and tell us something about it. We'd love to hear all about it.' You can impress them with your knowledge of these countries. But if you want to tell them about the places you have been, you must know where these countries are in the first place. If you want to know about the places to which you have travelled, you should learn some geography. Now it is the right time to learn. If you can take advantage of being here to gain some geographical knowledge, you'll be able to answer their questions without any problems when you get back home. For your extensive knowledge, other people will think highly of you. If you want to learn geography, I have maps and globes for you to learn from. After studying them, you'll know which direction we sailed after we left our country for France, and how long it took us to arrive here by boat and how far China is from France." On hearing his words, up to 30 labourers were willing to sign up for the class.

188. 天天服务之情形

余与张君翕如，在青年会服务，极为自由。然除其一人天天饭后即出外，赴附近之各华工队中演讲，下午有事时或演讲，或上课，始归外。其余之事，均余一人常在家为之。如整理棚之内外，及一切坐次后，替工人写信，或替翻译书写告示，未到下午，即须再为工人预备饮料。

下午时工人一还，坎停立即售卖货物及饮料。一到上课时间，即复摇铃上班。每晚上班两次，然后食晚饭。晚饭后，复学赞美诗。以至诸事皆毕，方算坎亭之账目。此即张君与余服务时之大概情形也。

Our Daily Work

Mr. Zhang and I had lots of freedom while working for the YMCA. Every day after breakfast he would go out to give speeches to labourers in nearby brigades of Chinese labourers. He would return in the afternoon in time to give talks or teach lessons. I needed to do all the other things in Brigade 102 such as tidying up the inside and outside of the large tent, arranging seats, writing letters for labourers, writing notices for the interpreter, and preparing drinks for labourers early in the afternoon.

孙干：欧战华工记
Records of Chinese Labourers in European War by Sun Gan

As soon as the labourers came back from work in the afternoon, I began immediately to sell goods and drinks in the canteen. When it was time for class, I rang the bell and gave lessons to the men. I taught twice a night and then had dinner. After dinner, we sang hymns again. After everything had finished, I began to deal with the accounts of the canteen. This was how Mr. Zhang and I worked every day.

189. 总华工青年会

一百零二队之青年会，不但其供给工人之物件，为总华工青年会为之代办。即办理之方法，总青年会亦不时派人观察。坎亭之款项，亦归总青年会管理。即平日工人之领受，总青年会之游行，干事之领教，亦实在不少。

Chinese Labourers YMCA

The YMCA of Brigade 102 not only provided labourers with various goods, but it also acted as an agent for the General YMCA of Chinese Workers. Its work was also inspected from time to time by staff sent from the General YMCA. The accounts of the canteen were also overseen by the YMCA. Everything from the wages paid to labourers, the expenses for the parade of the General YMCA, and the the salary given to secretaries, were all administrated from the head offices of the YMCA.

华工日记
Chinese Labourer's Diaries

190. 青年会游行干事王正叙到会演讲

青年会干事王正叙者，为外交家王正廷之三弟也。一日，到一百零二队对工人演讲。余将工人招集后，王氏曰："今天与大家得机会谈话，敝人觉得十分快乐。大家在此作工，都很有成绩。除作工尽了本分以外，听说还读些书，明些理，学些本事，以备后来应用。譬如识认些字，即渐渐有些学问，处处不用求人；学些算术，既会算账，将来更能作买作卖，以谋生活。现在凡有学问，能作买卖的人，皆是趁早预备下的。现在大家知道，英国是一强国，殊不知彼之国势，样样都是趁早预备下的。譬如英之一切武器，大家是常见的。即如彼之海船，共有一万余只，天天在海洋上往来游行。而我们中国之海船，虽有四五只，亦不能游航世界，可以说是直然没有。若以英国之国力，与我们中国比，孰胜孰败，孰弱孰强，那就不用说了。现在很望大家好好作工，好好求学，多攒些钱，多长些学问，以后有了实在本事，一定是比现在还好的多。到那时，不但现在教你读书的张先生同孙先生觉着光彩，即您们亦得到实际上的帮助哩。"言罢一时掌声如雷，众工人亦遂散去矣。

Speech by Wang Zhengxu, Parade Officer of YMCA

Wang Zhengxu, a secretary of the YMCA, was the third younger brother of Diplomat Wang Zhengting. One day, he came to our YMCA to give a speech to labourers of Brigade 102. After I gathered the labourers, he said, "I am very glad to have this opportunity to talk with you. I know all of you work very hard here. I also hear that you are learning to read, to increase your knowledge and learning some skills that will benefit you greatly in the future. As you can read, you'll gradually acquire more knowledge so that you needn't always ask others for help. As you also learn arithmetic, you can not only settle accounts but also do business in the future to make a living. Today, all those who have knowledge and can do business start preparing for it early. You all know that Britain is a powerful country, but you never know that Britain has prepared everything as early as possible. For example, Britain has all types of weapons as we've seen here. It still has more than 10,000 British ships sailing on the sea every day. However, China has only four or five ships, none of which can sail around the world. So it may as well be said that we have no ships at all. It is evident which country is superior and more powerful in terms of military strength when it is compared with Britain. Now I hope you all work hard, study hard, save more money and learn more things. In the future, when you've acquired more skills and ability, you'll be much better off than you are now. Not only will your teachers, Mr. Zhang and Mr. Sun, be very proud of you, but you are actually helping yourselves and will benefit a great deal from this learning." The applause was thunderous when he finished speaking. Afterwards all the labourers returned to their own tents.

191. 青年会干事张君教授工人注音字母

张君翕如，以所招之汉文学员及算术学员各两班、地理一班之数总

华工日记
Chinese Labourer's Diaries

觉不多，一日又招注音字母一班，人数三十余人。察其报名之学员，多为脑力较差，不能胜汉文、算术之烦难者。然此班之人数，虽不及他班，而人人能按日出席，或将来亦有可观也。

Secretary Zhang of YMCA Teaching Labourers Phonetic Scripts

Mr. Zhang Xiru also began a phonetic script class and received another 30 students because he always thought the total number of students was not enough with only two Chinese classes, two arithmetic classes and one geography class. He found that most of the labourers were too illiterate to learn the difficult and complex courses of Chinese and arithmetic, but they attended the phonetic script class every day. Although the students in this class were not as many as those in the other classes, he believed that some of them would become very capable in the future if everyone could be present at the class on time.

192. 体育之分班

一日，张君曰："一百零二队中之工人，共有四百余，而常到青年会中实在上班者仅百余人。若按诸学科，我们所定的功课，多是属乎用脑力者，而关于身体活动之功课殊少。就工人方面观之，提倡运动身体之学课则易，提倡用心思脑力之学课则难。譬如汉文、算术、地理、注音字、英文等等，皆用脑力之学科，工人学之则难；兵操、拳术、摔跤、

孙干：欧战华工记
Records of Chinese Labourers in European War by Sun Gan

打秋千等不甚用脑力之学科，工人学之则易。现在我们所办在室内上班之学科，皆系用脑力者也，工人之来学者虽不少，然视全队人数，仍算不多。倘再将以用身体之学科，加以提倡，而工人之来学者，一定更多也。"余曰："张君，汝真学过教育学与心理学者。若复按汝所说，而提倡体育，则是队之工人之幸福更大。但不知如何安排为相宜也？"彼又曰："提倡体育亦必须按工人之习尚。如中国之拳术，为工人平素多习之者，若就其所好而使之习，谅必不难。其余如兵操、摔跤，我们以后陆续一一加以提倡，定有效力。现在我们先再搜求拳术教师也。"余曰："可。"自是以后，凡在和工人上课及谈话时，便询何人会打拳。既觅得会打拳者数人，然后商议其中之技术最精良者作为教师。以后遂又商议招学员两班，共数十人，按日上班焉。

一日，张君欲提倡拳术班之招生，遂招集众工人演讲。工人既至，彼对工人曰："吾人之能有高寿者，全赖诸有好身体。吾国之长拳，即锻练身体方法之最良者也。世界各国之人，莫不羡慕吾国之拳术者。吾侪现在在此，读书识字者有之，学习地理、算术者有之，若人人再学上几套长拳，锻炼强壮之身体，岂不更为有益乎？不知大家亦乐意否？倘大家都乐意时，须先共同探寻拳术教员，何人可胜任也。"言至此，工人纷纷欲学习拳术，而想报名者很多，不一刻人数而足两班矣。报名既毕，而张君在场中自耍长拳一套。及完毕时，观者莫不鼓掌叫好也。

Grouping of Physical Education Classes

One day, Mr. Zhang said, "There are more than 400 labourers in Brigade 102, but only about 100 of them are actually learning with us. Most of the classes we offer are aimed at improving people's intellectual capabilities but few for their physical wellbeing. As far as the labourers are concerned, it is easy to improve physical exercises but difficult to promote the study of mental and intellectual subjects. For example, classes like Chinese, arithmetic, geography, phonetics, and English are all subjects for mental training and difficult for labourers to learn, while classes such as military training, boxing, wrestling, and gymnastics are subjects that require little intellectual capabilities and are easy to learn. The subjects we have offered in the classrooms are all intellectual training ones. Although many labourers are attending them, the number is still too small considering the large number of labourers in the whole brigade. If we advocate courses of physical exercises, I believe more labourers will join us." I said, "You're really an expert in education and psychology. If we offer physical education as you have suggested, the labourers in our brigade will gain much more benefit from it. But I don't know how to organise them properly?" He continued, "The physical education classes must be offered on the basis of labourers' habits and interests. For example, many labourers usually practice Chinese boxing. If we can offer trainings according to their interests, it won't be difficult to encourage them to learn. As for military training and wrestling, we can offer them one after another in the future. I believe all of them will have good effects. For now, our task is to look for boxing teachers." I agreed, "Good." From then on, whenever we taught in class or talked with labourers, we would ask them whether they knew anybody who was experienced in Chinese boxing. In this way, we found several labourers who were good at boxing and selected the most skilled ones as the teachers. Then we talked about recruiting two classes with dozens of labourers and having lessons every day.

To recruit students for the Chinese boxing classes, Mr. Zhang got the labourers together one day to give a speech. After the arrival of all labourers, he said to them, "To live a long life, one must have good health. Chinese long boxing is the best way to build up our body. People all over the world admire Chinese boxing very much. Now, some of our labourers here are learning to read and some are learning geography or arithmetic. Wouldn't it be even more beneficial for everyone here to learn a few sets of long boxing to keep yourselves healthy and strong? Would you like to do it? If everyone is willing to learn, the first thing to do is to find someone who is competent enough to be the boxing teacher." Upon hearing his words, many labourers said they would like to learn Chinese boxing and wanted to sign up for it. Soon we recruited two classes. After the registration, Mr. Zhang himself gave a performance of long boxing on the spot and was loudly applauded by the audience.

193. 摔跤班、陆军班打秋千、爬绳等设置

青年会对体育之组织，除拳术有两班天天下午按时上班锻炼以外，又组织陆军之训练一班。摔跤者，打秋千者，爬绳者，各一群，各都安置，有负责之人，每日按时监督管理。所以当时观一百零二队中，工人之活泼异乎他队。不但以前之赌博恶习绝无而仅有，即工人智识之程度及作工之效率，亦蒸蒸日上也。然是队之好现象，今后之可惧者为事变靡常，若一遇迁徙，则一切之设备，同统作废，每到另一地方，复另建设。不然上班运动之等等一切，均无房舍可住，又焉希望再得到处所，办理社会教育也？

Setting of Swinging and Rope Climbing for Wrestling Class and Army Class

In addition to the two Chinese boxing classes held in the afternoon each day, the YMCA also organised an army training class, which was divided into groups of wrestlers, swingers and rope climbers. For each group there were people in charge who supervised and managed the training sessions every day. As a result, labourers in Brigade 102 were much more active than those of other brigades at that time. Not only had the former bad habit of gambling been eliminated, but the intellectual education and efficiency of labourers had also improved significantly. However, what worried us considerably was the changeable situations in the future. If we moved to another place in the future, all our facilities would be given up and we would have to reconstruct everything in the new place. Otherwise, there would be no buildings for all our classes and training. In that case, how could we hope to find a place for social education?

194. 附设英文班

欧战招募华工，英浸礼教会中，明白中国话者，与有力焉。招工既为英政府，青年会干事又为英浸礼会中之人居多，故在法时，吾侪一举一动，竟与英人办事。所以英语一项，颇关重要。青年会又为中英两国人交际之处，青年会之干事，不能不会也。

吾对英语素无根底。然想不但余一人在此际正该借青年会设法研究，即对众工人，亦有提倡之必要。一日，余与张君商议，遂请北平王翻译，由本队办公之暇，担任英语班教授。会中又从本队工人中，招英语学生数十人，而开课上班矣。虽然，余之事务忙甚，而无须臾之暇以温习之，是以虽身充英语学生，而心因不忍废公而务私，故终未得到好的学问也。

孙干：欧战华工记
Records of Chinese Labourers in European War by Sun Gan

Opening of English Classes

In recruiting Chinese labourers for the European War, those who knew Chinese language in the British Baptist Church had made a great contribution. Because the recruitment was conducted by the British government and most of the YMCA officials were from the Baptist Church, nearly all our work in France was associated with the British. Therefore, English language was particularly important for us. Besides, the YMCA was also the main liaison place between the Chinese and the British. Therefore, English was a must for Chinese officials of the YMCA.

I knew nothing about English, but I thought it was very necessary to take this opportunity to advocate learning English in the YMCA, both for me and the ordinary labourers. I consulted about it with Mr. Zhang one day and then we decided to invite our brigade interpreter, Mr. Wang from Beiping, (Peking) to be the teacher of our English class in his spare time. We then recruited dozens of labourers from our brigade for the English class. Unfortunately, because I was usually too busy to have time to review the lessons and unwilling to abandon my public duties for private affairs, I was not a good student and, as a result, failed to learn English very well.

195. 华工于停战后之工作

自欧战停，众同工之作工为何？仍为修道路、捡残器、装卸车、

华工日记
Chinese Labourer's Diaries

平地沟。其地该使之整齐者，使之整齐；该使之洁净者，使之洁净。虽然战场地面之大，无一不需人力之整顿，其需时之久，需人之多，概可想见也。

Post-war Work of Chinese Labourers

What did the Chinese labourers do after the European War ended? They still engaged in repairing roads, clearing broken weapons, loading and unloading vehicles, and filling in trenches. They also helped to level the ground across the battlefields that had been completely wrecked by shellfire or mine explosions. Everything in the battlefields had to be rectified by manpower. With such a vast area of battlefields, one could imagine the great number of labourers and hours of labour required by the post-war work.

196. 华工亦仿德之俘掳镌刻炮弹廓

欧战时，德人之被法人掳去也，自民国三年至民国七年夏季，为数不止几万人。至民国七年冬停战以后，不但华工之工作渐减轻，即德人被掳于英者，其工作亦渐轻也。然人类好动，一有闲暇，而即思寻其他之事。其时有德人将大炮之炮廓，以刺刀作锯锯之，上镌以花纹，以细砂擦之，使放光泽，而为笔筒，然后售于法人之私家。有一个为全副者，有二个为一对者，或有以四个为一套者。以尺寸之大小，花样之新奇，花纹之疏密，而定其价钱之高低。贱者五六佛郎，贵者

孙干：欧战华工记
Records of Chinese Labourers in European War by Sun Gan

数十佛郎。德人倡之，华工效之。但一百零二队中，约得价亦不止数千佛郎也。

Labourers Imitating German Prisoners to Engrave Cartridges

From 1914 to the summer of 1918, tens of thousands of Germans were captured by the French during the European War. After the armistice in the winter of 1918, the workload was gradually reduced not only for Chinese labourers but also for the German captured by the British. However, because being active was human nature, people would try to find something to do once they were idle. At that time, some Germans made brush barrels out of the used cartridges by sawing them with a bayonet, carving patterns on them, rubbing them with fine sand to make them shiny, and sold them to the French. A single brush barrel constituted a complete one; two constituted a pair; and four constituted a set. The price was set depending on the size as well as the complexity or novelty of the pattern, with the lowest price at five to six francs and the highest at dozens of francs. Labourers in Brigade 102 earned thousands of francs by imitating the Germans to engrave cartridges.

197. 赴巴黎之初志

余来欧西，非抱功名富贵之心，乃以共和国民之资格，借助协约，

华工日记
Chinese Labourer's Diaries

以观察太西之文明也。兹时值欧战告终，对同工之尽义务，又半年有余。一日，忽想法之京城，虽号称欧洲人位之第三，然其街市之繁华，建筑之玲珑，却为第一。此距巴黎，仅数百里，若机会一过，定难再来。于是于民国八年七月十二日晚，语至友黄君世恩曰："余请游巴黎，汝愿之乎？"彼曰："在兄则可，在他人均不可。"余曰："有说乎？"对曰："有。吾辈天天非作工不行，谁不作工，不但自己不得工钱，大小工头均负有责任。强为还要处罚。兄现在青年会中，所作之工，与本队英人无关。兄赴巴黎，正其时矣。"

My Initial Ambition to Visit Paris

My original purpose for coming to Western Europe was not to achieve fame and fortune, but simply to observe the Western culture as an educated traveller from the Republic of China, a member of the Entente countries. Since the end of the European War, I had served our Chinese labourers for over six months. One day, the idea of travelling to Paris suddenly occurred to me. Known as the third largest city in Europe, Paris actually deserved the first place in terms of its bustling streets and exquisite buildings. It was only a few hundred miles away from where we worked. If I did not take this opportunity to travel to Paris, it would be nearly impossible for me to ever visit again. So, on the evening of 12 July 1919, I said to my friend Mr. Huang Shien, "I'd like to visit Paris, do you want to go with me?" He replied, "None except you can do it." I asked why and he said to me, "All of us have to work every day. If we don't work, not only we will lose our wages, but the foreman will become involved in it. We'll be severely punished and if we insisted on going. You are now in the YMCA and your work has nothing to do with the

孙干：欧战华工记
Records of Chinese Labourers in European War by Sun Gan

British officers in our brigade. So I think it is the best time for you to go to Paris now."

198. 余游花都之始

余因前上文呈于欧战驻法英之总司令部，未允余由法赴英，入校求学。后遂又欲赴巴黎参观，商之张君翕如。彼虽未加可否，但也不至反对。余想此次来法，虽已两阅寒暑，见不少之兵士及武器，闻不少之枪声与炮声，然对于素称花都之巴黎，世界各国之人莫不羡慕，而余尚未游及之，乃为一大憾事。乃预备英语地图及川资等，于七月十三日早饭后，由青年会辞行，至二十余里之遥，天将午时，至一车站，买票上车，向西南行车。与法之一文士相遇，彼亦欲赴巴黎者。相谈虽不达深意，而大致亦能明白。约五点钟时，至巴黎之北车站，一同下车，握手相别。停车场约有数里之阔，轨道之多，一时不能辨其数目，盖其地为众火车之集中点也。既至票房门口，见其卖票处所，共分若干间。虽人数至多，而出入按次，有条不紊。

Beginning of My Tour to Paris

I had written to the offices of the Commander-in-Chief of the European War in France and Britain, but my request being sent to Britain from France for further study was refused. Later, when I wanted to visit Paris, I discussed it with Zhang Xiru. Although he did not say yes, he did not object either. I thought that although I had seen many soldiers and weapons and heard much gunfire and explosions during my two years in France, it was still a pity that I had not travelled to Paris, a well-known Capital of Flowers in the world. So I left the YMCA after breakfast on 13 July taking with me a British map and some money for the journey. After walking a few miles, I arrived at a station at noon, where I bought a ticket and got on a southwest-bound train. I met a French student who was also travelling to Paris. Although it was hard for us to fully understand each other, we had a rough idea of what each other said. When we arrived at the Gare du Nord in Paris at about five o'clock, we got off together and shook hands to say goodbye to each other. The train station seemed miles wide and there were too many tracks for me to count because it was a place where many trains gathered. The ticket office was divided into several rooms. Although there were a lot of people, they all took turns to come in and go out.

199. 巴黎之建筑

民国八年七月十三日晚五点半，余初到巴黎街市中时，即见街之两旁，崇楼峻宇，悬挂法之国旗，如火如荼，又如云霞。及至街里，日将暮时，恰为一十字路口，周转一回视，而知世界之人称巴黎为花都，真名不虚传。

余在街口细观其街道之阔，约五六丈，并非十字街，实系四通八达之街衢也。街之中央，为一来一往之电车轨。轨之两旁，则为摩托车之来往。所行者，摩托车外，又为马车及脚踏车之路。再向外，为人行之

孙干：欧战华工记
Records of Chinese Labourers in European War by Sun Gan

徒步街道。人行道外，始为市肆楼房。人行道之中央，栽树一行，数武一株。树之高低疏密，整齐划一。树株之间，又有简单之小便所与树相间，不远一座。其中置自来水管，遂便遂洗，毫无恶臭。人数拥挤之多，车马驰骋之快，欲横过一街，从街之左而达于街之右，非目快腿速者，不能行也。及余欲归之时，环顾其街，不知何者为来路。因其街道之宽窄，房舍之高低，华丽之雕画，均为划一也。余遂至近旁之咖啡馆中，喝咖啡一壶，然后寻得一旅馆，盘旋而升十余层楼而宿焉。当余在十字路口环顾之时，日尚未落，而电灯已尽燃，明亮若白昼，由此可知巴黎建设之一斑矣。

Architecture in Paris

I arrived in the centre of Paris on 13 July 1919 at 5:30 p.m. and I saw many towering buildings on both sides of the street, with the French flag flying over them like a raging fire or clouds. Later, as I walked along the streets at the nightfall, I looked back from a crossroads and found that Paris really deserved its reputation as the Capital of Flowers.

From the corner of the street, I realised that it was not actually a crossroads but a street about 40 yards wide and leading off in all directions. In the middle of the street were tracks for the coming and going of trams, and on either side of the tram tracks were lanes for motor vehicles. Outside the lanes for motor vehicles were lanes for carriages and bicycles, outside of which were pavements for pedestrians. Shops and buildings stood outside the sidewalks. In the middle of sidewalks stood rows of trees of nearly the same height at the same intervals. Occasionally between the trees, there were situated simple looking toilets, which did not stink at all because pipes were installed to provide water for the flush after use. There were so many people on the streets and the vehicles moved so fast that one could not cross the street from one side to the other without good eyesight and fast steps. Nearly all the streets were the same width and all buildings were of the same height and construction. As a result, I failed to find my way back when I wanted to go back. I went to a nearby café and drank some coffee. Afterwards, I found a nearby hotel for the night, where I climbed up over ten floors before I could find my room. When I looked arounds at the crossroads, the sun had not yet set, but the lights were already on, which made the whole city as bright as daytime. From all of this we could see the high development of infrastructures in Paris.

200. 巴黎分上中下之三层

巴黎为法国北境盆地之中心，塞纳河由东南而西北去，马路、铁路异常整洁，人烟日密，高楼峻房因之日多。于是由邱陵修来火车道之及市者，则以铁柱高架之，而有高出在平常之住房以上数层者。此层可便于居高楼住户之往来，可谓之上层巴黎。居于平地者，可谓之中层巴黎。然交通过繁，而汽车、电车、摩托车及人力车、马车，不但规模都大，而行驶又更速。虽街道宽阔，而仍觉来往不便。所以以后有效蚂蚁之穿地者，将巴黎市之地下数丈深处，凿有若干之隧道，使电车无昼无夜，行于其中。其隧道每隔里许，凿一透洞，通于上面，以便乘车者之出入也。余乘是等车时，曾由塞纳河之东而入，从地中隧道乘车数站，穿过河底，至塞纳河之西而始出，然为时不逾两点钟。此可谓之下层巴黎也。

孙干：欧战华工记
Records of Chinese Labourers in European War by Sun Gan

Three Layers of Paris

Located in the centre of the basin in northern France and with the Seine River flowing through from southeast to northwest, Paris had unusually clean roads and railways, a large population and rapidly increasing high buildings. Railway from the hills was constructed by erecting high iron pillars across Paris, which were several feet higher than normal houses. Specially designed for the convenience of residents in the high-rise buildings, this layer of Paris could be called the Upper Paris. The layer at the ground level could be called the Middle Paris, which had many more vehicles and heavier traffic. With large numbers of automobiles, trams, motorcycles and carriages coming and going at fast speeds, it was often difficult to travel even though the streets were already wide enough. So came the third layer of Paris which was built underground. By imitating ants' building their nests underground, tunnels were excavated at the depth of over thirty feet for trams to travel day and night. A hole leading to the ground was excavated every a few miles apart in the tunnel for passengers to get in and out. I once entered a tunnel from the east side of the Seine River and got out from the about two hours later after traveling several stops underneath the city. This was called the Underground Paris.

201. 旅馆住一夜

民国八年七月十三日晚八点钟，余到巴黎一旅馆中，入门后不数武，即随其店伙，盘旋而登楼，虽高二十余层，住于一房间内，尚不及楼之半。房间之内，如电灯、电铃及脸盆、手巾、肥皂、镜子、牙刷、牙粉等等一切，无不应有尽有。房间之门外，另有便所一间，其中之自来水随手而到。观其设备，可谓清洁而便利。其被褥枕席，皆为上等材料之所作者，宜乎每人每夜自四元至八元之房价也。

Staying a Night in a Hotel

At 8 p.m. on 13 July 1919, I arrived at a hotel in Paris. When I entered the hotel, an attendant came and led me up a large circular staircase to my room. The hotel was 20 Storeys high and I lived in a room located halfway up the building. Everything was available inside the room, including electric lights, electric bells, a washbasin, towels, soap, mirrors, toothbrush and toothpowder. Outside the door of the room, there was a washroom, where the tap water came out when people's hand approached. All the facilities were clean and convenient. The bedding, pillows and mattresses were all made of superior materials, suitable for the room rate of four to eight yuan.

202. 游康靠尔

康靠尔者，乃巴黎繁华区之一胜境也。七月十四日，为法国之国庆日。吾于是日早起，支旅馆房价十佛郎，而出旅馆欲乘电车而赴康靠尔。然至大街，即见大街之人，轰轰烈烈，而来往摩托车行驶之迅速，真令人

孙干：欧战华工记
Records of Chinese Labourers in European War by Sun Gan

有欲停不得，欲进不能之概。街中之电车，每两辆作一行，一同行每开约行八九丈而即一停，每停约分半钟，而即又开，此乃以便客旅之上下也。虽距八九丈之遥，而停一次，然前者刚去，后者又来。来路如此，往路亦如此，双轨道上之电车，一来一往，一刻不停，交通之便利，为何如也！

余上电车，见车中前有一法人掌开车，二人在车之中，一掌收款及卖票，一管存款而管账。车之上空，有来往电线二条，欲使电车开时，掌开车之人，将车前端之长杆直竖之，上触空中之电线，则电气由杆而下，以引车前之机关转动，车乃随之立即前行。欲使电车停止时，亦掌开车之人，将直竖之引电杆拉下，使其不与空中之电线接触，而车前之电力立断，电车随之而停止矣。

余因初次见电车，更不知其售票之手续，又不明法人之语言，是以甫上车时，即见他人每票支铜元二枚。余亦随之买一票而支铜元二枚。到一站时，他人下车，余亦随之而下车，有时余在街中且走且问，有时对电车时上时下，此皆因地理不熟，不懂言语之故所致也。然傍午始达康靠尔之塞纳河东岸，其地旷场宽阔。塞纳河上之桥，该为水门汀所制成者，无处而不坚固，无处而不整洁。塞纳河东之旷场中，花圃无数，其最可观者，为二喷水池。池之中各有高台一座，高台之上又分三层，各层俱有奇花异草。自远望之，如一水塔然。水自池之周围各个石狮口中出，向池中塔之顶喷去。水落塔顶，然后由顶端之奇花异草上徐徐流下，淅淅沥沥而入于池。然虽满盈，而终不外溢，亦一大观也。

余复前行，经过凯旋门及许多花卉园后，至其众议院之旁。见约三丈余高之赭石耸立，始知为古代法人自埃及运来之方尖石，其形恰如一宝剑朝天而竖，诚法人巨大之纪念物也。及至康靠尔时，街衢为人所塞，而法人正于是日，开庆祝大会。其一切设备及其情形均不得见，惟闻炮声隆隆而已，惜哉！当时街旁之树上下亦人山人海，街中之售坐票者，每一人有值三百佛郎者也，猗欤盛矣！于是余不得已，而探寻寓巴黎之中国青年会去矣。

华工日记
Chinese Labourer's Diaries

Touring Concorde

Concorde was a prosperous district of Paris as well as a place of great beauty. 14 July was the National Day of France. That morning I got up early and after paying the hotel bill of ten francs, I intended to go out to Concorde by tram. However, when I came out, I found the streets were crowded with bustling people and roaring motor vehicles. The motorcycles travelled so fast that I was confused as to whether I should stop or walk forward. The trams in the street, every two in a row, would stop for one or two minutes for passengers to get on or off after travelling only about 25-30 yards. After each stop, they would go on again. Thus, although it was 25-30 yards away, there were passengers coming and going at each stop. It was the same in both directions. The trams on the two tracks just kept coming and going all the time. How convenient the transportation was in Paris!

When I got on the tram, I saw a driver at the front and two conductors in the middle of the tram, one giving out the tickets and the other collecting the money. Above the tram were two electric wires. When the driver wanted the tram to move, he would erect the long pole at the front end of the tram to make it contact the wire in the air. In this way, electricity would go down along the pole to start the engine at the front of the tram and the tram would move forward immediately. To stop the tram, the driver would lower the vertical pole to make it lose its contact with the wire in the air. In this way the engine in the front of the tram would lose power and stopped.

It was the first time I had ever seen a tram and I did not know how to buy a ticket. I did not understand the language either. So when I got on the tram, I observed that the other passengers gave two copper coins for their tickets. I did the same, paying two copper coins for my ticket. Seeing the others getting off

孙干：欧战华工记
Records of Chinese Labourers in European War by Sun Gan

at a stop, I got off too. Sometimes I walked through the city streets, stopping occasionally to ask for directions, while at other times I just got on a tram and then got off again at the next stop. I did this because I was not familiar with the city and did not understand the language. Just before midday, I finally arrived at the Place de la Concorde on the east bank of the Seine River, where there was a very large open space. The bridge over the Seine River was made of cement and it was very strong and remarkably clean everywhere. In the open area on the east side of the Seine River, there were numerous flower beds and two most spectacular fountains. In each pool stood a high platform, above which stood another three layers filled with various exotic plants and flowers. Viewed from a distance, it was like a water tower with the water being sprayed from the mouth of stone lions situated around the pool into the upper tower in the pool and then slowly flowed down through the exotic flowers and plants and dripped into the pool again. Although the pool was full, the water in it would never overflow. It was really a wonder.

I continued my sightseeing and arrived nearby the House of Representatives after passing through the Arch of Triumph and many beautiful flower gardens. On seeing an 80-feet-high red granite column standing there in front of me, I knew that it was the Obelisk that had been brought from ancient Egypt by the French. Like a sword standing upright in the sky, it was an impressive monument. When I arrived at La Place de la Concorde, the streets were crowded with people. It turned out that the French were holding parties to celebrate their national day. I did not see any parades or the fine carriages, but I heard the sound of guns and artillery. What a pity! At that time, even on the trees beside the streets there were numerous people. The ticket sold in the middle of the street was worth 300 francs, which was due to the great number of visitors. So I decided to go to the YMCA building in Paris.

华工日记
Chinese Labourer's Diaries

203. 到寓巴黎之中国青年会

余游花都之时，适值其国庆日，是亦幸事。可惜言语不通，又无同伴，故未得见其纪念之仪式也。然不得不往寓于巴黎之中国基督教青年会，以便寻得一乡道。思想至此，逐以英语询问法人者数次，法人均答以不知。及最后遇一美国人，美国人立即从囊中取出纸笔，将中国基督教青年会之坐落，在某街某巷并将经过之街道，一一画出，而加以英之注解以指示余。余受其图以后，遂就其所画之视线，不到半点钟，而果寻得青年会矣。斯时也，余知美国人之对图画一科，亦必习之有素也。既至青年会，拜见其主任全绍文未遇，而见北平之石干事。叙谈良久，被彼指示，遂又得赴维塞亚之梗概矣。

China Youth Association in Paris

It was a lucky thing that my visit to the flower capital coincided with the National Day of France. But I did not witness the commemorative ceremony due to my inability to understand their language and my lack of companions. So I decided to go to the YMCA in Paris in order to find a guide. Along the way I asked several Frenchmen in English for directions, but none had any idea of where the YMCA was. Finally, I met an American, who immediately took out a pen and a piece of paper from his pocket and drew the precise location of the YMCA, including the name of the alley and the street number. He also drew all the streets I would pass along and marked them all with names and directional instructions in English. With his picture, I found the YMCA in less than half an hour. At that time, I realise that Americans also had a good knowledge of drawing and writing. Unfortunately, when I arrived at the YMCA, I could not find the secretary named Quan Shaowen, but I met Secretary Shi from Beiping. We talked for a long time and from him I also learnt about the way to the Palace of Versailles.

204. 乘地里电车

七月十四日十二点半钟，由中国青年会出，逾街二，至一十字道口，借问巡警而下隧道。斯时余想，既然不知其规矩，不明其手续，在何处候车，从何处买票，若一入地，谅必黑暗异常，如入地狱然也。适值一法少妇亦欲下隧道而乘车，彼乃在前领导余。余既入，见其中处处电灯明亮异常，随处一一指点帮助，而始知地里电车，乃下层之巴黎也。其建筑地里电车之法，即由其地上各街之十字路口，先挖隧道盘旋而下，至数丈深后，辟之使大，即为一站。不但一处如此，处处皆是如此，使各街口上下皆通，然后将下面凿为若干平行之洞，使之互相通达，复敷以车轨。虽然至深，洞中之墙壁，其坚固之状，非言语能形容之也。余乘三站，下车随他人而出，观其方向，始知已由塞纳河东，逾河而至河西矣。

Taking the Underground Tram

I left the YMCA at 12:30 on 14 July. After walking past two streets, I arrived at a crossroads where I asked a policeman for directions, where I went down into the tunnel. At that time, I knew nothing about its rules, procedures, where to wait for the train, and where to buy tickets. I thought it would be very dark in the tunnel just like being in the hell. There happened to be a Frenchwoman who was also getting down the tunnel to take the train. So I followed her. I saw there were extraordinary bright lights everywhere. With the help of the Frenchwoman, I got my ticket and boarded a train, knowing that I was on the underground Paris. The method of constructing the underground train was to dig tunnels that circled down at the intersections of streets on the ground, and then to make them bigger at the depth of tens of yards as a stop. This was done only in one place but everywhere so that all the streets were connected both on and under the ground. Parallel holes were dug out to connect each other and then rails were laid. Deep as it was, the walls within the holes were very solid, quite beyond any word. After taking the train for three stops, I got off with lots of other people. Looking around, I realised that we had arrived on the west side of the Seine River from the east of it.

205. 世界之最高电台

余至巴黎，本拟参观其名胜，又适值其国庆日，路易十四之皇宫，欲往一观，非是日均不开放也。余至维赛亚车站，欲买票而不见其票房。欲待之，又恐误车。反复思之，总觉以不失其皇宫开放之机会为上策。于是，虽未买车票，而先上车矣。法人之在车中等候者，几乎满座，各在谈天。忽全车之人，一齐肃立，余不知其故，亦不得不随之而起。余

孙干：欧战华工记
Records of Chinese Labourers in European War by Sun Gan

甫起之际，见一妇人，携一网包入。既而妇人坐定，大家亦陆续而坐。始知西人之看待妇女，皆同其孱弱，而处处让之。非若吾国之乘火车者，虽壮年男子，一人占据二人地位，其余无地位者，虽老弱亦不顾也，又何论及妇女耶！

至开车后，向西南行，约六七里，即见世界最高之电台，高矗云霄。电台之构造，座为方形，约占地数十亩。座之高约有七八丈，由座而上，亦为方形，均以铁梁构成之。其顶峻极于天，挂有国旗，远望之飘飘然奇观也！至下二点钟，而达维塞亚。法之妇女，代余办理补票手续毕，遂出站。

Highest Radio Station in the World

When I arrived in Paris, I had planned to visit its most famous sights. Because that day happened to be the National Day of France the Palace of Louis XIV was open only on that day, I decided to have a visit to it. When I got to the Versailles Station, I wanted to buy a ticket but failed to find the ticket office. I intended to wait for a while, but I was afraid that I would miss the train. After careful consideration, I decided it would be the best policy was not to miss the chance of visiting the palace. So I got on the train without buying the ticket. Nearly all the seats were occupied and the Frenchmen on the train were all busy chatting. Suddenly, all people on the train stood up. Although I did not know why, I just followed them and stood up too. Just as I rose to my feet, I saw a woman with a pack enter the carriage. When the woman sat down, everyone else sat down one after another again. From this, I began to know that Westerners treated women as gentle people and gave courtesy and precedence to them everywhere. This was quite different from train passengers in China, where one person would occupy two seats even though they were strong young men, never considering the old and the weak, let alone women.

The train started to move off, heading for the southwest. After the train travelled a couple of miles, I saw the tallest radio station in the world, soaring high into the sky. It had a square pedestal which was about 70 to 80 feet high and covered an area of about 1600 acres. The building on the pedestal was square too, all made up of crossed iron beams. With its top high in the sky and the national flag of France flying, the radio station was really a wonderful sight. I arrived at Versailles at about two o'clock in the afternoon. After paying for ticket extension with the help of a Frenchwoman, I eventually left the station.

206. 路易十四之皇宫

七月十四为法之国庆日，余于民国八年是日下午二点，自巴黎趁火车而达维赛亚路易十四之宫殿前门，见有极高峻之铁栏。及入门，为一数十亩之大旷场。行至旷场之后，则入二门。二门之内，其庭堂面积较小于前。惟其二铜像立于左右二高台之上，巍巍峨峨，其骁勇若赫赫然自天降者，盖为路易十四及其始祖之肖像也。又前进，始为路易十四之宫殿。观其雕梁画栋，规模之宏大，廊牙回环玲珑之技巧，自远望之，直如黄花一丛，丰艳异常者也。谁能不以天宫目之耶？余自其楼前，委曲婉转，而至宫阙之后，遂上升至一高台，台中之椅，不止数千。高台之旁，又有长方池塘一鉴，面积约有数亩。其中莲花虽不多，而其澄清之水，不涌不泻，诚明光若镜者也。立此高台，向后望之，则远为若断若续之海，有小舟之来往于其中。近为曲折回环之花圃，及参差错落之

孙干：欧战华工记
Records of Chinese Labourers in European War by Sun Gan

亭阁。两侧又为一望无垠之森林也。

斯时也，余想宜乎普法战后之和约，德帝成立之宣布，及威廉一世之即位，皆就此地以行之也。吾由是台而下，复往前行，拟观一切之花卉，于是盘回往复，层层下降，所见之瑶草琪花，左左右右，莫不令人步步称胜也。瑶台垒阙，随处栖憩焉。直至下四点钟，余逐出宫门，乘车而还巴黎。然此去尚未得窥全豹者，以其未曾入宫殿之内，以览其蕴藏之一切也。

Palace of Louis XIV

I arrived at the front gate of the Palace of Louis XIV at 2 p.m. on 14 July 1919, the National Day of France. The front gate was surrounded by high iron fences. Inside the gate was an open space with an area of several acres. After walking across the open space, I arrived at the second gate, inside which was a smaller courtyard where stood two towering bronze statues on high platforms. They were the statues of Louis XIV and his first ancestor, whose valiancy and majesty were very impressive. A few steps forward from there was the Palace of Louis XIV, a richly ornamented building with carved beams and a richly painted facade. The magnificent scale and exquisite workmanship throughout the winding corridors made it like a cluster of gorgeous yellow chrysanthemums. It was just like a heavenly palace! From the front of this building, I wound my way to its rear and then climbed up to a high platform where there were thousands of chairs. Beside the high platform, there was a rectangular pond with an area of several acres. Although there were some lotus flowers in the pond, the clear water was very quiet and bright, shining like a mirror. Standing on this high platform, I looked back and found in the distance there was an intermittent sea, where ships and boats came and went, while closer to me there was a flower garden with winding corridors and various pavilions. A vast forest stretched out on both sides of the palace.

At the same time, I thought it was really an appropriate place for the signing of the peace treaty after the war between France and Prussia, the announcement of the founding of the German Empire and the enthronement of William I. Coming down the platform, I went on to enjoy all the flowers. I walked back and forth as I climbed up and down the stairs. The beautiful flowers and green grass all along the way amazed me as I took each step. With so many ornamental buildings and pavilions, people could take a rest almost anywhere. I strolled in the palace until it was four o'clock in the afternoon when I was told it was time to leave the Palace. I departed through the entrance and returned to Paris again by train. Unfortunately, I did not get to see the entire palace as I did not go inside the palace and see everything in them.

207. 巴黎市之摩托车

余自参观维塞亚后归时，已下五点余钟。自己想到，天既向暮，路又不熟，语言更不适用，当以何法以行也？于是坐于塞纳河岸之桥栏上，观来往如织之摩托车，每至桥边而即一停，于一停之际，旅客有上车者，有下车者。余乃知巴黎市上之摩托车，往来之人可任意雇赁也。不然，此处来往之客不能任意上下也。车能任意雇赁，现在天已将晚，余可就近一试。

孙干：欧战华工记
Records of Chinese Labourers in European War by Sun Gan

余思至此，遂行至桥上。时值一车甫停，余乃登车而坐，司机之人，回首向余咕咕噜噜，余终不解其语。余遂答之曰："余欲往巴黎市之北车站也。"须臾车开，至六点余钟，而果至巴黎市之北车站矣。余支给以两佛郎之车价而下车。其车前面之旋转机，系指其所行道路之远近，以标其价目之多少者也。

Motorcycles in Paris

When I returned from my visit to Versailles, it was already five o'clock in the afternoon and it was nearly dark. Since I was not familiar with the city and I could not speak French, how could I find my way to my place? I sat on the railings of the bridge over the Seine River and watched the coming and going of motorcycles. I found that the motorcycles would stop every time they came to the bridge, where passengers getting on and off sometimes. I knew that motorcycles in Paris could be hired for journeys. Otherwise, visitors could not be able to come and go as they pleased. Since everyone could hire the motorcycles and it was late, I decided to try it myself.

At this thought, I got up and went onto the bridge. Just as I came there, a motorcycle happened to stop there. So I went up and got onto it immediately. The driver of the motorcycle looked back at me and said something, but I did not understand what he was saying. So I said to him, "I want to go to the railway station of Gare du Nord Paris." Soon the motorcycle started and we arrived at the railway station a few minutes past six o'clock. I gave the driver two francs and got off the motorcycle. There was a revolving machine at the front of the motorcycle that recorded the distance travelled on the road and also the amount of fare to pay for the journey.

华工日记
Chinese Labourer's Diaries

208. 巴黎普通之饭店

巴黎市上，食物也，果品也，或摆为摊，或沿街叫卖，茶房酒肆随处皆有，大致与吾国相同。七月十四日晚，余自维塞亚至巴黎，遂至一普通饭店，作一尝试。既入其店，观其煎熬燔灸之法，与夫米、面、油、盐、酒、酱、糖、醋、肉类等之材料，与吾国无甚大异。其为菜也，或鲜或干，或炸或蒸，亦每相间。不过中国饭馆中多用箸与匙，而彼皆用叉与刀也。此亦饮食习惯之不同耳。一入馆，即闻谈笑之声，观其欢呼之状，尤胜于我国人数倍也。

Ordinary Paris Hotels

In Paris, food and fruits were sold either at stalls or by hawkers along streets and there were tea houses and wine shops everywhere, which was much the same as in our country. On the evening of 14 July, I went into an ordinary restaurant to see what it was like after returning from Versailles. As I entered the restaurant, I noticed their methods of cooking were by frying, boiling, roasting or steaming, and also their choices of ingredients included rice, flour, oil, salt, wine, sauces, sugar, vinegar, and meats. This was not very different from those of our country. The dishes they cooked, whether they were fresh or dry, fried or steamed, were also similar to ours. However, in Chinese restaurants chopsticks and spoons were often used whereas in French restaurants, knives and forks were used. This was also the difference in eating habits. As soon as I entered the restaurant, I heard the talks and laughter of the diners, whose noise and excitement were several times louder than those of the people in our country.

209. 自巴黎归

民国八年七月十四日晚，宿巴黎市北之旅馆中。翌晨早起，支法之纸币二十佛郎，合祖国洋银八元。到一饭馆，买饭少许，通常之饭，即面包猪肉，或牛肉或牛奶油等。食后，往北车站。买车票时，人虽甚多，却井井有序。上车后向东北行，将十二点下车。下午两点，到青年会矣。凡吾同工，无不相来问讯。张君翕如更使人达知本队队长，使其放心。

Return from Paris

On the night of 14 July 1919, I stayed in a hotel located in the north of Paris. The next morning, I got up early and paid twenty francs of paper money, equivalent to eight silver yuan of Chinese currency. I then went into a restaurant for breakfast, where a variety of food including bread, pork, beef and cheese were offered. After breakfast, I went to the Gare du Nord Railway Station. Although many people were waiting to buy tickets there, they remained in good order. The train I took travelled toward the direction of northeast and arrived at my destination at 12 o'clock at noon. By the time I returned to the

YMCA, it was already two o'clock in the afternoon. All my fellow labourers came to me to enquire about my trip. Zhang Xiru even sent labourers to inform the captain of our brigade of my safe arrival and tell him not to rest assured.

210. 社会教育之效力

余自花都归队,仍帮助青年会办理社会教育,如汉文也、算术也、地理也、注音字母也、拳术也等等一切。虽有时为师者不暇为之上班,而工人自行集合而上班。较深之班,亦可代理教授较浅者,岂非办社会教育之效力耶!每晚于上班之后,仍请工人之会唱者,或唱二簧,或唱笛梆,或唱西皮,或说大鼓京腔,工人莫不个个高兴也。

Effect of Social Education

After I returned to my brigade from Paris, I continued to help the YMCA with its social education such as the teaching of Chinese, arithmetic, geography, phonetics, boxing and other games. Sometimes the teachers were too busy working for the British to take classes, but labourers would still gather on their own to attend the class. In such cases, students from the advanced class would teach students in the preliminary class. Wasn't this the perfect system of social education! Every evening when the class started, those who were good at singing were invited to sing songs from Chinese local operas such as *Erhuang*, *Dibang*, *Xipi*, and *Peking Dagu*. All of the labourers were very happy.

孙干：欧战华工记
Records of Chinese Labourers in European War by Sun Gan

211. 看英人演剧

英人亦恒演剧于其青年会场，而请华工往观。其会场较中国青年会为大，然观其表演也、乐器也、服装也，均非东亚人所习见常闻。每次往观，辄少兴趣，卒至乘兴而往者，往往败兴而返。由此可知，西人之对东亚之音乐与戏剧，亦一定不能发生兴趣也。

Watching British Plays

The British also often stage plays at the meeting place of the YMCA and Chinese labourers were invited to attend. Compared with our Chinese local operas, the venue for the British plays were larger and the performances, musical instruments and costumes were all strange to East Asians. Chinese labourers seemed to have little interest in them. Every time the labourers went to see a show of English plays, they usually went there excitedly but returned dissatisfied. It could be assumed from this that the Westerners must show no interest in the music or plays of East Asians either.

华工日记
Chinese Labourer's Diaries

212. 看华工玩藏艺

吾曾办理青年会，本基督耶酥救世之主义，使社会之人，由其已能之事，欢乐而发展之，而及其未能；由其不正当之事，渐渐趋于正当。所以华工之中，何人有一技之长，务希使之供献于大家，使大家得益，令大家欢喜。华工队中，大约百分之七十系农夫，百分之十系商人，百分之十是兵士，百分之七是匠艺，其余百分之三是说书者、唱戏者、玩杂耍者、打拳卖艺者、读书者等等。青年会既为大家服务，为大家娱乐，所以常常搜罗会说书者、唱戏者、玩杂耍打拳卖艺者，请到会中，各奏其所能，各现其技艺，务期大家一见而欣赏之也。

一日下午，于闲暇之时，请一会玩藏艺者，至一旷场中。其人手持毛毯一床，两手捻两端，使毯下垂，以表现毯中毫无藏物也。更使正面反面反覆看毕，彼乃在场中来往两趟，就地打一跟头，立刻起立，而其手中遂端清水一大碗，凡围观者没不称奇也。

Watching Magic of Chinese Labourers

From my working experience in the YMCA, I learnt that the YMCA was based on Jesus Christ's doctrine of salvation so that people in society could joyfully develop what they could do and achieve what they previously could not or make them come on the right track from wrongdoings. Therefore, we tried to encourage anyone among the Chinese labourers who had a speciality to share it with all labourers so that it would benefit and delight all. In our brigade of Chinese labourers, about seventy percent were farmers, ten percent businessmen, ten percent soldiers, and seven percent craftsmen. The remaining three percent were storytellers, opera singers, jugglers, street acrobats, book lovers and others. Aiming to serve and entertain all labourers, the YMCA often tried to recruit people who were good at storytelling, opera singing, vaudeville playing and street performing to join the association and asked them to show their skills for the pleasure of the labourers.

One afternoon, we invited a labourer good at magic to an open field in our spare time to perform some tricks. Holding a blanket, he entwined both ends of it with his hands to make it hang loose, attempting to show everyone that nothing was hidden inside it. After asking some of the audience to check both the front and back of the blanket a couple of times, he walked back and forth in the open field twice. He then performed a full somersault on the ground and rose to his feet immediately but now with a bowl of water in his hand. The audience were truly amazed and applauded loudly.

213. 青年会总干事全绍文先生到会演讲

华工队中，青年会干事固天天对工人服务，而总青年会之总干事及巡行干事，亦常常到各华工队中帮助演讲也。华工一百零二队中，吾与张君翕如天天服务以外，亦常常有人从总青年会来，帮助演讲。

一日，有青年会总干事全绍文先生到队中演讲。工人齐集后，全先生曰："吾此次之来与大家相见，心中觉得十分荣幸。但余知大家心中都想说什么了。"继则曰："大概都想说的话,就是我们何时还家呢?我们来到法国,时候已经不少,不但我们想着还家,看看家中老的少的,亲戚朋友,就是家中老少亲朋,也都想念我们。说我们家中游法国的人,都在外边受了不少的苦,费了不少的力。幸尔欧战告终,究竟他们何时归家,使我一家老少,再得团圆呢?您想咱们此次来到法国,虽然受些寒冷,挨些饥饿,然而为国家增上不少的光荣。因为咱们国家倘若不加入协约,不着大家来此费心劳力,此次大战告终,我们国家定吃无限之亏啊!现在我们既加入了协约,华工弟兄们帮着打了胜仗,而不但我们国家当时得到平安,即华工之功劳亦乘此扬名世界。不独德奥之赔款不用归还,即英法等国之赔款,亦因大家来此作工而退让。所以大家此次之来,对国家,对世界,是很有光彩的啊!大家现在在此,仍然得好好作工。能用功的,还是好好用功,以待英国以后将我们好好送还中国,那就是人人所盼望的。英人送还大家之日期,我们虽然尚不知道,我想大概不出两三个月。现在大家可平心静气,等到平安回到中国再见面吧。"

全先生说罢,众同工一时掌声雷动,个个欢欣。盖因自到欧洲冒险二年余,现在听说对欧战胜利,国家得些光彩,即回家日亦尚不远,所以人人闻此信息,一时欢欣,不胜雀跃之至焉。

Address by Quan Shaowen, Secretary-General of YMCA

In each brigade of the Chinese Labour Corps, not only did the local YMCA representatives serve the labourers every day, but the Secretary-General and other officials from the General YMCA also often came to different brigades of Chinese labourers to made addresses. In Brigade 102 of Chinese Labour Corps, Zhang Xiru and I served the labourers every day. Besides,

Records of Chinese Labourers in European War by Sun Gan

people from the General YMCA also came to address the labourers.

One day, Mr. Quan Shaowen, Secretary-General of the YMCA, came to our brigade to address the labourers. He said, "It's a great honour for me to speak to you all today. I know what you want to say in your hearts." He continued, "You all want to ask when we shall return home. We've been in France for a long time. I know that all of us want to return home soon. I also know that our families, relatives and friends miss us very much. They say that those who travelled to France have suffered many hardships and toiled hard whilst living abroad. Fortunately, the European War has ended, but when will they come home and reunite with us again?" He then said to us, "In France, although we've suffered times of cold and starvation, we've also won a lot of honour for our country. If our country had not joined the Entente countries and we hadn't volunteered to work here, our country would probably have suffered a great loss when the war ended. Now that our country has joined the Entente countries and we Chinese labourers have helped win the war, our country has got peace at the moment and the contribution of Chinese labourers to the victory of the war has also become well-known all other the world. Our country now needn't return the reparations for Germany and Austria. Even the reparations for English and France have been reduced because of our work here. Therefore, our work here this time has brought honour not only to our country but also to the world. For now, we still need to work hard here. If we can work, we should work hard so that the British will organise your return back home to China as soon as possible. This is what everyone is hoping for. Although we don't know the date when the British will send us home, I believe it will be in only two- or three-months' time. Now, though, we must all remain calm and wait for our safe return to China."

On hearing these words from Mr. Quan, all my fellow labourers applauded and rejoiced. Since leaving home for Europe, we had risked our lives in Europe for over two years. Now we were told to have made great contributions to the victory of the European War and brought glory to our country, which meant that we would soon return to our country. Therefore, on hearing the news all the labourers were overjoyed for quite a while.

214. 华工感激青年会干事

在法华工一百零二队之工人，自从听总青年会干事全绍文先生演讲，英人将送华工回国后，不但本队队长相继亦公告，明示其事，即本队中青年会干事张君翕如于诸班上课之时，亦欲结束其所教之课程。于是工人因之各动故乡之思，纷纷酝酿还家之期为时不远矣。然工人对于青年会干事张君，知将欲离别，而不得长久同处，于其汉文、算学、地理、拳术、注音字等等功课，均不得再有研究，再有进步，所以每见张君益觉亲密。自是以后，工人于工作之暇，每日不论早晚，一有余暇，不用青年会招集，按时自即相率而至。其对于青年会感情之浓厚，不言可知。既而有人焉提议敬送祝辞对联各一副，以志欧战时在法作工，受张干事之陶冶，而嘱余为之作其辞。余因自己才浅，再三推辞，而终不得。遂为之作祝词一短篇、对联一副，其文如下：

颂曰：翕如先生，奉天姓张。离别祖国，远涉重洋。栉风沐雨，来欧战场。劳其心血，启我天良。谆谆教诲，善诱有方。汉文算术，指导颇详。注音地理，日就月将。吾侪虽愚，进步非常。长我知识，为国增光。先生之风，山高水长。

孙干：欧战华工记
Records of Chinese Labourers in European War by Sun Gan

对联：

恺悌堪为纲，尽忠国家有道义；
仁慈能施编，爱戴华工多恩情。

一日，一百零二队全体工人开一大会，工人先齐集一处，然后将以绸子书就祝词一幅及对联一副，共往青年会所恭送于张君。张君亦以茶点款待，热闹一场。当时张君亦一一握手而散。

Gratitude of Chinese Labourers towards YMCA Secretaries

After listening to the address by Mr. Quan Shaowen of the YMCA, all labourers of Brigade 102 of Chinese Labour Corps in France knew that the British would send them back to China soon. Following Mr Quan, the brigade officers also made some announcements. Mr Zhang Xiru, our YMCA secretary in Brigade 102, told us in his class that he would finish the subjects he taught soon. As a result, the labourers' homesickness was aroused quickly and all began to think that it would not be long before they could return home. Another concern for many labourers was that Mr. Zhang, our YMCA secretary, would soon leave us and no further lessons would be given in Chinese, arithmetic, geography, boxing or any other subjects. The labourers had grown so fond of Mr. Zhang that they did not want him to leave. From that day on, the labourers arrived at the classes on time every day no matter how late it was after they had finished their own work, without the calling of the YMCA. From it we could also see the strong feelings of workers towards the YMCA. Later, some of the

华工日记
Chinese Labourer's Diaries

labourers suggested that we write Mr Zhang a couplet and a short message to thank him for the friendship and education he had given us whilst working in France during the European War. I was asked to write something for him on everyone's behalf. However, due to my lack of talent and learning, I declined several times but had to accept it later. I wrote a short thank you message and a poem as follows:

The thank you message read as follows:

Master Xiru was born in Fengtian in a family of Zhang. Leaving his motherland, he travelled across the oceans all along. Despite the wind and rain, he arrived at the European War battleground. Great pains he took to enlighten the goodness with which we were born. With great patience and earnestness, he instructed us to go on. For Chinese and arithmetic, he explained in detail for us to catch on. For geography and phonetic scripts, he taught for months with dance and song. Great progress has been made though the student is as slow as a moron. Enriching our knowledge and winning honour for our country he insisted on. His influence is as mountain high and as river long.

Couplet:

With friendliness serving as the principle, he considers it a moral obligation to be loyal to our country.

With benevolence applied to organisations, he deems it universal fraternity to love the Chinese labourers.

One day, all labourers of Brigade 102 held a meeting. The labourers gathered and then walked together to the YMCA to send the letter and the couplet, which had been carefully prepared on a silk fabric, to Mr. Zhang. He entertained us all with refreshments and we had a good time together. When we left, Mr Zhang shook hands with each of us one by one.

孙干：欧战华工记
Records of Chinese Labourers in European War by Sun Gan

215. 受张君翕如之赠送纪念品

欧战告终，协约与联盟两方条约议成。战场之平垫，武器之整理，均大致就序。工人方面，亦各思还家。所以人人都想于回家时，可以何物为纪念品也。是时也，张君翕如亦往巴黎买到花都名胜画若干张，一巨幅赠送于余。其中如凯旋门、法众议院之大楼、世界最高之无线电台等等，凡属巴黎之著名之古迹，莫不有之，以表其与余离别之厚意也。

Souvenir Presented by Zhang Xiru

The European War came to an end after the Triple Entente and the Central Powers negotiated and reached an agreement. The battlefields were being levelled off and the weapons were recovered and sorted out. Everything was beginning to get back in order. The Chinese labourers were all thinking about returning home and began looking for souvenirs to take with them. Mr Zhang Xiru went to Paris and bought a number of landscape paintings, a large one of which he presented to me as a gift and a token of our friendship. In the painting there were many of the famous Paris landmarks such as the Arc de Triomphe, the French House of Representatives and the world's highest radio station.

华工日记
Chinese Labourer's Diaries

216. 为余书荐信以备回国后作事之用

一日,张君翕如问余曰:"孙先生回国后愿再与弟在一处,同作工可乎?"余曰:"弟前不知耶稣是何许人,基督教是何主义,迄今始知耶稣救主、救人、救世之大概。吾国现在衰弱已极,皆因人人不能效法救主耶稣牺牲自己之心力,而救国救人。若果人人如先生之从耶稣救主,则真能使人人渐渐知道爱国此等工作。弟实在佩服,实在愿同先生在一处。但是弟家中,不但父母年寿高大,即子女年幼,亦正待需人教养,恐因以上所说,致余不得与先生同在一处也。"彼又曰:"汝家中在经济方面状况如何?"余曰:"虽不宽裕,亦能支持耳。"张君曰:"余写一信,汝携之归,以备无事作时,持之到各处之教会,找点工作,借以糊口,余可作一担保也。"余曰:"先生费心,余先谢谢是等厚意。"翌日,彼遂写英文荐信一封与余。爱余如是,余焉得不感激之耶!

Recommendation Letter for My Future Work in China

One day, Zhang Xiru asked me, "Mr. Sun, would you like to continue working with me when we return to China?" I replied, "I didn't know who Jesus was or what Christianity was. Till today I've only know something about how Jesus would be the saviour of mankind and of the world. It is because our people failed to follow the example of Jesus to sacrifice themselves to save the nation and its people that our country is now so weak. If everyone believed in Jesus Christ, they would gradually be made more aware of how to love each other and their country. I really admire you and would like to work with you, but in my family I still have my elderly parents to take care of and younger children to bring up. Therefore, I'm afraid I will not be able to work with you." Then he asked again, "How about the financial situation in your family?" I answered, "We are not very well off, but we are still able to support ourselves." Mr. Zhang then said, "I'll write you a letter of recommendation. You can take it home in case you are in need of a job in the church for a living. I will be your reference." I replied, "Thank you for your kindness, Mr Zhang." The next day, he wrote me a letter of recommendation in English. He was so kind to me. How grateful I was to him!

217. 临别赠言

当欧战告后之八九月,各华工队皆酝酿还家。一百零二队中之青年会,亦整理一切什物运往他处,所有工人之功课亦渐结束。一日,与张君闲谈,张君曰:"孙先生对于西人之文明,视吾祖国为何如?"余曰:"西人之科学与教育程度,吾国之人非不能之。不过还须复有数十年之时日也。所难能者,惟西人之信仰耶稣及其品格,乃为吾国复有数十年尚不能及之也。"张君曰:"你知道我们祖国之人,处于现代,可谓危险已极。然非国人跟从救主耶稣不能认识上帝,又焉得有纯洁之信仰,以锻炼其纯洁之思想耶!至于身体方面,头脑之清楚,耳目之聪明,亦为吾人所当注意。西人从来各个人都有纯洁之信仰,又有常常沐浴之习惯,

华工日记
Chinese Labourer's Diaries

所以其发生均有高尚之品格。以后加以良好之教育，其程度焉得不出世界人之上？君返国后，望不但贵府老幼都借着耶酥认识上帝，即西人之每两日洗澡一次，亦当效法。万望先生注意，不知以为然否？因为人若认识上帝，思想即无邪僻。思想既无邪僻，志操始克纯正矣。身若时常洗涤秽垢，即不沾染秽垢。既不沾染，魂魄一定清爽矣。一国之中，人人志操纯正，气魄清爽，其国其家，方得自然之乐趣焉。深愿先生熟思而实行之也可！"余曰："斯言至善，吾夙有志愿学也。"

Farewell Words

In the August and September following the end of the European War, all brigades of Chinese labourers were planning to return home. The YMCA in Brigade 102 also sorted things out to have them transported elsewhere. All classes for the labourers were gradually coming to an end. One day, I chatted with Mr. Zhang and he said, "What do you think of the western civilisation in comparison with that of our motherland?" I said, "It is not impossible for Chinese people to achieve such levels of science and education as that of the westerners, but it'll take decades of time. The only thing that will be difficult to achieve is the faith of the Westerners and their character, which I think is beyond the reach of our country for many more decades." Mr. Zhang said, "You know, people of our motherland in modern times are in great danger. However, if our people don't follow the Saviour Jesus and don't believe in God, how could they have a pure faith and exercise a pure mind? Physically, we Chinese should also pay attention to the clarity of mind, the sharpness of eyes and ears. Westerners have always had the pure faith and a habit of bathing frequently. Thus, most people have a high moral character from birth. Besides, they receive good education later in their lives. How is it impossible for them to stand out in the world? I hope that when you return to China, all your family can know God through Jesus Christ and can even follow the practice of taking a bath every other day. I hope you can do that. Do you agree with me? For if one knows God, his mind will be away from evil things. Only when one has no evil mind can he have noble moral integrity. If you wash away dirt regularly, you won't be contaminated by dirt. Without contamination, your soul must be pure and clean. If everyone in a country is noble in moral integrity and clean in soul, both his family and his country can enjoy the pleasure of nature. I sincerely hope you'll think this over and practice it well!" I then said to him, "What you say are words of the utmost wisdom and I've been inspired to learn from them."

218. 至友黄君之赠纪念品

民国八年八月，华工各队均预备送工人还中国。工人多半亦都惦念家乡，是以自买金镑者有之，买金戒溜者有之，买金表者有之，买电光表者有之，买物送朋友者亦有之。一日，黄君世恩问曰："吾曹还家，当以何物为可带归以作纪念，买金钱乎，买戒溜乎？"余曰："纪念物之可带者，可于两方面定之：第一方面，凡在中国能买到者不带也；第二方面，凡于公众国家无利益者亦不带也。"黄君曰："余之意亦然。现今大家之所购者，如金表、戒溜、金镑等物，到祖国有钱均能买也。如德造之钢盔，在祖国恐买不到，乃是余之所欲带者也。但不知君之欲带之纪念物为何？"余曰："德之氯气炮帽，为国人之所当知而仿造者，是余所

华工日记
Chinese Labourer's Diaries

愿带者也。"黄君曰:"余更为君刻镌花笔筒一对,兄愿带欤?"余遂道谢其费心。数日后,黄君果以铜炮廓,上刻花纹笔筒一对赠于余,以备带归以作纪念品矣。

Souvenir from My Friend Mr. Huang

In August 1919, the eighth year of the Republic of China, all brigades of the Chinese Labour Corps were being prepared to travel back to China. Most of the labourers missed their hometowns and many had bought gold sovereigns, gold rings, gold watches, wrist watches, or other things as gifts for their friends. One day, labourer Huang Shien asked me, "What do you think we should buy as souvenirs to take home? Sovereigns? Or gold rings?" I said, "The things to take home as souvenirs should be based on two principles. The first one is that we never take anything that can be bought in China. The second is that we should never take anything that is of no interest to the public or the country." Mr. Huang said, "I agree with you. I see that most people buy gold watches, gold rings and sovereigns that can easily be bought in China if they have enough money. I think the steel helmet made by the Germans cannot be bought in our motherland. This is what I plan to take with me. What are the souvenirs you intend to take with you?" I asked. "I want to take the chlorine gas hood worn by the Germans, which is something the Chinese should know about and try to produce by themselves." Mr Huang then said, "I've also made a pair of engraved cartridge brush barrels for you. Would you like to take them home some the same to take home with you?" I thanked him for his kind offer and the trouble he had taken. A few days later, Mr Huang gave me a pair of cannon shell cartridges, beautifully engraved, for me to take home as souvenirs.

孙干：欧战华工记
Records of Chinese Labourers in European War by Sun Gan

219. 迁至喀李近郊装卸火车

民国八年八月下旬，张君翕如辞本队而去，临行时，众同工人等皆恋恋从行，彷徨不忍去。至翌日，余等亦迁往法极北境喀李市近郊之火车站装卸火车。既至，见火车站之旁靠近处有一煤油灌注场，观其煤油灌注房，亦为在吾祖国之所未见者。其建设为高三四丈，宽两丈余，长十余丈之大厦一所。内上层为两丈余高之一大铁筒，筒下均以铁梁架高之。大铁筒之上面，又有若干之小铁筒，从大厦以外，入而通于大铁筒之内。盖为煤油自他处来，经其中而入大铁筒者也。大铁筒之下，又有一丈余高，较细之小铁筒数根。每一小铁筒之上面，又有细铁管若干，上通入大铁筒之内，盖使承大铁筒内之煤油，由细铁管而下入小铁筒者也。小筒之下面，又各有细铁管若干条，自小铁筒出，下通近地处，末端安一水龙头，以便向煤油筒中灌注。

大厦内之四面，靠近墙壁，有一长木床，床中尽贯以圆轴若干条，一一排列。最初之轴较高，以后之轴逐渐稍低，使从头置物其上，则较高之轴一动，物即立移而至较低之轴上。是轴亦动，而物又移于更低之轴上。于是轴上之物，借众轴旋转之力，卒将其送至大厦之外，不用人力。所以大厦内之装油场，一开工时，每一水龙头下，需取筒工一人，灌油工一人，送油工一人。以上共需三人，全场若以三百水龙头计算之，则需工人共必千余。俱将所装就之油筒置于靠墙之轴床上，使其自行驱于场外，以便装入火车，运往战场或其他处。观其由屋内运而向屋外运物法，亦善矣哉！

以上所说，尽为煤油灌注场之设置如是也。至于能供千余人天天之灌注与战场之燃烧，其油之来源与其储藏，更为吾曹不得而知之也。

华工日记

Chinese Labourer's Diaries

Loading and Unloading Trains in the Suburb of Calais

In late August of 1919, the eighth year of the Republic of China, Mr Zhang Xiru left our brigade, when all labourers saw him off and were reluctant to part with him. The following day, all of us were also transferred to the railway station in the suburb of Calais at the northern border of France to load and unload trains. When we arrived there, we saw a kerosene filling yard nearby the railway station. The kerosene building was also something we had never seen in our homeland. It was a high-rise building with a height of about 40 feet, a width of over 20 feet and a length of more than 100 feet. Inside the building, the upper layer was a large iron cylinder of over 20 feet in height, which was elevated by iron beams below. On top of the large iron cylinder there were several smaller iron cylinders, which came from outside the building into the big iron cylinder. It turned out that the kerosene being supplied from elsewhere flowed through the small cylinders into the big one. Under the big iron cylinder, there were several smaller iron cylinders about 10 feet in height. On top of each there were a number of thin iron pipes, which were connected to the large iron cylinder so as to make the kerosene in the large cylinder flow through the thin pipes into the smaller cylinders. Under the smaller cylinders there were some thinner iron pipes that led down to ground level where faucets were installed to allow the kerosene to be poured into barrels.

On all sides of the building, there was a long, flat, wooden bed-like board close to the wall, inside which a number of circular shafts were orderly arranged. The first shaft was the highest and the other ones were slightly lower than the previous one. Therefore, the things put on the higher shaft would move to the next one immediately when the higher shaft moved. When this shaft moved, they were transferred to the next lower one. Thus, with the rotation of these shafts, the things on them would be transported outside the building without any use of manpower. Therefore, in the oil filling yard within the building, only three labourers were needed under each faucet: one to supply an empty barrel, one to fill it with oil and one to remove the barrel once filled. If there were a total of 300 faucets, more than a thousand labourers would be required. All the barrels were then placed on the shaft bed near the wall so that they could be transported out of the yard and loaded on trains to battlefields or other places. How clever the way of transporting things from inside to the outside of the building was!

What I have described here was just the setting up of the kerosene filling yard. As for the sources and storage of the fuel provided for the perfusion of thousands of people and the burning of it in battlefields, we had no idea at all.

220. 法妇女之作工

余在欧战时，不独尝见法之妇女相率成群往野外耘田，而大城市之工厂中，工人动辄数千，妇女常居大半也。余在喀黎灌煤油场作工时，见场中之妇女作工，个个敏捷。观其管理之法，亦将全厂之工人分为数部分，每部分有一老媪，执行管理监视，或点名、领款、进退等事。虽是妇女，作工极有秩序，不但毫无喧哗习气，更是异常仔细。虽与吾中之平常农家之妇女同是劳力，但毫无卑鄙之举现于声色，卒不失其高尚之态度。此亦受教育有程度之故欤！以吾国妇，深居闺阁之内者较之，谁为有益于其国耶？

华工日记
Chinese Labourer's Diaries

Working Frenchwomen

During the European War, not only did I see groups of women working in fields in rural areas, but I also saw them working in factories in large cities where there were often thousands of women labourers. When I worked at the kerosene filling yard in Calais, I found that all the women working there were quite agile. I noticed their method of management. All the workers in the factory were divided into several departments. In each department, an elder woman was in charge, responsible for calling the roll, getting the money, advancing, withdrawing and other duties. Although they were women, all worked in a very orderly manner with great care and without any noise. They were ordinary workers just like the women that worked in the fields, but they showed no contempt or any improprieties but only noble attitudes. Was this also because they were all well-educated? Compare with the women in China confined to only their own rooms, who were more beneficial to their countries?

221. 回脑于哀预备回国

在喀黎住一礼拜有余，而后趁火车回华工总分发所脑于哀时，在民国八年九月上旬也。一日，总工局传令到野外旷场中听谈话，及数队工人排队而至。一英人曰："大家来此作工帮忙，不知不觉已经两年有余。现在英政府欲急急打算以专船送大家回国。然而大家乘船，将来或到法之南部马赛，或到法之北部黎哈夫，尚不一定也。因为船之有无，正在

孙干：欧战华工记
Records of Chinese Labourers in European War by Sun Gan

等信息耳。至于大家回国，所带之物件，凡属于平日英人之发给者，均许大家携带，毫不禁止。而非英人所发给者，均在禁止之例。最近英司令有令云：'一切军用药品及武器，任何人不准随便携带。华工之将送回国者，更当一一检查之。'现在大家将各人所带之行李，可按次解开，摆在地上，以俟派人检验。"言讫，众工人纷纷将各人之行李解捆，英人三五成群，一一检验。至余之面前，即欲将黄君赠余炮弹廓所刻之笔筒，及德国之氯气帽持去。余绝对不允，彼亦无可奈何而去。以后至黄君世恩处，取其包内之德国钢盔，黄君亦坚持不允，彼亦作罢。盖因吾两人所带之物，虽属军器，而于行路或乘车坐船时，均不致发生危险也。检验完毕，各队按次排队而回。

Returning to Noyelles and Preparing to Return Home

After staying in Calais for more than a week, we returned to the General Distribution Station of Chinese Labourers at Noyelles by train in early September 1919. One morning, the General Bureau ordered us to gather in an open field. Shortly afterwards, several brigades of labourers arrived in line and a British officer came to address us. He said, "It has been more than two years since you came here to work and to help us. The British government is now eager to send you home by a special transport ship. However, it is not decided whether you will board the ship in Marseilles in the south of France or Le Havre in the north of France. We're still waiting for further information about the ship. As for the items that you will be allowed to take back to your home country, you may take with you only the things that the British distributed to you. None of those items are forbidden, but anything that is not distributed by the British is strictly prohibited. The British Commander-in-Chief has ordered, 'No one is allowed to carry any military medicines or weapons with him. All Chinese labourers to be sent back to their home country shall be inspected one by one.' Now, all of you should open your luggage and put it on the ground in front of you for inspection." With his words, the labourers had to put down their luggage and the British officers in groups of three or four commenced to inspect one by one. While they were inspecting my luggage, the British officer asked me to throw away the cannon-shaped engraved brush barrels Mr. Huang had given to me and the German chlorine gas hood. I refused to do so resolutely and eventually he had to give up. Later on, when they came to Huang Shien, they wanted to take away the German helmet from his luggage, but Mr. Huang would not agree, and they finally gave up too. I thought it was because the objects of mine and Mr. Huang would not pose any danger on the train or ship although they belonged to the category of military items. After the inspection, all brigades lined up and returned to their camps.

222. 代学注音字者领文凭

余当为青年会副干事之时，张君翕如即提倡注音班，使同工们学习注音字母。至张君欲离开一百零二队时，张君再三嘱托，以后若至脑于哀时，务要代学注音字母之诸位学员，到总青年会领取文凭。斯时也，吾曹既到脑于哀，不得不征求凡学过注音字者，愿否到总青年会领取文凭也。既征得数人同意，遂到青年会代为交涉，经总青年会另行考试一次以后，果发下文凭，可惜为数不多，仅几人而已。

孙干：欧战华工记
Records of Chinese Labourers in European War by Sun Gan

Diploma for Learners of Phonetic Scripts

When I worked in the YMCA as a deputy secretary, Zhang Xiru set up a phonetic class for labourers to learn phonetic scripts. Just before he left Brigade 102, Mr. Zhang told me repeatedly that I must go to the General YMCA to get the diplomas on behalf of the students in the class as soon as I returned to Noyelles. Therefore, after we had arrived at Noyelles, I asked all the labourers who had learned the phonetic scripts whether they would like to receive their diplomas from the General YMCA. With the consent of several of them I went to the YMCA to negotiate on their behalf. After another examination by the General YMCA, diplomas were issued. But it was a pity that only a few of them got their diplomas.

223. 在欧战时华工墓田

吾曹既到脑于哀，知将回国，所以人多表显高兴。而中国青年会又有特设之戏院一所在脑于哀庄外，凡到此地之华工，除每日三餐外，即为听戏。一日，余与同工数人，往脑于哀庄旁华工之茔田一观。见墓田前门，虽不十分高大，然铁栏亦极整齐。即入其内，知看墓田之人仍为华工。其中之坟墓，一一排列，虽不同欧人墓上均竖有十字架，然竖十字架者，间亦有之。惟不如有花圈者之多也。死亡者共亦千余人，较之在本国之死亡率，尚减少数倍。此坟墓之设，亦吾国在欧战所留之永久纪念也。

华工日记
Chinese Labourer's Diaries

Cemetery of Chinese Labourers during the European War

When we arrived at Noyelles and knew that we would soon return to China, most people were very delighted. The YMCA had set up a special theatre outside of the village of Noyelles and most Chinese labourers came to the theatre except for three meals every day. One day, some of my fellow labourers and I went to the cemetery for Chinese labourers nearby Noyelles. Although the front entrance of the cemetery was not very large and tall, the iron railings surrounding it were very neat. When we entered the cemetery, we learnt that those who tended the cemetery were Chinese labourers too. The graves were arranged in rows. Although not all of them were marked with a cross like those of the Europeans, there were some graves upon which the crosses were erected. But for most graves, there were wreaths in front of them. More than 1,000 Chinese labourers lost their lives in the European War, which was several times fewer than the death rate in our country. This cemetery was also a permanent memorial to our country in the European War.

224. 在黎哈夫等船

在脑于哀住一礼拜后，忽传令工人各负行李，排队往车站上火车。既乘火车，委曲婉转向西北方行，而至法之北海滨之黎哈夫矣。既下车，到黎哈夫以南十余里处一山林中宿焉。观其地既非村庄，又不近城市，

孙干：欧战华工记
Records of Chinese Labourers in European War by Sun Gan

盖为英人自欧战开始以来，特在此亦深建筑小房，以便英兵由英之海峡渡过时，以屯驻者。余等到此，住扎系数日，颇觉凉爽。

一日向暮，忽传令各船已靠岸工人各负行李，徒步行至黎哈夫码头上船。人人高兴非常，一时欢声盈耳，遂各个摒挡一切，不一刻而开拔。约北行五六里，天即昏黑，而人亦因行之过急，口喘汗出，衣尽湿透。各队秩序，一时紊乱。前队之在顶前者，因疲乏而行走迟迟。至半夜时，而退坠于后队之后。有勇往直前决不休息者，亦有且息且行者，亦有在路旁躺卧而酣睡者，有喊叫不止者，亦有为其行李所累骂不绝口者。余则且息且行，直行至翌日三点多时，始知一夜之行程，既到黎哈夫。而因船未靠岸，又由他路返回原驻之营房也。

余既至原营，见所还之同工，人数之归来者，尚不及半数耳。是夜也，足穿者为很重之皮靴，肩荷者为大捆之行李。行不数里，而汗流浃背，舌干口渴。欲求水饮而不能，欲不追随而不敢，宜乎骂吵之声震天，人物躺卧遍地也。余当时欲诉不得，欲笑不能，只有忍气吞声而已。然是夜之所为，英人用心何在，不得而知。

Waiting for Ship at Le Havre

After staying for one week in Noyelles, an order came suddenly that we take our luggage and proceed to the railway station to board the train. After we got aboard, the train wound its way to the northwest and finally arrived at Le Havre on the north coast of France. After getting off the train, we stayed overnight in a mountain forest more than six miles south of Le Havre. This place was neither a village nor a city, but the British had built small houses here ever since the beginning of the European War so that British soldiers could stationed here temporarily before they crossed the English Channel. We

华工日记
Chinese Labourer's Diaries

stayed there for several days and the weather was quite cool.

One day, an order came suddenly before sunset that all ships had arrived at the dock. Labourers were told to carry their luggage and walk to the dock at Le Havre on foot. Everyone was delighted and for a moment our ears were filled with laughter. With everything ready, we set off soon. After walking northwards for a few miles, it became dark, and we began to pant for breath and our clothes had been soaked by sweat for the quick marching. Brigades were in a state of disarray for a while. Because of fatigue, the brigade at the front began to walk slowly and by midnight the front brigades had fallen behind the rear ones. Some labourers went on courageously without any rest; some rested for a while and then continued; some even lay on the roadside and slept soundly; some kept shouting all the time; and some swore endlessly about their luggage. I walked and rested alternately. At about three o'clock the next morning, we arrived at Le Havre. Till then we realized that the journey would otherwise take a whole night. Because the ships had not yet arrived, we had to return to our original barracks by another route.

When I arrived back at the camp, I found no more than half of the labourers had returned to the barracks. On that night, we had heavy leather boots on our feet and carried large bundles of luggage on our shoulders. After walking a few miles, we became sweaty and thirsty but had no water to drink. We were too tired to follow the brigade, but we did not dare to rest. All we could do was just to swear and shout loudly or to lie on the ground everywhere. At that time, I wanted to complain, but I did not know to whom; I wanted to laugh, but I had no strength. I had to swallow this humiliation. We could not understand the intentions of the British for all this on that night.

孙干：欧战华工记
Records of Chinese Labourers in European War by Sun Gan

225. 由黎哈夫上船

民国八年九月十五日早饭后，传令上船。整队而行，天将午，即越过黎哈夫市，而到码头。甫进码头，见路旁有桌一张，桌后有若干纸包一垛，桌旁立有七八十岁之大老二人对吾曹拱手曰："辛苦辛苦！现在余等为大家预备一点船上用的东西，谁愿用的，可以捎带一点，以备远涉重洋之用也。"此盖英国教会之牧师为华工等送行者也，同工取者为数却甚寥寥。当日下午五点上船就序，至晚八点海潮来。十六日早三点，船由码头向西开行矣。

Boarding at Le Havre

After breakfast on 15 September 1919, we were ordered to board the ship. We went in line and by midday we had crossed the city of Le Havre and arrived at the port. As soon as I entered the port, I saw a table beside the road and a stack of paper parcels on the table. Behind the table were two elders in their 70s or 80s who said to us, "God bless you! We've prepared something for your voyage. Anyone that wants to take a little with them for the journey across the ocean may take some." They were priests of the Church of England who had come to see the Chinese labourers off. However, few of my fellow labourers took the paper parcels. Everything was ready onboard the ship by five o'clock in the afternoon and the tide rose at eight o'clock in the evening. At three o'clock in the morning of 16 September 1919, our ship began its voyage westward from the port.

226. 通直布罗陀海峡

　　船自黎哈夫开向西行一昼夜而入大西洋，时值风浪大作，又南行。四天之内，甫受风浪飘簸之苦。一夜闻船向东行，及天将晓，余自舱出见两岸相距不过十余里之遥时，风浪已息，水平若镜，为直布罗陀之海峡也。船往前行，值日将升，北为托里克，南为斯巴得拉角。一望突出海中，如在目前，俨然一门户焉，宜乎为素握海上霸权之英人所贵也。闻英得直布罗陀已二百余年，现为地中海西方出入之门户，驻有重兵于此。

Sailing through the Strait of Gibraltar

　　After sailing westward from Le Havre for a day and a night, our ship entered the Atlantic Ocean when a great storm appeared. Then our ship sailed southward. For the next four days we suffered strong winds and high waves. Knowing that our ship had been heading eastwards for a whole night, I came out of the cabin at dawn and saw that the two sides of the seashore were only a few miles apart. The storm had stopped, and the sea was as smooth as a mirror. I knew it was the Strait of Gibraltar. Our ship continued to go ahead as the sun was rising, shining on Spain in the north and Africa in the south. Standing out into the sea just like a gate in front of us, the Strait had been greatly valued by the British, who had always enjoyed the dominance of the seas. It was said that Britain had taken the control of Gibraltar about 200 years ago. As a gateway to the western Mediterranean Sea, the Strait of Gibraltar was stationed by the British troops.

227. 赛得港（亦曰薩伊特港）船上工人之谈话

自过直布罗陀海峡，东行六昼夜间。有时遥望南方，有陆地或即南非洲极北之阿尔及耳又或为必色耳与吕彼亚之古利奈。有时遥望北面，有陆地或为西西里岛，或为突尼司以北之笨角。然不靠岸，地面情形，无从而知。

六昼夜，东达赛特港。赛特港者，地中海之东门户者，苏彝士运河北首之第一商港也。吾乘之船一到是港，则见船桅林立，如义大利船、希腊船、法国船、美国船、英国船，一望无际。其商场之大，人工之多，不言可知。船之最多而不可数者，为英国船；最少仅二支者，为日本船。其余余不甚明了者，如埃及船、土耳其船、俄国船、罗马尼亚船、西班牙船、葡萄牙船等。时同工一人向余顿足曰："观此地之商港，各国之船均有之。堂堂中华，何以航行世界之船一无所有？吾国政府，岂不可叹耶！"

Labourers' Talks at Port Said

Since our ship passed through the Strait of Gibraltar, we had sailed eastbound for six days and nights. Looking southwards into the distance, I could see the land of Algiers or Bizerte of Tunisia at the northern tip of Africa. Looking to the north, I could see the island of Sicily or the Horn to the north of Tunisia. But I could not tell the ground situations because our ship would not stop at the shore.

After sailing another six days and nights, our ship arrived at Port Said, the eastern gateway of the Mediterranean Sea and also the first commercial port in the north of the Suez Canal. As soon as our ship arrived at the port, I saw endless ships of different countries, such as Italian ships, Greek ships, French ships, American ships and British ships. One could imagine how large its trading area was and how many workers were there. The country which had the largest number of ships was Great Britain, who had a countless number of ships there, while the country which had the smallest number of ships was Japan, with only two ships. There were also ships from other countries such as Egypt, Turkey, Russia, Romania, Spain and Portugal. Seeing this, one of my colleagues stamped his feet and said pitifully to me, "I find there are ships from nearly every country in the world in this commercial port, but why does a country as large as China not have a single ship sailing the world? How sad it is for our government!"

228. 在赛得港（亦名薩伊特港）船上望见工人之敬神

苏彝士运河，当欧、亚、斐交通之冲，船只之多，不言可知。船只既多，每到一船，因上水焉，上炭焉，装卸货物焉，样样需时日，所以每到一船，少必停泊三五日，多则迟延十数日，始克复往他处。余等乘

孙干：欧战华工记
Records of Chinese Labourers in European War by Sun Gan

船到此，既不能随便下船，在舱中又无事可做，故饭后多到舱外闲眺。一日，余同工数人，正在船上四望，见各船之旁，工人纷纷或上或下，或担或负，搢搢然争相工作。其工人之服装，有穿短衣者，但不如穿大褂者之多。于纷纷忙碌之际，时有人趋其工厂之旁，向西南方跪拜。此人拜返，彼又往焉。盖随时随处敬拜神灵，土俗然也。

Ship Workers' Worship at Port Said

As an important passage connecting Europe, Asia and Africa, the Suez Canal had very heavy traffic and a large number of ships sailed through it every day. Because of the great number of vessels and the great amount of time it took to add water and coal or to load and unload cargoes, every time a ship arrived, it would stay here for three or four days or even as long as ten days before it sailed again to another destination. When our ship arrived here, we were not allowed to go ashore. Having nothing to do in the cabin, I often went on deck and just looked around after meals. One day, several of my fellow labourers and I were looking around from the ship, we saw many workers were getting on or off their ships, shouldering or carrying things. Some workers wore short coats, but most of them wore long ones. Then we saw some of them walked close to their warehouses and knelt down facing the southwest. After one man finished, another man would follow. We were told that it was the customs of the local people to worship their gods whenever and wherever they were.

华工日记
Chinese Labourer's Diaries

229. 过苏彝士运河

法人雷塞布所凿成之苏彝士运河，盖因苏彝士运河适当亚洲、欧洲、斐洲之冲。其河之长，自南端苏彝士起，至北端之隆伊特港，长凡一百六十九公里，深九公尺以上，其中往来之船只，每年约在二十万吨以上，其多可知也。

余乘船出地中海东门赛得港，即入苏彝士运河焉。其时在船上，见河身之宽窄，有宽至十余丈者，有宽数丈者。两岸均为沙滩，两岸岸崖之高，有二三丈者，亦有仅一丈有余者。当时余在船上向东望之，平沙无垠，有时南风一吹，则如雪花纷纷，间有石垛沙滩，盖为当年修挖是河时之掘出者也。岸之西侧则为铁路，铁路以外又为干高叶大之椰子树，亦而居温带之人之所未见者也。自早至晚，开船约十余点钟，而达运河南端之苏彝士矣。将出运河之时，则见岸青石山崖壁立，船从崖下过时，状如石门，尤为险要。

Crossing Suez Canal

The Suez Canal built by the Frenchman Lesseps was an important channel for ships from Asia, Europe and Africa. Starting from Suez in the south and to the port of Said in the north, the Canal is over 120 miles long and about 30 feet deep. With an annual weight of over 200,000 tons of shipping, one could imagine how many vessels passed through the canal every year.

孙干：欧战华工记
Records of Chinese Labourers in European War by Sun Gan

Our ship entered the Suez Canal after it sailed out of the port of Said, the Eastern Gateway to the Mediterranean Sea. From onboard the ship, I could see that the Canal was over 100 feet wide in some places but only several feet wide at other places. On both sides of the Canal were sandy beaches and the banks were between 10 and 40 feet high. At that time, I looked eastward from the ship and saw the vast area of sands. Sometimes when the south wind blew, the sand would be blown everywhere like snowflakes. Occasionally, along the sandy beaches there were piles of rocks which were left by the excavators when the canal was being built or repaired. On the west side of the bank was a railway and outside the railway were coconut trees with tall trunks and large leaves, which had never been seen by people living in temperate zones. After the ship sailed for about ten hours from the early morning until evening, we reached the port of Suez at the southern end of the Canal. As we were getting out of the Canal, I saw a green bank among mountains and steep cliffs. Our ship was passing below the cliffs, which looked like a gate of rocks and added dangers to the ships passing through the Canal.

230. 过红海时之感想

余乘船自薩伊特港，过苏彝士运河，而至苏彝士，始知是运河之开凿时，南段多青石而北段多砂石也。于当一八五九至一八六九年时，土耳其人与埃及，各费尽其多少血汗也。

在苏彝士住一日后，又开船南行，而渡红海矣。当其过红海时，遂想到《旧约·出埃及记》十四章二十一节至二十八节，曾云摩西向

华工日记
Chinese Labourer's Diaries

海伸杖，耶和华使用大东风，使海水一夜退去。水便分开，海就成了干地，以色列人下海中走干地，水在他们的左右作了墙垣。埃及人追赶他们，法老一切的马匹车辆和马兵都跟着下到海中。到了晨更的时候，耶和华从云火柱中向埃及军兵观看，使埃及的军兵混乱了，又使他们的车轮脱落，难以行走。以致埃及人说我们从以色列人面前逃跑罢，因耶和华为他们攻击我们了。耶和华对摩西说，你向海伸杖，叫水仍合在埃及人，并他们的车辆马兵身上。摩西就向海伸杖，到了天一亮，海水仍旧复原。埃及人避水逃跑的时候，耶和华把他们推翻在海中，水就回流淹没了车辆和马兵。那些跟着以色列人下海法老，全军连一个也没有剩下。

由此可知，摩西圣人之信心，可谓至诚为上帝所拣选能领以色列族出埃及，作出多么伟人的事。余亦秉上帝之性灵，越过红海，于国家于社会，毫无裨益，又焉得无愧于心耶！斯时也在船中，只能想东为巴力洗分，西为比哈洗绿之两地相对而已也。

Thoughts on Crossing the Red Sea

Starting from port of Said, our ship arrived at Suez through the Suez Canal. Until then I knew that when the Canal was initially dug, the southern section was covered with bluestone rock while the northern section was covered with sandstones. From 1859 to 1861, both the Turkish and Egyptians spent much labour and money in building the Canal.

After one day's stay in Suez, our ship set sail again toward the south, heading for the Red Sea. When we crossed the Red Sea, I thought of what was said in the Old Testament. According to Verses 21-28 in Chapter 14 of Exodus, "Moses stretched out his hand over the sea and the LORD caused the sea to

孙干：欧战华工记
Records of Chinese Labourers in European War by Sun Gan

go back by a strong east wind all that night, and made the sea dry land, and the waters were divided. The children of Israel went into the midst of the sea upon the dry ground and the waters were a wall unto them on their right hand and on their left. The Egyptians pursued, and went in after them to the midst of the sea, even all Pharaoh's horses, his chariots and his horsemen. And it came to pass, that in the morning watch the LORD looked unto the host of the Egyptians through the pillar of fire and of the cloud, and troubled the host of the Egyptians, and took off their chariot wheels, that they drove them heavily. So that the Egyptians said, Let us flee from the face of Israel for the LORD fights for them against the Egyptians. The LORD said unto Moses, Stretch out thine hand over the sea, that the waters may come again upon the Egyptians, upon their chariots, and upon their horsemen. And Moses stretched forth his hand over the sea, and the sea returned to his strength when the morning appeared. The Egyptians fled against it and the LORD overthrew the Egyptians in the midst of the sea. And the waters returned, and covered the chariots, and the horsemen, and all the host of Pharaoh that came into the sea after them. There remained not so much as one of them."

From this, we could see that the faith of Moses was so sincere that he was chosen by the Lord to lead the Israelites out of Egypt. What a great thing he had done. It was also with the spirit of the Lord that I was crossing the Red Sea at this moment. If it did no good to our country and to society, how could I have a clear conscience? While being on the ship at this time, I could only imagine the Baal-zephon in the east and the Pi-hahiroth in the west facing each other.

231. 南斐洲之山岳

亚斐利加洲本为平均高于海面六百六十尺之高台地，从陆外四周观之，断崖壁立。余乘船渡红海时向西望之，则见山岳起伏，重岗叠岘。然观其形，虽层层相间，或白或黄，或赭或赤，如水成岩之构成，而其上却草木不生，惟一片砂石而已。

Mountains in South Africa

The continent of Africa was a plateau with an average height of 660 feet above sea level. From distance, it looked like a land with many steep cliffs. When crossing the Red sea on the ship, looking westwards, I saw many rolling mountains and overlapping hills. However, although its appearance, with the colours of white or yellow, deep ochre or red, was alternately layered just like the composition of the sedimentary rocks, there was no vegetation at all but only a vast area of sand and rock.

232. 刚入印度洋

由红海乘船东南行，五日出红海过巴备满德海腰。六日出亚丁湾而

孙干：欧战华工记
Records of Chinese Labourers in European War by Sun Gan

入印度洋，时民国八年十月初旬也。一日，船长下令招工人入船中之机器房中，作添炭、除秽、拭机器等工，每人每日工价洋五角。同工等咸云："吾侪既有英人供给食宿，复能作工得钱。"应募者，人颇不少。

翌日饭后，余游于舱外，与胶东同工某谈天。忽闻怦然作声，余曰："有人坠入海矣。"某急斥余曰："吾人出门在外，千万不可仓卒从事。"余虽闻其言，恐时间一迟，有误人命。又急呼曰："若有人坠入海中了。"某更止余曰："先生，弟不误汝。千万不可妄言多事，以致惹出意外，于己不利。"其言未毕，余果见有一人随浪浮沉。余遂厉声向船上大众曰："海中有坠入之人矣！"众皆轰然来观。余遂又大声亟呼，并使人告知船长。及船长至，船已前行数里，幸水平浪静，尚能望见之。斯时也，同工等都从舱出，集于船上面，齐呼快快营救。英人亦令船工扯桅，放划，船亦下淀停泊。是时也，船因骤停旋转之故，使海面浮然变色，与前之水色波光迥异，是以船上之人多半眩晕，呕吐。而船工正在乘小划下海往救之际，忽闻风声飒飒，顷刻间海浪齐作，不但在高至桅顶之人望不见人，即划舟而至其坠处，亦杳无踪迹矣。及往营救者还，众工人一见未将坠海之同工营救出险，遂群起质问英人。英人亦追询斯人坠海之故，最末始知为在船内机器房中作工，因房中热甚，自趋于船面，跳入海中者。众同工一时言语极为激昂，英人亦嫌中国人皆属无用。盖因船上所备之救生用具至多，何以当时一见，不能由船上掷下一二，以救其性命也？争执良久，半日后船乃东开。

First Entry into the Indian Ocean

We sailed from the Red Sea towards the southeast and by the fifth day we had sailed out of the Red Sea and crossed the Bab al-Mandab Strait. On the sixth day, we crossed the Gulf of Aden and entered the Indian Ocean. It

华工日记
Chinese Labourer's Diaries

was already October of 1919, the eighth year of the Republic of China. One day, the Captain ordered our labourers to come into the engine room and told us that they were recruiting workers to do jobs such as adding charcoal, removing stains, and cleaning machinery. The pay would be 50 cents per day for each worker. All my fellow labourers said, "It's worth doing since our food and lodging are provided by the British and we can also get money for doing work." Therefore, many people applied for the job.

After dinner the next day, while I chatted outside the cabin with one of my fellow workers from the Jiaodong Peninsula, we heard a loud sound suddenly. I said, "Someone must have fallen into the sea." He warned me saying, "When we are away from home, we should not rush to get ourselves involved in others' affairs." Although I heard what he said, I was afraid that a life would be lost if it was too late. So I shouted hurriedly, "Someone seems to have fallen into the sea." He stopped me again and said, "Sir, I say this for your own good. Don't shout out or get yourself involved in business that might not be good for you." Before he finished his words, I saw a man drifting along the waves. So I shouted loudly again to people on the ship, "Someone has fallen into the sea!" Lots of people came to see what happened. I shouted for help again and sent people to report to the Captain. When the Captain came, our ship had already moved forward several hundred yards away. Fortunately, there was no storm and we could still see him. By this time, all my fellow labourers had got out of their cabins and gathered on the deck of the ship, shouting for quick rescue. The British sailors also ordered the crew to pull the mast, set down the lifeboat, and stopped the ship. At the same time, because of the sudden stop and the rotation of the ship, the sea surface changed colour, which was quite different from the previous colour. As a result, many of the people on the ship began to feel dizzy and threw up. Just as the boatmen were rowing out to save the drowning man, some large waves came suddenly in an instant. Not only did the people at the top of the mast lose sight of him, but they also lost sight of the boatmen rowing the boat to save him from where he fell into the sea. When the rescuers returned, all the labourers began to question the British sailors the moment they realised that their fellow worker had not been rescued. The British also inquired about the reason why he had fallen into the sea. Soon, it became clear that he jumped into the sea because he felt too hot while working in the engine room of the ship. For a while, the labourers spoke indignantly and excitedly and the British thought that all Chinese were useless. Since there were so many lifesaving devices on board, why couldn't they throw one or two to save his life? After a long dispute, the ship continued to sail eastward half a day later.

233. 航海者旗语

印度洋当欧洲、亚洲、斐洲、澳洲四者之冲。余乘船自红海出，一入印度洋，即见船只往来，络驿不绝。有时此船与彼船前后相望，有时两船雁行而行，日有所见，迥异在太平洋时，二十余日而不见另有一船也。船与船遇，动隔数里，言语不闻则用旗语。旗语者，一人手持两小旗，向对方之船摇摆，或左或右，或上或下，或单或双，作等等旗势。对方亦持旗作势答覆。故虽远隔数里，亦能互通其意也。

Flag Language of Navigators

The Indian Ocean is a most important ocean that connects the continents of Europe, Asia, Africa and Australia. Once I sailed into the Indian Ocean after setting out from the Red Sea, I saw many ships coming and going on its surface. Sometimes the ships sailed in line one after another while at other times the ships sailed side by side in the way wild geese did. I could see many other ships every day, which was quite different from what it was like when we sailed on the Pacific Ocean. At that time we had never seen any other ships for over 20 days. When ships met each other, they were usually miles apart. Although people on different ships could not speak to each other directly, they could use flag language to convey messages. By flag language, we mean that a person on one ship waved two small flags in his hands to the left or to the right, up or down, single or double, or other signals to people on the other ship to convey messages. People on the other ship would also respond by waving their flags in the same manner. In this way, even though they are miles away from each other, the ships could still make communications with each other.

234. 飞鱼

印度洋中鱼类至多，有随船平行而跃者，有游泳水面而如蛇者。然在海面常见者厥为飞鱼。飞鱼形状，恰如燕子，故亦称之曰燕子鱼。秋初之时，人到野外草丛中，每前行，草内之蚂蚱则纷纷向两旁乱飞。印度洋中之飞鱼，一见船来则纷然飞去，其状亦犹是也。其飞或一二里，或三四里而更落。或因其虽然有翅，究不如飞禽之有毅力欤。

Flying Fish

We encountered great varieties of fish in the Indian Ocean. Some kept jumping parallel to our ship while others swam on the surface like snakes. However, the most common fish we saw on the sea were flying fish. Shaped like swallows, flying fish were also known as swallow fish. Just as the locust would fly to either side in a hurry when people passed through the wild grass in a field, the flying fish in the Indian Ocean flew away in the same way at the sight of our ship. But They would stop after flying for 500 yards or so, perhaps because their wings were not as strong as birds.

235. 海蛰

印度洋中除见种种鱼以外，惟海蛰为最多。海蛰之形状，其小者仿佛淡白色之葵花一朵，中为粉红色，边缘为白色；小者如杯，大者如盘，印度洋中到处皆是。

Jellyfish

Jellyfish are the most common creature in the Indian Ocean apart from the great variety of fishes. The small jellyfish are like sunflowers in shape, but they are pink in the middle and white at the edge. They could be as small as a cup or as big as a plate and they were everywhere in the Indian Ocean.

华工日记
Chinese Labourer's Diaries

236. 印度洋中华工第二次坠海

凡常乘船航海之人，都知船中之臭味难堪。余等趁华工专船归国时，行至印度洋，因近赤道而更热。一日，有一同工早起携其席褥出舱，而至船上面之小屋顶上卧焉，直至天八点，尚未醒也。有顷，分饭之时间到。号令一响，其人闻之则由屋顶而下。然屋之后檐适近于船边之栏杆，彼由屋檐下时，正是船身亦向外歪，将其送于船外之海水中矣。

斯时也，船上华工，因前次之人坠海，英人谓当时急以救生器掷下。今华工既知是法，故闻人坠水，齐将救生器掷于海中，当时近船海面几尽为救生器所掩。既而船工立将船上所带之小划放下海面，将坠水之人捞起，拔至船上，已无知觉矣，越二日其人始复苏。

Chinese Labourers' Second Fall into the Indian Ocean

Anyone who often sailed on the sea knew that the stench in a ship could be terrible. When our ship sailed across the Indian Ocean, the weather became very hot for its gradual approach to the equator. One day, one of our fellow labourers got up early and took his mattress out of the cabin. He lay on the roof of a small room and did not wake up until eight o'clock. Shortly afterwards, it was time for breakfast. On hearing the whistle, he began to climb down the roof. However, the eave at the rear of the room was close to the railings on the edge of the ship. As he climbed down, the ship happened to lean outward too. As a result, he was sent outside into the sea by the ship.

At that time, the Chinese labourers remembered what the British sailors had said to them when the worker had fallen into the sea last time. Realising that they should throw lifesaving devices into the sea when there was an emergency, the Chinese labourers began to throw the lifesaving devices into the sea the moment they heard the shouting that someone had fallen overboard. Soon the surface of the sea alongside the ship was almost covered with lifesaving devices. Then a boatman lowered a small rowboat to the sea. When the man who had fallen into sea was finally picked up and returned safely to the ship, he had lost his consciousness. It was only two days later that he regained his consciousness.

237. 航海常用之救生器

语云："工欲善其事，必先利其器。"此航海者，亦预备救生器也。余航太平洋、印度洋时，所常见船上之救生器。有以下数种：

一、救生带。将极轻之软硬木，大如土坯者六七块，以长白布条裹之，然后将各块稍离，再以细线将各块之四周密缝，使之巩固不动，末以线带缝于长布条之两端。倘遇不测，或触暗礁，或遇冰山，或遭火灾，或船被击坏时，乘船者即将所备之救生带紧束腰间，以期坠水不沉。盖因软硬木质轻，至水中而易浮也。

二、救命圈。将极轻之草干后，束为直径二尺许之一大圈，外用白布裹之，将布合之缝密，密缝之外，再加桐油涂好，其上若系以绳，作

华工日记
Chinese Labourer's Diaries

三角状。倘有人坠水，随手可以将救命圈掷于海面，使遇险者握之，即不致沉溺。此圈一具，可救二人或三人。

三、救生箱。以极轻铁质之薄页，造为高一英尺之空箱，宽长三尺或五尺，再大再小，亦可任意。务使严密，水不透入。外以坚固之木框装好，使在框内不致稍有活动。木框之各撑拴以坚固之麻绳，箱空而轻，浮而不沉。凡船均预备，其用之大，非前二者之所能及也。

Lifesaving Devices Commonly Used in Sea Voyages

As an old saying goes, "sharp tools makes good work." Lifesaving devices were very important for sea voyages. The lifesaving devices the commonly used on ships I had ever seen while sailing on the Pacific and the Indian Ocean could be classified as follows:

I. Lifesaving-belts Six or seven pieces of cork wood, as big as adobe bricks, were wrapped in long white cloth strips. Then each piece was slightly separated, and the edges of each piece was stitched closely with thin threads to make it firm and immovable. At each end of the cloth were stitched long tails of cloth. In the event of accidents caused by a reef, an iceberg, a fire or a wreck, the passengers on the ship could fasten the lifesaving belts tightly around their waists so that they would not sink. It was because the cork wood was very light and would remain buoyant in water.

II. Lifebuoys Dried light straw was tightly bundled into a large circle with a diameter of about two feet, which was then wrapped with white cloth. The seam of the cloth was stitched tightly and then coated with China wood oil over it. If it was tied with a rope, it would be triangular in shape. If someone fell overboard, a lifebuoy could be thrown into the sea so that the person in danger could hold it to prevent by himself from sinking. One lifebuoy could save two or three people.

III. Lifesaving boxes   A thin sheet of very light iron was used to make an empty box one foot high, three feet wide and five feet long or of any other sizes. The box must be watertight so that no water could get in. The box was then fitted with a strong wooden frame so that it would not move inside the frame. Strong hemp ropes were then tied around each support of the wooden frame so that the box remained light, buoyant and floated on the surface without sinking into the water. Every ship was equipped with lifesaving boxes, whose great use could not be matched by the former two types of lifesaving devices.

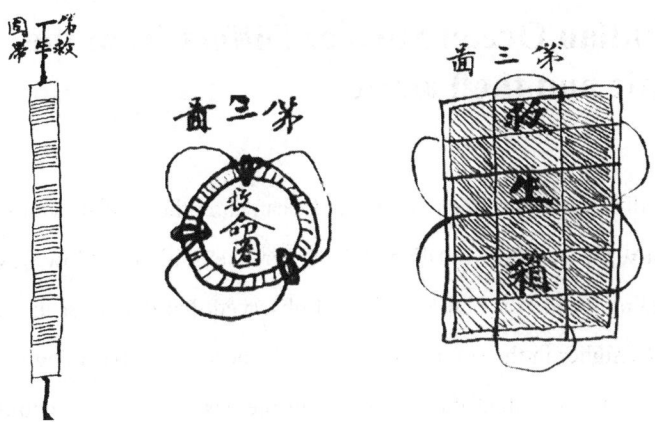

238. 印度洋洋面与大西洋、太平洋不同

印度洋洋面之现象与他洋中之不同者有数事焉：

一为水显然有高有低。一日，余站船之栏旁，见海中之水，南方高而北方低，如一层台阶。然东西望之，其长不见端际，非一时如是，船行二日，均如是也。

二为洋面之水，有平且光明之长线各处散布，如陆地中之有道路然。长者、短者、宽者、窄者，亦他洋之所无也。

三为洋面之水间，有如锅中欲沸之平浪，向四外周围反滚，昼夜不停。于风平浪静之时，环顾之如天中之有一星，然纵有小浪微波来侵，立被内滚外逐，而恢复其常态也。

四为有时现蠹天蠹地之云柱自洋面起，始起较细，愈高而愈粗大。及至高空，则与天上之云合而为一，或有谓之为飓风者。

以上数事，均为太平洋与大西洋所未曾得一见者也。

The Indian Ocean Surface Differs from the Atlantic and the Pacific

The differences between the Indian Ocean and other oceans as follows:

Firstly, the water obviously had the difference of high and low waves. One day, standing beside the ship's railings, I observed that the water in the Indian Ocean was higher in the south and lower in the north, just like a flight of stairs. However, when I looked into the water in the east and west, I could see no end of the smooth water. Such a phenomenon was not something temporary. It remained the same throughout the two days of our sailing on the Indian Ocean.

Secondly, smooth and bright long lines of water scattered everywhere on the surface of the ocean just like roads on the land. These lines, long or short, wide or narrow, were not found in other oceans.

Thirdly, the surface water of the Indian Ocean rolled outward day and night like small boiling waves in a pot. Looking around it while the ocean was

孙干：欧战华工记
Records of Chinese Labourers in European War by Sun Gan

calm, I found it was like a star in the sky. Even when small waves came, the water was rolled outward quickly and then restored to its normal state.

Fourthly, sometimes pillars of clouds would rise from the surface of the ocean, which started thin but became larger and larger as they rose. When they rose into the sky, they merged with the clouds. Some people call them hurricanes.

All of these things were what we had never seen while sailing on the Pacific and Atlantic oceans.

239. 西兰岛之所见

余等自苏彝士起椗东南行，东不见西乃山矣。十日后即到六万六千方公里之西兰岛焉。尝见吾国历史所载，三宝太监下西洋时，曾路过其地，将吾汉族之威德宣示于此。以致其后世，执玉帛而贡吾国者若干年。及一七九六年时，又为英人所治服，甚可惜也。

船尚未进其南方之加尔港，见两岸树木葱茏，高下一色。虽时将近严冬，然林壑犹如盛夏。林间之鸟，五色俱备，飞舞上下，鸣声悦耳，景色宜人，有非笔墨所能形容万一者。

既入港，始知港湾之大，容船之多。大船之间，有无数之小船，船身既极渺小，船上皆为破烂不堪之草棚。裸体一家或大人，或小孩，或妇女，都仅于其胁间围半截裤衩，盘旋于欧、亚、斐、澳四大洲往往来来之大船间，贩卖珊瑚、珍珠、鹦鹉、翡翠、凤梨、槟榔、杏梅等等，以为生涯也。此外又见多数之印度人以长形红巾裹其首，铣其足，往来于白人之左右服事，惟谨俨状，一奴隶情形，颇为可怜。

华工日记
Chinese Labourer's Diaries

Sights on Island of Ceylon

Starting from Suez, we travelled in a southeast direction but did not see Mount Sinai in the east. Ten days later, we arrived at the Island of Ceylon with an area of 25,000 square miles. I had read from books of Chinese history that Zheng He, also known as "Eunuch Sanbao", had stopped at this place when he voyaged to the Western Oceans and declared our sovereignty over the island. As a result, the later generations of this island kept paying tribute to our country with their jade objects and silk fabrics for several years. But the British took control and administered the island in 1796.

Before our ship entered the port of Galle in the south, we could see the lush trees lining both banks. Although winter was approaching, the forests and valleys looked as green as they were in midsummer. Birds of different colours flew up and down in the forests and sang sweet songs. The sight was so pleasant that its beauty was quite beyond words.

Only when we entered the harbour did we realise how large it was. It could accommodate many large ships, between which were countless small boats with small hulls and shabby thatched huts. The families on the boats including men, women and children, were all nearly naked, with only short underpants around their waists. They came and went between the big ships from Europe, Asia, Africa and Australia, selling their corals, pearls, parrots, thorn birds, pineapples, betel nuts, apricots, plums and so on. In addition, we also noticed that most Indians wrapping their heads with long red scarves and wearing nothing on their feet served the white people cautiously like slaves, constituting a quite miserable sight.

孙干：欧战华工记
Records of Chinese Labourers in European War by Sun Gan

240. 热带人下海逐钱

珊瑚、珍珠皆生长于热带之海底中，热带之人能缒入海底而寻取之，其习惯然也。余等乘船到印度以南西兰岛之加尔港后，住二日，船停港湾之中，吾曹不得随便下船，遨游闲眺于船边而已。

第二日傍午，有一同工告余曰："此地之人多善游泳，盍试之？"余曰："何以试之？"彼遂取铜元一枚，向本船侧之小船旁掷去。小船船工见之，立跃入水，不一刻欣欣然持铜元出矣。余亦取铜元再三试之，均随铜元入水取出。其敏捷娴熟一非余陆地人所能想知也。

Tropical People Diving into Sea for Money

Corals and pearls usually grew on the tropical seabed and people in the tropical regions customarily dived into the sea to look for them. After arriving at the port of Galle on the island of Ceylon in the south of India, we stayed there for two days. Because our ship had anchored in the harbour and we were not allowed to disembark, what we could do was only to roam around the decks and admire the views from the ship.

On the afternoon of the second day, one of my fellow workers came to me and said, "The local people here are excellent swimmers. Why not we go and test them?" I asked, "How could we test them?" He took out a copper coin and threw it at the side of a nearby boat. Seeing this, the boatman jumped into the water immediately and soon got out of water happily holding up the copper coin. I also took out several copper coins and threw them into water. Again and again the boatman dived down and got them out quickly. The swimming skill and agility of these people was beyond our imagination.

241. 到赤道下之新嘉坡

前在法国黎哈夫之时，天气颇觉寒冷；半月后乘船到红海中，便觉天气渐热；由印度洋而达西兰岛之十余日间，虽觉一路天气炎热，尚堪忍受；自船由西兰岛而东开，则炎热不可忍受矣。夜间在舱中睡时，真若在笼蒸。一到早晨，则人人都趋于舱外。虽然船身甲板之厚，一经日光照耀，船中之人，立即如灸如熨。人在船中，终日昏昏而已。惟日将落时，稍觉清凉。斯时也，船上所预备之洗澡盆，大者、小者、以铁制者、以木制者为数颇多，而吾侪轮流日日洗涤不已，为减少热度之一法。

Sailing to Singapore Near the Equator

It was very cold when we were at Le Havre in France, but it gradually became hot half a month later as we sailed onto the Red Sea. Although it was hot during the ten days from the Indian Ocean all the way to Ceylon, it was still tolerable; however, after our ship sailed eastward from the island of Ceylon, the heat became unbearable. Sleeping in the cabin at night was just like being steamed in a food steamer. Everyone would rush out of their cabins in the morning. Even though the ship's deck was very thick, it became so hot once the sun shone that people on the deck immediately felt as if they were being grilled or ironed. As a result, everybody on the ship felt faint all day long. Only when the sun set did it become slightly cooler. At that time, bathtubs of various sizes, mostly iron or wooden ones, were put on the deck for bathing. To take a bath every day was one of the only ways for us to reduce the unbearable heat.

242. 新嘉坡望月

余于欧美所到之处，自然有诸多事物与祖国迥不相同。然于日月或高低，无甚大异也。惟归途至新嘉坡时，昼间太阳甚高，大热异常，令人忍所不能忍。至于夜间，则见紫薇星低甚，而月亮当正午时，偏于人首之北方矣。

Watching the Moon in Singapore

While I was in Europe, I found there were many things that were quite different from those in our motherland, but there was no big difference in the rising and setting of the sun and the moon. When we passed by Singapore on the way back to China, the sun was very high in the sky during the daytime, and it was so unusually hot that it was nearly unbearable. But in the evening, the North star was very low whereas the moon was almost hanging overhead at midnight.

华工日记
Chinese Labourer's Diaries

243. 热带之产物

由西兰岛起淀，两日后即抵新嘉坡。新嘉坡港湾极大，船只极多。船既入港则见小船往来，非运货物，即作买卖者。观地上植物多为干高叶大之椰子与香蕉，其贩卖之菜蔬与果食，如王瓜、白菜、烧瓜、瓠子等，均甚多且鲜嫩也。海中之产物，有红珊瑚，状如蜂房或如浮屠；白珊瑚状如菌形，其色外白而内绿，形状有如树林。其小者无论，大者有高于人者。至于禽兽如猕猱、猿猴与翡翠、鹦哥等等，不但常闻其嘤嘤之声，而更见其飞舞于贩者之手上也。闻世之以贩卖鸟兽为业者，未有如此地之盛者矣。

Tropical Products

Our ship arrived in Singapore two days after it left Ceylon. The harbour of Singapore was very large and there were many ships and boats there. When our ship entered the harbour, I saw many small boats coming and going in the harbour, transporting goods and doing business. Most of the plants on the land were coconuts and bananas with their big dry leaves and tall trunks. Many vegetables and fruits were sold, such as Japanese snake gourd, Chinese cabbage and squashes. All of them were all plentiful and tender. There were also products of the sea including red corals, which were shaped like beehives, and fungi-shaped white corals, which were white outside and green inside like forests. Some corals were small, but others were larger and taller than a man. There were also many animals, such as macaques, apes, thorn birds, and parrots, being sold. We could not only hear their voices, but we could also see them dancing on the hands of vendors. Even places especially for the trading of animals and birds were not as prosperous as it was in this harbour.

244. 英人对华工之演讲

船至新嘉坡，停一礼拜，在此七日之中，饱尝赤道之炎酷。一日，日已西坠。英人由船上最高层之楼房中出，向众工人曰："汝等现在很好，在欧洲住了两年，天天盼望还家，来到现在，不久就要到家了。"一工人答曰："吾们知道，吾们快要到家，可是汝英国人为何不管我们呢？我们现在穿了你们英国给我们的衣裳，一回到中国去，人人都要因穿这种衣服而被耻笑，你们的衣服在我们中国可以说直然不可以穿。若现在趁着尚未回到中国，拿中国人所穿的裤褂给我们换换，您说可行不可行呢？"

英人曰："你们现在穿的衣服，以前在法国时，就有许多上官，为你们开会，早已规定住了。使你们华工各工，人人穿了在欧战帮忙发给你们的衣服回国。回到中国，中国之人一见了你们穿的衣服，就知道你们是加入欧战，回国有功的啊！我敢保现在你们穿着所穿的衣服，官府的人见了必然赶快招待你们，保护你们。即回家所经过铁路，随便坐火车无用花钱。因为你们大家此次到欧洲帮助协约，打胜了仗，直接着挣了些钱还算小事，间接着为国家帮忙，使中国国家在国际地位上提高了不少。假如欧战中国不有你们华工大家出来加入，到欧洲作工帮忙，那直怕是不但中国在国际间失去地位，而欠各国之欠款，亦必得立逼偿还

华工日记
Chinese Labourer's Diaries

呀！现在单就你们穿的衣服说，西洋衣服一双皮靴值洋六元，两床毛毯值洋八元，一身大氅值洋二十余元，若联裤褂雨衣及零碎物合计，共值四十余元。若更换为中国衣服，一双鞋袜值洋不过两元，一套裤褂值洋不过四元，连零星算之，共总方需洋七八元耳。"

一工人又曰："余等穿这种衣服，一到中国。中国之人，人人耻笑，人人害怕。现在在此，你们虽然说的条条有理，到了那时，我们都不能见你们英国人，你们亦就不管我们的闲事了，总不如现在把穿的西洋衣服，给我换为中国衣服哩。"

英人曰："现在虽然送你们大家回家，可是按你们的合同，所载三年尚不满期。在此期限以内，如有什么事故发生时，可到周村招工局报信。吾们英国人，仍旧照管呀！"英人言至此，好像尚有若干可向工人报告之事，只因工人之质问太无程度，遂不言而去。

British Speech to Chinese Labourers

Our ship stayed in Singapore for a week, during which we suffered greatly from the heat of the equator. One day, as the sun was setting in the west, a British officer came out of the highest part of the ship and spoke to the labourers, "I have good news for you all. While living in Europe for the past two years, you have often looked forward to returning home. The good news is that you will be home soon." One of the labourers shouted, "We know that we are going home but why do you British ignore us? We are still wearing the clothes that you gave us, but we will be laughed at for wearing such clothes when we get back to China. In the eyes of our Chinese, it is very inappropriate to wear your style of clothes. Can we change these British clothes into Chinese ones before we arrive back home in China? Is it all right?"

孙干：欧战华工记
Records of Chinese Labourers in European War by Sun Gan

The British officer responded, "When you were still in France, many senior officers had held meetings to discuss the clothes you should wear on returning to China. At that time, it was stipulated that Chinese labourers should wear the clothes they were given while serving during the European War for their return journey home. That way, when you are back home in China and the rest of the Chinese people see the clothes you wear, they'll know that you've joined the European War and done great credit to your country. I believe that you'll be well treated and even protected once the government officials see the clothes that you wear. It is probable that you won't even need to spend money to buy your tickets when you take the train home. It is because you have helped your country in the European War by going to Europe to assist the Entente countries. Of course, we've won the war with your help and you've earned some money. But more importantly, you've helped your country directly and greatly enhanced China's international status. If China had not have you Chinese labourers join us in the War and to work alongside us in Europe, I'm afraid your government would not only have lost its position in the international affairs, but it would also have had to pay back the debts it owed to other countries. Now as far as the clothes you wear are concerned, a pair of leather boots is worth six yuan; two blankets are worth eight yuan; and a coat is worth over 20 yuan. If we take the shirt, trousers and raincoats and other small things into account, the total value will be more than forty yuan. However, as far the Chinese clothes are concerned, a pair of shoes and socks are worth less than two yuan; a set of trousers and jacket is worth less than four yuan, even if we take other small things into account, the total cost is only seven or eight yuan."

Then another labourer shouted, "If we arrive in China wearing such clothes, everyone in China will laugh at and be afraid of us. What you say here and now seem to be reasonable, but we're afraid that once we arrive at home, we won't have any chance to see any British officials at all and you won't care about our business anymore. It would be better for us to take off these foreign clothes now and change into our own Chinese style of clothing."

The British officer said, "Although we are sending you all home now, your three-year contracts haven't terminated yet. So within this period, if anything happens, you can still report to the Zhoucun Recruitment Bureau. We, the British people, will still take care of you!" He seemed to have other things to tell the labourers, but he left without saying anything more because of the questioning of the labourers.

245. 做饭奇速

余自由青岛东行，见船上之造饭，无甚可观。即由过美洲后，又上船过大西洋时，亦未曾见船上造饭之情形。迨归回中国之船到新嘉坡时，天气既热，洗澡者、口渴者既多。船上之一切规矩，亦渐渐松懈。一日晨，余偕同工某在船上游览至饭房之旁，见饭房之内，阒其无人。时将近六点半矣，而七点钟即为开饭之时间。余问同工曰："吾曹七点即吹哨开饭，何现在将近六点半，饭房中尚无一人也？"同工曰："开饭既有定时，岂能误事？"旋有两人以大苇筐抬南瓜与牛肉半筐至。有顷，又有数人以苇筐亦抬大米至。其时，余语同工某曰："吾二人可在此观其造饭，能否不误时刻也。"

抬米者一人将米放下，先将其锅上之水龙首一拧，水即下流，又将锅下之汽门一转，热力即至。一锅如是，一行十锅，按次进行添水通汽，

孙干：欧战华工记
Records of Chinese Labourers in European War by Sun Gan

及返回时，第一锅中之水，不但已满，而且已滚。其人又挨次将水龙关闭，而所有之汽锅，亦无不俱沸矣。其余三人，下米者下米，做菜者做菜。为时不及半点，而米饭菜羹尽皆焖熟矣。斯时也，余始知汽之热造饭之速，实有出人意外者。不然，千余人之饭食，若以煤炭薪柴，半点钟时，何克有济耶！

Quick Cooking

When I first sailed eastward from Qingdao, I once saw men cooking meals onboard, but it was not very impressive. When I took the ship across the Atlantic after crossing the Americas, I did not get the chance to see how meals were cooked onboard. On this ship, however, when we arrived at Singapore on our way back to China, due to the hot weather most people took baths on the decks and everyone was always thirsty, the rules onboard had gradually become more relaxed. One morning, one of my fellow labourers and I walked to the kitchen on the ship and we found no one in it. It was nearly six-thirty, and we would normally have our meal at seven o'clock. I said to my fellow labourer, "We'll have our meal at the seven o'clock whistle. It's already nearly six-thirty. Why is there no one in the kitchen yet?" My fellow worker said, "The meal is always served at a fixed time. How could they make a mistake?" Soon after, we saw two people carrying a big reed basket of pumpkins and beef. A moment later, several other people carrying baskets of rice came too. At that time, I said to my fellow labourer, "We can watch them cooking here to see whether they'll get the meal ready before seven o'clock."

The person carrying the rice put it down and turned on a tap over the pot, from which water began to flow over the rice. Next, he turned a valve underneath the pot and a flame came and heated the pot. When the first pot was ready, he did the same to all ten pots that were in a row. He returned to the first pot when the water in it was boiling. He then turned off the valve under each pot in turn when all the steam pots had been boiling. The other three people, who were responsible for putting rice or pumpkins or meat into pots, also did their work. Within less than half an hour, the rice and dishes were prepared and ready. Only then did I know the rapid speed of cooking with steam pots, which was something we had not realised before. Otherwise, how could thirty minutes be enough time to cook the food for more than a thousand people with coal or firewood!

246. 新嘉坡停泊时所见港湾之买卖

新嘉坡本为欧、亚、澳、斐诸洲交通必经之地。船只之多，货物之繁，各洲之人类，各洲之钱币，形形色色，莫不有之。况地居热带，如南洋群岛之香料，西兰、印度之茶叶，销售于各地。其海中所产之珍珠珊瑚，又为贵重之物。观其贸易，每日自早至晚，无时不轰轰烈烈。其来之人种除马来人外，未有如吾中华人之多者。虽其主权为欧人，其实欧人之居其地者，极寥寥也。

Trading at Harbour of Singapore

Singapore was a transportation centre through which ships from Europe,

孙干：欧战华工记
Records of Chinese Labourers in European War by Sun Gan

Asia, Australia and Africa must pass. Here you could find numerous ships, various goods, different races, and all kinds of coins from every continent. Tropical goods, such as spices from the South Sea Islands and tea from Ceylon and India, were sold everywhere. The pearls and corals found in the sea were also precious items. The trade in Singapore was a daily affair and always vigorous from morning until night. The majority of people at this trading centre were Chinese except the Malaysians. Very few Europeans lived there although the Europeans had sovereignty over the island.

247. 剪发者技巧

新嘉坡既在赤道之下，其酷热无待于言。吾人久居其地，头晕目眩，终日昏昏。同工某，邀余理发。理发者快而且巧。其修耳，能将耳中之耳髓掏尽，而人尚不之觉也。他处理发，无及之者。技亦巧矣！

Haircutting Techniques

Because Singapore was near the equator, it was very hot all year around. We all felt dizzy or faint after staying there for a long time. One day, one of my fellow labourers invited me to have a haircut. The barber was quick and very skilful. He could get all earwax out of ears before the client was even aware of him doing it. No barber in any other place could match him. What a skilful barber he was!

华工日记
Chinese Labourer's Diaries

248. 余于过新嘉坡时所买之物

吾侪所乘之船在新嘉坡住停之时，较他处为多。盖装煤添水之工人，较他处为忙。至一礼拜将尽之时，同工等都纷纷买物，有买大猿者，有买小猴者，有买翡翠者，有买鹦鹉者。余因不喜以动物为嬉，故买红白珊瑚一篮，仅费洋两元；买凤梨二个，槟榔果二个，共费二元；买水果若干个，费洋一元。将带之归国，以开家人之眼界也。凤梨一物，盖取其两端绿碧之叶若凤之头尾，中间黄色之实其味若梨。槟榔果之壳，可为饭勺，其肉可食，其汁如乳之甘，便为可饮。至翌日早，船果开向东北矣。

My Purchase in Singapore

We spent more time in Singapore than we had in anywhere else because there were more boats and ships waiting to be filled with coal and water. By the end of the week, my fellow workers began to buy things such as big apes, little macaques, jade and parrots. I did not like to play with animals, so I bought a basket of red and white corals with only two yuan, two pineapples and two coconuts with another two yuan, and several other fruits with one yuan. I planned to take them home for my family, which would open their eyes to the world. The pineapple had green leaves at both ends just like the head and tail of a phoenix while the yellow pulp in the middle tasted like pears. The shell of the coconut could be used as a food spoon and its pulp could be eaten while its juice was as sweet as milk. Early next morning, our ship began to head for the northeast.

凤梨　果榔槟　瑚珊

249. 婆罗洲旁之大风浪

船自新嘉坡出向东北行，次日风浪大作，凡船面上之一切用物，无不倾斜偃仰。人则更不敢外出，幸炎热之气顿减于前。逾一昼后，船飘簸尤甚，欲出入于船面者，非循牵船上所系之大索，不敢徒行一步也。

其时东望之，遥遥见一百三十余万方里波萝洲大岛之沿岸，山峦之多，重岗叠巘。在隐约中，又一昼后夜，越过斐律宾南部之帕拉氏恩岛而至吕宋以西时，于夜间约一点钟，忽闻船底发巨大之振动。如大钉之戳旋轮，如大锤之砸船底，相间发响，继续不断。船中之人无不惶恐万状，不敢作声。

余询诸英人，英人曰："是船机关本为二轮，第一轮旋转，第二轮不动，以作预备。现在之响，即旋转之轮已坏。虽然，有第二轮以代替之，尚无大碍也。"自是以后，风浪渐杀，然人心终觉有所不安。又越一日

华工日记
Chinese Labourer's Diaries

夜，船已近台湾海峡，忽又回向西南行去。盖因船轮破裂，将往香港修理也。西南行一日夜后，船即渐渐绕山回转，至天将近午时，船由极峡之港经过。见两岸上之铁丝网下，各有巨炮一门，料已近香港，料为鸦片战争后，英人之设备也。

Storms Near Borneo

After leaving Singapore, our ship sailed all the way towards the northeast. The next morning, a sudden storm sprang up on the sea. Everything on the ship shook violently and no one dared to go out onto the deck. Fortunately, it was not as hot as it had been previously. In the evening, our ship shook even more violently. People who had to walk on the deck had to hold firmly onto the thick ropes that where fixed in place especially for the rough weather.

Looking eastward at that time, we could see the distant outline of the coast of Borneo, an island with an area of over 300,000 square miles and with many hills and mountains. Another day passed and at about one o'clock in the morning when our ship was passing on the east side of Luzon after we just sailed by the Palawan Island in the south of the Philippines, we suddenly heard a great vibration at the bottom of the ship. It sounded as if a big nail had been poked into a wheel or a big hammer was being smashed against the bottom of the ship. The noise continued on and off and all people on the ship were nearly scared to death and no one dared to make any sound.

I asked a British officer what had happened, and he said, "The ship usually has two propellers. The first propeller keeps rotating while the second remains motionless as a precaution. The noise we heard came from the first propeller because something went wrong. But it is all right because we can have it replaced by the one propeller." Ever since then, the storms and high waves ceased gradually, but most people still felt uneasy. A day and night later, our ship came near the Taiwan Strait when it suddenly turned and sailed towards the southwest. Due to the propeller of the ship being broken, it had to sail to Hong Kong for repair. After sailing southwest for a day and a night, the ship began to sail slowly back around some mountains and at about midday, our ship passed through a narrow port. Seeing giant cannons underneath the wire entanglements on each side, we arrived at Hong Kong and the cannons must be what the British had left after the Opium Wars.

250. 船到香港

余于未到香港以前，常思香港租于外人，租期九十九年，心中郁郁，不胜浩叹。今身入其境，更不禁为之咨嗟太息！港内之一切建筑，无一而不坚固，无一而不整齐。港湾之北，则为一高山，楼阁台榭，各色相间，上下罗列。不惟白昼望之海光山色秀丽可爱，即一到夜间，山腰往来之汽车，或与灯光，或与月光，艳映交辉，闪烁互应，繁华之盛，实为中国内地之所未见者也。

港内船只总不如新嘉坡之盛，而英国之船只实不为少。盖英在远东之势力，均集中香港一隅也。除英国船外，各国之船，间亦有之。更有吾中国之船数艘，上挂以青天白日之旗帜，为吾华北人之初次见之者也。

余等所乘之船，因破坏而停于港内修理，为期定一礼拜。在此一礼拜之内，有时有住居香港之汉人来船中游览，有欲对吾谈话者，但因余既不懂香港话，彼又不晓北京官话，是以始虽欲谈，终以扞格不入而罢。

华工日记

Chinese Labourer's Diaries

闻其地常常有中国人，因本国语言不统一，而反以英语谈话，彼此乃互通其意者。语言歧异，腾笑邻国，良有以也。

Arriving in Hong Kong

Before I arrived in Hong Kong, I could not help feeling sorry and sighing deeply every time I thought of the fact that it was rented to outsiders for ninety-nine years. Now I was actually here, I could not help but marvel at its beauty. All buildings in the harbour were well built and tidy. To the north of the harbour was a mountain with architecture of various types such as towers, pavilions and terraces on the slopes and on the top. In the daytime, people could see the picturesque scenery of the sea and the mountain. At night, the automobiles travelling to and fro along the mountainside, together with the lights and the moonlight, gave an even more beautiful sight. Nowhere in the mainland of China could be found such prosperity.

The ships inside Hong Kong harbour were not as numerous as those in Singapore, but there were really many British ships. This was because the British influence in the Far East mainly concentrated in Hong Kong. Along with the British ships, there were also ships from other countries occasionally, including several Chinese ships with the flying blue-sky-and-white-sun national flags. It was still the first time that many of us from northern China had seen the national flag of the Chinese navy.

Due to the damage our ship had to stop in the harbour for repairs for one week. During this period, some Chinese residents in Hong Kong visited our ship and intended to talk to us. However, because I knew nothing about the Hong Kong dialect and they knew nothing about Beijing Mandarin, we had to give up our attempt to talk with each other. It was said that due to different dialects in China, some Chinese people living here often spoke English rather than their own language to achieve an understanding of each other. Thus, it seemed justified for people to talk in another language due to the great differences in the dialects of their own country.

251. 过台湾海峡

民国八年阴历十一月初六日，吾曹所乘之船，自香港开出，第二日渡过台湾海峡。第四日即阴历十一月初九日，风浪又起。船身东倒西歪，摇荡颇甚。其时海中不见别有轮船往来，只见许多帆船三五成群，想系沿海等省之渔船也。

翌日拂晓抵东海，风平浪静。直至十一日午时，船即由东海而西，向扬子江口上溯，至傍晚则停泊于吴淞口矣。盖因船大水浅，而船不能前行至上海也。内有英人数名，欲下船而不得，只好在此等候上海来船迎接。所以是船在此又停泊二日也。斯时天气转变，较黎哈夫上船时，寒冷为更烈矣。

Sailing across the Taiwan Strait

On 6 November 1919, our ship set out from Hong Kong and sailed across the Taiwan Strait the next day. On the fourth day of our voyage, the storms began again and the ship swayed violently from left to right. At that time no other ships except many smaller sailboats clustered in twos and threes could be seen. These sailboats were probably the fishing boats of the coastal provinces.

At dawn the next day, our ship reached the East China Sea where the wind and waves were calm. Then at about midday on 11 November our ship began to head west from the East China Sea toward the estuary of the Yangtze River. We had to anchor at Wusongkou at dusk because our ship could not continue to Shanghai for its large size and the shallow water. Several of the British on our ship, who had planned to disembark in Shanghai, had to wait for smaller boats to come from Shanghai to pick them up. Our ship stayed there for another two days. During this period, the weather changed and it became even colder than it was when we boarded the ship at Le Havre.

252. 返国华工到青岛

民国八年阴历十一月十三日，吾等自吴淞口起淀，十四日在东海中，船梆冰块凝结渐厚。十五日晨，余在船上遥遥望见山东角之崂山上，一片雪白。余等在船上，因寒气逼人，都将所有衣服，穿着于身。

十五日下三点，达青岛。临下船，即见码头上驻有兵士若干，盖俟余等下船以维持保护者也。及余等下船，军警一齐前来，处处监视，不准随便行动，只许在指定处所等候火车。斯时也，同工等多纷纷不平曰："余等在欧洲时，英人曾对余等云：'华工远涉重洋，到欧洲战场，代替国家加入协约作工，苦则苦矣。然现在协约战胜联盟，其于中国，功勋可谓不小。以后回国，国家一定特别优待，或嘉奖也。'今国家既不优待，更无嘉奖，竟而禁止自由，殊为失望。"余晓之曰："为秩序计，军

孙干：欧战华工记
Records of Chinese Labourers in European War by Sun Gan

警实亦不得不然。亦可见吾曹华工之无程度也。今吾曹既安然返国，华工二字更彪炳全球，垂竹帛而万世不朽矣。他何求哉！"同工果顿然改悟，反忿忿而欣欣矣。

Chinese Labourers' Arrival in Qingdao

On 13 November 1919, we started sailing again from Wusongkou. The next day, as we sailed on the East China Sea, I saw the ice were getting increasingly thicker and continuously hit against the outside of our ship. On the morning of 15 November, I could see the snow-covered Laoshan Mountain in the eastern part of Shandong Province in the distance. Due to the bitterly cold weather, we had to put on all our clothes inside the ship to keep warm.

At three o'clock in the afternoon on 15 November 1919, we arrived at Qingdao. As we disembarked, I noticed some soldiers were stationed on the wharf to maintain order. As soon as we got off the ship, many military guards came and surrounded us. We were monitored everywhere we went and had no freedom to move about but to wait for the train at a designated place. On this moment, many of my fellow labourers became angry and said: "When we were in Europe, the British told us 'Chinese labourers travelled all the way to the battlefields of Europe and participated in the war as representatives of your country. Although the work here was hard, you've made great exploits to your country now that the Triple Entente had defeated the Central Powers. Your country will give you special and preferential treatment or awards when you return home.' But our country gives us neither preferential treatment nor awards. We're even deprived of our freedom. It really disappoints us." I tried to comfort them and said, "The military guards are doing this for the sake of maintaining order, which reflects what we Chinese labourers lack to a certain degree. Since we've returned to our country safe and sound and the name of Chinese Labourers has splendidly known throughout the world and will be remembered eternally in the history. What else should we ask for?" On hearing my words, my fellow labourers suddenly awakened to the truth and became rejoiced again instead of being resentful.

253. 余自青岛趁火车到张店又自买票到博山

　　余等于十五日晚，受军警指挥，在祁寒旷场中，饥渴殊甚。七点半临上车时，每人给馍馍三个。十六日早六点到张店站，同工由张店下车者十数人，赴博山者仅莱芜县之三人与余而已。方欲登车，路警止之曰："须俟晚间夜车也。"斯时余想，于此天气严寒之际，等至深夜，再坐车到博。不独余一人食宿维艰，三同人将往何处宿耶？余遂征求大家意见，孰愿自出车价，买票上车，三人均应声愿意。余遂趋于票房买票四张，于当日上午十点半钟，同同工三人至博山矣。莱芜同工当日南去，余下午三点即平安抵余之家乡——柿岩庄矣。

Taking Train from Qingdao to Zhangdian and Then to Boshan

On the evening of 15 November 1919, we were arranged by the military police to stay at the open field of Qihan, extremely thirsty and hungry. At 7:30

p.m., just before we got aboard the train, we were given just three steamed buns each. At 6 o'clock in the morning on 16 November 1919, we arrived at Zhangdian Railway Station and dozens of our fellow labourers got off. Only four of us were left to continue our last leg of the journey to Boshan, including three from Laiwu County and me. Just as we were about to get on our train, a policeman stopped us and said, "You should wait for the night train." At that time, I thought if I waited until midnight for the train, it would be very hard for me to find accommodation in such cold weather. My three fellow labourers were faced with the same situation and did not know where to find accommodation. I asked them if they would agree to buy tickets at their own expense so that we could get on the train right now. They all agreed. So I hurried to the ticket office and bought four tickets for the train. At 10:30 a.m. we arrived at Boshan, where we four parted with each other. My fellow labourers left for Laiwu and I arrived safely at my home of Shiyan Village at 3 o'clock in the afternoon.

254. 五大洲之与欧战

五大洲者，即亚细亚、欧罗巴、亚斐利加、阿美利加、澳大利亚也。欧战发生后，五洲之人均加入焉。战地不但在欧洲全部，而斐洲南部、东部，及亚洲之西部亦与焉。

观赴欧助战之人，有生于热带者，如南非洲之黑种人是也；有生近于寒带者，如英吉利与加拿大人是也；有生于温带者，如中国人、美利坚人、日本人、法兰西人、意大利人、葡萄牙人是也。此次欧战，德意

华工日记
Chinese Labourer's Diaries

志与俄罗斯俱由专制一变而为共和。使寒带、温带、热带之人，都被牵连，彼此往来，如开大会于法兰西焉。

今大战既告终矣，世界各国对于"优胜劣败，弱肉强食""恃德者昌，恃力者亡"，果由此而知其孰轻孰重，何去何从，则欧战三年未始非世界和平之大关键也！

Five Continents and European War

The five continents refer to Asia, Europe, Africa, America and Australia. After the European War broke out, people from each of the five continents became involved. The battlefields of the World War spread not only across the whole European continent but also to the south and east of Africa and the west of Asia.

Among the people sent to help in the European War were those who were born in tropical zones such as the black people of South Africa, those who were born in the cold temperate zones such as people from England and Canada, and those who were born in temperate zones, such as the Chinese, Americans, Japanese, French, Italians, and Portuguese. The war transformed Germany and Russia from autocracies into republics and got people from the cold, temperate and tropical zones worked together in France and strengthened the exchange between their countries.

Now the European War has ended. If countries around the world can learn from it that "survival of the fittest" is not the best way to resolve problems and that "those who rely on virtues will thrive and those who rely on forces will perish", and then make their decisions accordingly, the three-year-long European War might also be regarded as the key to world peace.

孙干：欧战华工记
Records of Chinese Labourers in European War by Sun Gan

255. 华工之略述

语云："霸者之民，驩虞如也；王者之民，皞皞如也。"华工者，出于中华民国之能作工之人民也。吾国自前清末叶，在上者心口不一，不能行王道之实，以致世道日下，人心不古。逮民国元年以后，不惟国内之人民咸惟利是趋，而门户一开放，一切新学说，亦乘虚而入。而读书之文士，往往只知讲优胜劣败，弱肉强食。而一般人民，又焉得不惟蒽之怀也。英人所招惟蒽之怀之工人，其中石匠也、木匠也、裁缝也、理发也等等一切工匠之外，农夫也、教员也、学生也、商人也，此皆华工队中之最善良者也。至于滥竽其中之市侩也、流氓也、散兵也、土匪也，既不认字，又不明理，既至法国分散于各地，又岂能不出杀人放火、奸盗邪淫种种之事乎？虽然，倘从其国帑中支其一二，遣忠实之人，引诱之，教导之，告诫之，儆醒之，工人亦未尝不能悔改，而转为善如王者之民，皞皞如也。

Brief Review of Chinese Labourers

As the saying goes, "Powerful kings with remarkable achievements make their people happy, while virtuous kings with mighty merits make their people content". Chinese labourers are people of the Republic of China who are capable of hard work. In our country, the rulers have not implemented the practice of a benevolent government since the last years of the late Qing Dynasty, leading to the day-to-day degeneration of morals of both individuals and the public in general, mainly because of the inconsistency between the words and behaviours of our rulers. Since 1912, the first year of the Republic of China, most people in our country have been driven solely by profit, and with the implementation of the "open door policy", many new ideas from foreign countries have also begun to pour into our country. While the intellectuals believe only in the survival of the fittest, why should we expect common people not to follow likewise? Many of those people recruited into the Chinese Labour Corps are artisans such as stonemasons, carpenters, tailors and barbers, as well as farmers, teachers, students and businessmen. They are the kindest people in the brigades of Chinese labourers. However, among the Chinese labourers there are also some bad guys like philistines, hooligans, disbanded soldiers, and bandits, who are usually illiterate and lack common sense. When they were sent to different places in France, it was inevitable for them to commit various crimes such as murder, arson, theft, or rape. If our government had allotted a small amount of national funds to employ some righteous people to encourage, instruct, warn and enlighten them, perhaps these labourers would have repented and amended their way of life so that they could be transformed into the "content people of virtuous kings".

256. 对吾政府之略述

政府者，国家行政之官员，以正当之事，治理全国人民之所居住之者也。吾国政府之中，多系讲博爱，讲自由，尚平等，尚牺牲者居之，其人之中，忠实者虽然不少，而内则对建设，对教育，或言论洋洋大篇，

孙干：欧战华工记
Records of Chinese Labourers in European War by Sun Gan

或公文层层如柱；外则其出也衣服辉辉煌煌，作福作威；入则便嬖满堂，酒肉实腹。又何暇如信耶稣救主，见利禄而不享，知为义而更用力者也？不然官府之食民之食者为谁，官府之衣民之衣者为谁？茶也、酒也、小妾也、大姨也，非剥削平民之脂膏以偿之，不足以安其嗜欲。又何况与言华工之赴欧助战，关系中国存亡之远大问题耶！望观吾《欧战记》后而注意，爱国者效法耶稣救主之爱天国也可。

Brief Review of Our Government

Government refers to the place where the administrative officials of a state govern its whole people in rightful and legitimate affairs. In our government, most officials emphasise fraternity, liberty, and equality. Although there are some faithful officials among those who advocate sacrifice, most of them will make long speeches or establish excessive rules and formalities on domestic affairs such as construction and education. They wear luxuriant clothes and behave domineeringly outside, while at home they indulge themselves in wines and delicacies with many servants in the hall. How can one expect these officials to see benefits without enjoying them and to know what righteousness is and work hard to achieve it as reverently as Christians believe in their Savior Jesus Christ? Otherwise, for what would those same officials who provide food and clothes for people get their profits? For tea or wine, mistresses and wives? It is hard to satisfy their greed without exploiting the common people, let alone the issue of sending Chinese labourers to the European War that concerns the survival of the Chinese nation! I hope that patriots, after reading my *Records of European War,* will follow the example of Jesus Christ who devoted his life to the love for the Kingdom of Heaven.

华工日记
Chinese Labourer's Diaries

257. 东亚民性与欧美民性

民性者，天赋与人合理生活之良知也。《圣经》上云，吾们人类自亚当始祖犯罪后，传至挪亚。经过洪水，其子三人闪、含、雅弗，散居于东西各地。经年既久，其相离愈远。以后迁至亚洲之人，自轩辕氏，及经尧、舜、禹、汤、文、武、周公，尚知天理为本。孔孟修身，齐家，治国，年代既久，则民性习焉而相远，中国现代之民性殆尽远古耶！势观历史，源远流长相传，年代愈久而天理愈彰著者。

现代欧美之民性逐兴，原不及我国悠久繁茂于前，盖因亚洲基督教传入欧美，民性振发耶矣，吾人应当处处学而奋进直追。我国居世之地位，虽远不及欧美，待发我之后生也！

《欧战记》终。

National Characters of East Asia, Europe and America

National character refers to the innate nature and the conscience of national life of a nation. According to the *Bible*, since the first man Adam was driven out of the Garden of Eden because of the original sin, human beings were descended to Noah. Noah had three sons, Shem, Ham, and Japheth, who scattered in the east and west of the earth after the flood. As the years passed by, they became more and more separate from each other and some of

孙干：欧战华工记

Records of Chinese Labourers in European War by Sun Gan

them moved to Asia. Since Xuanyuan, through the Emperors Yao, Shun, Yu, Tang, Wen, Wu and Duke of Zhou, people in ancient China began to form the essence of Chinese national character. Confucius and Mencius advocated the cultivation of personal morality, the regulation of one's family and the rule of the whole country. After years of development, the characters and customs of different countries became more and more diverse. The national character of modern China is quite different from what it was in ancient times. From a historical perspective, the national character descended from generation to generation. The more ancient it was, the more manifest the essence of national character was.

In modern times, the European and American nations, which had been lagging behind our nation, developed rapidly. The rise of their national characters, to a large extent, was due to the fact that Asian Christianity was introduced into European and American countries. People in our country should try to learn from them and strive to catch up with them. Although at present, the position of our nation in the world is not as high as those of European and American nations, our younger generations should take the responsibility and make our nation great again in the world.

End of *Records of Chinese Labourers in European War*

马春苓：游欧杂志

Miscellaneous Records of Travel to Europe
by Ma Chunling

华工日记
Chinese Labourer's Diaries

马春苓（1886—1962），字芳洲，一字赞臣，号廷襄，山东省潍坊市临朐县胡梅涧村人，出国前在当地任小学教师，1917年10月应英国招募和同村10名村民启程赴欧。马春苓应募华工除了挣钱养家糊口、维持生计外，还为圆自己的环游之志，"今日之举，既能增军事之新学识，又得偿游历之夙志愿，时哉弗可失矣！"

马春苓于1917年12月抵达法国，驻扎在法国加莱、勒哈弗尔等地，主要负责修路、运粮、伐木、运输战略物资等战勤保障工作。一战结束后，被派至比利时等地清理战场，直到1919年12月回到家乡。马春苓在欧期间写成《游欧杂志》，按时间顺序记录自己的真实经历和所见所闻，详细描述了华工在欧洲战场的分布与劳作情况，分析招募华工原因及战争始末，还以诗歌形式表达自己的见闻与情志，《吊比国街市》："荒野蓬蒿千宅绿，颓楼牖户万家通。昔年黎庶堂前燕，遁入战壕铁屋中。"反映了战争的惨烈及其造成的深重灾难。《游欧杂志》也成为后人研究一战华工历史宝贵的第一手史料。

回国后，马春苓先后在北朱、胡梅涧、大广饶、姬家河等地任小学教师，前后历教职四十余年。

Ma Chunling (1886-1962), with the courtesy name of Fangzhou and the literary name of Tingxiang, was born in Humeijian Village, Linqu County, Weifang, Shandong Province. He worked as a teacher in a local primary school before going to Europe. Ma Chunling, together with another 10 villagers, was recruited by Britain and set out for Europe in October 1917. He applied for recruitment as a Chinese labourer not only for the purpose of earning money to support his family and to make a living, but also for the purpose of realising his ambition of travelling around the world. According to his own words, "It can not only increase my military knowledge but also fulfil my long-cherished dream of travelling abroad. It is really too good an opportunity to miss!"

马春苓：游欧杂志
Miscellaneous Records of Travel to Europe by Ma Chunling

After his arrival in France in December 1917, Ma Chunling was stationed in Calais, Le-Havre and other places of France successively, mainly responsible for building roads, transporting grains, felling trees, transporting strategic supplies and other war support service work. At the end of WWI, he was also sent to Belgium to clean up battlefields. He returned to his hometown in December 1919. He recorded, in chronological order, his personal experiences and what he had seen and heard while he was in Europe in his diary *Miscellaneous Records of Travel to Europe*, which described in detail the distribution and hard work of Chinese labourers in European battlefields, analysed the reasons for the recruitment of Chinese labourers and the whole process of the First World War, and expressed his sentiments in the form of poetry. For instance, in the poem "Lamenting over Belgian Markets", he wrote, "Wildly growing are weeds in the wilderness and deserted houses, and in ruins scattered declining buildings and broken windows. Those swallows once nesting under the roof of ordinary households, are now escaping into the iron houses and entrenchments to seek shelters." This poem reflects the cruelty of the war and the great sufferings it brought about to the local residents. *Miscellaneous Records of Travel to Europe* has become a valuable first-hand historical document for later generations to study the history of the Chinese labourers in WWI.

Since his return to China, Ma Chunling worked as a primary school teacher for over 40 years in the villages of Humeijian, Daguangrao and Jijiahe successively.

华工日记
Chinese Labourer's Diaries

马春苓生平自述

余名春苓，字芳洲，兄弟二人，余居长。父叔平公年五十余始生余，爱如掌上珠，六七岁即教之读，十四岁命就外傅学制艺。十五岁娶妻田氏，次年八股成篇，出应童子试，大慰父望。每思常依膝下，不意先父遽然去世（寿七旬），时余年十七，弟春芝才十有四岁。余读书持家，异常劳悴，至二十岁，辍读授童蒙于本村。清末停科举，立学校，士子无由进取，余乃于民国二年考入县立师范学校，肄习教学新法，毕业后任本村小学教员。田氏生四女无子，弟又析居，余教授之余，兼事耕作，终岁勤劳，仅能糊口。

民国五六年，胸大饥，时欧战方酣，英人来募华工助战。余遂投笔而往，历二年余，战事告终，乃得东归，时民国八年十二月廿五日也。明年任北朱完小教员，校长每以"循循善诱、诲人不倦"称余。次岁，本村父老敦求回里，教授村中子弟，后经派充大广饶、姬家河、大张德诸村小学教师，然因家务羁绊，里人要求，在外不过一二年，即仍回本村服务，前后历教职四十余年。在故里之日居多，一时村中学子，尽属吾徒，大有桃李满门之概！

民国十二年，弟因家产荡尽，携眷谋生抚顺市，而老母在堂，奉养之事，归余一人。今弟已卜居于彼，其夫妻虽没，而子孙绳绳、宗道蒸蒸，亦不幸中之幸也！十三年，余卅八岁矣，子嗣尤虚，田氏劝余纳副室公氏，联生三子，长传宗，次传家、传宝，甚慰余怀！廿一年，老母辞世（寿八十三岁），茕茕中依礼以葬。

一九三八年（民国廿七年），日寇进犯，蒋介石率大军退避重庆，以

马春苓：游欧杂志
Miscellaneous Records of Travel to Europe by Ma Chunling

致杂派队伍，蜂拥而起，借抗日之名，涂炭人民。所到之处，抢掠一光。至一九四二年，岁又连饥，人民四散奔逃，余亦与公氏率三子（时四女皆于归）赴辽宁逃生，田氏留守。时余已五十有七，子时幼稚，不得已与儿辈勉强入工厂为佣，借以糊口。越两年余，岁渐好转，始相率归里，仍充本村教师。

一九四五年旧寇投降，共产党收复失地，消除杂派队伍，民赖以安。蒋贼率军东归，抗击共产党，余遂派长子传宗（年十八岁）参加八路军，抵抗蒋贼。一九四八年，共产党解放全中国，人民方得安居乐业。四九年，田氏病故（年七十）。翌岁，余卸教职，遂得赋闲。

回忆一生经历，早岁丧父，操心劳力，日夜不得宁处，中年遭时世坎坷，饥荒交迫，为仰事俯畜而西奔东逃，备历艰辛。今年已七十，犹本康健，子亦成立，五四年又参加农社，土地劳力所获，一家生活亦觉充裕。

Biography of Ma Chunling

I am Ma Chunling and Fangzhou is my courtesy name. I have one younger brother. I came into this world when my father was already in his 50s. Taken as an apple of my father's eye, I was taught to read at the age of six or seven and sent out to learn how to write eight-legged essays with my teacher. I got married at the age of fifteen. In the following year, due to my ability of writing good eight-legged essays, I passed the qualification test for imperial examinations, which greatly pleased my father. When my father died suddenly at the age of 70, I was 17 and my brother Chunzhi was only 14. From then on, I had to support my family while keeping on studying, which made me greatly exhausted. So at the age of 20, I had to stop my study and began teaching children privately in our village. At the end of the Qing Dynasty, the imperial examinations were abandoned and new schools were set up. In the second year of the Republic of China I was admitted to the Normal School of Linqu County, where I began to learn new methods of teaching. After graduation I became a primary school teacher in our village. My wife and I had four daughters. With no sons to help and my only brother living separately, I had to make a living by doing farm work while still serving as a teacher all the year round. Life was very hard.

In the fifth or sixth year of the Republic of China, when a great famine took place in Linqu and the European War was becoming more and more intense, the British came to recruit Chinese labourers to work for the war. So I quitted my teaching and went to Europe, where I worked for more than two years. On 25 December of the eighth year of the Republic of China, I returned home after the war in Europe had ended. In the following year, I began to work as a teacher in Beizhuwan Primary School, where I was highly praised by the principal for "being good at teaching and tireless in teaching". At the request of my fellow countrymen, I returned to teach children in my home village the following year. Later, I was assigned to teach in primary schools in the villages of Daguangrao, Jijiahe and Dazhangde. However, due to the household duties and my wife's request, I returned to teach in my home village again after working in other villages for one or two years. Thus, for most part of my 40 years of teaching career, I stayed in my own home village. As a result, nearly everyone in the village was my student at one time or another.

In the twelfth year of the Republic of China, after all his family properties were used up, my brother took his family to Fushun, Liaoning Province, to make a living. I had to take all the responsibility for taking care of my elderly mother. The family of my brother later settled down in Fushun, where both my brother and his wife spent the rest of their lives and their descendants continue to live happily to this day. This, in a sense, can be said to be the contribution my brother made to our family even if he failed to fulfil the filial duties to our mother. In the thirteenth year of the Republic of China, I was thirty-eight years old and because we had no sons all the time, my wife persuaded me into marrying a concubine, who later gave birth to three sons in succession. The eldest son was named Chuanzong and the other two, Chuanjia and Chuanbao respectively; all of whom were a great comfort to me. In the twenty-first year of the Republic of China, my mother died at the age of 83 and we buried her according to the rituals of that time.

In 1938 (the 27th year of the Republic of China), due to the invasion of Japanese, Chiang Kai-shek and his army retreated to Chongqing, resulting in the emergence of various warlords, which brought about great misery and suffering to people in the name of fighting against the Japanese invaders. Everything was plundered wherever they went. In 1942, due to successive famines people had to flee from their homes. I, together with my three sons and their mother, fled to Liaoning Province for a living while my wife stayed at home (my four daughters were all married by that time). Because my sons were still very young, I had to work in factories with young people at the age of 57 to make a living. It was only about two years later that the situation began to turn better. I took my family back home and worked as a teacher again in my village.

In 1945, the Japanese aggressors surrendered. The Communist Party of China regained the lost territory and eliminated the warlord factions, enabling people to have a safe life. Later, Chiang Kai-shek led his army back to the east to fight against the Communist Party. I sent my 18-year-old eldest son Chuanzong to join the Eighth Route Army to fight against Chiang. People

华工日记

Chinese Labourer's Diaries

could not live in peace and work in happiness until the Communist Party liberated the whole of China. My wife died in 1949 at the age of 70. I also resigned from teaching in the following year to enjoy a life of leisure.

To support the whole family after my father's death, I was forced to work hard and take care of the family without rest both day and night at a very young age. To avoid starvation during the great famines and make a living in the hard times of my country, I had to leave home and flee to different places, living a hard life in my middle-age. Looking back on those years, I feel satisfied with my present life. Now I am 70 years old and still in good health. All my sons have grown up and have their own families. We joined the agricultural cooperatives in 1954. With what is earned from the land and labour, our family is now living a happy and abundant life.

马春苓：游欧杂志
Miscellaneous Records of Travel to Europe by Ma Chunling

序

余尝披览地图，以见其世界之大，万国之众，水陆山原之异势，飞潜动植之殊态，以及人民风化，土地气候，莫不千差万别。若仅拘于一区，则眼帘障蔽，身外之事，一无所睹。虽朝夕讲诵地理，而授者听者，皆恍惚无证，反求诸己，亦多有未之敢作者。兴念及此，遂慨然有环游之志。而困于资斧，志未遑也。丁巳（民国六年）岁，余承乏大广饶庄国民学校教席。时欧战方亟，我国亦列入联盟。英人与政府订约募华工以助战，人民陆续应募者，已数万余众。余奋然曰："今日之举，既能增军事之新学识，又得偿游历之夙志愿，时哉弗可失矣！"遂于十月假节，告辞东君，投笔应募。兹将往返时日路程，暨经历之事项，见闻之大概，按时记录于下，以示不忘云尔。

民国六年九月三十日，自校旋里，次日为十月朔，躬奉时羞，致祭先茔，再拜先父墓前，告以赴欧之事。

初二日置酒堂前，招饮胞弟暨诸叔兄等，告以游历之举。诸兄皆曰："欧战方剧，危险万分。汝兄弟异居，堂上有七旬之母，应门无五尺之童，一切家务，招顾伊谁？"余曰："否否。母氏虽老，犹异常康健。吾弟居家，尽可代尽孝养。三载之期，转瞬即至。些须家事，有诸兄在，谅无差虞。余志已决，请与兄痛饮一次，以俟后会可也。"渠辈知吾志坚，遂不复拒，各开怀畅饮，至晚而罢。

初三日早起，拜别母亲，以家事付托内人，整装起行。内人曰："君志已决，妾碍难挽留，然三年归期，宁可必乎？"余笑曰："英人信义素著，三年送还，载在招募条约，虽一日不能迟延。卿宜善事老母，谨理

华工日记
Chinese Labourer's Diaries

家务。客况之措置,夫自斟酌处理,勿劳我妻过虑也。"早饭毕,同侣有族叔祥桂,族侄传诗、传礼、传兴等,来邀余偕行,遂相与携装北上。晚六时,至益都东谭家坊车栈而止宿焉。

初四日早十时,同至英国招工分局报名。英人检阅一次,咸蒙许可,即将姓氏籍贯,注于簿册。同日报名者尚百余人。晚饭后,皆留宿局中。

初五日早六时,自谭家坊登车。迤逦东南行,至下午二时,已达即墨之沧口。车中玻窗轩厂,东望崂山,玲珑秀丽,绵亘万里。南瞰沧海,洞明镜清,舳舻相接,诚大观也。与同侣下车,至招募总局。复验讫,各易戎服,寄居第十一号房。一院之中,伙友不下千余人,同食同宿,真热闹哉。

初九日上午八时,正欲排队演操,闻有自谭家坊来应募者,就问之,遇见族兄维坤、服侄传浩、堂侄传福偕至。迨渠验毕,余亦散队,聚首谈心,备形亲切。因询家况,对述明晰,心中悬念顿释,透彻异常,亦良遇哉!

二十二日,同袍七营,共三千四百三十人,起程赴欧。上午七句钟,由沧口登车,沿海而南,转瞬间见山麓之下,筑有高埠。房舍连亘,时属新式,铁路中通,三面俱为港湾,乃堡岛也(在青岛西北二里许)。甫下车,见轮船一艘,泊于岛右(该船长三百二十步,宽卅二步。船舱六层,船楼二层,汽锅三口,烟囱一座,为航舶之中次者)。

遂整队鱼贯而上,既入舱,则行装用具已分列床上。方检点整理,忽闻机声阵阵,友人曰:"舟启椗矣。"于是登甲板,凭栏而望。见碧浪连天,波涛汹涌,纵一叶之所如,凌万顷之茫然。而掀波劈浪,稳如磐石,于以叹西人格致之功,诚所谓精义入神者欤!是为志。是日也,下午一时,由堡岛东南行,及明日下五时,晚饭毕,凭栏远眺,见东北一带,山势迤逦,约数十里。舟子告余曰:"此朝鲜西南界也。"翌日即至日本矣。

二十四日复南行,至上八时折而东,泊于日之长崎口。是地三面环

马春苓：游欧杂志
Miscellaneous Records of Travel to Europe by Ma Chunling

山，西连大海，山上林木青葱，蔬菜湛然，屋宇环列，自山根直达其巅，各抱地势，钩心斗角，蜂房水涡，真不知其几千万落。晚间电灯齐燃，朗若曙星，高低灿烂，不辨西东，登楼纵目，几终仙境在即矣！

是日下七时，由长崎起椗东行。至次日下四时，忽见远山杳冥，帆船往来。翻译（英人募中国之精通英语者为翻译员，每队二人）遥指曰："此日本横滨也，过此则为太平洋矣。"

二十六日，出日本而东，行凡旬有余日，惟见碧浪滔天，弥望无际。岛屿不见，飞鸟绝迹。彤霞密布，朔风砭肌，直令人惕然而惊，亦惨然而凄。惟伏处舱中，欹枕专卧而已。

十一月十二日，晨起登船头东望，风平浪静，水光如镜，一轮红日，涌出海面，云霞掩映，幻奇丽于无穷，较之登泰岱，东观日出，更为亲炙矣。未几远山趋跄而来迎，群鸟翱翔以欢呼。金知距岸匪遥，至夜半，果抵北美洲堪拿大海岸而泊焉。

十三日舍舟登陆，至一处，地名汛哥佛（温哥华）。为堪拿大西南隅之一大岛也，是地四面环海，突起峡屿，山势崎岖，林木丛杂，人烟寥落，不成村里，惟依海滨山麓，架板屋而居焉。宅隅隙地，辟为田园，其中麦苗初出，残果犹存，气候恰似晚秋，但阴雨连绵，罕见天日，盖其地势使然欤。

二十八日早十时，由汛哥佛岛登舟，下三时起椗东行，约四时余，即至汛哥佛海关。停泊半宿，次日早二时，舍舟登车，沿堪拿大铁路东上，初惟高山浚谷，沿溪穴嶂而进，逾威尼比克而东，则平原万里，白雪尺许而无垠。市埠甚稀，而楼房极其壮丽。行凡旬日，不见城邑，居民但附近车栈，三两家或五六家簇聚而已。以视吾国之间阎扑地，鸡犬相闻者，奚啻天壤。昔年华盛顿独立美国，弃此地犹敝屣，良有以也。

十二月初七日，至大西洋西岸哈勒法海口。下车，复登汽船。初九日过午，开船东行，九艘并列而进，华工二艘，间有货船，余惟兵舰护

华工日记
Chinese Labourer's Diaries

送。此虽英人防御之严，而同事诸人，未尝无戒心焉。（时德国暗伏潜水艇于大西洋各航路，踪迹联军船只，突起沉之，为害最烈。）余喟然曰："大义所趋，死生一之，又何惧乎！今日之役，惟因德国肆虎狼之威，以陵夷西土，致于全球集怒，共兴问罪之师。吾国既入协约，自当军助战而民助力。吾等受政府承允于役西土，不须破斧缺枪，亦自有名有利。既无所悔，夫复何惧。鞠躬尽瘁，三年有日。至于成败利钝，岂吾蚩蚩者所能逆睹。"

十八日晚七时，至英格兰利勿波口岸下船，即乘汽车东南行。逾伦敦城至英伦海峡西北岸。夜半下车，次于行营。翌日平明，步行十余里，前至口岸，路见青松苍翠，红梅鲜妍，景物气候，颇与中国无殊。遂驾小明轮快船东渡。约两时许，即抵法国沙省西界，复舍舟登车。晚六时，开车东南行。至夜分，乃抵驻法华工队总分发处奴埃地，得与族弟汝彝相会。各诉离情，相对嘘唏，热情未已，离愁复续。不数日，复大队拨往加莱省西北鄙在勒艮木工厂，乃登车东北行约二百里许，始达其地而结营焉。时十二月廿三日也。

二十四日，本队长复分派我第一连华工百二十余人，往报白工厂开始作工。该地系加莱西北部之大镇，在在勒艮木东北十余里。其东南偏方修支路，为预备战线之基，故分派本连于此，以运输材料也。

民国七年二月初二日，报白工程告竣，乃复还在勒艮木旧营，曾于作工之暇，吟诗一首，以明心曲：

> 一为迁客去西欧，回望山东两泪流。
> 骨肉时牵万里梦，韦韝怎奈五更愁。
> 心驰利欲复何悔，学限管蠡志未酬。
> 那得杜公千日酒，恍然睡觉已三秋。

马春苓：游欧杂志
Miscellaneous Records of Travel to Europe by Ma Chunling

夜梦旋里与梅亭相会

偷闲跋涉旋胸城,遥见梅亭笑靥迎。
满腹愁肠诉不尽,猛惊院吏晓钟声。

服兄春魁,字梅亭。与吾为莫逆友,最相知心。自去岁分袂以后,几无宿不与相会,故作绝句一首,以志想念之情。

书怀

卷怀经史莫搜罗,破上微躯受折磨。
日锁愁眉空自苦,轻敲铺板且长歌。

呜呼,日营工作,筋疲力困。夜避飞炸,心惊胆裂。回望故国,关山万里。前计归期,迢迢三年,其苦况诚不忍言。虽然,吾人旅此,如枊虎瓶鱼,即插翅亦难奋飞。虽日夜忧虑,亦将奈何?惟苦处寻乐,随遇自安,以保我微躯。至于吉凶祸福,概诿夫天命而已!

咏欧女细腰

西洋美女巧梳妆,蚕发蜂腰裙带长。
倘入郢都宫里去,定然喜坏楚灵王。

咏法女肥乳

玉容不屑粉脂香,新剥鸡头炽而昌。
倘入长安宫里去,也应馋杀小三郎。

欧洲属白种人,其妇女之白皙,自不待言。但英人面色颇红,鼻亦特巨。法人面色纯白,鼻亦较小,尤为美观。然其褐发卷曲,翠睛圆润,瘦腰纤细,肥乳突峙,则是欧女特色。故作绝句二首,以志其尤。

华工日记
Chinese Labourer's Diaries

清明日野游集句

独怜幽草涧边行,送尽东风过楚城。
况是清明好天气,何人不起故乡情。

清明翌晨集句

无花无酒过清明,总是关山离别情。
蝴蝶梦中家万里,夜来还到洛阳城。

六月二十三日,工厂工作闲暇,下午分工,余与联璋冯世侄(砚兄聿岫之少子,与余同隶一营),共累道木(修铁路所用之木枕)十数块。须臾事竣,相与仰卧木垛之上,偶得一联云:"斯离坝上斯离铺(英语谓道木为斯离坝,安眠为斯离铺)。"倩联璋对之。适英团长乘马至工厂,查视工人勤惰。余二人忙起效劳,联璋应机对曰"好尔厮休好尔题(英语谓马为好尔厮,止步停立为好尔题)。"盖恐其久驻,有妨我二人安眠故也。即境生情,遂感而应,其心机灵敏,可概见矣。

七月二十八日由在勒艮木移于敖锥(在在勒艮木西北三十余里)作工二十余日,至八月二十二日复移于茏汪省(在加莱省西南)西北鄙之子弹工厂。

Preface

From the map, I once observed the large size of the world, numerous countries, vast oceans, various landforms, diverse animals and plants, and different peoples, customs, landscapes and climates. If one were confined to only one place, his eyes would be blocked and see nothing new outside his own area. I taught my students geography every day, but even though they

马春苓：游欧杂志
Miscellaneous Records of Travel to Europe by Ma Chunling

listened to me attentively, they were still confused and frustrated for lack of real-life evidence. When seeking the cause in myself, I did not dare to give the evidence most of the time for my own lack of personal experiences. Frustrated by this situation, I began to dream about travelling around the world. However, my dream has never come true for lack of money. In the sixth year of the Republic of China, I took a teaching position in the Primary School of Daguangrao Village. During that time, the European War was becoming more intense and our country also joined the Entente countries. The British and Chinese governments signed a contract to recruit Chinese labourers to work for the war. Many people applied for the recruitment and in only a few days tens of thousands of people were recruited. I was excited and said to myself, "I will choose to work for the European War. It can not only increase my military knowledge but also realise my long-cherished dream of travelling abroad. It is really too good an opportunity to miss!" So I quitted my teaching job to apply for the recruitment in October. To help remember this period of my life, I recorded everything in chronological order, including the dates of departure and returning, the voyages, and what I had experienced during this time.

On 30 September of the sixth year of the Republic of China, I returned home from school. The next day was 1 October, the day to honour the memory of the dead. I prepared some seasonal food as offerings to sacrifice at the graves of my ancestors and then told my father about my intention of travelling to Europe in front of his grave.

On the following day, I invited my younger brother and cousins to have dinner together and told them about my decision to travel to Europe. All my cousins said, "The European War is so fierce now, it is too dangerous to go there. You and your brother live in different places and your mother is already in her seventies. But in your family, there is no servant to answer the door. Who would do all the household work and who would take care of her?" I said, "No, no. Although my mother is elderly, she is still in excellent health. My brother stays at home and he can take care of her for me. Three years is not a long period. As for the household affairs, I believe they can be handled properly with the help of all of you. I've already made up my mind. Let's drink to our heart's content today and look forward to our meeting again in the future." Knowing that it was impossible to change my mind, they did not refuse my proposal again and we drank freely with great joviality until the night fell.

On 3 October, I got up early. After bidding farewell to my mother and putting the household affairs in my wife's charge, I packed up my luggage and got ready for departure. My wife said to me, "Since you've made up your mind, I know I should not get in your way. But is it true that you will return after three years?" I replied to her with a smile, "The British are famous for their integrity, now that the three-year service is contained in the recruitment contract, they will send us back home without a single day of delay. You should take good care of our mother and the housework, I can take care of myself outside, please don't worry about me at all." After breakfast, I set out to the north together with my kinsmen of Uncle Xianggui and Nephew Chuanshi, Chuanli and Chuandian. At six o'clock in the evening, we stopped at a hotel in Tanjiafang in the east of Yidu and stayed there for the night.

At ten o'clock on 4 October we went to the British Recruitment Bureau to sign up for recruitment. All of us passed the British inspection and then we put down our names and places of birth on the registration book. More than 100 other people also came to sign up for recruitment. After supper, we all stayed at the bureau.

At six o'clock on 5 October, we got on a train from Tanjiafang and travelled windingly eastward. At two o'clock in the afternoon, we arrived

马春苓：游欧杂志

Miscellaneous Records of Travel to Europe by Ma Chunling

at Cangkou in Jimo. From the glass window of the train, we could see the beautiful long-stretching Laoshan Mountain in the east and the vast area of sea with clean water and grand convoys of ships in the south. We got off the train together and arrived at the General Recruitment Bureau. After a re-inspection, all of us were given uniforms to change into and we lived in Barrack-Room 11. With more than one thousand fellow labourers living and eating together in a yard, it was very boisterous.

At eight o'clock on 9 October, while we were getting ready to queue up for drills, we heard that there were applicants from Tangjiafang. Among them I encountered my kinsmen of Cousin Weikun, Nephew Chuanhao, and Nephew Chuanya. When they finished the inspections, our drill also finished. We talked together cordially. When I asked about things in my family, they told everything in detail. Hearing their words, I felt a sudden relief. It was really a good encounter.

On 22 October, seven battalions with a total number of 3,430 Chinese labourers started their journey to Europe. At seven o'clock in the morning, we got on a train from Cangkou and travelled southward along the coast. Soon we saw a high wharf at the foot of mountains, where the railways ran through rows of new-style houses with harbours on three sides. It was a port island about three quarters of a mile away in the northwest of Qingdao. As soon as we got off the train, we saw a ship berthed on the right side of the island. It was about 1,600 feet long and 160 feet wide. With six storeys of cabins, two stories of forecastles, three steam-boilers and a high chimney, it was a second-rate ship.

We embarked on the ship one after another. When we got into the cabin, we put our luggage onto our respective beds. Hardly had we finished sorting things out when we suddenly heard the sound of the engines. One friend told me, "The ship has set sail for voyage." I went up to the deck and leaned against

华工日记
Chinese Labourer's Diaries

the railing. As far as my eye could reach were roaring waves and all around us was boundless sea. Sailing forward through the surging waves, our ship remained as stable as a gigantic rock. I could not help admiring the advanced technology of the Westerners, who had grasped the essence of nature. That was why I recorded all of this. At one o'clock in the afternoon, we sailed southeast all the way from the port island. After eating our meal at five o'clock the next day, we leaned against the railings and looked into the distance. In the northeast were mountain ranges stretching dozens of miles. A sailor told me, "This is the southwest border of Korea." We arrived in Japan the following day.

On 24 October, we kept sailing southward until eight o'clock in the morning when we changed our direction toward the east and later stopped at the port of Nagasaki in Japan, which was surrounded by mountains on three sides and the sea on the west. On the mountains were luxuriant trees and green vegetables. Numerous houses scattered along the slopes, from the foot all the way up to the top of the mountain like honeycombs. When all lights turned on at night, the houses at different heights were all as bright as the morning star, which might make one lose his directions among them and gave him the illusion that he was in a fairyland.

At seven o'clock that day we started our sailing again eastward from Nagasaki. At four o'clock the next day, we suddenly saw great mountains in the distance and shuttling sailboats. An interpreter (for each brigade of Chinese labourers, the British appointed two English speaking labourers as interpreters) pointed to the distance and said, "This is Yokohama of Japan. We'll enter the Pacific Ocean after we cross it."

On 26 October, we sailed out of Japan and continued our voyage eastward. We sailed on the ocean for over ten days and all that we could see was the boundless ocean with surging waves. There were no islands around

马春苓：游欧杂志

Miscellaneous Records of Travel to Europe by Ma Chunling

and no birds in the sky. The dense rosy clouds and the piercing north winds made us watchful, fearful and miserable. We had to stay inside our cabins and lay on our beds.

On 12 November, I went to the deck and looked eastward after I got up in the morning. With no waves and no winds, the ocean was very calm, just like a huge mirror. A red sun rose from the ocean surface and magnificent rosy clouds changed their shapes in the sky. Such a view was grander than the sunrise view on the top of Mount Tai. A few moments later, I spotted some mountains in the distance and groups of birds flying in the sky. I knew that we would soon arrive at land. As expected, our ship arrived and berthed at the coast of Canada in the North of America at midnight.

On 13 November, we disembarked and went ashore. We went to a place called Vancouver, a large island in the southwestern corner of Canada. It was surrounded by sea on all sides with prominent gorges and islets. The rough mountains and thick forests showed few signs of human habitation. Wooden houses with residents could only be found at the foot of the mountains along the coast. The spaces between the houses were cleared up as fields, where grew wheat seedlings and trees with remnant fruit on. It was late autumn, but sunshine was seldom seen because of the cloudy and rainy weather, which I thought was due to its unique terrain.

At ten o'clock on 28 November, we embarked again and set sail eastward from the island of Vancouver at about three o'clock. At four o'clock, we arrived at the customs of Vancouver, where we stayed for half a night. At two o'clock the next morning, we got on a train and travelled eastward along the railways of Canada. At first, the train travelled among deep valleys and high mountains but then, after it passed through Winnipeg, it began to travel on a boundless great plain covered with thick snow. There were fewer marketplaces,

华工日记
Chinese Labourer's Diaries

but the buildings were very imposing. We travelled on the train for nearly ten days without seeing any cities or local residents. What we saw were just a few hotels clustered nearby the railways. There seemed to be a world of difference from the closely-connected and densely-populated towns and villages in China. Thus, it seemed justified for George Washington to discard this piece of land when he founded the United States independent from the Great Britain.

On 7 December, our train arrived at the seaport of Halifax on the western coast of the Atlantic Ocean. We got off the train and embarked onto a ship again. On the afternoon of 9 December, nine ships sailed eastward side by side, among which two were ships carrying Chinese labourers, two were cargo ships, and the others were escorting warships. Although the British defended our ships carefully, many of our Chinese labourers were on alert all the time. The hidden German submarines that followed the ships of the allied forces in various routes across the Atlantic Ocean would emerge suddenly to launch attacks on the passing ships, bringing about the most serious damage to them. I sighed, "Even if something happens, it is for justice that we lose our lives. There is nothing to fear at all. This European War was originally caused by the German aggression of the land of Western Europe. But their aggression resulted in the rage of the whole world and people of different countries have united to fight against it. Now that our country has joined the Entente countries, it is naturally the duty of both our armed forces and our civilians to give a helping hand. We left for Europe to work in the west because our government made a promise to help. We won't need to fight with 'all cauldrons smashed and all boats sunk' and can get some fame and fortune. Now that we don't regret it, there is nothing we can fear at all. What we should do is just to spare no efforts in our work during the three years abroad, which I believe will soon pass by. As to the success or failure of the War, it is something we can't predict or reverse."

马春苓：游欧杂志
Miscellaneous Records of Travel to Europe by Ma Chunling

At seven o'clock on 18 December, we arrived at the port of Liverpool, England. As soon as we got off the ship, we continued our journey by coach toward the southeast. We soon arrived at the northwestern coast of the English Channel after passing through London. At midnight, we got off the coach and stayed in the field headquarters. At dawn the next day, we set out for the port and arrived there after walking about five miles. Along the road, we saw green pine trees on either side of the road and red plums in blossom. It seemed that both the scenery and the climate had nothing different from those in China. Later, we got onto clippers to cross the channel. About two hours later, we arrived at the western border of the Seine Maritime region of France, where we got on a southeast-bound train. The train departed at six o'clock in the evening arrived at the General Distribution Station of Chinese Labourers in Noyelles late that night. At the camp I met Ruzhu, a younger brother of my clan. We talked happily about our respective experiences and then we started to sob uncontrollably, knowing that we would soon part from each other. A few days later, our brigade was ordered to go to a factory in Legenmul in the northwest border of Calais. After travelling on a train for over 60 miles, we finally arrived and settled in the camps. It was 23 December.

On 24 December, the Captain assigned over 120 labourers in the first company of Chinese labourers to work in a factory in Baobai, which was a large town in the northwestern part of Calais and was located over six miles to the northeast of Legemul. Our company was dispatched here to transport materials for the building of access road in the southeast as the foundation for the future battlefront.

After the completion of the project in Baobai, we returned to the old battalion in Zailegenmu on 2 February 1918. I wrote the following poem which best expressed my innermost feelings at that time:

华工日记
Chinese Labourer's Diaries

As soon as I left my home heading for Western Europe,

Looking back, running tears on my cheeks I couldn't help.

Distance gave me more worries about my family in dreams,

And leather boots failed to cease my sorrow at deep nights.

How could I regret for the ambitions I had long cherished,

Which my limited experience render unable to be achieved.

How eager I wish I could get drunk with wines every day,

So that I'd get up to find three years had elapsed already.

Meeting Meiting in Hometown in Dreams

In dreams back to Linqu I trudged over a long distance,

And saw Meiting coming to me with a smile on his face.

Before we could tell our deep sentiments to each other,

Awakened I was by the sudden bells from the officer.

Meiting was the courtesy name of my cousin Chunqui who was my closest friend. Since we separated from each other last year, almost no night have passed without meeting him in my dreams. This poem was written to express my deepest missing of him.

Sentiments on Books

Take all these Confucian classics away and search no more,

For I'd be greatly afflicted with even the slightest suffering.

Instead of being indulged with frowns and sorrows every day,

Sentimental verses I chanted while gently tapping bed planks.

马春苓：游欧杂志
Miscellaneous Records of Travel to Europe by Ma Chunling

Alas! In the daytime, we worked to exhaustion while at night we escaped the air raids in fear. Looking in the direction of our motherland, we sighed over the great distance away. Counting days for return, we still had three long years according to our contracts. The hardships we bore were beyond words. Just as tigers in cages or fish in bottles, we were unable to escape even if we had wings. Although we were worried and anxious day and night, we could do nothing about it. What we could do was just to seek joy in troubles and make the best of it so as to protect ourselves. As to what would happen to us, be they blessings or misfortunes, we could only resign ourselves to our destinies.

On Slender Waists of European Women

Western beauties take great care of their figures,
With curly hair, slender waists, and long skirts.
Provided they were sent to Yingdu the palace,
It would greatly please King of the Chu State.

On Plump Breasts of French Women

Fair faces and plump figures they keep, even with no makeup,
And over their head is flaming thick hair like the cockscomb.
If sent to the palace of Chang'an as the emperor's concubines,
They would make happy Xuanzong Emperor of Tang Dynasty.

The Europeans belonged to the white race and thus the European women had very fair countenance. Most British were reddish in face with a big nose. However, most French were pure fair in face with a smaller nose, which made them particularly attractive in appearance. Curly brown hair, blue eyes, slender waists and plump breasts were the characteristics of European women, so I composed the above two verses to record their uniqueness.

A Cento on Field Walking on the Day of Qingming

Walking along tranquil valleys with my favourite wild grass,
In the ruthless season I bid farewell to the last gust of wind.
On the Day of Qingming with such a mild sunny weather,
It was no wonder people's homesickness came naturally.

A Cento on the Next Day of Qingming

The Day of Qingming we spent with neither wines nor flowers,
But inseparable to us were always separation and homesickness.
Like a dream was the past and our home a great distance away.
We always returned to Luoyang our dearest home every night.

On 23 June, the work in the factory was not so busy. In the afternoon, I was ordered to work on dozens of railroad sleepers together with Feng Lianzhang, one of my fellow labourers in the same battalion, and also the youngest son of one of my senior fellow students Feng Yuxiu. In a while we finished the work. So we lay together on a pile of wood to have a rest. Suddenly, I came up with the first line of a couplet, "A good sleep on sleepers," and invited Liangzhang to give the other line. But just then, the regimental commander riding on a horse arrived to inspect labourers. As we were getting up to work, Liangzhang uttered the other line of the couplet, "A sudden halt to horses", implying that our sleep would be stopped if the commander should stay longer. Such a response to the immediate situation reflected to some extent his quick wit.

马春苓：游欧杂志
Miscellaneous Records of Travel to Europe by Ma Chunling

On 28 July, we moved from Zailegenm to Aozhui, which was located over ten miles to the northwest of Zailegenmu and where we worked for more than twenty days. On 22 August, we were transferred again to work in a bullet factory in the north-western border of Rouen Province, which was located in the southwest of Calais.

华工日记
Chinese Labourer's Diaries

论英募华工作工于法国之理由

法国北连北海，西北隔英伦海峡与英国为邻。东北隔比利时与德国之西境相接。德人既吞比国，复进据法国东北诸省，英人不能不为唇亡齿寒之虞，故兴倾国之师以助法御德，凡子弹粮草，及一切战具皆输自英国。招我华人，助彼运输，故驻法华工，多分扎于法国北鄙焉。

On Reasons for Britain's Recruitment of Chinese Labourers to Work in France

France was connected with the North Sea in the north, bordered on Great Britain in the northwest across the English Channel, and was connected with the western border of Germany across Belgium in the northeast. After the German troops had occupied Belgium, they marched to occupy several provinces in the northeast of France. It was the fear for the shared fate with France that Britain helped France to resist the German aggression with forces of the whole country. All bullets and provisions as well as weapons were transported from Britain. Chinese labourers were recruited to help them with transportation. That was why most Chinese labourers were stationed in the northern borders of France.

马春苓：游欧杂志
Miscellaneous Records of Travel to Europe by Ma Chunling

华工分驻区处之大概

勒哈弗为沙省（在法国西北鄙）滨海口岸，东南通巴黎，西接英伦海峡（塞纳河自巴黎西北流，由勒哈弗入海），街市延袤，商业繁盛。茏汪在勒哈弗南二百余里，亦滨江商埠，白龙在勒哈弗北百余里，亦滨海港湾。奴埃在白龙东二百余里，为华工分发总处。哈里在加莱省北鄙，为法国滨海商埠，登客在哈里东北百余里，亦滨海口岸。敖追、报白、在勒艮木均为加莱内地，介于哈里、登客之间。三道门在报白南二十余里，亦加莱市埠，为战线西界。又东南百余里，有一大镇，地名哈木提意日斯，为北省东北边境，适当战线之冲。又东北则为比利时境。欧战以来，凭为战场，四年之间，得失数次，城镇村市，尽成丘墟，良可慨也。

Survey of Distribution of Chinese Labourers

Le Havre was a coastal port in the province of Seine Maritime in the northwestern border of France. Neighbouring Paris on the southeast and the English Channel on the west, Le Havre, through which the Seine River runs north-west from the northwest of Paris to the Sea, was a prosperous port with boisterous markets. Rouen, located over 60 miles to the south of Le Havre, was a riverside commercial port. Boulogne, located over 30 miles in the north of Le Havre, was also a coastal port. Noyelles, located over 60 miles to the east of Le Havre, was the General Distribution Station of Chinese labourers. Hali(Calais),

华工日记
Chinese Labourer's Diaries

located on the northern border of Calais Province, was a coastal commercial port. Dunkirk, located over 30 miles to the northeast of Hali, was also a coastal port. Aozhui, Baobai and Zailegenmu were all located in the hinterland of Calais between Hali and Dunkirk. Saint-Omer, located over six miles to the south of Baobai, was also a port of Calais as well as the western border of the battlefront. Armentieres, located over 30 miles in the southeast of Calais, was a large town on the northeastern border of the Nord province and a centre of the battlefront. Farther in the northeast was the territory of Belgium, which became the main battlefield repeatedly occupied by the Germans and regained by the Belgians during the four years of the European War. All villages and towns were turned into ruins.

马春苓：游欧杂志
Miscellaneous Records of Travel to Europe by Ma Chunling

论该处之气候、风土、物产

以上所陈诸地，皆属法国北部，庇北连北海，西北接英伦海峡，西靠大西洋，故其气候纯系海洋性，冬无祁寒，夏无酷暑，阴雨倍于晴明。谷类之中，惟殖来牟、元麦、豌豆、蚕豆等。麦种于季冬，而熟于孟秋，岁获一季。此外多种植糖萝卜，园蔬以蔓菁、地蛋、白菜、葱、芹为大宗。果实以苹果、葡萄、栗子为最多，其余各种瓜菜蔬薪亦间有之。惜阴气盛而阳和鲜，总不如我国土产之甘且美也。地势多平原，并无峻山巨川，惟土岭绵亘，森林丛杂。人民居处，因职务而异其地。士子萃处学校，工商罗列街市。至于农民，则各因耕种之便，星布原野。田园牧场，环宅四周。田畔浚溪，以备水涝。背山临溪，作彼攸宇。各自为家，不成村里。柴门棘垣，不设墙户。板桥曲通，石砌幽净。既便耕作，又合卫生，良足羡欤！

余初来法国，即分派加莱省西北部诸工厂，去战线尚百余里，故未冒子弹之险，并未遭颠沛之苦。惟夜间敌国飞机潜入内地，抛掷炸弹，以毁战线后路之营盘、粮草厂、子药局。凡晴明之日，无夕不至。英人常备机械，射电光飞空四烛，迹其所至，发快炮击之，或驾飞机，拨机关枪敌之。弹壳如雨，为害最烈，故各营之中，皆备地穴或沙屋以避之。如炸弹掷下，离四五十步，或能无恙，一夜之间，常奔避数次，故在该地驻七八月，未尝解衣而寝。自移茏汪以来，去战线逾远，飞机亦不易及，始得安枕而卧。因于晚间灯下，将法国风土情形，为耳目所接触者，略记梗概，以备参考云。

十月初八日上午十一时，正在工厂作工，忽闻各处舟车工厂及机器

华工日记
Chinese Labourer's Diaries

局时发动汽笛，呜呜而鸣，英人亦鼓掌欢跃。未几，法国童叟妇女，排列队伍，执旗鸣鼓，游行街市，观其貌若极形欢忻者。余等初不知为何事，散工而归，适舒先生（江苏人，留学美国，现任照料华工青年会干事员）在营，集问之。渠曰："德国败绩，停战请和。联军得胜，不久凯旋。故各国人民，悬旗张彩，以相庆贺耳（既停战则危险可免，生还有望，故恐惧忧愁之怀顿释）。异日和议告成，汝等即全体旋归，不俟三年满期矣。"众闻其言，不觉恐怀驰然，愁思涣然，乡心油然矣。

东初冯先生题茏汪码头景致

沮水负山地势雄，滨临渤溟起英风。
金汤巩固成天堑，盘石奠安赖战功。
万缕炊烟迷市肆，一声汽笛走艨艟。
工余兄弟同眺望，多少楼台指顾中。

余移茏汪，与东初冯砚兄列营而居，常相会谈，借遣旅闷。欧战告停后，先生偕余同游江诸，感而此赋（东初名聿屿，红庙王舍人）。

On Local Climate, Customs, and Produce

Located in the northern part of France, which was connected with the North Sea in the north, the English Channel in the northwest, and the Atlantic Ocean in the west, all the places mentioned above had the oceanic climate with no severe cold in winter and intense heat in summer, but with more rain and less sunshine. Grains such as wheat, barley, highland barley, peas and beans were grown in these places. Wheat was planted in winter and harvested in autumn. In addition to grains, vegetables such as turnips, potatoes, cabbages,

马春苓：游欧杂志
Miscellaneous Records of Travel to Europe by Ma Chunling

onions and celeries, and fruits such as apples, grapes and chestnuts were grown widely in these places. Other fruits and vegetables could also be found occasionally. However, due to the abundance of rain and less sunshine, most of them were not as sweet as those in our country. With few high mountains and large rivers, most of the areas were plains and undulating hills with thick forests. People with different careers lived in different places: scholars concentrated around schools; merchants crowded around marketplaces; farmers scattered in fields surrounded by farm houses and pastures for the convenience of farming. Beside fields were dredging ditches to prevent flood. Near the rivers and against hillsides were houses with wooden gates and thorny fences. People lived in their own houses which were separate from each other rather than connected with each other into a village. With slab bridges and winding lanes, the countryside was both clean and quiet for living and convenient for farming, which was greatly admired by us.

I was assigned to work in factories in the northwestern part of Calais province, which was over 30 miles away from the battlefront. So I hardly suffered the risk of gunfire and the hardships of drifting from one place to another. But the enemy aeroplanes frequently came behind the lines at night and dropped bombs to blow up the camps and factories of provisions, bullets and ammunition in the rear of battlefronts. Not a single fine night passed without the arrival of the enemy aeroplanes. The British would follow their trace with the help of searchlights and fought back with fast cannons or shot with machine guns from their own aeroplanes. With showers of shells and bullets, the air raids often resulted in some serious damage. Therefore, barracks usually had underground shelters and sand shelters to avoid the bombs. One might be safe if the bombs were forty or fifty steps away. Sometimes, we had to run away several times during one night. Therefore, for the seven to eight

华工日记
Chinese Labourer's Diaries

months we lived there, we had always slept with our clothes on at night. We could not have a good sleep at night until we later moved to Rouen, a place far away from the battlefront and out of the reach of enemy aeroplanes. This also meant that I now had the opportunity to write down a brief survey of the local climate, customs and products, as well as what I saw and heard in France for later reference under the candlelight on these nights.

At eleven o'clock on 8 October, I suddenly heard the sound of sirens coming from factories, vessels, vehicles and machines as well as the rejoicing applause of the British while I was working in the factory. In a short while, countless French children, women and the elderly came out to parade along streets in lines by waving flags and playing drums in a state of ecstasy. But we did not know what had happened. After returning to the camp from work, we went up to Mr. Shu, a YMCA secretary with the Chinese labourers from Jiangsu Province and who had studied in America, and asked him about the matter. He told us, "The Germans have failed and asked for an armistice. The allied forces have won the war and will soon return triumphantly. Now that no war means more life and fewer dangers, people of various countries feel greatly relieved from their fears and sorrows. So they're celebrating the armistice with colourful flags. Once the agreement on peace is signed, perhaps we can return to our country without waiting for the expiration date of three years." Upon hearing his words, we felt a sort of involuntary nostalgia and homesickness as well as a long relief.

Lines Composed by Feng Dongchu on Rouen Port

With imposing terrain of low wetland and high mountains,
It bordered on the sea and enjoyed a status of importance.
Boasting consolidated fortresses, it was made a natural chasm,

马春苓：游欧杂志
Miscellaneous Records of Travel to Europe by Ma Chunling

And firm rocks laid solid foundation for battle achievements.

Wisps of smoke from kitchen chimneys shrouded markets.

Various warships departed with the sound of steam whistles.

In their leisure our fellow labourers looked into the distance,

And in an instant they found numerous towers and buildings.

When I moved to Rouen, I lived next to the barrack of Feng Yuyu, a fellow student of mine from Wangshe Village of Hongmiao with a courtesy name of Dongchu. We often met to have talks with each other to get rid of the depressive feelings. After the armistice of the European War, we visited the port of Rouen together and the above poem was composed after that visit.

华工日记
Chinese Labourer's Diaries

述欧战颠末

初，塞（塞尔维亚）败土（土耳其），修旧怨也，即进据地中海马其顿岸线。德（德意志）为欧后进强国，每欲东拓疆土，故先结土（土耳其）奥（奥地利），觊并巴岛（巴尔干半岛）。因塞据咽喉，素疾之。今又得马其顿，更不利于彼。逐约奥，迫令退还土国。时奥王老，太子主政。塞人集恨奥储，逐于一九一四年六月二十八日乘便刺之。殪。奥大恚。乃于七月二十五日向塞宣战。俄（俄罗斯）素结塞以图巴岛，塞危，则伊染指地中海之计亦空，逐助塞敌奥。德既疾塞，又忌俄之南略，遂于八月一日向俄宣战。法（法兰西）素仇德，因结好英（英吉利）俄，每欲报复而无由，故乘衅而起。土布（布加利亚）诸国，助德奥以敌俄塞。德出倾国之师，大举西下。法之东鄙，有阿尔卑斯山脉，横亘南北，路途险峻，而守御又严，德兵不得逞。比（比利时）境平坦，且乏守备（比受列强担保，故不设御外侮之兵），德乘虚越道而进。比集内兵御之，屡战皆北。英大怒，于八月十四日，起兵助战。而意（意大利）日（日本）等国，亦入英法联盟。德益兵南下，势甚猛烈。

二十三日，大破联军于雪里老（比地），进至孟斯。该地系比、法交界，为铁路要塞。德乘胜力攻，法军败退。旬余日，至巴黎（法国京城）东北之马恩河。法统帅霞飞与福熙将军死力拒守，德兵稍却，京师仅得不陷，时九月九日也。德见法京难下，逐分兵取加莱省开赉士港，以绝英援。福熙飞兵先至，合英军破之。法命福熙为总司令，指挥联军，相持年余。德军追踵相接，势如怒涛疾飚，联军力拒不能支。一九一六年秋，德军直抵凡尔登，联军屡挫，退走松末河，巴黎大震。福熙决河淹

马春苓：游欧杂志
Miscellaneous Records of Travel to Europe by Ma Chunling

下游，德兵不能进，京师稍定。美（美利坚）人素抱和平主义，不忍民族相残，出与列强媾和，德执拗不允，反用潜行艇沉其商船于地中海。美大怒，约中国共入协约，供给联军。一九一八年春，德破俄灭塞，并吞比境，倾师南下，两攻凡尔登，三逾松末河。联军屡战屡挫，全欧震惊。美见势不敌，遂于七月一日兴师来援。时德军已进旧法京，福氏整饬军旅，背城借一。德军以巴黎指日可破，预为庆宴，阵前所遗酒瓶（西人皆用瓷瓶盛酒）多于弹壳（炮子皮也）。既而进攻，竟三进三挫。福氏出奇兵，薄德军于许亥莱要塞，大破走之。联军厚集，并力追击，于九月七日，直抵兴登堡阵线。该线为德国内堑，布置险固，联军乘胜力攻，月余不能破。布、土惧众寡不敌，相继投降。德人困于征役，复粮食缺乏，民不堪命，上下挟贰，集怨德皇，群起攻之。威廉第二（德皇帝）只身奔荷（荷兰国），德军无主，望风奔溃。遂破兴登堡阵线，进薄莱茵河。十一月初九日，奥降。德革命军遂主持和议，宣布停战，时十一月十日也。牵连十数国，鏖兵四五年之大战争，乃于此告终焉。

自咏

自读格言悟果因，廿年未涉别园春。
任他比法风光好，难浼平生洁白人。

余童时读《朱子家训》，至"见色而起淫心，报在妻女"之句，常掩卷筹思。上考往古，下征近今，凡渔色之人，其偿还诚未有出其闺阃者。世风愈下，报应愈速，天理昭彰，固如是也。余恪守明训，见他人妇女，如对神明，懔然不敢萌异念，如是者已廿有年。今来欧境，虽非我种族，亦同为人类，移其地即易其心，将何以为人。且廿年清白，复失身于一旦，他日旋归，何以对我綦巾乎？故比法妇女虽如云如荼，类皆玉容仙姿，究非我思存焉。遏人欲以彰天理，华夷罔间。境遇不涽，愿我少年共勖之。

华工日记
Chinese Labourer's Diaries

除夕旅怀
慈亲缺事隔年赊，万虑萦怀乱似麻。
爆竹屠苏风味杳，徒教游子益年华。

战时不得私用火药，故无爆竹之声；营中禁酒，故乏屠苏之味。

除夕怀旅人
无依无靠过新年，一样孤衾倍寂然。
稚子休题乃父事，今宵为母定安眠。

妻以夫为天，纵大家团聚，而夫主不在，总算无依无靠耳。孤衾寂寞，能不倍于曩昔乎？惟然，妻念其夫，出自衷情，何待人题？纵使稚儿箝口，诚不知果能安眠否耶？今宵定欲安眠，则他宵之未曾安眠也明矣。然今夕何夕，阖家饮宴，庆贺新节，岂安眠时也？乃言定安眠者，其无心年节也，又可知矣。不言己之思家而托室人怀己，推情断理，揣摩逼肖，使读者蓦然神驰矣。

On the Story of the European War

At the beginning, Serbia occupied the Macedonian coastline in the Mediterranean in revenge for the old grudge formed after Serbia defeated Turkey. Germany was an emerging power in Europe with a constant ambition to expand its territories eastward. So it first formed an alliance with Turkey and Austria, who coveted the Balkan Peninsula and hated Serbia for its central strategic position in Europe. Serbia's occupation of Macedonia constituted another disadvantage for Germany. So together with Austria, Germany forced

马春苓：游欧杂志
Miscellaneous Records of Travel to Europe by Ma Chunling

Serbia to return the territory to Turkey. At that time, the Austrian king was old, and it was the prince who was in charge of the government. Serbia hated the prince of Austria and assassinated him on 28 June 1914. The death of the Austrian prince enraged Austria and it declared war against Serbia. Russia had been on good terms with Serbia with the intention to take the Balkan Peninsula. If Serbia was in danger, Russia's plan to occupy the Mediterranean would fall short. So Russia helped Serbia to fight against Austria. Germany hated Serbia on one hand and feared Russia's southward aggression on the other. Germany declared war against Russia on 1 August. France had a long hatred for Germany and also declared war, together with Britain and Russia. Turkey and Bulgaria joined Germany and Austria to fight against Serbia. Germany then marched westward with all its forces, but the German aggression was frustrated due to the long distance, strong defence and the Alps stretching from south to north in the eastern border of France. The territory of Belgium was mostly plain and its defence was weak because, guaranteed by other major powers, it did not have forces to defend against aggressors. So the German troops marched forward via Belgium, which mobilised its few soldiers to defend, but was defeated repeatedly. This enraged Britain, which mobilised its forces to join the war on 14 August. Italy and Japan also joined the alliance with Britain and France. After strengthening its forces, Germany made a more fierce southward attack soon.

On 23 August, the German troops defeated the allied forces at Charleroi, Belgium and stormed to Mons, a railway fortress at the borders of Belgium and France. The German troops continued their attacks triumphantly and the French troops were defeated. In more than ten days, Germany had reached the river of Marne in the northeast of Paris, the capital of France. Under the desperately brave defence of General Joffre and General Foch, the German troops withdrew

华工日记
Chinese Labourer's Diaries

a little and Paris was successfully defended. It was 9 September. Seeing that it was difficult to take Paris, Germany changed its strategy by dividing its forces to occupy the port of Calais to cut off British assistance. But the attack was defeated by the joint forces of General Foch and the British army. France appointed Foch as the Commander in Chief to command the allied forces and the confrontations continued for over a year. But later, under the overwhelming attacks of the German troops, the allied forces failed to resist them. In the autumn of 1916, the Germans arrived at Verdun and the allied forces had to retreated to the Somme River after repeated frustrations, which shocked Paris. Foch broke the dam to flood the lower reaches, which prevented the advance of the Germans, and Paris became safe temporarily. America, adhering to pacifism and unable to bear the killing between nations, came forward to make peace between the powers. But Germany did not agree and sank an American commercial ship in the Mediterranean. Infuriated by this, America, together with China, joined the Entente countries and provided support to the allied forces. In the spring of 1918, Germany broke the defensive line of Russia and occupied Serbia. After capturing the whole territory of Belgium, all the German troops began to march southward and launched two attacks on Verdun and crossed Somme River three times. The allied forces were defeated time and again and this shocked the whole of Europe. Under such circumstances, America joined the fighting on 1 July. At that time, the Germans had already entered the capital of France and Foch consolidated his troops to make a last big defence. Believing that Paris would soon be occupied, the Germans held celebrations in advance. The wine bottles—Westerners used porcelain bottles to contain wine—that were discarded by the Germans in the battlefield were more in number than the shell cases. Soon after, the Germans launched three large attacks, but they were defeated each time. With his ingenious military moves, Foch forced the Germans to retreat to Xuhelai fort. The defeated Germans had to withdraw from there. On 7 September, the allied forces followed up their victory with more attacks and compelled the Germans to retreat to the Hindenburg battle line, a strategically consolidated deep trench in the territory of Germany. However, the allied forces failed to break it through until another month of continuous attacks had passed. Turkey and Bulgaria both feared that they would finally be outnumbered and surrendered to the allied forces. The citizens of Germany, who had long suffered from heavy taxes and military service, coupled with a lack of food supplies, were living in misery and finally directed their anger at the Emperor of Germany, who was then under the attack from both inside and outside of Germany. William II, the Emperor of Germany, fled alone to the Netherlands. Without any commander, the German army soon broke up and soldiers escaped to all directions. The allied forces eventually broke through the Hindenburg battle line and advanced towards the River Rhine. On 9 November, Austria surrendered. The German revolutionary army came into power and asked for an armistice, declaring the end of the War on 11 November. The Great War, which had involved dozens of countries and lasted four to five years, eventually came to an end.

On Myself

During my twenty years of reading and reflections,
I never went to others' gardens for different springs.
However beautiful women in Belgium and France are,
As a pure and innocent person I keep not being tempted.

In my childhood, every time I read the sentence in *Zhu Family Instructions* that "Lusting after beautiful women will bring retribution on one's own wife and daughters", I closed the book and fell into reflections. From ancient times to today, all philanderers would receive punishment for their misbehaviours on their own wife and daughters. With the worse moral degeneration of the world, the retribution of a person was becoming quicker and quicker because God's justice was always manifest. In the past 20 years, I followed the instructions of the Zhu family. Every time I saw other women, I treated them as gods, not daring to have dirty feelings for them. I held the same attitude towards European women because they were also people like you and me, despite the different race they belonged to. It was impossible for me to change my attitude toward women just because I was in a different place. Besides, if I should show interest in other women, how could I face my wife when I returned home? Therefore, although there were many beautiful women in Belgium and France, I had no interest in them. Wherever one was, in China or in foreign countries, he should behave consistently and keep his morality and integrity by suppressing his desires. This poem was written as a mutual encouragement for both myself and all young people who were living in complex situations.

Sentiments on Chinese New Year's Eve in Europe

On thought of my long absence in attending upon my mother,
Deep in my heart I could not help feeling guilty and worried.
Without the sound of firecrackers and the smell of Tusu wine,
One year older became I after this lonely Eve in a foreign land.

Because gunpowder was forbidden for private use during war time, there were no firecrackers to set off. Because alcohol was not allowed in barracks, there was no smell of the Tusu wine at all.

马春苓：游欧杂志
Miscellaneous Records of Travel to Europe by Ma Chunling

Sentiments of Travellers on Chinese New Year's Eve

Without family reunion and joyous celebration,

The Eve for travellers was far lonelier than ever.

For their mothers to have a good sleep tonight,

Children refrained from mentioning their father.

The husband was the backbone for the wife. Even if there was a family reunion, the wife would still feel lonely and helpless. Sleepless on bed, her loneliness would become several times deeper, but it was natural for the wife to miss her husband. Even if no one mentioned him, her loneliness would not get reduced. If this night she could have a good sleep, there must be other nights when she kept awake all night. But this night was the New Year's Eve when the whole family had dinner together to celebrate the coming of another New Year. How could it be a time for her to sleep soundly? To say that she would have a good night's sleep, I mean that she was in no mood for any festivals; let alone the New Year's Eve. Rather than expressing my homesickness and my missing home, the poem expresses the feelings of the wife who missed her husband greatly. Its fine feelings and vivid descriptions would not only arouse readers' emotions but also enable them to experience the feelings of the Chinese labourers in Europe.

华工日记
Chinese Labourer's Diaries

砚兄冯东初识

民国八年二月二十三日,由茏汪移于乜哎铺,收拾战场内遗弃军械。该地系比国西南边境,与法之哈木题意日斯紧相接连。北四五十里即八比伦齿,是处离海稍远,雨水颇稀,天气较寒,三月犹冰。节逾谷雨,树木始萌,至四月尚不成荫。不及晚秋,即黄而陨矣。惟丰草嫩绿,三冬犹芳,韶华灿烂,孟夏始荣。固不殊乎法地,民风物产,亦仿佛法土,在他年固亦繁华之区也。自经战乱之后,诚有不堪言者。屋无完壁,木无完株,弹穴渊布,瓦砾山差,尸横遍野,阴风惨凄。其铁网纠绊(凡战壕前后,皆用铁豆条为蒺藜,拖缠铁柱之上,内外数层,以为藩御),战壕逶迤,荒草没顶焉。有《黍离》流离死绝,民少孑遗。停战半载,尚无栖迟,老叟悲叹,稚妇涕洏。我等眷言顾之,亦凄焉出涕矣。因忆唐彦谦诗云:"禾麻地废生边气,草木春寒起战声。"亦曰此物此志耳。

春夜集句
柳条藤蔓系离情,竹影当窗乱月明。
一去紫台连朔漠,夜来还到洛阳城。

清明书怀
荒烟蔓草曲桥西,人自伤心鸟自啼。
客岁曾吟白下句,今朝又赋清明题。

马春苓：游欧杂志
Miscellaneous Records of Travel to Europe by Ma Chunling

其二
离家两次度清明，旧泪未干新泪倾。
子母各天人万里，夫妻一榻月三更。

端阳日题
清明乍过又端阳，佳节重逢意倍伤。
弱柳无能牵恨去，娇花适足惹愁长。

六月十三日，由乜哎铺南移二十里，营于法国列黎城之西北，与加莱城东西相望，亦北省重镇。驻二十日，至七月初四日，复移比国伊普斯地。该地在巴比伦东南二十余里，适比法英美与德军鏖战之冲，蹂躏破坏，尤为特甚。自停战以来，各国派队收埋阵亡兵士。直至于今，荒野间犹白骨累累。人谓自古兵争，未有如欧战之惨者，诚然欤！（古人云："一将功成万骨枯。"于此益信）

吊比国街市
荒院蓬蒿千宅绿，颓楼牖户万家通。
昔年黎庶堂前燕，遁入战壕铁屋中。

停战以后，燕子因楼榭颓坏，不可以居，故寻得战壕内所遗铁屋，以营巢生儿。诗言遁入者，若为避难而然，亦趣语也。

吊阵亡兵士坟茔
十架亭亭魂有因，荒丘累累奠谁陈。
可怜路畔遗残骨，犹是深闺梦里人。

（西人营葬皆用十字架插于坟前，以为标志。）

华工日记
Chinese Labourer's Diaries

八月初十日，北移于巴比伦，驻十七日，复还伊铺斯，营于北郊。是时华工返国者，已四万余众。余因来欧较后，不得与彼辈偕行，乡念如焚。又值重阳在即，益觉无聊，遂口占一绝以写怀：

中秋始度又重阳，亲舍云根忆故乡。
预料归期蓦不远，但逢佳节倍凄凉。

九月十二日，雨雪寸许，时天气霸发，水渐成冰。至二十日，复雨雪终日。

二十二日，分发总局华工督办，电召本队回奴埃，预备归国。队长宣布命令，阖队欢欣异常。白叟拍掌而相庆，黄童舞蹈以欢呼，歌声笑语，彻夜不休。余以见乡思之殷，人人有同情也。

二十三日五时，早起，整理行装。六时，晨餐毕，整队起行，至伊普斯车站，乘二等客车，七时发轫，西南行百余里，而抵法境。复易法国火车。晚二时，开轮西北行，折而南。八时，至奴埃总局。明日，督办费公宣布政府公令，再三申谢华人助战之功，且谓今战事已毕，诸君得早日凯旋，特于月薪外，各加6月饷银，以示褒奖。

十月初三日，归国事务，办理妥协。晚九时，登车西南行。至翌日早八时，抵勒哈弗尔口岸，因船只未凑，遂次于行营以俟之。

十三日，英舰坎饶炼（船名）于勒哈弗尔海口停泊。早十二时，华工四千人，一同登舟。晚六时，起椗西南行。出英吉利海峡，而入大西洋。把舵西进，历八昼夜，至二十一日晚十时，乃抵坎拿大东境哈勒法克斯海口停泊。翌晨，划舟就岸。晚四时，下船即登汽车。七时，复发轫而西。方华工之登岸也，坎拿大总督派委欢迎，使士子赠以香烟，妇女授以苹果，再三致意，极其热诚。于以见英人之感激华工，良非浅鲜也。

十一月初一日晚八时，至坎拿大西鄙温古华海口。该地系太平洋沿岸之一大商埠，与美国旧金山南北相望，市厂繁盛，商旅云集。华商侨

马春苓：游欧杂志
Miscellaneous Records of Travel to Europe by Ma Chunling

寓者，颇不乏人，惟多系南方人士，与我言语不同，相见但以意通殷勤而已。翌日早九时，下车即登汽船。十一时，发机西南行。晚四时，至温古华岛之东南隅，就岸下船，复次于来时旧营。时序同前，故景物依旧，惟昔往今返，胸怀顿殊，因作五律一首以志喜：

> 回忆来营日，于今已二年。
> 山容全似昨，水势复同前。
> 景物皆依旧，胸怀殊不然。
> 归舟如有便，旋里廿余天。

二十三日枕上作

> 温古山头宿旧营，寒帷夜夜纳涛声。
> 归船久盼三周尽，未识何时得起程。

二十九日晚，团长传令言："顷接无线电报，英邮船明日即至。诸公可预备登程。次日早八时，各整行装，同至码头等候。"晚二时，果见轮船一艘，自南而至，须臾抵岸，遂架木桥，两路并登，顷刻而尽。五时，即发机西上。

十二月初一日，饭后登甲板游览，见执事人员，皆系粤产，因往来邮送华工，与北人习处，颇晓北语，偶与谈话，类能应答。回想出洋时，船上粤人，相对如聋哑，或有问答，惟以纸笔相授受。由今拟昔，便利悬殊，但若辈对语，吾人仍茫然莫辨。因忆欧美语言通国一致，虽远隔万里，款接如一家，而我中国南北异音，方言各殊，能不为交通之阻障哉！吁，可慨也矣！

初六日早饭后，散步甲板，见风和日丽，乘客麇集，歌者舞者，弹者鼓者，欢娱之声，彼此相闻。回忆出洋时，人人不服水性，类时呕哇昏倒，呻者吟者，叹者泣者，愁惨之声，满舱皆是。由今视昔，悲欢奚

华工日记
Chinese Labourer's Diaries

窨天壤。流览移时，胸襟畅适，遂登船所，凭栏俯视，猝见群鱼跃出，飞行水面。陡忆荀子《劝学篇》尝有瓠巴鼓瑟、流鱼出听之事，动物亦与人同乐，往往然也。

十三日早十时，抵日本横滨口岸。因昨夕舟中失慎，货舱被焚，故停泊于此。卸出余烬，整理舱舍，五日始竣。

十八日晚一时，由横滨起椗西南行，适雨雪交集，云雾迷漫。船轮缓缓前进，汽笛呜呜不休。因探路者不能远望，恐有来舟冲撞故也。至夜分，天霁月朗，舟始驶行。二十日早，经长崎口，折而西北，至二十三日早八时，乃抵山东之青岛而泊舟焉。舟既附岸，遂各整理行装，鱼贯而下。方排队简阅，瞥见汽车自东来，连绵三十余辆。车既戾止，即陆续共登。时栈房时表，已下午一句钟矣。待至四时，始开车东上，折而西，逾仓口以达胶州。时渐黄昏，城垣且模糊不可辨认，驶行一夜，至翌日黎明而抵潍邑。复展轮西行，十一时而达益都车栈。

二十四日午，由车栈步至益邑东关，睡于逆旅。时天气严寒，积雪寸余，晚间冻云复合，白雪纷落。明晨开门一望，雪已没胫。惟因年关伊迩，乡心孔急，切不计道途之艰阻，而一意起程焉。

二十五日早餐毕，与同侣五六人，由益南旋。时冰雪遍野，道途艰劭。负笥担囊，踯躅前趋。因念昔我往矣，霜露初敷。今我来斯，雨雪在途。于是过赤涧，经石村，逾朐城，登涤垠（岸也），乃瞻衡宇，载欣载奔。子弟欢迎，老母依门。扶亲入室，两泪流痕。田园既芜，青毡犹存。吾想夫自亚赴欧，水陆倭迟。方逾二载，贲然来斯。既历三洲，游兴已随。联军奏凯，战功永垂。橐有赢余，俯仰无亏已矣乎，心猿意马暂收驻，绛帐旧业重就绪。名利二字且让人，耕读两途莫失予。

胞弟大人手足：

兄自离家，屈指年余。堂上老母，全赖吾弟竭力奉侍，感何可言！惟念弟一向放荡，致家业倾颓，倘复不知悔改。将来人口日增，家产日

马春苓：游欧杂志
Miscellaneous Records of Travel to Europe by Ma Chunling

戚，弱妇雏儿，其何以糊口乎！兄虽羁旅异国，未尝不朝夕乃心于弟也！夫人生在世，贵能立志。兄前因连年歉收，度日维艰，不得不忍痛将祖父遗产割弃，以济眉急。自是寝食不安，昼夜筹思，无计还珠。遂不惮千辛万苦，履尾批鳞，而为此举。吾弟年过而立，非复往日童稚无识所可比。家道落寞，更非俦昔席有祖产所可拟。若再不图立志，前途艰窘，何堪设想！兄与汝谊属同胞，情系手足，痛痒关切，何忍坐视。故不惮剖肝沥胆，万里上书，惟吾弟乎听焉。

民国八年清明后二日由法国诚弟书

First Acquaintance with My Fellow Student Feng Dongchu

On 23 February 1919, we were transferred from Rouen to Jieanpu, a place in the southwestern borders of Belgium and bordering on Armentieres, to clear away the abandoned weapons on battlefields. About ten to 15 miles away in the north was Babilunchi, which was far away from the sea and had less rainfall. The weather was very cold and there was still ice in March. Trees began to grow leaves after the solar term of Grain Rain and could not make a shade even in April. All leaves would turn yellow and be gone before the late autumn. However, the grass grew well all the year round and kept green even in winter with the best time in the summer. It seemed that France, together with its colourful customs and abundant produce, must be a country of prosperity, but everything was in a state of chaos and destruction after the war. No houses or trees remained intact; trenches and shell holes were everywhere; chilly winds blew over mountains covered with rubble and fields littered with dead bodies. Among tall weeds were endless miles of barbed wire and meandering trenches.

华工日记
Chinese Labourer's Diaries

There were no crops in the fields and a multitude of people lost their homes or were killed in the war, leaving only a few lonely widows and parentless children. Six months passed by after the armistice, but homeless people still could not find places for shelter. The elderly people sighed mournfully, and young widows shed tears. Seeing their misery, we Chinese labourers could not help but shed tears too. The scene reminded me of the lines of Tang Yanqian's poem, "Enveloped in desolation were abandoned fields short of crops, Echoing with battles were withered vegetation in a chilly spring", which might be the best reflection of this scene in Europe.

A Cento on Spring Nights

Willows and vines held travellers back from departure,
Bamboos by the windows swayed wildly in moonlight.
Like Zhaojun left Chang'an for the vast desert of Hun,
Travellers would return to dearest Luoyang in dreams.

Sentiments on Qingming Festival
I

Walking near a bridge deserted by men and infested with weeds,
I as a traveller cried heart-brokenly as sorrowfully sang the birds.
Despite the lines composed last year on desperate homesickness,
My great sorrow was written into this year's verse on Qingming.

II

Sentiments on Qingming Festival

Two Qingming Festivals have passed since my departure from home,
New tears of this year were shed upon the undried ones of last year.

马春苓：游欧杂志
Miscellaneous Records of Travel to Europe by Ma Chunling

Great distance has not only made the separation of mother and son,
But also gave rise to numerous sleepless nights of husband and wife.

On Dragon Boat Festival

Dragon Boast Festival came as Qingming Festival went by,
Which caused my grief over family separation every time.
Like weak willows was resentment over my incompetence,
Just as tender flowers aroused my long feelings of sadness.

On 13 June, we moved six miles south from Jieaipu and camped in the northwest of Lille, a place of strategic importance in the Nord province of France that faced the city of Calais. We were stationed there for twenty days and then on 4 July we moved to Ypres in Belgium, which was over 6 miles to the south of Babylon. As a key battlefield area for the fierce fighting between the German armies and the allied forces of Britain and France, Ypres was devastated almost into complete ruins. Since the end of the war, each country had sent teams of labourers to bury the dead bodies of their soldiers. Even at that time the ground was still littered with the bones and bodies of the dead. It was true that the European War had brought much greater destruction than any other wars in the history of the human beings. Hence, I believed more and more that "A general's success is built on the death of millions of others", just as it was said by the ancients.

Lamenting over Belgian Markets

Wildly growing are weeds in the wilderness and deserted houses,
And in ruins scattered declining buildings and broken windows.
Those swallows once nesting under the roof of ordinary households,
Now escaping into the iron houses in entrenchments to seek shelters.

华工日记
Chinese Labourer's Diaries

Unable to find places to build nests due to the collapse of the buildings after the armistice, swallows could only fly into the iron dugouts inside the trenches to nest for breeding. The word "escaping" used in this poem not only indicated the swallows' state of taking refuge but also for the purpose of witticism.

Mourning at Graves of Soldiers Killed in the War

Upright erected crosses are thou eternal souls,
With offerings displayed on countless graves.
While buried roadside are thine remnant bones,
Thou remain dearest in dreams of those at home.

(In the West, when a dead person was buried, people usually set up a cross in front of his grave as a mark of respect.)

On 10 August, we moved further north to Babylon, where we were stationed for seventeen days, and then moved again to the northern suburb of Ypres. At that time, over 40,000 Chinese labourers had already returned to China, but due to my late arrival in Europe I could not return together with them. But I had a burning homesickness in my heart and became even more melancholy as the Double Ninth Festival was drawing near. So I composed the following poem:

With the passage of Middle Autumn came Double Ninth Festival,
Following the floating clouds returned my thoughts to hometown.
Although I thought the date for my return would come very soon,
Still in my heart was greater loneliness every time came a festival.

On 12 September, the sleet fell heavily. Due to the piercing winds, it

马春苓：游欧杂志
Miscellaneous Records of Travel to Europe by Ma Chunling

became extremely cold, and the water was gradually frozen into ice. It kept sleeting for another whole day on 20 September.

On 22 September, our brigade received the order from the General Distribution Camp of Chinese Labourers that we return to Noyelles and prepare for our departure to China. When the Captain told us the news, the whole brigade became overjoyed. With applause and dancing as well as laughter and songs, our celebration lasted the whole night. Hence, it could be seen that all people, be they white or yellow, old or young, had strong feelings of nostalgia.

At five o'clock on the morning of 23 September, we got up early and to get our luggage packed. At six o'clock, the whole brigade set out after breakfast. At the railway station in Ypres, we got on a second-class passenger train which started its travel south-westward at seven o'clock. After travelling for about thirty miles, we entered the territory of France and then changed onto a French train that departed at two o'clock in the morning, first heading northwest and then toward the south. At eight o'clock, we arrived at the base depot in Noyelles. The following day, Supervisor Fei read a governmental decree and repeatedly thanked all Chinese labourers for their work in the war. He said that all of us could return home early and triumphantly now that the War had come to an end. Each labourer would be given another six months' payment as a mark of appreciation in addition to their usual salary for this month.

On 3 October everything was ready for our return to China and at nine o'clock that night, we got on a south-west bound train and arrived at the port of Le Havre at eight o'clock the next morning; however, because there were no ships available at that time, we stayed in a camp at the port awaiting ships to arrive.

On 13 October, the British ship berthed at the port of Le Havre. Four

华工日记

Chinese Labourer's Diaries

thousand Chinese labourers embarked at twelve o'clock at noon. At six o'clock in the afternoon, the ship started her south-westward voyage. After sailing out of the English Channel, the ship entered the Atlantic Ocean. At ten o'clock on the night of 21 October, we arrived at the port of Halifax in the east border of Canada after sailing westward for eight days and nights. We went ashore in small rowing boats the next morning. At four o'clock in the afternoon, we disembarked from the ship and boarded a train. At seven o'clock, we started out westward once again. As we disembarked from the ship, we were warmly welcomed by the Canadian governor and the local people, who gave us gifts such as cigarettes and apples and expressed their thanks repeatedly. Hence, it could be seen that the British really appreciated the efforts of Chinese labourers very much.

At eight o'clock in the evening of 1 November, we arrived at the port of Vancouver in the western border of Canada,. With its thriving markets and numerous trading merchants, it was one of the largest commercial ports along the coast of the Pacific Ocean, facing America's San Francisco in the south. There were also many Chinese merchants living in there, but most of them were from the south of China and we could only exchange simple thoughts with them due to our different dialects. At nine o'clock the following morning, we boarded a steamship as soon as we got off from our ship. At eleven o'clock, we set sail toward the southwest. At four o'clock in the afternoon, we arrived at the southeastern corner of the island of Vancouver and disembarked from the ship again. We had arrived at the same place that we had visited when sailing to Europe. Because the time of the year was nearly the same, there were few changes in scenery or surroundings. But the last time we were on our way to Europe away from our homeland, while this time we were on our way back to our homeland. Therefore, the feelings inside us were quite different from those of the previous visit. I wrote a poem to record my rejoicing at returning home.

> Two years of time has passed by since we arrived before.
> Mountains and rivers remain unchanged with no less and no more.
> Regardless of the identical scenery our sentiments aren't the same at all.
> With ships available in twenty days we'd be back home at family's call.

Lines Composed on the Night of 23 November

> In Vancouver we were accommodated in the former camps,
> With chilling quilts and roaring sea waves night after night.
> Three weeks passed in our waiting for homecoming ships,
> We just wondered when our homeland could be within sight.

On the evening of 29 November, the brigade commander told us, "I've just received a radiogram. The British ocean liner will arrive tomorrow. You can get everything ready for the voyage. When all our things are packed, we'll go to the port at eight o'clock in the morning and wait for the liner." At two o'clock in the afternoon, we saw a ship arriving at the port from the south. After the ship stopped and the wooden gangway was laid down, we quickly boarded it in two organised lines. At five o'clock, we set sail toward the west.

On 1 December, I went onto the deck after the meal and met some officers of the ship, all of whom were Cantonese. Because they often transported Chinese labourers to or from Europe, they had spent so much time together with labourers from the northern part of China that they knew some of our dialects and were able to exchange a few words with me occasionally. This reminded me of the time when we first met Cantonese on the ship while

华工日记
Chinese Labourer's Diaries

travelling to Europe. Unable to speak their dialects, we, just like the deaf and the dumb, could not communicate with the Cantonese at all without the help of paper and pen. But now things had changed, and we could talk a little with each other. However, we were still at a loss when two or more Cantonese spoke together in their own dialect. I then thought of the language of Britain and America. English was the common language throughout their countries. As a result, however far two persons were from each other, they could communicate just as one large family. In China, there were great differences between the dialects of northerners and southerners, which would eventually block the communications between them. Alas, what a pity it was!

On 6 December, it was fine and clear. I went to take a walk on the deck, where happily gathered many passengers who were singing, dancing or playing the drums. It reminded me of the scene on the deck on our way to Europe. At that time, we were still unaccustomed to travelling on water and the whole ship was filled with the sound of vomiting, groaning, weeping or sighing. In comparison with the sorrows at that time, the present joy made a great difference. After wandering around for a while, I felt at ease. So I leaned on the railings and looked down into the water. Suddenly, I saw a school of fish leap out of the water, flying over the surface of water. At this sight, I suddenly thought of a story in *Encouraging Learning* by Hsun-tzu that while the fish in streams jumped to listen to Hu Pa playing the zither. It seemed that animals wanted to share the happiness together with human beings.

At ten o'clock on 13 December, our ship arrived and was berthed at the port of Yokohama, Japan, because the cargo was destroyed by the fire due to carelessness last night. It took us five days to unload the ashes and clean up the cabins.

At one o'clock in the afternoon of 18 December, we set out from

马春苓：游欧杂志
Miscellaneous Records of Travel to Europe by Ma Chunling

Yokohama and continued sailing toward the southwest. The sea was enveloped by thick cloud and mist due to heavy sleet. The lookouts could only see a short distance and our ship had to travel slowly and kept the foghorn blaring all the time for fear that she might collide with other ships. At midnight, it cleared up and the moon shone brightly in the sky. Till then, our ship began its regular sailing speed. On the early morning of 20 December, our ship changed its route and began to sail toward the northwest after passing Nagasaki. We finally arrived at Qingdao, Shandong Province. We then got all our things packed and disembarked from the ship in an orderly manner. As soon as we lined up, we saw over 30 coaches coming from the east. After they stopped, we got on the coaches one after another. It was already one o'clock in the afternoon. The coaches began to move eastward at first, but it turned to the west after a while and finally arrived at Jiaozhou via Cangkou. Then the night fell and the city walls gradually became indistinct and unrecognisable. After travelling a whole night, we arrived at Weiyi in the early morning of the following day. From Weiyi, we continued our journey to the west and arrived at Yidu station at eleven o'clock in the morning.

On the noon of 24 December, I walked from the station to Dongguan Street in Yiyi and slept in a hotel. At that time, with thick snow on the road, it was very cold, and it began to snow even more heavily during the night. On the next morning, when I opened the door, I found all roads were completely covered by snow. Because the Spring Festival was just around the corner, I had a particularly strong wish to reunite with my family. So I was determined to set out for home regardless of any obstacles or hardships along the way.

On 25 December, I headed southward from Yidu together with five or six fellow labourers after breakfast. It was a hard journey because all the ground was covered with heavy snow at that time. We stumbled forward with sacks

华工日记
Chinese Labourer's Diaries

and suitcases on our shoulders. I remembered it was in the early autumn over two years ago that I left for Europe, but today on my return it was in winter with heavy snow on the ground. I walked past the village of Shicun and the city of Linqu. After climbing up the bank, I could see our house and I was so excited that I started to run hurriedly. My brother and my sons came up to meet me and my mother leaned against the door anxiously. While I supported my elderly mother into the house, tears ran down my cheeks. Although the field went nearly bare, the wingceltis trees were still standing there. Thinking of my thrilling travel from Asia to Europe by both land and sea, I could hardly believe that I had finally returned home again after more than two years. My dream of travelling abroad had been realised and I had been to three continents. The allied forces won the war at last and their exploits would never be forgotten. With money in bags and nothing lost, I settled for my ambition and began to prepare for my teaching career again. I gave up fame and fortune and continued my farming and teaching as usual.

My dear brother,

I have been away for more than a year. During this period, you have taken the whole responsibility for taking care of our elderly mother. I appreciate your dedication to our family. But there is one thing I feel worried about you. I know you have been living an uninhibited life. I am afraid that your family property might be squandered if no impenitence was made. With the increase of your family size but the decrease of your family property, how would you make a living for your wife and children in the future? I have felt worried for you every day and night although I am physically confined to Europe. I believe the most important thing in life is to have plans for the future. In the previous years I had to reluctantly sell some of our grandfathers' properties due to the

Miscellaneous Records of Travel to Europe by Ma Chunling

hardships in life caused by the continuous famines in order to solve the urgent need for living. But ever since then, I have spent countless sleepless nights trying to come up with a plan to get them back. That is why I came to work in Europe in spite of the perils and hardships. My dear brother, you have grown up and cannot behave as an ignorant child anymore. With the family decline, we do not have as many ancestral properties to inherit as we did before. If you do not start making plans as soon as possible, you cannot even begin to imagine what a hard life you will have in the future. We are brothers. How could I turn a blind eye to your suffering? So I write this letter from such a great distance to show you my inner-most concerns for you. I hope you will listen to my advice.

Written to my brother in France on the second day after the Qingming Festival of 1919

顾杏卿：欧战工作回忆录

Reminiscences on My Work during European War
by Gu Xingqing

华工日记
Chinese Labourer's Diaries

顾杏卿（1893—1986），上海人，著有《欧战工作回忆录》，讲述自己作为华工翻译赴欧洲的经历。1917年，还是一名在校学生的顾杏卿被招募到一战华工队担任翻译，像许多年轻人一样，当时的他认为那是踏出国门、换取美好未来的跳板。1917年4月17日，顾杏卿离开青岛港，跨越太平洋，穿过加拿大，从大西洋西海岸乘船前往英国。7月，抵达法国滨海努瓦耶尔（索姆），在枪林弹雨中为驻法华工担任翻译，维护华工权益，1919年回国。而后到美国留学，1923年在美国西北大学获得艺术与科学硕士。顾杏卿最初并无意将自己对战场上的观察、记录和回忆公之于众，直至中国抗日战争时期，他才决定将笔记整理出版，希望以华工在欧洲战场的经历勉励同样饱受战争蹂躏、遭受战争苦难的同胞。新中国成立后，顾杏卿任上海外语学院（今上海外国语大学）英文教授。

2018年11月11日，为纪念第一次世界大战停战100周年，法国在巴黎凯旋门前隆重举行纪念仪式。仪式上，华裔高中女生用普通话朗读了顾杏卿《欧战工作回忆录》之《休战日之狂欢》一节，引发国际社会广泛关注。

Gu Xingqing (1893-1986), born in Shanghai, is the author of *Reminiscences on My Work during European War*, which tells about his personal experiences as an interpreter for the Chinese Labour Corps during the First World War. It was in 1917 when he was still a student at school that he was recruited to work as an interpreter in a team of Chinese labourers. Like many other young people, he thought it as springboard for travelling abroad and a better future. He left Qingdao wharf on 17 April 1917 and sailed for Britain all the way by first crossing the Pacific Ocean through Canada to the western coast of the Atlantic Ocean. He arrived at Noyelles-sur-Mer (Somme), a coastal town in France in July and since then he had served as an interpreter for the Chinese labourers amidst the gunfire and tried to protect the rights and

顾杏卿：欧战工作回忆录
Reminiscences on My Work during European War by Gu Xingqing

interests of Chinese labourers. After he returned to China in 1919, he went to the United States for further study and obtained a master's degree in art and science from Northwestern University in 1923. Originally, Gu Xingqing had no intention to make his observations, records and recollections in battlefields to the public. It was not until the war against Japanese invasion commenced in China that he decided to sort out and publish his manuscripts in the hope of encouraging his suffering Chinese compatriots with Chinese labourers' experiences in European battlefields in WWI. He worked as an English professor in Shanghai Institute of Foreign Languages (today's Shanghai Foreign Studies University) after the founding of the People's Republic of China in 1949.

On 11 November 2018, a ceremony was held in front of the Arch of Triumph in Paris, France, to commemorate the 100th anniversary of the armistice of WWI. At the ceremony, a high school Chinese girl recited in Mandarin the "Rejoice of Armistice Day", from Gu Xingqing's *Reminiscences on My Work during European War*, which sparked widespread international attention.

华工日记
Chinese Labourer's Diaries

自序

余幼时，耳食海外文明，羡慕久矣，且尝见同胞出国求学，不绝于途，益动我远游壮志。然为境遇所困，惟有咨嗟叹息而已。讵知天下事有出人意料者，值一九一七年春，欧战方殷，英、法两国忽在我华招募华工，并广聘译员。余闻之，不禁色然喜曰："时哉不可失，余之远游机会至矣！"乃毅然应聘，随十余万华工出国，途经日本、坎拿大之温哥华、落矶山、大西洋而至法兰西、比利时。迨抵目的地，始知此次英、法招募华工，实为参战之故。既已深入虎穴，生死即置度外。虽中途备受鱼雷潜艇之恐怖，前线屡遭空军之袭击，日处枪林弹雨中，惊心动魄，安之若素，卒至化险为夷，竟庆生还，此足以自慰者也。古人有云："有志者，事竟成。"余于此行而益信。环顾前后，出国为时数载，而此数载之中，最足以昭告国人者，为吾十余万华工，离祖国，涉重洋，冒锋镝，历艰险，出死入生，参加欧洲大战，以博无上之荣誉，此实为吾国外交上一页光荣史也。然观夫欧战之残酷，将使人民无噍类，又深懔乎佳兵不详。呜呼！科学愈进步，人类愈不幸，是则深可慨焉！用是不揣谫陋，追溯既往，爰成《欧战工作回忆录》。幸海内读者，有以教正之。

民国二十五年十一月
顾杏卿序于镇江

顾杏卿：欧战工作回忆录
Reminiscences on My Work during European War by Gu Xingqing

Preface by the Author

I had long admired overseas civilisations ever since I heard about them when I was very young. Later, I saw endless streams of our compatriots go abroad to pursue further study, which further strengthened my own ambition of going abroad. However, trapped by circumstances, I could only sigh for my destiny. But things took place unexpectedly sometimes. In the spring of 1917, when the European War became even more intense, Britain and France began to recruit Chinese labourers and interpreters. Hearing the news, I could not help bursting into laughter, "What a great opportunity for me to realise my ambition of going abroad! I must seize this opportunity." I applied for the recruitment resolutely and set out together with one hundred thousand Chinese labourers. We arrived in France and Belgium via Japan, Vancouver of Canada, the Rocky Mountains, and the Atlantic Ocean. However, we did not know that we had been recruited to take part in the war until we arrived at our destinations. Since we had already arrived at the battlefields, we gave no thought to our personal safety. Under the terror of torpedoes and submarines as we crossed the oceans and the frequent attacks of the enemy air forces at the front, we lived a dangerous life among bombardments and bullets every day. However, we took it very calmly. Eventually, we returned home alive after undergoing so many hazards, which is a great self-consolation for us. Just as the saying goes, "where there is a will, there is a way." I believe this even more after my experiences in Europe. Looking back, during these years of stay in Europe, I believe the most important thing I could proudly give to my fellow countrymen is that the over one hundred thousand Chinese labourers who left our country for Europe and risked their lives in the war, had won great honour for our nation. It is indeed

华工日记
Chinese Labourer's Diaries

a glorious page in the history of diplomacy for our country. However, I have also seen how cruel the war was, causing so many ordinary people to lose their lives. I also feet deep awe for the various weapons that were used in the war. Alas, the more advanced science and technology is, the more unfortunate human beings will become. This is really something that makes us give our sentiments. Therefore, I have recorded my past experiences in these years in *Reminiscences on My Work during European War*, hoping that readers at home and abroad will find it useful.

November 1936
Gu Xingqing at Zhenjiang

顾杏卿：欧战工作回忆录
Reminiscences on My Work during European War by Gu Xingqing

1. 远别祖国

一九一七年春，余因体弱养疴于华北，既不能攻读，又不能服务，心灵上顿感痛苦。某日忽闻英公使署，有征聘华工译员之举，余认为出国漫游之绝好机会临矣，于是毅然应聘。虽体弱如故，亦不遑顾及。

余既应聘赴法，数日内即须成行，故亟亟整理行装，从事远征，并于启行前一日，赴各友处告辞。而至友之来余寓话别者，慰勉备至，使余感激莫名。教会会长英人史培志之以"自由""正义""和平"，勉余为服务宗旨，实为确切不移之座右铭。至友周菊人君以"少年须具冒险精神，方可建功立业"相勖，尤使余感动不置。是夜，念邻室徐、林二友处，尚未得闲一往，拟作最后之告别，然彼等皆入睡乡，怅然而返。独坐斗室，万籁无声，往事前程，萦绕脑际。酣梦未成，东方已白，起身盥洗，略进早点，赴站候车，同行者已先后莅站。送行之人，拥满月台，于晨光熹微中，挥巾不已，有无限惜别之情。其中有一老人，泪浕浕下，双目红肿。睹此情状，诚令人心酸不已。人生于普通之离别，已足使柔肠九转，而况远别祖国，赴万里重洋之外乎？

是日启行，按预定路程，先往济南，再转青岛搭轮放洋。余等至济南，时已日暮，乃投宿逆旅。翌晨，方乘胶济车行。其时胶济铁路，大权操诸日人，在站购票及乘车时，均系日人指挥。所有旅客一一列队，依次前进，秩序井然。迨余等车抵青岛，已有多数华工，先余辈而至。闻此辈华工，每日从事操练，以备送往法境战线服务，余闻而愕然者久之。

下车后至待发所，见有工人数千，在场操练，英人教以简单之步伐。闻彼等抵所时，须先沐浴，然后经医生检查体格，有无肺痨、花柳及沙

华工日记
Chinese Labourer's Diaries

眼等传染病。不合格者，给资遣回；其查验合格者，改换服装，签订合同，编列号码，留待出发。翌晨（四月六日）五时，余见英方官员，正在发给津贴及衣帽等物，汗流浃背，倍觉忙碌（依照普通规定，华工一人，除在中国每月付十元给其家属为赡养费，及在法日予一法郎工资外，上船时又各给二十元津贴。所有华工衣服食物等件，概由雇主发给），分发事毕，即命排成列队，以便出发。每四百人一大排，排长以在中国各商埠回国投效之商人或教士充之。

临行时，所中职员，醵资备多量爆竹燃放，用以表示欢送远别同胞之意。是时工人亦全体新装，肃立致谢，且均喜形于色，抱有乘长风破万里浪之气概焉。余在同侪中年最幼，时尚未满二十，参此壮游，颇足自豪。第因同轮者思家情热，亦不禁顿生别离家国之感。然转念此行，大可增加识见，方庆幸之不暇，何郁郁以自苦？乃以此旨互相告勉，同往者精神为之一振。

Leaving Motherland

In the spring of 1917, I recuperated in Northern China due to my delicate health. Unable to either study or work, I felt great distress in my heart. One day, news came that the British consul office was recruiting Chinese labourers to work as interpreters. Deeming it a good opportunity to travel abroad, I went determinedly to apply for it, irrespective my delicate health.

As I had applied for going to France and had to leave in a few days, I decided to pack my belongings immediately to get ready for the trip. I visited some of my friends to say goodbye on the day before my departure. When my best friends came to my home to bid me farewell, they gave me such great comfort and encouragement that I was deeply touched. The president of the church, an Englishman with the Chinese name of Shi Peizhi, encouraged me to take "freedom", "justice" and "peace" as the aim of my service, which later became my steadfast motto. Mr. Zhou Junren, one of my best friends, encouraged me with the idea that "Young people can only accomplish their goals with an adventurous spirit", by which I was deeply moved. That evening, thinking that I had not said goodbye to my friends Xu and Lin who lived next door, I decided to visit them. However, they had already fallen asleep and I returned in disappointment. Sitting alone in my small room, with everything in stillness, I could not help but think about my past and my future. I hardly slept all night. I got up at daybreak and ate something after I washed my face. Then I went to the railway station, where my companions had arrived successively. The platform was crowded with people who came to see us off. Seeing them waving their hands in the morning light, all of us had infinite feelings of reluctance to part. Among them stood an old man whose eyes had become red and swollen with tears running down his cheeks. Such a scene really caused our heart to ache. Ordinary partings in life could make people heart-broken, let alone leaving our motherland for foreign countries so far away!

So we left that day. According to the schedule, we would first go to Jinan and then to Qingdao where we would get on a ship to cross the ocean. When we arrived in Jinan, it was already dusk. So we were lodged in hotels and set off the next morning by train along the Jiaozhou-Jinan railway. At that time, the Jiaozhou-Jinan railway was under the control of Japanese, who commanded when we bought tickets and got on the train. All the passengers lined up and boarded the train one by one. When we arrived in Qingdao, there were already a great number of Chinese labourers there who had arrived earlier than us. It was said that the Chinese labourers drilled hard every day while waiting to be sent to the battlefields to serve in France. This shocked me for a long time.

华工日记
Chinese Labourer's Diaries

After getting off the train, we went to the Preparatory Coolie Station, where I saw thousands of Chinese labourers were drilling and the Englishmen were teaching them the simple steps. I heard that when they arrived, they were required to take a bath first and then have a physical check by doctors to see whether they had infectious diseases such as tuberculosis, venereal disease or trachoma. Those who failed to meet the requirements would be sent back. Those who were qualified would change clothes, sign contracts, be given number bracelets and get ready for departure. At five o'clock the next morning (6 April), I saw the British officers were busy giving out allowances and clothing. According to the general rules, the family of each Chinese labourer shall be paid ten yuan every month as separation payment and each Chinese labourer shall receive one franc each full day in France as his pay. Besides, when they were aboard the ship, they shall be given 20 yuan each as their allowances. All clothes and food shall be supplied and paid for by the British. After the distribution of allowances and clothing, the Chinese labourers were ordered to stand in line for departure. Every 400 people made up a platoon and the platoon leaders were missionaries or merchants who had worked in various Chinese trading ports and chosen to return to offer their services.

On the day of departure, staff in the recruitment bureau would set off firecrackers bought with money they had raised to see off their departing compatriots. At that time, all the labourers in their new clothes would stand solemnly to express their gratitude, with delight on their faces and the spirit to ride waves and winds. Under the age of 20, I was the youngest among my companions and I took great pride in taking on such a grand mission. But at the same time, because of the intense homesickness of people in the ship, I could not help having the sad feelings of leaving my family and motherland. Now that the trip could greatly expand our horizons, why should we feel sad about such a grand opportunity? So, I comforted my fellow labourers with these words and they cheered up again.

2. 道经日本

十七日晨，船始启椗。风平浪静，如履平地。十九日晨，抵日之长崎，解缆停舶，即有日医官登船检查。二十一日晚九时，船又开行，工人中长于音乐者颇众，故途中管弦杂奏，颇不岑寂。二十三日下午一时，抵日之横滨，余上岸一游，街道整洁，店铺林立，书肆尤多，所有店员，十九皆女子。来往车辆，除电车外，以人力车为多，车夫休息时，皆读报纸，由此可知日本教育之普及。当时日本虽已加入欧战，究与战地距离遥远，故国内仍安静异常，毫不受战事之影响。

二十四日晚，船又启椗，翌晨风浪骤作，船身摇撼特甚，至睡铺前后倾欹，左右转侧，目为之眩，头为之晕。且气候暴冷，更使身体不适，饮食莫能进。航行之苦，实难忍受，故同行者有云："设余一旦返故乡，誓必终身蛰居乡里以事耕种，优游岁月。决不慕此虚荣，而受此无谓痛苦。"余闻之，不禁哑然失笑。

Travelling via Japan

On the morning of 17 April, the ship began to set sail and all went smoothly on the calm and tranquil sea. On the morning of 19 April, our ship arrived in Nagasaki, Japan, and moored there for Japanese medical officers to come aboard for inspections. At 9 o'clock in the evening on 21 April, our ship set sail again. Many labourers were good at music and they played various musical instruments along the way, which made the voyage not lonely at all. At 13 o'clock on 23 April, our ship arrived in Yokohama, Japan. I went ashore for a tour. In the very clean streets there were many shops, especially bookstores. Nine out of ten assistants of these shops were women. In addition to trolley buses, most of the vehicles travelling in the streets were rickshaws. When taking a rest, all the rickshaw pullers read newspapers, which showed the popularisation of education in Japan. At that time Japan had joined the European War, but because it was far away from the battlefields, it was very quiet, seeming not to be affected by the war at all.

On the evening of 24 April, our ship sailed again. The next morning, a sudden storm blew in and the whole ship rocked so violently that everything was thrown back and forth, left and right or up and down. As a result, we became dazzled and dizzy. And for the sudden cold weather, we all felt uncomfortable and unable to eat anything. The hardships of the voyage were so unbearable that some of our fellow travellers said, "If I could return to my hometown, I would swear to live there in the countryside for the rest of my life, doing farming work leisurely. I would never envy such vanity and suffer this unnecessary pain." Hearing these words, I could not help laughing.

3. 赴坎途中

舟行十九日（五月六日），船主云："此去离坎拿大Vancouver埠，只

顾杏卿：欧战工作回忆录
Reminiscences on My Work during European War by Gu Xingqing

有数日矣。苟能风平浪静，则又减少一日行程。"余等正苦舟行日长，闻之皆怡然自乐，盖众人企望登岸之心，十分急切。舟行又一日余，遥望群鸟飞旋空际，盖离岸已不远矣。众皆喜悦，不可言状。

五月七、八两日，天空忽起大雾，虽伸手可见五指，但三尺以外已无法辨认。因此舟行极缓，每隔二分钟，必鸣笛一次，以防与他船互撞。雾之大，为余有生以来所仅见。如是者一日半，雾始消失，浪静风平。余等至此，精神一爽。数日不思饮食之余，亦觉饥肠辘辘，乃狂啖午餐以果腹。翌晨举目遥望，高山隐现，询诸船役，则谓离岸已近，数小时水程可达，余闻之不禁雀跃。

On the Way to Canada

On 6 May, when we had been on the sea for 19 days, the ship owner said, "It's only a few days' voyage from here to the port of Vancouver, Canada. Provided that there are no storms, we can arrive one day earlier." We were suffering greatly from the long and dull voyage at that time. Hearing his words, all of us became happy again, revealing our eagerness to get ashore. After another day of voyage, we could see in the distance flocks of birds flying in the sky. It was obvious that we were not far from the port. All became excited, and our delight was beyond words.

On 7 and 8 May, heavy fog suddenly appeared in the sky. Although one could see his five fingers in front of him, he could not see anything more than three feet away. Our ship went very slowly and whistled every two minutes to avoid colliding with other ships. It was the heaviest fog I had ever seen in my life. The fog continued like this for another day and a half. Then it began to disappear and the sea became calm again. Only at that time did we all begin to feel high-spirited again. I had not felt like eating for several days, but now my stomach was crying out for food. So at lunch I ate lots of food to satisfy my hunger. The next morning, when I looked into the distance, I could see the indistinct outline of mountains. When asked, the sailors on the ship told me that the coast was near and we could arrive there within a few hours. On hearing the news, I nearly jumped for joy.

4. 坎境一瞥

五月九日晨，乃安抵温哥华，计海行已二十余日。余辈在舟中，但见黯淡之苍天，与澎湃之怒潮而已。迨登彼岸，衷心安慰，无可言喻。余见舟已傍岸，乃与美人马君，共雇汽车游览该处。马君年虽七十余，仍在船上服役为医，精神矍铄，实为常人所不及。

温城商业繁茂，为坎拿大铁道之终点，由此海口航行，可以直达中国、日本及澳大利亚。数十年前，荒无人烟，今则崇楼层叠，船舶云集，一跃而为坎拿大西岸之第一良港，称最重要之新兴市场。该处街道平整可观，交通则有电车、汽车。汽车之多，不下于吾国之人力车。电车座位不分等级，稳妥舒适。店铺林立，有所谓五分、一角及一角五分店铺者，即铺中所售各种物件，至贱者五分，而最贵者则一角五分也。价目虽贱，然日用之物，应有尽有。在吾国尚未有与此相类之店铺，然在坎拿大全国共有七十所，在英国共有六十处。店员均为妙龄女子，人往购物，彼必道谢。游览时曾往邮局寄信，见有禁止吐痰通告一纸，违者须罚茄金五十元。夫随地吐痰，吾国人向不注意。彼国禁止极严，吐痰之害，于此可见。马君于该地最熟悉，乃导余往游斯丹来公园

顾杏卿：欧战工作回忆录
Reminiscences on My Work during European War by Gu Xingqing

（Stanley Park），园地甚大，长宽各二英里，园中树林甚密，松柏尤茂，天然胜境也。

游园后往咖啡店饮茶，侍者为一妙龄女郎，见余饮时，格格作捧腹笑。余询何故，则曰："朱古律糖亦饮料之一也。"盖是时，余命取咖啡茶后，再命取朱古律糖故。余盖初涉重洋，履此异地，宜乎不识茶之种种名称，此犹外人在我国茶馆，既饮红茶，又需要淡茶相仿佛云。

余与马君饮毕出外游览时，途遇侨胞数人，均广东籍。彼等见余为同胞，如旧相识然，又知余乃初莅该地者，特趋前与余握手，并以国语询余曰："君是否赴法参与华工翻译职务者？"余曰："然。"并询彼曰："君等何能先知？"曰："顷间傍岸之船，闻载有华工甚多。君既似初来者，谅搭是船至此无疑。且此船不载其他旅客，故能知君之行踪也。"侨胞言语之间，除屡露赴法之不利外，更详述经大西洋而赴法途中之种种危险。余固初出国者，身临异地而聆此危言，心颇忐忑不安。然细察华侨行为，实系君子者流，所说似可深信。但余既立志赴法，一切利害皆不之顾，只求赴目的地耳。

翌晨即见三千余华工，由英兵率领登岸，改乘特备之专车进发，以期早达目的地。第闻此地定例，凡华工入境，须纳人头税，计每人茄金五百元。兹则英政府早已与茄政府商定临时办法，即华工之赴法路过茄境时，免除缴纳人头税，而以华工不能自由登岸为条件。故船傍温岸，华工一律伏居船中，不得上岸。迨专车至，始由负管理责任之英兵，督率上车。其车厢两端，均有英兵看守，是以在车华工，仍不能在车中随意往来。随车之英医，每晨巡视车厢各一次，查察华工是否患有疾病。然每日巡查所得，华工患有胃病者甚多，断为缺少运动所致。但余以为处此囚车式之火车中，亦所难免耳。

余在车上所有饮食起居，尚称满意。晨间为余治寝具者，乃一黑人，其面貌一如炉炭砚墨。余初见时，以为若人之污秽，至斯而极。然细察之，亦甚清洁，不过皮肤特别黧黑耳。

451

华工日记
Chinese Labourer's Diaries

余等所乘之车，为英政府所特备者。车行一星期，除车头加煤进水外，从未一靠任何车站。不然沿途各地风土人情，与夫习俗惯例，正可增余识见不鲜。兹则昙花一现，等于过眼烟云。即有所见，亦不过若干特异之点，映于眼帘已耳。途中一路风景绝佳，令人欣赏不已。

回忆幼年读书时，地理教授曾问余："落矶山何在？"余瞠目不知所答。今在车中忽见巍然陈列于我眼帘者，正名闻世界之大落矶山也。是山远望，但见满山积雪，恍似一片白银世界。"岭表明霁色，城中增暮寒"，此地有焉。时在夏季，有此奇异之雪景，颇觉洋洋可观。据熟悉此地情形者言，是山终年积雪，以致毫无生物产生。至山中有无矿质，至今亦尚未有发现者。车行是山之隧道，凡五英里，闻为世界最长之隧道，辟此隧道之工程，其伟大可想而知矣。又据某英人语余，当开凿隧道时，以平均计，日必死伤工人三四名。非丧生于大石之坠落中者，即因呼吸山中之毒气而致窒息以死者。综计二年余之工作期内，工人之无辜牺牲，何可胜数，余闻之悚然。

每站设有饮食店，以便列车到站时，旅客下车购物（车上无售物者）。沿铁路一带房屋，纯系木制，未见用砖砌者，即车站办公室亦多为木质。余异而询之，始悉此地富森林，木材可以随意取用，不必花费分文也。

A Glimpse of Canada

On the morning of 9 May, we arrived in Vancouver safe and sound. Till then we had been on the sea for more than 20 days. When we were aboard the ship, all we ever saw was blue sky and surging waves. So when we set foot on the land, we became so delighted that such heartfelt pleasure was beyond description. Mr. Ma, an American doctor on board, and I hired a car to have a

顾杏卿：欧战工作回忆录
Reminiscences on My Work during European War by Gu Xingqing

tour around this place. Although Mr. Ma was more than seventy years old, he was still healthy and energetic, much fitter than most ordinary people of his age.

Vancouver, a prosperous commercial city, was the terminus for the Canadian Railway and ships departing from its port could head directly to China, Japan and Australia. Decades ago, it was still desolate and uninhabited. But now, with high buildings and gathering ships, it became the main port on the West Coast of Canada, known as the important emerging market. The streets were neat and smooth, filled with trolley buses and cars. The number of cars on the streets was no less than the number of rickshaws in our country. The seats on the trolley buses, with no class differentiation, were safe and comfortable. Among the numerous shops were the so-called five-cent, ten-cent, and fifteen-cent stores. In these stores, every item was sold from five cents for the cheapest and fifteen cents for the most expensive. Despite the low prices, all kinds of things for daily use were available in such stores. There were no such shops in our country yet. However, there were apparently seventy in Canada and sixty in Britain. Shop assistants are all young women, who always said "thanks" to each person going shopping there. During the tour, I went to the post office to send a letter and found a notice prohibiting spitting. The violator must pay a fine of 50 dollars! In our country, no people ever paid any attention to it while in Canada spitting was strictly prohibited, which indicated the great harm of spitting. Mr. Ma was most familiar with the area and he took me to Stanley Park, which was very large, two miles in length and width. Filled with very dense trees, particularly pines and cypresses, the park is a natural attraction.

After the tour in the park, we went to a coffee shop for a drink. The waitress was a young girl and when she saw how I drank, she giggled. I asked

453

for the reason, she said, "Chocolate sugar is also part of the drink." It turned out that I had asked her to take coffee first and then ordered chocolate sugar. Since it was the first time I had been in a foreign country, I did not know the various names of drinks, just as a foreigner in the tea house in our country would ask for milk while drinking the black tea.

When Mr. Ma and I left the coffee shop, we met several our fellow countrymen who lived abroad and all of them were from Guangdong Province. Knowing that I was also a Chinese, they treated me like an old acquaintance. When they learnt that I was a stranger in this place, they walked forward to shake hands with me and asked me in Mandarin, "Are you going to France to serve as an interpreter?" I said "Yes" and asked them, "How could you know it?" They answered, "We hear that a ship carrying many Chinese labourers stopped at the wharf right now. You look like a newcomer, so we think you must also have arrived on that ship. We also hear that this ship will not take any other passengers. That is why we can guess where you are going." During our talk, they mentioned some disadvantages of going to France and recounted the various dangers of crossing the Atlantic Ocean on the way to France. It was the first time I had ever gone abroad and on hearing these comments in a foreign place about the dangers of travelling to France, I felt rather upset. What they said seemed believable because they seemed like decent gentlemen in words and behaviour. However, as I was determined to go to France, I would continue to my destination regardless of all the frightening risks and potential dangers.

The next morning over 3,000 Chinese labourers, led by British soldiers, disembarked from the ship and took a special train to get to their destination as quickly as possible. According to the local regulations, each Chinese labourer should pay 500 Canadian dollars as the poll tax when entering the country. In view of this, the British government and the Canadian government had already

顾杏卿：欧战工作回忆录
Reminiscences on My Work during European War by Gu Xingqing

reached an agreement on a provisional measure. Chinese labourers crossing Canada on their way to France were exempt from poll tax on the condition that they were prohibited from disembarking their ships. Therefore, when our ship stopped at the coast of Vancouver, no Chinese labourers were allowed to go ashore and had to stay on the ship. When the special train arrived, they were led by the British soldiers responsible for their management to get on the train. Even when they were on the train, they could not move freely because both ends of each carriage were guarded by British soldiers. The soldiers on the train also inspected the compartments every morning to check whether Chinese labourers had any diseases. The results of the daily inspections showed that many Chinese labourers had stomach problems, which was probably for the lack of physical exercises. In my opinion, diseases were inevitable now that we were imprisoned in this prison-like train.

I was satisfied with the food and lodging on the train. The person in charge of my bedding was a man whose face was as black as charcoal or ink. At the first sight of him, I had thought he was an extremely filthy person, but after closer scrutiny I found he was actually very clean and the fact was that his skin was black.

The train we took was one specially provided by the British government. For a whole week, the train travelled without stopping at any station, except when the locomotive was coaled or watered. Otherwise, it would have been a good opportunity for me to learn about the local people and their customs along the way. But the reality was that all was as transient as a fleeting cloud. Even if when I did manage to see something, what came into our sight was only something different from our own. Fortunately, I could enjoy the excellent views outside the window all the way.

When I was a schoolboy, my Professor of geography once asked me,

华工日记
Chinese Labourer's Diaries

"Where are the Rocky Mountains?" At that time, I did not know the answer. But now the imposing mountain ranges of the world-famous Rocky Mountains were passing by in front of us outside the window of the train. Although they were far away, I could still see through the window that the snow-covered mountains were like a world of silver. Such a scene reminded me of a poem by Zu Yong, a poet in the Tang Dynasty, who described the sunset glowing among trees after snow while the city grew colder at dusk. It was summer at that time and I was deeply impressed by such a wonderful snow scene in the summer. According to some people familiar with this place, there were no living creatures in the mountains at all because they were covered with snow all the year round. No minerals of any kind had yet been discovered in the mountains. The train travelled through a tunnel which was five miles long and was said to be the longest tunnel in the world. One could imagine how difficult it was to build such a long tunnel in the mountains. An Englishman told me that when the tunnel was excavated, three or four labourers on average were killed or injured every day. They were either killed by the fall of large boulders or suffocated by breathing in poisonous gases from within the mountains. I was horrified to hear that countless workers had lost their lives in building the tunnel during the two years of this project.

At each station there was a catering store, from which passengers could buy the things they needed when the train pulled in (there was no selling of goods on the train). All the houses along the railway were built with wood rather than bricks and even the station offices were made of wood. Later, after enquiring, I learnt that it was because wood could be used for free as this area was rich in forests.

顾杏卿：欧战工作回忆录
Reminiscences on My Work during European War by Gu Xingqing

5. 大西洋中之脱险

五月十八日，车抵坎拿大东岸蒙特利奥（Montreal）城，为坎拿大工商业最繁盛之区。计自温城车行至此，已五千四百余英里。稍停，车即开行至海列发克斯（Halifax），乃舍车登轮。时前线紧急，德国实行其"无限制"潜艇政策。敌人潜艇，出没无常，海上船只，奉有英海军部命令，晚间行驶，一律不许燃火，以避敌艇袭击。

此次航行大西洋，先有英二等巡洋舰一只，随轮护送。待舟离英约有四日水程，英海军部又派出驱逐雷艇七艘迎护。据同舰之英军官谓余曰："舟经此处，巡视偶一不慎，辄遭鱼雷之险。敝国（英国）为尊重贵国（指我国）尊严，爱护多数华工起见，政府特命令海军部派遣多数军舰迎送，以资保护。"余于感谢之中，寸心实觉惴惴不安也。

迎送余等之军舰，每小时速力能行三十海里。余等乘船为商轮，行驶极缓，常见该项军舰，忽焉前进，忽焉后退，忽焉后退而又前进，竭卫护之能事。

余等乘船，首尾均装大炮，有英海军官日夜驻守。并有英军官若干人，特在舱面教授各华工使用舢舨与救命圈种种方法，用以预防不测，并指授行驶小舢小艇之术。船上所置小艇，均储干粮、饼干之类，并嘱："如遇危险，凡任工头者，须令工人先行下艇。在此数日内，晚间不可解衣而卧，以防万一之危险。"

某日深夜，余正熟睡，忽为人声所惊醒。急询何事，同室之王君子安云："不必询问，速起速起！"余聆其言，为之大惊，立由床上一跃而起，拟将置在身旁之救命圈捆扎身上。时虽夏季，竟寒冷如严冬，又在

华工日记
Chinese Labourer's Diaries

黑暗之中，一时竟不易摸索。余此时恐怖万状，不可言喻。余乃于恐怖之黑暗中，徐徐将救命圈置之身上，并奔赴邻室，以探究竟。所有同人等，均默坐无言。未几，王君谓我曰："船已抛锚，余闻炮声已有三次矣。"当吾人寂静无声时，似闻有炮声隆隆。然事后询问经过事实，始知曾有敌国潜水艇之桅杆出现水面，适被英军官所见，发炮攻之，敌艇始遁去。华工中之胆怯者，往往发生无谓之惊惶与忧虑。余兴之所至，时入统舱，与华工辈讲解故事，以资娱乐。盖如此方法，一以自解愁闷，一以劝慰枯寂之华籍同胞也。

越数日，船长（英人）语余曰："船抵目的地，仅二日行程矣。但船之最危险时期，亦在此数日中。"请余转告华工："自此时至登岸时止，每晚须和衣而睡，及练习小舢舨之行驶术与救命圈之使用法。更有一语，请告彼等特别注意，设一旦船临险地，务当镇静行事。设或鼓噪无常，心神错乱，虽有急救方法，亦将无从施展。"予闻语唯唯，即将此意一一为之转达。然余之心房中，此时竟如千万辘轳，无一刻安宁也。万一遇险，亦在意中。念及死之最凄惨者，莫甚于沉溺汪洋之水中，葬身鱼腹，家莫闻知，犹以为乘风破浪，正在前进中也。余等于此三日中，朝夕未曾安眠。环顾是时之船长，竟日夜不寐，奋勇从事。西人之勇敢任劳，实予吾人以深刻之认识也。

六月一日下午六时左右，余船已安抵英之利物浦（Liverpool）埠。行将系岸时，余为同事所推举，特草一英文长函致船长，表示途次驾驶有方，化险为夷，代表同胞感谢之意。船长得函，异常欣喜，并谓余等曰："予将此函深藏箧中，留作永久纪念。盖余与贵国人士通函，此实为破天荒第一遭也。"迨船泊已定，余等乃与船长及诸船员，一一握手道别登岸。在余等联袂登岸时，早有英之士女，前来欢迎，脱帽狂呼者有之，扬巾呐喊者有之。所以有此盛况者，该地人士自接有三千华工到埠之消息，英政府为亲睦华工起见，与该埠市长等，特先致意于该地人民，行此欢迎盛典。盖不如此，不足以鼓励华工之兴奋而赴前线工作也。

顾杏卿：欧战工作回忆录
Reminiscences on My Work during European War by Gu Xingqing

Escaping Danger in Atlantic

On 18 May, the train arrived at Montreal, a city on the east coast of Canada and also the most prosperous industrial and commercial area of Canada. The train had run more than 2,500 miles since it left Vancouver. After a very short stay in Montreal, the train continued to Halifax, where we got off the train and embarked on a ship. At that time, Germany implemented its "unrestricted" submarine policy because of the desperate situation line. The enemy submarines appeared and disappeared on the sea with regularity. Therefore, all ships on the sea had to strictly obey the orders of the British Navy that no lights were allowed on ships after dark to avoid the attack of enemy submarines.

While crossing the Atlantic Ocean, our ship was first escorted by a second-class British cruiser. When we were four-day sailing away from Britain, seven mine destroyers were sent by the Admiralty to meet and escort our ship. A British officer on the ship told me, "It is a dangerous place for ships, any careless patrol will stand the risk of being torpedoed. The British government has issued special orders for the Admiralty to send more warships to meet and protect the ship in order to show dignity and respect to your country and take good care of the Chinese labourers." On hearing his words, I felt fearful and anxious, but my heart was thankful to the British.

The warships sent out to meet and escort our ship could travel 30 nautical miles per hour, while the ship we were on was a commercial ship and it travelled very slowly. We could see the warships travelling backwards and forwards from time to time, fulfilling their duty of protection.

On the bow and stern of our ship there were cannons guarded day and

华工日记
Chinese Labourer's Diaries

night by soldiers and officers of the British Navy. On the deck, several British officers taught the Chinese labourers' various methods of using sampans and life-saving rings as precautions and told them about the skills of handling the small sampans (rowing boats), which were stored with solid food and biscuit rations. They also ordered that "in case of emergency, all foremen should order the labourers to get onto the boats immediately and nobody should undress to sleep for the next few days".

Late one night, I was sleeping soundly when I was suddenly woken up by people's shouting. I asked my roommate Wang Zi'an what had happened, he just said, "Don't ask why, just get up quickly." Shocked by his words, I jumped up immediately and reached to fasten my life-saving ring which was always beside me. It was already summer, but it felt as cold as winter, I groped for my life-saving ring in the dark for a while but could not find it. My panic at that time was beyond words. I finally found the life-saving ring and fastened it to me in the darkness and terror slowly and rushed to the next room to see what the matter was. All my fellow labourers sat there in silence. After a while, Mr. Wang told me, "The ship has broken down, and I have heard the sound of cannons three times." In silence we seemed to have heard the sound of cannons. Later, I asked a British officer about the details and knew that a British had seen the mast of an enemy submarine emerging on the water surface and the ships had launched attacks on it with their cannons, which scared away the enemy submarine. Seeing the unnecessary panic and worries of some timid Chinese labourers, I went into their cabins and told them stories for entertainment. In this way, I helped myself to relieve my own depression on the one hand and to comfort the lonliness of our fellow labourers on the other hand.

A few days later, the Captain (an Englishman) said to me, "Our ship will

顾杏卿：欧战工作回忆录
Reminiscences on My Work during European War by Gu Xingqing

arrive at the destination in another two days, but this is the most dangerous period for us". He asked me to tell all the Chinese labourers, "From now on to the time of landing, all of you must sleep in your clothes every night and practice the operation of sampans and life-saving rings". There's another important thing that you should tell them to pay special attention to. "If our ship is really in danger, be sure to keep calm. If people were in great panic and noise, even if we have methods to save them all, there would be no way for use to use." I agreed and went to convey his message to all the labourers in detail. However, I felt thousands of butterflies in my stomach and was unable to rest. I made preparations for the worst-case scenario because anything could happen after all. But it would be the saddest thing for us to be drowned in the ocean to feed the fishes while our families at home would know nothing about it, believing that we were travelling safely on to our destination. For the following three days, none of us dared to ha e a good sleep at all. Looking around, I found our Captain had been engaging in work bravely day and night, without sleeping for a minute. From this, I gained a deeper understanding of the courage and sense of responsibility of Westerners.

At about 6 p.m. on 1 June, our ship arrived safely in the port of Liverpool, England. Before disembarking, I was elected by my fellow labourers to write a long letter in English on behalf of all Chinese labourers to thank the ship's Captain for his great courage and skill in fending off various dangers. The Captain was overjoyed to receive the letter and said to us, "I'll keep this letter in my suitcase as a treasured souvenir. It is the first letter I've got from the people of your country." When our ship was berthed, we shook hands with the Captain and his crew one by one to say goodbye. When we set our feet on land, there were lots of British people there to greet us. They shouted their greetings and waved their hats or scarves. It turned out that the British government, together with the mayor of Liverpool, had asked the local residents to organise this grand welcoming ceremony to show their respect for and friendliness towards the three thousand Chinese labourers when they got the news of our arrival. The purpose, of course, was to give encouragement to Chinese labourers who were to work on the front line.

6. 驻英福克斯登（Folkestone）

  同船来此之大队华工，亦于此欢呼声中，离舟登岸，并由英政府指派之干事人员，担任招待。盖此次华工之由英赴法，名虽华工，实际上为赴前线服务耳。英军得此战斗上助力，或可优占胜势。彼国政府与该地人民之热烈欢迎，自属应有之表示。

  翌晨即由利物浦上车，凡途中所经市镇，辄有英人扬巾狂呼。车行十二小时，乃抵英吉利海峡之福克斯登地方。福克斯登为由英赴法轮埠之一，此地工厂林立，人烟稠密，惟因时受德飞机之蹂躏，市面已呈萧条之象。英陆军部在此郊外，建有华工休息之营舍，占地甚广，派中校军官管理其事，并挑选华工数百名，留以担任一切杂役。车行抵此，即由该管理者指挥招待，并供应一切。凡华工之由英赴法者，即以此地为休息营舍。

  余等与众华工，本拟在此暂宿一宵，即搭轮赴法。奈医官查验结果，患有耳腺炎病者，竟有一千四百名以上之多，被扣而居此者，凡一月有余。余则因此而得饱览此地之风景，不可谓非旅途中之眼福也。

  此千余人，在常人之目光，一无患病之征象，外表与寻常人无异。现被英医官验得有疾，可见英医查验之严密矣。吾人在英，敌人飞机，

顾杏卿：欧战工作回忆录
Reminiscences on My Work during European War by Gu Xingqing

时由敌境飞至城中，抛投炸弹，其声如雷，无不惊惧。华工初见飞机，不禁喜甚，昂首仰视，以为翱翔如鸟，兴趣盎然。后经一次之爆炸，始觉危险之堪虞。某日之夜（时间约在晨间二时），余正熟睡之际，忽闻英军官扣帐声甚急，为之惊醒。并大声疾呼曰："速起！速起！"继又大呼不可燃火。余惊问何故，英军官又大声呼曰："速出！速出！事急！无须穿衣。"余乃赤足而出。时虽夏季，然此时之风紧气冷，一如我国之冬季。余出帐后，即有同营之队伍，强曳余至附近树林中。在黑暗中，询以何事急急如此。话犹未毕，轰然爆炸声已至。次晨阅报，方知英人死者七十六人，妇女幼稚之受伤者百七十四人。余辈以急急奔避，未伤毫末。余辈居此危险地者，约一月有余，每日除操练外，一无所事。余乃利用暇时，阅书报以消遣。报纸所载，除战事消息外，颇多盗劫与离婚等新闻，洵见战时社会状态之纷乱也。

Staying at Folkestone, Britain

The Chinese labourers on the ship came ashore in the cheers of the local people and were then entertained by British officers appointed by the government. The Chinese labourers, despite its names, were actually sent to France via Britain to serve at the front. With the help of the Chinese labourers, the British army were likely to gain some advantages in battles. Therefore, the hospitality of the British government and the warm welcome from local residents did not come as a surprise.

The next morning, we set off from Liverpool by train. In every city and town along the way, we could see people cheering and waving their scarves. After a 12-hour journey, we arrived at Folkestone of the English Channel, one of the main shipping ports to France and a densely populated area with

华工日记
Chinese Labourer's Diaries

large numbers of factories. However, due to the bombardments by German aeroplanes, it had already taken on a look of depression. Camps were built on the large area of its outskirts for the Chinese labourers to rest. A lieutenant colonel was in charge of the camp and several hundred Chinese labourers were chosen to do all the chores. Chinese labourers were supplied with everything they needed. All of the labourers who were about to go to France from Britain were required to rest in these camps.

According to the plan, the Chinese labourers were supposed to stay at the camp for only one night and would then take ships to France the next day. But more than 1,400 Chinese labourers were diagnosed with otitis and we were thus detained for over a month. This gave me the opportunity to enjoy the beautiful local scenery, which was a real blessing for me.

In the eyes of ordinary people, the Chinese labourers had nothing different from healthy people because there were no obvious symptoms at all. But they were diagnosed with illness by the British doctors. From this we could feel the thoroughness of their medical examinations. While staying at Folkestone, the enemy's aeroplanes often flew from their own territory to the city and dropped bombs into the city. The thundering rumble terrified everyone. At the first sight of the aeroplanes, the Chinese labourers were all very excited and looked up at the bird-like flying machines with great interest. However, after experiencing an explosion, they began to realise the great danger of the aeroplanes. One night, I was suddenly awakened from my deep sleep by the British officer's knock at the tent at about two o'clock in the morning. He shouted hurriedly in a loud voice "Get up! Get up!", and then told us not to light the fire. When I asked why, the officer shouted again, "Get out! Get out! It's urgent! No clothes." So I ran out with bare feet. Although it was already summer, it was still very cold just like in winters of China. As soon as I rushed out of the camp, I was pulled into nearby woods by our fellow labourers. In the dark, I asked what had happened but my words were interrupted by a loud explosion. From the morning newspaper the following day, I learnt that 76 Englishmen were killed, and 174 women and children were injured during the explosion. Fortunately, we were all spared as we had left in time. We stayed at this dangerous place for more than one month, doing nothing but training. I spent my spare time reading newspapers for recreation. Besides news about the war, there was a lot of news on robbery and divorces, showing the disorder and restlessness of society during wartime.

7. 抵法老爱儿（Noyelles）

七月七日，为我国华工与余等离英赴法之第一日。晨间三时，即起身，整理行装，以备下轮启行。钟鸣六下，所有华工，先行整队下船。余与英军官等，至九时许，始行下轮，十时许轮始起椗出口。

轮行四小时，过英海峡，抵法之白龙（Boulogne），为法西北境重要之大城市，遥望岸上，营幕累累，军械重重，盖是地已入军事重心区域。招募华工原意，本为分发各工厂充当工人，然以现在情形证之，殆将使我华工，咸临前线工作也。

抵法后，起岸登车，向华工总分发处事务所报到。惟所乘火车，为法政府所供给，向皆装载货物牛马，战时因输送太忙，载人之客车万不敷用，乃即以此项货车装运兵士。车中既无灯火，又无椅橙，所供食品，只有坚硬之饼干。我华人参与欧战工作，度困苦生活者，即以此为起点。和会之得占一席地于日后，或即种因于是。华工为祖国争国格，

华工日记
Chinese Labourer's Diaries

为同胞争光荣，于此可见一斑。沿途每过一站，停顿时间甚久，以便来往不绝之兵车及载货车先行。但余辈在车急切渴望者，即能早时到达目的地，以脱离车上之困苦。然处此军事运输繁忙之际，余辈亦莫可如何，诚如法人所谓："此因战争故也。"车行约十二小时，乃抵老爱儿地（Noyelles），是地华工云集，为华工之总招待与总事务所所在地。

华工未进营之先，须由所中英军官点名后，始得鱼贯而入。营门外有英国宪兵持枪守卫，华工不能自由出入。营舍本空地，乃英军租于法人者。方圆数百亩，四周围以坚固之铁网。工人所住者，全系行军所用帐幕。每一帐幕约有英尺一丈余之大，可宿十五人。既抵老爱儿，由带领华工之英官员，将所带队伍，一律交与华工督办处办理，而彼等则须前往伦敦一行，投英陆军部报到。由部考验其平日旅华之经验，然后加以陆军官衔，改穿制服，再返法国老爱儿，听候英人华工督办差遣委用。或派往已经成立之华工队伍，充当中尉或队长之职。但道中与华工相处既久，感情较深，一旦分离，颇为怅然。当握手道别时，彼此多有泣下沾襟者，足见同受患难之人，其精神上之结合本诸天性也。噫，感情之足以动人也如此！

老爱儿位于法国北部索姆河（Somme）之口，法国极小之一村落也。顾以地居铁路沿线之中心，故为法北部南往巴黎京城必经之道，且该地与英国远征第五军总司令部驻扎之阿不畏儿城（Abbeville）相距仅八法里，军令之传达，队伍之调遣，极形便利。因而华工至法者须先会集于此，然后分发法、比各战地工作。余辈抵此后，亦受英军医之检查。因英政府对于身体之检查，极加重视。工人中有患沙眼、耳腺炎及肺症者，莫不悉被留居医院。其经检查及格者，始重行编队。每队五百名，由英军官五人，下士二十人统率，并置译员一人或二人。又置中国工头二十人，队长一员，以陆军少校或上尉任之。军官及下士一律戎装，与军人无异，惟不备枪耳。

吾侪目击此状，不觉如坠五里雾中。盖余辈初为工作应募而来，而在祖国并未见有军官率领工人者。今睹斯状，引起我人之惊异，自在意

顾杏卿：欧战工作回忆录
Reminiscences on My Work during European War by Gu Xingqing

中。但我华工同舟来法者，彼此极行亲密，形同骨肉，难舍难分。故当局每将同来者，编成一队，但间有少数，因检查不及格而被摈弃者，一旦分袂，不胜依依，令人发生生死离别之感。盖此辈工人，从未远离本乡，一旦跋涉重洋，来此海外，咸认为最可亲近者，惟此同伴耳。

英政府在老爱儿地方，为吾华工特设大医院一所。凡华工有患重病及传染病，或工作时为炮弹炸伤者，均一律送至该院医治，或休养院中。所有英医官二十余人，均曾在吾国行医，因此对于吾华人患病，颇有经验。且多通华语，似无杆格不通之虞。

至该院组织，规模宏敞，予戚杨君永贵在该院服务，曾导余周览全院。内容完备，有开刀室、验尸所、外科及内科病房、隔离病室（专为传染病人所设）、眼科病室及花柳科病室、配药室、爱克司光线室等等。英人格莱上校（Lieut. Col. G. D. Gray）（前任英国使馆医官）为该院主任，学问渊博，心地慈祥，克尽厥职，颇为人所称道不置。

该院尚附有疯人院（患者约一百余人），其中大多数因受炮火之惊骇而顿失常态之工人。此外因思家过度，神经错乱成疯者，亦不在少数。患者既精神失其常态，故入院监禁，一如囚犯，当然无自由可言。总计全院病人，约有三千余，为数至足惊人。

余与英人华工副督办波顿少校（Purdon）晤谈后，督办为英人法亚法克上校（Fairfax），即被派至四十九队服务。该队工人均与余同舟来法者，故彼等闻之，咸来问候，欢欣之状，莫可言喻。中以山东籍者居多，年龄均在二十与四十之间，有军人、工匠、伶人、教员等等，而以农夫占大半。渠等均未出国门一步，而能抱此大无畏精神，背井离乡，远渡重洋，历此空前未有之危险，来充参战之华工，究为何故乎？实为生计耳。然而吾华工之勇敢，亦足以自豪矣。

余等守候约二星期，队长始接到上峰出发命令。余乃奉命通知总工头，转令各工头，传达各工人。各工人闻信之下，莫不喜形于色。静极思动，人同此情也。

华工日记
Chinese Labourer's Diaries

Arrival at Noyelles, France

7 July was the day we left the UK for France. We got up at three o'clock in the morning to prepare for the voyage. At six o'clock, all the Chinese labourers boarded the ship. The British officers and I did not get onto the ship until nine o'clock and the ship departed at about ten o'clock in the morning.

After 4 hours, we crossed the English channel and arrived in Boulogne, a very important large city in the northwest of France. Looking into the shore, we could see countless barracks and armaments, indicating that it was a military center. The original intention for the recruitment of Chinese labourers was for them to work in various factories. But it seemed that all Chinese labourers were to be sent to work close to the front lines.

Upon our arrival in France, we boarded a train to report to the General Distribution Centre of Chinese Labourers. The train we took was originally a freight train for carrying cows and horses. Because of the busy transportation in wartime, passenger trains were rarely available, so the French government used freight trains to transport soldiers. There were no lights, no chairs or benches, no other food except hard biscuits. This was the starting point for the hard life of the Chinese labourers during the European War. It was probably because of this that China won a seat in the post-war negotiations. What the Chinese labourers had achieved then was a proud and glorious accomplishment for China and the Chinese people. At every station, we would stop for so long a time that trains full of soldiers and cargo could go forward first. Though eager to reach our destination as quickly as possible to get rid of the pain we were suffering on this train, we could actually do nothing about this busy traffic. "It is all caused by the war," as was usually said by the French people. About

12 hours later, we finally arrived in Noyelles, where the Chinese labourers gathered and the General Reception and Service for the Chinese Labour Corps (CLC) in France was located.

Chinese labourers were given a roll-call before they made their way into the camp. With the British military police on guard outside, they were not allowed in or out freely. The camp was built in an open space rented from the French people by the British army. Hundreds of acres of the land around it was enclosed by barbed wire. The tents, used by marching soldiers, was about ten feet wide and could accommodate 15 people. While all Chinese labourers were led to the Supervisors Office for more formalities, the British officers who had travelled all the way from China to Europe with us, had to report to the War Office in London, where they would be conferred different ranks of army according to their experiences in China. Afterwards, they should wear the uniform and return to Noyelles at the disposal of the Supervisors Office. Some of them would probably be assigned to be in charge of brigades of Chinese labourers as Captain or Lieutenant. As they said goodbye to the Chinese labourers, with whom they had stayed for so long a time, both the British officers and the Chinese labourers felt quite upset, many of us even burst into tears. This touching affection really demonstrated that in times of trouble people tended to be spiritually united.

Before they were distributed to different battlefields, all the Chinese labourers would arrive in Noyelles, a very tiny village on the Somme estuary in the north of France. As a centre along the railway lines, Noyelles was the only access to Paris and was also only 8 miles away from Abbeville, where the general headquarters of the Fifth Army of the British Expeditionary Force were situated. Noyelles boasted great convenience in both order delivery and army dispatchment. Therefore, all Chinese labourers were sent here after arriving in

华工日记
Chinese Labourer's Diaries

France and then distributed to work in different places in France and Belgium. As the British government attached great importance to medical checks, we were also given a thorough physical check by military doctors when we arrived at Noyelles. Labourers diagnosed with trachoma, otitis or lung diseases were all kept in the hospital at the camp until recovery. Healthy labourers were reorganised. Each brigade was composed of 500 labourers, commanded by five British officers and twenty Corporals. For each brigade, there were one or two interpreters as well as twenty Chinese foremen and one senior officer with the rank of Captain or Lieutenant. Officers and Corporals wore uniforms just the same as other military men, and the only difference was that they were not equipped with guns.

Such an arrangement confused us greatly. We were only told that we would work in France when we were first recruited in China. Never before had we seen that military officers led labourers to work in our own country. Therefore, it was natural for us to feel puzzled with an arrangement like this. During the long journey from China to France, Chinese labourers who had travelled on the same ship had formed close relationships like brothers. Although most of them were reorganised into the same brigade, a few of them were excluded for failing to meet the physical requirements. When the time for separation came, the labourers could not help having a feeling of parting forever. It was because these Chinese labourers, who had never left their hometowns before, considered their voyage companions as their closest friends now that they had travelled abroad for the first time.

The British government set up a hospital for Chinese labourers at Noyelles. All the severely sick, infectious, or injured Chinese labourers would be sent there for treatment or rest. There were over twenty British doctors in the hospital and all of them had rich experience in treating Chinese patients for their previous medical practice in China. What's more, most of them could speak Chinese and therefore seemed to be able to have good communications with their Chinese patients.

The hospital was large in scale and complete in departments. My relative Yang Yonggui worked in this hospital and he once showed me around it. There were all the necessary departments such as operating room, mortuary room, medical and surgical wards, isolation wards (set exclusively for infectious patients), ophthalmology room, venereal disease room, pharmacy, X-ray room, and so on. The director of the hospital was Lieut. Col. G. D. Gray (a former medical officer at the British Embassy) who was well known for his profound knowledge, warm heart, and commitment to his job.

There was a lunatic asylum in the hospital, where more than 100 patients were receiving treatment. Most of them had lost their sanity as they were panic-stricken by the constant shellfire of the War. Still a great number of labourers lost their sanity due to extreme homesickness. For their insanity, these mentally ill labourers were detained in the hospital like prisoners, without any freedom. The total number of patients in the hospital was approximately three thousand, which was rather surprising.

After a meeting with Major Purdon, the British deputy supervisor of the CLC (Captain Fairfax was the supervisor at that time), I was assigned to work in Brigade 49, whose labourers were also those that had travelled on the same ship with me to France. On hearing of my arrival, all the labourers came to greet me with happiness. Among the labourers of Brigade 49, most were from Shandong Province with the age ranging from 20 to 40. Some of them were soldiers, craftsmen, actors and teachers, but the vast majority were farmers. Why did these people who had never been away from their hometowns and villages go overseas to join the European War as labourers, regardless of the unprecedented risks? They did all this to make a living, to provide for their families. The courage they had shown in this endeavour really deserved respect.

We stayed at Noyelles for two weeks before the Captain received an order from his superiors that we move on. He asked me to notify the Head Foreman to inform the other foremen, who then in turn delivered the order to their platoons of labourers. All the labourers were excited as they could finally get moving after having stayed here for so long.

8. 驻比怕勃伦基城（Pomperinghe）

时至深夜，始列队出发。抵站上车后，车即开行，但开往何地，无一知悉。待车抵目的地，始知为比之怕勃伦基城，英军驻扎比境之总司令部在焉。队长不知营地何在，乃出其所带之军令及地图，翻阅一过，始命全队一律在站候命。彼与余及一中尉，同乘军用摩托车，四处寻觅。沿途所见者，全系来往荷枪之军队、架炮之炮车，及红十字救护伤兵车耳。经数小时，始发现空旷营地一方。该地四周，围有坚固之铁丝网。前面仅有一大铁门，可通出入。其中仅有临时木造军用厨房一间，余无他屋。队长觅得营地后，通知全队入营。迨全队开到，先令盖搭帐幕及置放军灶，然后分发粗硬之军用饼干及干酪充饥。但各人到此，均觉疲乏不堪，多有不食而睡者矣。是夜月明如昼，仰视天空，所谓"露从今夜白，月自故乡明"，思家之念，油然而生。然终因疲乏而睡，讵料好梦方酣，忽被门外汽笛声所惊醒。俄顷，天空间轧轧之声不绝于耳。仰观云际，德飞机三五，盘绕其上，隐约可辨。我方侦敌电光，照耀如同

顾杏卿：欧战工作回忆录
Reminiscences on My Work during European War by Gu Xingqing

白日，亟将高射炮，向上轰击如连珠，然终未获中一机。余等至是，拟即逃出营门，以避危险。然铁门紧闭，竟不得出。须臾，又闻炸弹之下坠轰炸声，地面为之震动。余等更恐怖万分，但既无路可逃，亦只有静待死神之下降已耳。是时之余，亦以昂藏七尺之躯，遭此无谓之牺牲，不免有负来日之壮志。愁思万种，莫展一筹，亦惟有听诸天命而已。

敌机既去，余倦极入睡。中夜忽再来袭，又被惊醒，竟夜不得安睡。且抛投炸弹，满布恐怖，直至清晨始止。然朝暾既上，不得不起而工作。盖前方军士不能一日无粮秣，不能一日缺军需，而兵士所携有限，消耗甚易，子弹告竭，即束手待毙，运输实战事之命脉。故工作极度紧张，不容稍缓。

次晨，英下士等笑谓余辈曰："尔等昨晚饱受惊慌矣。"谈笑中似有表示此种遭遇，实不足注意之状，一若昨晚无事件发生者。余等闻此，精神为之一振，英军官见余时，亦谈笑自若。

依照华工队之组织，除留十二人组成一卫生队，专司营中清洁外，又命十二人为一巡警队，维持营中秩序。更派厨司十二人，理发匠一人，补鞋匠一人，各任其专门工作。即将全队工人，分成四小队，每队有一中尉率领出外工作，并令各人携带防毒面具，以备万一。是日工作之地，乃屯集炮弹之暗藏所也。所内藏有要塞、野战、过山、各种大小炮弹极夥，输出输入，皆以军用摩托车或军用火车装载之。无论何人，禁止在内吸烟，违者军法从事，盖防疏忽或致爆炸之虞也。

Staying at Poperinghe, Belgium

We did not started off to the railway station until deep into the night. As soon as we got on the train, it left the station, but no one knew where it was going. It was not until we arrived at the destination that we knew it was

华工日记
Chinese Labourer's Diaries

Poperinghe in Belgium, where the British Army Headquarters were stationed. Not knowing where to find the camp, the Captain took out the military order and a map to read while the whole brigade was ordered to wait at the station. The Captain, a Lieutenant and I drove a military motorcycle to look around. What we saw as we drove around were armed soldiers, gun carriages and Red Cross ambulances with wounded soldiers. A couple of hours later, we finally found the empty camp. It was surrounded by strong barbed wire fences with an iron gate for access. There were no other buildings except a temporary wooden military kitchen. After finding the camp, the Captain sent orders for the rest of the brigade to follow. When the whole brigade had arrived at the camp, the Captain ordered labourers to set up tents and military stoves. Then hard biscuits and cheese for military use were distributed to labourers as food. Extremely exhausted, many labourers went to sleep without eating anything. That night the moon was shining as bright as day. Looking up at the bright moon, I thought of the lines of Du Fu, a famous poet in the Tang Dynasty, that "Tonight we start the season of white dew, The moon is just as bright as in my homeland". A strong feeling of nostalgia came over me. Soon I fell asleep due to extreme fatigue. But my good sleep was disturbed by a sudden whistle outside the door. Soon afterwards, our ears were filled with the rumbling of German aircraft in the sky, which could be faintly seen hovering over our heads. The sky was lit as bright as daytime by the British searchlights and the anti-aircraft artillery fired into the sky continuously, but they failed to hit any of the aircraft. Seeing this scene, we had intended to run out of the camp to a safe place, but we could run to no place because the iron gate was closed. We soon heard the explosions of the bombs dropped from the sky and the ground shook violently. We were all greatly horrified. As there was no way to escape, we could do nothing but wait for death. I thought to myself, if I were

Reminiscences on My Work during European War by Gu Xingqing

so killed in this air raid, how could I fulfill my great aspirations? Sentiments of melancholy and pity overwhelmed me, but I could do nothing but accept my destiny.

Finally, the enemy aircraft were gone and I managed to fall asleep again. At midnight, we were awakened by the attack of the German aircraft again. For the rest of that night, I was in mortal terror of bombs, making it impossible for me to sleep at all. But when the sun rose, we had to get up and go to work because soldiers at the front could not afford to run out of supplies or ammunition at any time. Since what they carried with them was limited, they would be faced with death helplessly once their supplies were used up. Therefore, transportation was essential during wartime and we always worked under great pressure and no time could be wasted.

The next morning, the British Corporals, said to us smilingly, "You guys must have been knocked about a great deal last night." From the way they spoke and their smiles, there seemed to be no sign of worry as if nothing special had happened during the night. On hearing their words, we all cheered up and when the British officer came to see me, I could talk and laugh again quite naturally.

According to the organisation of the Chinese Labour Corps, in each brigade, 12 labourers were selected to form a cleaning team, responsible for the sanitation of the whole brigade and another 12 labourers were picked out to form a patrol team, responsible for the maintaining the order of the whole brigade. In addition, there was also a twelve-labourer cooking team, a barber and a cobbler in each brigade. The other labourers were divided into four squads, each of which was led to work outdoors by a lieutenant. Each labourer was also ordered to wear a gas mask in case of emergency. That day we worked in a place where stored a great number of shells of various types and sizes such as shells for garrison artillery, field artillery, and mountain artillery. They were transported in or out by military motorcycles or trains. No smoking was allowed and anyone who violated the rule would be punished according to military law. The purpose was to prevent negligence or the risk of causing an explosion.

9. 大战中之摩托车

大战中摩托车之供军用，为战争时一大利器，实非常人所可意想者。在宣战后之第一月，交战各国用于阵地之各式汽车，殆不下二十五万辆。战事开始时，各国政府向民间征用汽车甚多，其数累有增加。余日常所见摩托车之多，触目皆是，载炮也，运兵也，输送军火、食粮、辎重也，救护伤兵也，随时随地所设临时修理工场之各项器具，亦均由摩托车运输。摩托车有利于战争，由此可知。然其应用尚不止此，盖我人所知者，对于战事运输，火车甚属重要，惟铁轨一旦被毁，火车即不能于短时间内前进，势必停顿，贻误军机。而汽车道则不然，即使一旦被毁，随时修缮较易且速，于短时间内仍可前进无阻。常见英法军队一面浩浩荡荡前进，而兵工队在后方仍奋勇从事修缮，未见军队因汽车道被毁而停止前进，亦未见因敌人之轰击而不进也。彼西人之勇敢，自可钦佩，而得摩托车之一大助力，亦一昭彰之事实也。即战事开始时，德军攻击比利时，以至进逼巴黎，亦莫非利用此摩托车以运输兵械耳。故摩托车对于战事效用之广，有如上述。

顾杏卿：欧战工作回忆录
Reminiscences on My Work during European War by Gu Xingqing

Motorcycles in the War

One could never imagine that motorcycles could become such a convenient transport for military troops. In the first month after the declaration of war, more than 250000 vehicles were being used in the battlefields. At the beginning of the war, quite a sizable number of cars were commandeered from the residents by the government, and the number kept increasing. What I saw everyday was an overwhelming number of motorcycles being used to carry artillery shells, transport soldiers, munitions, food supplies and equipment to the front, to help the wounded soldiers, and to transport all appliances needed by the temporary repair shops set up anytime and anywhere as well. It could be seen that motorcycles were very useful in wartime, and their use was not only limited to what I mentioned above. The importance of trains to wartime transportation was known to everyone, but once the railway tracks were destroyed, trains would be hindered for a while and military operations might be delayed. In contrast, the motorways were quite different. Automobiles could still move forward even if roads were destroyed, as the damaged roadways could be repaired easily and quickly. Quite often, the British and French troops were marching on while the construction brigades were bravely mending the roads behind. The troops were neither stopped by the damaged roads nor hindered by the enemy attack. Evidently, motorcycles proved to help fueling the courageous and admirable deeds of the Westerners. From the very beginning of this war when Germany attacked Belgium till it closed in on Paris, the transportation of men and materials all depended on motorcycles, whose use was indispensable.

10. 战地生活

华工饮食，每日三次，午餐在野外席地而食，其余早晚两餐，均在营中。在外因不便煮饭，故仅食面包，佐以牛油充饥。

华工之饮食，颇得英人美满之考虑，因若辈来自我国南北两地，南人食米，而北人食面，且华工在家所惯食者，未必尽能得之于法地。故英人所供给之食物，未必全为华工所喜，如最初发给之乳酪及麦片，华工均不能惯食，后乃改给以乳油及米粉等，以适合华工之生活。若非经英人之考虑周详，安能得此美满之饮食哉。

每一工人食粮均有定额，然并不分发各个人。每日由队长派人向大粮栈领取，交与厨司，依定额每人应得之量，计肉（羊或牛）四两，米十两，面包十两，面粉六两，蔬菜（马铃薯及葱）八两，糖一两，火腿二两，硬壳油一两半，乳酪一两，茶八分之三，盐四分之一，牛油一两（以上均以英两计算）。由此可知所发食物既夥，亦可适口。至于肉食，常以兔肉代之，当系牛羊缺乏之故。

除军粮外，每人每周得领烟草及纸烟等物，但余不嗜此，持以赠人。至英军队中，再另给糖酒（rum）一种，俾作战时增加其精神，兴奋其勇敢云云。

英为一大工业国，故平时食物，多运自海外。至欧战因更须供给在比、法之军队，于是食物之需要更殷。德人熟知此故，乃采用潜艇政策，暗中封锁，使食物无可到达英岸。但英人既视食物之接济为紧要，于是不惜冒大险，渡重洋，源源载物而归，生命之丧失，船只之击沉，皆置之不顾。工人有时偶感食物之不足，即出怨言。余与同事戴君步云及总

顾杏卿：欧战工作回忆录
Reminiscences on My Work during European War by Gu Xingqing

工头张君连荣为之解释一切，务使各人体恤英人购买食物之艰难困苦也。余经此次工作，而知足食足兵之古训为不诬矣！

至我人日常生活中，颇感不自由者，厥为通信问题。凡寄递信件，照例无须贴用邮票，果属便利。然非先经英军官严密检查，不准置邮。故华文信件须先寄至老爱儿，受检查后，始准寄往中国。至英文信件，先经本营官员检阅，方送邮局，再由驻局之英检阅官，复行查阅核准后，方能发出。信中如载所驻地点，及有关战情内容者，一概不许寄出。故所书家信，仅能略道寒暄，无关紧要之语，实际情况，不能吐露只字。英军官及军士信件，亦受同样之检查，其目的无非严守战地消息，不使军情有所泄漏于敌人耳。

我华工同胞，固非军士可比。但我华工队因附属于驻法英国远征军之下，为英输送队之一种，故虽不受英军法之管束，然须服从英军纪律。工人中设有抗令及侮辱长官者，轻者罚镁，重者亦须受军法裁判，甚至有处以死刑者。余尝闻交战国军人，有因违抗长官命令临阵脱逃而被判枪毙者。余队中有一工人，因殴打长官，被判死刑。该工人为二四二三二号，系卫潘汉克地方（Wippenhoek），用铲击中尉汉特莱（Lieut. Hadley）（此军官年二十许，善华语，生于吾国），被判死刑。幸邀总司令之特赦，减轻为五年惩役。按英国军法裁判，例须队中长官，先禀告上校，要求批准，再由上校禀呈总部，然后由军法官三人，赴请求之队中审判之。审判之前，法官及证人等，依照习俗，均须起立，手持基督教之《圣经》接吻。吻后，各人手持《圣经》宣誓，借以表示所作证言，既诚实不欺，判决罪名亦为公正无私之意。誓毕，开始行其裁判。

Life in Battlefields

Chinese labourers had three meals each day, with lunch eaten in the open air and breakfast and dinner in the camp. When cooking was not possible outside, only bread with butter was available.

Food had been thoughtfully considered by the British. In spite of that, what was supplied in meals might not always cater to the taste of the Chinese labourers who had different eating habits as they came from either the south or the north of China. The southerners enjoyed rice while the northerners preferred noodles. Besides, it was almost impossible to get the food they preferred in France. For example, the labourers did not take readily to the cheese and oatmeal cereal that they were initially given. Later, cheese and oatmeal were replaced by cheese and rice to suit the taste of some Chinese labourers. If the British had not carefully considered these changes, it would not have been possible for the Chinese labourers to enjoy their favourite food.

Decent food rations were allocated to labourers, but they were not distributed to each person directly. Every day, the Captain received food from the Grain Depot and then gave it directly to the chief cook. Each individual was given four ounces of meat (mutton or beef), ten ounces of rice, ten ounces of bread, six ounces of flour, eight ounces of vegetables (potato and onion), one ounce of sugar, two ounces of ham, one point five ounces of shell oil, one ounce of cheese, three eighth of an ounce of tea, a quarter of an ounce of salt, and one ounce of butter. These were enough provisions to feed and satisfy the labourers. For the lack of beef and mutton, the meat ration was usually supplemented with rabbit.

Along with the food, each person could get some supply of tobacco or cigarettes every week, which I gave to others as I did not enjoy them. In the British army, a kind of rum was added to cheer up the labourers' spirit and increase their courage in battles.

Britain was a major industrial country, so food was usually shipped

顾杏卿：欧战工作回忆录
Reminiscences on My Work during European War by Gu Xingqing

from overseas. To support the Belgian and French army in the European War, food became even greater. The Germans were well aware of this and adopted a submarine policy to blockade food from reaching the British shores. The British, however, saw the need for food as a matter of urgency and took great risks in crossing the ocean to return with their loads, ignoring the loss of lives and the sinking of ships. The labourers sometimes complained when they felt that there was not enough food. When the labourers complained about the occasional lack of food, I, along with my colleague Mr. Dai Buyun and the Chief Foreman Mr. Zhang Lianrong, would try to explain the reasons, making them aware of the difficulties the British had in supplying and transporting food. From this experience, I came to understand the importance of what was emphasised by the ancient maxims: that an army marches on its stomach.

One thing in life in which we enjoyed no freedom was about letters. As a rule, no stamps were required for all letters, which was very convenient for labourers. However, no letters could be posted without being checked by the British officers. All Chinese letters were first sent to Noyelles, where they were strictly examined before they were sent off to China. All English letters would be first reviewed by officers at the camp before they were sent to the post office, where they were re-examined by British officers. No letters containing the location of the camp or any information about the war were allowed to be sent off. Therefore, to keep secret of the military situation and avoid giving away any information to the enemy, there should be nothing about the real conditions except some greetings or small talks in the letters home. Even the British officers and soldiers were not exempt from this type of examination.

Although Chinese labourers were not soldiers, they were one of the British transportation brigades affiliated to the British Expeditionary Force. Thus, they should obey the disciplines of the British army even though they were not controlled by the British military law. Those who defied or insulted the officers would be fined and those who committed more serious offences would face charges under the strict British military law, even the death penalty. I often heard of soldiers in the warring nations being shot because they disobeyed an order or ran away from the enemy. One labourer in my brigade, No. 24232, who worked in Wippenhoek, was sentenced to death because he assaulted a British officer with a shovel. The officer was the 20-year-old 2nd Lieutenant Hadley who was born in China and could speak fluent Chinese. Fortunately, he was given a five-year imprisonment under an amnesty from the commander-in-chief. Under the British military law, cases would first be reported to the Colonel for approval, and then delivered to the general headquarters for three officers to conduct a trial. According to their customs, the trial opened with all the judges and witnesses standing up to kiss the *Bible* in their hands, then swearing on the *Bible* to tell the truth and to ensure justice and impartiality of the decision. After the pledge, the trial began.

11. 大战中之飞机

余队驻在怕勃伦基城工作时，敌之侦察飞机，日间则从事侦察及摄影工作，晚间则改以爆炸机抛掷炸弹。每值皓月当空，敌机辄来侵犯。故当月明星稀、皎洁可爱之夜，反增恐怖之心。敌之爆炸机，亦时至伦敦、巴黎各地，恒掷巨量炸弹于伟大之建筑物。伤亡人口，牺牲财产，难以估计。战神之足以毁坏物质文明，古今一例。

某晚，敌机正飞空侦察时，某队有一工人，偶站营幕外，燃火柴以

顾杏卿：欧战工作回忆录
Reminiscences on My Work during European War by Gu Xingqing

吸烟。讵料此星星之火，适为敌机所见，立即瞄准投下巨大炸弹，以至全幕工人十四名均受死伤。该工人为个人吸烟而丧性命于俄顷，并危及同幕者生命。若该工人者，亦可为罪魁祸首也已。

每值敌机将到，例用汽笛狂鸣，借以警报。八月二十七晚，五十九队队长得警报后，遥闻机声，度敌方必有猛烈攻击，急将营中铁门大开，大声疾呼。工人于仓猝间，尽力奔避，不旋踵营内果中弹而炸，全队工人幸免于难而得不死，咸赖该队队长机警营救之功也。

战器中功用最大，而能发挥最大力量者，莫如飞机。此为各军事家所公认，亦为余在欧战中观察所得者。盖大战时之飞机，最能活动。敌方之大炮、敌人之铁甲车，虽属战争利器，未能常施其威力于战线之外，惟飞机则不然。远如法、比、英各大都市，近如前线后方，不分昼夜，往来飞翔，侦察轰炸，冀以消灭士气，破坏物力，伤失对方人民战斗之志，减少对方士兵战斗之力。此外尚有一种最大功用，为常人所不及知者，为交战时作军队之眼线是也。因士兵日夜蛰伏壕沟，对方攻击之由何方而来，吾方应向何方猛攻，对方炮弹之由何地而来，吾方应向何地射放，颇有辨别不清之处，胥惟借飞机之报告是赖。故各飞机均备有摄影箱及无线电机，随时随地，均可通知作战军队，使有所适从。至于炮队，若无飞机之侦察报告，必至无从射放。盖飞机之于炮队，尤属重要，因大战时必以炮战为决胜之战斗也。由此观之，飞机于战事上之价值，可想而知矣。

Aeroplanes in the War

While in Poperinghe, we were constantly bothered by enemy scout planes that conducted reconnaissance and took photos in the daytime, while in the evening they were modified as bombers to drop bombs. A moon-lit

华工日记
Chinese Labourer's Diaries

evening was more horrible for us because the enemy would always attack with aeroplanes. The enemy aeroplanes also targeted London, Paris, and other places, dropping large numbers of bombs on significant buildings, causing uncountable casualties and losses of properties. The damage of the war to human civilizations was unprecedented.

One evening, while an enemy plane was scouting, a worker happened to be standing outside his tent lighting a cigarette, which was spotted by the plane. He immediately became the target of the enemy attack and fourteen labourers in the tent were either killed or injured by the bombs from the enemy aeroplane. The labourer should be blamed for this careless behaviour which claimed his own life as well as his fellow labourers'.

Every time enemy aircraft approached, a loud siren would sound the alarm to everyone. On the evening of 27 August, the Captain of Brigade 59, thinking that the enemy would give a violent raid after hearing the sound of the alarm, raced to open the iron gate and ordered everyone out. Thanks to the alertness of the Captain, all the labourers in the brigade were spared as they managed to rush out to avoid the bombardment of the camp that followed only a moment afterwards.

Among all the vehicles, aircraft could be best exploited in wars, as was known to strategists and proved by my observations. Aircraft, unlike other powerful weapons, such as artillery and armoured cars, were not limited to working within the limits of the battlefields. They flew over France, Belgium, Britain, and other metropolises as well as over the front and rear of the battle lines, scouting and bombing day and night in the hope of demoralising the troops, damaging the resources, draining the spirit of the people, and reducing the army's combat strength. Aircraft could become the eyes of the belligerent powers, a function unknown to the common people. Living in the trenches day and night, our soldiers found it impossible to identify the enemy assaults. Only through the aircraft could we tell where the enemy attack and the artillery shells came from so that we knew where to direct our own forces and artillery fire. This explained why every aircraft was equipped with a camera box and wireless radio communication, with which it could inform the troops of the whereabouts of the enemy attack in time. Obviously, the artillery forces could not locate the targets without the scouting reports from the aircraft. As the artillery units usually played a decisive role in the war, aircraft could not be ignored. All the above discussions proved what aeroplanes mean to the War.

12. 战地见闻

怕勃伦基为英在比战线后方之重要之根据地：军需物品，堆积如山；工人众多，输送迅速。军人连续过此，或开往前线作战，或由战线归来休息，不绝于途。余于暇时，信步出游，偶至比人开设之咖啡店，遇一军官，彼备述前方战壕生活，据云："日夜潜伏其中，秉勇敢精神毅力对敌，虽弹如雨下，毫不胆怯。实早置生命于度外，效死战场，为国争光，男儿之天职也，何惧之有？"吁！西人之爱国心理，有如此者。

既而又曰："吾人久处壕内，生活艰苦，不易忍受，实为事实。身污不得沐浴，疲乏又难安睡，日在尘土中过活，因此周身肮脏。食物之难求清洁，亦所难免。倘值大雨，水深腰际，其中痛苦，有难以言语形容者！然吾辈一无沮丧之气，茹苦含辛，常戏言相投曰：'谈笑足增勇毅之战斗精神，危惧反足以消减士卒之壮志。'故我等于战壕中，置敌方枪炮于不顾，习以为常，处之泰然。我等每晨必须受长官检阅，事先须各自

华工日记
Chinese Labourer's Diaries

修面，刷衣，擦枪，整纽扣，擦皮鞋，检阅时间，计约五分钟。盖其目的，不外维持清洁，减少疾病，奉守军纪，于生命危险之中，犹整饬军容，以鼓励生机，保持勇敢，引起同仇敌忾、为国争光之心理耳。"

工作之暇，余与比、法人民谈及战事，知战前德人准备作战计划，已有数十年。而在联军方面，尚无大准备，尤以英国为甚。战争之初起，联军大败，幸有英军之援助，比、法二国得免并吞。其在战前，敌探满布比、法全境，若辈均用科学方法，精密组织之。迨至开战后，在战事方面观察，更可显出敌人战前侦探之效力。盖敌方辄利用所探得之密报，以达其军事目标。即如联军之军力，及其军队之移动，彼皆借探密报，知之甚详。且在法、比境内时，每于形迹可疑之家庭中，查见无线电报之仪器，均有极巧妙之方法，隐秘于人所不能窥见之处。闻其密报方法，间有用窗户上之灯光，或开闭窗户，以暗示敌人，可谓精巧严密之至矣。

时队中有在前线作战之军官，每喜以作战法引为谈资。余又因而闻得一二，转述于次：

据云：近世战争，炮兵占最重要部分。在战线上，每次步兵前进，先须用大炮向敌方，铲除敌人之铁丝网及电网，并毁灭四周布列之机关枪及大小炮，庶步兵前进无阻。因此，欲占取敌人之壕沟，备足军火，亦属重要，否则生命之牺牲，不堪胜言。但步兵之前进，每次仅有数百码之遥，如若过远，则被敌方未毁之炮所铲灭。是以在战术上，欲占据敌人防地数英里，非一朝一夕所能得，即非经数旬或数月之战斗不为功。

最大之炮弹，不能穿达数码以下之深土，所以在三四十尺泥土以下，若用木料及三合土建一个堡垒，大炮力量亦即不可及也。是以防守者，虽在敌人炮攻时，竟可安居其中，如饮食，如睡眠，悉如常时。有开留声机，借以娱乐者。

关于敌人具屈强抵抗之决心，有一事足述者。为某日，英国某上校，占居某地高屋一所，约四十分钟后，德人之大炮弹，忽落于屋之四周，密如雨下。某上校不胜骇异，急命部下搜觅室内各地窖，发现一更深者，

顾杏卿：欧战工作回忆录
Reminiscences on My Work during European War by Gu Xingqing

见有德军人三名匿居在内，且有一军官，明知本人生命危险，正用电话指挥炮队如何轰击。彼等瞥见某英军官，料为重要指挥官员，一见我人（英人）入窖时，彼即起立，态度自若，毫无惊惧，静待彼最后命运之来临，其勇敢实可钦佩也。

此外尚有一德军官，匿于礼拜堂中，而该堂内外，遍埋地雷，设一爆裂，全村之半，立即炸成瓦砾之场。幸我人（英人）发见该军官正在暗中摸索，以备发放，遂举枪歼之。

至近代之战争性，如在广大之地面作平面战争，实为不可能。盖生命之牺牲，至为浩大也。故在 Marne 一战将终止时，双方军队，均忙于掘壕作战，以避敌人眼目。当此时也，新式大炮，互相攻击，惟有泥土足以保护若辈之生命耳。自此次一战之后，在法及欧东之一部分，由山至海，所防备者，仅为战壕。双方军队伏于壕内，有如田鼠然，不使敌人窥见，以免危险。某军官所言，盖战争之常识也。

What I Saw and Heard in Battlefields

Poperinghe was an important British base in Belgium, in the rear of the front line, where there were mountains of military supplies, numerous labourers and rapid transportation links. Soldiers went in and out of this place constantly, either on their way to the front lines or coming back from battlefields for a rest. Once in my spare time, I walked aimlessly and ran into a coffee shop that was owned by the Belgians, where I came across an officer who gave me an account of his life in the trenches. He said, "We hide in the trenches day and night and fight against the enemy bravely and determinedly. Under a constant hail of bullets and shells, we fight without any signs of cowardice. What we think of is our responsibility to protect what is right and good and to win glory

华工日记
Chinese Labourer's Diaries

for our country even at the sacrifice of our own lives. So we'vee nothing to be afraid of." Alas! What strong patriotism the Westerners have!

After a while, he continued, "It is true that the life in trenches for a long time is hard for people to endure, we have no opportunity to take a bath to wash away the dirt on our bodies and it is impossible for us to have a good sleep, even if we are exhausted. Living in the mud all the time, we're dirty all over. When it rains heavily, we are living in muddy water up to our waists, the pain is beyond words; however, we'll be soaked in water as deep as our waists and the pain is beyond words. However, we're never frustrated and often joke that 'talking and laughing can increase the fighting spirit of bravery and fortitude, while the fear of death can only reduce the ambition and morale of the soldiers.' Therefore, we've become accustomed to living in the conditions and can remain calm in the trenches regardless of the enemy's shellfire and bullets. Every morning we are inspected by the Captain, which takes about five minutes. So we have to shave our beards, brush our clothes, clean our guns, adjust and polish our buttons, and polish our leather shoes ready for the inspection. The purpose of the inspection is to maintain cleanliness, reduce diseases, and maintain military disciplines. If we can maintain a good military appearance in the danger of life, then we can keep our vitality and courage so as to stimulate a bitter hatred of the enemy and win glory for our country."

In my talk with the Belgians and French in my spare time, I learnt that the Germans had been preparing for this war for decades in advance. But the Entente countries, especially Britain, had hardly any preparation at all. When the European War first broke out, the allied forces of Belgium and France were almost defeated. Thanks to the help of the British army, Belgium and France managed to avoid being annexed. Before the war, German spies were sent throughout Belgium and France and adopted a scientific approach to gathering information, with precisely organised methodology prior to their invasion. The extent of the enemy's pre-war spying became evident at the commencement of the war. The secret reports obtained by the spies were used by the enemy to successfully achieve its military objectives. For example, the enemy knew the exact strength of the allied forces and the movements of their troops. In every house in France and Belgium suspected of being used by the spies, could be found wireless telegraph equipment hidden in very ingenious ways and in places very hard to find. I heard that the spies employed very sophisticated or ingenious means to send their secret messages. For example, they used lights on windows and the opening or closing of windows to send information to the enemy.

At that time, I came across some officers who had fought line and liked to talk about military strategies. The following was what I heard:

It was said that artillery played the most important part in modern wars. In the front line, every time before the infantry advanced, the artillery was used to attack the enemy so as to eliminate their barbed wire entanglements and power grid, and to destroy the machine guns and cannons deployed around them. In this way, the infantry could advance without hindrance. To occupy the enemy's trenches, it was also important to prepare enough arms and ammunition beforehand. Otherwise, numerous lives would be lost. The infantry could only advance a few hundred yards at a time. If they went too far, they would be wiped out by the enemy's undamaged artillery. Tactically, the occupation of the enemy's defences miles away could not be fulfilled overnight, but rather it would take weeks or months of fighting.

The most powerful shells still could not penetrate the deep soil several yards deep under the ground. So, if a fortress was built at the depth of 30 or

华工日记
Chinese Labourer's Diaries

40 feet underground with wood and concrete, it would not be damaged even by the power of the largest cannons. Thus, a defender, even under the attack of the enemy's artillery, could live safely in their fortress, eating and sleeping as usual, or even playing the gramophone for entertainment.

There was one story worth mentioning about the unyielding resistance. One day, a British colonel occupied a large house in a certain village. About 40 minutes later, storms of German artillery shells suddenly fell around the house. The colonel was so astonished that he ordered his men to search for cellars inside the house. At last they found a deeper cellar where three Germans were hiding. Among them was a German officer who was commanding, with a telephone, his artillery to bombard the house, even though he knew that his life was in great danger. When they saw the arrival of a British officer, they knew that he must be an important commanding officer. Seeing the British entering the cellar, they stood up with great calmness and no fear at all, waiting for the coming of their final destiny.

Another German officer was said to have hidden in a chapel, the inside and outside of which were planted with mines. If one of the mines had blown up, half of the village would have been turned to rubble. Fortunately, a British soldier found him. Just as he was fumbling in the dark for the switch to blow the mines, the British soldier raised his gun and shot him dead.

In modern times, wars, such as a plane war, on the vast ground was impossible due to the great number of casualties. Therefore, after the battle at Marne, both sides of the European War were busy digging trenches to avoid being seen by the enemy. With new types of powerful cannons attacking each other, only the earth could protect the men's lives. Therefore, in France and in parts of eastern Europe from the mountains to the sea, the only defence was to dig trenches. To escape dangers, the armies of both sides hid in trenches like field mice in case they were to be seen by each other. What the officer said was the common sense of war.

13. 大战中之民众

一般普通民众，日常战争所抱之态度，以缺乏军事学识，遂无助战之能力。于是袖手旁观者有之，远而避之者有之，徒于战事胜利时喜形于色，挫折时咨嗟兴叹而已。此均不明近代战争性所致，实无可非议也。在大战期间，常有数百万军士，在前线作战，另有数百万民众，在后方从事作战上需要之各项工作。若辈虽不亲临战场，然与身临战地者无异。何也？盖开战后，无论各界，均应间接加入战线，惟不若军人为前方真实之战斗也。如农产物之请求增加，利器之准备完全，一切应用物品之充实，以及文字之宣传，不断之接济，凡此种种，皆为后方之要著。此等工作，与壕沟中继续不断之战斗相较，虽重要性各有不同，但为增进战事上之效力计，则其重要性，无异于直接战争也。试以面包一项而言，每天须烘制数百万枚，又妇女必日夜缝合沙袋，以备战壕随时不测之用。即军鞋一项，亦须无数男若女为之修补及赶制，工作亦甚紧张。是以后方民众，有功于前方战事，诚非浅鲜。余观于欧战一役而益信。

Civilians in the War

The general population often thought that they could do nothing to assist the ordinary war for lack of military knowledge. So they would either stand

华工日记
Chinese Labourer's Diaries

by or just stay away from it, only feeling delighted at the victory of war or getting frustrated by the failure of war. Such an attitude toward war derived from people's ignorance of the nature of modern warfare. However, this should not be criticised. During the wartime, millions of soldiers fought on the front line while millions of the civilian population were engaged in a variety of jobs needed by the war in the rear of battlefields. Even though they had never been to the battlefield, what they did actually had no difference from fighting at the front. Why? Because all walks of life should join in the battlefront against the enemy indirectly after a war broke out. The only difference was that they were not fighting in the same way as the soldiers in the battlefield. For example, to meet the increasing demand for agricultural products, to make full preparations of sharp tools, to provide sufficient supplies for the troops, and to do written propaganda work or relief work were all tasks of great importance for the war effort. Compared with the continuous fighting in trenches, the work in the rear was of a different kind of importance. But considering its function in enhancing the effectiveness of the fighting, it was as important as the direct combat at the front. For example, millions of loaves of bread had to be baked every day and women must sew sandbags day and night for their constant use in the trenches. Also, numerous men and women had to work intensively to manufacture or repair countless pairs of military boots. Thus, it was clear that the civilian population also made an important contribution to the war. This realization was further deepened by my experience in the European War.

14. 军官与华工

　　查我华工队中之官员，考其来历，有在吾国传教之牧师，有在吾国营业之商人，有由军队奉调而来者。至若辈待遇华工，以各员性质之优劣，及资格之不同，自有区别。态度从容，和蔼慈善，而令人悦服者有之；声色俱厉，粗暴成性，而一无官员资格者亦有之。以余队而言，先后官员，共约十余人，内有一名马太斯（Matthews）者，系来自英军队中，曾参战而受伤多次。今英政府特免其前线军役，而命其服务于华工队，以示优异。该军官对待诸工人，毫无骄色，待人浑厚，温言慰勉。如工人无力工作时，准予给假休养，群情爱戴，工人咸称之曰马大人。

　　另有一军官，生长吾国，善操华语，但暴躁性成，动辄詈骂。倘工人表示无力工作，彼毫不怜惜，必报告队长，使其受罚。最可笑者，敌机来时，彼即惶惧，首先逃避，匿于沟渠，跪求上帝，宽恕其罪，以保生命。但至翌日，旧态复萌，咒骂如故，殊堪发噱。此人毫无修养，殆未受高等教育使然欤？余队尚有良善官员二。一名汉莱荪（E.J.Harrison）中尉，彼曾著一书，名《日本之战争精神》，极为外人所赞赏。一名少布莱（C.S.M.Sharpley），彼曾在上海麦伦书院任童子军教练长，其父母死于歇浦，葬于上海。彼在工人前自称华人，温和谦恭，绝无傲气，故工人亦均爱之如同胞。彼爱华人，一若爱其本国之同胞然。人为有感情之动物，信然。

　　至英军官之良善与否，与华工工作成绩之优劣，颇有连带关系。未有队官良善，而工作成绩不佳者；亦未有队官不良，而工作仍佳者。某英教会领袖尝语余云："余时闻人言，成绩不佳之工队，究其原因，由于

华工日记
Chinese Labourer's Diaries

不得适宜之官员所致者多。由于队中募有不良之工友者，实居少数。"然在战事进行中，所有前线作战之军队，均须胜任之军官充当之。至在后方指挥华工队之军官，已非上乘，故不能得适当之处置也。

对于官员之待遇，在老爱儿地方，贴有大字中文之通告。凡工人或工头如受不公正之待遇，必须控诉英官员者，得直接禀告督办，以便处置。督办亦常派善操华语之英参谋，巡察各队，秘密询问工头及工人英军官有无虐待之事情。如确有其事，一经查明属实，即将虐待工人之军官查办，或调往前线作战，作为惩罚。因此队中官员亦有所警惧，乃不敢擅作威福。夫华工在军队生活中，尚受军法之保障，于此而益知法之足以保障人权矣。

Military Officers and Chinese Labourers

The officers in the brigades of Chinese labourers came from either former priests who had done missionary work in our country or former merchants who had done business in our country or former soldiers who had served in the army. They treated Chinese labourers quiet differently depending on their temperaments and qualifications. Some were calm, amiable and quite charitable in manner, while others were strict, rude and unqualified for any officials. Our brigade had a dozen of officers successively, among whom was Matthews, a man from the British army who had participated in the war and had been injured many times. The British government granted him special exemption from serving line and sent him to serve in the Chinese Labour Corp for his excellence. He treated all the workers politely and with no arrogance at all, he was kind, sincere, and ready to help all the time. If a worker was too weak to work, he would give him a leave for rest. As a result, he was respected

顾杏卿：欧战工作回忆录
Reminiscences on My Work during European War by Gu Xingqing

by the Chinese labourers and was nicknamed as "Master Ma".

Another officer in our brigade was one who had grown up in our country and spoke good Chinese, but he was bad-tempered, rough and abusive. If labourers said they were too weak to work, he showed no sympathy for them at all and would report to the Captain to have them punished. What we found amusing about him, though, was that he was extremely frightened when enemy aeroplanes approached. He would run to hide in a ditch and kneel down to pray for God to forgive his sins and protect his life. However, he would become as cruel as before the following day, yelling at and cursing the labourers. How ridiculous he was! Why was he so uncultured? Was it because he had never received any higher education? There were two other good officers in our brigade. One was Lieutenant E. J. Harrison, who had written a highly-acclaimed book entitled *The Fighting Spirit of Japan*. The other was C. S. M. Sharpley, a former boyscout coach at Shanghai Mailun Academy, whose parents died in Xiepu and were buried in Shanghai. Considered himself as a Chinese in front of the Chinese labourers, he was modest and courteous to everyone. As a result, the Chinese labourers loved him as much as they loved their countrymen. Likewise, he loved the Chinese labourers as much as he loved his own countrymen. It was true that human beings had feelings.

There was a close relationship between the quality of British officers and the work achievements of Chinese labourers. Brigades with good officers had good performance in work while brigades with poor leadership had poor performance in work. An English Church leader once said to me, "I often hear people say that most brigades with poor performance have unsuitable officers. After all, only a small number of labourers in a brigade are bad ones." However, all troops fighting in the front should have competent leaders during wartime. The fact was that the officers who commanded the Chinese labourers in the rear were not the best ones. Therefore, it was reasonable that they would not gain the best performances.

As for the treatment of officers, there were notices written in large Chinese characters posted in Noyelles. If a worker or a foreman wanted to complain about unfair treatment by a British officer, he should report directly to the superintendent for disposition. The superintendent would often send English staff officers who were good at speaking Chinese to periodically inspect brigades and ask foremen and labourers about whether they had been maltreated by the British officers. Once they were found to have maltreated the labourers, the officers would be investigated and transferred to fight in the front as punishment. As a result, most officers working with brigades of the Chinese Labour Corps were very careful and did not dare to abuse their powers. From the fact that the lives of Chinese labourers were protected by military law, I became increasingly aware that laws could protected human rights.

15. 舌人情操

吾华工队译员，共约四百余人，如夏奇峰、蔡善身、杨永经、戴步云、吴泽湘、沈向高、余光超、毛华棵、陈俊德、何事耕、魏光征、古伟青、赵卓甫、刘国光、王琢芝、陈安慈、宋文奎、林逸仁、张荣森等，大多为年约二三十岁之青年学生，来自我国各大学校（如约翰、沪江、南洋、金陵、清华、北大等校）。余在法遇有清华学生二名，彼等不愿赴美留学，甘愿冒险来法任华工译员者，实因参加欧战，为难得之机会。

军人服从领袖，日常礼节，异常重视，惟对于译员则不然。因余辈

顾杏卿：欧战工作回忆录
Reminiscences on My Work during European War by Gu Xingqing

既非军人，又非官员，除行晋接普通常礼外，并无军礼之拘束。故余辈之出入，及游行散步，或与英官谈话，一无麻烦，尚觉自由也。

在华工队中任译员甚非易事，因吾国工人来自各省，语言不一。如奉天、热河、河北、河南、安徽等处，山东尤以泰安、青州、济南居多。官员方面，亦来自英之各处，如爱尔兰（Ireland）、苏格兰（Scotland）及伟尔斯（Wales）等地，同属英人，语音亦不一致，尚有含糊而不清晰者。设置译员，原使明瞭双方言语，免致隔膜，但事实亦有困难之处。各队中一无华籍官员，因此译员自居于中国官员之地位，任指导及保护之职，并常为华工辩护。因华工被审时，持有充分理由而苦不能申述，故得有译员在旁，代为据情解释申辩，务使得公正裁判，以免冤屈。侨工受译员之护佑，实非浅鲜。

Sentiment of Interpreters

In the Chinese Labour Corps, there were over 400 interpreters, such as Xia Qifeng, Cai Shanshen, Yang Yongjing, Dai Buyun, Wu Zexiang, Shen Xianggao, Yu Guangchao, Mao Huake, Chen Junde, He Shigeng, Wei Guangzheng, Gu Weiqing, Zhao Zhuofu, Liu Guoguang, Wang Zhuozhi, Chen Anci, Song Wenkui, Lin Yiren, and Zhang Rongsen. Most of them were young students in their 20s or 30s from various universities in China, such as John University, Lujiang University, Nanyang University, Jinling University, Tsinghua University and Peking University. While in France, I encountered two students from Tsinghua University, who gave up the opportunity to study in America and volunteered to be interpreters for Chinese labourers at the risk of their lives because they believed it was a rare opportunity to participate in the European War.

华工日记
Chinese Labourer's Diaries

Soldiers should obey the orders of their officers unconditionally and were required to strictly follow the daily formalities, but interpreters were exceptions because we were neither soldiers nor officers. We were not so strictly bound by military formalities except for some regular etiquette. Therefore, we could enjoy the freedom of leaving and entering the camp, going for a walk, or talking with the British officers.

But it was not an easy thing to serve as an interpreter in the Chinese Labour Corps because our labourers came from many different provinces and had different dialects. For example, most of our labourers came from provinces such as Fengtian, Rehe, Hebei, Henan, and Anhui. Labourers from Shandong Province were mostly from the Taian, Qingzhou and Jinan in particular. The British officers also came from various parts of the United Kingdom, such as Ireland, Scotland and Wales. Although they all spoke English, they spoke with such strong accents and sometimes with vague and unclear pronunciations that it was difficult to understand them. The original purpose of employing interpreters was to make communications between both sides by bridging the gap between their languages, but in reality, there were many difficulties. As there were no Chinese officers in the Chinese Labour Corps, the interpreters took the role of directors and protectors and often defended for Chinese labourers. When Chinese labourers were tried, they could not make clear explanations for their actions even if they had sufficient justifications. So interpreters were needed to stand by and make explanations and defence on behalf of them so as to seek fair judgment and avoid any injustice. It is not unusual for interpreters to represent overseas workers, but it was not always a simple task.

顾杏卿：欧战工作回忆录
Reminiscences on My Work during European War by Gu Xingqing

16. 死里逃生

余队在法工作，约有三载，然并不常驻一地。各地调动，先后约有十余次之多。至迁调之原因，有时因处境危险，工人自动要求迁居他处；有时因敌人猛进，英兵后退，不得不迁往后方，以避危险。每次迁营命令，无不突然而来者。军令一到，立即他迁，且命令之发出，无分昼夜。余忆及一九一八年三月之某晚四句钟，余等正在酣睡时，忽英军工团司令之迁营命令到达，只得立刻起程，列队出发，乘军用小火车，向后方退却。时敌人行将攻入该地，已间不容发矣。然每次离营之前，无论如何紧急，队长必命营中卫生队，将全营场地扫除一周，务使全场清洁，而后列队开拔。英人之重视清洁，与整齐严肃之精神，亦由此可见一斑。

余队虽常在战线后方工作，但距离前线仅有数英里之遥，故敌炮敌机轰炸之危险，随时可以发生。迄今回忆前情，犹觉不寒而栗。

某日，余队驻在比境时，正与同事戴君步云畅谈国事，忽屋顶洞穿，飞下炮弹碎片若干。始知德又用大炮轰击矣，乃皆向邻近比国民家地窖中奔避。时有比国夫妇二人，各抱小儿（一年约四五岁，一年约二三岁），极形恐怖。屋外炮声隆隆，余即语彼夫妇曰："余等为战事工作而来，不得已而留此。但君等何以尚居此险地，不速离耶？"乃夫若妇以法语答曰："囊橐空虚，何以遁为。身无分文，即出亡亦将饿死。"言语凄恻，若不胜其唏嘘也者。

某月，余队所驻地点，距离比国火车站甚近（其时期及地点，曾有记录，因一·二八闸北之战遗失），敌人每逢午夜后，常用大炮轰炸车站，所幸无一击中者。敌机亦时来投弹，故每夜余被惊醒者必数次。日间服务辛苦,夜间又不得安睡,此种困苦生活,实非身居局外者所能想象万一。

某晚二时,一弹正落在余睡幕之后,顿时炸成大洞,面积巨大如桌。余被惊醒,周身如覆重物,盖为实弹炸力,震动泥土塌下所致。所幸余队均睡于地下,当时预将睡处掘土甚深,上面覆以帐幕,以避风雨。因此炮弹炸裂,碎片散布全营,故一无死伤者。队长梅克歪伦(MacFarlane)为一热心天主教徒,据其侍从云,彼闻炮弹炸裂声后,即起身跪地祷告,然后奔至余处慰问。余死里得生,实为万幸。倘该弹正落在余幕中时,余必被炸成齑粉矣。

一九一八年三月间,余队驻在比境之尔能汉斯脱(Reninghelst)时,适为月之十六夜间。余疲极熟睡,好梦正甜,忽被落在营外之炮弹声所惊醒。立即起床出营,继又闻炮弹落地声。亟尽力奔逃,待抵距离数英里之英军青年会时,犹闻炮声不绝,乃复向前奔。其时手中仅携一绒毯,月明如昼,更深夜寒,但闻犬吠之声不绝于耳。此情此景,凄惨欲绝。一路飞奔,仍不稍懈。人虽疲劳,竟忘其苦。后幸觅得空屋一小间,入内安睡,以天气严寒,终不得合眼。乃起身回营,奔至半途,遥见工人络绎于途,时正午夜后二小时也。据同伴云,敌人仍用炮轰营前之木工厂,恐已毁矣。余乃随队而行,寻得草墩一所,疲极而睡。仅数小时,东方已白,再回营中,已八句钟矣。

Narrow Escape

Our brigade had been working in France for about three years, but we were not always encamped in the same place. We had moved from one place to another at least ten times. Sometimes due to the dangerous situation, we moved to another place at the request of the labourers themselves. At other times, we

顾杏卿：欧战工作回忆录
Reminiscences on My Work during European War by Gu Xingqing

were forced to move further to the rear to avoid the dangers due to the enemy's rapid advance and the withdrawal of the British armies. Each time, the order to move came very suddenly. As soon as the military order arrived, we would have to set off immediately, whether it was in the daytime or the middle of the night. One day in March 1918, an order from the commander of the British engineering corps came at four o'clock in the morning when we were still sound asleep. We were ordered to move our camp and start off immediately. We set off in line and then took a military train to the rear. It was urgent because the enemy was about to invade the place we had encamped. However urgent it was, our Captain always asked the sanitation team to clean up the whole camp before we left for a new place every time. From this detail we could see that the British attached great importance to cleanliness and tidiness even in the case of emergency.

Our brigade usually worked in the rear of the frontline, which was only a few miles away. So bombardments and air raids could happen at any time. I could still feel the shudder of horror even today.

One day, when we were stationed in Belgium, I was talking about the affairs of our nation with Mr. Dai Buyun. Suddenly, the roof was pierced through by pieces of flying shrapnel. We realised immediately that we were being bombarded by the German guns again, so we all ran to find shelter in the cellars of a Belgian resident's house in the neighbourhood. Inside the house there were a frightened couple, each holding a child in their arms (one of four or five years old and the other only two or three years old). Outside the house we could hear the rumbling sound of gunfire. I said to the couple, "We have to stay here for the work of the war. But why don't you leave this dangerous place as quickly as possible?" The couple replied in French, "How can we escape with nothing left? With no money at all, we'll starve to death on the way even

华工日记
Chinese Labourer's Diaries

if we leave." Hearing their words, I began to feel more sadness with each breath because of their pitiful situation.

One month, we stayed at a place near a railway station of Belgium (The records of the specific location and period were unfortunately lost during the Zhabei Battle of 28 January). Every day, the enemy bombarded the station with artillery after midnight. Fortunately, no one was injured during the bombardments. The enemy aeroplanes also dropped bombs at times and I was disturbed several times every night. Although we were very tired after a day's hard work, it was impossible for us to have a good night's sleep. Such hardships were really beyond the imagination of an outsider.

One night, a bomb fell just behind the tent I was sleeping in at about two o'clock in the morning. It exploded and caused a hole with the size of a large table. I was awakened with a start and felt as if my whole body was covered with heavy objects, which turned out to be the broken earth caused by the bomb's exploding force. Fortunately, at that time we all slept beneath the level of the ground with tents covering us to shelter from the wind and rain. When the bomb exploded, its small fragments spread throughout the whole camp but did not cause a single casualty. Captain MacFarlane was a zealous Catholic and according to his attendant, he got up from his bed and knelt down to pray immediately after hearing the explosion. Then he rushed to our tent to console us. It was a blessing that I could escape death narrowly. If the bomb had fallen right into my tent, I would have been blown into pieces.

On 16 March 1918, we were stationed in Reninghelst, Belgium. I was very tired and was in a deep sleep when suddenly I was awakened by the sound of shells exploding around our camp. I got up and ran from the camp immediately and then heard the sound of shells falling to the ground again. I did my utmost to flee as quickly as possible. When I arrived at the British

YMCA a few miles away, I could still hear the ceaseless gunfire and so I continued running away. At that time, I only had a blanket with me. The moon was as bright as day, but it was very cold at late night. I could hear the continuous barking of dogs. What a miserable scene it was! I kept running, not daring to stop for quite a while. Tired as I was, I forgot all about the pain and bitterness. Fortunately, I found a small empty house later and slept in it. But it was so cold that I could not fall asleep at all. I got up and headed back to our camp. Halfway back, I met some other labourers on the way in the distance. It was exactly two o'clock after midnight. My companions told me that the enemy were still bombarding the carpentry factory in front of our camp, which must have been completely destroyed. I walked together with them until we found a sheltered grass mound, where I fell asleep because of exhaustion. A few hours later, the sun rose in the east. When we eventually returned to the camp, it was already eight o'clock in the morning.

17. 炮轰机炸

次夜同事戴君，约往巴斯察波（Boeschepe）居住（在比、法二国间之一小镇）。据云，彼有女友（比人）名球孟（Germaine）者（余曾晤及），已由伊波斯城（Etaples）迁往彼地以避危险。现借宿法籍人民家中，该法人仅有一子，以身许国，作战于韦尔顿（Verdun）。沿途步行相谈，不觉已抵该女友家。戴即高声叩门，其时适值深夜，彼女友已早入睡乡，嗣为叩门声所惊醒，乃出外开门。立谈少许，该女友即领导余二人至另一法人家寄宿。余与戴君同睡，甚觉舒适。迄今回思当夜之安睡情况，可

华工日记
Chinese Labourer's Diaries

谓余在法最舒适之一夜。

酣睡至晨，余二人乃相偕回营。时余队仍工作于营前之木工厂中，忽一敌弹飞落厂中，余立时出厂。余即通知营中队长，正在出厂之际，忽又飞来一弹，落在余之近旁，幸未爆炸。迨见队长嘱余镇静毋恐，并谓余曰："避弹之法，最好卧伏壕沟内，或有掩避之处。缘敌弹倘正落在身旁，实无幸免之理。即落在丈余外，或再稍远，则炮弹爆裂后之铁皮及被弹力轰起之石块，亦足以丧生命。"余闻而颔之，行至营外，见各工人正向各处奔逃，秩序大乱，余亦偕同前奔。此时余侪四周，均有炮弹落地，危险万状，然炮弹无情，安可不避。各工人见余，亦均追随余后奔避，至日中已离数英里之遥。时各人饥肠辘辘，余乃为彼等购买咖啡，借以解渴。不料法人竟拒绝出售，余即用法语尽力解释误会，始允出售。除购咖啡外，并购大面包十枚，每枚约计二佛郎，以分飨四十余工胞。又请比国居民，特为彼等煮咖啡茶。工人对余，均甚感激。盖欧战时之比、法二国，食物甚感缺乏。因军民二界，食物均有定额，所谓有钱即可购物之一语，实不适用于此时矣。是晚工人露天席地而睡，余则借宿于比国民家。

余队在法，虽屡受炮轰机炸之虚惊，然始终无一人受伤，实为幸事。但他队则不然。某晚深夜间，有一炮弹正落五十二队之一帐幕中，炸死全幕工人十四名。幕中尚有一人，适往如厕，因免于难。某日午饭后，四十八队正在列队，以备出发工作时，忽一炸弹直落队中，队中工人多名，当即炸毙，译员一人亦受重伤。翌日，余特往该队慰问，见各工人及官员，双眼红肿，均极伤心，余亦为之泪下。又一日，余在爱亚（Aire）之地，会与二十六队译员谈及彼队所遇之危险，据云，彼队在顿克（Dunkirk）工作时，敌人常用飞机掷弹及用水陆大炮轰炸，死伤甚多，惨不忍言。

念吾华人，为求生计而来欧，其不幸者，或死于病，或死于弹，欲求生活而反丧失其生命，夫岂余辈初料所及哉？余等在欧，日夜思虑者，

顾杏卿：欧战工作回忆录
Reminiscences on My Work during European War by Gu Xingqing

除想协助克服强敌者外，即为吾身能否安全回返祖国一问题。自念苟能一旦安抵故里，得再与家人戚友等重行叙晤，余愿亦良足矣。各人身处危险时期之感想，莫不如此，人非木石，谁能无情？万里他乡，不知何日始能重见故国河山也。

华工来欧前，曾与英招工局订有合同，载明在铁路、道路、船坞、矿厂等处工作。今在比、法二国，被派至前线工作，实非诸工胞所料及者。但既已来欧，亦无可奈何。遇危急时，惟有一方设法避免，一方请求工团司令迁居安全地带而已。

然在欧战期间，华工不幸而死于危险者，约计二千余人，受伤及患重病死者，尚不在内。法政府特在老爱儿地方，辟地以葬华工，为留永久之纪念。黄土一抔，魂羁异国，伤哉！

吾华工虽常处于危险境遇中，然遇战事紧急时，仍冒险而勤于工作。虽为联军出力，实亦为祖国争光。华工在欧战中获得劳绩，亦可为我民族吐气矣。

Bombardments and Air raids

The next night, my colleague Mr. Dai asked me to accompany him to stay in Boeschepe, a small town located on the border of Belgium and France. It was said that his girlfriend, Germaine, a Belgian girl whom I had met before, had moved there from Etaples to escape danger and was living at the house of a French couple, whose son had gone to fight in Verdun. We talked as we were walking and soon arrived at the house his girlfriend was living in. Mr. Dai knocked loudly at the door, it was late at night and his girlfriend, who had already gone to bed, was awakened by the knock and opened the door for us. We stood there talking for a few minutes and his girlfriend then took us to the house of another French family where we could stay. That night, Mr. Dai and I slept together comfortably in their house. Looking back on the peaceful sleeping of that night, I believed it to be the most comfortable night I had ever spent in France.

The next morning, after our good night's sleep, Mr. Dai and I went back to our camp. At that time, the labourers of our brigade were working in the carpentry factory in front of the camp when a bomb from the enemy fell into the factory. I ran out of the factory to inform our Captain at the camp. But just as I was leaving the factory, another bomb fell very close to me. Fortunately, it did not blow up. When I saw the Captain, he told me to keep calm and said, "The best way to avoid bullets is to lie in a ditch or a shelter. No one could escape death if an enemy shell fell right beside them. Even if it landed three yards away or even further. The iron sides of the shell and the stones blasted by the bomb's explosive force would still be powerful enough to kill people." I nodded and walked out of the camp. Just then, I noticed all the workers running away in disorder, so I ran away with them too. Bombs and shells were exploding all around us. It was extremely dangerous and there was no place to hide. Other workers saw me and started running in the same direction. By noon, we had run several miles away. All of us were very hungry and thirsty, so I decided to buy coffee for them to quench their thirst. Unexpectedly, the Belgians initially refused to sell coffee to us, but they finally agreed after I had tried my best to explain the misunderstandings in French. Besides coffee, I also bought ten loaves of bread at the price of two francs each. I distributed the bread to over forty workers and asked the Belgians to make coffee for us. The workers were very grateful to me. Food was very scarce in France and Belgium during the wartime. There were specific rations for both soldiers and civilians. Therefore, the saying that money could buy everything was not true at that time. That night the workers slept in the

顾杏卿：欧战工作回忆录
Reminiscences on My Work during European War by Gu Xingqing

open air and I slept in a Belgian house.

Although greatly frightened by the enemy's repeated bombardments, no one in our brigade was injured during the bombardments. We were really extremely fortunate, but other brigades did not have our good fortune. One late night, a shell fell onto one of the tents of Brigade 52 and all of the 14 workers in it were killed. Only one man escaped death because he happened to be in the toilet at that time. On another occasion, the labourers of Brigade 48 were standing in line ready for work after lunch when a bomb fell right into the middle of them. Many of the labourers were killed instantly and one interpreter was seriously injured. The following day, I went there to offer our condolences and saw that the labourers and the officials there were in great grief with red and swollen eyes. I could not help shedding tears myself. One day, when I talked with the interpreter of Brigade 26 in Aire about the dangers they had encountered, he said that his brigade was often attacked by the enemy artillery and aeroplanes and numerous people were killed in the bombardments and air raids.

Most Chinese came to Europe for the sake of livelihood, but unfortunately many died of illness or were killed by bullets. They would not have expected to lose their lives when they decided to leave for Europe to make a living. How could we have expected such an outcome? While in Europe, I would think day and night about how to help defeat such a strong enemy and whether or not I would return to my motherland safe and sound. If I could return home safely and reunite with my family and friends one day, I would feel great satisfaction. Anybody in great danger would surely feel the same as me because we were all human beings rather than emotionless trees and stones. When could our Chinese labourers in Europe see the rivers and mountains of our motherland again?

华工日记
Chinese Labourer's Diaries

Before Chinese labourers came to Europe, they had all signed contracts with the British Recruitment Bureau which stated that they shall work in places such as railways, roads, docks, and mines. But instead they were sent to work line in Belgium and France, which was something they had not expected. Now that they were already in Europe, they could no nothing but settle for it. When dangers or crises arose, the only way to escape from them was to request the commander of the brigade to move us to a safer place.

Even so, more than 2,000 Chinese labourers were killed during the European War and many more suffered injury and serious illness. The French government set aside a piece of land in Noyelles as the burial place for Chinese labourers and as a permanent memorial to their contributions during the European War, but how sad it was for these Chinese labourers who had to remain in a foreign land forever.

Although we were often in dangerous situations, our Chinese labourers still worked hard and risked their own lives when they were needed in the war. Even though they were working for the British and French forces, they were actually doing it for their motherland. The merits and accomplishments achieved by Chinese labourers had won respect and honour for all of the Chinese people.

18. 华工劳绩

一九一八年三月，德军施总攻击时，英、法联军之阵线，非常危险。如白龙、加来各埠及法国北部，皆有朝不保暮之势。幸吾华工在后方，

顾杏卿：欧战工作回忆录
Reminiscences on My Work during European War by Gu Xingqing

日夜挖掘战壕，输运子弹，故联军得以凭借防守。平均每一英兵，每日能掘战壕一百二十尺，而华工则倍之。我工胞以耐劳苦著称，此可谓欧战史上我华工助战之极大成绩也。其余如修理坦克炮车，制造飞机，修缮军用铁道及汽车道路，建筑野战病院，或在船坞上下船货，搬运子弹食物，以供英军之用，无不勤奋异常，为英军官所赞扬。当敌人施总攻击时，前线需用军火及食料，急如星火。于是华工分为日夜二班工作，晚班每于下午六时列队出发，直至次晨五时停工，辛苦万状，故因此患病者甚多。于是总部特许每日百分之十休息在营，并准许在营之四周一英里半内，在下午二时至四时间，由工头率领出外散步，借以运动身体。较之以前一出大门即须受罚，优待多矣。

余队所有工作，与其他各队无甚区别。惟一九一八年春间，大战正殷时，协约联军二方面每日死于大炮、炸弹、地雷等种种之杀人利器者，擢发难数，故余队及邻队之工作，即转而为埋葬战死之军士及官员之工作。吾华工将无数毛毯包裹战士之尸身（不用棺木），一一埋之于地穴。埋葬时仅由天主教神父或耶稣教牧师，行一简单之教会葬仪，费时仅数分钟。葬毕覆以泥土，插一十字形之木架，姓名死期，一一为之载明。此情此景，不禁为之目睹心伤焉。然于吾华工之因伤或病至死者，埋葬时遵照华俗，一律用棺，足见英政府亦重视吾国数千年相传之葬礼也。

Merits and Accomplishments of Chinese Labourers

When the Germans launched a general attack in March 1918, the front line of the allied forces of Britain and France was in great danger. For example, many ports in northern France such as Boulogne and Calais were in a very precarious situation. Thanks to the efforts of our Chinese labourers who dug

华工日记
Chinese Labourer's Diaries

trenches and transported bullets day and night in the rear, the British and French forces were able to defend their fronts. On average a Chinese labourer could dig 120 feet of trench a day, which was twice that of the British soldier. Chinese labourers became famous for their hard work, which might be the greatest achievement for Chinese labourers in the history of European War. Chinese labourers also showed great diligence in other types of work, such as repairing tanks and gun carriers, building aeroplanes, repairing railways and roads, building field hospitals, loading and unloading goods in docks and carrying munitions and food for the use of the British forces. Their excellent performance was highly praised by British officers. When the enemy's general attack was launched, ammunition and supplies were urgently needed at the front. So during that time Chinese labourers worked on a two-shift basis. Every day labourers of the night shift started work at six o'clock in the evening and stopped at six o'clock the next morning. It was a really hard time and many labourers fell ill during that period. Due to the levels of sickness, headquarters authorised 10% of Chinese labourers to rest in the camp each day. They were also allowed to take a walk between two and four o'clock in the afternoon for physical exercise. Supervised by the foremen, Chinese labourers were also allowed to take a walk during two to four o'clock in the afternoon within a mile and a half round their camp for physical exercises. It was a much more preferential treatment for Chinese labourers in comparison with the previous regulation that they should be punished if they took even one step out of the gate!

The work of our brigade was the same as that of other brigades. But in the spring of 1918, as the war became increasingly fierce, people who were killed by shells, bombs, mines and other kinds of weapons in the British and French forces each day became too numerous to count. Our brigade and another neighbouring brigade were ordered to bury the dead bodies of soldiers and officers. Our Chinese labourers wrapped countless soldiers' dead bodies with blankets (without coffins) and then buried them in the ground one by one. Upon burial, only a simple funeral was performed by a Catholic priest or a Jesuit priest, which took only a few minutes. They were then covered with earth and a cross-shaped wooden frame, with the names of the dead and the dates of death, was set upon the ground. Such scenarios made everyone very sad, and some could not help crying. When our Chinese labourers died of injury or illness, they were buried in coffins in accordance with Chinese customs. Therefore, it could be seen that the British government also showed a great respect for the tradition of our Chinese funerals that had been passed down for thousands of years.

19. 战地青年会

战地生活，枯燥异常。耳所闻者，枪炮轰炸声也。目所见者，各种杀人利器也。然欲调节战地生活，则有法、比女子所开设咖啡店于各战地，然亦不足供军人之消遣及娱乐。是以英国救世军队，有见及此，特在战地开辟会所，招待军人。而法政府并专为其军队备有影片、戏剧等等，以供娱乐。法之著名伶人及歌唱大家，均欣然担任服务，甚受彼辈之欢迎。因军人年龄皆在十八左右，均属青年，得此调节自足以增进其兴奋也。回顾我华工，十之八九，既不能阅读书报，又无正当娱乐之可言，且偶或出外散步、游玩，又不准与比、法人所设之咖啡店（英军令二七四五号禁止各有色工人入内），故我华工生活之单调，不堪胜言。

华工日记
Chinese Labourer's Diaries

乃有借赌博,暂为工余唯一之娱乐者,是不可以为训。但至一九一八年,始有华工青年会之设立,干事人员各国皆有,如英、美、法、丹、瑞、华等国人士,均系义务职,然吾国干事居其多数,大半为英、美之留学生,如蒋廷黻、李权时、全绍文、陈湘涛、陈立廷、王正序、程其保、王志仁、梅景周、吴维德、全绍武、傅葆琛、温万庆、郑道儒、邝光林、林凤岐、钟宝璇、舒鸿等是。彼等半途辍学往欧为同胞服务,实行其博爱主义,至足钦佩。该会一切用费,大都捐自英、美两国,计建造六十会所。所中一切布置,共费英金七万磅。会中事业,注重教育、娱乐及宗教。教育方面,设有英法文、算术、历史、地理及国文班,并演讲时事、西方风俗及战时常识。娱乐则有电影、演讲、足球、弈棋、拳术、蓄音机等。此外又由该会编刊《华工周报》,借以互通消息,联络情感。主编者为傅若愚、陆士寅、晏阳初诸干事,并组设小商铺,以便工人之购物。每逢星期,宣讲教道,开设查经班,使得宗教上之认识,心灵上之安慰,并又特编六百汉字,以便工人易于识字实用。余队工人自愿加入研读此六百汉字者,计有一百三十人,读地理、算术者,约六十人。自该会创设后,一班华工在青年会训导之下,非但知识得以增进,且生活亦感兴趣;对于赌博,咸觉无益而乏味,竟收绝对不犯之效果。此亦提倡正当娱乐,有以使然。中国社会上正当娱乐提倡之不可缓也明矣。

Battlefield YMCA

Life in the battlefields was extremely dull and boring. All that people saw and heard were just killing weapons and bombing sound. To enrich the life in battlefields, some French and Belgian women set up coffee shops in various areas. But it was not enough for the recreation of soldiers. In view of this situation, the British Salvation Army established battlefield clubs to entertain soldiers. The French government also prepared films and plays to entertain the troops. Many famous French actors and singers undertook the task of entertaining the army and were greatly welcomed by soldiers. Since most soldiers were youths at the age of 18 or so, they were easily satisfied with these entertainments. However, things were more difficult for Chinese labourers. The majority of Chinese labourers were unable to read and had no proper form of recreations. When they went out for a occasionally, they were forbidden to enter the coffee shops opened by the French and Belgians (Coloured workers were forbidden to enter these places according to the military order of No.2745). Therefore, the boredom and dullness of Chinese labourers' lives were beyond words. As a result, gambling, although it should not be advocated, became popular as the sole form of recreation in their spare time. It was not until 1918 that the YMCA for Chinese labourers was established. The secretaries of the YMCA were volunteers from different countries, such as Britain, America, France, Denmark, Sweden and China, but most were overseas Chinese students living in Britain or America, including Jiang Tingfu, Li Quanshi, Quan Shaowen, Chen Xiangtao, Chen Liting, Wang Zhengxu, Cheng Qibao, Wang Zhiren, Mei Jingzhou, Wu Weide, Quan Shaowu, Fu Baochen, Wen Wanqing, Zheng Daoru, Kuang Guanglin, Lin Fengqi, Zhong Baoxuan, Shu Hong and others. Dropping their studies halfway and coming to Europe to serve their compatriots, these students practiced their philanthropy with their own actions, which really deserved our admiration. Sixty clubs were established by the YMCA, with a total expense of 70,000 pounds, most of which were from donations in Britain and America. The YMCA focused its work on education, entertainment and religion. In education, the YMCA opened classes of English and French, arithmetic, history, geography and Chinese, and organised lectures on current affairs, western customs and wartime knowledge. In entertainment, the YMCA provided theatre, public speeches, football, chess, Chinese boxing, and radios. Besides, a newspaper *Chinese Labour Weekly* edited by Fu Ruoyu, Lu Shiyin and Yan Yangchu was established to exchange information and make friendly contact. YMCA shops were also set up to provide small items of convenience. The YMCA organised preaching of religious teachings every Sunday and set up classes for *Bible* study to improve their religious awareness and to provide additional spiritual comfort for the men. It also compiled a special textbook with 600 Chinese characters for people to read and use to study. As many as 130 labourers in our brigade voluntarily signed up for the study classes of the 600 Chinese characters, and another 60 signed up for the study of geography and arithmetic. Under the guidance of the YMCA, the Chinese labourers not only had their knowledge improved but also had their interest in life stimulated and as a result, many completely abandoned the bad habit of gambling, thinking of it as meaningless and boring. This clearly advocates the proper promotion of entertainment. From it we could also see that it was time for Chinese society to promote proper entertainment.

20. 爱国热忱

华工之在祖国，国人皆以下等阶级视之，欧洲白人亦以苦力呼之。然华工爱国之心，实未尝较受有高等教育者稍逊。余为此言，实非虚语，谨以事实，以证予言之不谬。

某队有一华工，不惜将二年之积蓄，悉数交于王正廷代表（王氏当时

顾杏卿：欧战工作回忆录
Reminiscences on My Work during European War by Gu Xingqing

适为巴黎和会中国代表），请资助最有利于吾国者。其爱国心可见一斑。

欧战停止后，在比国之英军人，某日特开国际大运动会，并请各华工队加入。计吾华工队前往参加者，共有十二队之多，约共六千人。待抵场地，仅见各国国旗飘扬空际，独无吾国国旗。各华工于非常愤怒之下，立即退出会场，各自回营。当时译员夏君奇峰及予之亲戚杨君永经，均在场目睹此爱国举动者也。

当凡尔赛举行和会时，美国大总统威尔逊赴欧出席和会，轮抵法国勒哈佛尔（LeHavre）（系法国西部海港）时，我华工队曾派代表多人，整队至该处欢迎，予威尔逊氏一极良之印象。当和会未开时，日本四处活动，主张中日直接解决山东问题，并迫我代表，承认日本承继战前德国在华一切权利。我华工队闻之大愤，曾派代表致书，并赠一手枪于陆徵祥，书云："苟签字承诺日本之要求，请即以此枪自裁，否则吾辈必置尔于死地……"陆君于是未敢签字承诺。凡此种种亦可见吾华工爱国之热忱矣。

Patriotic Enthusiasm

Although Chinese labourers were seen as a lower class in China and were called coolies by the white people in Europe, they showed no less patriotism than those who were highly-educated. My words were not ungrounded and the following facts are evidence that I was telling the truth.

A Chinese labourer from one of the brigades gave all his savings in the past two years to Wang Zhengting, the Chinese representative at the Paris Peace Conference in 1919 and asked him to give financial support to those who would benefit China the most, which showed his great patriotism.

One day after the end of the European War, the British soldiers in

华工日记
Chinese Labourer's Diaries

Belgium held an international sports meeting and Chinese labourers were also invited to participate in it. A total of about 6000 participants from 12 brigades went to attend the sports meet. When they arrived at the venue, they found national flags of all the countries flying in the air, but there was no national flag of China among them. The Chinese labourers were so infuriated that they immediately left the venue and went back to their camps. At that time, Xia Qifeng, an interpreter, and Yang Yongjing, a relative of mine, witnesses the patriotic act of the Chinese labourers on the spot.

When the peace conference was held at Versailles, President Wilson of the United States went to Europe to attend it. When he arrived in Le Havre, a seaport in western France, many representatives of Chinese Labour Corps were sent to the port to welcome him, which gave Wilson a very good impression. Before the beginning of the peace conference, Japan moved around, advocating that China and Japan should directly solve the issue of Shandong. It forced the Chinese representatives to recognise Japan's inheritance of all the rights Germany had enjoyed in China before the War. On hearing the news, our Chinese brigades became very angry. They immediately asked their representatives to write a petition and sent it to Lu Zhengxiang along with a pistol. The petition said, "If you sign and agree to the Japanese requirements, then kill yourself with this pistol, or we would kill you…" As a result, Mr. Lu did not dare sign and make the promise. From these incidents, it is easy for us to see the patriotism of Chinese labourers.

顾杏卿：欧战工作回忆录
Reminiscences on My Work during European War by Gu Xingqing

21. 可歌可泣

中国之参战，虽未曾直接出兵助战（唯一九一八年九月，曾派兵若干，至海参威协助捷克军而已），然不无有几分实力之赞助者，厥为华工，此人所共知者也。但若辈虽为华工，尚有令人闻之可歌可泣者。此为人所不尽知，然亦为国人所不可不知者也。聊纪一二，以告国人。

新婚遥怨 一九一八年中秋日（在欧每年英政府特准放假三天，即端午、中秋、旧历新年各一天），一百二十队中，有一年约二十岁工人，自经于营舍之厨房内。平时常有人闻其自言自语曰："三年太久，三年太久。"（凡赴法工人签有合同，三年为期）此或为其自杀之原因。按该工人，为一新婚之青年，婚后仅数日，即行离国。待抵法地，始悉英人招工赴法，目的为在欧战服务，非一时所能回国。且为合同所束缚，若欲私自逃归，既不识途径，且囊无川资。佳节已届，遥望家乡，苟得团聚天伦，何等快乐。而今孑然一身，飘流海外，回国之日，杳杳无期。思念至此，惟求一死为快，因此自萌短见，遂牺牲一生幸福矣。

游子思亲 五十八队中有一监工某，当彼在中国启程后，伊妻即吞服吗啡自尽。先是某念国内无法生活，故急思赴法谋生。伊妻百般苦劝，终不置听，气愤之极，即行自杀。迨该工头在法接得此项噩耗，急欲回国，未蒙准许，彼自念既不能归，家中尚有老母，乏人照顾，于是恳切哀求，终不见允。悔恨之余，徒叹不听妻言，致失行动自由，因之神经错乱，致病疯狂，卒被送至老爱儿疯人院拘禁，良可悯矣。

念子殉生 一九一八年七月之某日，余队有一年老之工人，年约五十许，忽被救护车由厂送回营中。待军医到营，开其眼，已不能动，

华工日记
Chinese Labourer's Diaries

抚其身，已失去知觉，二小时即死，其致死原因为中暑病。按该工人是日午饭后，大饮冰水，复仰卧于烈日之下，待醒后即行大吐。顷刻间，人已昏迷，卒致不起。至该工人赴法唯一之目的，在希望寻觅其爱子。一俟寻获后，即同行回国。不料爱子未获，而渠竟先赴黄泉矣。伤哉！

Heroes and Tears

Although China did not directly send troops to assist in the European War (except that in September 1918, the Chinese government sent troops to Vladivostok to help the Czech Army), the Chinese labourers also made a great contribution to the victory of the War, which was well known throughout the world. Although they were just Chinese labourers, among them took place something both heroic and tragic, capable of evoking praises and tears. This was unknown not only to the world but also to the people of China. The following are only some of those tragic and touching stories happened to Chinese labourers.

Distant Resentment of Newlywed: A young man of about twenty years of age from Brigade 120 of the Chinese labourers killed himself in the camp kitchen on the Mid-Autumn Festival Day of 1918. (The British government gave us special permission to have three days off every year on the Dragon Boat Festival, Mid-Autumn Festival and Spring Festival.) Some of his fellow labourers had heard him saying to himself, "Three years is too long! Three years is too long!" (Every Chinese worker had signed a three-year contract before he left for France.) This might be the reason for his suicide. It was said that the young worker was a newly married young man who had left home only a few days after his marriage. Only after arriving in France did he learnt that they were recruited by Britain to serve in the European War and could not return home for a short period of time because they were bound by their contracts. Even if he had tried to escape, he neither knew the way back home, nor had the money for the voyage. With the approach of the Mid-Autumn Festival, gazing into the distance, he became more eager to go back home and enjoy the reunion with his family. But now, he was alone in a foreign country and did not know when he would return to his motherland. Thinking of this, he just wanted to end his life as soon as possible. He thus killed himself, ending his young life and sacrificing his lifelong happiness.

A Traveller Missing His Wife: There was a foreman in Brigade 58 of the Chinese labourers, whose wife killed herself by taking morphine after he had left China. Considering the difficulty of making a living in China, he had decided to go to France to earn some money. His wife did not want him to leave for France and tried to persuade him to give up the idea, but he would not listen to her. She was so angry that she committed suicide. When he received the news in France, the foreman was eager to return home but got no permission. Knowing that if he could not go back, there would be no other person to take care of his old mother, he earnestly begged for permission but failed. He regretted not listening to his wife's advice and finally resulting in his loss of freedom. In great remorse, he became insane and was sent to the lunatic asylum in Noyelles for detention. What a pity it was!

Death in Seeking Son: One day in July 1918, an old worker in his fifties in my brigade was suddenly sent back to the camp by ambulance from the factory. When the military doctor arrived at the camp to see him, he found that his eyes had already been unable to move and his body had become still without any consciousness. Two hours later, the old man was pronounced dead and the reason for his death was heatstroke. It was said that the worker had drunk a lot of ice water after lunch and then laid on his back in the hot sun. When he woke up, he began to vomit violently. Only in an instant, he lost his consciousness and fell down to the ground. The only purpose of the labourer's going to France was to look for his beloved son. Unexpectedly, he died first before he could find his only son. How sad it was!

22. 华工艳事

　　华工在法娶法女事，在英募华工队中，未有所闻。然与法女由认识而交友者，亦间有所闻。惟在法华工队内，华工娶法妇生子女者，不在少数。法募华工，大半系机工，所入多倍于英募之华工，且其日常起居生活，自由较多，又加接近法女工之机会更多，彼等与法女双方因好奇之心，始而生热趣，继而生情感，及情感日深，于是每多由爱情而结婚。但其后因华工之娶法女者日众，因此引起法政府之注意。在一九一九年十一月十日，法国内务总长鲍慕司为华工与法妇联婚事，有黄祸通告，略谓："华工皆多苦力，家境贫寒。饮食起居，不堪言状。吾大法民国之妇女，何不嫁与凯旋之法国兵士，而欲与黄种苦力联婚？殊失吾强国名誉。望法国贵女，速起反对，以免日后黄祸之发生。"但大战时间，法国甚感男子之缺乏。大半壮男，或死于战，或受重伤，亦成废人。女子因不参战，故死伤究属少数，因此全国人口，女多于男。倘法政府坚持每一法女须嫁法人，势所不能。此通告因不顾当时之实况，竟亦无补于事。然法女究非无识者，既见政府之通告，咸有戒心。凡嫁华人，其唯一条件，为不使其离国。而华工因谋生计故，亦愿久留法国，以随法妇人而生活也。可慨！可慨！

顾杏卿：欧战工作回忆录
Reminiscences on My Work during European War by Gu Xingqing

大战期间，所有男子既均赴前方作战，故留于战线后方者，除从事军事工作者外，当然仅有年老之男女、妙龄之女子，与残废及小儿而已。依照战时军人休息定律，兵士作战九个月，可回家休养一星期。然终因前线紧急，军士竟有连战三年，未得请假回里者。其最不幸者战死于前线，或受伤而死于医院，终不得一归家乡。因此战时之法国女子，未嫁者多不得与本国人成为情侣。已嫁者，有送别良人赴战线后，数年间未获一晤，即幸得一晤，其后亦有难以重逢者。彼姝者子，顿感怀春。于是法女因前途暗淡，甚觉独身之无聊，渐致不耐寂寞而恣行浪漫生活。此皆由万恶之战争，有以造成此当然结果也。

英国法官Justice Darling云"战争影响于我国人民之德行，数倍于物质上之损失，而尤以养成妇女浪漫行为尤甚"等语。由是观之，英国虽非直接战地，然尚如此，况在战地之法国人民乎？

Love Affairs of Chinese Labourers

In brigades of Chinese workers recruited by the British government, it was something unheard of for a Chinese worker to marry a French woman in France. However, in brigades of Chinese laborers recruited by the French government, quite a few of them had married French women and had their children. Most of the Chinese labourers recruited by France were mechanics and their income was several times of that of Chinese labourers recruited by Britain. They also had much more freedom in their daily lives and had more chances to approach French women workers. At first, Chinese labourers and French women showed interest in each other mainly out of curiosity, but gradually they began to get to know each other a little better. After spending more time together, they fell in love and eventually, their love was so strong

华工日记
Chinese Labourer's Diaries

that many of them got married. But later, with more and more Chinese labourers got married with French women, the French government became concerned and as a result the Minister of the Department of Internal Affairs in France made an announcement about the "Yellow Peril" on 10 November 1919. It read something like this: "Most Chinese labourers are just coolies from poor families, who had terrible life in China. Why not our French women marry the French soldiers returning triumphantly from the front instead of the yellow coolies? It is really a disgrace for our country. We hope that our French women oppose this immediately so that we can avoid the yellow peril in the future." However, the reality was that there was a great shortage of men in France because of the war. Most of the young men in France were either killed in the battles or seriously injured and disabled. Because women did not participate in the War, only a small portion of them were killed or injured in the War. As a result, among the whole population of the country, the number of women far exceeded the number of men in France. In such a situation, it would be impossible for the French government to insist that every French woman should marry a French man. Thus, for its ignorance of the reality at that time, this announcement did not help much. But the French women did not disregard it completely either and they became more guarded against Chinese labourers after the announcement was made. From then on, the only condition under which Chinese could marry a French woman was that he promised not to leave France. For the Chinese labourer in France, for the sake of making a living, they were also willing to stay in France and live with the French women forever. Alas, what a shame!

During the war, all men went to fight. So all that stayed in the rear of course were only old people, young women, the disabled and children except some men engaged in military work. According to the wartime regulations, a soldier could return home to rest for one week after fighting in the front for nine months. But due to the emergency on the front line, many soldiers did not get the opportunity to return home for three years or more. Most unfortunately, many thousands of soldiers were killed in the front or died in hospitals from serious wounds and never had the chance to return home again. As a result of this, during the wartime, after seeing their beloved to the front, the unmarried French women were unable to find French men to get married to, and the married French women did not get to see their husbands for years or would never meet their husbands again if they were fortunate enough to have seen them once. For those young women, they would begin to think of their loved ones when they saw other men on the streets. However, due to the bleak future, those French women got bored with being single. They found such loneliness unbearable gradually and began to get involved in love affairs. All these affairs were due to the evils of war of course.

Justice Darling, a British judge, said, "The effect of the War on the morals of our people was several times greater than the material losses. The most profound effect was the cultivation of women's tendency toward romantic affairs." From his words, we could see how deeply the war affected the behaviour of women in Britain, even if it was not the direct battlefields. So it is not hard for us to imagine how greatly the women in France, the main battlefield of the European War, were affected by the War.

23. 民间交际

华工在欧，与西人日有接触，每日工作，任管理及指导者，皆彼西人。工厂中同伴工作者，均为比、法两国人。工人出外购物，或游览时，

华工日记
Chinese Labourer's Diaries

相过从者，皆比、法士女也。法之各地及比境佛莱特斯（Flanders）随处见有华工散居其间，比、法人初遇华工时，似觉诧怪。相处日久，遂不为异。华工亦然，日久亦习知西人性情，乐与周旋。加之华工抵法不久，能操英、法语者甚多，所谈虽不足成语，然能使英、法人闻之明瞭，已属不易。华工居法有年，工余之后，常赴比、法人家游玩。余在比、法人家，曾遇华工多次，彼与主人翁闲谈一切，或饮其家之特制啤酒（按法人之饮啤酒，即如吾国人之饮茶，各家全备），情甚亲密。彼主人或男或女，殷勤招待，一无轻视吾苦力之表示。而吾华工举止有礼，毫无粗鲁之态度。华工常取营中所发之香烟，贻赠彼等。盖比、法人甚喜吸烟，然因战时限于法定之数额，往往不能如愿购吸。工作时，华工每喜与和善之欧人谈笑。彼欧人突以为奇，因普通欧人于未见华人前，以为华人乃不知诙谐之民族。今见中国之最低级苦力尚能嬉戏，一如白人，始悉彼理想中无风趣之华人，并非真确。我华工以全体而论，在欧所予白人印象甚佳。彼英、法人常言华工为世界上最快乐之儿童，由此可知彼国人士对华工之心理得美满见解矣。

Social Communication

While in Europe, Chinese labourers had contact with Westerners every day. In their workplaces, the managers and supervisors were all Westerners. Their fellow workers in the factories were all people from Belgium and France. When they went out shopping or sightseeing, the people passing by were all nationals of Belgium or France. In various parts of France and Flanders of Belgium, Chinese labourers could be found working everywhere. When the Belgians and French first encountered Chinese labourers, they felt that Chinese people were very strange. But after getting along with them for a

顾杏卿：欧战工作回忆录
Reminiscences on My Work during European War by Gu Xingqing

long time, the Westerners would find Chinese people were not strange at all. The same was true of the Chinese labourers. After a time, they came to learn of the temperaments of the Westerners and were able to get along with them quite well. In addition, not long after the Chinese labourers arrived in France, many had learnt to speak some English and French. Although their English and French might not always be good enough, it was really not too hard for them to make themselves understood by the British and French. After living in France for some years, the Chinese labourers often went to visit the homes of some French and Belgians. I had met Chinese labourers in homes of the French and Belgians many times. They chatted with the hosts about everything under the sun or drank the special homemade beer (Just as we used tea to entertain our guest, the French people would offer beer as drink). They seemed to be very friendly with each other. The host or hostess warmly entertained our Chinese labourers without any contempt for them being coolies and our Chinese labourers always behaved politely and showed no attitude of rudeness. Chinese labourers often brought with them a gift of the cigarettes distributed to them in the camps. The French and Belgians enjoyed smoking very much but because of the limited quota in wartime, they often could not buy and smoke as much as they wished. While working, Chinese labourers would like to speak with the friendly Europeans. At first, the Europeans were very surprised because they thought that the Chinese had no sense of humour at all before they saw any Chinese. Seeing that even the lowliest of Chinese coolies could behave just as white people did, they came to learn that their notion of the Chinese people as being uninteresting or having no sense of humour was not true at all. The Chinese labourers as a whole left a good impression on the white people in Europe. The British and French often said that Chinese labourers were the happiest children in the world, from which we could see that the Europeans had a positive view on Chinese labourers.

24. 休战日之狂欢

一日，午前十一句钟，余辈正在Rouen油厂工作之时，忽闻教堂钟声、工厂汽笛声以及厂外欢呼声与歌唱声同时并作。余辈惊问何故，始知敌人业已签订休战条约，战事从此可以终止矣。此何日也，即余永久不忘之一九一八年十一月十一日也。是日各地工作，各地战事，自十一点起，一律停止。余返营午膳后，乃即出外，欲一观当日法人庆祝休战之盛况。迨行至街市间，已人山人海，男女老幼，军士人民，各色人种，混在一起，互相携手，时或唱歌，时或欢呼。其尤甚者，不顾一切，彼此狂吻。且有法女纷向男子接吻者，以示喜庆之诚意。其尤可异者，在万人欢呼歌唱之中，竟有哭泣者，此实喜极而涕之表现，亦有念家人之伤亡，由悲痛而号哭者。此情此景，虽觉惊奇，然静心细思，亦无足异。何也？盖彼法人久困于凶暴之战争中，日夜忍受种种精神及肉体上之痛苦，自不待言。今一旦得获解除，其情不自禁之快乐，自非言语所可形容此种种狂欢之状也。

Carnival on Armistice Day

One day, at eleven o'clock, an hour before noon, we were working at the Rouen Oil Factory when we heard the sudden burst of church bells, factory sirens, and cheers and singing outside the factory. We felt greatly surprised and asked each other what had happened. It turned out that the enemy had signed a truce and that the war was over. What day was this? The date was

11 November 1918, a date I would never forget. All work and all fighting in all places stopped from eleven o'clock on that day. After we had lunch in the camp, I went out to see how the French were celebrating the truce. When I walked to the town, I found that the streets were already crowded with large numbers of people. Both men and women, the old and the young, soldiers and civilians, and people of all colours sang and cheered, hand in hand. Some people were even kissing each other desperately. Some French women sent their kisses to men to show their joy and sincerity. Among the cheering and singing crowds, there were also people who burst into tears as a result of extreme joy. There were also people who who cried in grief for the deaths of their family members. Although surprised at the sight of this situation, on reflection I thought that it was normal under the circumstances. After all, the French had been trapped in this violent war for such a long time and endured all kinds of spiritual and physical sufferings day and night. Now realising that it had finally come to an end, they could not help but feel ecstatic. They were so happy that words failed to describe their carnivals for such joy.

25. 德国致败之由

欧战自一九一四年八月初爆发后，直至一九一八年十一月十一日始告休战，计四年零三月之久。在此长久时期中，德国始终未被协约国之一兵一卒侵入寸土，其大屠杀之恐怖战场，终在法、比两国境内。是德国之乞和，实非军事上之失败，乃外交上以及其他方面之种种原因而失败。爰略述其致败之由若干点如下：

华工日记
Chinese Labourer's Diaries

比利时拒绝假道 欧战发生前数年，德国已充分预备。故宣战后，预料在英国未及动员前，德国军队可以假道比国，长驱入法，一月之内即可占领巴黎。则英国必不致加入战团，而德国胜利，唾手可得也。孰知比虽蕞尔小国，不受德国之威胁利诱，对德国之假道，竟坚决拒绝，死力抵抗，实出德国意料之外。德国虽于一星期内完全占领比国全境，然在此短短七日内，畀予英、法两国以动员时机，竭力预备，从容布置。故比国之不辞牺牲，拒绝假道，实为联军胜利之第一功也。

义大利脱盟联协 欧战发生前，义大利本为同盟国之一，经英、法之外交家动之以利，乃脱离同盟，而加入协约，此亦为德国失败之一大原因也。

潜艇政策之失败 一九一七年，德国施行潜艇政策，以极少数人与极多数人相拼，以极小之艇与极大之船只相拼，故其损失小而收效大。以为联军方面之运输船只，感牺牲太大，必不敢再航行于海面，则协约方面之后援绝，而粮草断不能支持，势必降服无疑也。孰知世界第一之英国海军，被击沉之船只虽多，而制造新船之速度，竟超过被击沉之数。牺牲虽大，仍得在洋面上往来运输不绝，初非德国预料所及。吾故曰英国为欧战之中坚，协约国之胜利，英国之功最大也。

德国外交之失败 欧战爆发时，德国以为英国不致加入战团，疏于对英外交。迨至一九一七年实行潜艇政策时，实冒天下之大不韪而为之，于是素以洁身自守之美国，亦起而加入协约方面，此则完全为德国外交上之大失败也。

Reasons for Germany's Defeat

Breaking out in early August 1914 and finally coming to an end on 11 November 1918, the European War lasted four years and three months.

Throughout its whole period, Germany had never been invaded by any troops of the Triple Entente. The brutal massacres mostly took place in the battlefields of France and Belgium. Therefore, the Germany's asking for peace was actually not a military defeat, but rather a defeat caused by diplomatic and other factors. The main reasons for the defeat of Germany are outlined as follows.

Belgium's Refusal to Permit Germany to Invade France via Its Territory: Germany had made full preparations many years before the breakout of the European War. Therefore, when it declared war, it had expected that the German troops could get to France directly by way of Belgium and occupy Paris within a month before Britain had time to mobilise its troops. In that case, Britain would not have joined the fighting corps and Germany could achieve its victory easily. Germany had never anticipated that, small as it was, Belgium would refuse to let the German troops pass through its territory and began to resist courageously despite various threats and temptations of Germany. Such a result was quite out of the expectations of Germany. Although the German troops occupied the entire territory of Belgium within a week, it gave opportunity for Britain and France to mobilise their troops and make necessary preparations for the War. Therefore, Belgium's resolute refusal to let the German troops invade France by way of its territory was indeed the first contribution to the victory of the Triple Entente.

Italy's Withdrawal from the Central Powers and Joining the Triple Entente: Before the European War, Italy was one of the Central Powers. But later with the persuasion of diplomats of Britain and France, it withdrew from the Central Powers and joined the Triple Entente. This was another important reason for the final defeat of Germany.

Failure of the Submarine Policy: In 1917, Germany implemented a submarine policy to fight against a large number of people with a very small number of people and against the huge ships with small submarines so that it could attain great results with only small losses. It had thought that considering the great loss, the transport ships of the Triple Entente forces would not then dare to sail on the sea again. Then with the backing forces being cut off by the Central Powers, the allied forces of Britain and France were bound to surrender once the supply of food and munitions stopped. However, it did not anticipate that although many of the British ships were sunk by the German submarines, the British navy, known as the most powerful navy in the world, could make ships at such a great speed that the newly-made ships soon outnumbered the sunken ships. Therefore, despite the great losses, the British ships still kept transporting supplies on the ocean, which was quite beyond the expectations of Germany. It could be said that Britain, as the backbone of the European War, made the greatest contribution to the victory of the Triple Entente.

Failure of German Diplomacy: When the European War broke out, Germany thought that Britain would not join the fighting corps and neglected its diplomacy with Britain. In 1917, when the submarine policy was introduced, Germany was actually risking the condemnation of the whole world. As a result, the United States, which had kept neutral at first, joined the Triple Entente and plunged into the War. This was a major failure in the diplomacy of Germany.

26. 华工荣誉

常人侈谈战事，往往注重军队及枪炮、飞机等种种利器，以为战场取胜之道，端赖乎是。故非有雄壮之军队，精制之枪炮及最新式之武器，

顾杏卿：欧战工作回忆录
Reminiscences on My Work during European War by Gu Xingqing

从何取胜？此种观念，虽有理由，殊不知后方工作，所关甚大。设对于后方工兵之工作，漠然视之，断不能有利于战事。盖战无工兵，难操必胜之算。所谓工兵乃军中之血脉，诚非过言。故欧战中若无华工自始至终，日夜不间断之工作，力助联军，则联军之胜利与否，尚难断定。前英大元帅，欧战时英远征军总司令海格大将（Sir D. Haig）曾在英之圣安得烈大学（St. Andrew's University），对参战前线工作之华工赞扬云："华工在欧，虽饮食起居，远不如欧人之丰富舒适，然仍能精神奋发，克苦耐劳。其工作效率，余虽不敢断言完全胜过白人，然至少能与工作最优之白人相等。彼中国人大多数皆能如此勤劳，加之地大物博，蕴藏既富，耐劳多力，将来中国，势必有一日与吾白人竞争于世界。"云云。此言确有见地，实非过赞，愿我大中华民族其共勉之。

欧战后，英、法政府念吾华工有功于战事，特给每一华工及译员，参战奖牌一枚，借以感谢。吾华工不远万里而赴欧参加战事工作，虽受尽艰辛困苦，能得此奖励而生回者，亦可以稍自慰安矣。

此次我华工被募而来，乃接替联军壮丁，在后方担任各项工作。若辈壮丁，悉被遣送前方作战。因此联军多募一华工，即可多得一作战之兵士。而我中国人，勤苦素著，故前后共被英、法招募来欧者，计吾国工人及机匠，约十七万五千人，分南北两帮，南帮多浙人，北帮多直、鲁、豫人。附属于驻法、英国远征军者，有十二万五千人；美国远征军者六千人；派往菲洲及米波大米者，计有四千人；而为法政府招雇者，计有四万人，总共计约十七万五千人。此十余万工人耐苦勤劳，始终勿懈，故颇为西人所赞誉。若将此种耐苦精神，发挥而光大之，中国其庶几有豸。

Honour of Chinese Labourers

When talking about war, people tend to focus on the strength of the army, guns, aeroplanes and other weapons, on which they think the victory of battles depend. In their view, it is impossible to win wars without a strong army, refined guns and the newest weapons. This view is justified, but what people do not realise is that the work in the rear of battlefields is also of vital importance. If the work of the engineering brigades in the rear were not taken seriously, it would never be conducive to winning the war. This is because any battle would be difficult to win without the work of engineers in a war. It is never understated to say that military engineers are the lifeblood of the army. Without the continuous work of Chinese labourers' day and night from the beginning to the end to help the allied forces, the victory of the Entente countries in the European War would have been hard to achieve. Sir Douglas Haig, the former Marshall Commander-in-Chief of the British Expeditionary Force during the European War, once spoke highly of the Chinese labourers working line. Giving a speech at St. Andrew's University he said, "Our experience with the Chinese labourers in France has shown us that in all classes of routine work, both skilled and unskilled, Chinamen can labour as efficiently, if not more efficiently, than the best European workmen, and with a persistence without rival. They are content with a far smaller wage, accustomed to less food, and expect fewer comforts. If all Chinese people are as hardworking as the Chinese labourers, then coupled with its vast territory and rich resources, China is bound to become powerful enough to compete with the western people in the world of commerce one day in the future." These visionary words were not over-praise, and I would like to share them with every one of our Chinese nation.

After the European War came to an end, considering the great contributions that Chinese labourers had made during the war, the British and French governments gave every Chinese labourer and interpreter a war medal, as a token of gratitude. This medal was something of a consolation and comfort to those who came back alive, despite the great hardships they had experienced while working for the war effort in Europe.

Chinese labourers were recruited to carry out various kinds of work in the rear, taking over the work of young men of the allied nations, who were all sent to the front to fight. Therefore, one more Chinese labourer recruited meant one more soldier at the front. Because our Chinese had been known to be industrious and hardworking, about 175,000 Chinese labourers and craftsmen were recruited by Britain and France. They were divided into two groups: one in the north and one in the south. Most of the people among the southern group were from Zhejiang Province while most of the northern group were from the provinces of Hebei, Shandong and Henan. Among all the Chinese labourers, 125,000 were affiliated to the French and British Expeditionary Forces; 6,000 were affiliated to the American Expeditionary Forces; and 4,000 were sent to Africa and Mesopotamia. There were also 40,000 that were recruited by the French government. The total number of Chinese labourers was about 175,000. For their persistent hard work, Chinese labourers were highly praised by the Westerners. If this spirit of hard work was maintained by everyone, China might find solutions to its various issues in the future.

27. 军犬寻尸

欧战告终，协联方面既已休战，战事工作当然停止。然战场凌乱不堪，急需整理。英、法政府乃调各华工队，任此清理工作。但战场上未曾

华工日记
Chinese Labourer's Diaries

爆炸之炮弹及炸弹,遍地皆是,稍一不慎,即遭危险。故战后工作之危险,实不亚于战时。例如英所募某队华工,在比地掘洞置锅烹茶时,各工人皆环立四周,待饮甚急,不知地下藏有未经爆发之炸弹,未知详察,忽闻轰然一声,工人多名均被炸成齑粉。血肉横飞,惨烈之状,目不忍睹。

战地清理工作,除收拾炮弹、炸弹及铁丝网等外,尚需发掘英人尸骸,以备英人运回迁葬。然战场广大,寻觅死尸,亦非易事。乃利用红十字犬搜寻,此种犬类嗅觉敏捷,如寻觅有得,则狂吠不止,唤起人之注意,俾人可前往起掘。但因战场广大之故,清理至数月之久,尚未竣事,亦可见工程之浩大。直至一九一九年十月,余队方得回国之命令。至是英募各华工队,乃于清理工作告竣后,完全遣回矣(惟法之技术华工,与法政府订有合同五年。因战后之法国,建筑工程甚属需要,故多被继续雇用,从事建设)。华工乘船回国之集合地,为法之勒哈佛尔(Le Havre)。该城华工云集,盛极一时。至回华途程,则仍由大西洋赴坎拿大,而由坎乘船渡太平洋抵中国。此时渡洋之一切情景,自与战时不同。各人心中既无危险之忧虑,又得安返故里,一种愉快之情状,喜形于色,有非笔墨所能形容者。

Army Dog Searching for Dead Bodies

All fights ceased after the armistice was signed between the Triple Entente and the Central Powers at the end of the European War. However, the battlefields were still in a great mess and required to be cleared away immediately. So the British and French governments dispatched Chinese labourer brigades to do the work of clearing battlefields. Because the battle ground was still littered with numerous shells and bombs that had not exploded, the post-war work was no less dangerous than that of the wartime and any

顾杏卿：欧战工作回忆录
Reminiscences on My Work during European War by Gu Xingqing

carelessness would lead to great disasters. For example, while a brigade of Chinese labourers recruited by the British worked in a Belgian battlefield, they set up the teapot by digging a hole in the ground, unaware that there were unexploded bombs hidden below. The men just stood around waiting for the tea to boil, when suddenly a loud explosion was heard and many of the labourers were blown into pieces. Their flesh and blood were everywhere and the scene was too horrible to look at.

In the battlefields, Chinese workers not only needed to do such work as clearing away shells, bombs and barbed wires, but they also needed to excavate the dead bodies of British soldiers for them to be transported back to Britain for burial. However, it was not an easy job to locate bodies in such large battlefields. For this purpose, sniffer dogs of the Red Cross Society were used to help search for dead bodies. These dogs had an excellent sense of smell and would bark continuously once they had found the dead bodies. Attracted by their barks, labourers would rush to excavate these dead bodies. But the battlefield had so large an area that the clearing work had not been completed after several months, which also reflected the difficulty and hugeness of the project. It was not until October 1919 that our brigade finally received the order to return to China. By that time, all the other brigades of Chinese labourers recruited by the British government had been sent to China after the completion of much of the clearance work in the battlefields. But the skilled Chinese labourers recruited by the French government had to remain in France because they had signed a five-year contract with the French government. Due to the urgent need for construction workers in France after the end of the European War, most of them continued to be employed and engaged in the post-war re-construction of France. Before embarking for China, most Chinese labourers were sent to Le Havre, which became extremely prosperous for a time with so many Chinese labourers gathering there. On our return journey to China, we took the same route as the one for coming to Europe. We first sailed across the Atlantic Ocean to Canada, where we changed our ship and then sailed across the Pacific Ocean to China. However, things seemed quite different from what it was like during the war. With the excitement of a safe return and no worries about dangers, everyone felt very happy and the kind of happiness shown on their faces was beyond description.

28. 归途遭遇

船经坎拿大，大受坎政府不自由之待遇，仍与前赴法经过时无异。当时适有中国政府英顾问福开森（John Ferguson）君，途经坎拿大，目击此状，代鸣不平，即在坎报诘责坎拿大政府。兹将一九一九年十月三十日温哥城之Daily Colonist报所登载者，译述如下：

中国总统政府政治顾问福开森，返华途经此城，见坎拿大待遇华工，深抱不平。据云："余深知中国为世界最大之市场，倘坎拿大有意增进在华之商业，而思参与此中国大市场之利益，彼必能改变其对待华人之方针与态度。此辈华工，现由法返国。在法战地时，曾在战线后方，从事战时重要工作，以便有训练之军士，得免除其劳役，开往前线，为国作战，以增加联军之战斗力。彼等为联军出力，故英、法两国，特许彼等在英、法两国行动自由。然坎政府则不然，竟在海利发克斯（Halifax），先驱逐经过坎国之二十万华工出船，置之于火车，横越坎境，一如铁笼中之野兽。然后再由车中驱出至栅中，而由栅再驱之上船，送之回国，如牛羊

顾杏卿：欧战工作回忆录
Reminiscences on My Work during European War by Gu Xingqing

然。敢问坎拿大希望此辈华工返国后，对坎拿大之制造品或坎拿大之出产品，作何等之宣传？坎国如此待遇华工，岂不知羞辱华工为可耻乎！"

次日温报（Vancouver Sun）更载有坎拿大斯迪华脱（J. W. Stewart）大将，发表之谈话，而深对坎国政府表示不满云："即坎拿大移民律不许华工以自由，然该律未曾禁止坎民，或以香烟，或以糖食，款待此辈有功于欧战者。余之参战中曾有数万华工助我工作，深觉彼等天性温和，冒险从事，毫不推让，甚得联军兵士之友爱，且有多数人竟为联军牺牲其生命者。"云云。可知公道自在人心，又可知受此不平等之遭遇，亦天之所以策励吾人欤？吾同胞其猛省之！

Encounters on the Way Home

When our ship passed through Canada, we received the same unfair treatment from the Canadian government as we did on our way to France. John Ferguson, a British adviser to the Chinese government, happened to pass through Canada at that time. Witnessing the unfair treatment, he denounced the injustice on our behalf by reprimanding the Canadian government in Canadian newspapers. The following was the main idea of what was reported in the newspaper of *Daily Colonist* in Vancouver on 30 October 1919:

John Ferguson, a political adviser to the government of the Republic of China, was outraged by the injustice the Canadian government gave to Chinese labourers when he passed by Vancouver on his way back to China. He said, "I know that China is the largest market in the world. If Canada would like to promote its business in China and share the interests of the Chinese market, it should change its policy of and attitude towards the Chinese. These Chinese labourers are now

华工日记
Chinese Labourer's Diaries

returning to China from France. When they were in France, they undertook important work in the rear of the frontline during the War so that the disciplined soldiers were able to go to the front and fight for their country in order to increase the combat effectiveness of the Entente Countries. Now that they worked and contributed to the Entente Countries during the war, these Chinese labourers were given special permission to move freely by the British and French governments. However, in Halifax, they were unfairly treated by the Canadian government. More than two hundred thousand Chinese labourers were first ordered to get off the ship and then placed onto the train as if they were beasts in cages. Then they were ordered to get out of the train into the fenced compounds, embarking the ship from the fenced areas as if they were cattle and sheep. I would like to ask the Canadian government, how could it expect these Chinese labourers to promote Canadian products? Doesn't the Canadian government know it is shameful to humiliate Chinese labourers with such treatment?"

The Canadian Brig. General J. W. Stewart also expressed his dissatisfaction with the government of Canada in a speech in the next day's *Vancouver Sun*. "Even if the Canadian immigration law does not give freedom to Chinese labourers, it does not forbid ordinary Canadians to entertain those who have made great contributions to the European War with cigarettes or sugar. In the battles I fought, there were tens of thousands of Chinese labourers that helped us in the war. I know that they are gentle in nature and are ready to risk their own lives in the war. They were very friendly to the soldiers of the allied forces and many of them even sacrificed their lives for the allied forces." From these words we could see that justice was in people's hearts. How couldn't we know whether this unfair treatment could also spur our Chinese? Our fellow countrymen should think of it deeply!

顾杏卿：欧战工作回忆录
Reminiscences on My Work during European War by Gu Xingqing

29. 天伦之乐

余辈所乘之船，离坎之温哥华城后，直驶青岛，各人因归家心切，在船竟不觉时间久长。虽渡太平洋时略有风浪，亦不觉其苦。舟抵青岛，余等下船后，有立即乘车返家者，有须转轮回里者。各人一旦重归故土，心中快乐，有非言语所可喻者。余因须换轮，乃宿青岛一宵。翌日，始乘轮返申。待舟抵沪埠，急雇车回家。家人骤见余回，惊喜若狂。余亦见祖父母、父母、叔父母、弟妹等，均安好如故，更使余不胜欣慰。盖当余在欧时，彼此远隔重洋，思念虽殷，难通款曲，更不知何时可赋归欤。盖家人日夜所望者，即为余得早日平安返家。今果如愿以偿，久别重逢，团圆之乐，自非楮墨所能描写者矣。

Happiness of Family Reunion

After leaving Vancouver, Canada, our ship sailed all the way to Qingdao. Everyone was so eager to return home that none of us felt the long time of our voyage and none of us felt the hardships of the rough seas during storms while we were crossing the Pacific Ocean. Soon our ship arrived in Qingdao. Some of us returned home by train immediately after disembarking, while others, including myself, had to transfer to other ships. The happiness one feels on returning to his native land was quite beyond words. I had to transfer to another ship, so I spent a night in Qingdao and took a ship to Shanghai the next day.

华工日记
Chinese Labourer's Diaries

As soon as the ship arrived in the port of Shanghai, I hired a car to get home quickly. Seeing my sudden return, my family became overjoyed with happiness at the surprise. I was also very happy to see that my grandparents, my parents, my uncles and aunts, my siblings and all of my cousins were all healthy and happy. When I was in Europe, we were so far away from each other that it was difficult to express our heartfelt emotions even though we were missing each other so much, let alone when I would be able to return home. All that my family had longed for day and night was that I could return home early and safely. Now what they had longed for eventually came true, the joy of reunion after such a long period of separation was really something beyond words.

30. 欧战杂感

大战损失之巨 此次欧洲大战实为人类空前未有之大惨剧，其损失之巨，实堪惊人。某报曾例以建筑，作财产之计算比较，颇能使人对于欧战之巨大损失，更多认识。兹特抄录于左，以供众览而有所警惕焉。

此次欧战之结果，除兵士死伤三千万，及人民生命之死伤、精神之耗费不计外，仅以财产损失一项而言，已达美金四千万万元之巨。如将此款用之于建筑房屋，以每所占地五英亩，每亩价一百元，房屋建造费二千五百元，家具一千元计，建成后除可容美、坎、奥、英、法、比、德、俄诸国人民居住其中外，尚余可建二万人以上之城市，五百万元之图书馆，及一千万元之大学各一。再集所余之零星杂款，以之存入银行，如以常年五厘计，每年之利息，亦足支付年俸一千元之教员十二万五千人，看护者十二万五千人。

顾杏卿：欧战工作回忆录
Reminiscences on My Work during European War by Gu Xingqing

大战前之准备 一般人民皆视战前之准备，问题简单，以为只须将枪炮飞机等利器备就后即可作战。实不知衣食之供给，交通之布置，战时运输之计划，兵士之训练，原料如煤、铁等物之备足，完成一切在在需要充足周密之设计。如何可称足以应战，乃一绝大问题，非一朝一夕之事。所谓养兵千日，用兵一旦，如欧战前德人之攻法准备，亦无时或息也。

大战之科学化 协联两方，均以科学先进竞称，故利用科学从事战争，理所当然。德飞机之改进，英坦克之发明，无不借科学之发达，开杀人之新路。故毒瓦斯死光等等，练术之士，莫不早夜研究，以期完成残酷之杀戮为宗旨。或云："将来之战争，不复以争地争城为取胜之道，而以歼尽敌人军队，消灭敌国军备，使敌人战斗力完全丧失，为战争主要目的。"实非过言。

大战之全民性 我国人民有以战争为政府之事，与己莫不相干。故远离战地则取旁观态度，祸延眉睫则出于逃避之一法。对于人民与国家间之关系，淡焉置之。实不知人民利害与战争之胜败互相联系，胜则利，败则害，此事所当然者也。故欧战时，彼交战国人民，其先无不热烈赞助政府，予以精神物质之协助。举凡军器之制造，军用品之供给，食用之节省，宣传之普及，在在足以表示彼人民助战之热忱。增加战力，鼓励勇气，实非浅鲜。同盟方面之德国，其所以难于支持而乞和停战者，系因人民对于彼政府不满，与食用之发生恐慌，遂群起革命而反抗之故也。

大战中之女子 大战期间，女子所受之痛苦，实不亚于男子，对从事战争努力，亦不下于作战之男子，实可证明男女平等，权利义务亦相等也。当余在欧战时，感觉最深者，厥为来往客车中所见之妇女幼孩，非领披黑纱，即面露忧色。一望而知其若夫若父，已疆场效命，为国捐躯矣。但同时所见者，即战线后方许多工作，凡战前为男子所担任者，今大战时皆以女子代之。如电车、摩托车之驾驶员，邮局之信差，弹药

华工日记
Chinese Labourer's Diaries

厂之工人，店铺及公司经理等等，无一非女子任之。盖战事发生，向为男子所经营之事业，今已被征而十室九空，不得不由彼女子起而代之。然工作之成绩，亦殊不亚于男子也。

英军营中，时见服军装之少妇，往返不已。若辈即为英政府组织之女子军，借以辅佐英军后方工作，其一种饱满之精神，竟与军人无异也。

大战中之精神 军士在战场中，虽日处于危险万分之境，但日常生活秩序井然，即饮食起居，虽与下等动物无异，其耐劳精神，仍始终不懈。而人民则于恐怖、忧虑、缺乏、不安、家破、人亡之中，亦极力助战，刻苦度日，一无难色，此种精神有足多者。

忍耐 军士人民日处危险，境遇困苦，已如上述。然仍时抱乐观之态度，日常谈笑如故。即大战多日不休，毫无怨色。对于一切痛苦危险，悉持以忍耐之心。

服从 战时军令森严，长官命令，不得违抗批评。盖军令重在绝对服从，故战时之征募新兵命令，人民均无异言，一律加入行伍。如遇人民抗募者，则罚以监禁之罪，但未闻有逃避、冀免军役者。

合作 彼人民之于政府，随时随地，皆合作协助。如政府征发军用品，人民尽量供给之。军粮缺乏，人民自动节省饮食，而补充之。军队之间合作尤甚，盖稍一散漫，即关全军生命。例如当一九一八年三月，英之第五军队阵线，在阿米恒斯（Amiens）突被德军冲击，其危急情状，实有全军覆亡之虞。法之福尔斯（Folles）大将，立即率领法之新军，赶往营救，英军始得脱险。

勇敢 军士人民于大战时，勇敢精神，实足为我人钦仰，尤以凡尔登（Verdun）战役，最为显著。当时德全副精力，皆集于此地而为总攻击，而法亦以全力来相抵御。卒之德军之死伤及被俘者竟达三十万人之多，损失之巨，为开战以来所罕见。法国因困守死地，损失亦属不赀。然双方勇敢之精神，于此可见一斑矣。

亲善 古昔战争，苟掳敌犯，杀戮殆尽，至为残忍。近代战争，较

顾杏卿：欧战工作回忆录
Reminiscences on My Work during European War by Gu Xingqing

为文明，所有俘虏，囚之于营，只使其无自由行动而已。而欧人尚以敌犯所受之待遇，仍不免非常恶劣。然余在大战时所见者，适为相反。余队在一九一九年之九月，曾迁居德犯之英营中，其中洗浴室、盥漱室、厨室、大运动场等种种设备甚为完全。彼敌犯日常生活之舒适，由此可想而知。据云，优待俘虏，自有目的。盖敌犯一经善待，必有报告寄往敌国。敌兵阅后，战场上如遇有确实无法抵抗时，必自愿投降，或竟不战而降，所谓以德服人者此也。

友爱 此次英、法所募之华工，虽不足以代表我国之全体民族，但实足代表中国大多数之人民。盖华工大半均系农人，而农人又占我国人口百分之八十以上。华工之在欧，同胞间患难相共，即对于彼邦人士，如有困难之处，亦莫不尽力救助。兹略引事实一二，以资佐证。

一九一八年三月某日，余目睹英兵五十名左右，精神疲乏，饥饿垂毙，由前线归来，经过余队时，向我营中华工乞食。我华工人虽因当时全法食物缺乏，粮额业已减少，每一面包，十人分食。然华工博爱心重，自愿节食，分赠饥饿之英兵。一九一八年春间，大战正属剧烈，当敌兵大举进攻时，各工程队均已退出险地，但我华工仍有不顾危险，与英兵朝夕相处，助其煮饭等工作。吾华工友爱之精神，于此可见一斑。

大战中所得之教训 一般主张和平主义者，辄以战争为酷残，摧文化，荡民居，故有起而提倡解除或减少世界各国军备，以实行世界和平者。此种论调，似是实非。盖欲维持和平，惟有日常备战，虽我不犯人，但一旦人欲犯我，其将奈何？故余敢言世界一日不灭，战争亦一日不止。美之威尔逊氏，曾倡言以战争停止战争，作为欧战最大之目的。虽不免过于崇拜战神，蔑视和平，但际此世界战云漫涨之时，列强野心日亟之秋，我人为自卫而备战，为御侮而备战，为保存民族而备战，为公理人道而备战，显非不当。盖守土争存，舍死抗敌，为世界和平国际信约而战，谁云不宜。愿我国人，速起图之，其毋忽焉。

华工日记
Chinese Labourer's Diaries

Miscellaneous Thoughts on the European War

Great Loss of the War: As an unprecedented tragedy in human history, the European War brought about a great loss to human beings. A newspaper once reported the cost by calculating the buildings destroyed in the War, which could give people a better understanding of the alarming number of losses. The report was recorded below for the reference and vigilance of the public.

Except for the 30 million casualties of soldiers as well as the countless casualties of civilians and spiritual losses, the cost of the European War is $400 billion only in terms of the property loss. Suppose this amount of money is used to build houses, each of which has an area of five acres. And suppose each acre of land is $100, each house's building expense is $2,500 and the furnishing expense is $1,000. Then, we can build houses which, after completion, will accommodate all the people of America, Canada, Austria, Britain, France, Belgium, Germany and Russia. The remaining money is still enough to build a city with more than 20,000 residents, a library of $5 million, and a university of $10 million. Then if we collect and deposit the rest of the miscellaneous funds into the bank and suppose the annual interest is 5%, the received annual interest every year will cover the payment of 125,000 teachers and 125,000 nurses with an annual salary of $1,000.

Pre-war Preparations: Ordinary people often regard preparations before war as something easy, believing that the war could be fought as long as weapons such as guns, cannons and aeroplanes had been well prepared. They do not realise that sufficient and thorough planning is needed for such things as the supply of food and clothing, the lines of transportation, the planning of wartime mobilisation, the training of soldiers, and the sufficient supplies of raw materials such as coal and iron. The full preparation for a war is a huge task and not something that can be completed overnight. Just as an old saying goes, "An hour use of the army requires a thousand days of training," the Germans' pre-war preparations for the attacks in the European War were not done in one day.

Scientific Weapons of the War: Both the Triple Entente and the Central Powers of the European War were famous for their advanced science in the war. It was natural that both of them took advantage of their advanced science during the war. The improvement of German aircraft and the invention of British tanks are both good examples of employing advances in science to kill people. Other weapons such as poisonous gas and the death ray of laser were all studied by specially-employed scientists day and night in advance so as to achieve their purpose of cruel mass killing. According to some people, "The future wars will no longer depend on the occupation of cities and lands but on the annihilation of the enemy's army and armaments. The primary purpose of war will be to reduce the enemy to complete impotence." Such words are surely no exaggeration.

Nationwide Involvement of the War: Some people in our country will consider the war as the sole business of government and having nothing to do with the common people. So they will stand by when the battlefields are far away from them and will escape when the battlefields are a few steps away from them. They take lightly the relationship between the state and its people. They never realise that the interest of the people is closely related to the result of a war. It is self-evident that the victory of a war will bring benefit to the people of a country, whereas the failure of a war will bring only harm to them. Therefore, during the European War, the people of all the belligerent countries gave their governments utmost support both materially and morally. Their

华工日记
Chinese Labourer's Diaries

enthusiasm in helping their government could be found in the manufacture of arms and ammunition, the provision of military supplies, the production and saving of food, and the spread of propaganda. It was not uncommon to see their people volunteer to serve in the army and boost the morale of the entire nation. However, things were different for Germany, one of the main Central Powers, at the end of the European War. Dissatisfied with their government and panicked by food shortages, the German people started a revolution to revolt against their government, which led to Germany's asking for an armistice eventually.

Women in the War: The suffering of women during the European War was no less than that of men and the contribution women made was no less than that of men, which best illustrated the equality between men and women, in terms of both rights and obligations. When I was in Europe, I was greatly impressed by the women and children wearing either black veils or looks of great sadness on passenger trains. It could be known that they had either lost their husband or their father who had died while fighting for their country. At the same time, I saw many jobs previously undertaken by men in the rear were done by women. For example, women were seen to work in various fields such as motorcycle drivers, messengers for the post office, workers in ammunition factories, and managers of shops and businesses. This was because most men had been recruited into the army after the start of the war and women had to take the place of men to engage in the undertakings that men had done before the war. The work performance of women, as could be clearly seen, was by no means worse than that of men.

Young women in military uniforms could often be seen come and go in British camps. They were the women army personnel organised by the British government who helped the British army and worked in the rear. Their

顾杏卿：欧战工作回忆录
Reminiscences on My Work during European War by Gu Xingqing

energetic spirit was as good as any male soldiers.

Spirit Displayed in the War: Officers and soldiers went about their daily life in an orderly manner despite the great dangers they faced in battlefields. Even though they lived a life without sufficient food and decency just as animals did, they displayed a great endurance for hardship and great perseverance in front of difficulties. The civilians also did what they could to assist in the fight, despite their fear, anxiety, insufficiency, uneasiness and loss of their beloved ones and their homes. They worked hard to overcome all difficulties they encountered, never showing any signs of discouragement. There were many other cases where such spirit was displayed during the war.

Endurance: Just as it was described above, officers, soldiers and civilian population all suffered a great many dangers and hardships every day during the war, but they kept an optimistic attitude all the time and would just talk and laugh as usual. Even when the fight lasted for days, they had no complaints at all. They seemed to be able to endure all of these pains and dangers.

Obedience: Military discipline was extremely strict during the wartime. Once an order was given by the officers, no one would be allowed to disobey or criticise. Perhaps it was due to the total obedience to military orders that people would enlist in the army without any disagreement when their recruitment orders were received. Anyone that resisted recruitments would be punished with imprisonment. Bbut no one was heard to have escaped their military service.

Cooperation: Whenever and wherever possible, the people would cooperate and assist their government. When the government collected military supplies, the people tried their utmost to provide them. When there was a shortage of army provisions, the people saved food voluntarily to supplement them. The cooperation between different armies was even closer because any

华工日记
Chinese Labourer's Diaries

carelessness would have resulted in the destruction of the whole army. For instance, when the British Fifth Army was suddenly attacked by the Germans at Amiens in March 1918, the French New Army, led by General Fayolle, hurried there to the rescue. Thanks to the help of the French army, the British army escaped its fate of total destruction.

Bravery: The bravery of the officers, soldiers and the civilian population during the war, particularly in the Campaign at Verdun, really deserved our admiration. At that time, Germany launched a massive attack by concentrating all its forces around Verdun while France also resisted the attack with all its forces. More than 300,000 German soldiers were killed or captured in the battle and Germany suffered an unprecedentedly huge loss since the beginning of the European War. France also suffered a great loss while desperately defending its land, with over 400,000 casualties. The spirit and bravery of both sides was evident during this war.

Goodwill: In ancient times, all enemy captives of a war were usually killed, which was very brutal. In modern wars, all enemy captives or prisoners of the enemy are imprisoned in camps, which only limited their freedom of movement. It is said that Europeans thought such treatment of enemy prisoners was still cruel, but what I saw during the European War was just the opposite. In September 1919, our brigade was moved into a British camp for German prisoners, where I saw there were complete facilities such as toilets, washrooms, kitchen, and a large sports field. So one can imagine how comfortable the daily life of these German captives was. Of course, there are good reasons for the kind treatment of prisoners. Once the enemy captives are well treated, they might send reports about the fair treatment they receive to their countries, which would be read by other enemy soldiers. So, later in the battlefield when resistance is impossible, the enemy soldiers will be willing to surrender, or they might surrender without any fighting. It might be the so-called winning people with goodwill.

Fraternity: Although the Chinese labourers recruited by Britain and France might not be enough in number to represent the whole Chinese people, they could definitely represent the majority of people in our country because most of them were that accounted for more than 80% of the population of China. They helped each other in trials and tribulations while working in Europe. They had also done their utmost to lend a helping hand to those from other countries when they were in trouble. The following are just a few examples to show the fraternity of the Chinese labourers.

One day, in March 1918, I saw about 50 extremely starved and exhausted British soldiers asking Chinese labourers for food while passing by our brigade on their way back from the front. At that time, the food ration of Chinese labourers had been greatly reduced due to the shortage of food all over France, and each loaf of bread was shared by ten labourers. However, out of fraternity, our fellow Chinese labourers gave the bread they had saved to these starving soldiers. On another occasion, when the enemy launched a large-scale attack in the spring of 1918, most engineering brigades had withdrawn from the dangerous frontline areas, but some of our Chinese labourers did not leave. Regardless of the great dangers, they stayed there together with the British soldiers day and night, doing various jobs such as cooking meals for them. From these examples we can have an insight into the fraternity of Chinese labourers.

Lessons from the European War: People advocating world peace, often argue that countries in the world should be disarmed or reduce their armaments to maintain world peace because war is cruel and will bring about great destructions of cultures as well as people's houses. True as it might seemingly

华工日记
Chinese Labourer's Diaries

be, such an argument of these pacifists is actually wrong. For countries in the world, the only way to maintain world peace is to be well prepared for war in daily life so that they we are able to defeat any enemy that dare to make an aggression. In my view, as long as the world exists, wars will never cease. The American President Wilson once advocated that stopping war by war as the greatest objective of the European War. Of course, such ideas might be taken as a type of war worship and contempt for peace. However, there is nothing wrong for us to get ourselves well prepared for self-defence, for resistance to invasion, and for justice during this world war launched by one of the great powers in Europe. No one will think it inappropriate for us to fight bravely against an enemy for the purpose of defending our own land and for reaching international agreements on world peace. Therefore, it is of my hope that Chinese people could be awakened to this realization and get well prepared for the war.

蒋镜海：旅欧文集（摘要）

Collected Works on Travel to Europe (Abstracts)
by Jiang Jinghai

华工日记
Chinese Labourer's Diaries

蒋镜海(1880—1964),字鉴秋,山东省东营市广饶县李鹊镇沟头村人,自幼聪颖,能干好学。清光绪三十一年(1905年),清朝"废科举,办学堂",蒋镜海考入了乐安官立高等小学堂,学制4年,毕业时成绩名列全校第二,后考入济南单级师范养成总所。

他思想进步,反对帝制,提倡男女平等,反对妇女裹脚和男子留辫子。1912年,与县劝学员长宋文山一起,创办乐安县单级师范养成所,所长宋文山,旋以蒋镜海分任。蒋镜海热心教育,在财力吃紧的情况下仍努力工作,培养人才。

1917年,蒋镜海应募华工,赴法国服役3年多,在华工队89营担任营长。他曾负责起草公文《纪念驻法华工善后实业学校筹办宣言》《祭欧战效力捐躯诸同胞文》等。在法国期间,蒋镜海与他人合力创办旅欧同人会,并执笔"同人会简章",号召会员捐款捐物,以疗贫济国,支持办学,振兴实业,充分展现了其谋求国家富强的爱国热情。

回国后,蒋镜海在家乡创办沟头小学,实行义务教学10余年,为本村培养了大批人才。其中李锡禄、李桂林都是早期的共产党员。1940年,蒋镜海到周村基督教会的培德中学担任语文教员两年,借授课之机宣传爱国思想,教育学生抵制日寇,拒当汉奸,深受学生爱戴。

解放后,他自学中医,热心为群众义务看病,特别是对眼科深有研究,为好多群众医好了眼疾。写有《子书聊解》《学医悟要》《为人修养法》《愚学集》《旅欧文集》等。

Jiang Jinghai (1880-1964), with the literary name of Jianqiu, was born in Goutou Village, Lique Town, Guangrao County, Dongying City, Shandong Province. He was intelligent and studious from childhood. In 1905, the 31st year of the reign of Emperor Guangxu of the Qing Dynasty, when the "Imperial Examinations were abolished and Schools were established", Jiang Jinghai was admitted to Le'an Government Higher School where he studied for four years.

蒋镜海：旅欧文集（摘要）
Collected Works on Travel to Europe (Abstracts) by Jiang Jinghai

After graduating from there as a top student with the second place in academic performance, he was admitted to the Jinan Single-level Teacher Training Institute.

Progressive in thought, he was opposed to monarchy. Calling for equality between men and women, he was opposed to women's foot-binding and men's pigtails. Together with Song Wenshan, chief of Department of Inducement of Le'an County, he founded Le'an Single-level Teacher Training Institute in 1912, with Song Wenshan as the director and himself as the co-director. Keen on education, Jiang Jinghai devoted the rest of his life to the cultivation of talents by working hard even under tight financial budgets.

Jiang Jinghai was recruited as a Chinese labourer in 1917 and was sent to France where he served for more than three years as the leader of Brigade 89 of the Chinese labourers. He once drafted the official documents of "Declaration on Preparations for the Establishment of the Rehabilitation Industrial School in Memory of Chinese Labourers in France" and "Elegiac Address to Chinese Compatriots Who Had Served in European War". During his stay in France, Jiang Jinghai, together with others, co-founded the Tongren Society for Chinese Labourers in Europe and wrote the "General Regulations of Tongren Society", calling for its members to donate money and materials to help the poor and support the country to establish more schools and to revitalise its industry, fully demonstrating his patriotic enthusiasm for increasing the strength and prosperity of our country.

After returning to China, Jiang Jinghai founded Goutou Primary School in his hometown, where he taught for nothing for over ten years and cultivated many talents for his village. Among them, Li Xilu and Li Guilin were the early members of the Communist Party. In 1940, Jinghai was transferred to Peide High School as a Chinese language teacher, where he taught for two years.

华工日记
Chinese Labourer's Diaries

During this period, he took the opportunity of teaching to spread his patriotic ideas on his class and taught his students to resist the Japanese aggressors and to refuse to become traitors. He was deeply loved and respected by his students.

After the liberation of China, he taught himself the traditional Chinese medicine and treat diseases of the masses keenly on a volunteer basis. With good expertise especially in ophthalmology, he cured the eye diseases of many people. He wrote many works in his life, including *Interpretations of Works of Ancient Philosophers*, *Understanding the Essence of Medicine*, *Self-cultivation of Individuals*, *Collections of Superficial Learning*, and *Collected Works on Travels to Europe*.

蒋镜海：旅欧文集（摘要）
Collected Works on Travel to Europe (Abstracts) by Jiang Jinghai

旅欧华工十二月歌

　　正月里梅花开迎接新春，闻听说大英国来招工人。修铁道保马路整理房舍，决不派战斗事扛炮当军。有去的养家费每月十块，路途上不用愁自费分文。四乡里贴报单决不失信，慌了那贪财迷那些穷人。十块洋合京钱廿余吊，我家中有几口能度光阴。

　　二月里菜花开百草青青，招工局补名的人多如蜂。华工册有名的一验就准，无名的烦托人亦不应承。看起来验妥的有福贵子，验不准命该是在家受穷。这一趟怕的是祢衡曹府，众人说学美髯赴宴江东。我不听众兄弟胡言乱语，总不如到外洋也算鲜明。

　　三月里桃花开满园发红，院内的华工人吵闹哄哄。找乡亲访朋友问兄那县，又看见喝酒的结拜弟兄。无智人花银元买拜义子，小儿孩认仁父欲把人坑。众兄弟胡谈论余心焦躁，想起辈古人训记在心中。父母在不远游游必有处，我今日外国去孝心不成。这就是君子穷时运不到，舍祖国走外洋忠也不忠。

　　四月里春风和养蚕又忙，华工人坐轮船到了老洋。水连天天连水心中害怕，身背着救命袋好不悲伤。闻听说德国口甚是难过，众兄弟老和少两泪汪汪。洋鬼子妙计多且莫害怕，十四只海洋舰保护无妨。伍子胥过昭关皋公相助，我好似汉刘备携民渡江。

　　五月里石榴花迎接端阳，下轮船英国人变了心肠。他将俺派在了辎重军队，两阵前掘战壕运动快枪。工程苦甚劳力粮或不到，饿的这华工人眼前发慌。这个说打洋人吃些羊肉，那个说把司令拉到厨房。这个说锅底下烧了队长，那个说把两个熬成菜汤。众工人齐呐喊就要动手，有

华工日记
Chinese Labourer's Diaries

老者他言道此事不祥。听我劝学刘邦荣城忍耐,万不可效霸王自投乌江。

六月里三伏天荷花水浮,华工人在外洋两泪扑簌。想起了中国的甜瓜美酒,兄弟们凉亭上正好歇伏。趁此时调藕丝饮酒乐甚,我今日空守着一把水壶。孔夫子他也曾绝粮七日,子路说君子人亦有穷乎。看起来法国境秦地相似,何人是蔺相如伟大丈夫。

七月里七月七秋风又高,英国军法国兵都打败了。霎时间大炮响惊动天地,洋官长传下令不许走逃。大炮子打坏了帐篷三个,我只得钻地洞去把命逃。老洋熊同翻译亦来逃难,将二人推出外骂声好娇。圣贤书你不读洋话通好,误中原投外洋亦有今朝。只想着来此地身受富贵,哪知道少后成盗马投曹。

八月里中秋节十五月圆,按合同也就该歇工一天。兄弟们聚成堆都把牌看,带道的进房来又把令传。年幼人记号码上街挂号,剩一人在房内安眠清闲。亦有人来面前求写书信,看起来这个人何时得闲。这个去那个来接连不断,忙一天未住手日落西山。忙乱事良心人替俺代办,俺也就放下笔敬他袋烟。都言道先生恩何日得报,冰雪冷不在这一时之寒。洋散真他在旁看着欢喜,华工中许多人诗文成篇。

九月里菊花黄寒风又凉,可叹俺华工人缺少军装。合同上言明是一概都有,为甚么天冷了不换衣裳。也有人披麻袋去上工厂,洋人嫌不给他弄脸增光。记号码罚暂歇工所为何事,早打死这总办理也应当。骂官长不办事要你何用,老天爷知道了你罪难当。为人首得把这公事苦办,光知道吃好的多领佛郎。

十月里北风催天降大雪,闻听说欧战事和了条约。大小船挂胜旗众人皆喜,却不晓华工人几时回国。黑鬼子昨一日对俺言讲,他言道三工牌亦是至多。法国里众百姓庆贺新节,青年会众洋人又把乐作。回营盘兄弟们言论此事,总就是这年前未必说妥。一棚里十五人七言八语,忽然间来队信号码是我。急慌忙拆信封仔细观看,书内云敬启者华工回国。法国钱扣银元两佛郎半,有恩饷六个月一百元多。要紧的诉几句余言不

蒋镜海：旅欧文集（摘要）
Collected Works on Travel to Europe (Abstracts) by Jiang Jinghai

赘，后具名愚世兄顿首拜托。

十一月严冷天流水成冰，写一封安家信寄至家中。问父母身康健合家安好，嘱荆室在高堂仍把孝行。见此信汝莫要朝思暮盼，团圆期等来春花红草青。罗氏女盼秋胡桑园相会，王宝钏守寒节得了正宫。虽然是穷工人不敢高比，薛平贵起初时也是当兵。心怀志在外国不敢出口，回中国练人马招聚英雄。欲治外先治内古人明训，制飞艇造炸弹抖抖威风。

十二月腊梅开又是一年，华工人思家乡双泪不干。中国里老和幼团圆之日，我今时一个人外国过年。烦先生问官长此事怎办，青骆子哈夫社他便开言。磕捕听不在队我是代理，窃皮带真无有一个铜元。众工人闻此言俱都不悦，看亭内康先生他把话言。众弟兄你莫要伤心愁叹，青年会我今年大发财源。营门口五色旗我去制办，捎来的戏盒子宫调俱全。大家伙在一块庆贺新节，免去了思家意愁闷赌钱。我不贪众弟兄佛郎分半，只望着善人牌把我名添。

Songs of Twelve Months for Chinese Labourers in Europe

In the first month of the lunar year, while the plum blossom opened to greet the approach of the Spring Festival, Great Britain came to recruit labourers, who would be sent to build railways, maintain roads and rebuild houses but never to be sent to carry weapons or fight in battles. Ten yuan every month would be given to the family of those who agreed to go, and they need not worry about any money along the way. Posters were put up everywhere in the neighbourhood to show their sincerity, which greatly shocked the money-mad men in poverty. Ten yuan was a large sum of money, which was enough to support the life of my family.

华工日记
Chinese Labourer's Diaries

In the second month of the lunar year, while rape flowers blossomed and grass grew, numerous people swarmed to the Recruitment Bureau to place their names. All those with names on the Chinese labourers list were accepted while any person whose name was not on the list shall never be accepted. Those accepted seemed to be lucky dogs whereas those rejected seemed destined to be poor at home. Some said the trip forebode disasters rather than blessings, like Mi Heng in the mansion of Cao Cao while others said I should learn from Guan Yu who went alone to the banquet held by Lu Su. Despite advice of various types from my friends, I decided to go abroad to find out for myself.

In the third month of the lunar year, while peach blossoms bloomed all over the garden, the Chinese labourers in the yard were boisterously gathered. Busy with going to different places to visit relatives and friends, I saw people who were drinking together become sworn brothers. A silly man spent money to buy a foster son whereas the child recognised him as a benevolent father with the intention to entrap him. Hearing the words of my friends, I became restless and anxious and recalled the precepts of the earlier generations. Those whose parents were still alive should not travel to far-off places and if they had to, then they should have a certain destination. Now that I am leaving for foreign countries, it was impossible for me to be filial to my parents. This illustrated the fact that a man of noble character could not be a lucky one while he was in poverty and I wondered whether it was being faithful or not for me to leave our motherland for foreign countries.

In the fourth month of the lunar year, while spring breeze blew and people were busy with raising silkworms, Chinese labourers boarded a ship onto the ocean. Seeing the sky and waters meet on the horizon, I could not help feeling scared in heart. With a life-saving bag on my back every day, feelings of sadness came over me. Hearing we were crossing a German port, I felt very

蒋镜海：旅欧文集（摘要）
Collected Works on Travel to Europe (Abstracts) by Jiang Jinghai

sad, and all my brothers were in tears. Foreign people were full of cunning tricks, but there was nothing to be afraid of because we were protected by fourteen naval vessels. Just as Wu Zixu went through Zhaoguan pass with the help of Donggaogong, I was just like Liu Bei of Han Dynasty who crossed the Hanjiang River together with his people.

In the fifth month of the lunar year, while the pomegranate flowers greeted Duanyang Festival, the Englishmen changed their mind as soon as we disembarked from the ship. I was sent to the army services corps and geared up to dig trenches at the front. The work was hard but not enough food was given and some Chinese labourers fainted from their hunger. Some said we should kill foreigners and eat their meat, and others said we should bring the commanding officers to the kitchen to have them cooked. Some said we should burn the Captain in the fire under the pot, and others said we could boil the two into vegetable soup. Many labourers yelled aloud to take actions when an old man wisely said that such a matter would be ominous. He advised us to learn from Liu Bang who endured hardships in Pengcheng and never to imitate Xiang Yu who killed himself in the river of Wujing.

In the sixth month of the lunar year, while the lotus blossoms floated on dog days, Chinese labourers in foreign countries were in tears. Thinking of sweet Chinese melon and tasty wine, my fellow labourers were taking a rest in the pavilions. While I should have been preparing lotus root fibres and happily drinking wines at home, I was now holding an empty kettle in my hand. Confucius also once did not eat anything for seven days, and Zilu asked whether even noble persons also had times of such plight. It seemed that France had a similar situation to that in the Qin Dynasty, but who was Lin Xiangru, the great man of the time.

In the seventh month of the lunar year, while the autumn wind began to

华工日记
Chinese Labourer's Diaries

blow violently, both the British and French troops were defeated. Suddenly, the sound of artillery shocked the heaven and earth, and the foreign officers ordered us not to flee. The cannons destroyed three tents of us, and I had to escape into the tunnels. A foreigner and the interpreter also came in to seek refuge, but they were pushed out and scolded by us severely. It served you all right, who had betrayed our motherland and came to work for foreigners by learning foreign languages rather than reading the books of sages. You had intended to become rich by serving foreigners here, how come you knew you would turn away from your nature and become guys as bad as a thief.

In the eighth month of the lunar year, we had a day off according to the contract for the day of the Mid-Autumn Festival. While our labourers were playing cards together, someone came in to deliver orders. Young people went out to register their numbers in the street and I was left alone in the room. Sometimes people would come, asking me to write letters for them, and it seemed impossible for me to spare time for rest. People came and went one after another, while I kept writing all day until the night. For those people with conscience who helped to do my other work, I also paid my respect for him by putting down my pen and giving him a pack of cigarettes. All said they would pay me the debt of gratitude one day but as the coldness of ice and snow came not only from the cold of a single day. It delighted the foreign sergeant who watched them all the time that many of the Chinese labourers could create poems impromptu.

In the ninth month of the lunar year, chrysanthemums blossomed, and a cold wind blew, but we Chinese labourers had no uniforms to wear. It was clearly stated in the contract that clothes of all types would be provided, but why not change our clothes since it became so cold? Some wore sacks when going to factories to work, while foreigners resented us, considering it as a

蒋镜海：旅欧文集（摘要）
Collected Works on Travel to Europe (Abstracts) by Jiang Jinghai

shame to lurk. For what should they put down their numbers and stopped their pay as punishment? The chief official deserved to be killed as soon as possible. We could not help but to curse, since you did not do things for us, what was the use of having these officials? Even God would consider you as guilty if HE knew. As leaders you should be thoughtful towards us and tried hard to do things for us, but you only knew to eat well and get more francs.

In the tenth month of the lunar year, with the northern wind came heavy snow and news that the European War had ended, and a treaty had been signed. All were delighted to see victory flags flying over ships large or small, but we didn't know when Chinese labourers could return home. A black told me yesterday that we could return home within three days at most. The French people celebrated it as a new festival, and foreigners in the YMCA also made merry all day long. My fellow labourers talked about it in the camp, saying that we would possibly return before the New Year. While the fifteen people in our tent were heatedly talking about it, a sudden message came that there was a letter addressed to me. In a hurry, I opened the envelope and read it carefully, saying that the revered Chinese labourers would soon return to China. Two and a half francs were deducted and the wages for the six months were over one hundred yuan. No further words of unimportance need be stated here, at the end of the letter was the signature of my elder brother.

In the eleventh month of the lunar year, it was so cold that ice would come from flowing water and to home I wrote a peace letter. There was no need to miss me day and night since we would get a reunion in the spring. Looking forward to reuniting with husband, Luo Fu and Qiu Hu met each other in the mulberry field. Living alone in a cave for many years, Wang Baochuan finally united with her husband and became a lady. Although as poor labourers we dare not compare ourselves to those in high status, Xue Pinggui was a soldier at first like us. Great ambitions we also had, but we dare not speak them out to others. After returning to China, we would gather heroes by recruiting followers. Our ancestors told us that to resist foreign aggressions required a good governance of the state first, so we would make airships as well as bombs to make our country powerful.

In the twelfth month of the lunar year, with the blossom of wintersweet came another year, but with homesickness all Chinese labourers became depressed. On the day of family reunion of old and young in China, we now spend it alone, and our Spring Festival is in the country of France. As the representative, I asked officers about the celebration of the Spring Festival, and a low-rank officer began to say in response, I am the deputy since the Captain is away, but not a single copper coin do I have in my pocket. Hearing his words, more disappointed became our workers, when Mr. Kang rose to his feet and began to speak. "Please don't be sad, my dear brothers. I've earned money in great amounts in the YMCA this year. I will buy five-coloured flags to hang at the entrance, and you can all enjoy yourselves with many operas. Together we shall celebrate the Festival, and no one will be homesick or gamble because of loneliness. I would not like you to share the expenses, but only to add my name to the list of charitable persons."

记事

一、旅欧经过之地点和时间

民国六年十月廿二日，由青岛上船（三天）至日本之长崎，（十二

蒋镜海：旅欧文集（摘要）
Collected Works on Travel to Europe (Abstracts) by Jiang Jinghai

天）过太平洋至英属之坎拿大之维多利亚岛，（又四点）至验合同处。由湾扣而上火车，（十一天）至哈拉肥斯，下车登船，十一天过大西洋。至英国之大海口利物浦（英格兰地），上火车，约六点钟夜行至佛哥思屯，又上船，两点钟至法岸之白浪。又十点上火车至挪叶（民国六年十二月十八日晚），即华工总分发处，亦名大院。驻三天，至利哈夫。

至民国八年三月廿八日（即阳历四月一号），又移至扒得克勒道之哈勒破他府之扒格炮木之西，拉撒而，月余又移至炮木之东波泥。

二、英人之不知耻也

民国八年七月十九号，法人菜园葱、蒜、芸豆等被人偷窃甚多，园主告之法国巡捕。巡捕领园主先至136队各工人寝室，搜寻一遍而一芥无有。寻至英人寝处则葱、蒜等等连叶带蔓而翻出十三袋之多。甚矣，英人之不知耻也！

三、聚会之抒情

近三年，劳劳碌碌，公务之余，即与欧美诸学士不时叙谈，研究诗书、道德。异乡寂寞之苦，借资消减。今公毕回国，仓忙已甚，聊赋俚语，略表离悃。无意无词，音韵颠倒，尚希原谅为幸。诸同乡、同志均此一笑。即请，道安并贺众位年祺：

光瞻道德神州耀，远望岳华祖国山。
孟子书中言利国，桥翁圯上教为梁。

四、关于大战中比国受辱之实事

比利时至小之国也，其面积一万一千四百英方里，其人口不过七百五十万。德意志至大之国也，其面积有二十万八千七百八十英方里，其人民不下六千五百万。比国处于德、法之间，德、法既宣战，德人即欲长驱其军，过比境以攻法。比国中立之邦也，不肯假道于德，以得罪于友邦，德军竟侵入比境。比人拒之甚力，然力弱人寡，至其结果，比国全境为墟。无辜之庶民，受杀戮及惨酷之待遇。德军焚烧其家室，污辱其妇女，屠宰其童稚。其幸而得免者，被执为俘虏，运之于装送牛马之车中以入德，饥不能得食，渴不能得饮。德人众庶且团聚各车站候车，而讪笑之，凌辱之。及至德，分发于田间、矿中，使劳力如奴隶，稍有违意，鞭笞随之。嗟夫！此无辜之众，固非甲胄之士也，未尝有害于德也，而犹如此。德人加于比人之痛苦，宜百世仍铭于心矣。后如有为德人说项者，吾人当答曰："唯唯，然比利时不可忘也！"

五、恭颂华工队四道队长吴屯田先生德行

先生中华之能干人也，世居山东寿光县，历代书香，累世簪缨，为一邑望族。先生在华，经营商业，富有阅历，素有游历世界之大志。遂于民国六年冬，率领华工，效力欧战，枪林弹雨之中，军需无缺；飞艇雷火之外，军规惟公。欧战告终，世界文明，华工之力居多。今公毕回国，照料我辈，安抵中原，先生之德我多多矣。爰为之歌曰：

北斗高高兮，仰我福星；大洋滔滔兮，御浪乘风。携众以渡，安抵华中。山水远近以无忧，温饱中外而不穷。同气同声，相求相应。共患共难，如弟如兄。呜呼美哉兮，先生之德，海阔天空。

六、恭颂旅欧华侨诸同胞功德

欧洲战争，为有世以来最大之一战局也。彼德人思执牛耳于天下，逞其野心，蚕食列邦。我国加入战团，以固国本。我辈效力欧战，为国增光。不避枪林弹雨，何畏电火飞艇。直接助战，宿露卧风。卒致欧战告终，还我文明。联邦各国，中原策工。伊谁之力，吾数十万华工其承承，呜呼美哉，诚无愧为世界一功！

蒋镜海：旅欧文集（摘要）
Collected Works on Travel to Europe (Abstracts) by Jiang Jinghai

Record of Events

1. Places and Time of Our Travel to Europe

On 22 October 1917, we boarded a ship in Qingdao and three days later we arrived in Nagasaki, Japan. We sailed across the Pacific Ocean and arrived at the British Victoria Island in Canada and four hours later we arrived at the Contract Inspection Office. We then took the train from Vancouver and arrived at Halifax on 28 November where we got off the train and embarked again to cross the Atlantic Ocean. On 7 December we arrived at the seaport of Liverpool, England, where we took the night train and arrived at Folkestone at 6'oclock in the morning. At two o'clock, we boarded another ship and arrived at Boulogne-sur-Mer on the French coast. At 10 o'clock, we took the train and arrived at Noyelles on the evening of 18 December 1917. Noyelles, also known as the Compound, was where the General Distribution Office of Chinese Labourers was located. We stayed there for three days and then moved to Le Havre. Till then, 58 days had passed since we left China.

On 1 April 1918, we moved to Lazare, the west of the Bagepangmu in Halepaotafu, and a month later we moved again to Boni, the east of the paomu.

2. Shame of the British

On 19 July 1918, many vegetables such as onions, garlic and kidney beans were stolen from a vegetable garden of a Frenchman and its owners reported it to the French police. Together with the owner, the policemen searched the brigades of Chinese labourers first, but they found nothing. Then they went to the British tents and found as many as thirteen bags of onions and garlic together with vines and leaves. What a shame it was for the British!

华工日记

Chinese Labourer's Diaries

3. Poem for a Gathering

In the past three years, I had often alleviated my loneliness of staying in foreign countries by talking with European and American scholars about poetry and morality after I completed my work and official duties. I became even more engaged in routines after I had returned to China. To express my sincere feelings of departure, I wrote a poem in my spare time which has no novel diction and regular rhyme. I hope my countrymen could enjoy it irrespective of its imperfections. Here is the poem with my sincerest wishes:

> Looking at the divine state of morality with great reverence,
> We seemed to see Mount Hua of our motherland in the distance.
> Just as Mencius instructed to do things beneficial to our country,
> Our labourers constructed solid bridges over the destroyed ones.

4. Humiliation of Belgium in European War

Belgium was a very small country with an area of 11400 square miles and a population of only 7.5 million, whereas Germany was a very large country with an area of 208780 square miles and a population of no less than 65 million. Located between Germany and France, Belgium was the only way that German troops had to cross to attack France after they had declared war. As a neutral country, Belgium refused to let the German troops cross its territory and offend its friendly neighbour of France. So the German troops invaded Belgium unexpectedly. Although the Belgians fought back courageously, the whole Belgium was reduced to ruins for its weak military forces. Innocent civilians were slaughtered or subjected to cruel treatment. The Germans set fire to their homes, raped their women and slaughtered their children. For those who were fortunate to survive, the Germans transported them as prisoners

蒋镜海：旅欧文集（摘要）
Collected Works on Travel to Europe (Abstracts) by Jiang Jinghai

in trucks normally used for the transportation of cattle and horses over to Germany. They would not be given any food or water during the whole journey and were made fun of or humiliated by Germans that gathered at the railway station waiting for trains. When they arrived in Germany, they were distributed to work in fields and mines as slaves. If they showed any signs of disobedience to the Germans, they would be severely flogged or whipped severely. Alas! The Germans were so cruel to the innocent civilians who were not soldiers and were harmless to Germany. The sufferings and humiliations Germany had imposed on the Belgian people should be remembered forever. Later, if some people should speak up for the Germans, we should reply, "Oh, but never forget what they did to Belgians!"

5. Virtues of Wu Tuntian, Leader of the Brigade of Chinese Labourers

Mr. Wu was a capable Chinese man who came from a prominent family in Shouguang County, Shandong Province. For generations, their family had been scholars and officials. While in China, Mr. Wu was a businessman with rich experience and great ambitions of travelling around the world. So in the winter of 1917, the sixth year of the Republic of China, he led the Chinese labourers and served in the European War. Under his leadership, there was no shortage of military supplies and all were fairly treated according to regulations during the war. Chinese labourers made great contributions to the end of the European War and the preservation of world civilisations. On our way back home after the War, Mr. Wu took care of us and guaranteed our safe arrival in China. For his great virtues, I composed a song for him:

Like the Big Dipper high in the sky, I looked up to my lucky star. In vast oceans violently surging, together we sailed through waves and wind. Under the leadership of you, we arrived back in China without any woe. It is because of the company of you, that we never felt distant and poor. In the same breath and voice, you took good care of us. Going through sufferings and hardships, we stay together like brothers. Alas! Your virtues were as vast sea and high skies.

6. Merits of Chinese Labourers in Europe

The European War was one of the biggest wars in the world's history. Germany began to encroach on other countries to fulfil its ambitions to be the leader of the world. For this reason, our country also joined the War to defend and consolidate itself. Our Chinese labourers served in the European War and won glory for our country. Working under the rain of bullets as well as the attacks of aircraft, they assisted directly in battles while often sleeping in the open air during the War. They worked hard until the end of the European War and restored ancient civilisations. Among the Entente countries, China sent over one hundred thousand labourers, who made a great contribution to the end of the European War. Alas, their hard work in the war made real contributions to the world's peace.

旅欧同人会简章

序言

语云："独立难支，众擎易举。"自古富国强兵者，未有不合群力群策而能成其大功也。况兹战局初和，百废待举，而今后人种无形战争之激烈当千百倍于有形，则合群力群策之社会更不可少也。我中国人心不

蒋镜海：旅欧文集（摘要）
Collected Works on Travel to Europe (Abstracts) by Jiang Jinghai

固，团体如沙，贫者不安其贫，而甘心斯滥；富者自恃其富，乃纵意乎奢。维时不无社会发生，然多循华，或为会魁，利用窃攘私名，致使列国凯觑，欧风逼我，列强挟利，美雨侵人，几乎酿成剖豆瓜分之势，可胜言哉！同仁等因事赴欧，目击列国诸社会所主办公布诚，平时则教民守业，各安其生，而不预闻国事，战时则全体奋力报效不顾其身。于是乎，知列国之强，强在社会也。回首宗邦，犹自凶凶扰扰，民不聊生，其故为何？无合群力群策之良社会耳。因思国之存亡，匹夫有责，乃不自揣浅陋于客中，发起斯会，命曰"同人"，取其人同之义也。会中骨髓为疗贫济国一捐。本会同人平时月出微资，以资储蓄，积滴为海，集腋成裘。日后会友苟遭经济困难，本会通其缓急；家贫身故，本会抚其妻孥。培养英才则兴学校，提倡实业则立工程，经商富国，筑路便民。俾母子之相生循环不已，希人材之迭出发达无穷。至于国家有事他邦，则共出斯捐助其屯甲。而本会同人，亦许从戎报效，决死疆场。故此种之捐，小用则疗贫，大用则济国。可以修身齐家，可以治国平天下。然则何为其然也？曰无他，合群力群策而致耳。

一、宗旨：疗贫济国，遵从政府。

二、命名：在欧时暂为"旅欧同人会"，返国后删去"旅欧"二字，曰"同人会"。

三、目的：期在中国各府州的外蕃行省所有同人会。

四、会友：凡中华民国之民而愿守本会章程，经本会友介绍者，皆可以为本会会友。

五、资格：会友以有专门职业者为合格。

六、宗教：本会不限宗教。

七、利权：本会会友皆可享受本会所有之利权。

八、证书：本会会友皆执有本会所发给之证书。

九、违例：凡不守本会章程之会友，本会有开除之权。在欧时不按该合同殷勤作工者，本会亦不认为会友。

十、捐款：见疗贫济国捐简章。

疗贫济国捐简章

一、捐款：在欧时每名会友按月捐三佛郎，返国后按月捐大洋三角，其款直接交本会主事，或交与各属介绍人，由介绍人转交主事均可。然交款后有本会主事亲笔收条，分给各捐款人以为凭证。

二、储蓄：主事收得之款，随时亲交司库，由司库将该款存入银行，非因公众公议其款，不得擅动分文。

三、用途：分甲乙丙丁四种。

甲：接济会友。本会会友若遭艰难大故，一时经济周转不灵，可向会中支借，言明偿还确期，不取利息。会友家贫身故，本会有抚恤其妻孥责任。

乙：开设学校。本会发达时，在各道县、镇设立同人小学，教养本会会友之子女。其中英俊颖异者，可拨入各属省城之同人中学。之出类拔萃者，得入北京同人大学。大学毕而尚有心向学，本会助款出洋养成大器。不愿出洋或不能卒读者，可于本会之工商各业为觅生计。

丙：振兴实业。本会所存之款，决不能不使其子母相生，以图国家丰富，故矿务、工厂、道路、船坞各大业在所必兴，既可挽回国家之权利，又可谋会友之幸福。是以各实业厂之执事人员，皆以本会会友或同人学校学生充之。

丁：维持政府。一日国家有事他邦，本会之款可以借于政府修兵屯田，待时平之后，仍向政府索还。至于战时，本会同人亦宜投戎报效，以固邦基。

四、账目：日用账目，主事宜按月报告，以免误会。

五、银钱事重私弊：必多宜防患于未然，财政清理员决不可少。该员既为会众公举，自有清理款项权衡。

蒋镜海：旅欧文集（摘要）
Collected Works on Travel to Europe (Abstracts) by Jiang Jinghai

十一、职员：由本会会友投票选举，职员之额数及掌职之时间，归本会会众议定，在欧时本会职员皆尽纯全之义务。

十二、中央地点：返国后挂在北京、上海、汉口、广州、库伦五处设立模范机关，复向各该处渐次推广。

十三、通信：暂以华工第八十九营为临时通信处。

十四、存案：本会在欧时当先在华工本部存案，而后返国后，亦宜在政府存案。

十五、删改：此简章统系草创，其不完善之处应多，本会会友时有删改之权。

General Regulations of Tongren Society for Chinese in Europe

Preface

As an old saying goes, "It is hard for an individual to maintain the overall situation, but it is easy to achieve success if many people work together." Since ancient times, the rich and powerful countries have achieved their success by collective efforts and wisdom. Because many things were waiting to be resolved since the end of the European War and the invisible wars between different races will be far greater than the visible ones, collective efforts and wisdom were becoming more and more essential in societies. Being unsolidified, our Chinese people are just like a plate of sand, among which the poor are not content with their poverty but ready to abuse their poor conditions while the rich are indulged in extravagance counting on their fortunes. Previously, there were also societies and associations of some kind, but most of them followed Chinese rules or their leaders attempted to usurp the country,

华工日记
Chinese Labourer's Diaries

leading to the aggression of various countries, the coercion of European countries, the threat of western powers and the invasion of Americans. The result is the miserable fact that China has nearly been divided by western powers. My colleagues went to Europe for good reason and witnessed how the societies of European countries functioned in an open and sincere way. At ordinary times, the societies instruct their people to live in peace without participating in state affairs but to spare no efforts to serve their countries in wartime. Since that time, my colleagues have learnt that the strength of these European countries lies in their orderly societies. However, it is quite a different scene In China. The society is still full of disturbances or riots, and the people are still living in destitution. But why? I believe it is because our society does not have a tradition of using collective efforts and wisdom. Considering that every person should be responsible for the fate of his country, I have decided to start this society regardless of my limited knowledge and ability, and of the fact that I am living in a foreign country. I name it "Tongren Society" because the meaning of *Tongren* in Chinese is the righteousness of benevolent people. Members of the society only need to set aside a small part of their salaries every month for their fees. After all, many a little makes a mickle. If its members suffer financial difficulties later, the society will help them through their difficulties; if its members become too poor or dying, the society will give support to their wives and children. The society will set up schools to cultivate talents and undertake projects to advocate the development of industry, do business to make our country rich, and build roads to bring people convenient travels. In this way, the inheritance from mothers to their children will form an endless cycle while the constant nurturing of rare talents will constitutes an infinite development. When our country has wars with other nations, the society will make donations for army weapons and supplies.

蒋镜海：旅欧文集（摘要）
Collected Works on Travel to Europe (Abstracts) by Jiang Jinghai

Members of the society are encouraged to enlist in the army to serve the country and fight bravely in the battlefields. Thus, the society's donations can not only help alleviate the poverty amongst the people, but they can also provide help for our country; they can not only cultivate one's moral character and manage one's family affairs, but they can also help to govern our country and pacify the world. But how could we do that? The answer is nothing but the collective efforts and wisdom.

  1. Mission: To alleviate poverty, benefit the state, and comply with the government.

  2. Name: "Tongren Society for Chinese in Europe" while in Europe and "Tongren Society" while in China.

  3. Objectives: To unite all Tongren Societies in foreign countries or states, outside the provinces of China.

  4. Membership: Any citizens of the Republic of China willing to abide by the regulations of the Society can become its members with the recommendation of other members.

  5. Qualifications: Members should have specialised professions.

  6. Religion: The Society has no limitations of religion.

  7. Rights: All members have the rights and interests of the Society.

  8. Certificate: All members hold certificates issued by the Society.

  9. Violation: The Society shall have the right to dismiss any member who does not abide by the regulations of the Society. The Society shall not take any member who fails to work diligently under this contract while in Europe.

  10. Donation: Each member shall donate three francs a month while in Europe and three *Jiao* of silver dollars after returning to China. The money shall be handed directly to the chairman of the Society or handed over by his introducers. Upon receiving each payment, the chairman shall give a receipt

with signature, which shall be given to each donor as proof of donation.

11. Savings: The money received by the secretaries shall be handed to the Treasurer in person at any time. The Treasurer shall deposit the money in banks. No money shall be used without public consultation.

12. Purpose:

A: To help its members. Members who are suffering difficulties or in temporary financial problems can borrow money from the Society by stating the precise repayment date and no interest shall be required. For members who are in great poverty or have been dead, the Society has the responsibility to provide help and assistance for their wives and children.

B: To open schools. When it is developed, the Society shall set up Tongren primary schools in counties and towns to educate the children of its members. The gifted and exceptional students in primary schools can be transferred to Tongren high schools in provincial capitals. Those outstanding high school graduates shall be admitted to Beijing Tongren University. The Society shall provide funds for those university graduates who are determined to pursue further studies abroad. For those who do not go abroad for further study or who fail to graduate, the Society shall offer opportunities for them to find a livelihood in its industries and commerce.

C: To develop industry. The money deposited in banks shall not be prohibited from accruing interest. To make our country richer, the Society shall develop various industries such as mining, factories, construction and dockyards, which are able to regain the rights of our country and to further the well-beings of its members. Therefore, the directors or managers of various industrial factories shall be undertaken by members of the Society or students from Tongren Universities.

D: To maintain the government. If the state has wars with other countries, the Society shall lend money to the government to make weapons and to produce food. The Society shall ask the government to return the money after wars come to an end. In wartime, it is also advisable for our colleagues to join the army to serve our country and consolidate the foundation of our country.

13. Accounts: The directors shall report the daily accounts every month to avoid misunderstandings.

14. Prevention of irregularities in money matters: Preventive measures shall be taken to ensure indispensable Financial clarity.

15. Clerks: Office clerks shall be elected by the members of the Society. The number of clerks and the period of their employment shall be agreed upon by all members of the Society. They shall perform their full duties while in Europe.

16. Central Locations: After returning to China, the Society shall set up model agencies in Beijing, Shanghai, Hankou, Guangzhou and Kulun and then spread to other places gradually.

17. Correspondence: The 89th Battalion of the Chinese Labour Corps shall be the temporary correspondence address until further notice.

18. Registration and Files: The Society shall be registered in the Central Department of Chinese Labourers while in Europe and then in the Government after returning to China.

19. Deletions and Corrections: The General Regulations is only a draft and there might be some imperfections in it. Members of the Society have the right to make deletions and corrections.

华工日记
Chinese Labourer's Diaries

祭欧战效力诸同胞文

维中华民国八年十月十六日，谨以茶点果品，致祭于我侨胞诸兄弟之灵曰：

呜呼！欧战四载，血染半球。抛无数头颅，掷亿万性命，始得了结此空前绝后之一大战局。凡我联邦莫不顶礼相庆，曰驱除德奥，扶持世界之公理，还我大同之文明。世界乐业，国际公平，此无他，战士之力也。而我之所以享此利益者，实我阵亡诸先烈士之所赐也。我加入战团，宜出师百万，直接交锋，方无愧联军之真相。而华军未至，欧战告终。幸赖我侨胞诸先烈，鞠躬尽瘁，大名已成。联盟各国，中原策功。伊谁之力，侨胞其承。诸君虽死，寄于我生。枪林弹雨，不避险踪。杀身成仁，国士堪称。捐躯殉难，勋标烟凌。义气昭昭，明若日星。豪光万丈，气满太空。为国死难，一世英雄。魂挽祖国，闵岳亦同。试执天下而相问，无负尔之耿忠。呜呼，美哉！后侨胞而死者，谁不慕尔之休风。噫，苍梧野莽，生于诸凭。岐周圣主，卒于郫郢。死正邱首，厥惟太公。大丈夫死得其当，何暇计地分中外，土坟黄青。嗟夫，死者长逝矣，生者有何能。君留欧西，我还亚东。悲愤交集，感慨之情，同声一哭，泪洒襟胸。忧忧悃悃，奠尔之灵，来格来临，冥冥之中。呜呼！哀哉！尚飨。

蒋镜海：旅欧文集（摘要）
Collected Works on Travel to Europe (Abstracts) by Jiang Jinghai

Elegiac Address to Chinese Compatriots Who Had Served in European War

On 16 October 1919, the eighth year of the Republic of China, with tea and fruits as the sacrifice, we held a memorial ceremony for our compatriots who died in the European War.

Alas! Four years of the European War has stained the world's hemisphere with the blood of young soldiers. This unprecedented world war only came to an end at the expense of the loss of millions of lives. The nations of the Entente countries celebrated the hard-won victory, saying that they had expelled Germany and Austro-Hungary, upheld world justice and restored the civilisation of human beings. Both world's peace and international justice were achieved by the brave fighting of soldiers. And the peace and justice I enjoy today was the result of the bravery of martyrs who had died in battles. It was advisable that our country joined the war by dispatching ten million soldiers to fight directly with the enemies. However, the war came to an end before the arrival of Chinese armies. Thanks to our martyrs, who spared no effort working in the war and achieved great fame through their dedications. Among all the countries in the alliance, China made its contribution by sending to Europe you, our beloved Chinese labourers. Though you were dead, you have saved our lives and your spirit would live in our hearts forever. You fought bravely without withdrawal from various dangers under the rain of bullets. Dying to achieve virtues, you are considered our heroes and martyrs, who sacrificed your lives to achieve great virtues. With obvious righteousness, you were as bright as stars, whose brightness shines throughout the universe. You died for your country and shall remain our heroes for all time. Wherever you are, your souls remain close to the motherland. No one else in the world could be more loyal than you. Alas, how noble! Your Chinese compatriots that live because of your sacrifice admire your high virtues. Ah, among the wild grass in Cangwu was the birthplace of virtuous emperors, but the emperor of Qizhou died in Piying and only Jiang Taigong was buried in his hometown after death. If death is a worthy sacrifice, it makes no difference whether you die in your own homeland or in foreign lands. The dead have gone forever but what can the living do? You stay in Western Europe while we return to Eastern Asia. With our mixed feelings of grief and indignation, we could not stop our tears from falling. With great sincerity we came to pay homage to your souls, why seemed to have stayed here because of destinies. Alas! Please enjoy the sacrifice.

起草公文

纪念驻法华工善后实业学校筹办宣言

自从欧战发生，公理侵陷，涂炭已极，天人共愤。列强联军义举，共讨恶魔，挽扶公理。故我十五万华工，以友谊助战来欧。昼荷锹铲，夜卧沟垒。处于枪林弹雨，死伤无计，犹坚忍工作，绝无悔色者，为社会灭强权，争公理耳。幸天厌乱，德奥败北，公理复兴。吾祖国得参入议和，争回各种利权，与德奥庚子赔款，时赖吾华工之力也。故陆、王两专使，侨务局诸公及青年会等念及死义孤儿，度日维难，迭上条陈，拟请政府格外垂怜。业蒙钦许，决定由德奥庚子赔款中，每年提出十万元，作华工善后开端。于山东曲阜孔林开设一华工实业学校，使孤儿残幼有谋生之机，华工子弟有求学之路。望诸大君子踊跃捐输，表示爱国

蒋镜海：旅欧文集（摘要）
Collected Works on Travel to Europe (Abstracts) by Jiang Jinghai

热诚，政府、国人无不感激资助，则华工前途有厚望焉！

筹备委办　孙子严　丁振岗　同启

Drafting Official Documents

Declaration of the Preparation of an Industrial School Commemorating Chinese Labourers in France:

Since the European War began, justice in the world had been abandoned and the misery and sufferings had reached an extreme, causing the indignation of both people and nature. The allied forces united to fight against the devils and defend the justice in the world. Out of friendship, 150,000 Chinese labourers came to Europe to assist in the war effort. They excavated trenches with spades and shovels in the daytime and slept beside the trench walls at night. Countless labourers were killed or injured under the constant shellfire. But others continued to work with perseverance without regrets because they fought for power and justice for the society. Fortunately, Germany and Austro-Hungary were defeated, and justice was restored. For the contributions the Chinese labourers, our country also participated in the negotiations and contended for various rights and interests as well as the reparations by Germany and Austro-Hungary. In view of the difficulties faced by families and children of the Chinese labourers that lost their lives during the war, Envoy Lu and Envoy Wang, officers of the Overseas Chinese Affairs Bureau and the YMCA, presented petitions to the government asking them to give special consideration to the families of dead Chinese labourers who had difficulty in making a living. With the approval of the government, it was decided that 100000 yuan would be offered annually from the German-Austrian Boxer's

华工日记
Chinese Labourer's Diaries

indemnity, as the beginning of the rehabilitation for Chinese labourers. A Chinese Labourers Industrial School was to be established at Konglin in Qufu, Shandong Province, to ensure the children of Chinese labourers have a place to study and to help provide them with future employment. We hope that all people will also donate enthusiastically to express their patriotism. The government, as well as the people, will be very grateful for your support. In this way, the Chinese labourers will have a bright future.

Sun Ziyan and Ding Zhengang
The Preparatory Committee Office

诗歌、赋词

华工多虱赋（以题为韵）

茹毛饮血，宿露栖霞。只图哺啜，不事桑麻。三载悠游裤内，每时潦倒天涯。胯下低藏，无异汉臣韩信；釜中空乏，宛如齐使子华。原夫华工之来西欧也，披星戴月，沐雨栉风。自南徂北，自西徂东。惨目兮狼烟笼碧，痛心兮烽火飞红。只闻炸弹淋漓，处处纷争地利；徒见艇飞上下，人人都讶天工。

而其多虱也，噬脐兴叹，搔首频歌。除恶不能务本，歼凶难免余波。兄弟联床，不料连茹于我；友朋共衾，熟思滋蔓及他。觅来切肤之衣，纷纷不少；检视周身之缕，累累孔多。

且虱之为物也，其体甚微，其形则不一。行动可寻，隐藏难觑。潜行衣上，皮毛与日月争光；缓步缝中，首尾共衣裳一色。美矣，祖公起舞，胸中不忘雄鸡；惜乎，王猛高谈，手底只扪伏虱。

蒋镜海：旅欧文集（摘要）
Collected Works on Travel to Europe (Abstracts) by Jiang Jinghai

嗟夫，困苦咸尝，坚辛毕遇。痛痒关心，坎坷击目。景同吴氏箫吹，迹比苏家羊牧。罹此勿妄之灾，众者袖手而旁观；虽云疥癣之忧，谁肯降心以相助。远离祖国，竟图阁上麒麟；回首神州，共逐原中狡兔。观华工之飘零异域，愿吟感颂之诗，恨臭虫之剥食愚民，欲作驱除之赋。

世界文明我为先

中华大国四千有余年，神农轩辕自古传。创造指南车，勘定蚩尤乱。世界文明唯有我先。

同胞立志灭日本

我东邻日本国地方不多大，人又少地又窄三岛立国家。军政警农工商存心藏诡诈，世界上人最恨日本矮鬼娃。到今朝他甚想逞强在东亚，拒德美联英法扰乱我国家。众同胞齐努力想法把它打，除灭了这倭贼富强大中华。

客中忆母

高堂谁为劝加餐，屈指慈龄泪暗弹。
抚子至今无苦节，承颜何处觅微官。
遍游亚美欧非澳，一世辛甜淡辣酸。
寸草春晖知莫报，前途努力敢偷安。

寄内

衣单不耐五更寒，举首前途泪不干。
蓬梗飘零无定向，家书勉强说平安。
萧条客旅人先瘦，惶恐春晖景已残。
卿自聪明知孝道，堂前努力劝加餐。

华工日记
Chinese Labourer's Diaries

生日感怀

徒增马齿客心惊，廿五年前剑未横。
枉说功名欺白发，空谈经济误苍生。
琴书现已飘零惯，生计还无一事成。
欲赋万言舒愤懑，灯前搅笔泪先倾。

赠留法诸同事

从来历史不堪闻，聚聚离离百感纷。
骥尾追随休忘我，童头领袖有诸君。
死生豪杰前途共，成败英雄末路分。
漫说斯文无济事，都能横笔扫千军。

赠别马第元

临行欲话泪满满，珍重前途努力先。
此去何时能复会，初交也算是因缘。
同君漂泊千重海，伴我萧条九十天。
总为客中朋友少，落花流水也情牵。

赠别吴俊章

交情深浅有何殊，相济刚柔我不如。
世味亲尝浓也淡，欢场惯兄实也虚。
重逢当在三年后，患难而今五月余。
握别将欲心事写，临岐意乱不成书。

即事

涛声月色映松林，何处天涯是故人。
纵得闲吟终少兴，倘能沽酒不辞贫。

蒋镜海：旅欧文集（摘要）
Collected Works on Travel to Europe (Abstracts) by Jiang Jinghai

山头号角声惊耳，帐背流泉冷逼身。
如此隆冬冰似铁，前军死战又经春。

寄母

雁宇传来自亚洲，灯前披读泪先流。
慈恩菽水何由报，夙志戎衣尚未酬。
曾为谋生游北冀，又因学剑客西欧。
可怜风浪似经历，犹是飘零一叶舟。

杂感

旧事回想迹已陈，谁家后果与前因。
干戈不已怜斯土，湖海难堪老此身。
遗老至今思楚客，故园何处觅秦人。
囊中依旧贫如洗，不负侨民与母亲。

题像片

且凭泥爪志游踪，话别从前感慨同。
协约条条遗痛史，乡园草草失英雄。
扫平四岛心才死，阅历重洋眼界空。
笑我疏狂如野鹤，也叨末座伴诸公。

题小照（二首）

其一

且留小照志斯游，海外英豪一并收。
疾首夷人凌圣旗，伤心倭贼秽神州。
知机临事甘奴婢，苦学随时做马牛。
早识诸君衔国恨，从戎投笔尽来欧。

其二

相逢一语即心倾，交似联床十载情。
海外风波似阅历，欧西雷火各纵横。
论兵目下无孙子，忧国胸怀似祖生。
自幸何缘攀骥尾，姓名从此共群英。

赠别朱梦侠（二首）

其一

天涯患难已经年，自幸追随有凤缘。
正好寒宵谈学业，忽惊雨夜对离筵。
前途早卜鹏程九，到老还夸骥路千。
自愧赠交无宝剑，聊将俚语写鸾笺。

其二

知有前期在，同君醉乙瓯。
形骸参聚散，踪迹各沉浮。
颠簸空搔首，存亡看后头。
才从实处用，学向浅中求。
勤俭营生计，辛甜共友筹。
故园方岌岌，尤勿负神州。

赠别（四首）

其一

书香继世属君家，壮志从戎尤足夸。
颇恨与君相见暮，约逢佳会抵中华。

其二

苦读寒窗十数秋，欲图阁上麒麟游。
此番不幸来西亚，只伴鱼虾糜鹿俦。

蒋镜海：旅欧文集（摘要）
Collected Works on Travel to Europe (Abstracts) by Jiang Jinghai

其三

万里从军海外游，恨无家报时常投。
谨将尺素忙呈上，惟盼高人注意收。

其四

就将文人常作俦，可怜名士不能留。
与君临别无他赠，聊赋俚词借报酬。

欧战场感怀

欧战和平后，荒凉纵目初。
草青愁暗淡，骨白乱废墟。
树木多枯槁，楼台尽土丘。
东西千里外，南北万家余。
烽火三秋苦，人烟四野无。
坎坑深处处，何日得安居。

舟中元旦

为客西欧已数秋，年前奉诏转神州。
今朝正好千樽酒，元旦难堪一叶舟。
拱手已辞旧岁去，鞠躬又报新春投。
虽然未偿天伦乐，观海斯时借此游。

太平洋中阴历年

其一

阴历年添旅梦愁，依然做客他乡游。
太平洋内无情水，莫向西南祖国流。

其二

茫茫太平水无涯，举首宗邦不见家。

华工日记
Chinese Labourer's Diaries

每日身中身似醉，忽逢阴历旧年华。

其三
他乡为客泪如麻，满目苍苍不见涯。
惹起思家阴历节，恨不一日到中华。

其四
从戎数载最凄凉，阴历年来客断肠。
早知他乡无乐土，依然今夕太平洋。

其五
回忆家中旧历年，桃符万户总新鲜。
可怜无数太平客，只愿中流舟不前。

其六
举首宗邦望亚东，家家万紫共千红。
太平洋内客心感，欢乐谁云到处同。

无题

其一
半生沦落走西东，不当书生当华工。
漫说胸怀鸿鹄志，转教燕雀笑英雄。

其二
荏苒韶光廿四年，堪叹书剑两茫然。
医生沦落白人手，呼作马牛有谁怜。

Verses and Poems

Lice on Chinese Labourers

They lived a life of savages and slept in the open air. They went to Europe

蒋镜海：旅欧文集（摘要）
Collected Works on Travel to Europe (Abstracts) by Jiang Jinghai

for the purpose of having something to eat and not work in the field. For three years they worked hard outside their country but remained down and out. Just as Han Xin in the Tang Dynasty who was humiliated by others, they had to be submissive to foreigners. Just as Zi Hua in the Spring and Autumn Period who was an envoy of the Qi State, they did not have enough food to eat for most of the time. On their way to West Europe, these Chinese labourers travelled day and night regardless of the bad weather. In Europe they frequently migrated, from south to north or from east to west. They witnessed the terrible flames of the war and the agonizing gunfire of battles. They were accustomed to the sound of bombs with which both sides fought for favourable geographical positions and to the sight of aeroplanes which flew up and down in the sky to everyone's amazement.

There were many lice on Chinese labourers, who sighed at their sufferings and were cursing as they scratched. As it was impossible to eliminate all in the process of obliterating the evil critters, it was inevitable to leave behind aftermaths in the process of getting rid of lice. When our beds were connected, the lice on my colleagues came to me incessantly. When my friend came and slept alongside me, I was afraid that the lice would spread to him. So I check my underwear and found there were actually a great number of lice. Then I examined all of my clothes and found a lot of holes on them.

As a small creature, lice were tiny in size but irregular in the body shape. It was easy to find their traces when they were in action, but they were difficult to find when they remained under cover. While they were sneaking on the surface of clothes, their hair was hard to notice under the sunshine; while they were strolling along the seams, their heads and tails were the same colour as the clothes. It was admirable that Zu Ti got up to do a sword dance when he heard the crow of the rooster; but it was pitiful that Wang Meng talked about

华工日记
Chinese Labourer's Diaries

the state affairs with his hands catching lice on his clothes.

Alas, Chinese labourers had experienced all kinds of bitterness and hardships. The pain and itching led to the discomfort of the mind, whereas ridges and pits resulted in dissemination of the eyes. Their situations were just like those of Wu Zixu, who played *xiao* in streets for food, and Su Wu, who herded flocks of sheep as a shepherd. Lice victims suffered greatly from this horrible problem, but others just stood by and did not offer any help. They said that it was only the trouble of scabies, but few would stand up to help. Far away from the motherland, we were searching the Kirin in the pavilion, but lice are more cunning than rabbits on the plains in the Yuan Dynasty. Seeing the miserable life of Chinese labourers, I would like to chant poems of praise, and hating the disgusting lice that sucked the blood of workers, I would like to write a poem of delousing.

China, One of the World's Earliest Civilisations

With a history of over four thousand years, China has the ancient legends of Emperor Shennong and Emperor Xuanyuan, who created the south pointing chariot and settled the wars against Chi You, the god of war. Thus, China has one of the earliest civilizations in the world.

Compatriots' Determination to Wipe Out Japanese Aggressors

As our neighbour in the east, Japan is a three-island country with a small area and population. Deceitful are its people in all walks of life and people in the world hate the Japanese most. At present, attempting to become a dominant power in East Asia, it invaded our country together with Britain, United States, France and Germany. Making concerted efforts to become rich and powerful, all Chinese compatriots are determined to wipe out the Japanese aggressors.

Missing Mother in Foreign Land

Unable to stay home and accompany you to have dinners,

Thinking about your age I cannot help but burst into tears.

While bringing me up, you've lived a bitter and frugal life,

But I failed to wait upon you by becoming a petty official.

I was determined to travel to every continent in the world,

And experience the sweet and sour taste of life without fear.

Even now I still have no way to repay your love and care,

But in the future, I'll do my utmost to be an obedient son.

To My Wife

The few clothes I wore could not bear the cold before dawn,

As I thought of the future, tears couldn't help rolling down.

Wandering alone from place to place aimlessly all the time,

I pretended to be safe and happy every time I wrote home.

As a stranger in turbulent foreign land, soon I became thin,

And in great fear spoiled were the landscapes in springtime.

To our parents, you were clever enough to know filial piety,

Please try to persuade them to eat more food to stay healthy.

Birthday Sentiments

I was greatly shocked to know that I was another year older again,

For my military dream I had not achieved in the past twenty-five years.

Do not say in vain that fame could be achieved only with grey hair,

And it did harm to commoners to give empty talks about economy.

华工日记
Chinese Labourer's Diaries

The singing art of *Qinshu* had been accustomed to the wandering life,

But up to now nothing has been achieved as a means of a livelihood.

I'd intended to express my indignations with ten thousand of words,

But my tears began to pour as I stirred my brush before the lamp.

A Farewell to My Colleagues in France

For most of the time history is something unbearable to be heard of,

Because the gatherings and departures give us a multitude of emotions.

Please don't forget me in the process of following well-bred persons,

And among the elder leaders of high status were you, my colleagues.

Whether it is life or death, we share a common future with heroes,

Success or failure, people have their own destiny in the world's eyes.

We could not say that men of letters can do no good to things at all,

For with their pen, they can wipe away millions of troops in an instant.

A Farewell to Ma Diyuan

Before saying parting words, I had tears in my eyes,

Please hold dear your future by always working hard.

Perhaps we would never have chances to meet again,

But even first acquaintances also had it own causes.

Travelling a great distance together over land and seas,

We accompanied each other for ninety depressed days.

Though few friends I made among people overseas,

I was reluctant to part with them for short periods.

A Farewell to Wu Junzhang

There is no difference in the depth of our friendship,

蒋镜海：旅欧文集（摘要）
Collected Works on Travel to Europe (Abstracts) by Jiang Jinghai

For I admire your combined strength and gentleness.

Strong tastes become weaker with familiarity and time,

True feelings may become false for those who enjoy cabarets.

Reunion is expected to be three years from now,

We have shared weal and woe for over five months.

I try to write about my desires and concerns on parting,

But with mixed feelings I could hardly write anything.

Improvisation

With sea waves, moonlight and pine forests,

Where in the world can I find my old friends?

Having no mood to enjoy even the idleness,

With wine I would not care how poor I was.

From hilltops came the harsh sound of horns,

Behind the tent flowed the freezing streams.

In such a deep winter with ice as thick as iron,

Warfare will continue through another spring.

To Mother

Upon receiving the letter from home in east Asia,

With tears in my eyes, I read it in great eagerness.

I wonder how I can return your love and support,

For my wish to be a soldier has not been fulfilled.

I had travelled to Beijing and Hebei to earn living,

And then to Western Europe for military learning.

After experiencing great waves and storms at sea,

I am still like a boat adrift, floating around the world.

华工日记
Chinese Labourer's Diaries

Random Thoughts

Sweet memories of the past have now gone forever,

For what reasons I came here I can hardly remember.

Pathetic looks this land for the cruelty of the ceaseless war,

I grew old after undergoing these intolerable hardships.

But old people still missed relatives living in a foreign land,

Where could I find my kinsfolk in the homeland.

Still with little money in my pocket as ever before,

I lived up to expectations of expatriates and my mother.

On Portrait

From traces of the past, we knew your ambition to travel afar,

And couldn't help but sigh with sentiments while saying goodbye.

The signing of the peace treaty made us forget miserable history,

While the lush grass in the cemetery reminded us of our heroes.

Until we brought peace to the continent we would never cease,

And came empty visions after we experienced long voyages.

As an unrestrained wild crane, people would likely laugh at me,

But what I wanted was only to be buried here and accompany thee.

On Portrait (Two)

I

I kept the portrait of you to inspire my travel,

To make friends with all our overseas outstanding figures.

With bitterness I hated the humiliation of the foreigners,

And grieved over the aggression of Japanese invaders.

I worked as a slave in order to learn ways of governance,

蒋镜海：旅欧文集（摘要）
Collected Works on Travel to Europe (Abstracts) by Jiang Jinghai

And to acquire knowledge at any time through hard work.

I knew that all of you with the hatred of our home,

Would give the pen for the sword to serve in Europe.

II

With only a few words we found each other congenial,

The friendship between us seemed to be that of a decade.

We both experienced overseas incidents of various kinds,

And in west Europe fought under the gunfire in the battlefields.

They talked about the art of war as adeptly as Sun-Tzu,

They showed concerns for our country's destiny like Zu Ti.

Grateful to have the opportunity to meet and follow them,

My name was also included in the list of heroes since then.

Farewell to Zhu Mengxia

I

For years we had gone through thick and thin together,

And it was a great luck that I could be your follower.

Talking about schoolwork on a cold dark night as a learner,

I realised we'd parted after the rainy night with each other.

A bright prospect I would have predicted as you earlier,

Great expectations you wished me even as a senior.

Ashamed of being unable to present you a sword as a souvenir,

I wrote this small sincere poem from my heart as a farewell letter.

II

For knowing that we were good friends,

We together drank to our heart's content.

Physically we would meet and then depart,

华工日记
Chinese Labourer's Diaries

Our own ups and downs we could control.

Without ways to settle the present turbulence,

We should try to conserve our own survival.

Talents came only from the practical use,

Learnings derived from those more shallow.

Diligent and thrifty we have a better living,

And share the sweetness of our friends.

In precarious situations our motherland still was,

Remember never to betray our country always.

Farewells

I

Born into a family of scholars for generations,

You joined the army for your lofty aspirations.

What a pity it was that I had not met you earlier,

So we appointed to meet on your arrival in China.

II

By studying hard for more than ten years,

I had intended to be one of the military officers.

But for this unfortunate trip to West Europe,

We've only fish, shrimp, and elk as partners.

III

As a soldier in an overseas army far away from home,

Eager for letters from home I wrote from time to time,

Very cautiously I presented my letter for delivery,

Just wishing that it would be received by my family.

蒋镜海：旅欧文集（摘要）
Collected Works on Travel to Europe (Abstracts) by Jiang Jinghai

IV

I often kept company with men of letters,

But it was a pity that the celebrities were to go.

With nothing as a gift while parting from you,

As a reward I composed this small poem so.

Thoughts on European Battlefields

At the beginning of peace after the European War,

As far as eyes can reach stretch the desolate lands.

Green as it seems, the grass is sad and gloomy,

The ground is scattered with white bones in ruins.

The number is great, and the scene is haggard,

With all the buildings being blasted into ruins.

From east to west they extend thousands of miles,

With over ten thousand homes north to south.

Flames of war lasted in here for three autumns,

And not a single person to harvest the fields.

Everywhere are trenches and ditches of various types,

And I wonder when people shall live a life a peace.

New Year's Day on Ship

After having worked for several years in Western Europe,

We set sail to return to the land of divinity a few days ago.

Today by drinking thousands of bottles of excellent wine,

We celebrated the New Year's Day on the ship in sorrow.

Bidding a farewell to the past year with hands cupped on chest,

We saluted the coming of another new year with a bow.

华工日记
Chinese Labourer's Diaries

Unable to get together with family to enjoy the reunion,

We could still have a good ocean sightseeing though.

Lunar New Year in the Pacific Ocean

I

On Lunar New Year strong became nostalgia of travellers,

Who were still staying at places far away from home alone.

Alas, how ruthless the waters of the Pacific Ocean remain,

Which'll never flow Southwestward to the land If our own.

II

So boundless was the vast water of the Pacific Ocean,

Looking up we found invisible homeland still remain.

As if intoxicated we stayed inside the ship every day,

And suddenly came Chinese Lunar New Year once again.

III

With bitter tears in the eyes of labourers in foreign countries,

In no way could they see the end of the vast grey water in Oceans.

Thinking of the Lunar New Year brings in great homesickness,

They wished to be back in China with their family the next day.

IV

The most lonely moment during the many m years of serving the armies,

Lunar New Year became a heart-breaking day for all labourers overseas.

Although they had known there existed no paradise in other countries,

They would be still sailing on this evening in the Pacific Ocean waters.

V

Upon recollecting the Chinese Lunar New Year in our homeland,

Memories of peach charms hung on every household were fresh.

蒋镜海：旅欧文集（摘要）
Collected Works on Travel to Europe (Abstracts) by Jiang Jinghai

Poor countless travellers on ships crossing the Pacific Ocean,
Merely wished we would stay there motionless and never rush.

VI

Looking up onboard at our country in the east of Asia,
We could still see the blossoms of thousands of flowers.
But sad felt the travellers on the ship in the Pacific Ocean,
As it was hard to find the same happiness in alien places.

Untitled Poems

I

At nearly the middle age of my life, I sailed abroad
To become a Chinese labourer rather than a teacher.
Despite the great ambitions deep in my inner heart,
The hero was laughed at by the ordinary birds.

II

Although twenty-four years of the youth elapsed quickly,
What a pity it was that he was good at neither books nor swords.
When the doctor was reduced to a servant of the foreigners,
Where was the sympathy for his becoming a servile labourer?

附 录

回忆祖父蒋镜海

蒋德山

祖父蒋镜海，字鉴秋，生于1880年10月1日，逝于1964年1月17日，广饶县李鹊镇沟头村人。自幼聪明，能干而好学，但家境贫困，无力供读。艾家村一财主，见祖父聪明伶俐，便叫他来自己办的学校中读书。几年后，正赶上清朝"废科举，办学堂"的好机会，他于光绪31年（1905）考入了乐安官立高等小学堂，读书四年，毕业时名列全校第二名。但毕业不分配工作，为了谋生，他在本镇董家村教小学。小学是个人所办，只管饭，没有工资，生活非常困难。

1917年，第一次世界大战期间，英法两国招募十多万华工支援欧洲前线。祖父认为这是为国争光的光荣使命，毅然报名参加华工招募。我们村共有4人参加，其他3人李汉书、蒋博山、蒋宝龄都是文盲。到法国后，因为我祖父有文化，被任命为总4道89营营长。该营主要负责抬担架、运伤兵、挖战壕、运弹药，有空还得种田、收割庄稼、生产粮食，其工作异常艰苦。有时因战事紧张，华工吃不饱，穿不暖，天冷了不发棉衣，天热时掏去棉花当单衣穿。战时一有空闲，祖父及其他华工就学习法语，还担任教员，教华工识字，替华工写家信，一天下来难得闲。幸运的是，战后祖父与同村其他3人都安全回来了。

祖父对我讲过一次危险的经历：当时德国军队进攻，法国军队与华工都向后撤退，几天后，法国军队重新占领该地区，华工随着军队驻扎。一天中午，华工89营烧水做饭，突然一声爆炸，锅饭飞上天，周围人员

华工日记
Chinese Labourer's Diaries

有的炸死，有的炸伤，我祖父离得稍远一点，没有受伤。原来德国撤退时在灶下埋了炸弹，生火做饭被引爆，炸死华工6人，炸伤4人。华工回国时，祖父写了一篇祭文，名《祭欧战效力捐躯诸同胞文》，纪念牺牲的同胞，文中写道："嗟夫，死者长逝矣，生者有何能，君留欧西，我还亚东，悲慨激情，同声一哭，泪洒襟胸，忧忧悃悃，奠尔之灵。"祖父还写了大量诗词，特别是《旅欧华工十二月歌》，把华工经历的生活状况，工作战斗，苦难日子表现得淋漓尽致，读之感人肺腑。

1918年11月，第一次世界大战结束，华工陆续回国。祖父回国后，适逢省府出公文招考区长，祖父因成绩优异被录取，在临淄县三区任区长3年。但他看不惯北洋政府的腐败风气，为官很多不关心百姓疾苦，任满后便托辞回家，不再任官，在本村当小学教师。1937年日军侵华，本村学校被迫解散，祖父到周村教会中学任教，教授古典文学，同时向学生开展爱国教育。据当地人说，此校学生没有一个当汉奸的。解放后，爷爷又自学中医，为群众免费看病，受到乡亲们的称赞。

Recollections of My Grandfather Jiang Jinghai

Jiang Deshan

My grandfather, Jiang Jinghai, with the literary name of Jianqiu, was born in Goutou Village, Lique Town, Guangrao County on 1 October 1880, and died on 17 January 1964. He was intelligent and studious from early childhood, but his family was too poor to support him for schooling. Seeing that my grandfather was clever and quick-witted, a rich man in Aijia Village invited my grandfather to study in a school founded by himself. A few years later, the Qing Dynasty launched the campaign of "abolishing imperial examinations and establishing schools". Taking this as an opportunity, my grandfather was

Recollections of My Grandfather Jiang Jinghai

admitted to Le'an Government Higher School in 1905, where he studied for four years and ranked second in the school when he graduated. However, there was no guarantee of a job assignment upon graduation at that time. So, to make a living, he taught in Dongjia Village Primary School in Lique Town, a privately-own school where, in return for teaching, he was provided with three meals a day but without pay. Life at that time was very difficult for him.

During the First World War, Britain and France recruited more than 100,000 Chinese labourers to support the European front in early 1917. My grandfather thought this was a glorious opportunity to win honour for our country and applied for it immediately. Four people in our village were recruited, among whom Li Hanshu, Jiang Boshan and Jiang Baoling were all illiterates. When they arrived in France, due to his higher level of literacy, my grandfather was appointed as the leader of Brigade 89 of the Chinese labourers. They were mainly responsible for carrying stretchers, transporting wounded soldiers, digging trenches, and transporting ammunition. Besides, they also had to till land, harvest crops, and producing food. Life was extremely hard for them. Sometimes they did not have enough food to eat or proper clothes to wear due to the difficult circumstances caused by the war. They were not given cotton-padded clothes when it became cold or they had to wear the cotton-padded clothes as the unlined ones by taking out the cotton when it was hot. Life was always busy for my grandfather during the war. But once he had some free time, my grandfather would either learn some French with other Chinese labourers or teach Chinese labourers to read, and write letters for them. Fortunately, my grandfather and the other three people from the village all came back safely after the war.

My grandfather once told me about a dangerous experience in the War. It happened at a time when the German army launched an attack and both the

华工日记
Chinese Labourer's Diaries

French army and the Chinese labourers retreated to the rear of the front. A few days later, the French army reoccupied the area and the Chinese labourers were still stationed with them. One day, an explosion broke out suddenly when Brigade 89 of Chinese labourers were cooking at noon. The cooking pot was blown up into the air and workers around were either killed or injured. My grandfather escaped the tragedy because he was a little far away. It turned out that he Germans had buried some bombs where the stove was set up when they retreated. Thus, when the labourers set fire to cook, the bombs were all detonated, killing six and injuring four of the Chinese labourers. To commemorate them, my grandfather wrote an elegy entitled "Elegiac Address to Chinese Compatriots Who Had Served in European War" when he returned home to China. It reads, "The dead have gone forever but what can the living do? You stay in Western Europe while we return to Eastern Asia. With our mixed feelings of grief and indignation, we could not stop our tears from falling. With great sincerity we came to pay homage to your souls, why seemed to have stayed here because of destinies." My grandfather also wrote numerous poems, especially the touching "Songs of Twelve Months for Chinese Labourers in Europe", which vividly depicted the living conditions, the work, the fighting and the sufferings of Chinese labourers in WWI."

At the end of the First World War in November 1918, Chinese labourers returned to China in quick succession. When my grandfather returned home, he applied for the selection of district governor by Shandong Provincial Government. For his excellent performance, my grandfather was admitted and served as the district governor in Linzi County for three years. He hated the corruption of governmental officials who showed disregard for the life of ordinary people. So when his term came to an end, he resigned and returned to his home village, working as a teacher in the village primary school. When the

回忆祖父蒋镜海
Recollections of My Grandfather Jiang Jinghai

Japanese army invaded China in 1937, the village school was forced to close, and my grandfather was transferred to Zhoucun Christian Middle School, to teach classical literature and gave students patriotic education at every opportunity. According to the local people, none of the students graduated from that school ever became traitors to China. After the liberation, my grandfather taught himself traditional Chinese medicine and gave free medical treatment to the masses. He was always highly regarded by his fellow villagers.

我的爷爷是一战华工

马京东

我的爷爷马春苓（1886—1962），字芳洲（一字赞臣），号廷襄，山东省潍坊市临朐县东城街道胡梅涧村人。爷爷去世时我刚出生10个月，关于我爷爷的很多故事，都是通过家人的口述和爷爷的日记了解到的。

爷爷六岁时就跟着曾祖父读书，十六岁八股成篇，通过了童子试，十七岁父亲去世，耕读持家，异常艰辛。二十岁辍读教私塾。由于清末停止科举考试，成立新学校，我爷爷于1913年考入临朐师范学校，毕业后任小学教员。虽整日对学生讲诵地理，对外面世界却并不了解，所以爷爷一直抱有环游世界增加新学识的理想。他在日记中写道："余尝披览地图以见其世界之大，万国之众，水陆山原之异势，飞潜动植之殊态，以及人民风化，土地气候，莫不千差万别。若仅拘于一区，则眼帘障蔽，身外之事，一无新睹。虽朝夕讲诵地理，而授者听者，皆恍惚无证，反求诸己，亦多有未之敢作者。""余念及此，遂慨然有环游之志。"

1917年第一次世界大战进入最残酷的阶段，欧洲陷入全面混战，协约国人力资源面临极大匮乏，此时英法将目光投向了中国，决定招募华工从事战场劳务工作。爷爷得知这一消息后毅然报名，爷爷在日记中写道："吾国既入协约，自当军助战而民助力。""今日之择，既能增军事之新学识，又得偿游历之夙志愿，时哉弗可失矣！"

爷爷于1917年10月3日拜别家人，同本村十几个华工一道出发，从青岛乘船赴欧洲战场。在大西洋搭载华工的船只经常遭到德国潜艇的攻

华工日记
Chinese Labourer's Diaries

击，很多华工命丧大海。爷爷在日记中写道："惟见碧浪滔天，弥望无际。岛屿不见，飞鸟绝迹。彤霞密布，朔风砭肌，直令人惕然而惊，亦惨然而凄。""德国暗伏潜水艇于大西洋各海路跟踪联军船只，突起沉之，为害最烈。"当时爷爷也是恐惧不已，但是仍然强打精神，鼓励同胞"大义所趋，死生一之，又何惧乎！""今日之役，吾等受政府承允，于役西土，不须破斧沉枪，亦自有名有利。既无所悔，夫复何惧？"

爷爷和同行华工途径日本、加拿大、美国、英国、比利时，漂泊两个月零二十天，于1917年12月23日到达法国加莱，还没来得及舒展疲惫的身体，爷爷和其他华工就立即被送往工厂去做工，运输材料和修路，工作条件极其艰苦，劳动强度非常大。爷爷在日记中写道："呜呼！日营工作，筋疲力困。夜避飞炸，心惊胆裂。回望故国，关山万里。前计归期，迢迢三年。其苦况诚不忍言。虽然，吾人旅此，如锁虎瓶鱼，即插翅亦难奋飞。虽日夜忧虑，亦将奈何，惟苦处寻乐，随遇自安，以保我微躯。至于吉凶祸福，概诿夫天命而已！"

爷爷在法国工作的地方是加莱省西部诸工厂，去战线尚有百余里，故未冒子弹之险，并未遭颠沛之苦。但夜间常有敌国飞机潜入内地，抛掷炸弹，销毁战线后方之粮草弹药供应。英国军队发快炮回击，或驾飞机发射机关枪，弹壳如雨，为害最烈。所以各营常备地穴、沙屋，以避炸弹。一夜之间，常奔避数次，故在该地驻七八月，未尝解衣而寝。

虽然一战于1918年11月11日结束，但爷爷和其他华工又被分派到法国和比利时打扫战场，清理废墟。爷爷在日记中写道："自经战乱之后，诚有不堪言者。屋无完壁，木无完株，弹穴渊布，瓦砾山差，尸横遍野，阴风惨凄。其铁网纠绊，战壕逶迤，荒草没顶焉。有《黍离》流离死绝，民少孑遗。停战半载，尚无栖迟，老叟悲叹，稚妇涕洏。我等眷言顾之，亦潸焉出涕矣。"1919年7月4日，我爷爷又被派到伊普斯清理战场，该地在巴比伦东南二十余里，是法英美与德军鏖战之要冲，蹂躏破坏尤为特甚。自停战以来，各国部队收埋阵亡兵士直至于今，荒野间尤白骨累累。人谓自古兵争,未有如欧战之惨者,诚然欤。爷爷感慨之余作诗两首。

吊比国街市

荒院蓬蒿千宅绿,颓楼牗户万家通。
昔年黎庶堂前燕,遁入战壕铁屋中。

吊阵亡兵士坟茔

十架亭亭魂有因,荒邱累累奠谁陈。
可怜路畔遗残骨,犹是深闺梦里人。

战争结束后近一年时间里,华工们都被分派到各地打扫战场,清理废墟,帮助英、法、比重建家园,很多华工清理战场时被哑弹炸死,终究没能回到家乡。

1919年10月13日,我爷爷被批准回国。至12月25日,我爷爷与同伴五六人经由益都(今青州)回来,"时冰雪遍野,道途艰岖。负笥担囊,踯躅前趋。……于是过赤涧,经石村,逾朐城,登潊垠(岸也),乃瞻衡宇,载欣载奔。子弟欢迎,老母依门。扶亲入室,两泪流痕。田园既芜,青毡犹存。"爷爷回国后,继续教学至七十岁,前后共教学40余年,可谓桃李满天下。

爷爷作为一战华工赴欧助战历时两年多,他把当时华工在欧洲战场辛苦劳作的情景和一战悲惨的战况,写成《游欧杂志》一书,这本书是一战残酷战争的真实写照,为后人了解一战那段悲惨历史留下了宝贵的资料。

2018年是一战结束一百周年,11月我有幸随山东侨务代表团赴英、法、比参加一战结束一百周年华工纪念活动。当来到英、法华工墓园时,看到一排排墓碑面向东方,两万多华工同胞,为了捍卫世界和平,献出了

华工日记
Chinese Labourer's Diaries

自己年轻的生命,客死在了异国他乡,我不禁潸然泪下。14万华工的汗水、血泪和牺牲没有得到世界的重视,正如英国一战华工史作家赠予我的书上写道"华工是一战英雄,拯救了我们,却在巴黎和会上被出卖。"

战争是残酷的,战争永无赢家。一战华工为欧洲的自由和重建作出了贡献,他们的历史功绩值得我们永远铭记。法国前总统希拉克曾说:"任何人都不会忘记这些从中国远道而来的、在一场残酷的战争中与法国共命运的勇士,他们用自己的灵魂与肉体捍卫了法国的领土、理念和自由"。

我们可以告慰先辈的是,今天的中国,在中国共产党的领导下,各族人民团结奋斗,内政外交取得了丰硕成果,中国以更加昂扬的姿态日益走近世界舞台的中央。我们要铭记一战血的历史,珍视今天得来不易的和平生活,世界各国人民要和睦相处、共同发展,携手开创和平美好的未来!

My Grandfather Was a Chinese Labourer in WWI

Ma Jingdong

My grandfather Ma Chunling (1886–1962), with the courtesy name of Fangzhou (also Zanchen for a time) and the literary name of Tingxiang, was born in Dongcheng Street, Humeijian Village, Linqu County, Weifang, Shandong Province. He died when I was only ten months old. Therefore, many stories about my grandfather were learnt from what my family have told me and what I have read from his diary.

At the age of six, my grandfather began to study with my great grandfather. At the age of 16, he could write incredibly good eight-part essays and passed the qualification test for the imperial examinations. When he was

My Grandfather Was a Chinese Labourer in WWI

17, my great grandfather died and from then on he had to study and do farm work to support the family. Life was very hard for him at that time. At the age of 20, he stopped studying and began to teach private lessons. At the end of the Qing Dynasty, the imperial examination system was abandoned, and new schools were established. My grandfather was admitted to Linqu Normal School in 1913 and worked as a primary school teacher after graduation. Although he taught geography to students most of the time, he knew little about the outside world. Therefore, my grandfather had always dreamt of travelling around the world to increase his knowledge and broaden his horizons. He wrote in his diary, "From the map, I once observed the large size of the world, numerous countries, vast oceans, various landforms, diverse animals and plants, and different peoples, customs, landscapes and climates. If one were confined to only one place, his eyes would be blocked and see nothing new outside his own area. I taught my students geography every day, but even though they listened to me attentively, they were still confused and frustrated for lack of real-life evidence. When seeking the cause in myself, I did not dare to give the evidence most of the time for my own lack of personal experiences. Frustrated by this situation, I began to dream about travelling around the world."

In 1917, the First World War entered its most brutal stage and Europe fell into a state of full-blown chaos. The Entente countries were confronted with a great shortage of human resources and at that time, Britain and France decided to recruit Chinese labourers to work in the battlefields. My grandfather was determined to sign up for it resolutely the moment he heard the news. He wrote in his diary, "Now that our country has joined the Entente countries, it is naturally the duty of both our armed forces and our civilians to give a helping hand. This assistance to the European War will not only increase my military

华工日记

Chinese Labourer's Diaries

knowledge but also realise my long-cherished dream of travelling abroad. It is really an opportunity that cannot be missed."

On 3 October 1917, my grandfather left his family and travelled with a dozen of other Chinese labourers from the village to Qingdao, where they boarded a ship to the European battlefields. The ships carrying the Chinese labourers across the Atlantic Ocean were often attacked by German submarines, and many Chinese labourers lost their lives at sea. My grandfather wrote in his diary, "all that we could see was the boundless ocean with surging waves. There were no islands around and no birds in the sky. The dense rosy clouds and the piercing north winds made us watchful, fearful and miserable." He also wrote, "The hidden German submarines that followed the ships of the allied forces in various routes across the Atlantic Ocean would emerge suddenly to launch attacks on the passing ships, bringing about the most serious damage to them." Terrified as he was, my grandfather still tried hard to encourage his compatriots, saying to them, "Even if something happens, it is for justice that we lose our lives. There is nothing to fear at all." He added, "We left for Europe to work in the west because our government made a promise to help. We won't need to fight with 'all cauldrons smashed and all boats sunk' and can get some fame and fortune. Now that we don't regret it, there is nothing we can fear at all."

After a voyage on the sea of nearly 80 days, my grandfather and his fellow labourers arrived at Calais of France on 23 December 1917 via Canada, America, Britain and Belgium. Before they could stretch their tired bodies, my grandfather and other Chinese labourers were immediately sent to work in factories, transport various materials or to build roads. The working conditions were extremely hard, and the labour intensity was very high. My grandfather wrote in his diary, "Alas! In the daytime, we worked to exhaustion

My Grandfather Was a Chinese Labourer in WWI

while at night we escaped the air raids in fear. Looking in the direction of our motherland, we sighed over the great distance away. Counting days for return, we still had three long years according to our contracts. The hardships we bore were beyond words. Just as tigers in cages or fish in bottles, we were unable to escape even if we had wings. Although we were worried and anxious day and night, we could do nothing about it. What we could do was just to seek joy in troubles and make the best of it so as to protect ourselves. As to what would happen to us, be they blessings or misfortunes, we could only resign ourselves to our destinies."

Working in factories in the west of Calais, about 30 miles away from the battlefront, my grandfather had hardly suffered from the risk of gunfire and the hardships of moving from place to place. However, the enemy aeroplanes frequently came during the night, dropping bombs and destroying the army provisions and ammunition supplies in the rear of battlefronts. The British army fought back with artillery or fired machine guns from their own aeroplanes. With showers of shells, the air raids often resulted in very serious damage. Therefore, the camps usually had underground shelters and sand-covered buildings to avoid bombs. The teams of Chinese labourers would often have to run for cover several times during the night. Thus, for the seven or eight months they lived there, they had always slept with their clothes on at night.

Although the First World War ended on 11 November 1918, my grandpa and other Chinese labourers remained in France and Belgium to clear the battlefields and remove the debris. My grandfather wrote in his diary, "Everything was in a state of chaos and destruction after the war. No houses or trees remained intact; trenches and shell holes were everywhere; chilly winds blew over mountains covered with rubble and fields littered with dead bodies.

华工日记
Chinese Labourer's Diaries

Among tall weeds were endless miles of barbed wire and meandering trenches. There were no crops in the fields and a multitude of people lost their homes or were killed in the war, leaving only a few lonely widows and parentless children. Six months passed by after the armistice, but homeless people still could not find places for shelter. The elderly people sighed mournfully, and young widows shed tears. Seeing their misery, we Chinese labourers could not help but shed tears too." On 4 July 1919, my grandfather was sent to clean up the battlefields in Ypres, a place located about 6 miles to the southeast of Poperinghe which had suffered the most serious destruction because it was at the centre of devastatingly fierce battles between the French, British, Belgian, American and German forces. Since the armistice, the troops of various countries have been collecting and burying their soldiers who died in battles all across the surrounding countryside. It is said that there has not been a war as tragic as the European War ever since the beginning of time. My grandfather wrote two poems while he was filled with emotions:

Lament over Belgian Towns

Wildly growing are weeds in the wilderness and deserted houses,
And in ruins scattered declining buildings and broken windows.
Those swallows once nesting under the roofs of ordinary households,
Are now flying into the iron houses in entrenchments to seek shelters.

Mourning over Graves of Fallen Soldiers

Upright erected Crosses are thou eternal souls,
With offerings displayed on countless graves.
While buried roadside are thine remnant bones,
Thou remain dearest in dreams of those at homes.

我的爷爷是一战华工
My Grandfather Was a Chinese Labourer in WWI

For nearly a year after the end of the war, the Chinese labourers were sent to different places to clean up the battlefields, to remove munitions and rubble, and to help the French and Belgians to rebuild their homes. While cleaning up the battlefields, many Chinese labourers were killed by unexploded bombs, never to be able to return to their hometowns.

My grandfather was given permission to return to China on 13 October 1919. When my grandfather, together with five or six of his fellow labourers, came back home via Yidu (today's Qingzhou) on 25 December, "It was a hard journey because all the ground was covered with heavy snow at that time. We stumbled forward with sacks and suitcases on our shoulders. I remembered it was in the early autumn over two years ago that I left for Europe, but today on my return it was in winter with heavy snow on the ground. I walked past the village of Shicun and the city of Linqu. After climbing up the bank, I could see our house and I was so excited that I started to run hurriedly. My brother and my sons came up to meet me and my mother leaned against the door anxiously. While I supported my elderly mother into the house, tears ran down my cheeks. Although the field went nearly bare, the wingceltis trees were still standing there." My grandfather continued to teach after he returned home until he was seventy years of age. During the 40 years of his teaching career, he had cultivated countless students scattered all over the country.

As a Chinese labourer in WWI, my grandfather worked in Europe for over two years providing services during the war. He gave a detailed account of the hard work carried out by Chinese labourers in the European battlefields, and of the cruelty of the First World War, in his book entitled *Miscellaneous Records of Travel to Europe*. With its true portrayal of the cruelty of the First World War, this book provides us with precious materials for future generations to learn about the tragic history of WWI.

华工日记
Chinese Labourer's Diaries

2018 was the 100th anniversary of the end of the First World War. In November, I was honoured to travel to Britain, France and Belgium, together with the Shandong Province overseas affairs delegation, to participate in the commemorative activities for Chinese labourers on the 100th anniversary of the end of WWI. When I visited the cemeteries for Chinese labourers in Britain and France, seeing the rows of gravestones facing the east and thinking that over 2,000 Chinese labourers sacrificed their young lives in foreign countries in order to defend world peace, I could not help shedding tears. Sadly, the sweat, blood and sacrifice of 140,000 Chinese labourers have never been brought to the attention of the world. Just as one British writer wrote in his book on the history of Chinese labourers in WWI, "Chinese labourers are heroes during WWI, heroes who have saved us, but they were betrayed at the Paris Peace Conference."

War is cruel in nature and there are no winners in war. The Chinese labourers in WWI made contributions to the freedom and reconstruction of Europe, and their historical achievements are worth remembering forever. The former French President Jacques Chirac once said, "No one will ever forget these warriors who came all the way from China and fought side by side with the French people in the cruel war. They defended the territory, ideas and freedom of France with their body and soul."

Under the leadership of the Communist Party of China and with the united effort of people of all nationalities, today's China has achieved fruitful results in both domestic and diplomatic affairs and is approaching the centre of the world stage with a more high-spirited posture, which is something that we can console our ancestors with. We should bear in mind the cruel history of WWI and cherish today's hard-fought peaceful life. People all over the world should live in harmony and work together to create a peaceful and bright future!

后　记

　　2018年是一战结束100周年，为纪念一战华工为世界和平所做出的牺牲和贡献，山东省侨务代表团于11月5日至14日赴英国、比利时、法国举办一战华工系列纪念活动。随团前往的山东籍华工后代马京东向大家展示了爷爷马春苓手写本日记《游欧杂志》，引起社会各界尤其是学术界的极大关注，当地主流媒体争相报道，一时轰动。各界希望能够出版华工日记，让更多人了解一战华工历史。

　　在此后开展的一战华工历史研究和展览的过程中，我们还有幸得到了山东籍华工孙干、蒋镜海的日记手稿以及华工翻译顾杏卿著述的《欧战工作回忆录》，这些宝贵的文字记录，成为当今研究一战华工历史的重要史料。为方便海内外读者阅读，我们将其进行编辑整理，并以简体字和中英文对照的形式呈现出来。

　　在本书整理过程中，我们始终坚持尊重原作、呈现原貌的原则，文字尽量保持华工自身的书写习惯及当时时代环境下的语言风格，增加读者的亲历感和现场感。日记手稿中有个别错别字，适当予以修改，例如"嘹"改为"瞭"、"删刀"改为"铡刀"、"摔脚"改为"摔跤"、"炮弹廊"改为"炮弹廓"等。一些不影响读者阅读的别字和当时的通用字形尽量尊重原作未予改动，例如现在通用"廿"字作者手稿为"念"。日记中出现的国外地理名称，未予改动，例如"非洲人"写为"斐洲人"，"加拿大"写为"坎拿大"，"勒阿弗尔"写为"黎哈夫"，"新加坡"写

华工日记
Chinese Labourer's Diaries

为"新嘉坡"等，此类翻译与现在使用文字不同，或者作者限于知识结构书写有误，但是不影响读者阅读，所以未予改动，望读者理解。

本书的顺利出版，得益于专家学者的鼓励支持，得益于关注一战华工的同仁朋友们的倾情付出，更得益于华工后裔的无私奉献和协助。在此，感谢华工后裔孙光隆、孙肇永、马京东、蒋德山、蒋树平为我们提供先辈文稿，全权委托我们负责出版事宜；感谢李翔、David Moore对英文文稿的审校；感谢徐国琦、张岩、齐德智等学者给予我们的宝贵意见；感谢为出版此书付出努力的所有工作人员。

需要说明的是，由于《华工日记》书写时间久远，书写习惯差异较大，校对任务繁重，书中难免有疏漏甚至错误，还望读者谅解，感谢大家的指正。

编者

Afterword

2018 was the 100th anniversary of the end of World War I. To commemorate the sacrifices and contributions made by Chinese labourers in WWI for world peace, the overseas Chinese delegation of Shandong Province went to Britain, Belgium and France to hold a series of commemorative activities for Chinese labourers in WWI from the 5th to 14th November. Ma Jingdong displayed the manuscript of *Miscellaneous Records of Travel to Europe* by his grandfather Ma Chunling, a Chinese labourer in WWI from Shandong. It attracted great attention from all sectors of life, especially the academic community, and created a sensation with the reports made by the local mainstream media. People from all sectors of life hope to publish the diaries of Chinese labourers

后 记
Afterword

in WWI so that more people can learn about the history of the Chinese labourers during the First World War.

In our subsequent research and exhibitions on the history of Chinese labourers in WWI, we have also collected the diary manuscripts of Sun Gan and Jiang Jinghai, both of whom were Chinese labourers from Shandong Province, along with the *Reminiscences of My Work during European War* by Gu Xingqing, an interpreter from Shandong Province in the Chinese Labour Corps. These valuable written records have become important historical materials for studying the history of Chinese labourers during WWI. For the benefit of readers at home and abroad, we have organised the collected materials and presented them in simplified Chinese and English.

To give readers a sense of authenticity, we have adhered to the principle of respecting the original work and presenting the original appearance in the process of editing. We have tried to keep the writing habits of these Chinese labourers and the language style of that time as much as possible. For some mistakenly written characters in the diary manuscripts, we have made proper modifications. For instance, "嘹" was corrected as "瞭" (to watch from a higher place or a distance), "删刀" as "铡刀" (straw cutter), "摔脚" as "摔跤" (wrestling), and "炮弹廊" as "炮弹廓" (cannon barrels). But for those characters that will not affect the understanding of readers and those commonly-used characters of that time, we respect the originals as much as possible and have kept them unchanged. For example, the current character of "廿" (meaning twenty) was written in the manuscripts by the authors as "念". Also, some foreign geographical names in the diaries such as "斐洲人" for "非洲人" (African), "坎拿大" for "加拿大" (Canada), "黎哈夫" for "勒阿弗尔" (Le-Havre), and "新嘉坡" for "新加坡" (Singapore), are simply different translations from those of today or the authors' mistaken spelling due to their

华工日记
Chinese Labourer's Diaries

limited knowledge due to their limited knowledge. Since they will not affect readers' understanding, we have not made any corrections to them.

The publication of this book benefits a lot from the encouragement and support of experts and scholars, the efforts of our colleagues and friends who have being paying close attention to Chinese labourers in WWI, and the selfless dedication and assistance of the descendants of the Chinese labourers. We would like to thank Sun Guanglong, Sun Zhaoyong, Ma Jingdong, Jiang Deshan and Jiang Shuping in particular for providing us with the manuscripts of their ancestors and entrusting us with full authority for the publication. We would also like to thank Xu Guoqi, Zhang Yan, Qi Dezhi and other scholars for their valuable opinions as well as all the staff members for the effort they have made for the publication of this book.

It should be noted that due to the differences between today's writing habits and those of over a century ago when these diaries were written, there might be some omissions or errors in this book and any suggestions and corrections are welcome.

Editors